SAMS Teach Yourself

ASP.NET 2.0 in 24 Hours

Scott Mitchell

SAMS 800 East 96th Street, Indianapolis, Indiana, 46240 USA

Sams Teach Yourself ASP.NET 2.0 in 24 Hours

International Standard Book Number: 0-672-32738-4

Library of Congress Catalog Card Number: 2005937213

Printed in the United States of America

First Printing: March 2006

09 08 07 06 4 3 2 1

Trademarks

Warning and Disclaimer

Bulk Sales

Sams Publishing offers excellent discounts on this book when ordered in quantity for bulk purchases or special sales. For more information, please contact

U.S. Corporate and Government Sales
1-800-382-3419
corpsales@pearsontechgroup.com

For sales outside the U.S., please contact

International Sales
international@pearsoned.com

Associate Publisher
Greg Wiegand

Acquisitions Editor
Neil Rowe

Development Editor
Mark Renfrow

Managing Editor
Charlotte Clapp

Senior Project Editor
Matthew Purcell

Copy Editor
Chuck Hutchinson

Indexer
Aaron Black

Proofreader
Heather Arle

Technical Editor
J. Boyd Nolan

Publishing Coordinator
Cindy Teeters

Designer
Gary Adair

Page Layout
Kelly Maish

Contents at a Glance

Part IV: Site Navigation, User Management, and Page Layout

Part V: Building a Photo Album Web Application with ASP.NET

Table of Contents

Part II: Collecting and Processing User Input

Part III: Working with Databases

About the Author

As editor and main contributor to 4GuysFromRolla.com, a popular ASP/ASP.NET resource website, **Scott Mitchell** has authored several hundred articles on Microsoft Web Technologies since 1998. In addition to his vast collection of online articles, Scott has written five previous books on ASP/ASP.NET: *Sams Teach Yourself Active Server Pages 3.0 in 21 Days* (Sams); *Designing Active Server Pages* (O'Reilly); *ASP.NET: Tips, Tutorials, and Code* (Sams); *ASP.NET Data Web Controls Kick Start* (Sams); and *Teach Yourself ASP.NET in 24 Hours* (Sams). Scott has also written a number of magazine articles, including articles for Microsoft's *MSDN Magazine* and *asp.net PRO*.

Scott's nonwriting accomplishments include speaking at numerous ASP/ASP.NET user groups and ASP.NET conferences across the country. Scott has also taught numerous classes on ASP.NET and related technologies at the University of California—San Diego University Extension. In addition to teaching and writing, Scott also is a software developer. He works as an independent consultant and has authored and sold a number of commercial software applications.

Scott can be reached at mitchell@4GuysFromRolla.com; his blog is available at www.ScottOnWriting.NET.

Dedication

This book is dedicated to my dog Sam. You're such a good girl!

Acknowledgments

Writing a book is an arduous and draining endeavor, a feat that would not be possible without the untiring patience and undying support of my wife, Jisun. You make life unbearably fun and full of smiles.

Furthermore, neither this book, nor any of my others, would have been possible without my wonderful family. Their unwavering love and encouragement has made me the man I am today.

Thanks also to Neil Rowe, Mark Renfrow, Matt Purcell, and the entire editorial team at Sams Publishing.

We Want to Hear from You!

As the reader of this book, *you* are our most important critic and commentator. We value your opinion and want to know what we're doing right, what we could do better, what areas you'd like to see us publish in, and any other words of wisdom you're willing to pass our way.

As an associate publisher for Sams Publishing, I welcome your comments. You can email or write me directly to let me know what you did or didn't like about this book—as well as what we can do to make our books better.

Please note that I cannot help you with technical problems related to the topic of this book. We do have a User Services group, however, where I will forward specific technical questions related to the book.

When you write, please be sure to include this book's title and author as well as your name, email address, and phone number. I will carefully review your comments and share them with the author and editors who worked on the book.

Email: feedback@samspublishing.com

Mail: Greg Wiegand
Associate Publisher
Sams Publishing
800 East 96th Street
Indianapolis, IN 46240 USA

For more information about this book or another Sams Publishing title, visit our website at www.samspublishing.com. Type the ISBN (excluding hyphens) or the title of a book in the Search field to find the page you're looking for.

Introduction

As the World Wide Web continues its meteoric growth, websites have matured from simple collections of static HTML pages to data-driven dynamic web applications. For example, websites like eBay or Amazon.com are much more than simple HTML pages; they're actual applications that are accessed through the Internet. Although there are many competing technologies for building data-driven websites, this book shows how to use the latest version of Microsoft's popular ASP.NET technology for creating web applications.

ASP.NET web applications are composed of individual ASP.NET web pages. As we will see in numerous examples throughout this book, these ASP.NET web pages can display HTML, collect user input, and interact with databases. ASP.NET web pages contain a mix of both HTML markup and source code. It is the source code of an ASP.NET web page that allows for the more advanced features, such as accessing data from a database or sending an email from an ASP.NET web page. The source code of an ASP.NET web page can be written in any one of a number of different programming languages. For this book we will be using Microsoft's Visual Basic programming language. Don't worry if you've never programmed in Visual Basic or have never even programmed at all. Starting with Hour 5, "Understanding Visual Basic's Variables and Operators," we will spend three hours examining programming language concepts and the Visual Basic syntax.

To ease ASP.NET web page development, Microsoft provides a free development editor, Visual Web Developer, which is included on this book's accompanying CD. We will be using Visual Web Developer throughout this book to create our ASP.NET web pages. Visual Web Developer simplifies creating both the HTML markup and source code portions of ASP.NET web pages. The HTML markup for an ASP.NET web page can be quickly created by using the What You See Is What You Get (WYSIWYG) graphical editor. With this WYSIWYG editor, you can simply drag and drop various HTML elements onto an ASP.NET web page, moving them around with a few clicks of the mouse.

ASP.NET version 2.0 contains a number of improvements over version 1.0. With ASP.NET 2.0, Microsoft has made it easier than ever before to build data-driven websites. Starting in Hour 13, "An Introduction to Databases," we will begin our look at building websites that interact with databases. Hours 14 through 16 highlight a number of the new tools in ASP.NET 2.0 that facilitate creating database-aware web pages. Additionally, ASP.NET 2.0 and Visual Web Developer provide tools to help with building professional, easy-to-use websites. In Hour 19, "Defining a Site's Structure and Providing Site Navigation," we'll look at how to define a website's navigational structure and easily provide menus, treeviews, and breadcrumbs. Hour 21, "Using Master Pages to Provide Sitewide Page Templates," examines master pages, a new feature that enables web designers to create a web page template that can be applied to all pages across the site.

This book is geared for developers new to ASP.NET, whether or not you've had past experience with HTML or programming languages. By the end of this book, you'll be able to create your own dynamic, data-driven web applications using ASP.NET. In fact, in Hours 22 through 24 we'll build a completely functional online photo album web application, highlighting the lessons learned throughout the previous hours.

Conventions Used in This Book

This book uses several conventions to help you prioritize and reference the information it contains:

- *Did You Knows* highlight information that can make using ASP.NET 2.0 more effective.
- *Watch Outs* focus your attention on problems or side effects that can occur in specific situations.
- *By the Ways* provide useful information that you can read immediately or circle back to without losing the flow of the topic at hand.

In addition, this book uses various typefaces to help you distinguish code from regular English. Code is presented in a `monospace` font. Placeholders—words or characters used temporarily to represent the real words or characters you would type in code—are typeset in *`italic monospace`*. If you are asked to type or enter text, that text will appear in **`bold monospace`**.

Some code statements presented in this book are too long to appear on a single line. In these cases, a line-continuation character (an arrow) is used to indicate that the following line is a continuation of the current statement.

I hope you enjoy reading this book as much as I enjoyed writing it.

Happy Programming!

Scott Mitchell
mitchell@4guysfromrolla.com

PART I

Getting Started with ASP.NET

HOUR 1

Getting Started with ASP.NET 2.0

In this hour, we will cover

- What is ASP.NET?
- System requirements for using ASP.NET
- Software that must be installed prior to using ASP.NET
- Installing the .NET Framework, Visual Web Developer, and SQL Server 2005
- Taking a quick tour of Visual Web Developer
- Creating a simple ASP.NET web page and viewing it through a web browser

ASP.NET is an exciting web programming technology pioneered by Microsoft that allows developers to create **dynamic web pages**. Dynamic web pages are pages whose content is dynamically generated whenever the web page is requested. For example, after you log on, the front page of Amazon.com will show books it recommends for you, based on your previous purchases. This is a dynamic web page because it is a single page whose content is customized based on what customer is visiting the page. In this book we'll examine how to create dynamic ASP.NET websites quickly and easily.

Prior to ASP.NET, Microsoft's dynamic web programming technology was called Active Server Pages, or ASP for short. Although ASP was a popular choice for creating dynamic websites, it lacked important features found in other programming technologies. Microsoft remedied ASP's shortcomings with ASP.NET. Version 1.0 was released in January 2002 and quickly became the web programming technology of choice for many. In November 2005, Microsoft released the much-anticipated version 2.0 of ASP.NET. When designing ASP.NET 2.0, Microsoft focused on identifying common web development tasks and adding functionality to make such tasks a breeze.

Before we can start creating our first ASP.NET website, though, we need to install the .NET Framework, Visual Web Developer, and SQL Server 2005. The .NET Framework is the technology that ASP.NET needs to be able to function. Visual Web Developer is a sophisticated program for creating, editing, and testing ASP.NET websites and web pages. ASP.NET web pages are simple text files, so any text editor will do (such as Microsoft Notepad), but if you've created websites before, you know that using tools like Microsoft FrontPage makes the development process much easier than using a generic text editor like Notepad. This is the case for ASP.NET, as well.

The third and final piece we'll need to install is SQL Server 2005. SQL Server is a **database engine**, which is a specialized application designed to efficiently store and query data. Many websites interact with databases; any eCommerce website, for example, displays product information and records purchases in a database. Starting with Hour 13, "An Introduction to Databases," we'll see how to create, query, and modify databases through both Visual Web Developer and ASP.NET pages.

This hour will focus on getting everything set up properly so that we can start creating ASP.NET web applications. Although it would be nice to be able to jump straight into creating ASP.NET pages, it is important that we first take the time to ensure that the pieces required for ASP.NET are correctly installed and configured. We will create a very simple ASP.NET page at the end of this hour, but we won't explore it in any detail. We'll look at ASP.NET pages in more detail in the next hour and in Hour 4, "Designing, Creating, and Testing ASP.NET Pages."

What Is ASP.NET?

Have you ever wondered how dynamic websites like Amazon.com work behind the scenes? As a shopper at Amazon.com, you are shown a particular web page, but the web page's content is dynamic, based on your preferences and actions. For example, if you have an account with Amazon.com, when you visit Amazon.com's home page, your name is shown at the top, and a list of personal recommendations is presented further down the page. When you type a book's title into the search text box, a list of matching books appears. When you click on a particular book's title, you are shown the book's details along with comments from other users and an overall rating. When you add the book to your shopping cart and check out, you are prompted for a credit card number, which is then billed.

Web pages in websites whose content is determined dynamically based on user input or other information are called **dynamic web pages**. For example, any website's search engine page is an example of a dynamic web page because the content of the search page is based on the search criteria the user entered and the documents on the web server. Another example is Amazon.com's personal recommendations. The books and products that Amazon.com suggests when you view the page are different from the books and products suggested when someone else views these pages. Specifically, the recommendations at Amazon.com are generated by products you have viewed as well as previous purchases you have made.

The opposite of a dynamic web page is a **static web page**. Static web pages contain content that does not change. HTML pages, for example, are static web pages. That is, an HTML page on a website with the following HTML markup is considered static:

```
<html>
<body>
  <b>Hello, World!</b>
</body>
</html>
```

Such a page is considered a static web page because regardless of who views the page or what external factors there might be, the output will always be the same: the text `"Hello, World!"` in a bold font. The only time the content of a static web page changes is when someone edits the page and saves over the old version.

By the Way

Virtually all websites today contain a mix of static and dynamic web pages. Rarely will you find a website that has just static web pages because they are so limited in their functionality.

By learning ASP.NET, you will be learning how to create websites that contain dynamic web pages. It is important to understand the differences between how a website serves static web pages versus dynamic web pages.

By the Way

Competing Web Programming Technologies

ASP.NET is only one of many technologies that can be employed to generate dynamic web pages. ASP.NET is the successor to Active Server Pages (ASP), which was Microsoft's earlier dynamic web page creation technology. Other technologies include PHP, JSP, and ColdFusion.

Personally, I find ASP.NET to be the easiest and most powerful technology of the bunch, which is why I'm writing a book about ASP.NET instead of one of these other technologies. ASP.NET is head and shoulders above ASP. If you've created ASP scripts in the past, you'll no doubt find that you can do the same things you did in ASP by using ASP.NET but in a fraction of the time. Similarly, version 2.0 of ASP.NET provides numerous enhancements over version 1.0, including a vastly improved editor—Visual Web Developer—which is included on this book's accompanying CD.

If you have experience developing web applications with other web programming technologies, such as ASP, PHP, or JSP, you may already be well versed in the material covered in the next two sections. If this is the case, feel free to skip to the "Installing the ASP.NET Engine, Editor, and Database System" section.

Serving Static Web Pages

If you've developed websites before, you likely know that a website requires a **web server**.

A web server is a software application that continually waits for incoming **web requests**, which are requests for a particular URL (see Figure 1.1). The web server examines the requested URL, locates the appropriate file, and then sends this file back to the client that made the web request.

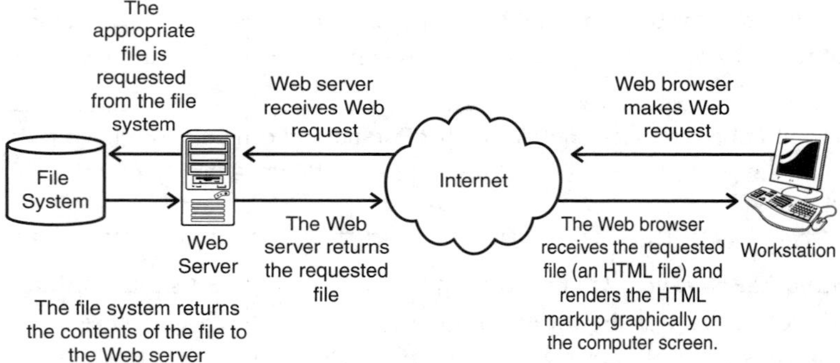
The appropriate file is requested from the file system
File System
Web Server
The file system returns the contents of the file to the Web server
Web server receives Web request
The Web server returns the requested file
Internet
Web browser makes Web request
The Web browser receives the requested file (an HTML file) and renders the HTML markup graphically on the computer screen.
Workstation

FIGURE 1.1 The web server handles incoming web requests.

For example, when you visit Amazon.com, your browser makes a web request to Amazon.com's web server for a particular URL, say `/books/index.html`. Amazon.com's web server translates this requested URL into an actual file residing on the same computer where the web server resides. The web server returns the contents of the file, which is then rendered by your browser.

This web server model is adequate for serving static pages, whose contents do not change. However, such a simple model is insufficient for serving dynamic pages because the web server merely returns the contents of the requested URL to the browser that initiated the request. That is, the contents of the requested URL are not modified in any way by the web server based on external inputs.

Serving Dynamic Web Pages

With static web pages, the contents of the web page are just HTML elements that describe how the page should be rendered on a user's web browser. Therefore, when a static web page is requested, the web server can simply send the web page's content, without modification, to the requesting browser.

This simple model won't work for dynamic web pages, where the content of the web page can depend on various factors on a per-visitor basis. To accommodate dynamic content, dynamic web pages contain source code that is **executed** when the page is requested (see Figure 1.2). When the code is executed, it produces HTML markup as its result, which is then sent back to the visitor's browser.

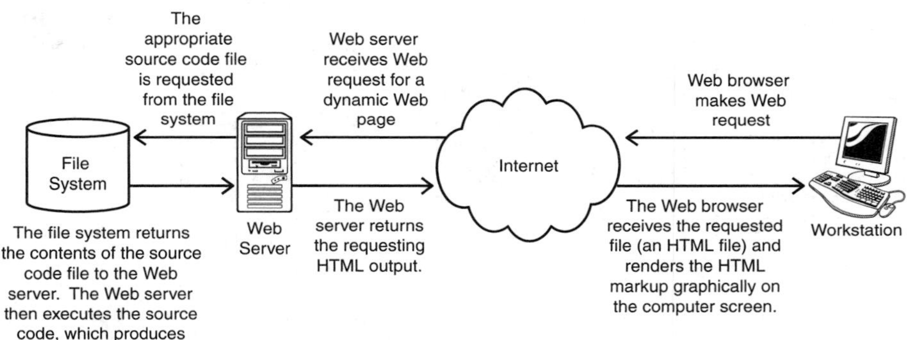
The appropriate source code file is requested from the file system
Web server receives Web request for a dynamic Web page
Web browser makes Web request
File System
Internet
The file system returns the contents of the source code file to the Web server. The Web server then executes the source code, which produces HTML output.
Web Server
The Web server returns the requesting HTML output.
The Web browser receives the requested file (an HTML file) and renders the HTML markup graphically on the computer screen.
Workstation

FIGURE 1.2 The content of a dynamic web page is created by executing the dynamic web page's source code.

This model allows for dynamic content because the content for a dynamic web page isn't actually created until the web page is requested. For example, imagine that we wanted to create a web page that displays the current date and time. If we wanted to do this using a static web page, someone would need to edit the web page every second, continually updating the previous time on the page to the current time. Clearly, this isn't feasible.

With a dynamic web page, source code can retrieve and display the current date and time. Say that one particular user visits this page on February 4, 2006, at 4:15:03 P.M. When the web request arrives at this time, the dynamic web page's code is executed, which obtains the current date and time and returns it to the requesting web browser. The visitor will see, displayed in the browser, the date and time: February 4, 2006, 4:15:03 P.M. If another visitor requests this page 7 seconds later, the dynamic web page's code will be executed, which will obtain the current date and time (February 4, 2006, 4:15:10 P.M.) and will return it to the requesting web browser, where it will be displayed.

Figure 1.2 is, in actuality, a slightly oversimplified model. Commonly, the web server and the execution of the dynamic web page source code are **decoupled**. That is, when a web request arrives, the web server determines whether the requested page is a static web page or dynamic web page. If the web page is static, the web page's contents are sent directly back to the browser that initiated the request (as shown in Figure 1.1). If, however, the requested web page is dynamic—say an ASP.NET web page—the web server hands off responsibility of executing the page to the **ASP.NET engine** (see Figure 1.3).

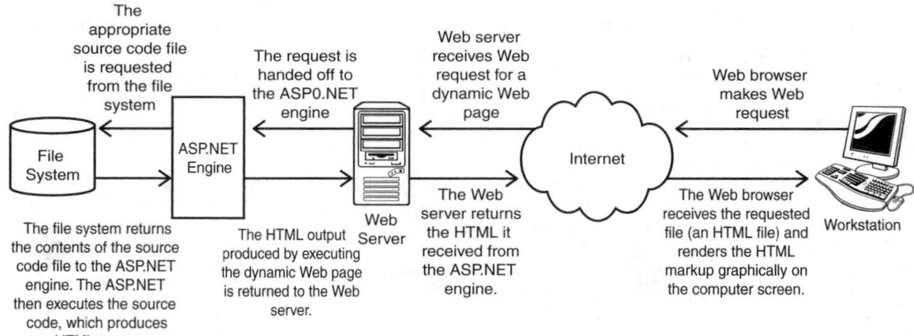
The appropriate source code file is requested from the file system
File System
ASP.NET Engine
The request is handed off to the ASP0.NET engine
Web Server
Web server receives Web request for a dynamic Web page
Internet
Web browser makes Web request
Workstation
The file system returns the contents of the source code file to the ASP.NET engine. The ASP.NET then executes the source code, which produces HTML output.
The HTML output produced by executing the dynamic Web page is returned to the Web server.
The Web server returns the HTML it received from the ASP.NET engine.
The Web browser receives the requested file (an HTML file) and renders the HTML markup graphically on the computer screen.

FIGURE 1.3 Execution of an ASP.NET web page is handled by the ASP.NET engine.

The web server can determine if the requested page is a dynamic or static web page by the requested file's extension. If the extension is `.aspx`, then the web server knows the requested page is an ASP.NET web page and, therefore, hands off the request to the ASP.NET engine.

> The ASP.NET engine is a piece of software that knows how to execute ASP.NET web pages. Other web programming technologies, such as ASP, PHP, and JSP, have their own engines, which know how to execute ASP, PHP, and JSP pages.

When the ASP.NET engine executes an ASP.NET page, the engine generates the web page's resulting HTML output. This HTML output is then returned to the web server, which then returns the HTML to the browser that initiated the web request.

Hosting ASP.NET Web Pages

After we've created ASP.NET web pages, to be able to view them, we need to request the ASP.NET page through a web browser. The browser then sends a request to the web server, which dispatches the request to the ASP.NET engine. The engine processes the page and returns the resulting HTML markup to the browser. When you're developing ASP.NET websites, the ASP.NET web pages you create will be saved on your personal computer. For you to be able to test these pages, then, your computer must have a web server installed.

Fortunately, you do not need to concern yourself with installing a web server on your computer. Visual Web Developer, the editor we'll be using throughout this book to create our ASP.NET websites, includes a lightweight web server designed for testing ASP.NET pages locally. As we will see in later hours, when testing an ASP.NET page, Visual Web Developer starts its **ASP.NET Development Web Server** and launches a browser that issues a request of the form: `http://localhost:`*`portNumber`*`/`*`ASP.NET_Page`*`.aspx`.

The `http://localhost` portion of the request tells the browser to send the request to your personal computer's web server, as opposed to some other web server on the Internet. The *`portNumber`* specifies a particular **port** through which the request is made. All web servers listen for incoming requests on a particular port. When the ASP.NET Development Web Server is started, it chooses an open port, which is reflected in the *`portNumber`* portion of the URL. Finally, the *`ASP.NET_Page`*`.aspx` portion is the filename of the ASP.NET page being tested.

Hosting ASP.NET pages locally through the ASP.NET Development Web Server has a number of advantages:

- **Testing can be done while offline.** Because the request from your browser is being directed to your own personal computer, you don't need to be connected to the Internet to test your ASP.NET pages.
- **It's fast.** Local requests are, naturally, much quicker than requests that must travel over the Internet.
- **Advanced debugging features are available.** By developing locally, you can use advanced debugging techniques, such as stepping through running code line-by-line.
- **It's secure.** The ASP.NET Development Web Server allows only local connections. With this lightweight web server, you don't need to worry about hackers gaining access to your system through an open website.

The main disadvantage of hosting ASP.NET pages locally is that they can be viewed only from your own computer. That is, a visitor on another computer cannot enter some URL into his browser's Address bar that will visit the ASP.NET website you've created on your local computer. If you want to create an ASP.NET website that can be visited by anyone with an Internet connection, you should consider using a **web-hosting company**.

A web-hosting company has a number of Internet-accessible computers for individuals or companies to place their websites. These computers contain web servers that are accessible from any other computer on the Internet. When setting up an account, you can ask the company to register a **domain name** for you. A domain name is the text that a person would enter into the web browser to visit your website. (For example, the domain name of Microsoft's site is microsoft.com. For my personal website, I might choose scottmitchellinfo.com.)

Did you Know?

> Of course, you can only choose a domain name that has not already been registered by somebody else. To determine whether your desired domain name is still available, visit http://www.netsol.com, where you can enter a domain name to check on its availability.

The benefits of using a web-hosting company to host your site include

- **A publicly available website**—With a web-hosting company, any visitor who has an Internet connection can visit your website!
- **Use of a domain name**—You can register a domain name and have it point to your website so that visitors can reach your website through a name like www.mysite.com.
- **Ability to focus 100% on building your website**—Installing a web server, applying the latest security patches, properly configuring domain names, and so forth can be tricky tasks. By using a web-hosting company, you are paying for this service, which allows you to concentrate on building your website.

By the Way

> You can choose from literally thousands of web-hosting companies, ranging dramatically in price, performance, features, support, and other qualities. A great place to start shopping for a web-hosting company is at a website like http://www.tophosts.com or http://www.hostindex.com. These websites catalog the thousands of web-hosting companies and allow you to search through their database looking for companies that match your price range, feature needs, and so forth.
>
> When you choose a web-hosting company that you'd like to do business with, be sure to contact the company and make certain it supports ASP.NET development.

After your web-hosting account is set up, you can move web pages to the computer where your account is hosted. Then you, or anyone else on the Internet, can visit these pages. If you upload a web page named `index.htm` and your domain name was bobshomepage.org, anyone could view the `index.htm` page by typing `http://www.bobshomepage.org/index.htm` into the browser's Address bar.

Getting Started with a Web-Hosting Company

Before you can create an account with a web-hosting company, you need to find a company that supports ASP.NET version 2.0. The easiest way to find such a company, in my opinion, is to check sites like TopHosts.com and HostIndex.com, which list thousands of web-hosting companies. You can search these sites' databases for web-hosting companies that meet certain criteria, such as cost per month, geographical location, web server platforms used, and other criteria.

Costs for web-hosting companies can range from a few dollars per month to hundreds or thousands of dollars per month, based on the features provided. Additionally, most web-hosting companies have a setup fee in the $25 to $100 range. On top of the web-hosting costs, you will probably want to register a domain name, which typically costs between $10 and $35 per year, depending on the domain name registrar used.

After you have picked out a web-hosting company and have double-checked that it supports ASP.NET development, contact the company's sales staff to create an account.

Develop Locally, Deploy to a Web Host

Because there are many advantages to hosting a site both locally and with a web-hosting company, often the best choice is to do both! I encourage you to develop, test, and debug your ASP.NET websites locally, through Visual Web Developer's built-in web server. After you have completed your site and are ready for visitors, then procure an account with a web-hosting company and deploy your site. This approach allows for the best of both worlds—an ideal development environment with the end result of a publicly accessible website!

Can I Host a Website from My Personal Computer?

Readers who have always-on broadband connections, such as through a cable modem or DSL, and a static IP address may be able to host a website from their personal computers. For more information on this option, contact your broadband provider.

If you want a public website, I personally recommend that you go with a web-hosting company. Setting up your computer to host a public website can be a difficult process and, if not done correctly, can leave your computer open to a number of security threats. For example, in July 2001 an Internet worm named Code Red spread quickly across the Internet, infecting Microsoft web servers. (A **worm** is a program that replicates and distributes itself over a computer network.) Specifically, the worm defaced web pages by adding the following text: `"HELLO! Welcome to http://www.worm.com! Hacked By Chinese!"` (For more information on the Code Red worm, see http://www.cert.org/advisories/CA-2001-19.html.) By setting up a public web server on your personal computer, you open yourself up to this sort of attack.

You can neutralize such threats by keeping abreast of the latest security patches from Microsoft, along with the know-how on how to best secure systems. Chances are, the professionals at the web-hosting company have more experience setting up, administering, and securing web servers than you and therefore likely provide a better line of defense.

Installing the ASP.NET Engine, Editor, and Database System

Recall that a browser doesn't know or care that your website uses ASP.NET pages. However, for a web server to be able to execute ASP.NET pages, it needs to have the ASP.NET engine installed, which is what executes the ASP.NET web page. If you want to install the ASP.NET engine, your computer must be running Microsoft Windows 2000, Microsoft Windows XP, Microsoft Windows Server 2003, or Windows Vista.

By the Way

> If you are running a version of Windows prior to Windows 2000, such as Windows NT, Windows ME, or Windows 98, you cannot develop ASP.NET applications on your computer using Visual Web Developer.

Even if your system does have the required operating system installed, you may need to take additional steps before you can start working with ASP.NET. For example, those using Windows XP need to have Service Pack 2 (SP2) installed. If you're uncertain whether your system meets the requirements, simply attempt the installation process. The installation program will inform you if there is some prerequisite for installation, such as Service Pack 2.

Three components need to be installed for us to work with the ASP.NET examples throughout this book. First, we must install the .NET Framework, which contains the core libraries required to process an ASP.NET page. The ASP.NET engine is part of this .NET Framework. Second, we'll need to install Visual Web Developer, which is the editor of choice for working with ASP.NET pages. Finally, we'll need to install SQL Server 2005, a database engine that is used extensively from Hour 14, "Accessing Data with the Data Source Web Controls," onward.

All three of these components can be installed through the single installation program included on this book's accompanying CD. To begin the installation process, simply insert the CD into your computer. This will bring up the installation program starting with the screen shown in Figure 1.4. Click the Next button to progress through the next two screens.

By the Way

> If your computer lacks the prerequisites, such as not having the latest service pack installed, the installation program will inform you of the problem with instructions on how to update your system. After you have updated your computer, rerun the installation program.

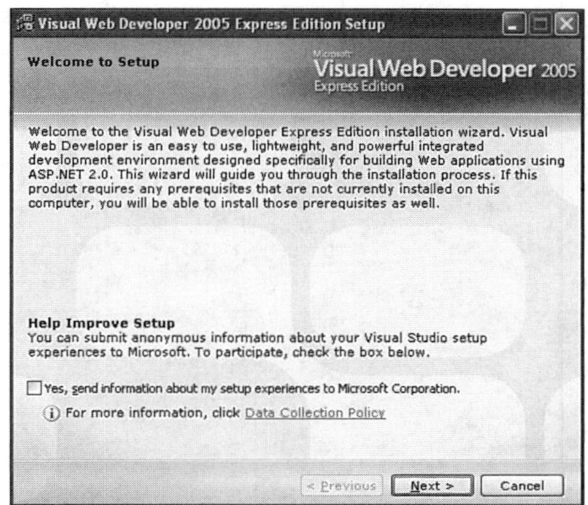

FIGURE 1.4
Start the installation process by inserting the CD into your computer's CD-ROM drive.

The book's CD is the installation CD for Microsoft's Visual Web Developer editor. Because Visual Web Developer is designed for developing ASP.NET websites, when you're installing the .NET Framework, which contains the core libraries needed for ASP.NET websites, it will be automatically installed. You can also install two optional packages, as shown in Figure 1.5.

The first optional package is Microsoft MSDN 2005 Express Edition. MSDN is Microsoft's collection of product documentation, whitepapers, code samples, and help files. While all of this information is accessible online through http://msdn.microsoft.com, I encourage you to install MSDN locally on your computer by selecting the check box.

The second optional package is Microsoft SQL Server 2005 Express Edition, which is a free database engine. While this package is optional in the sense that Visual Web Developer will install successfully with or without SQL Server 2005, the latter half of this book's examples rely on SQL Server 2005 being installed. Therefore, make sure that this check box is selected.

The next screen (see Figure 1.6) allows you to specify in what folder to install Visual Web Developer as well as what products will be installed and the disk space required. After double-checking that the correct packages are being installed, click the Install button to begin the installation process. The overall installation process will take several minutes. During the installation, you are kept abreast with what package is currently being installed as well as the overall installation progress (see Figure 1.7).

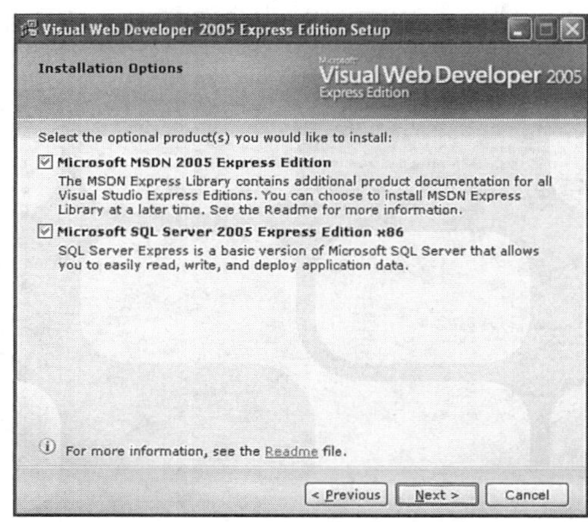

FIGURE 1.5
Make sure that you install SQL Server 2005 Express Edition.

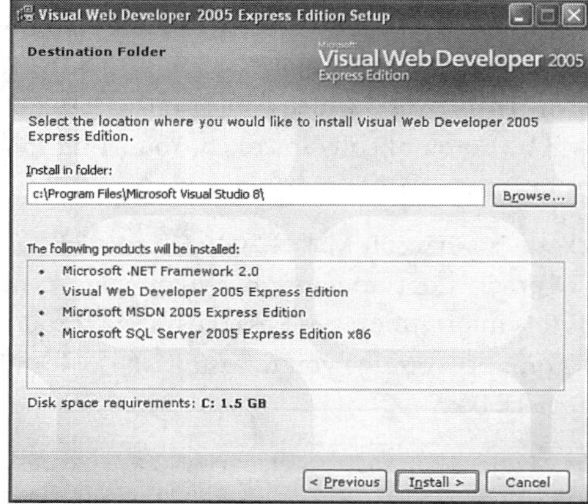

FIGURE 1.6
Specify the folder to install Visual Web Developer.

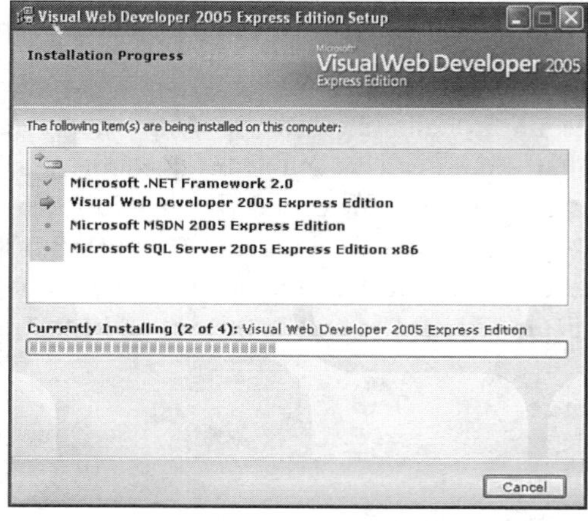

FIGURE 1.7
Monitor the installation's progress.

A Brief Tour of Visual Web Developer

When the installation process completes, take a moment to poke through Visual Web Developer. To launch Visual Web Developer, go to the Start menu, choose Programs, and click on Microsoft Visual Web Developer 2005 Express Edition. Figure 1.8 shows Visual Web Developer when it loads.

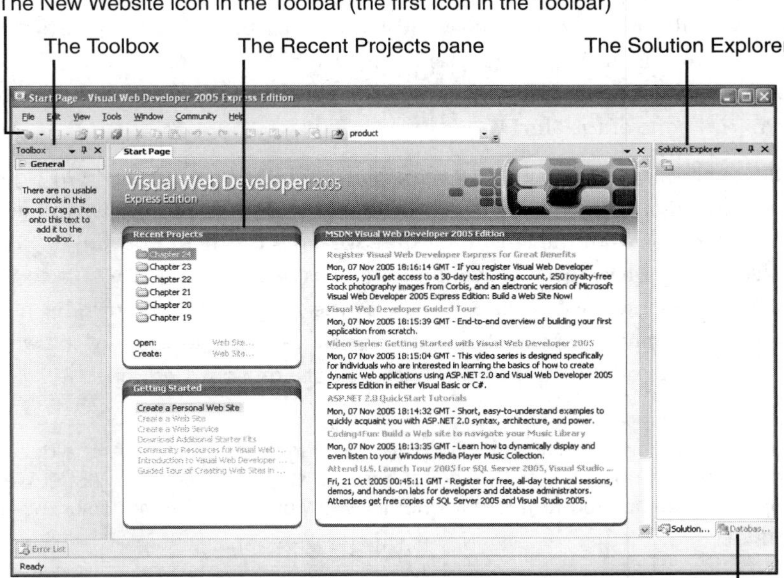

FIGURE 1.8 The Start Page is shown when Visual Web Developer is loaded.

When you open Visual Web Developer, the Start Page is initially shown. This Start Page includes a list of Recent Projects in the upper-left corner, a Getting Started section with some links for accomplishing common tasks in the bottom-left corner, and a list of recent articles on Microsoft's MSDN site in the right column.

On the left you'll find the Toolbox. In the Start Page the Toolbox is empty, but when you're working with an ASP.NET page, the Toolbox contains the plethora of ASP.NET Web controls that can be added to the page. (We'll discuss what Web controls are and their purpose in the next hour.)

To the right of the screen, you'll find the Solution Explorer. Again, on the Start Page this is empty, but when you load or create an ASP.NET website, the Solution Explorer will list the website's files. These files include database files, HTML pages, ASP.NET pages, image files, CSS files, configuration files, and so on. In addition to the

Solution Explorer, the right portion of the screen is also home to the Database Explorer. The Database Explorer lists the databases associated with the project and provides functionality for creating, editing, and deleting the structure and contents of databases.

Creating a New ASP.NET Website

To create and work with an ASP.NET page, we must first create an ASP.NET website. There are several ways to create a new ASP.NET website from Visual Web Developer. You can go to the File menu and choose the New Web Site option, you can click on the New Website icon in the Toolbar, or you can click the Create Web Site link in the Recent Projects pane of the Start Page.

All of these approaches bring up the New Web Site dialog box, as shown in Figure 1.9. Let's take a moment to create a website. For now, don't worry about all the options available or what they mean because we'll discuss them in detail in Hour 3, "Using Visual Web Developer." Leave the Templates selection as ASP.NET Web Site, the Location drop-down list as File System, and the Language drop-down list as Visual Basic. The only thing you should change is the actual location of the website. Place the website in a folder named `MyFirstWebsite` on your Desktop.

When creating a new website, you can enter the name of a nonexistent folder. If you enter the name of a folder that doesn't exist, when you click OK, Visual Web Developer will prompt you to find out whether you want it to automatically create the folder.

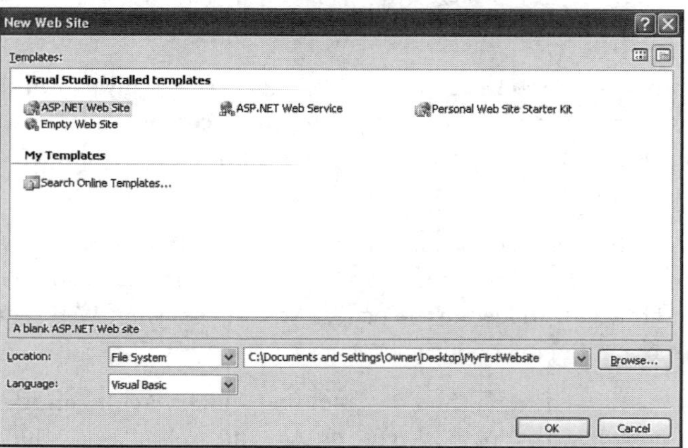

FIGURE 1.9
Create a new ASP.NET website in a folder on your Desktop.

After you create the new website, your screen should look similar to Figure 1.10. When creating the new website, Visual Web Developer automatically created an

App_Data folder, an ASP.NET page named `Default.aspx`, and a web configuration file (`web.config`). This folder and these two files are shown in the Solution Explorer.

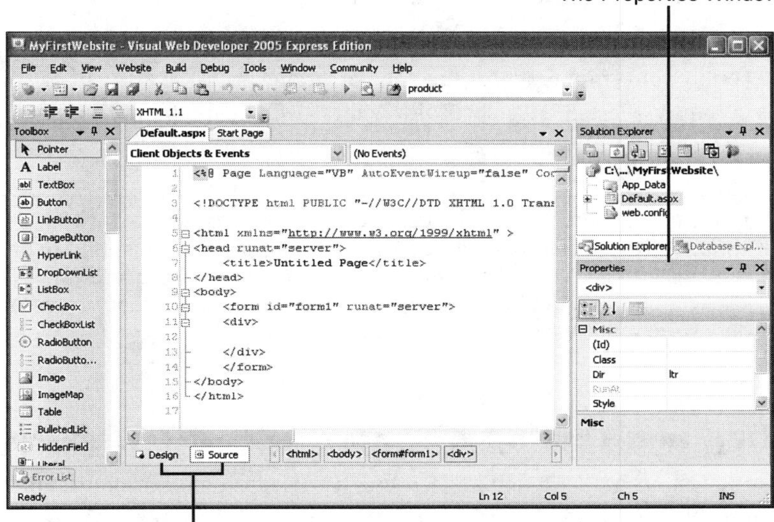

FIGURE 1.10 A new website has been created with an ASP.NET page, `Default.aspx`.

The `Default.aspx` page that was automatically created is opened, its contents being shown in the main window. Right now this ASP.NET page consists of just HTML. As we will see in future hours, in addition to HTML, ASP.NET pages can also contain Web controls and server-side source code. Typically, these portions of an ASP.NET page are broken up into two files: one that contains the HTML markup and Web control syntax, and another that contains just the source code. In fact, if you click on the plus icon in `Default.aspx` in the Solution Explorer, you'll see that there's another, nested file, `Default.aspx.vb`. This is the source code file for `Default.aspx`.

By the Way

> Don't worry if you're feeling a bit overwhelmed. The point of this hour is to give a cursory overview of Visual Web Developer. Over the next three hours, we'll look at the portions of an ASP.NET page and the steps involved in creating and testing ASP.NET pages in much greater detail.

When you're working with the HTML and Web controls in an ASP.NET web page, there are two views. The first view is the Source view, which shows the HTML page's underlying HTML markup and Web control syntax. The second view, called the Design view, provides a simpler alternative to specifying the page's content. Rather than having to manually enter the page's HTML by hand, as in the Source view, you can drag and drop HTML elements and Web controls from the Toolbox in the Design view. You can toggle between the Source and Design view for an ASP.NET page by using the Design and Source buttons at the bottom of the main window.

Beneath the Solution Explorer, you'll find the Properties window. This window displays the configurable properties for the page or whatever HTML element or Web control is currently selected. This particular window will be used quite often when we start creating ASP.NET web pages.

Did you Know?

> You can reposition the Properties, Toolbox, Solution Explorer, and Database Explorer windows by clicking on their title bar and dragging them elsewhere, or resize them by clicking on their borders. If you accidentally close one of these windows by clicking on the X in the title bar, you can add the window back by selecting the window from the View menu.

Creating and Testing a Simple ASP.NET Web Page

If we want to test an ASP.NET web page, a browser needs to make a request to the web server for the particular ASP.NET page. Let's test `Default.aspx`. Before we do, though, we need to add some content to the page, because right now the HTML markup will not display anything when viewed through a browser. From the Source view, place your cursor between the `<div>` and `</div>` tags of `Default.aspx` and add the following text:

```
<h1>Hello, World!</h1>
```

This will display the text `"Hello, World!"` in a large font. After entering this text, go to the Debug menu and choose the Start Without Debugging menu option. This will start the ASP.NET Development Web Server and launch your computer's default browser, directing it to `http://localhost:`*`portNumber`*`/MyFirstWebsite/Default.aspx` (see Figure 1.11). The *`portNumber`* portion in the URL will depend on the port selected by the ASP.NET Development Web Server.

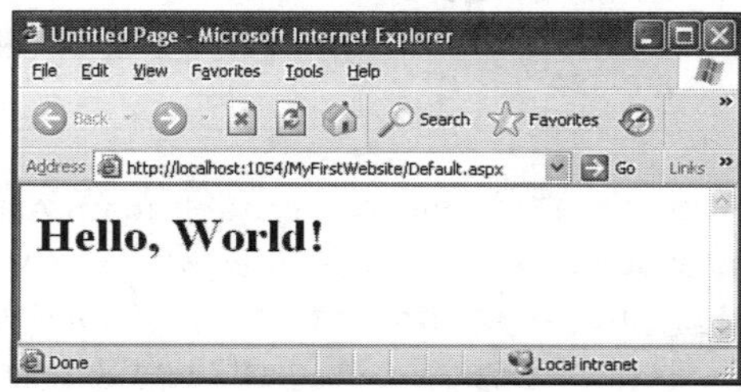

FIGURE 1.11
`Default.aspx`, when viewed through a browser.

This ASP.NET page isn't very interesting because its content is static in nature. It does, however, illustrate that to be able to view the contents of an ASP.NET page, you must start the ASP.NET Development Web Server and request the page through a browser. You can accomplish this automatically by going to the Debug menu and choosing Start Without Debugging.

By the Way

> You may be wondering what debugging is, and why I instructed you to start without it. We'll cover the differences between the Start Debugging and Start Without Debugging menu options in Hour 4.

Summary

Today virtually all websites contain dynamic web pages of one kind or another. Any site that allows a user to search the site's content, order products, or customize the site's content is dynamic in nature. There are a plethora of technologies for creating dynamic pages, one of the best ones being ASP.NET.

Throughout this book we'll be examining how to create interactive and interesting ASP.NET web pages. You'll be implementing the examples using Visual Web Developer, a free editor from Microsoft designed specifically for working on ASP.NET websites. In the "Installing the ASP.NET Engine, Editor, and Database System" section, we looked at how to install Visual Web Developer, along with the .NET Framework and SQL Server 2005, two additional components that will be needed for the book's examples. Finally, in the "A Brief Tour of Visual Web Developer" section, we poked around Visual Web Developer and created our first ASP.NET web page, testing it through a browser. In Hour 3 we'll explore the Visual Web Developer environment in much greater detail.

We have just begun our foray into the world of ASP.NET. Over the next 23 hours we'll explore the ins and outs of this exciting technology, culminating in the creation of a fully functional online photo album application.

Q&A

Q. ***What is the main difference between a static and a dynamic web page?***

A. A static web page has static content, whereas a dynamic web page's content is generated each time the page is requested. The dynamic content is typically generated from user input, database data, or some combination of the two.

For example, the official website for the National Basketball Association (www.NBA.com) lists the teams' schedules, the ongoing games' scores, players' statistics, and so on. The web pages simply display the content from some database that is updated after each game. A search engine site like Google displays dynamic content based on both its database of websites and the visitor's search term.

Q. ***You mentioned that with Visual Web Developer we'll be using the ASP.NET Development Web Server. Are there other web server systems available for serving ASP.NET pages?***

A. The ASP.NET Development Web Server is designed specifically for testing ASP.NET version 2.0 web pages locally. If you move your website to a web-hosting company, it uses different web server software. Most likely, it uses Microsoft's Internet Information Server (IIS), which is a professional-grade web server designed to work with Microsoft's dynamic web technologies—ASP and ASP.NET.

If you are running Windows 2000, Windows XP Professional, or Windows 2003, IIS may already be installed on your computer. If not, you can install it by going to Start, Settings, Control Panel, Add or Remove Programs, and clicking on the Add/Remove Windows Components option.

I encourage you not to install IIS and to instead use the ASP.NET Development Web Server unless you are familiar with IIS and know how to administer and secure it. The ASP.NET Development Web Server is more secure because it allows only incoming web requests from the local computer; IIS, on the other hand, is a full-blown web server and, unless properly patched and administered, can be an attack vector for malicious hackers.

Workshop

Quiz

1. What is the difference between a static web page and a dynamic web page?
2. What is the purpose of the ASP.NET engine?
3. True or False: ASP.NET web pages can be served from computers using the Windows ME operating system.
4. What software packages must be installed to serve ASP.NET web pages from a computer?
5. When should you consider using a web-hosting company to host your ASP.NET web pages?

Answers

1. The HTML markup for a static web page remains constant until a developer actually modifies the HTML markup in the web page. The HTML markup for a dynamic web page, on the other hand, is produced every time the web page is requested by a visitor to the site.

2. When the web server receives a request for an ASP.NET web page, it hands off the request to the ASP.NET engine, which then executes the requested ASP.NET page and returns its HTML markup to the web server. The ASP.NET engine allows for the HTML markup of an ASP.NET web page to be dynamically generated for each request.

3. False. ASP.NET pages can be served only from computers running Windows 2000, Windows XP, Windows Server 2003, or Windows Vista.

4. For a computer to serve ASP.NET web pages, the .NET Framework and a web server that supports ASP.NET must be installed.

5. You should consider using a web-hosting company if you want your ASP.NET website to be accessible via the Internet. Typically, it's best to develop the website locally and host it with a web-hosting company.

Exercises

This hour does not have any exercises. We'll start with exercises in future hours, after we become more fluent with creating ASP.NET web pages.

HOUR 2

Understanding the ASP.NET Programming Model

In this hour, we will cover

- A quick primer on HTML semantics and syntax, including a look at XHTML
- What content belongs in the HTML and source code portions of an ASP.NET web page
- Using Visual Web Developer to create new ASP.NET websites and web pages
- Adding Web controls to the HTML portion of an ASP.NET web page
- Specifying the functionality of an ASP.NET page through server-side source code
- Viewing an ASP.NET page through a web browser

Before we can start creating ASP.NET web pages, it is important that we have a solid understanding of the ASP.NET programming model. As we'll see in this hour, ASP.NET web pages are composed of two portions: a source code portion and an HTML portion. In this hour's first section, "Examining the HTML Markup Portion of an ASP.NET web page," we'll examine what belongs in the HTML portion of an ASP.NET web page. The source code portion of an ASP.NET page is discussed in the second section, "Examining the Source Code Portion of an ASP.NET Web Page."

In this hour, we'll also see Visual Web Developer in action a number of times. This practice will serve as a good introduction to the next hour, "Using Visual Web Developer," which takes a more detailed look at the editor we'll be using throughout this book.

Examining the HTML Markup Portion of an ASP.NET Web Page

As we discussed in the preceding hour, there are some fundamental differences between static web pages and dynamic web pages, the most profound one being that dynamic web pages contain a mix of HTML markup and server-side source code. Whenever a dynamic web page is requested, its source code is executed, generating HTML. This dynamically generated HTML is then sent back to the requesting client.

In this section, we are going to look at the HTML markup portion of a dynamic web page. In the next section, "Examining the Source Code Portion of an ASP.NET Web Page," we'll look at one of the more interesting parts of dynamic web pages—the source code.

Before we begin our examination of the HTML portion of an ASP.NET page, it is important to have an understanding of what HTML is, its syntactical rules, and how it is rendered in a web browser. This topic is tackled in the next section, "A Brief HTML Primer." If you are already well versed in HTML syntax, feel free to skip ahead to the "Creating the HTML Portion of an ASP.NET Web Page Using Visual Web Developer" section.

A Brief HTML Primer

HTML, as you may already know, specifies how data should be displayed in a web browser. For example, to have a web browser display a message in bold, you could use the following HTML:

```
<b>This will be in bold.</b>
```

HTML is composed of **elements** that specify how the data should be rendered in a web browser. An element is composed of a beginning tag and an optional ending tag, like

```
<elementName>... some content ...</elementName>
```

Here, `<elementName>` is referred to as the **start tag** and `</elementName>` is referred to as the **end tag**. The semantics of an HTML element apply formatting to the content between the start and end tags; the formatting applied depends on the element name. As we saw earlier, text is made bold by placing it between `<b>` and `</b>` tags. (The `<b>` element specifies that the content it contains be made bold.)

A plethora of HTML elements enable you to specify formatting in a web page. For more information on HTML and its myriad of elements, be sure to check out *Sams Teach Yourself XHTML and HTML in 24 Hours* (ISBN: 0672320762), or go online to http://www.w3schools.com/html/.

Not all HTML elements have a start and closing tag. For example, the `<br>` element, which specifies a line break, does not have a closing tag. Nor does the `<hr>` element, which displays a horizontal line. Similarly, you can use the paragraph element (`<p>`) without a closing tag like so:

```
This is one paragraph.
<p>
And this is another.
<p>
And yet another.
```

However, you can use starting and closing paragraph tags like so:

```
<p>This is one paragraph.</p>
<p>And this is another.</p>
<p>And yet another.</p>
```

Although the HTML syntax does not require that all elements have matching opening and closing tags, a stricter dialect of HTML, known as XHTML, does impose such requirements. The stricter XHTML syntax is easier and quicker for a browser to parse than the more flexible HTML syntax. For this and other reasons, many sites strive to make their content XHTML-compliant. In the upcoming section, "A Brief Look at XHTML," we'll talk more about XHTML's rules and its benefits.

Extraneous Whitespace

When a web browser renders HTML from a website, the whitespace in the markup—carriage returns, tabs, spaces, and so forth—do not affect the whitespace displayed in the browser. For example, consider the HTML shown in Listing 2.1, which contains several carriage returns, tabs, and extraneous spaces.

LISTING 2.1 A Snippet of HTML with Extraneous Whitespace

```
         <h1>Welcome to my Site!</h1>
<p>
<b>Welcome!</b>

You are                    now visiting my site!

<i>This is neat, I like
H
```

LISTING 2.1 Continued

```
 9: T
10: M
11: L
12: </i></p>
```

> **Watch Out!**
>
> The line numbers in Listing 2.1 are present simply to make it easier to refer to specific lines of markup in the listing. An HTML page would not contain these line numbers as part of its markup.

The HTML markup, when viewed through a browser, will compress the whitespace, as shown in Figure 2.1. Notice that any extra whitespace is reduced down to a single space. For example, each carriage return between the *H, T, M,* and *L* letters in the markup is rendered as a single space between each of the letters in the browser. On line 5, the multiple spaces and tabs between "You are" and "now visiting my site!" are compressed down into one space in Figure 2.1.

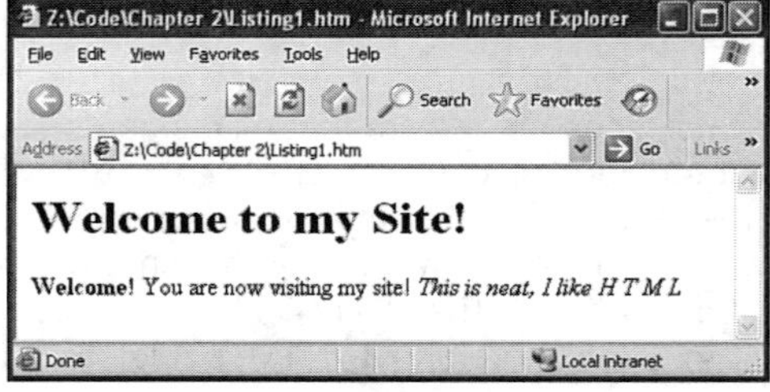

FIGURE 2.1 Extra white-space in the HTML is ignored by browsers.

Finally, note that some elements are rendered on a new line, whereas others follow after one another. For example, the content of the <h1> element appears on a separate line from the content of the <p> element. The <b> and <i> elements, however, have their content flow together on the same line.

HTML elements can be displayed in one of two ways: as *inline elements* or *block elements*. Inline elements do *not* introduce a carriage return after the closing tag, whereas block elements do. As you can probably guess from the rendered output in Figure 2.1, <h1> is a block element, while <b> and <i> are inline elements. (Although it might not be clear from the example, <p> is a block element.)

> **Did you Know?**
>
> You can find a complete list of inline and block HTML elements at http://www.htmlhelp.com/reference/html40/inline.html and http://www.htmlhelp.com/reference/html40/block.html, respectively.

With extraneous whitespace compressed by the browser, a natural question at this point is, "How do I position HTML elements?" That is, if no number of carriage returns or spaces affects the positioning of an HTML element, how do you create a web page where content appears to the right of other content or is indented?

HTML elements contain various **style attributes** that you can use to specify formatting information, such as padding, margins, positioning, and how the content flows relative to other content in the page. These topics are a bit beyond the scope of this book, but we will examine some techniques to position elements throughout this book. Additionally, Visual Web Developer can help in laying out elements, as we'll see next hour.

Nested Tags

HTML tags can be **nested**, meaning that one set of HTML tags can appear within another. For example, if you wanted to have a web page display a message in both italics and bold, you would use both the <i> and <b> tags like so:

```
<i><b>This is both italic and bold</b>, whereas this is just italic</i>
```

In this example, the <b> tag is said to be *inside* the <i> tag. (Throughout this book I will also refer to nested tags as one tag being *contained within* the other, or *enclosed within*.)

The semantics of nested tags are fairly straightforward. In our example, the <i> tag indicates that everything within it should be formatted using italics. Next, the <b> tag indicates that everything within it should be bold. Therefore, the text "This is both italic and bold" will be formatted using both bold and italics, while ", whereas this is just italic" will appear in italics.

There's no reason why the <b> tag must be inside the <i> tag and not the other way around. That is, you could also do

```
<b><i>This is both italic and bold</i>, whereas this is just bold</b>
```

The preceding two examples show how to use **properly nested tags**. Note that in our last example, the <i> tag that is contained within the <b> tag has both its starting and closing tag (<i> and </i>) before the closing <b> tag (</b>). An **improperly nested tag** is one whose start tag is contained within a tag, but its closing tag is not. The following HTML is an example of an improperly nested tag:

```
<i><b>This is both italic and bold</i>, but this is just bold</b>
```

Notice that the <b> tag's starting tag is contained within the <i> tag, but the <b> tag's closing tag is not. Therefore, the <b> tag is improperly nested.

Avoid using improperly nested tags because they make the HTML harder for humans to read. Also, as we will see later in this hour, various pieces of the HTML portion of ASP.NET web pages require that tags *not* be improperly nested.

Case Sensitivity

HTML tag names are *not case sensitive*; that is, the casing of the tag names is irrelevant. For example, a bold tag can be specified using `<b>` or `<B>`. The `<table>` tag can be specified using `<tAbLE>` or `<TABLE>`. Additionally, the case of the start and close tags need not match either. That is,

```
<b>This is bold.</B>
```

will have the same effect as

```
<B>This is bold.</B>
```

or

```
<B>This is bold.</b>
```

A Brief Look at XHTML

XHTML is a variant of HTML that has stricter syntax rules. Specifically, XHTML requires that its tags be properly nested tags and that all tags appear in lowercase. That is, to create an HTML table using the XHTML dialect, you must use `<table>`, not `<TABLE>` or any other casing variation.

Additionally, XHTML documents require that all tags have a matching close tag. That means to use the paragraph tag, you can't simply use `<p>`, but instead must use `<p>...</p>`. For tags that don't have a closing tag, such as `<br>` and `<hr>`, XHTML requires that you use the following variation:

```
<br />
```

and

```
<hr />
```

The `/>` is a shorthand notation to specify that there is no content between the starting and closing tags. Using `<`*`tagName`*` />` is synonymous to using `<`*`tagName`*`></`*`tagName`*`>`.

Finally, XHTML compliance requires that elements have **quoted attributes**. An **attribute** is a name and value pair that can optionally be placed within the opening tag, like so:

```
<p id="instructions" style="color:red;">blah blah blah</p>
```

Here, the <p> tag has two attributes: `id`, with a value of `instructions`, and `style`, with a value of `color:red;`. Note that the values of these two attributes are delimited by quotation marks ("). All elements with attributes must have quoted values in order for the document to be XHTML compliant.

By the Way

XML, which stands for **eXtensible Markup Language**, is a language that uses elements for describing data. XML has strict formatting criteria that XHTML adopts, such as case sensitivity, properly nested tags, and the requirement that all tags have closing tags. For more information on XML and XHTML, be sure to pick up a copy of *Sams Teach Yourself XML in 24 Hours* (ISBN: 0672322137) and *Sams Teach Yourself XHTML and HTML in 24 Hours* (ISBN: 0672320762).

Having a thorough understanding of XHTML is not vital when creating ASP.NET web pages. However, it is important to be familiar with the concepts for a couple of reasons. First, Visual Web Developer provides an easy way to validate your page's markup against various rules, including XHTML compliance, which we'll examine in the next hour. Second, ASP.NET's Web controls, which we'll be looking at in this hour, are denoted using XHTML in the HTML portion of the ASP.NET page. Additionally, when an ASP.NET page is requested by a browser, these Web controls are converted into XHTML, and it's that markup that's sent to the browser.

Creating the HTML Portion of an ASP.NET Web Page Using Visual Web Developer

The HTML portion of an ASP.NET web page is composed of both static HTML and **Web controls**. Web controls are programmatically-accessible chunks of HTML, enabling developers to modify the HTML sent to the browser based on programmatic logic. Web controls also provide a means by which user input can be collected. They serve as the bridge between the HTML and source code portions of an ASP.NET page. We'll examine adding and working with Web controls in more detail later in this hour; starting with Hour 8, "ASP.NET Web Controls for Displaying Text," we'll spend significant time examining the plethora of Web controls available at our disposal.

Visual Web Developer provides two means by which HTML content and Web controls can be added to an ASP.NET web page:

1. By typing in the HTML and Web control content by hand
2. By dragging and dropping HTML elements and Web controls onto the ASP.NET page using Visual Web Developer's **WYSIWYG designer**

By the Way

WYSIWYG stands for **What You See Is What You Get**. Visual Web Developer hastens web design by allowing designers to simply drag and drop HTML elements onto the web page. Similar WYSIWYG editors can be found in other editors like Microsoft FrontPage and Macromedia's DreamWeaver.

In my experience, I've found most developers already familiar with HTML prefer typing in the HTML and Web control syntax by hand, rather than using the WYSIWYG capabilities. Those coming from a background that did not include HTML exposure, however, usually find using the WYSIWYG designer to be a more intuitive and cost-effective approach. Regardless of your past experiences, I encourage you to try both techniques and settle on the one that you are most productive with.

To illustrate adding content to the HTML portion of an ASP.NET page, let's create a simple ASP.NET website with a single web page. To follow along, start Visual Web Developer by choosing Start, Programs, Microsoft Visual Web Developer 2005 Express Edition. Create a new website by going to the File menu and choosing New Web Site. This will display the New Web Site dialog box, shown in Figure 2.2. Create a new website by choosing the ASP.NET Web Site template with the Location drop-down list set to File System and the Language drop-down list set to Visual Basic. Finally, specify the folder to place the website files in the text box to the right of the Location drop-down list. (For this example I will be placing the website a folder named `Chapter2` on my Desktop.)

By the Way

The Location drop-down list indicates where the website will be saved. The examples in this book use the File System option, although other options are available. All of the examples that we'll be examining in this book will use Visual Basic as the server-side programming language. Therefore, when creating new websites to follow along with examples from this book, leave the Language option as the default (Visual Basic).

Next hour, "Using Visual Web Developer," we'll examine the New Web Site dialog box in much greater detail.

After you make the appropriate settings in the New Web Site dialog box and click the OK button, Visual Web Developer will create the following folders and files in the directory you specified:

- `App_Data`—This folder, which is initially empty, will contain any data-related files. We'll begin our look at creating data-driven ASP.NET applications in Hour 13, "An Introduction to Databases."
- `Default.aspx`—This file contains the HTML portion of the ASP.NET page.

- `Default.aspx.vb`—This file contains the source code portion of the ASP.NET page.
- `Web.config`—This XML-formatted file contains configuration information for the website.

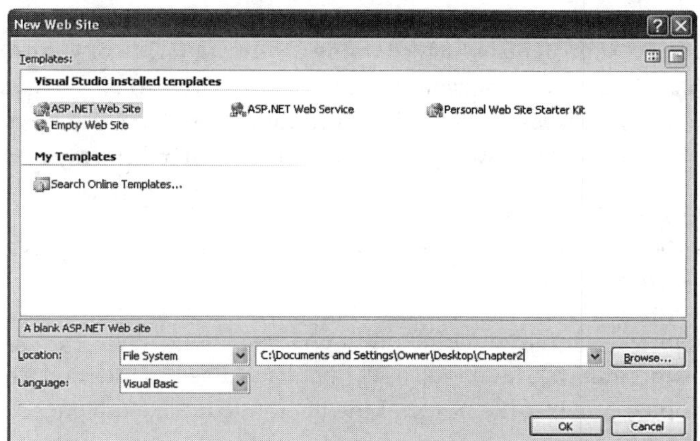

FIGURE 2.2
Choose to create a blank ASP.NET website.

Figure 2.3 shows Visual Web Developer after creating the new website. The Solution Explorer, shown in the upper-right corner, lists the files in the project. In the main window, Visual Web Developer has opened up the file `Default.aspx`, showing its HTML markup.

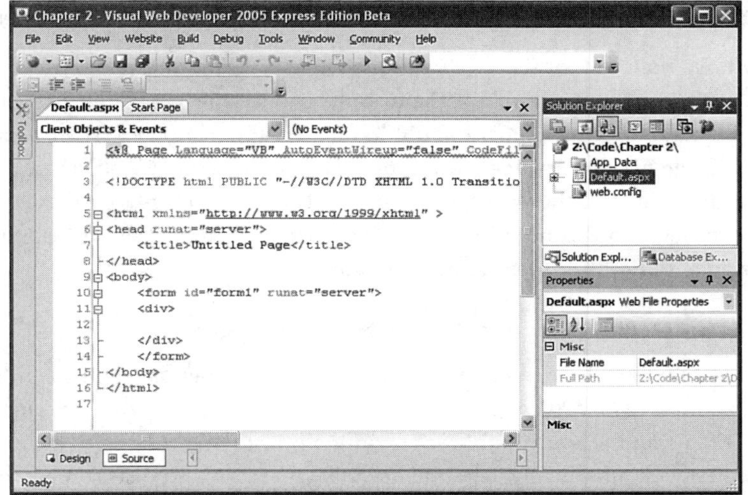

FIGURE 2.3
Congratulations! You have created your first ASP.NET website.

In the bottom-left corner you'll find two tabs: Design and Source. The Design tab displays the **designer**, which is the WYSIWYG editor. Using the designer, you can simply type in the content you want to appear on your ASP.NET page. If you want to add HTML elements or Web controls to the page, you just select them from the Toolbox on the left and drag them onto the designer. We'll see how to do this shortly.

The next tab is the Source tab, which contains the actual HTML of your ASP.NET web page. This tab is selected by default, as you can see the HTML content for `Default.aspx` on your screen. Notice that even though we have yet to add any HTML content to our ASP.NET web page, some HTML content already exists.

At the top of the page is the `@Page` directive:

```
<%@ Page Language="VB" AutoEventWireup="false" CodeFile="Default.aspx.vb"
➥Inherits="_Default" %>
```

This directive provides information about the ASP.NET page. The `Language` attribute indicates the programming language of the page's source code portion; the `CodeFile` attribute provides the name of the file that contains the page's source code. When we look at an end-to-end example later in this hour, you'll find that not all content in an ASP.NET page is sent to the requesting browser. The `@Page` directive is one such fragment; its contents provide information to the ASP.NET engine on the web server, and therefore it is not rendered to the client.

After the `@Page` directive, you'll find the default HTML content Visual Web Developer adds when creating a new ASP.NET page. This includes an `<html>` element, which has nested within it `<head>` and `<body>` elements. Inside the `<body>` element is a `<form>` element, and inside the `<form>` element is a `<div>` element.

You may have noticed that the `<form>` tag in Figure 2.3 contains a `runat="server"` attribute. This is not a standard HTML attribute. In fact, the `<form>` element in Figure 2.3 is not an HTML element at all! In an ASP.NET web page, HTML elements that contain the `runat="server"` attribute are a special form of Web control. We'll be discussing what, exactly, Web controls are and what is their place in an ASP.NET web page throughout this hour. Hour 9, "Web Form Basics," looks at this special `<form>` element and its purpose in greater detail.

Editing the HTML Content Using the Designer

To edit the ASP.NET web page's HTML content, you can either use the Design tab, which provides a WYSIWYG experience, or you can add content while viewing the page's HTML using the Source tab. Let's examine how to add content to our page using the designer. Specifically, let's add an HTML `<table>` that lists some popular Internet websites—Yahoo!, Google, MSN, and Lycos—along with their logos.

By the Way

The HTML <table> element creates a grid-like display, consisting of a set of rows and columns. The <table> element is commonly used to lay out the contents of a web page, although other techniques are available. For more information on laying out HTML content, including a look at using <table>, check out http://www.w3schools.com/html/html_layout.asp.

Start by switching to the Design tab. The first thing to add is an HTML <table>. Go to the Layout menu and select Insert Table. Choosing this option will show the dialog box in Figure 2.4. Here, you can either choose a standard template or create a custom table by entering the number of columns and rows you want to display, as well as the table's overall width and height. 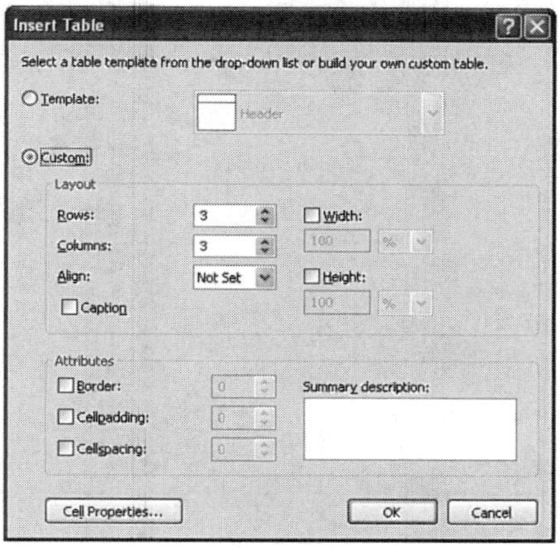

FIGURE 2.4 When inserting an HTML table, you can specify the number of rows and columns as well as the table's width and height.

Choose a table with two columns and four rows and an overall width and height of 300 pixels by 500 pixels. In the first column we will display the name of the website, and in the second column we will display the website logo.

To add the website names, simply click inside the first column of each row and type in the website's name. Figure 2.5 shows the table after the names have been added.

Notice that the name of each website is displayed left-justified in a fairly plain-looking font. Let's spruce things up a bit by centering the name of each website and displaying each name in a bold, Arial font.

To accomplish this, simply select the text of a particular website. Once it is selected, you can make the text bold by going to the Format menu's Font submenu and selecting Bold. Next, to center the text that is still highlighted, go to the Format menu's Justify submenu and select Center. Finally, to make the font of the still-selected text Arial, simply click on the list of fonts that is positioned beneath the

Cut, Copy, and Paste icons near the top-left corner. (The Cut, Copy, and Paste icons are the scissors, paper, and clipboard icons found directly beneath the View, Format, and Layout menu headers.)

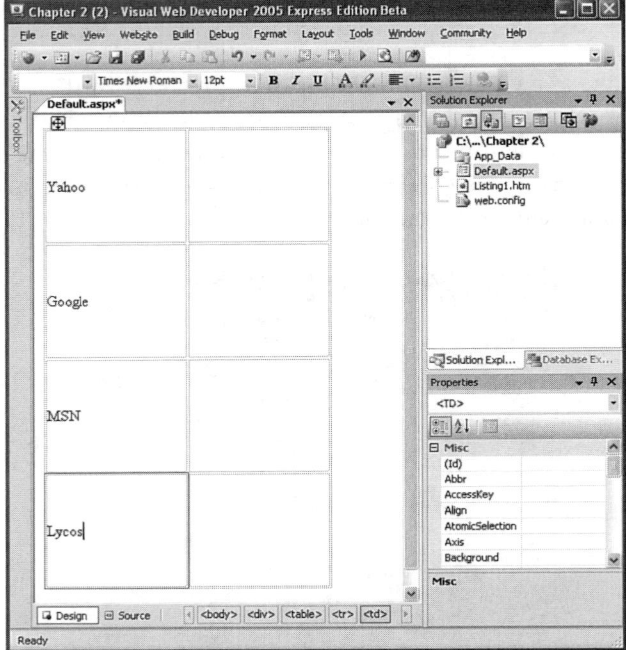

FIGURE 2.5
The first column contains the names of four websites.

Figure 2.6 shows Visual Web Developer after this formatting has been applied to all four website names.

Did you Know?

> In addition to setting the Bold and Center options through the Format menu, you can also make selected text bold by clicking the Bold icon in the toolbar or by pressing Ctrl+B. To center the selected text, you can click the Cent er toolbar icon.

Now, let's add the logos for each of the websites in the second column.

The **Toolbox** contains HTML elements and Web controls that can be dragged onto the WYSIWYG designer. By default, the Toolbox is shown on the left side of Visual Web Developer; if you do not see the Toolbox on your screen, you can display it by going to the View menu and selecting the Toolbox menu item.

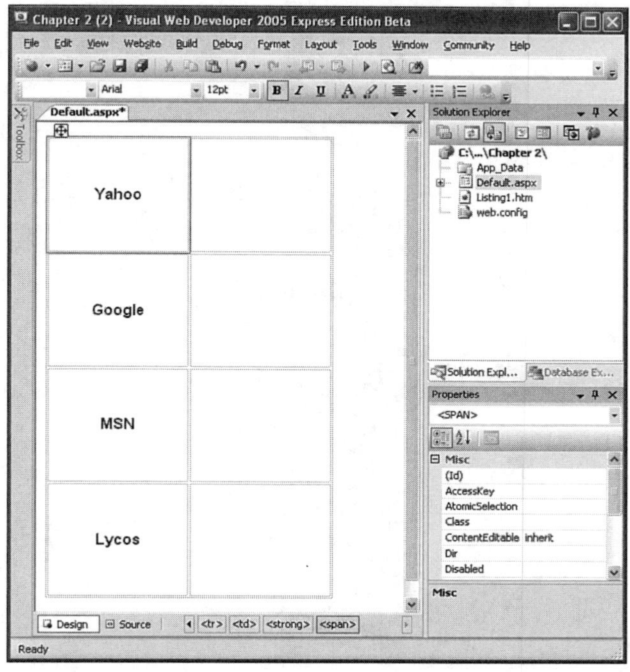

FIGURE 2.6
The website names have been centered, bolded, and changed to Arial font.

There are eight tabs in the Toolbox:

- Standard
- Data
- Validation
- Navigation
- Login
- WebParts
- HTML
- General

Each tab contains a number of elements underneath it. By default, the Standard tab will be expanded, which includes items such as Label, TextBox, Button, LinkButton, and so on. The Toolbox with the Standard tab expanded is shown in Figure 2.7.

The Toolbox contains both Web controls and standard, static HTML elements. The HTML elements can be found in the Toolbox's HTML tab; all other tabs contain Web controls. At this point in our discussion, we've yet to explore the differences between Web controls and static HTML elements. When we finish examining the HTML portion and then turn to the source code portion of an ASP.NET page, the differences will become clearer. For now, just understand that unless you are adding items from the HTML tab onto the designer, you are adding Web controls to the page, and not HTML elements.

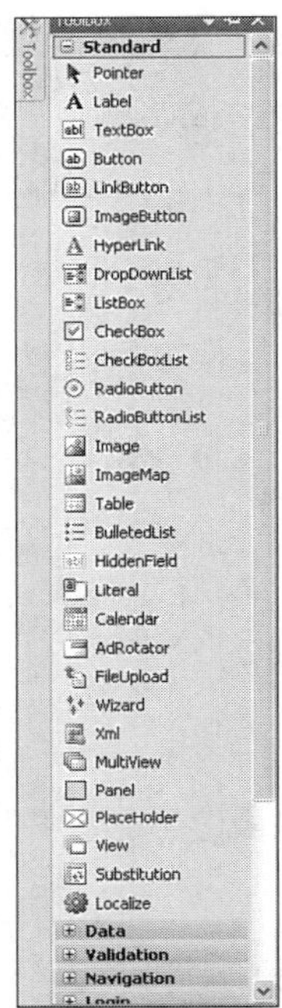

FIGURE 2.7 The Toolbox contains elements that can be dragged and dropped into the designer.

To add one of the items in the Toolbox to your ASP.NET web page, simply click on the item you want to add and, holding down the mouse button, move the mouse pointer over the location you want the item to be placed and then release the mouse button.

As you can see from Figure 2.7, one of the items in the Standard tab is an Image Web control. We'll use this Web control to add the website logos in the second column of the `<table>`. Start by dragging and dropping four Image Web controls into the designer, one in each of the second columns of each of the four rows.

Figure 2.8 shows what you should see after the four Image Web controls have been added to the designer.

Note that each Image Web control currently is displayed as a red X. The reason is that we have yet to specify the URL of the image. The Image Web control has an `ImageUrl` property that specifies the URL of the image. Before we can assign the `ImageUrl` property, though, we first need to have the appropriate image files present for our website. Go to each of the search engine's home pages, locate its logo, and save that logo to the same folder where you created your website. (To save an image in your browser, right-click the image and choose Save As.)

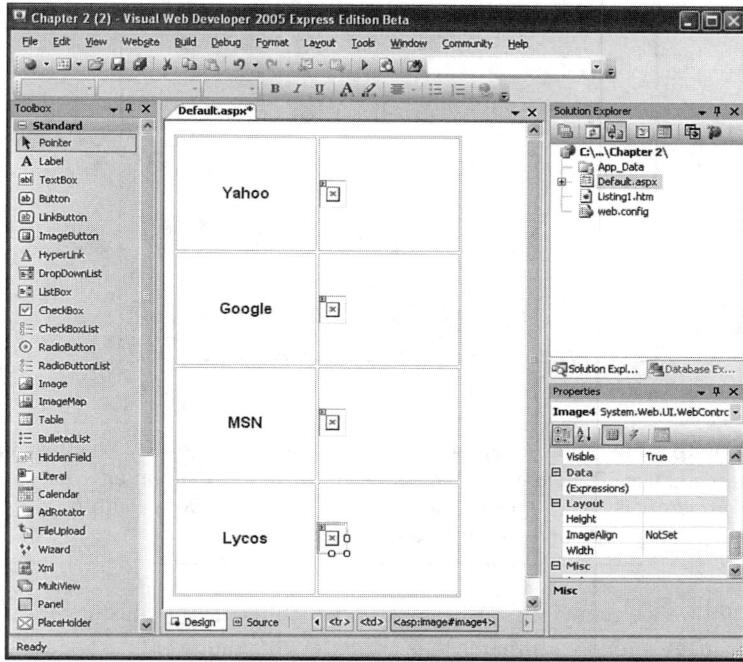

FIGURE 2.8
An Image Web control has been added to each row in the table.

Once you have downloaded the four logos to your computer, you can now edit the `ImageUrl` properties of the Image Web controls. The properties of a Web control can be viewed and altered through the Properties window, which resides, by default, in the lower-right corner. If you do not see the Properties window, go to the View menu and choose Properties Window.

To specify an Image Web control's `ImageUrl` property, click on the Image Web control in the Design view, which will load the control's properties in the Properties window. By default, the `ImageUrl` property's value is a blank string, meaning that no value for the `ImageUrl` property has been specified. You can either type in a value or click the ellipses to select a file.

Because we already have the image files in our website's root directory, click on the ellipses. This will display the Select Image dialog box, shown in Figure 2.9. From here, you can choose which image to display in the Image Web control. For each of the four Image Web controls on your page, select the appropriate logo.

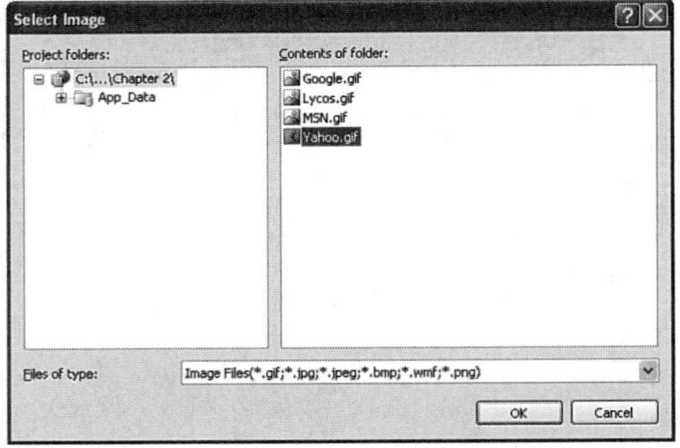

FIGURE 2.9 Choose the image to display in the Image Web control.

Did you Know?

After you have added the four images, you may notice that the images are taller or wider than you like. To adjust an image's height or width, you can alter its `Width` and `Height` properties. To specify that an image should have a width of, say, 100 pixels, simply set its `Width` property to a value of `100px`.

At this point we've created the HTML content, which includes both static HTML, such as `<table>`, along with Image Web controls. Note that we did not have to write a single line of HTML; rather, we simply chose various menu options, dragged and dropped Web controls from the Toolbox, and set properties via the Properties window.

To test your ASP.NET web page, go to the Debug menu and choose Start Without Debugging. Alternatively, you can press Ctrl+F5. This will compile your ASP.NET pages' source code portions and launch a web browser, taking you to the website's startup page. The project's startup page is the page the browser automatically navigates to when you begin debugging. When you create a new website, `Default.aspx` is made the startup page. You can indicate which ASP.NET page should be the startup page by right-clicking on that page in the Solution Explorer and choosing Set as Startup Page.

By the Way

Visual Web Developer provides you with two options to test your ASP.NET pages through a browser, both through the Debug menu: Start Debugging and Start Without Debugging. Both options compile your ASP.NET pages' source code portions and automatically launch a browser, taking you to the specified start page, but the Start Debugging option also has the effect of running the debugger. The debugger is useful if you are troubleshooting the source code portion of an ASP.NET page. If you just want to view an ASP.NET page, though, and are not diagnosing any programmatic problems, you can start without debugging. We'll talk about working with the debugger in future hours.

> Personally, I choose Start Without Debugging if I don't need to use the services of the debugger. It's a snappier experience since Visual Web Developer doesn't need to load the debugger. However, there's nothing wrong if you always want to start with debugging. If you do attempt to use Start Debugging, your configuration file (`Web.config`) will need to be updated to indicate that the website is in debug mode. If this update is needed, Visual Web Developer will inform you of this change and offer to make it on your behalf.

Figure 2.10 shows the ASP.NET web page when viewed through a web browser. Note that what the user visiting the page sees is what we saw in the designer; this is why the designer is referred to as a What You See Is What You Get (WYSIWYG) editor.

FIGURE 2.10 The ASP.NET web page when viewed through a browser.

Examining the HTML Content

Some Web designers feel more comfortable creating a web page by being able to view the page's HTML rather than using a WYSIWYG editor. Although entering the HTML through the Source view is usually not as easy or efficient as using the designer, entering the HTML through the Source view allows for finer control over markup, as well as its positioning and indentation.

To appreciate the time the designer saves, take a moment to switch from the Design tab to the Source tab. This lengthy markup is shown in Listing 2.2.

LISTING 2.2 The Markup Generated by the Designer

```
<%@ Page Language="VB" AutoEventWireup="false" CodeFile="Default.aspx.vb"
➥Inherits="_Default" %>

<!DOCTYPE html PUBLIC "-//W3C//DTD XHTML 1.0 Transitional//EN"
➥ "http://www.w3.org/TR/xhtml1/DTD/xhtml1-transitional.dtd">

<html xmlns="http://www.w3.org/1999/xhtml" >
<head runat="server">
    <title>Untitled Page</title>
</head>
<body>
    <form id="form1" runat="server">
    <div>
        <table style="width: 300px; height: 500px">
            <tr>
                <td style="width: 100px; text-align: center">
                    <strong><span style="font-family: Arial">Yahoo</span>
➥</strong></td>
                <td style="width: 100px">
                    <asp:Image ID="Image1" runat="server"
➥ImageUrl="~/Yahoo.gif" /></td>
            </tr>
            <tr>
                <td style="width: 100px; text-align: center">
                    <strong><span style="font-family: Arial">Google</span>
➥</strong></td>
                <td style="width: 100px">
                    <asp:Image ID="Image2" runat="server"
➥ImageUrl="~/Google.gif" Width="133px" /></td>
            </tr>
            <tr>
                <td style="width: 100px; text-align: center">
                    <strong><span style="font-family: Arial">MSN</span>
➥</strong></td>
                <td style="width: 100px">
                    <asp:Image ID="Image3" runat="server"
➥ImageUrl="~/MSN.gif" /></td>
            </tr>
            <tr>
                <td style="width: 100px; text-align: center">
                    <strong><span style="font-family: Arial">Lycos</span>
➥</strong></td>
                <td style="width: 100px">
                    <asp:Image ID="Image4" runat="server"
➥ImageUrl="~/Lycos.gif" /></td>
            </tr>
        </table>

    </div>
    </form>
</body>
</html>
```

First, appreciate the bulk of HTML that the designer automatically adds. It added the various <table>-related elements along with the style information (the bold, centered, Arial text). Without doubt, the designer knocked off several minutes of time it would have taken us to type this out by hand.

By the Way

> You can drag and drop elements from the Toolbox onto the Source view, and the Web control or HTML element will be automatically injected.

Next, study the syntax for the four Image Web controls (lines 17, 23, 29, and 35). The Google Image Web control (line 23) has the following markup:

```
<asp:Image ID="Image2" runat="server" ImageUrl="~/Google.gif" Width="133px" />
```

The Web controls have an HTML-like syntax: They are represented by opening and closing tags; the opening tag can optionally contain attributes; and, although not shown in the Image Web control example, Web controls may contain content within their starting and closing tags.

While there are a bevy of valid HTML elements, `asp:Image` is not one of them. In fact, none of the ASP.NET Web controls (all of whose tags have the notation `asp:`*`WebControlName`*) are valid HTML elements. This does not pose a problem, however, because the Web control syntax shown in our ASP.NET page in Visual Web Developer is *not* the markup that gets sent down to the browser that requested the ASP.NET page. Instead, the Web controls are *rendered* into valid XHTML-compliant markup. Rather than the browser receiving an `<asp:Image>` element, the Image Web control is rendered into an `<img>` element, which is a valid HTML element.

To see this in action, return to viewing `Default.aspx` through a browser. Then, from your browser, view the HTML source received. (For Internet Explorer, go to the View menu and choose Source.) This will open up Notepad with the contents of the HTML sent to your browser. Listing 2.3 shows the rendered HTML that was sent to my browser (Internet Explorer 6.0) when visiting `Default.aspx`.

LISTING 2.3 The HTML Received by the Browser When Visiting `Default.aspx`

```
<!DOCTYPE html PUBLIC "-//W3C//DTD XHTML 1.0 Transitional//EN"
➥ "http://www.w3.org/TR/xhtml1/DTD/xhtml1-transitional.dtd">

<html xmlns="http://www.w3.org/1999/xhtml" >
<head><title>
    Untitled Page
</title></head>
<body>
    <form name="form1" method="post" action="Default.aspx" id="form1">
<div>
```

LISTING 2.3 Continued

```
<input type="hidden" name="__VIEWSTATE" id="__VIEWSTATE"
➥value="/wEPDwUJODM3MDQ0NzEzZGQO7I8sK4vUD1hpvvsg1JT9Ms6ECg==" />
</div>
    <div>
        <table style="width: 300px; height: 500px">
            <tr>
                <td style="width: 100px; text-align: center">
                    <strong><span style="font-family: Arial">Yahoo</span>
➥</strong></td>
                <td style="width: 100px">
                    <img id="Image1" src="Yahoo.gif"
➥style="border-width:0px;" /></td>
            </tr>
            <tr>
                <td style="width: 100px; text-align: center">
                    <strong><span style="font-family:
Arial">Google</span>➥</strong></td>
                <td style="width: 100px">
                    <img id="Image2" src="Google.gif"
➥style="width:133px;border-width:0px;" /></td>
            </tr>
            <tr>
                <td style="width: 100px; text-align: center">
                    <strong><span style="font-family: Arial">MSN</span>
➥</strong></td>
                <td style="width: 100px">
                    <img id="Image3" src="MSN.gif"
➥style="border-width:0px;" /></td>
            </tr>
            <tr>
                <td style="width: 100px; text-align: center">
                    <strong><span style="font-family: Arial">Lycos</span>
➥</strong></td>
                <td style="width: 100px">
                    <img id="Image4" src="Lycos.gif"
➥style="border-width:0px;" /></td>
            </tr>
        </table>

    </div>
    </form>
</body>
</html>
```

While the markup in Listings 2.2 and 2.3 look nearly identical, there are some subtle and important differences. Starting from the top, the `@Page` directive on line 1 in Listing 2.2 is *not* in the rendered HTML output shown in Listing 2.3. Next, notice how the `<form runat="server">` on line 10 in Listing 2.2 has been transformed into

```
<form name="form1" method="post" action="Default.aspx" id="form1">
```

There's also a hidden form field that's been added to Listing 2.3 (on line 10):

```
<input type="hidden" name="__VIEWSTATE" id="__VIEWSTATE"
➥value="/wEPDwUJODM3MDQ0NzEzZGQO7I8sK4vUD1hpvvsg1JT9Ms6ECg==" />
```

We won't be discussing these transformations in this hour; instead, this topic is left for Hour 9, "Web Form Basics."

Lastly, note that the Image Web control syntax from Listing 2.2 has been replaced by standard `<img>` HTML elements in Listing 2.3, with the `ImageUrl` property transformed into the `src` attribute.

These changes highlight an important concept with ASP.NET pages: The markup present on the web server is not necessarily the markup that is sent to the requesting browser. When an ASP.NET page is requested, the ASP.NET engine handles the request, which involves making these changes as needed. Also, as we'll see shortly, the rendering process involves the execution of any server-side code that we've written for the page. This server-side rendering process, which occurs when any ASP.NET page is requested, is what makes ASP.NET a dynamic web technology. The resulting HTML sent down to the browser can be programmatically altered based on various criteria, such as database data, user input, and other external inputs.

Examining the Source Code Portion of an ASP.NET Web Page

Now that we've examined the HTML portion of an ASP.NET web page, let's turn our attention to the source code portion. While the HTML portion defines the layout of the ASP.NET page along with its static content, it's the source code portion where the content for the dynamic portions of the page is decided.

The source code portion for ASP.NET pages can appear in one of two locations:

- **In a separate file**—The ASP.NET page is composed of two separate files, *`PageName`*`.aspx` and *`PageName`*`.aspx.vb`. The *`PageName`*`.aspx` file contains the HTML and Web control syntax, while the *`PageName`*`.aspx.vb` file contains the source code. This is how our current sample web page is structured, with `Default.aspx` and `Default.aspx.vb`.
- **In a `<script>` block in the same file**—The HTML and source code portions can reside in the same, single file. In this scenario, the source code portion is placed within a *server-side `<script>` block*.

The examples in this book use the separate file technique, although either option is acceptable. Many developers prefer the separate file approach because it provides a cleaner separation between the HTML and source code portions. Furthermore, in the previous version of ASP.NET, there were several other advantages to using a separate file over the server-side `<script>` block.

If you find yourself working in a large ASP.NET project, you'll more than likely be using the separate file approach. Hence, we'll stick with this technique for the examples in this book.

By the Way

> ASP.NET web pages can have their source code portion written in one of two programming languages: Visual Basic or Visual C#. In this book all of our code examples will use Visual Basic.
>
> For more information on Visual Basic, consult Hours 5 through 7.

You can view the source code portion of an ASP.NET page that uses the separate file technique through any one of the following actions:

- Right-click on the ASP.NET page in the Solution Explorer and choose View Code.
- Click on the plus icon in the Solution Explorer for the ASP.NET page whose source code you want to edit. This will list its corresponding source code file, *PageName*`.aspx.vb`. Double-click on this source code file to display its contents.
- In the Source or Design view of an ASP.NET page, right-click and choose View Code.

Take a moment to view the source code portion for `Default.aspx`. You should find the following content in `Default.aspx.vb`:

```
Partial Class _Default
    Inherits System.Web.UI.Page

End Class
```

These three lines are the bare minimum code that must exist in an ASP.NET page's source code portion. Specifically, it's defining a *class* called `Default` that extends the `System.Web.UI.Page` class. Classes are a central construct of object-oriented programming, which is the programming paradigm used by ASP.NET. The next few sections provide an overview of object-oriented and event-driven programming; if you are already familiar with these concepts, feel free to skip ahead to the "Event Handlers in ASP.NET" section.

By the Way

It is vitally important to remember that the ASP.NET page's source code portion is *server-side* code. As we discussed in Hour 1, "Getting Started with ASP.NET 2.0," when an ASP.NET page is requested, the ASP.NET engine executes the source code and returns the resulting HTML to the requesting browser. Therefore, none of the ASP.NET page's source code is sent to the browser, just the resulting markup.

A Quick Object-Oriented Programming Primer

The source code portion of an ASP.NET web page uses a particular programming model known as **object-oriented programming**. Object-oriented programming is a programming paradigm that generalizes programming in terms of **objects**. A key construct of any object-oriented programming language is the **class**, which is used to abstractly define an object. Classes contain **properties**, which describe the state of the object; **methods**, which provide the actions that can be performed on the object; and **events**, which are actions triggered by the object. Objects are instances of classes, representing a concrete instance of an abstraction.

Whew! This all likely sounds very confusing, but a real-world analogy should help. Think, for a moment, about a car. What things describe a car? What actions can a car perform? What events transpire during the operation of a car?

A car can have various properties, like its make, model, year, and color. A car also has a number of actions it can perform, such as drive, reverse, turn, and park. While you're driving a car, various events occur, such as stepping on the brakes and turning on the windshield wipers.

By the Way

In object-oriented terms, an object's actions are referred to as its **methods**.

This assimilation of properties, actions, (hereby referred to as methods), and events abstractly defines what a car can do. The reason this assimilation of properties and methods is an abstraction is that it does not define a specific car; rather, it describes features common to *all* cars. This collection of properties, methods, and events describing an abstract car is a class in object-oriented terms.

An object is a specific instance of a class. In our analogy, an object would be a specific instance of the car abstraction, such as a year 2000, forest green, Honda Accord. The methods of the car abstraction can then be applied to the object. For example, to drive this Honda to the store, I'd use the Drive method, applying the Turn method as needed. When I reached the store, I'd use the Park method. After making my purchases, I'd need to back out of the parking spot, so I'd use the Reverse method, and then the Drive and Turn methods to get back home. During the operation of the car object, various events might occur: When I'm driving to the store, the "Turning the steering wheel" event will more than likely transpire, as will the "Stepping on the brakes" event.

Examining Event-Driven Programming

Another important construct of the programming languages used to create ASP.NET web pages is the **event handler**. An event, as we just saw, is some action that occurs during the use of an object. An event handler is a piece of code that is executed when its corresponding event occurs. Programming languages that include support for handling events are called **event-driven**.

When an event occurs, it commonly is said that the event has **fired** or been **raised**. Furthermore, an event handler, when run, is referred to as having been **executed**. Therefore, when an event fires (or is raised), its event handler executes.

For events to be useful, they need to be paired with an event handler. An event handler is a block of source code that is executed when the event it is specified to handle fires. The event handler for the car's Starting event, for example, might contain code that instructs the starter to start turning the crankshaft. When the stepping on the brakes event fires, code might execute that applied the brake pads to the brake drums.

You can think of ASP.NET web pages as event-driven programs. The source code portion of the ASP.NET web page is made up of event handlers. Furthermore, a number of potential events can fire during the rendering of an ASP.NET page.

Out-of-Order Execution

In ASP or PHP, two other dynamic web page technologies, the source code portion of a web page is executed serially, from top to bottom. That is, if the source code section contains five lines of code, the first line of code is executed first, followed by the second, then the third, the fourth, and finally the fifth. This programming paradigm, in which one line of code is executed after another, is known as **sequential execution**. With sequential execution, the code is executed from the first line of code to the last. With sequential execution, you know that code on line 5 will execute before code on line 10.

With event-driven programming, however, there are no such guarantees. The only serial portions of code in an event-driven program are those lines of code within a particular event handler. Often you can't make any assumptions on the order that the events will fire, and therefore you can't be certain the order with which the corresponding event handlers will be called. Furthermore, often you can't assume that a particular event will fire at all.

Looking back at our car analogy, imagine that our car has the following events:

- Starting
- Stopping
- Applying brakes
- Starting windshield wipers

During a car's use—driving from home to the store, let's say—some events will definitely fire, such as the Starting and Stopping events. However others, such as "Starting windshield wipers," might not fire at all. Furthermore, while we can assume that the Starting event will be the first event to fire and Stopping the last, we can't say with any certainty whether or not the "Applying brakes" event will come before or after the "Starting windshield wipers" event.

When creating an ASP.NET page, you may optionally create event handlers for the plethora of events that may transpire during the ASP.NET page's life cycle. When an event fires, its corresponding event handler—if defined—executes. Returning to the car analogy, we may want to have event handlers for just the Starting and Stopping events. The code in the event handlers would be executed when the corresponding events fired. For example, imagine that our Starting event has an event handler that had the following two lines of code:

```
Begin Starting Event Handler
  Send signal to starter to start turning the crankshaft
  Send signal to fuel injector to send fuel to the engine
End Starting Event Handler
```

When the Starting event fires, the Starting event handler is executed. The first line of code in this event handler will fire first, followed by the second. Our complete source code for the car may consist of two event handlers, one for Starting and one for Stopping.

```
Begin Starting Event Handler
  Send signal to starter to start turning the crankshaft
  Send signal to fuel injector to send fuel to the engine
End Starting Event Handler

Begin Stopping Event Handler
  Send signal to brake drums
  Decrease fuel injector's output
End Stopping Event Handler
```

Even though the Starting event handler appears before the Stopping event handler in the source code, this does not imply that the Starting event handler will execute prior to the Stopping event handler. Because the event handlers are executed only when their corresponding event fires, the order of execution of these event handlers is directly dependent on the order of the events that are fired.

The important point to keep in mind is that the order of the event handlers in the source code has no bearing on the order of execution of the event handlers.

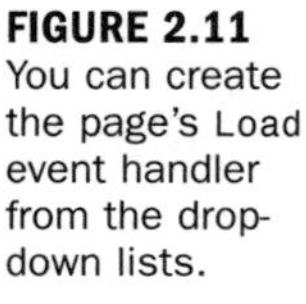

The code used to describe the Starting and Stopping events is not actual Visual Basic code, but is instead **pseudocode**. Pseudocode is not code recognized by any particular programming language, but instead is a made-up, verbose, English-like language commonly used when describing programming concepts.

Event Handlers in ASP.NET

When writing the code for an ASP.NET page's source code portion, you'll be creating event handlers that execute in response to a specific ASP.NET-related event. One example of an ASP.NET event is the page's `Load` event, which fires every time an ASP.NET page is requested. If you have code that you want executed each time the page is requested, you can create an event handler for the `Load` event and place this code there.

There are a couple of ways to create the event handler for the `Load` event:

- If you are viewing the ASP.NET page's HTML portion through the Design view, you can simply double-click somewhere in the Designer background. Just be sure to double-click the background, and not some existing Web control (like a Button or Image tag). If you double-click a Web control you'll create an event handler for one of the events of that Web control.
- From the source code portion, you'll find two drop-down lists at the top. From the left drop-down list, select (Page Events). Then, from the right drop-down list, select Load (see Figure 2.11).
- Lastly, you can simply type in the necessary event handler syntax for creating the event handler and associating it with the page's `Load` event.

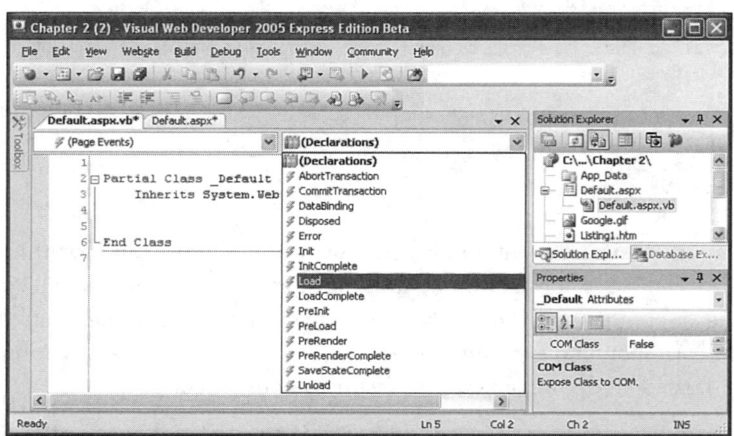

FIGURE 2.11 You can create the page's `Load` event handler from the drop-down lists.

Regardless of how you create the event handler, once you have done so, the syntax in your source code portion should resemble that in Listing 2.4.

LISTING 2.4 The `Page_Load` Event Handler Fires in Response to the Page's `Load` Event

```
1: Partial Class _Default
2:     Inherits System.Web.UI.Page
3:
4:     Protected Sub Page_Load(ByVal sender As Object, ByVal e As
➥System.EventArgs) Handles Me.Load
5:
6:     End Sub
7: End Class
```

Whenever the ASP.NET page is visited through a browser, whatever code you add between lines 4 and 6 will be executed.

Watch Out!

> You should *not* type the line numbers shown in Listing 2.4 into the source code portion. These line numbers are present simply to make it easier to refer to specific lines of code in the listing.

As we will see in future hours, many events can fire during the rendering of an ASP.NET web page. In addition to page-level events (such as the `Load` event), Web controls have associated events as well. For example, one of the ASP.NET Web controls is the Button Web control. When the user visiting the web page clicks the Button Web control, the button's `Click` event is fired; if an event handler is created for this event, the code within that event handler will execute upon the button being clicked. For now, though, we'll be working strictly with the page's `Load` event.

Programmatically Working with Web Controls

Earlier this hour, I mentioned that one difference between Web controls and static HTML content was that Web controls could be programmatically accessed, whereas static HTML content cannot. Furthermore, Web controls have a number of properties; for example, the Image Web controls added earlier had the `ImageUrl` property that indicated the URL of each search engine's logo. These properties can be read from and written to in the ASP.NET page's source code portion.

To illustrate this concept, let's enhance `Default.aspx` to contain some dynamic text at the top of the page. Specifically, above the `<table>` of search engine names and logos, let's add text that says, "Welcome to my site, it is now *currentTime*," where *currentTime* is the current date and time on the web server. (The web server in this instance is your personal computer.)

To accomplish this, return to `Default.aspx` and add a Label Web control above the HTML `<table>`. A Label Web control is designed to display dynamic text in an ASP.NET page and is covered in greater detail in Hour 8, “ASP.NET Web Controls for Displaying Text.” To add the Label Web control, you can either drag on the control from the Toolbox through the Design or Source views or, if you'd rather, enter the following syntax in the Source view by hand before the `<table>` element:

```
<asp:Label ID="Label1" runat="server" Text="Label"></asp:Label>
```

Once you've added the Label, change its `Text` and `ID` properties. Recall that this can be accomplished through the Properties window; if you are in the Source view, it may be quicker to just edit the attributes value directly in the HTML markup as opposed to using the Properties window, although either approach will suffice.

Specifically, clear out the `Text` property and change the `ID` to `currentTime`. Figure 2.12 shows the Properties window after these changes have been made.

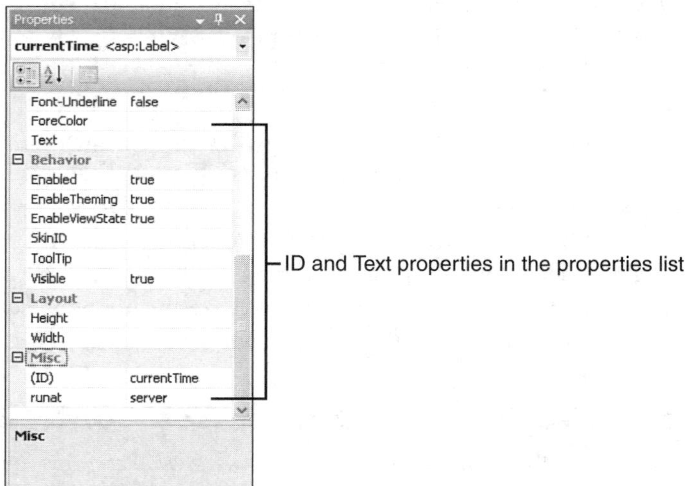

FIGURE 2.12
The Label's `ID` and `Text` properties have been altered.

Once this change has been made, the syntax for the Label Web control in the Source view should now look like so:

```
<asp:Label ID="currentTime" runat="server"></asp:Label>
```

In the source code portion of this ASP.NET page, we're going to programmatically set the `Text` property of the `currentTime` Label Web control to the current date and time. To accomplish this, return to the source code portion and, in the `Page_Load` event handler added earlier, enter the following line of code (referring back to Listing 2.4, you would add this on line 5):

```
currentTime.Text = "Welcome to my site, it is now " & DateTime.Now
```

Note that the Web control is referenced programmatically by its `ID` property value. That is, our Label Web control's `ID` property was set to `currentTime`; hence, we can programmatically set its properties using `currentTime.`*`Property`*.

Did you Know?

When you type `currentTime` into the source code view and follow it with a period (`.`), Visual Web Developer displays the set of available properties and methods for this Web control. This listing of available properties and methods is known as **IntelliSense**, and it saves oodles of time!

When viewing the drop-down list of allowable properties and methods, you can just type in the first few letters of the property or method you want to select. When the property or method you want to use is highlighted in the drop-down list, simply press the Tab key and Visual Web Developer will type in the rest for you.

If you do *not* see a drop-down list after entering `currentTime` and typing a period, Visual Web Developer could not find a suitably named Web control in the ASP.NET page's HTML portion. Take a moment to ensure that the Label Web control's `ID` property is, indeed, `currentTime`.

Take a moment to view `Default.aspx` through a browser (see Figure 2.13). Now, at the top of your page, you'll find the message "Welcome to my site, it is now *currentTime*." If you refresh your browser, the *currentTime* displayed will be updated. This illustrates the dynamic nature of ASP.NET pages, as we now have a page whose content is not static, but rather based on the current date and time.

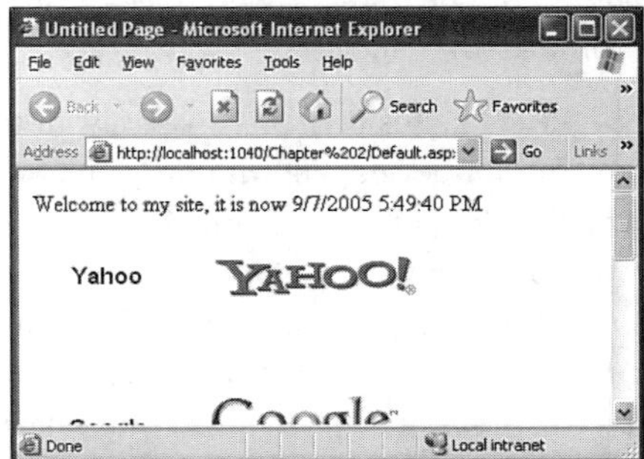

FIGURE 2.13 The ASP.NET page shows the current date and time.

As this example illustrated, a Web control's properties can be set either *declaratively* (via markup) or *programmatically* (via code). When a Web control property is specified through the Properties window or in the Web control syntax in the HTML portion, the property is said to be declaratively set. The `ID` property in our current example was set declaratively, as were the `ImageUrl` properties of the Image Web controls in the example that preceded this one. When the property value is set through the source code portion, it is said to have been set programmatically. In this example we set the Label's `Text` property programmatically.

Summary

We covered quite a bit of material in this hour, starting with an examination of the HTML portion of an ASP.NET web page. Here, we saw how to add an HTML `<table>` and other static content through the Design view, as well as how to drag and drop Web controls onto the page. We also saw how to change the appearance of HTML content in the designer by using the options under the Format menu. In addition to using the WYSIWYG designer, Visual Web Developer also allows you to enter HTML by hand via the Source tab.

After studying the HTML portion of an ASP.NET web page, we moved on to the source code portion. Here, we went over a crash course in object-oriented and event-driven programming. We then saw how to provide code that would be executed each time an ASP.NET web page is first visited.

The examples we examined in this hour and the previous one have been pretty simple ones with limited real-world application. In Hour 4, "Designing, Creating, and Testing ASP.NET Web Pages," we'll create a more practical ASP.NET web page with more involved HTML and source code portions. First, though, we'll explore the Visual Web Developer editor in greater detail.

Q&A

Q. ***Why are we building all of our ASP.NET web pages using Visual Basic as the server-side programming language?***

A. I chose to use Visual Basic for this book because it is, in my opinion, an easier language to comprehend for developers who may be new to programming than Visual C#. Visual Basic syntax reads much more like everyday English, whereas Visual C# uses more cryptic symbols. Furthermore, Visual Basic is not case sensitive, whereas C# is case sensitive, thereby making it more susceptible to typos and other frustrating errors. For this reason, languages that are not case sensitive are typically easier to pick up for those new to programming.

Q. ***When should I choose to use static HTML elements versus Web controls? That is, if I have to display static text, should I simply type in the text or use a Label Web control with its*** `Text` ***property set accordingly?***

A. For content that you know is going to be static, it's often wiser to use HTML elements as opposed to Web controls. Of course, if the content is dynamic, such as the text displayed in the Label Web control in our last example in this hour, you'll want to use a Web control.

Some developers, however, prefer to use Web controls for all content, even static content. In fact, we did this in our first example, using an Image Web control as opposed to a static <img> HTML element. If you are unfamiliar with HTML syntax, you may find it easier to use Web controls instead of having to research what HTML elements would be used (although many of the more common HTML elements are available through the Toolbox's HTML tab). There is a slight performance enhancement to using static HTML content instead of Web controls for static content, but don't let that minor impact sway your decision. Instead, use what you're most comfortable with. If you have an HTML background, you'll likely be more apt to use HTML elements for static markup; if you're new to HTML, Web controls may seem a more natural fit.

Workshop

Quiz

1. What does WYSIWYG stand for?
2. Is the following HTML properly nested?

```
<html><body>
<h1>My First Web Page</h1>
These are a few of my favorite <i>things:
<ol>
  <li>Jisun</li>
  <li>ASP.NET</li>
  <li>Basketball</li>
</ol></i>
</body></html>
```

3. What does the `@Page` directive do? Does it get rendered to the browser?
4. What is the name of the event handler you would use to have code execute each time the ASP.NET web page is loaded?
5. How can you add a Web control to an ASP.NET web page?

Answers

1. What You See Is What You Get.
2. Yes. There are no tags whose start tag appears after another tag's start tag (call that tag *t*), but whose end tag appears after *t*'s end tag.
3. The `@Page` directive supplies additional information to the ASP.NET engine, such as the server-side source code language used for the page and the location of the corresponding source code file. It is *not* rendered to the requesting browser.

4. The `Page_Load` event handler. Refer to Listing 2.4 to see an example of this event handler in the source code portion.

5. There are two ways. First, you can simply drag and drop the appropriate Web control from the Toolbox onto the designer. Second, you can enter the Web control syntax manually in the Source tab.

Exercises

The aim of these exercises is to help familiarize yourself with the Visual Web Developer editor.

1. The ASP.NET web page we created in the "Creating the HTML Portion of an ASP.NET Web Page Using Visual Web Developer" section contained an HTML `<table>` tag that was added by going to the Layout menu and selecting the Insert Table option. Once an HTML `<table>` has been added to a web page, you can easily set the table's various display properties.

   For this exercise, open up `Default.aspx` in the Design view and alter the `<table>` element's settings. If you click on the HTML table so that it is highlighted, you will find that its properties are displayed in the Properties window. (You can also select the <TABLE> element from the drop-down list in the Properties window.) For this exercise, set the `border` property to 3 and the `CellPadding` property to 5. Also, try setting the `BgColor` property. Notice that when you select this property from the Properties window, you can choose from an array of colors. You are invited to try setting the various HTML table properties to view their effect to the table in the designer.

2. For this exercise, add a message to the top of the `Default.aspx` web page that reads: "Here Are Some Popular Search Engines." This text should be centered, appear above the message that displays the current time, and be displayed in a bold, Arial font.

   To accomplish this, start by positioning the cursor in the designer immediately before the Label Web control. Press Enter a few times to create some space. Then type in the text **`Here Are Some Popular Search Engines`**. After you have entered this text, select it with the mouse. Then choose the Arial font from the font drop-down list near the upper-left corner. Next, make the text bold by going to the Format menu and selecting Bold. Finally, center the text by going to the Format menu's Justify submenu and choosing the Center option.

   As with exercise 1, you are encouraged to experiment with Visual Web Developer's formatting capabilities. See how the text looks with different fonts and formats. Note that you can add bulleted lists, numbered lists, and so on.

HOUR 3

Using Visual Web Developer

In this hour, we will cover

- Creating new websites and web pages
- Opening existing websites
- Customizing the editor through Visual Web Developer's Options menu
- Using techniques for laying out HTML content through the Design view
- Moving and resizing the assorted windows
- Accessing help through the installed documentation

In the preceding hour we looked at the ASP.NET programming model, noting how ASP.NET pages are composed of an HTML portion and a source code portion. Recall that the HTML portion of an ASP.NET web page consists of static HTML markup and Web control syntax; the source code portion, separated out into its own file, is implemented as a class with various event handlers.

In the past two hours, you got a cursory look at Visual Web Developer, the development environment we'll be using throughout this book to build ASP.NET pages. In Hour 1, "Getting Started with ASP.NET 2.0," we installed Visual Web Developer and received a quick tour of its features. In the preceding hour we delved a bit deeper into Visual Web Developer's interface, looking at how to create a new ASP.NET website and how to use the WYSIWYG Design view, the HTML Source view, and the source code editor.

Because we'll be using Visual Web Developer extensively throughout this book, it behooves us to take a moment to fully explore this editor. Visual Web Developer is a sophisticated and powerful programming editor, with a bevy of features and capabilities. As with any profession, it's important to have a solid grasp of the tools at your disposal.

Creating a New Website

When you start Visual Web Developer, you will typically want to do one of two things: either create a new website or open an existing website. A website is a collection of resources: static and dynamic web pages, graphic files, style sheets, configuration files, and so on. In addition to various files, a website may contain subdirectories, each of which may contain its own set of files and further subdirectories. A website is akin to a folder on your personal computer: It's a repository for files and subfolders.

To create a new website with Visual Web Developer, go to the File menu and select New Web Site or simply click the New Web Site icon in the Toolbar. Either of these actions will bring up the New Web Site dialog box, shown in Figure 3.1.

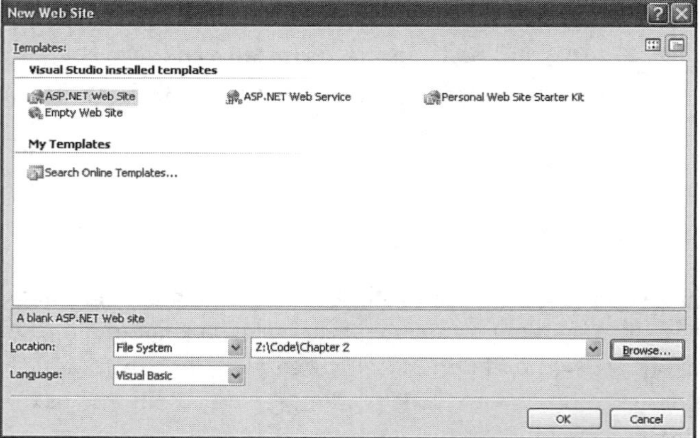

FIGURE 3.1 Create a new website from the New Web Site dialog box.

Choosing a Website Template

When creating a new website, you can choose among a number of available templates. For example, there's the ASP.NET Web Site template, the ASP.NET Web Service template, the Personal Web Site Starter Kit template, and an Empty Web Site template. Regardless of what template is selected, a website will be created; the differences among the templates is what default files the template includes with the website. For example, in the preceding hour we saw that creating a new website using the ASP.NET Web Site template creates a website with an `App_Data` folder and three files: `Default.aspx`, `Default.aspx.vb`, and `web.config`. Creating a website using the Empty Web Site template will create the website but will not add *any* default folders or files.

Did you Know?

> The website templates are available to hasten the startup involved in creating a web application. The Personal Web Site Starter Kit template, for example, will build a website with a number of existing pages and features to help you in creating a personal website. (For more information on this template, see http://msdn.microsoft.com/asp.net/archive/default.aspx?pull=/library/enus/dnaspp/html/pws.asp.)
>
> Be sure to try out the Search Online Templates feature in the My Templates section. This option, if selected, will look online for additional website templates created and distributed by Microsoft and others.

Although there is an array of website templates to choose from, all of the examples in this book will be created using the ASP.NET Web Site template.

Specifying the Website's Location

Websites can be located either on your personal computer or on a remote computer. Typically, personal computers do not double as web servers; that is, chances are the personal computer on which you're working right now does not host websites. Rather, you use your PC for your own ends—surfing the web, checking email, playing games, and so on. Publicly available websites are often hosted through **web-hosting companies**, which offer always-on computers with a persistent connection to the Internet. These computers' sole purpose is to host a website; they have web server software running on them and essentially sit around and wait for incoming requests. Upon receiving a request for a web page, they render the page and return the resulting markup to the requesting browser.

Often developers place a website on their own personal computer during the building and testing phases. The site won't be accessible over the Internet, but that's okay because the site is not yet ready for the public. When a functional site is complete, though, it can be moved to a remote web-hosting company so that the site can be accessed by anyone with an Internet connection. However, you can opt to create a new site on a remote computer from the get-go. All you need is an account with a web-hosting company.

Did you Know?

> A gaggle of web-hosting companies is available with various features and pricing plans. You can find these web-hosting companies through any search engine or through sites such as HostIndex.com or TopHosts.com, which serve as a directories of web-hosting companies.
>
> If you decide to host your ASP.NET website with a web-hosting company, be sure to check (and double-check) with the company to ensure that its servers support ASP.NET 2.0.

If you opt to host the website on your local computer you can host it in, potentially, one of two ways:

- **Through the file system**—With this approach, you provide a directory on your hard drive that serves as the website's **root directory**. All of the site's associated files and folders will be placed in that specified directory.
- **Through IIS, Microsoft's Web server**—If your personal computer has Internet Information Services (IIS) installed, you can host the website locally through IIS. IIS can be installed on Windows XP Professional and Windows 2003 Server; it is not able to be installed on Windows XP Home edition.

If you want to host the site locally, from the Location drop-down list, select File System. Next, click the Browse button to the right of the Location drop-down list. This will bring up the Choose Location dialog box shown in Figure 3.2.

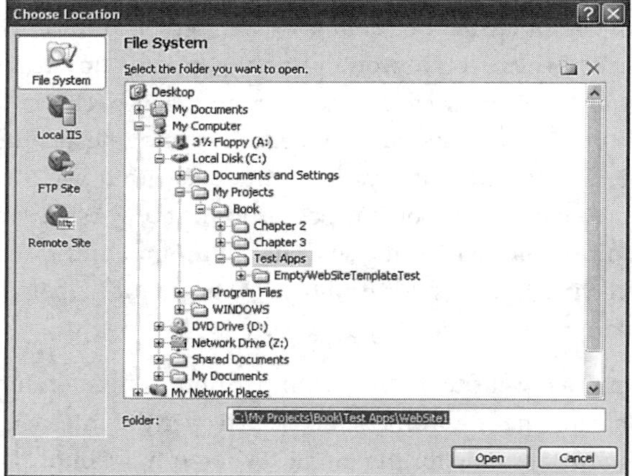

FIGURE 3.2
Choose the location where your website will reside.

The left column in the Choose Location dialog box lists the various locations the website can be saved.

> If your personal computer doesn't have Microsoft's IIS web server installed, you may be wondering how, in the preceding hour, we were able to view an ASP.NET page through a browser. This is possible because Visual Web Developer ships with a scaled-down web server referred to as the **ASP.NET Development Web Server**.
>
> This web server is designed solely for testing websites locally and will refuse any attempted access from outside your own computer. It is shipped with Visual Web Developer, so those developers who run Windows XP Home, which does not support IIS, can still create, build, and test ASP.NET applications.

To host the website on a remote computer, select either the HTTP or FTP options for location and specify the HTTP or FTP address. For the FTP settings, you'll need to provide the FTP server, port, directory, and username/password, if anonymous access is not allowed. Similarly, if you choose to use the HTTP setting when attempting to create the website, you'll be prompted for a username and password. Contact your web-hosting company for information on whether you should use HTTP or FTP access and what settings you'll need to use in order to connect.

All of the websites throughout this book will be created on the local file system.

Choosing the Source Code Programming Language

The setting chosen in the Language drop-down list specifies the programming language of your ASP.NET web pages' source code portions. Two options are available: Visual Basic and Visual C#. As discussed in the preceding hour, the Visual Basic language will be used for the examples throughout this book.

By the Way

> If you have a programming background in Java or C/C++, you may be more familiar with Visual C# than Visual Basic. Visual Basic is typically preferred by those with a background in the language or those new to programming.
>
> If you are interested in learning more about Visual C#, check out Microsoft's Visual C# Developer Center (http://msdn.microsoft.com/vcsharp/) along with *Microsoft Visual C# 2005 Unleashed* by Kevin Hoffman (ISBN: 0672327767).

To gain practice creating websites in Visual Web Developer, go ahead and create a new website using the ASP.NET Web Site template, the File System location with the website in a directory of your choice, and with the Language set to Visual Basic. As we saw in the preceding hour, this will create a website with an `App_Data` folder, a `Default.aspx` ASP.NET page (with a corresponding `Default.aspx.vb` file), and a configuration file, `web.config`. These files are listed in the Solution Explorer, which you can find in the upper-right corner. (If you do not see the Solution Explorer, go to the View menu and choose the Solution Explorer option.)

Opening Existing Websites

Now that we've created a website, let's see how to open this website at a later point in time. First, go ahead and close the website. This can be accomplished by closing Visual Web Developer altogether, or by going to the File menu and choosing Close Project.

After closing your website, reopen it by going to the File menu and choose the Open Web Site menu option. This will list the Open Web Site dialog box. This dialog box is nearly identical to the Choose Location dialog box shown in Figure 3.2.

Because you created your website locally through your personal computer's file system, open the site by selecting the File System icon in the left column and then navigating to the folder where you placed the website. Finally, click the Open button to open the website.

Opening the website will close the existing opened website (if any) and load the selected website's contents into the Solution Explorer. At this point you can work with the website as you normally would, creating and editing web pages' HTML and source code portions.

If you have recently worked with a particular website, there's a quicker way to open it with Visual Web Developer. The File menu contains a Recent Projects menu item that lists the most recently opened projects. Clicking on a project name from the Recent Projects list opens that project.

Working with Web Pages and Other Content

A website is simply a repository of related files and subdirectories. Websites typically contain files of the following types:

- **Static web pages**—An **HTML page** is a static web page. Unlike an ASP.NET page, it contains only HTML content—no Web controls and no source code. As its name implies, the content of these types of files is static, and cannot be altered based on user input, server-side data, or other criteria.
- **ASP.NET web pages**—ASP.NET pages are the dynamic web pages in your site. They are implemented as two files: `*PageName*.aspx`, which contains the HTML portion; and `*PageName*.aspx.vb`, which contains the source code portion.
- **Image files**—Most websites have various images, logos, and clip art. These image files typically are stored on the website, either in the root directory or in an Images subdirectory.
- **Configuration files**—ASP.NET websites contain a configuration file named `web.config`, which provides server-side setting information.
- **Style sheet files**—Style sheets are files that spell out display information. For example, in your site you might want all content to be displayed in the Arial

font and have content within <h1> tags displayed in italics. You can specify this aesthetic information through style sheet files. For more information on style sheets, refer to http://www.w3schools.com/css/.

- **Script files**—In addition to server-side source code, a web page may contain **client-side script code**. This is code that is sent to and runs on the end user's web browser. Often this script is packaged in a separate script file on the web server, which the browser requests as needed.

This list of file types enumerates the most commonly found file types on a web server but is hardly exhaustive. A rock band's website, for example, might also have MP3 files available for download. Additionally, numerous ASP.NET-specific files can optionally be added to your website to provide various types of functionality. We'll be learning about many of these different ASP.NET-specific file types throughout this book.

Adding Content to Your Website

When you create a new website using the ASP.NET Web Site template, the new website has the `web.config` file along with a single ASP.NET page, `Default.aspx` (which is really composed of two files, `Default.aspx` and `Default.aspx.vb`). You can easily add additional files and folders through the Solution Explorer. From the Solution Explorer, start by right-clicking on the website name; this will bring up the context menu shown in Figure 3.3.

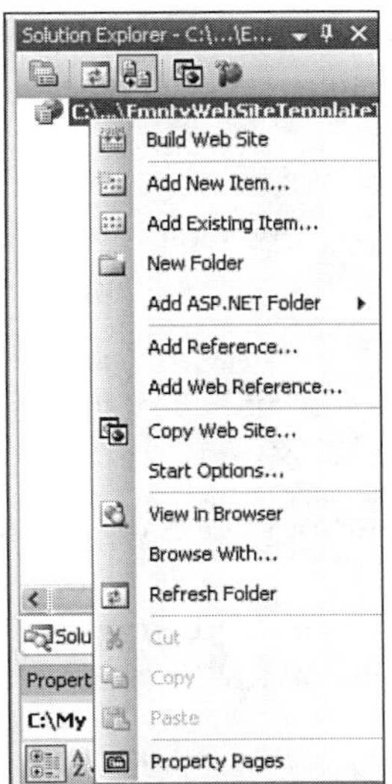

FIGURE 3.3
To add a new file or folder, right-click on the website name in the Solution Explorer.

To add a new folder to your website, select the New Folder item from the context menu. To add a new file, choose Add New Item. Selecting Add New Item will display the Add New Item dialog box (see Figure 3.4). The Add New Item dialog box lists the wide variety of types of files that can be added. Notice that there are file types for each of the popular file types enumerated earlier, in addition to many other types.

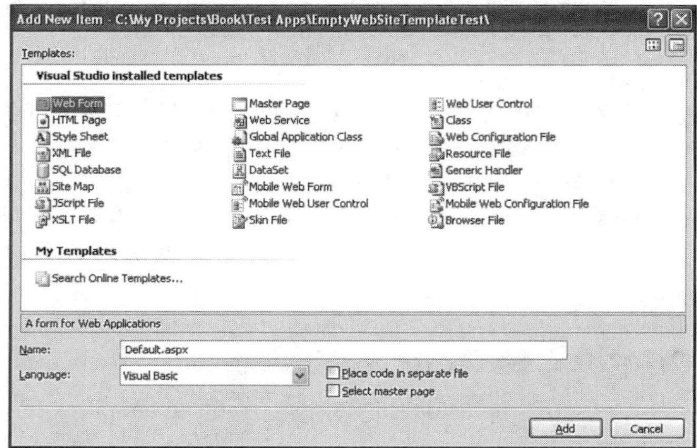

FIGURE 3.4 The Add New Item dialog box allows you to choose the type of file to add.

By the Way

To add a new ASP.NET page to your website, add an item of type Web Form.

At the bottom of the Add New Item dialog box, you'll find a series of options. The options displayed depend on what file type you have decided to add. For Web Forms, which are the item type name for ASP.NET pages, there are four options:

- **Name**—This indicates what the file will be named.
- **Language**—This dictates the language of the page's server-side source code portion.
- **Place Code in Separate File**—This specifies whether the source code portion should be implemented as a second file (`*PageName*.aspx.vb`) or if server-side `<script>` blocks will be used instead.
- **Select Master Page**—A **master page** is a site-wide template that can be applied to ASP.NET pages to maintain a consistent look and feel across the site. If you are using master pages, you can check this option to assign a master page to the newly created ASP.NET page.

> Master pages are a very useful way to create a consistent page layout across all pages in your site. We'll discuss the benefits of master pages, along with how to use them in your ASP.NET website, in Hour 21, "Using MasterPages to Provide Site-Wide Page Templates."

By the Way

The Language drop-down list value for the ASP.NET page's source code portion will be the same language choice you specified when creating the website. However, a single ASP.NET website can have web pages that use different programming languages for their source code portions. However, I recommend against this approach and encourage you to stick with a single, unified programming language choice across all ASP.NET pages for a given website.

Although ASP.NET pages will work just as well if their source code portion is in the `.aspx` page in a server-side `<script>` block or if it is relegated to a separate file (*`PageName`*`.aspx.vb`), keep in mind that all of the examples we'll be working through in this book use the separate page model. Therefore, when adding a new ASP.NET page to your website, be sure to check the Place Source Code in a Separate File check box. Doing so will create both the *`PageName`*`.aspx` and *`PageName`*`.aspx.vb` files.

> The Place Code in Separate File option in the Add New Item dialog box is "sticky." That is, Visual Web Developer remembers your selection. Unfortunately, this "stickiness" is not remembered across projects. That is, if you create a new ASP.NET website project, Visual Web Developer will revert back to the default—to have this option unchecked. Therefore, whenever adding a new ASP.NET page, take a quick moment to ensure that this check box is indeed checked.

Watch Out!

Let's practice adding a new ASP.NET page to our website. Imagine that in addition to `Default.aspx,` we also want to have a second ASP.NET page, `DisplayTime.aspx`. To add this page to your website, perform the following steps:

1. Go to the Solution Explorer and right-click on the website name.
2. Choose Add New Item from the context menu.
3. From the Add New Item dialog box (see Figure 3.4), select to add an item of type Web Form.
4. Enter **`DisplayTime.aspx`** for the page's Name, leave the Language setting as Visual Basic, and check the Place Source Code in a Separate File check box.
5. Click the Add button to create the new ASP.NET page.

You can follow these same steps to add other types of resources to your website. Of course, the options present in step 4 will differ depending on the type of item being added.

Adding Existing Content

Along with adding new content to your website, you can use Visual Web Developer to easily add existing content. You may already have an image file on your hard drive or an ASP.NET page from another project that you want to include in this project as well. If that's the case, you can add an existing item by right-clicking on the website name in the Solution Explorer and choosing Add Existing Item.

Choosing this option will display the standard file browsing dialog box. From here, you can navigate to the folder on your hard drive that contains the content you want to add, select it, and click the Add button. This will copy over the selected item to your website's directory, making it part of your website now.

Moving, Renaming, and Deleting Content

Along with adding new folders and files, from the Solution Explorer you can also move and delete content. To move content among the folders in your website, simply drag the file or folder from its existing location to a new file or folder.

To rename or delete a file or folder, start by right-clicking on the item in the Solution Explorer. This will bring up the context menu shown in Figure 3.5. As you can see from the figure, Rename and Delete menu items are available. Simply click on the appropriate menu item to rename or remove the selected file or folder.

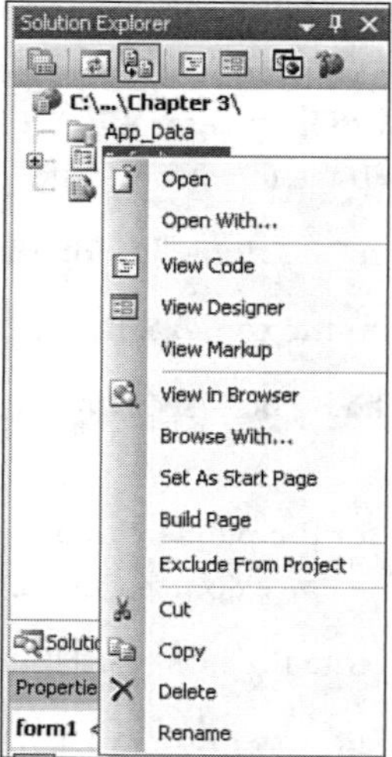

FIGURE 3.5 Select the appropriate menu item from the context menu.

Customizing the Visual Web Developer Experience

Like any robust programming editor, Visual Web Developer is highly customizable, enabling developers to configure the editor in a way that maximizes their productivity. Not only does Visual Web Developer give you fine-grained control over a variety of settings, but it also provides an easy way to export your unique settings to a single file. You can then re-create your environment at a new computer by importing your settings file. This makes it easy to move your settings from a desktop computer to a laptop; additionally, if you place your settings file on a website or keep it saved on a USB drive or web-based email account, you can easily re-create your development environment at *any* computer where you end up working!

In this section we'll examine how to customize Visual Web Developer. The bulk of the customizability is accomplished through the Options dialog box, which is available through the Tools menu. There are literally hundreds of settings, so we won't have the time to go through each and every one. Instead, we'll focus on the more germane settings. We'll also see how to alter the Visual Web Developer panes and their display settings, along with settings that aid with laying out HTML content in the Design view.

By default, the Visual Web Developer Options dialog box shows only the most pertinent options. To see all available options, check the Show All Settings check box.

By the Way

The screenshots throughout this book have been taken using the default Visual Web Developer settings. If you customize the environment to suit your preferences, there may be some disparity between your screen and the screenshots in this book.

Examining the Environment Settings

The majority of the customizable settings in Visual Web Developer are accessible via the Options dialog box, which you can display by selecting the Options item from the Tools menu. Figure 3.6 shows the Options dialog box when first opened.

The Options dialog box is broken down into various hierarchical categories, which are listed in the left column. Selecting an item from the list on the left displays its corresponding options on the right. As Figure 3.6 shows, the default category selected when opening the Options dialog box is the Environment category.

There are far too many categories and options available in this dialog box to exhaustively list them all; instead, let's just focus on the more pertinent ones.

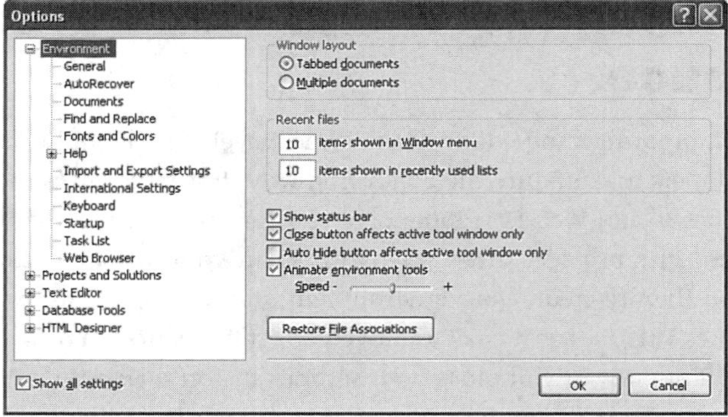

FIGURE 3.6
Customize your Visual Web Developer experience through the Options dialog box.

The Environment has two settings worth exploring. The first is the AutoRecover setting. While you are working on a website, Visual Web Developer will automatically save copies of modified files every so often, based on a setting you provide (the default is every five minutes). These backup copies are kept around for a specified number of days (seven, by default). The AutoRecover feature protects against losing hours of work due to an unexpected shutdown. If your officemate LeRoy happens to walk past your desk and kick the power cord out of the wall, in the worst case you'll not have the last five minutes of changes saved (assuming you left the AutoRecover frequency as the default). If you have AutoRecover enabled (which it is, by default), backup copies of your modified files will be saved periodically to the `\My Documents\Visual Studio 2005\Backup Files\<projectname>` folder.

The final Environment setting we'll look at is the Fonts and Colors settings, which is shown in Figure 3.7. The Fonts and Colors settings dictate the fonts, sizes, and colors of the text used in Visual Web Developer. You can alter the fonts and colors for a variety of settings: the Visual Web Developer text editor, the printed output, various debugging windows, and so on. Furthermore, for each variety of setting, there are multiple display items whose font and color can be customized. For example, the default fonts and colors for the Text Editor setting's Plain Text is black, 10pt, Courier New; its setting for the Selected Text is white with a blue background, 10pt, Courier New.

Many developers tweak the Fonts and Colors settings to make it easier to see certain types of tokens in their source code. For example, in the version of Visual Web Developer I use, I have Numbers displayed as purple, bold, 10pt, Courier New text, and Strings displayed as turquoise, 10pt, Courier New text.

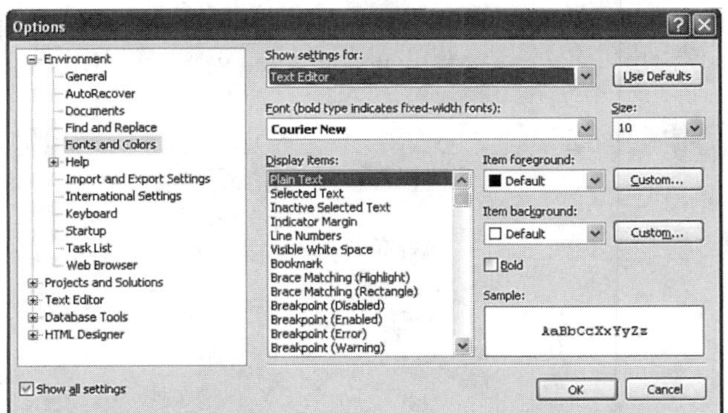

FIGURE 3.7 Specify the fonts, sizes, and colors of the text used in Visual Web Developer.

Configuring the HTML Design-Time Experience

The last settings item in the Options dialog box worth noting is the HTML Designer category. Expand this category and select the General item beneath it. On the right you should see an option titled Start Pages In with two options: Source View and Design View. Recall that when editing an ASP.NET page's source code portion, you can either work with the HTML content directly, through the Source view, or drag and drop HTML elements and Web controls onto the page from the Design view. By default, when you're creating a new web page or opening an existing one, the page is opened in the Source view. If you prefer the Design view, you can change the default behavior here.

The second setting in the HTML Designer category that merits discussion is the CSS Positioning item (see Figure 3.8). The key setting in this item is the Positioning options. If you check the first check box—Change Positioning to the Following for Controls Added Using the Toolbox, Paste, or Drag and Drop—you can indicate how items should be laid out on the designer. By default, this check box is unchecked, meaning that no positioning information is applied to Web controls or HTML elements added through the Design view. In the preceding hour we touched on this, discussing how extraneous whitespace is ignored in HTML, and to position elements, you need to use `<table>` elements like we did in the example in Hour 2, "Understanding the ASP.NET Programming Model," or other techniques that we have yet to explore.

One such positioning technique is **absolute positioning**. This technique gives each HTML element and Web control dragged onto the designer a fixed coordinate for its upper-left corner. These coordinates are sent down to the browser and are positioned accordingly. If you check the Change Positioning to the Following for Controls Added Using the Toolbox, Paste, or Drag and Drop check box and select the

Absolutely Positioned item from the drop-down list, you will be able to simply drag Web controls and HTML elements to the position you want on the designer.

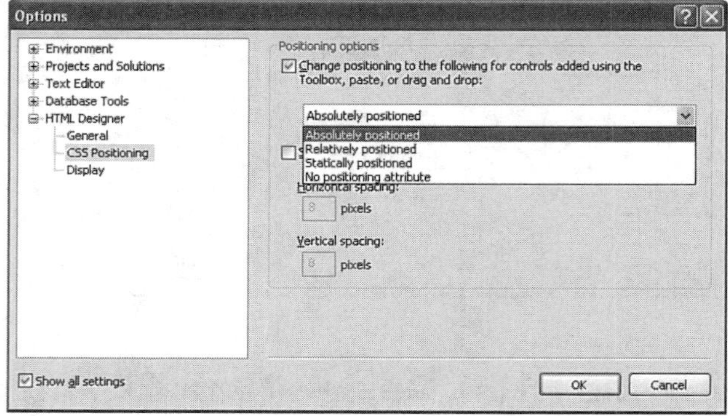

FIGURE 3.8
Control the HTML layout to a finer degree with absolute positioning.

Figure 3.9 illustrates this by examining the designer after configuring Visual Web Developer to use Absolutely Positioned elements. Specifically, I have added a Button Web control and then dragged it near the middle of the design surface. More precisely, the absolute position of the Button Web control is 119 pixels from the top and 100 pixels from the left, as can be seen in the lower-left corner of the Visual Web Developer status bar.

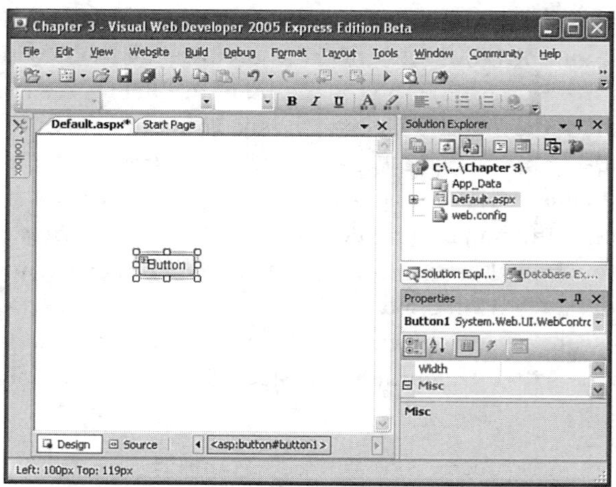

FIGURE 3.9
A button has been absolutely positioned to 119px from the top and 100px from the left.

While absolute positioned elements may seem like a godsend, making it supremely simple to move elements around to specific locations, it is important to be aware of the risks. For starters, when you position elements absolutely, you are making inherent assumptions about your visitors' screen resolutions. For example, imagine that you are designing your site on a monitor with a resolution that's 1,024 pixels wide and 768 pixels tall and you want a Button Web control to be placed near the right side of the page. You may drag the Button to have an absolute position of, say, 900 pixels from the left and 100 pixels from the top.

When a visitor reaches your site, his browser will place that Button 900 pixels from its left margin and 100 pixels from its top. But what if the visitor's monitor supports only a resolution of 800 pixels wide by 600 pixels tall? That Button you meant to be on the right side of the screen is now off the visitor's screen, so he needs to scroll to the right to see it.

Another disadvantage of absolutely positioned elements is that they do not flow nicely as their size increases. When we reach Hour 15, "Displaying Data with the Data Web Controls," we'll look at a Web control that displays database data. Since at design time we might not know how much data will be displayed (because that would depend on how much data is in the database, which will change over time), we may run into problems if we put a GridView on our page and, say, a Button beneath it. When there are but a few items in the GridView, the Button may be positioned nicely, but as time goes on and more data is added to the database, the GridView's dimensions will increase and eventually its larger size will cover up the Button beneath it.

I am not categorically saying that you should never use absolute positioned elements. They make perfect sense in a controlled environment, like an intranet, where you can be assured that your visitors all have a certain minimum resolution so you can design the site accordingly. However, don't simply opt to use absolute positioned elements because it seems simpler than learning the more intricate methods of positioning using HTML syntax. The time you save in bypassing learning positioning with HTML syntax is likely time that will be taken back from you when some of these common absolute position design issues arise.

By the Way

To learn more about positioning HTML content without using absolute positioning, refer to http://www.w3schools.com/html/html_layout.asp.

Did you Know?

When you have settled on the particular settings you find most conducive, take a moment to export your savings to a file. To accomplish this, go to the Tools menu and select the Import and Export Settings option. This will take you through a wizard where you can indicate what settings to export along with the filename and location to save the settings.

Once you have exported your settings, you can re-create your personalized settings on another computer by importing this settings file. This capability is useful if you develop on both a desktop and laptop, depending on whether you're onsite or not, or if you are a contractor who moves jobs every few months but want to maintain a consistent collection of settings.

Viewing, Moving, and Resizing Windows

The Visual Web Developer environment is made up of a bevy of windows that provide various tidbits of information. The window we've examined in most detail is the Solution Explorer, which lists the files and folders in the website. In the preceding hour, we saw two other windows: the Properties window, which listed the properties for the selected HTML element or Web control; and the Toolbox window, which listed the Web controls and HTML elements that could be dragged onto an ASP.NET page.

These are but three of the many windows available in Visual Web Developer. You can see a complete list of the available windows by going to the View menu.

Windows in Visual Web Developer each have a default position, size, and behavior. The position indicates where on the screen the window is placed and whether or not it is floating or docked. The Solution Explorer, for example, is in a docked position in the upper-right corner, by default; the Toolbox can be found in a docked position on the left. A docked window is one that's attached to a margin of the editor; when a docked window is shown, the content it displaces is moved elsewhere on the screen. A floating window is *not* attached to any margin; it floats above all other windows and content in the editor, covering it up rather than displacing it.

Each window also has a size. You can move your mouse to the margin of the window and click and drag to increase or decrease the window's width or height. Lastly, each window has a behavior: It's either pinned or unpinned (the unpinned behavior is sometimes referred to as Auto-Hide behavior). A pinned window remains displayed regardless of whether your mouse is over the window. An unpinned window is displayed when you move your mouse over the window and disappears when your mouse leaves the window's focus. You can toggle a window's pinned status by clicking the pin icon in each window's upper-right corner. Typically, I keep the Solution Explorer, Properties, and Toolbox windows pinned because they are commonly used; all other windows I'll make unpinned so they do not encroach on my screen's real estate.

In addition to being able to pin and unpin windows, you can also close a window. To remove a window from the screen, simply click the X icon in the upper-right corner of the window (it's next to the pin icon).

> If you cannot find a window onscreen where you expect it, you may have moved it or accidentally closed it. In any event, you can display the needed window by going to the View menu and selecting the appropriate menu option.

If you do not like the position of a window, you can easily move it. Simply click on the top of the window and, holding down your mouse button, drag your mouse to the location you want the window to appear.

A World of Help at Your Fingertips

ASP.NET is a rich, robust web development technology built on a platform known as the .NET Framework. This platform consists of hundreds of classes that provide the core functionality of the ASP.NET engine. Needless to say, it can take *years* to have a deep understanding of the framework and its capabilities.

Fortunately, Visual Web Developer provides a variety of documentation and help. The version of Visual Web Developer you have installed on your computer includes the MSDN Library for Visual Studio Express editions. The MSDN Library is Microsoft's colossal collection of articles, whitepapers, technical documentation, knowledge base content, and frequently asked questions and answers. To view the library, simply go to the Help menu and choose Search, Contents, or Index. This will launch the Microsoft Visual Studio 2005 Express Editions Documentation program, from which you can poke through the help.

Another neat feature of Visual Web Developer is its Dynamic Help. From the Help menu, select the Dynamic Help option. This will display the Dynamic Help window (which you can resize, position, and pin just like any other window). As its name implies, the Dynamic Help window shows context-sensitive help based on where your cursor is in the source code or HTML portions. For example, if you're in the Design view and you click on a Button Web control in your page, the Dynamic Help window will automatically display help links with titles like

- Button Web Server Control Overview
- How to: Add Button Web Controls to a Web Forms Page
- How to: Add ImageButton Web Controls to a Web Forms Page

There's also the Community menu, which contains menu items like Ask a Question and Check Question Status. These menu options plug into Microsoft's online forum site, which you can access directly through a web browser by going to http://forums.microsoft.com/msdn/.

In addition to the Microsoft online forum site, the Community menu item has links to other developer resource sites and tools to assist in searching online for answers, templates, samples, and controls.

Although a wealth of information is available through the documentation installed on your computer and through Visual Web Developer's Community and Help menus, a vast array of information is also available online. One tip to help your searches is Google's Microsoft-specific search, available at http://www.google.com/microsoft.html. This customized search page returns only results relating to Microsoft technologies and topics, which can help expedite your search for answers to your questions.

Summary

We spent this hour investigating Visual Web Developer in greater detail. It is important that you have a familiarity with this editor since it is what you'll be using throughout this book and beyond. While we will have ample opportunity to sharpen our Visual Web Developer skills throughout the future hours, I thought it worthwhile to take some time to more formally explore the tool.

Specifically, we looked at how to create and open websites in Visual Web Developer. Websites can be located either locally, on your personal computer, or remotely, with a web-hosting company. Visual Web Developer makes it easy to work with both sites locally and remotely, and even includes a lightweight, built-in web server that allows for developers using Windows XP Home to run ASP.NET websites locally. After you have created a website, you'll want to add various files and folders. This is easily accomplished through the Solution Explorer.

This hour we also looked at customizing the environment through the Options dialog box and by repositioning and resizing the many windows. We concluded with a quick synopsis of Visual Web Developer's extensive built-in help system. The Dynamic Help capabilities are especially useful for developers new to ASP.NET.

In this hour and the past two we've covered a lot of ground. We've looked at the fundamentals of ASP.NET and the .NET Framework; installed the .NET Framework, Visual Web Developer, and SQL Server 2005 Express Edition; dissected the ASP.NET programming model; created our first ASP.NET web page, complete with HTML markup, Web controls, and server-side source code; and explored Visual Web Developer. We're now ready to build a nontrivial ASP.NET web page, which we'll tackle in the upcoming hour. This exercise will help hammer home many of the key points mentioned through these first three hours.

Q&A

Q. ***I want to use a web-hosting company to host my ASP.NET website. How do I determine whether a particular web-hosting company can host my ASP.NET application?***

A. The easiest way to ascertain whether a given web-hosting company can host your site is to simply ask. Be sure to tell the company that you are creating an *ASP.NET 2.0* website using Visual Web Developer. For your ASP.NET site to be able to run on the company's servers, the web-hosting company will need to be running Microsoft's web server, IIS, along with the .NET Framework version 2.0. If these conditions are met, your site should run just fine.

Q. ***I have created a website on my local file system with the website located at folder X. I'd like to move the website to folder Y. Is this possible?***

A. Sure. To move the site, simply close Visual Web Developer and then move the website's folder from its current location to wherever else you'd like it to reside. After you have moved the files, reopen Visual Web Developer, go to the File menu, and choose the Open Web Site option. Browse to the *new* folder location and click Open. That's all there is to it!

Q. ***What are some online resources for ASP.NET information?***

A. There are a plethora of ASP.NET resources available free online. Your first destination should be the official ASP.NET website, www.asp.net. This site has links to virtually every ASP.NET resource site on the Net, along with a very active online forum site (http://forums.asp.net/) that has received more than 1,000,000 posts from hundreds of thousands of users.

Many of the larger ASP.NET resource sites have been around for many years, having started when there was no ASP.NET, only ASP. I run a popular online resource, 4GuysFromRolla.com, which has a messageboard, FAQs, and thousands of ASP/ASP.NET-related articles. Some other large and prominent ASP.NET sites include 15Seconds.com, ASPAlliance.com, and ASP101.com. There's also Microsoft's ASP.NET Developer Center, available at http://msdn.microsoft.com/asp.net/.

Workshop

Quiz

1. There are two local and two remote techniques through which a website can be created or opened. What are these four techniques?
2. True or False: IIS stands for Internet Information Service and is Microsoft's web server software.
3. True or False: The ASP.NET Development Web Server and IIS are the same thing.
4. When you're adding a new Web Form (ASP.NET page) to your website, there's a check box titled Place Source Code in a Separate File. How will the created ASP.NET page differ if you don't check this option versus if you do?
5. What are the advantages and disadvantages of having absolute positioned Web controls and HTML elements?

Answers

1. The two local techniques are through the local file system or through a local version of IIS, Microsoft's web server software. (Keep in mind that in order for you to use the local IIS option, your personal computer must have IIS installed. IIS is not installable on Windows XP Home edition, and, even if your operating system supports IIS, it might not currently be installed.) The two remote techniques are through HTTP or FTP. If you are using a web-hosting company, talk to the company to determine which approach to use and the various settings to use.
2. True.
3. False. IIS is Microsoft's professional grade web server software. ASP.NET Development Web Server is a lightweight web server that ships with Visual Web Developer to enable those who do not have IIS installed to be able to still develop, build, and test ASP.NET applications. IIS is designed to run real-world websites; the ASP.NET Development Web Server is designed solely for local-only, low-stress testing.
4. If you do *not* check the Place Source Code in a Separate File check box, only one file will be created for the ASP.NET page, `PageName.aspx`. Your source code portion will need to be placed within a server-side `<script>` block. Preferably, you'll check the Place Source Code in a Separate File check box, in

which case *two* files will be created: `PageName.aspx` and `PageName.aspx.vb`. In this scenario, the HTML markup and Web control syntax resides in the former file, while the source code portion resides in the latter.

5. Absolute positioned elements have the advantage that they're easy to place on a page: You simply drag and drop from the Design view. The disadvantage is that using absolute positioning makes implicit assumptions about the end user's screen resolution. Since you, as the developer, are laying out the site according to your screen's resolution, the results may look good for visitors who use a similar resolution but will likely look "off" for those visitors who use a much lower or higher resolution.

   Additionally, absolute positioned elements that can grow dynamically based on the data bound to them have an annoying knack of consuming more screen real estate than originally estimated, thereby potentially overlapping any elements beneath it.

Exercises

1. For more practice with Visual Web Developer, take a moment to create a new website. Along with the `Default.aspx` page, add some additional ASP.NET pages. In each page, add various content through the Design view or Source view, much like we did in the preceding hour. Tinker around with the editor, not worrying about whether you're doing things right or wrong. Just experiment.

   After creating a couple of pages, try marking each page as the start page (right-click on the ASP.NET page in the Solution Explorer and choose Set as Start Page) and then visit the page in a browser by going to the Debug menu and choosing Start Without Debugging.

   If you're feeling adventurous, try adding some image files from your hard drive to your website. Next, have them displayed in your ASP.NET pages using Image Web controls, much like we did in the preceding hour. Again, focus more on the exploration than whether you are doing things the right way. Take your time and have fun; it's the best way to learn!

HOUR 4

Designing, Creating, and Testing ASP.NET Web Pages

In this hour, we will cover

- Creating the design requirements for the financial calculator
- Creating the user interface
- Adding the needed Web controls to the ASP.NET web page
- Writing the code for the ASP.NET web page's source code portion
- Testing the ASP.NET web page

In the past three hours we've spent quite a bit of time talking in very high-level terms about ASP.NET web pages, the ASP.NET programming model, and Visual Web Developer. We've looked at how to configure our computer to serve ASP.NET web pages, and we've looked at the role of the web server. We've examined the HTML and source code portions of an ASP.NET web page. We've created some very simple ASP.NET web pages and have seen how to use Visual Web Developer to create these pages.

In this hour we turn from these high-level discussions to actually designing, building, and testing a nontrivial, useful ASP.NET web page that illustrates the concepts discussed in the past three hours. Specifically, we'll be creating an ASP.NET web page that serves as a financial calculator.

Specifying the Design Requirements

Throughout this book we will be creating a number of ASP.NET web pages, which involves creating both the ASP.NET web page's HTML and source code. When we're writing any piece of software, whether a Windows desktop application or a dynamic web page, there are a number of development stages. First and foremost, we need to decide what the purpose of the software is, along with what features and functionality the software should provide. After this, we must sit down and actually write the software. Finally, we need to test the software and fix any bugs or errors that arise.

These three steps—design, development, and testing—should always be performed when creating an ASP.NET web page, but too frequently, developers jump straight to the coding task without spending enough time in the planning stage.

This initial planning stage, sometimes called the **design requirements** stage, is vital for the following reasons:

- It lays down a road map for the software project. Having a road map allows us to determine how much progress we've made at a given point, as well as how much we have left to accomplish.
- The design requirements spell out precisely what the software will provide.

To get into the habit, we will spend a bit of time discussing what features will be present and what user interface will be employed in the ASP.NET web page we will be creating in this hour.

By the Way

> Without spending adequate time in the design requirements stage, you would be unable to accurately answer your boss when he asked, "How much longer will this take," or "How much progress have you made?" Additionally, agreeing on a list of feature requirements—a task typically performed during the design requirements stage—avoids any confusion at the conclusion of the project when your boss or client wonders why a feature they thought was going to be present was not.

Formulating the Features for Our Financial Calculator

An important step in the design requirements process is to list the features you plan on providing in your application. So far, I have just mentioned that we will be creating a financial calculator, but let's take the time to specifically define the features we want to provide.

For our financial calculator let's build a loan calculator designed to determine the monthly payments for a fixed-rate home **mortgage**. To determine the monthly payments required for a fixed-rate mortgage, we need three inputs:

- The amount of money being borrowed (the principal)
- The loan's annual interest rate
- The duration of the loan—typically 15 or 30 years (the loan's term)

The output of our financial calculator, along with these three inputs, gives us the features of our financial calculator. In a sentence: Our financial calculator will compute the monthly payment of a fixed-rate mortgage when provided the amount, duration, and interest rate of the mortgage.

Deciding on the User Interface

After we describe the features that the application will have, the next stage in the design requirements phase is to create a user interface. The user interface, or UI for short, is the means by which the user interacts with the application. How will the user enter these inputs? How will the results be displayed?

With large applications, the user interface portion of the design requirements phase can take quite a while and be very involved. For our financial calculator, however, the user interface is fairly straightforward and will exist on a single web page.

Essentially, our users need to be able to do two things: enter the three inputs discussed earlier and see the result of the calculation. These inputs can be entered via TextBox Web controls. The output of the financial calculator should show the mortgage's monthly cost.

Figure 4.1 shows the ASP.NET web page financial calculator when first visited by the user. Note the three text boxes for the three inputs. Additionally, there is a button labeled Compute Monthly Cost that the user is instructed to click after entering the required inputs.

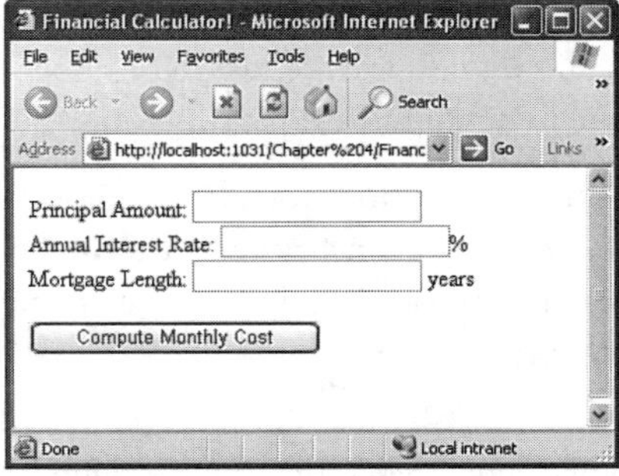

FIGURE 4.1
The user is asked to enter the three inputs.

Figure 4.2 shows the financial calculator after the user has entered the requested inputs and has clicked the Compute Monthly Cost button. Note that the output shows how much money the mortgage will cost per month.

To display the output of our calculation, we need to add a Label Web control to our ASP.NET page. This Label Web control will display the result of the calculation.

Therefore, we should place this Label Web control in the ASP.NET web page precisely where we want the final output to appear. As you can see from Figure 4.2, I have created the financial calculator so that the output appears below the input text boxes.

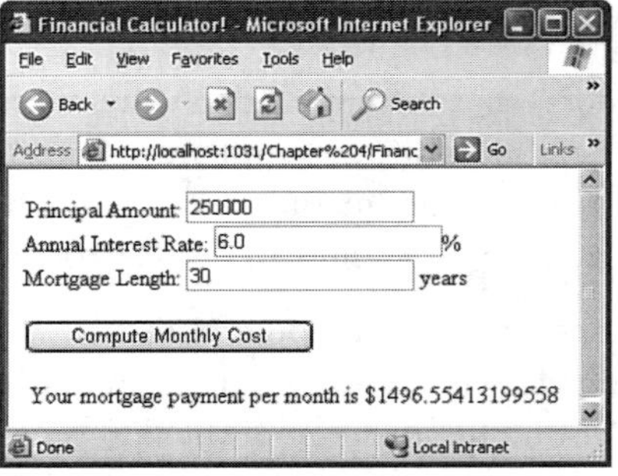

FIGURE 4.2 The monthly cost of the mortgage is shown.

Did you Know?

When creating a user interface for your web applications, you can use Visual Web Developer's WYSIWYG Design view to quickly create a mockup. Or, if you're more old-fashioned or there's a power outage, you can use a trusty pencil and pad of paper as the canvas for your UI ideas.

Creating the User Interface

Now that we've completed the design requirements phase and have decided what features our financial calculator will provide, as well as how the interface will appear to the user, it's time to actually start creating our ASP.NET web page.

The first task is to create the user interface (or UI), which is considered the HTML portion of our ASP.NET web page. To construct this UI, we'll add a TextBox Web control for each of the three inputs as well as a Button Web control that, when clicked, will perform the necessary computations.

By the Way

After creating the user interface, we will turn our attention to writing the needed source code to perform the financial computations.

To start creating the user interface, launch Visual Web Developer and create a new ASP.NET website on your computer's file system, just as we examined in the preceding hour. As we've seen, this will create a website with an ASP.NET page named `Default.aspx`. For practice, go ahead and delete this ASP.NET page and add a new page named `FinancialCalculator.aspx`. When you're creating a new ASP.NET page, remember that the item type to select is Web Form; also be sure to choose Visual Basic as the language and check the Place Source Code in a Separate File check box.

Adding the Three TextBox Web Controls

Let's start by adding the TextBox Web controls for our user's three inputs. While we've yet to examine using the TextBox Web control in any of our previous examples, it's fairly straightforward. Just like with the Image and Label Web controls we added to our page in Hour 2, "Understanding the ASP.NET Programming Model," adding a TextBox Web control to a page is no different. Simply drag the TextBox from the Toolbox onto the page, either from the Design view or Source view. After adding the TextBox to the page, you can configure its properties through the Properties window (or by typing them in directly in the Source view, if you prefer).

Watch Out!

> There is one caveat that's important to mention. When adding Web controls that collect user inputs—like TextBoxes, RadioButtons, DropDownLists, Buttons, and so on—you *must* place these Web controls within the page's **Web Form.** The Web Form is the name for that `<form runat="server">` markup we talked about in Hour 2. If you are dragging controls onto your page from the Design view, you need not worry about this because the controls will automatically be added within your page's Web Form. However, if you are adding the controls from the Source view, make sure you drag the Web controls onto the page somewhere between the opening `<form runat="server">` tag and the closing `</form>` tag.
>
> We'll be discussing *why* this is essential in detail in Hour 9, "Web Form Basics."

Before we drag a TextBox Web control onto the page, let's first create the title for the TextBox we're going to add. Because the first input is the amount of the mortgage, start by typing in this title in the `FinancialCalculator.aspx` page's Design view: `Principal Amount:`.

Next we want to add a TextBox Web control after this title. To accomplish this, make sure that the Web Controls tab from the Toolbox is selected; then drag a TextBox control from the Toolbox and drop it into the page after the `Principal Amount:` title.

Take a moment to make sure your screen looks similar to Figure 4.3.

By the Way

> Recall that an ASP.NET web page's HTML portion can be crafted using either the Design view or Source view. For most of the examples throughout this book I'll be using the Design view in the screenshots that highlight the progress. Feel free to use the view that works best for you, though.

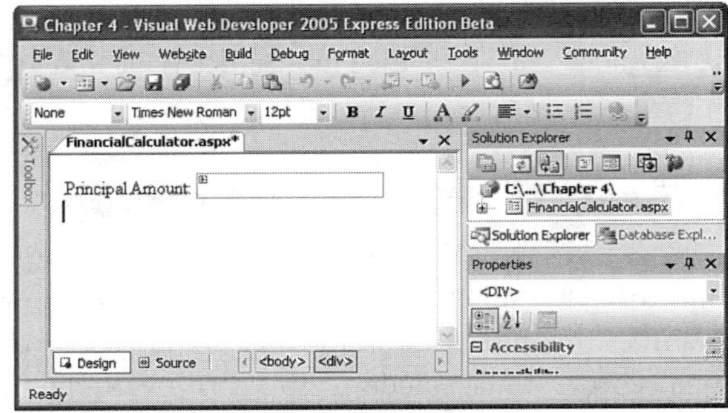

FIGURE 4.3
At this point you should have a title and a single TextBox.

Currently, the TextBox Web control we just added has its `ID` property set to `TextBox1`. Because we will later need to programmatically refer to this `ID` in order to determine the value of the beginning mortgage principal entered by the user, let's choose an `ID` value that is representative of the data found within the TextBox. Specifically, change the `ID` property to `loanAmount`.

Did you Know?

> To change a Web control's `ID` property, click on the Web control, which will load the Web control's properties in the Properties pane in the lower-right corner. Scroll through the Properties pane until you see the `ID` property. This is the property value that you should change. Note that in the list of properties in the Properties pane, the `ID` property is denoted as (ID).

Now let's add the second TextBox, the mortgage's interest rate. Add it just as we did the previous TextBox Web control by first creating a title for the TextBox. Type in the title `Annual Interest Rate:`. Next, drag and drop a TextBox Web control after this title and change the TextBox's `ID` property to `rate`.

Finally, add the third TextBox, the duration of the mortgage. Start by adding the title `Mortgage Length:`. Then drag and drop a TextBox Web control after the title. Set this TextBox's `ID` to `mortgageLength`.

Did you Know?

> You might want to type in some text after each TextBox Web control to indicate the units that should be entered into the TextBox. For example, after the "Annual Interest Rate" TextBox, you might want to add a percent sign so that the user knows to enter this value as a percentage. Similarly, you might want to enter the word *years* after the "Mortgage Length" TextBox. Figure 4.4 includes these optional additions.

Figure 4.4 shows the Design view after all three input TextBox Web controls have been added.

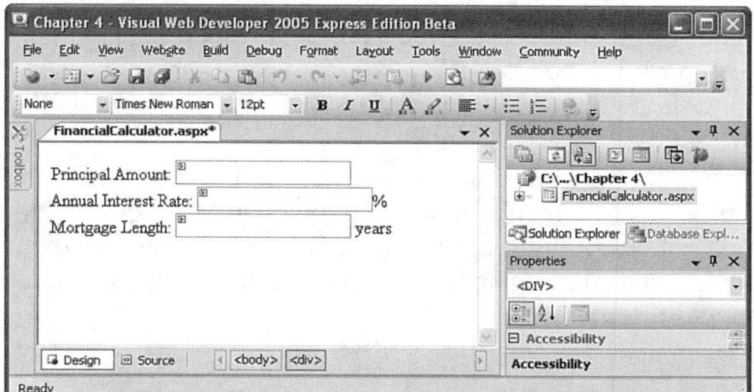

FIGURE 4.4
The Design view, after all three TextBox Web controls have been added.

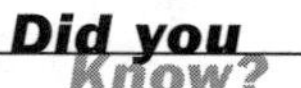

Figure 4.4 shows the TextBox Web control titles in the standard font. Feel free to change the font or the aesthetics of the HTML portion however you see fit. Likewise, you can adjust the font, color, border, and other aesthetic settings of the TextBox Web controls themselves through the Properties pane.

Adding the Compute Monthly Cost Button

After the user has entered inputs into the three TextBox Web controls, we want to be able to take that information and perform our financial calculation. As we discussed in Hour 1, "Getting Started with ASP.NET 2.0," though, there is a temporal, physical, and logical disconnect between the client—the end user's web browser—and the server—the web server software that renders the ASP.NET pages.

When the user visits the `FinancialCalculator.aspx` ASP.NET web page via her browser, she is receiving HTML that contains the user interface we created from the Web controls and static HTML. Once the user's browser has received our ASP.NET page's HTML markup, there's no communication between the client and the server until the client explicitly makes a request *back* to the web server. Therefore, for the calculation to take place, the inputs entered by the user must be submitted back to our ASP.NET web page (`FinancialCalculator.aspx`). Once our ASP.NET web page receives these user-entered values, it can perform the financial computation and return the results.

For the client to post the inputs entered by the end user back to the web server, an HTML `<form>` is used. This process typically commences when a submit button is clicked. We can add such a button by adding a Button Web control to our ASP.NET web page.

The intricacies involved in having the browser send back a user's inputs to the appropriate web page are handled for us automatically by the browser's built-in functionality and the HTML markup produced by the ASP.NET web page and its Web controls.

Although an in-depth understanding of this low-level plumbing is not a requisite, it is important to have, at least, a cursory understanding. For now, let me waive my hands and we'll not worry about what's happening behind the scenes; however, we will return to this topic, discussing the specifics involved with collecting and computing user input in Hour 9.

To add a Button Web control, drag the Button Web control from the Toolbox onto the page, dropping it after the last input title and TextBox. When you add a Button Web control, the Button's caption reads "Button." To change this, click on the Button, and then in the Properties window, change the `Text` property from `Button` to `Compute Monthly Cost`. This will change the caption on your button to "Compute Monthly Cost." Also, while in the Properties window, change the Button's `ID` property—listed in the Property window as (ID)—from the default `Button1` to `performCalc`.

Take a moment to make sure that your screen looks similar to Figure 4.5.

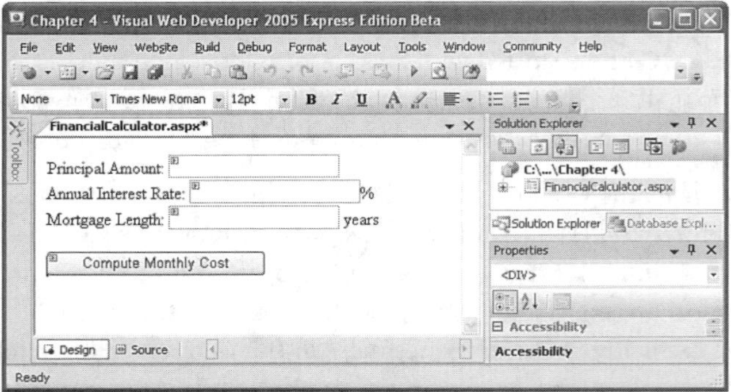

FIGURE 4.5
A Button Web control has been added.

Creating a Label Web Control for the Output

The final piece we need to add to our user interface is a Label Web control that will be used to display the output of our financial calculation. Because the Label Web control will display the output (the amount of money the mortgage costs per month), the web page's final result will appear wherever you place the Web control. Therefore, if you want the output to appear at the bottom of your ASP.NET web page, simply drag and drop a Label Web control after the existing content in the designer. If you want the output to appear at the top of the web page, place it before the existing content in the designer.

After you have added the Label Web control, you will see that it displays the message "Label". The Label Web control displays the value of its Text property, which is configurable via the Properties window. Figure 4.6 shows the designer with the Label Web control added.

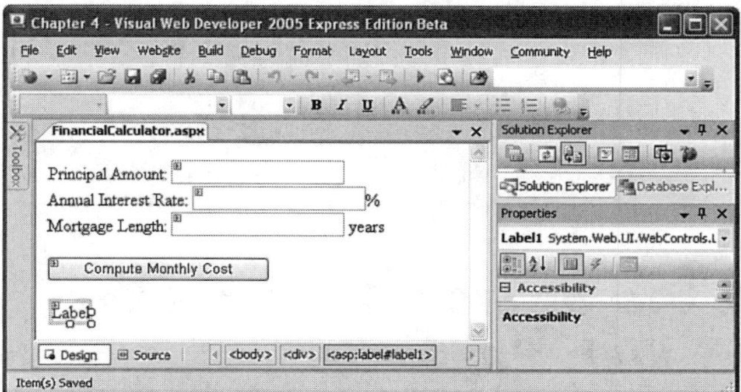

FIGURE 4.6
A Label Web control has been added to the ASP.NET web page.

Because we don't want this Label to display any content until the user has entered three inputs and the calculation has been performed, clear out the Label's Text property.

To clear out a property value for the Label Web control, first click on the Label Web control so that its properties are loaded in the Properties pane. Then, in the Properties pane, locate the Text property and erase the Text property's value by clicking it and pressing Backspace until all of the characters have been erased.

After you clear out the Label's Text property, the designer will show the Label Web control as its ID property, enclosed by brackets. Currently, the Label Web control's ID property is Label1, meaning that in the designer you should see the Label Web control displayed as [Label1]. Go ahead and change the ID property of the Label Web control from Label1 to results, which should change the Label's display in the designer from [Label1] to [results].

Figure 4.7 shows the designer after the Label Web control's property has been changed to results.

Completing the User Interface

At this point we have added the vital pieces of the user interface. If you want to add additional user interface elements at this time, perhaps a bold, centered title at the top of the web page, or a brief set of instructions for the user, feel free to do so.

Now that we have created the HTML portion of the ASP.NET web page, we are ready to create the source code portion. In the next section we will tackle this task.

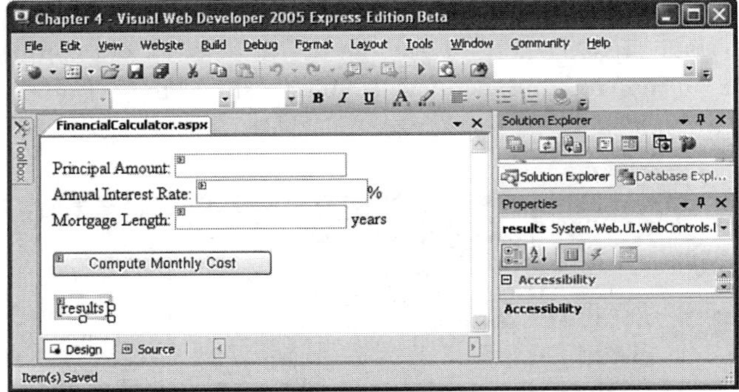

FIGURE 4.7 The Label Web control's `ID` has been changed to `results`.

Writing the Source Code for the ASP.NET Web Page

Now that we have completed the HTML portion of our ASP.NET web page, all that remains is the source code. The source code will read the user's inputs and perform the necessary calculations to arrive at the monthly cost for the mortgage.

In Hour 2 we looked at the page's `Load` event and the corresponding `Page_Load` event handler. This event handler, which you can include in your ASP.NET web page's source code portion, is executed each time the web page is loaded. We will not be placing the source code to perform the monthly mortgage cost calculation in this event handler, though, because we do not want to run the calculation until the user has entered the principal, interest rate, and duration values and has clicked the Compute Monthly Cost button.

Button Web controls have a `Click` event, which fires when the button is clicked. Therefore, what we want to do is create an event handler that is associated with the Compute Monthly Cost button's `Click` event. This way, whenever the Compute Monthly Cost button is clicked, the event handler that we provide will be executed. When we have this event handler, all that will remain will be to write the source code that performs the computation inside this event handler.

Creating an event handler for a Button Web control's `Click` event is remarkably easy to accomplish with Visual Web Developer. The quickest way is to go to the Design view and simply double-click the Button Web control. This will automatically create the necessary event handler and whisk you to the page's source code portion, where you should see the following source code:

```
Partial Class FinancialCalculator
    Inherits System.Web.UI.Page
```

```
    Protected Sub performCalc_Click(ByVal sender As Object, ByVal e As
➥System.EventArgs) Handles performCalc.Click

    End Sub
End Class
```

Note that the event handler is named `performCalc_Click`. More generically, Visual Web Developer names it *`buttonID`*`_Click`, where *`buttonID`* is the value of the Button's `ID` property. (Recall that after adding the Button Web control, we changed its `ID` from `Button1` to `performCalc`.)

Another way to create this same event handler is to go to the source code portion. At the top you'll find two drop-down lists. From the left drop-down list, select the Button Web control (`performCalc`) and then, from the right drop-down list, select the `Click` event. After you select the Click option, an event handler will be automatically created for the `performCalc` Button's `Click` event with the same code had you double-clicked the Button in the Design view.

Any code that you write within the event handler will be executed whenever the `performCalc` button is clicked. Because we want to compute the monthly cost of the mortgage when the `performCalc` button is clicked, the code to perform this calculation will appear within the `performCalc_Click` event handler.

Reading the Values in the TextBox Web Controls

To calculate the monthly cost of the mortgage, we must first be able to determine the values the user entered into the three TextBox Web controls. Before we look at the code to accomplish this, let's take a step back and reexamine Web controls, a topic we touched upon lightly in Hour 2.

Recall that when the ASP.NET engine is executing an ASP.NET web page, Web controls are handled quite differently from standard HTML elements. With static HTML content, the markup is passed directly from the ASP.NET engine to the web server without any translation; with Web controls, however, the Web control's syntax is rendered into a standard HTML element. Specifically, what's happening behind the scenes is that an object is created that represents the Web control. The object created is created from the class that corresponds to the specific Web control. That is, a TextBox Web control has an object **instantiated** from the `TextBox` class, whereas a Label Web control has an object **instantiated** from the `Label` class.

By the Way

Recall that a class is an abstract blueprint, whereas an object is a concrete instance. When an object is created, it is said to have been **instantiated**. The act of creating an object is often referred to as **instantiation**.

Each of these Web control classes has various properties that describe the state of the Web control. For example, the `TextBox` class has a `Columns` property that indicates how many columns the TextBox has. Both the `TextBox` and `Label` classes have `Text` properties that indicate that Web control's text content.

Did you Know?

> A complete list of properties, methods, and events for the Web control classes, along with a description and sample code, can be found in the Visual Web Developer help. If you have enabled Dynamic Help, you can simply click on the Web control that you want to learn more about, and the Dynamic Help window will be populated with technical documentation, articles, and other related information on that particular control.

The primary benefit of Web controls is that their properties can be accessed in the ASP.NET web page's source code section. Because the `Text` property of the TextBox Web control contains the content of the TextBox, we can reference this property in the Compute Monthly Cost button's `Click` event handler to determine the value the user entered into each TextBox.

For example, to determine the value entered into the Mortgage Amount TextBox, we could use the following line of code:

```
loanAmount.Text
```

When the ASP.NET engine creates an object for the Web control, it names the object the value of the Web control's `ID` property. Because `loanAmount` is the `ID` of the Mortgage Amount TextBox Web control, the object created representing this Web control is named `loanAmount`. To retrieve the `Text` property of the `loanAmount` object, we use the syntax `loanAmount.Text`.

By the Way

> Don't worry if the syntax for retrieving an object's property seems confusing. We will be discussing the syntax and semantics of Visual Basic in greater detail in Hours 5 through 7.

The Complete Source Code

Listing 4.1 contains the complete source code for our ASP.NET web page. Visual Web Developer has already written some of the code—the class declaration and the event handler—for you. You will, however, need to enter the code between lines 4 and 35 into the `performCalc` Button's `Click` event handler.

Did you Know?

Keep in mind that you should *not* type in the line numbers shown in Listing 4.1 as well. The line numbers are present in the code listing only to help reference specific lines of the listing when we're discussing the code.

Also, remember that IntelliSense can help expedite entering property names and alert you when there's a problem. For example, when referencing the `Text` property of the `loanAmount` TextBox Web control, we use `loanAmount.Text`. When you type the period (`.`) after typing in `loanAmount`, you should see a drop-down list of available properties and methods for the TextBox Web control. You can then type in the first few letters of the property or method you want to use and press the Tab key to autocomplete the rest of the property or method name.

Additionally, if you *don't* see a drop-down list, something has gone awry. Did you mistype `loanAmount`? Did you not set the corresponding TextBox Web control's `ID` to `loanAmount`?

LISTING 4.1 **The Computation Is Performed in the `performCalc` Button's Click Event Handler**

```
Partial Class FinancialCalculator
    Inherits System.Web.UI.Page

    Protected Sub performCalc_Click(ByVal sender As Object, ByVal e As
➥System.EventArgs) Handles performCalc.Click
        'Specify constant values
        Const INTEREST_CALCS_PER_YEAR As Integer = 12
        Const PAYMENTS_PER_YEAR As Integer = 12

        'Create variables to hold the values entered by the user
        Dim P As Double = loanAmount.Text
        Dim r As Double = rate.Text / 100
        Dim t As Double = mortgageLength.Text

        Dim ratePerPeriod As Double
        ratePerPeriod = r / INTEREST_CALCS_PER_YEAR

        Dim payPeriods As Integer
        payPeriods = t * PAYMENTS_PER_YEAR

        Dim annualRate As Double
        annualRate = Math.Exp(INTEREST_CALCS_PER_YEAR * Math.Log(1 +
➥ratePerPeriod)) - 1

        Dim intPerPayment As Double
        intPerPayment = (Math.Exp(Math.Log(annualRate + 1) / payPeriods)
➥ - 1) * payPeriods

        'Now, compute the total cost of the loan
        Dim intPerMonth As Double = intPerPayment / PAYMENTS_PER_YEAR

        Dim costPerMonth As Double
```

LISTING 4.1 Continued

```
30:         costPerMonth = P * intPerMonth / (1 - Math.Pow(intPerMonth + 1,
➥ -payPeriods))
31:
32:
33:         'Now, display the results in the results Label Web control
34:         results.Text = "Your mortgage payment per month is $" &
➥ costPerMonth
35:     End Sub
36: End Class
```

An in-depth discussion of the code in Listing 4.1 is provided toward the end of this hour in the "Examining the Source Code" section. For now, simply enter the code as-is, even if there are parts of it you don't understand. One thing to pay attention to, though, is in lines 10 through 12. In these three lines we are reading the values of the three TextBox Web controls and assigning the values to variables.

By the Way

If the source code in Listing 4.1 has you hopelessly lost and confused, don't worry. The point of this hour is to get you creating a useful ASP.NET web page. We will examine the source code for this page in more detail later in this hour. Additionally, we'll spend Hours 5 through 7 investigating the Visual Basic syntax in greater detail.

The mathematical equations used to calculate the monthly interest cost can be found at `http://www.faqs.org/faqs/sci-math-faq/compoundInterest/` . A more in-depth discussion of these formulas can be found at `http://people.hofstra.edu/faculty/Stefan_Waner/RealWorld/Summary10.html` .

Testing the Financial Calculator

Now that we have completed the HTML and source code portions of our ASP.NET web page, it's time to test the financial calculator. To view the ASP.NET web page through your browser, begin by marking `FinancialCalculator.aspx` as the start page. To accomplish this, run the page by going to the Debug menu and choosing Start Without Debugging (or by pressing Ctrl+F5 on your keyboard). This will compile your ASP.NET source code portion and launch a web browser pointed to `FinancialCalculator.aspx`.

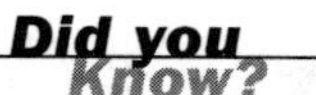

The Start Debugging option compiles the ASP.NET pages' source code portions, starts the Visual Web Developer **debugger**, and visits the page in a browser. The Start Without Debugging option compiles the code and visits the page in a browser *without* starting the debugger.

A debugger is a piece of software that can intercept running code, allowing a programmer to step through executing code one line at a time. Visual Web Developer's debugger is quite powerful and is a very helpful tool when your page's programmatic output isn't what you expected. For now, just use Start Without Debugging; in the section "Using the Debugger," we'll examine the basics of debugging an ASP.NET page.

When first visiting the page, you should see three empty TextBoxes and the Compute Monthly Cost button, as shown in Figure 4.8.

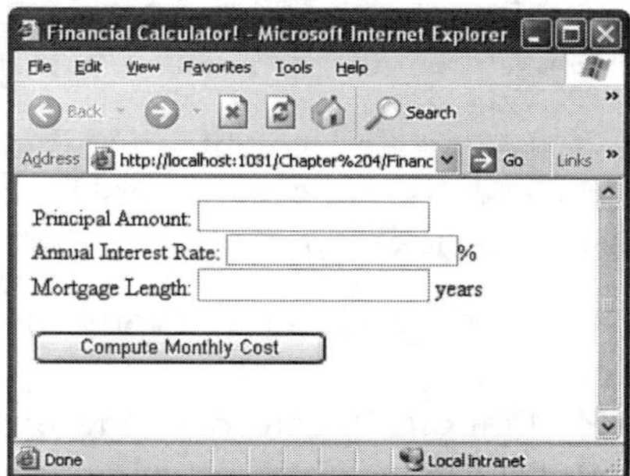

FIGURE 4.8
When the ASP.NET page is first visited, three TextBoxes await user input.

Now, go ahead and enter some valid values into the TextBoxes and then click the Compute Monthly Cost button. When this button is clicked, the monthly cost is displayed beneath the TextBoxes and Button, as shown in Figure 4.9.

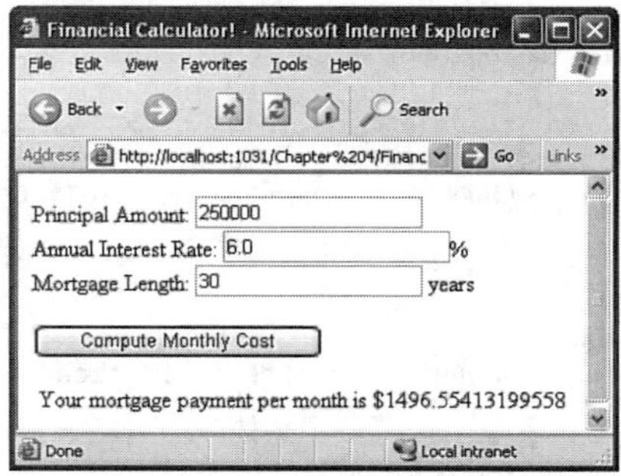

FIGURE 4.9
The output of the financial calculator is displayed when the Button is clicked.

Viewing the Rendered Source Code

When an ASP.NET page is requested by a browser, the ASP.NET engine on the web server renders the ASP.NET page and returns the resulting HTML markup to the browser. The Web controls are transformed into standard HTML elements, and the applicable event handlers in the source code portion are executed, potentially tweaking the resulting output further. (For example, in `FinancialCalculator.aspx` the `performCalc` Button control's `Click` event handler updates the `results` Label Web control's `Text` property, which affects the resulting HTML markup for the page.)

You can see precisely the page's rendered markup by viewing the page's source through the browser. All browsers allow you to view the markup they received; for Internet Explorer, go to the View menu and choose the Source option.

Viewing the resulting HTML markup can, at times, help with diagnosing a problem. Even if there are no problems, I encourage you to view the source often as you're learning ASP.NET to see how Web controls are rendered as HTML.

Let's take a moment to examine the HTML output generated by `FinancialCalculator.aspx`, both when the page is first visited as well as after the user has input values and clicked the Compute Monthly Cost button.

Listing 4.2 contains the HTML received when first visiting the ASP.NET page.

LISTING 4.2 The HTML Markup Received by the Browser When First Visiting the Page

```
<!DOCTYPE html PUBLIC "-//W3C//DTD XHTML 1.0 Transitional//EN"
➥ "http://www.w3.org/TR/xhtml1/DTD/xhtml1-transitional.dtd">

<html xmlns="http://www.w3.org/1999/xhtml" >
<head><title>
   Financial Calculator!
</title></head>
<body>
    <form name="form1" method="post" action="FinancialCalculator.aspx"
➥ id="form1">
<div>
<input type="hidden" name="__VIEWSTATE" id="__VIEWSTATE"
➥value="/wEPDwUKMTY1MDQyNjc5NWRkWCZG70mybehTLkL+AMJBTgTYIUg=" />
</div>

    <div>
        Principal Amount:
        <input name="loanAmount" type="text" id="loanAmount" />
        <br />
        Annual Interest Rate:
        <input name="rate" type="text" id="rate" />%
        <br />
        Mortgage Length:
        <input name="mortgageLength" type="text" id="mortgageLength" />
➥ years
```

LISTING 4.2 Continued

```
22:         <br /><br />
23:         <input type="submit" name="performCalc"
➥value="Compute Monthly Cost" id="performCalc" /><br />
24:         <br />
25:          <span id="results"></span></div>
26:
27: <div>
28:
29:     <input type="hidden" name="__EVENTVALIDATION"
➥id="__EVENTVALIDATION" value=
➥"/wEWBQKcrbH5AgKCs9T4CwKUhujeBAKYoa30AgLenfqNAb2wEvk+jxCQoSwPS9/KqKgwouro" />
30: </div></form>
31: </body>
32: </html>
```

The HTML received by the browser looks pretty similar to the HTML content in the ASP.NET page's HTML portion, save for a few exceptions. First, the `@Page` directive that is found at the top of the ASP.NET page's HTML portion is *not* rendered and sent to the requesting browser. Second, the Web Form—that `<form runat="server">`—is converted into a more detailed `<form>` tag (see line 8) and also includes some hidden form fields (see lines 10 and 29).

The TextBox, Button, and Label Web controls have also been transformed from their Web control syntax—`<asp:`*`WebControlName`*` runat="server" ... />`—to standard HTML elements. The TextBox Web controls have been converted into `<input type="text">` elements (lines 15, 18, and 21), the Label Web control into a `<span>` (line 25), and the Button Web control into `<input type="submit">` (line 23). Notice that the properties of the Web controls are translated into attributes in the controls' corresponding HTML elements. For example, the `ID` properties of the Web controls are rendered as `id` attributes in the resulting HTML elements.

After a user enters particular values into the three text boxes in his browser and clicks the Compute Monthly Cost button, the browser re-requests `FinancialCalculator.aspx`, but this time sends this user-entered information back to the web server with the request. Submitting user-entered values back to the same web page is referred to as a **postback** and is the most common way user-entered information is relayed back to the web server for the server-side code to process.

On postback, the ASP.NET engine can determine that the postback was caused by the Compute Monthly Cost button being clicked and therefore raises the `performCalc` Button control's `Click` event, which in turn causes the associated event handler to run. In addition, the `Text` properties of the three TextBox Web controls are updated to reflect the values entered by the user. The event handler for the Button's `Click` event runs (see Listing 4.1), computing the monthly cost for the mortgage based on the user's inputs. The `results` Label Web control's `Text` property is updated with this computed cost. Finally, the page is rendered, generating the HTML markup that is sent back to the client.

The resulting markup from the postback has changed slightly from the first time the page was requested because now the TextBox Web controls' `Text` properties have values (based on the user's inputs), and the `results` Label Web control's `Text` property is set to the monthly cost. Listing 4.3 shows the HTML received by the browser after the inputs have been entered and the Compute Monthly Cost button has been clicked.

LISTING 4.3 The HTML Markup Received by the Browser After the User Has Clicked the Button

```
<!DOCTYPE html PUBLIC "-//W3C//DTD XHTML 1.0 Transitional//EN"
➥ "http://www.w3.org/TR/xhtml1/DTD/xhtml1-transitional.dtd">

<html xmlns="http://www.w3.org/1999/xhtml" >
<head><title>
    Financial Calculator!
</title></head>
<body>
    <form name="form1" method="post" action="FinancialCalculator.aspx"
➥ id="form1">
<div>
<input type="hidden" name="__VIEWSTATE" id="__VIEWSTATE"
➥value="/wEPDwUKMTY1MDQyNjc5NQ9kFgICAw9kFgICCQ8PFgIeBFRleHQFNFlvdXI➥gbW9ydGdhZ2
UgcGF5bWVudCBwZXIgbW9udGggaXMgJDE0OTYuNTU0MTMxOTk1NThkZGQmhcYzmU7nNm+➥gvjipGZoNR
pn60g==" />
</div>

    <div>
        Principal Amount:
        <input name="loanAmount" type="text" value="250000"
➥id="loanAmount" />
        <br />
        Annual Interest Rate:
        <input name="rate" type="text" value="6.0" id="rate" />%
        <br />
        Mortgage Length:
        <input name="mortgageLength" type="text" value="30"
➥id="mortgageLength" /> years
        <br /><br />
        <input type="submit" name="performCalc"
➥value="Compute Monthly Cost" id="performCalc" /><br />
        <br />
         <span id="results">Your mortgage payment per month is
➥$1496.55413199558</span></div>

<div>

    <input type="hidden" name="__EVENTVALIDATION" id="__EVENTVALIDATION"
➥ value="/wEWBQKh8oS+BwKCs9T4CwKUhujeBAKYoa30AgLenfqNAT6xN1DkR5
➥CYWYqiT0Fwk8flqLpm" />
</div></form>
</body>
</html>
```

The HTML markup in Listing 4.3 has some very important differences from the HTML in Listing 4.2. The `Text` property of the three TextBox Web controls is now reflected in the corresponding `<input type="text">` HTML elements. Specifically, the value of the TextBox Web control's `Text` property has been emitted as a `value` attribute (lines 15, 18, and 21). Additionally, the Label Web control's `Text` property has been emitted as the inner content of the corresponding `<span>` tag (line 25).

The key points in this interaction are highlighted in Figure 4.10.

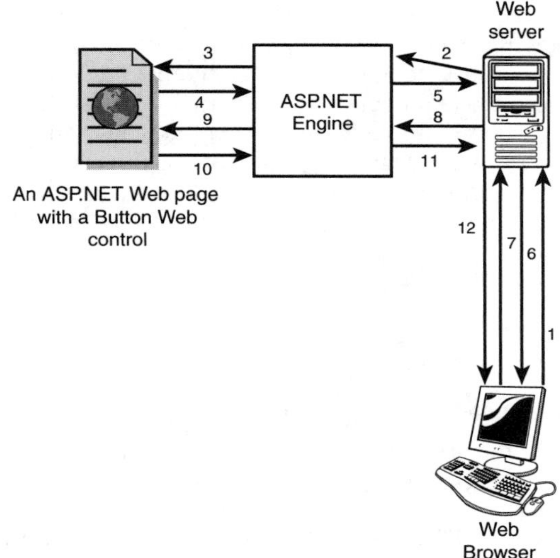

FIGURE 4.10 Server-side code is executed only when the client makes a request to the server.

SEQUENCE OF STEPS:

1. The Web browser requests the FinancialCalculator.aspx Web page from the Web server.
2. The Web server hands off the request to the ASP.NET engine.
3. The ASP.NET engine executes the FinancialCalculator.aspx ASP.NET Web page.
4. The ASP.NET Web page's source code and Web controls are rendered as HTML.
5. The ASP.NET Engine returns the resulting HTML to the Web server.
6. The Web server returns the resulting HTML to the Web browser, which displays the Web page.

7. The User clicks the button, which posts back the ASP.NET Web page, rerequesting the FinancialCalculator.aspx Web page from the Web server.
8. The Web server hands off the request to the ASP.NET engine.
9. The ASP.NET engine detects that the request is a postback, and the postback occurred because the button was clicked. Therefore, the Button's Click event is fired.
10. The ASP.NET Web page is converted into HTML markup, just the in step 4.
11. Same as step 5.
12. Same as step 6.

It's important to understand that the only way the code in an ASP.NET page's source code portion can run is when a request is made from the end user's browser to the web server. For pages on which the user is prompted to supply the inputs, the server-side code does not execute until the user submits the form, which typically involves clicking a submit button (which is rendered by using a Button Web control). This process will be discussed in greater detail in Hour 9.

By the Way

> In your testing, when you click the Compute Monthly Cost button, your browser is re-requesting the `FinancialCalculator.aspx` page, sending along your inputs. This entire interaction is likely happening in a split second on your computer, so you might not even realize this step is taking place. It just looks instantaneous: You click the button; the mortgage cost immediately appears on the page.
>
> The reason there is seemingly no delay in your testing is that in this case the client—the web browser—and server—the web server software and ASP.NET engine—reside on the same machine, your personal computer. Typically, the client and server are separated physically, connected via the Internet. Your user experience is so snappy because there is no network lag time; in a real-world use setting, though, there will be a short delay between clicking the button and seeing the result, with the actual delay time depending on a host of variables (whether the client has a low or high bandwidth connection to the Internet, the responsiveness of the web server, the route across which the request and response must travel over the Internet, and network congestion).

Testing Erroneous Input

Part of testing is testing not only expected inputs, but also unexpected ones. For example, what will happen if the user enters into the Mortgage Length TextBox a value of "Jisun"? Obviously, this is not a valid number of years.

Entering such an erroneous value will cause a runtime error, as shown in Figure 4.11.

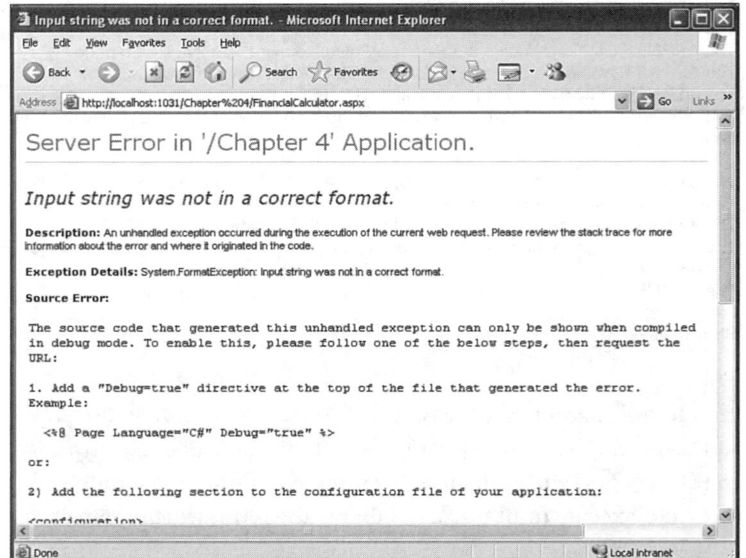

FIGURE 4.11
A runtime error will occur if the input is not in proper format.

Errors such as those shown in Figure 4.11 are an eyesore. Rather than displaying such error messages when the user enters erroneous input, it would be better to display a simple error message next to the TextBox(es) with erroneous input, explaining that the input is not in the right form.

The process of ensuring that user input is in the correct format is known as **input validation**. Fortunately, input validation is incredibly easy with ASP.NET. We'll examine ASP.NET's input validation features in Hour 12, "Validating User Input with Validation Controls."

> **By the Way**
>
> Earlier in this hour we discussed the importance of planning the user interface and functionality of an ASP.NET web page prior to creating the page. It is important to plan not only how the ASP.NET web pages should work, but also how the ASP.NET web page should behave when things don't necessarily go according to plan.

Examining the Source Code

While we've yet to take an in-depth look at the Visual Basic language, I believe it will still prove worthwhile to take a moment to go over the source code for the ASP.NET page we just created. We've already discussed the "filler" code inserted automatically by Visual Web Developer—the class definition and `Inherits` statement, as well as the event handler—so let's concentrate on the code within the event handler. This is the code that is executed when the user clicks on the Compute Monthly Cost button. Its aim is to read in the user's inputs and calculate and display what the monthly mortgage costs.

The first line of code in the event handler (line 5) is a **comment**. In Visual Basic, comments are denoted by an apostrophe (`'`); all other content after an apostrophe is ignored by the ASP.NET engine. Comments serve a simple purpose: to make source code more readable by humans. Throughout the code examples in this book, you'll find helpful comments littered throughout, making it easier for you to read and understand what's happening.

After the first comment are two **constants**. A constant is a value that cannot be changed programmatically. The two constants here—`INTEREST_CALCS_PER_YEAR` and `PAYMENTS_PER_YEAR`—define how often the interest is compounded and how many pay periods will occur throughout the life of the loan. By default these are both 12, indicating that the loan compounds every month and payments are made once per month. Next, on lines 10 through 12, the values from the three TextBox Web controls are read into **variables**. A variable is a construct that holds some value. The variables defined here are named `P`, `r`, and `t`, and are of **type** Double.

The type of a variable indicates what sort of information it can hold. A Double is a predefined type in the .NET Framework that can hold a vast array of various numbers of varying precision.

After these TextBox Web control values have been read in, we apply the mathematical formulas needed to compute the monthly payment due.

On lines 14 and 15 the variable `ratePerPeriod` is created and assigned the value of the interest rate each time it's compounded. Following that, the number of pay periods is recorded and stored in the `payPeriods` variable. Next, the annual interest rate is determined as well as how much interest per payment is due (and then how much interest is due per month). Finally, the cost per month is computed on line 30. The resulting output is then assigned to the `Text` property of the `results` Label Web control.

The source code in Listing 4.1 is fairly readable, although the mathematical formulas might seem foreign. But I hope you'll agree that if you simply read through the lines of code, one at a time, it is clear what is happening. For example, on line 18, `payPeriods = t * PAYMENTS_PER_YEAR`, we are taking the value of `t` (the loan's term) and multiplying it by the number of payments made per year. This gives us the *total* number of payments made throughout the life of the loan. The point is, with Visual Basic's English-like syntax and semantics, even to someone with little to no programming background, it's possible to pick up the gist of the code by simply reading through it.

Don't worry if you still feel lost and bewildered by Listing 4.1. Your code-reading acumen will greatly improve over the next three hours as we delve into the syntax of Visual Basic. By the time you finish working through Hour 7, "Working with Objects in Visual Basic," you'll have the Visual Basic background necessary for understanding all of the examples throughout this book.

Using the Debugger

Over the course of creating ASP.NET pages, you'll undoubtedly run into problems where the page's source code portion isn't behaving as you'd expect. Perhaps a particular block of source code is not running when you expect it to, or the output you're seeing is different than what you'd expect. In such circumstances, your best friend is the **debugger**. A debugger is a special piece of software that can intercept a running program and provide the programmer a deep level of introspection into the inner workings of the program. Unfortunately, we don't have the time or space to delve into the depths of debugging; instead, we'll just concentrate on some of the more common debugging tasks.

To use the debugger when testing an ASP.NET page, you need to go to the Debug menu and choose Start Debugging. If this is the first time you've attempted to debug this particular website, the Debugging Not Enabled dialog box will appear, as shown in Figure 4.12. If you need to debug an ASP.NET website, the site must be configured to support debugging; by default, a new ASP.NET website project is *not* configured to support debugging. The Debugging Not Enabled dialog box warns you of this and offers to automatically alter the `web.config` configuration file to enable debugging support.

You can also start debugging by pressing F5 or the green play button icon in the toolbar.

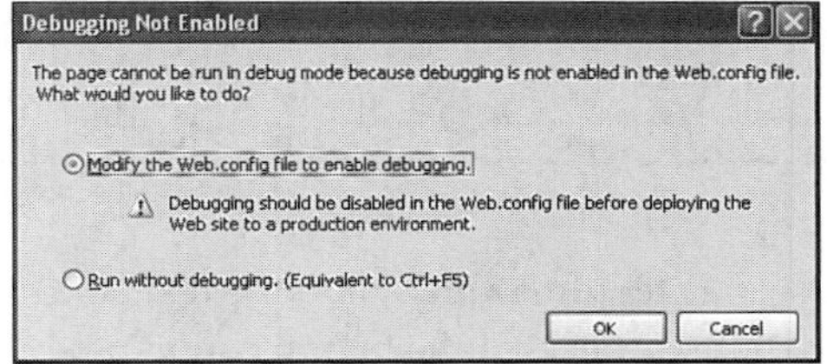

FIGURE 4.12 The Debugging Not Enabled dialog box warns you that the application is not configured for debugging.

Opt to have the `web.config` file updated so that the website supports debugging by selecting Modify the `Web.config` File to Enable Debugging and click the OK button. This will fire up the browser, loading the `FinancialCalculator.aspx` page, just as in Figure 4.8.

At this point you can't even tell that the debugger is running because there's nothing different shown in the browser. The difference is that now you can add one or more **breakpoints** to your ASP.NET page's source code portion. A breakpoint is a marker in the source code that, when reached, causes the program to halt, letting the debugger take over. When a breakpoint is reached, control automatically reverts to Visual Web Developer, allowing you to step through the execution of the code one line at a time, viewing the value of variables.

Let's set a breakpoint. Leave the browser running and return to the `FinancialCalculator.aspx` page's source code portion in Visual Web Developer. Let's add a breakpoint to the line of code that reads `Dim P As Double = loanAmount.Text` (line 10 in Listing 4.1). To accomplish this, place your cursor on this line of code and press F9; alternatively, you can click in the light gray, left margin next to this line of code. In either case, a breakpoint will be set, which will display a red circle in the margin and highlight the line of code in red. Figure 4.13 shows the page's source code portion in Visual Web Developer after this breakpoint has been set.

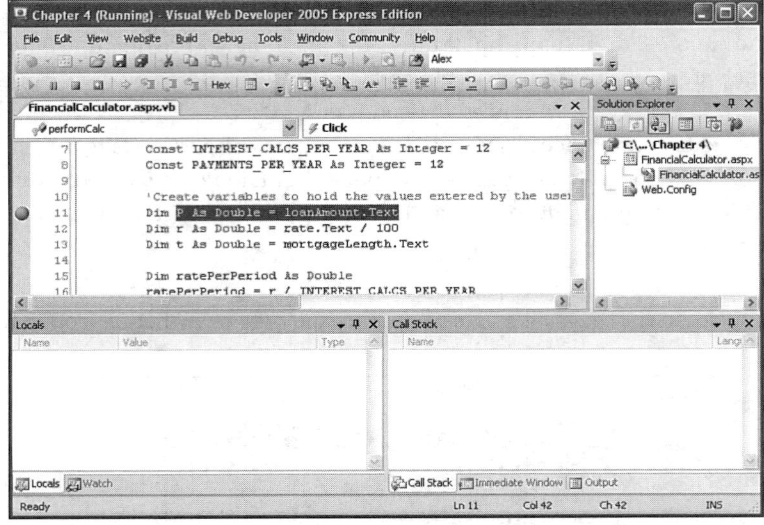

FIGURE 4.13
A breakpoint has been set.

Now return to the browser, enter some values into the text boxes, and click the Compute Monthly Cost button. Clicking the button causes a postback, which returns control to the ASP.NET page's source code portion, invoking the Button's `Click` event handler to execute. As this execution occurs, eventually the `Dim P As Double = loanAmount.Text` line of code is reached, where we have our breakpoint. When this line is hit, the program halts and the debugger takes over. In Visual Web Developer, the current line of code being executed is highlighted yellow (see Figure 4.14); this current line of code is the line where we set the breakpoint moments ago.

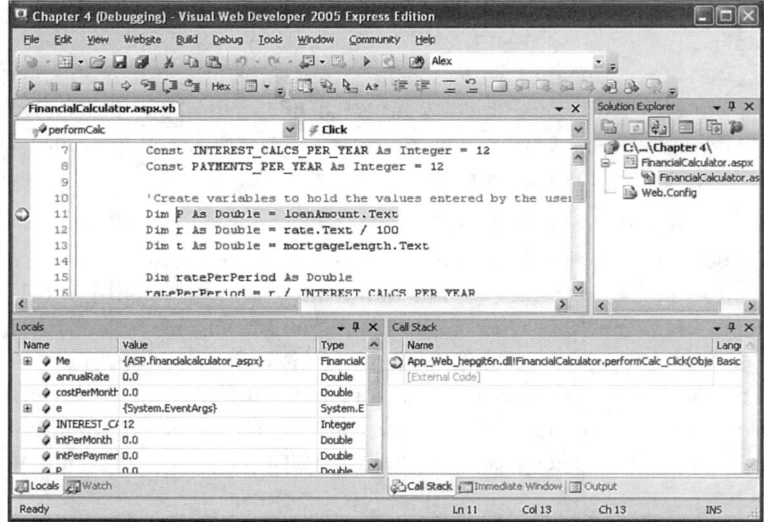

FIGURE 4.14
The breakpoint has been reached, halting program execution.

When a breakpoint is hit and program execution is halted, the debugger takes over. From the debugger we can inspect the values of various variables. For example, in the lower-left corner of Figure 4.14, you'll find the Locals window, which shows all of the current variables and their values. Many of these variables have their default values. For example, the variables `annualRate`, `costPerMonth`, `intPerMonth`, and so on all have values of 0. The reason is that we've yet to reach the lines of code where these variables are assigned a value. As we step through the executing program, these values in the Locals window will be updated accordingly.

To progress the flow of the program's execution, go to the Debug menu and choose Step Over, or simply press F10. This will move you to the next line of code. Press F10 a couple of times and note how the yellow highlighted line moves further down the lines of code, updating the values in the Locals window. If you want to run until the next breakpoint, press F5, or go to the Debug menu and choose Continue. Doing so in our example will return control to the browser because no more breakpoints will be reached.

Did you Know?

In addition to using the Locals window, you can determine the value of a variable by simply hovering your mouse pointer over the variable's name in the source code portion. There are also additional debugging windows that can be of help. The Watch window allows you to specify particular variables or expressions whose value you want to monitor. A complete list of debugging-related windows can be found in the Debug menu's Windows submenu.

To stop debugging altogether, go to the Debug menu and choose Stop Debugging.

The preceding explanation is but a brief overview of the debugging capabilities offered by Visual Web Developer. Before you explore Visual Web Developer's debugging capabilities in more detail, I first encourage you to become more familiar with creating ASP.NET web pages. When you're ready, however, you can learn more about the debugging process at Microsoft's *Walkthrough: Debugging Web Pages in Visual Web Developer*, available online at http://msdn2.microsoft.com/en-us/library/z9e7w6cs.

Summary

In this hour we saw how to create our first useful ASP.NET web page. We started by outlining the features we wanted to include in our ASP.NET web page, including the output and needed inputs. We then briefly discussed what the user interface should look like.

Next, we implemented the user interface by completing the HTML portion of the ASP.NET web page. With Visual Web Developer, this was simply a matter of typing in the TextBox labels and dragging and dropping the needed TextBox, Button, and Label Web controls onto the page.

After the HTML portion, the source code portion was entered. The code to perform the calculation was inserted in an event handler for the Compute Monthly Cost Button's `Click` event. This had the effect of having the entered code executed whenever the user clicked the Compute Monthly Cost button.

Following the design and development stages, we tested the ASP.NET web page by visiting it with a Web browser and entering some values for the three TextBoxes. This hour concluded with discussion of the source code portion of the ASP.NET page.

Q&A

Q. ***How do I associate "event code" with a Web control that I've placed on a Web Form? Can I always just double-click the Web control in the Design view?***

A. In this hour we saw how to have the Button Web control's `Click` event associated with an event handler provided in the source code section. One way to accomplish this is by simply double-clicking the Button Web control in the Design view. This causes Visual Web Developer to inject some code into the page's source code portion. For the Button Web control, a `Click` event handler is added.

However, a Web control may have a number of different events, meaning we can, potentially, have numerous event handlers in our ASP.NET page's source code. Each Web control has a **default event**. When the Web control is double-clicked in the designer, an event handler is created for this default event. (Note that the Button Web control's default event is the `Click` event.)

Adding an event handler for an event other than a Web control's default event requires that you go directly to the source code portion and pick the Web control and event from the two drop-down lists at the top. This is a technique we discussed briefly in both this hour and in Hour 2.

Q. ***What would happen if I placed the financial calculation code in the*** `Page_Load` ***event handler instead of the*** `Button_Click` ***event handler?***

A. Recall that the source code in the `Page_Load` event handler executes every time the ASP.NET web page is requested. When the user visits the page for the first time, she has yet to enter the loan principal, interest rate, and duration. Therefore, in attempting to compute the calculation, we will get an error. Specifically, the code will try to perform numerical calculations on a user-inputted value that has yet to be provided.

Because we want to perform the calculation only *after* the user has provided the required inputs, the source code for the calculation is placed in the Button's `Click` event handler.

Workshop

Quiz

1. Why is the design requirements phase of software development an important one?
2. How can you add a TextBox Web control to an ASP.NET web page using Visual Web Developer?
3. Why did we add a Label Web control to our ASP.NET web page's HTML portion?
4. What will the ASP.NET web page's output be if the user enters invalid characters into the TextBoxes? For example, if under the Mortgage Amount TextBox, the user enters "Sam"?
5. How do you add an event handler for a Button Web control's `Click` event with Visual Web Developer?
6. When using a TextBox Web control, what property is referenced to determine the value entered by the user?

Answers

1. The design requirements phase outlines the specific features for the software project and also outlines the user interface. It is an important stage because, by enumerating the features, you and your boss and client can easily determine the current progress of the project. Furthermore, there is no ambiguity as to what features should and should not be included.
2. There are two ways to add a TextBox Web control. First, you can simply click the TextBox Web control from the Toolbox and drag it onto the page. Second, from the Source view, you can manually type in the TextBox's syntax:

   ```
   <asp:TextBox runat="server" ID="ID"></asp:TextBox>
   ```

3. A Label Web control was added to the ASP.NET web page's HTML portion to indicate where the output of the financial calculator would appear.
4. If the user provides invalid input, a runtime error will occur. Refer to Figure 4.11 for the error message the user will receive.
5. To add an event handler for a Button Web control's `Click` event, simply double-click the Button in the Design view that you want to add an event handler for. You can alternatively create the event handler by selecting the appropriate

Web control and event items from the two drop-down lists at the top of the source code portion.

6. The `Text` property contains the value entered by the user. To reference this property in an ASP.NET web page's source code portion, we can use

```
TextBoxID.Text
```

Exercises

1. In this hour we saw how to use Visual Web Developer to create an ASP.NET web page with three TextBox Web controls, a Button Web control, and a Label Web control. Using this knowledge, let's create an ASP.NET web page that will prompt the user for his name and age. After the user provides this information and clicks the submit button, the ASP.NET web page will display a message for the user, depending on his age.

   This ASP.NET web page will need to have two TextBox Web controls, a Button Web control, and a Label Web control. Set the TextBox Web controls' `ID` properties to `name` and `age`. The Button Web control should have its `Text` property set to `Click Me`. Set the Label Web control's `ID` property to `results` and clear out its `Text` property. Then create an event handler for the Button Web control's `Click` event. Recall that this is accomplished by simply double-clicking the Button in the designer.

   Now, in the `Click` event handler, determine what message to display, based on the user's age. The code for this will look like:

   ```
   If age.Text < 21 then
     results.Text = name.Text & ", you are a youngster!"
   End If

   If age.Text >= 21 AND age.Text < 40 then
     results.Text = name.Text & ", you are an adult."
   End If

   If age.Text >= 40 then
     results.Text = name.Text & ", you are over the hill!"
   End If
   ```

   After you have entered the preceding source code into the Button Web control's `Click` event handler, save the ASP.NET web page and test it by visiting it through a browser.

2. For more practice with Visual Web Developer, take a moment to enhance the user interface of the `FinancialCalculator.aspx` web page we created in this hour. Some suggested enhancements include displaying the TextBox Web control titles in a more appealing font, adding some text at the top of the web page explaining the purpose of the financial calculator, and so on.

HOUR 5

Understanding Visual Basic's Variables and Operators

In this hour, we will cover

- What a programming language is
- What variables are and how to declare them
- How to assign values to variables
- What data types are and why they are important
- Visual Basic's operators and how to use them
- Typing rules

As discussed earlier, ASP.NET web pages are composed of two portions: an HTML portion, which contains HTML markup and Web controls; and a source code portion, which contains the ASP.NET web page's server-side source code. Using Visual Web Developer, you can write this source code section in one of two programming languages: Visual Basic or Visual C# (often referred to as just C#).

Most beginning developers find Visual Basic a much easier language to pick up than C#, mainly because Visual Basic's syntax and structure are much closer to everyday English than C#'s. Therefore, all of the source code portions of ASP.NET web pages discussed throughout this book use Visual Basic as the programming language.

If you are new to programming, you likely found the source code portions of the example in Hours 2 and 4 to be a bit daunting. Don't worry; in this hour and the next two, we'll take an in-depth look at Visual Basic. By the end of these three hours, you'll be able not only to make sense of source similar to that in previous hours, but also to write similar code on your own.

If you've had programming experience with Visual Basic for .NET in the past, you may need to just skim the contents of the next three hours because it is geared toward those who have had limited programming experience. If you have had experience with Visual Basic 6.0 or VBScript—versions of Visual Basic before Microsoft introduced the .NET Framework—I encourage you to read these three hours because there have been some important changes in the syntax and semantics from Visual Basic 6.0 and VBScript.

The Purpose of Programming Languages

When computers were first designed in the early twentieth century, they were created to carry out mathematical computations that, at the time, were performed by humans. Computers were preferred over man because they could perform the calculations faster, could work around the clock, and were not susceptible to error. That is, a computer doesn't forget to carry the one when subtracting two numbers, an error every human has likely made at some point.

Computers then, as computers today, were built to accept a sequence of **instructions** and to carry out these instructions in the order in which they arrived. This made computers ideal for solving problems that could be broken down into a sequence of simple steps. For example, addition of large numbers can be broken down into simpler addition problems by first adding together the ones place in both numbers, then the tens place, and so on, carrying over a digit into the preceding column if needed.

For a computer to solve a problem, though, it first needs to be told the sequence of steps to perform. Think of a computer as a very obedient young child, one who can understand only simple words and commands and will always do whatever you instruct. If you want this child to, say, go to sleep, you would have to tell him first to go to his bedroom, which might require that you first tell him to start walking toward the stairs. Then you would need to give instructions to step up the first step, then the second, and so on. After that you might need to tell him to walk down the hall to his room. You would then need to tell him to open his door, to walk into his room, to lie down in bed, and finally, to fall asleep.

The verbal commands you give the child must be fairly simple ones the child can understand. That is, if you said, "My beloved nipper, I implore that you acquiesce to slumber," the child would wonder what in the world you were saying. Similarly, when you're providing instructions to a computer, the instructions must conform to a specific syntax and structure.

Specifically, computers understand commands only from particular **programming languages**. A programming language is a language with a well-defined syntax and semantics.

There are multitudes of programming languages. When creating ASP.NET web pages, however, we are restricted to using .NET-compatible programming languages, such as Visual Basic and C#.

By the Way

> There are many .NET-compatible programming languages, such as JScript.NET, COBOL.NET, Visual C++, and others. However, ASP.NET web pages are most typically created with either Visual Basic .NET or C#. In fact, Visual Web Developer provides support for using only one of these two languages.

Concepts Common to All Programming Languages

Although many programming languages are in existence, they all share some common features. These features include

- **A means to store data temporarily**—In Visual Basic **variables** are used to store data. We'll be discussing variables in the next section, "Declaring and Using Variables."
- **A set of operators that can be applied to the data stored in variables**—One such operator is +, which sums the values of two variables. We'll look at the operators available in Visual Basic in the "Visual Basic Operators" section.
- **A variety of control structures that can be used to alter the flow of instructions based on the value of variables**—The control structures in Visual Basic are covered in the next hour, "Managing Program Flow with Visual Basic's Control Structures."
- **A way to modularize source code into reusable units**—In Visual Basic, code can be compartmentalized into subroutines and functions, as we'll see in the next hour.

In this hour we will look at how the features of the first of these two universal programming languages are implemented in Visual Basic.

Declaring and Using Variables

A **variable** is a location in the computer's memory where you can temporarily store information, such as a number or a string.

By the Way

> In a programming language, a **string** is a sequence of characters and is delimited by the double quotation marks. An example of a string would be
>
> `"Hello, world!"`

Variables have three components to them:

- A **value**, such as 5, or `"Hello, world!"`
- A **name**, which is used to refer to the value of the variable
- A **type**, which indicates what types of values can be stored. For example, a variable of type `Integer` could store values like 5 and –858. A variable with type `String` could store values like `"Hello, world!"` and `"Jisun is a toad"`.

Did you Know?

Because a variable's type dictates what data can be stored in the variable, a variable's type commonly is referred to as its **data type.**

Think of a variable as a specific type of box into which you can place things of a certain type. Each box has a name that you give it, which you can use to reference the value in a particular box. For example, as Figure 5.1 shows, a box named `age` can accept an integer value. Inside this box we can place values like 24, 97, –3,829,294, or any other valid integer value.

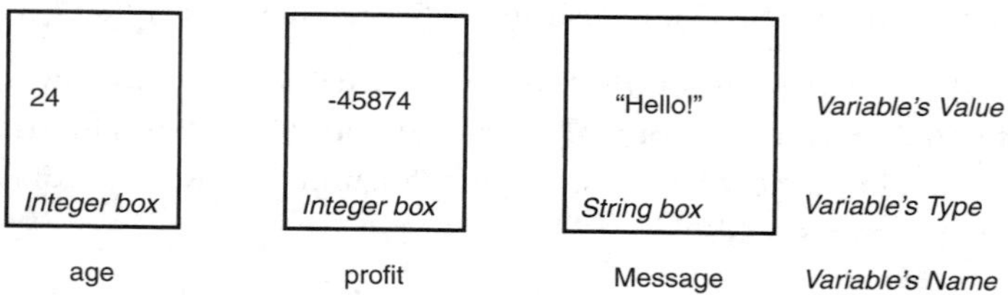

FIGURE 5.1 Think of a variable as a named box that can contain a certain type of value.

Assigning Values to Variables

The name and data type of a variable are **immutable**. That is, once the variable's name and type have been specified, they cannot change during the program's execution. The variable's value, on the other hand, is **mutable**, meaning that it can change over the course of the program's execution.

Variables alter their value through **assignment statements**. An assignment statement assigns a value to a variable using the = operator and has the following form:

```
variableName = value
```

This statement assigns *`value`* to the value of the variable *`variableName`*.

By the Way

> We will discuss the = operator (often referred to as the **assignment operator**) in the "Visual Basic's Assignment Operators" section.

Declaring a Variable

To use a variable, you must first **declare** the variable using the Visual Basic `Dim` statement. When declaring a variable, you must provide both the name and data type of the variable and optionally may include the value. For example, to create a variable named `age` that accepts values of type `Integer`, you would use the following `Dim` statement:

```
Dim age as Integer
```

More generally, the `Dim` statement has the following form:

```
Dim variableName as type
```

We'll examine the `Dim` statement in much greater detail in the "Examining the `Dim` Statement" section. First, though, we need to look at the rules for naming variables, as well as the available variable types.

Rules for Naming Variables

Each programming language imposes its own set of rules for naming variables. For Visual Basic, variable names can start with an alphabetic character or an underscore character, followed by zero to many underscores, alphabetic characters, or numeric characters.

By the Way

> Variable names in Visual Basic may be anywhere from one character long to 16,383 characters long. They are *not* case sensitive, meaning that the casing does not matter. Therefore, the variable name `Age` is equivalent to the variable names `AGE`, `age`, `aGe`, and so on.

Some examples of *valid* variable names are

- `Age`
- `message2`
- `xyz123abc`
- `txtPassword`

Watch Out!

> If a variable name begins with an underscore, it *must* be followed by at least one other character. That is, you cannot have a variable simply named _.

Some examples of *invalid* variable names are

- `3Age`—Invalid because a variable name cannot start with a numeric character.
- `_`—Invalid because if a variable name begins with an underscore, it must be followed by at least one other character.
- `234`—Invalid because a variable name cannot start with a numeric character.

When you're naming your variables, it is important to choose names that make sense given the information the variable will store. For example, if you are going to use a variable to store the product of two numbers, you might want to name that variable `product`, or some other descriptive name, rather than using something ambiguous, like `x` or `variable3`.

Examining Variable Data Types

Recall that the data type of a variable dictates what type of value can be stored in the variable. For example, a variable of type `Integer` can store only values that are integers (negative and positive whole numbers).

If you have worked with ASP, ASP.NET's predecessor, you've likely had experience with VBScript, a watered-down version of Visual Basic 6.0, which was the version of Visual Basic that predated Microsoft's .NET platform. With VBScript, variables were **loosely typed**.

Loosely typed variables are variables that are declared without an explicit data type. Their type is inferred by the value assigned to the variable. For example, in VBScript you could write code that looked like so:

```
1: Dim x
2: x = "Hello, World!"
3: x = 4
```

Note that the `Dim` statement on line 1 does not contain a type (that is, it does not read: `Dim x as String`). The type of `x` is dynamically inferred by the value assigned to it. Therefore, on line 2, when `x` is assigned the value `"Hello, World!"`, which is a string, `x`'s type is considered to be of type `String`. On line 3, however, `x` is assigned the value 4, which is an integer. After line 3, `x`'s type now is considered to be of type `Integer`.

The opposite of loosely typed is **strongly typed**. In strongly typed languages, *all* variables must be declared to be of a certain type. After a variable has been declared to be a certain type, it can be assigned only values that correspond to that type.

By the Way

> With loosely typed languages, any value can be assigned to any variable, and the value being assigned determines the variable's type. With strongly typed languages, a variable's type is explicitly specified, and only values corresponding to the variable's type may be assigned to the variable.

Visual Basic is a strongly typed language. Therefore, all variables must be given an explicit data type, and the set of values that can be assigned to a given variable is limited by the variable's type.

Because each type has a predefined set of values that can be assigned, it is important to give your variable the proper type. For example, in Hour 4, "Designing, Creating, and Testing ASP.NET Web Pages," we looked at an ASP.NET web page that calculated the monthly cost of a home loan. The variables used to hold the intermediary computations were of type `Double`, which is a numeric type that stores numbers with decimal places. Had we chosen to use integer variables, the calculation would have come out incorrectly because we were dealing with decimal numbers.

Specifically, the interest rate involved in the calculation, which might be 0.065 (for a 6.5% interest rate), could not be expressed as an integer. Rather, we would have to use 0 or 1 (or some other whole number), which would clearly produce an incorrect answer. For this reason, using the correct type is important.

In general, when declaring a variable, you use the following syntax:

```
Dim variableName as type
```

Integer Types

Integers are whole numbers that can be either positive or negative. For example, 34, 76, –3,432, and 234,124 are all valid integers, whereas 12.4 and –3.14159 are not.

There are three types of integer data types, each differing in the range of integers it can contain. The most common integer type is type `Integer`, which can accept values ranging from –2,147,483,648 to 2,147,483,647. To create a variable of type `Integer`, use the following syntax:

```
Dim variableName as Integer
```

If you need to store larger or smaller integer values, you can use the `Long` data type, which accepts integer values ranging from –9,223,372,036,854,775,808 to 9,223,372,036,854,775,807. To create a variable of type `Long`, use the following syntax:

```
Dim variableName as Long
```

If you need to store much smaller integer values, you can use the `Short` data type, which can store integers ranging from –32,768 to 32,767. To create a variable of type `Short`, use

```
Dim variableName as Short
```

Nonintegral Numeric Types

Integer variables cannot store numbers that have decimals. However, very often calculations involving numbers with decimals need to be performed. To provide for this, Visual Basic offers three **nonintegral numeric data types**.

> **By the Way**
>
> A nonintegral numeric data type is a data type that has a specific number of significant digits but can have the decimal place moved to improve the accuracy of the decimal portion.

The first nonintegral numeric data type is `Single`, which can accept values ranging from –3.4028235E+38 through –1.401298E–45 for negative values and from 1.401298E–45 through 3.4028235E+38 for positive values.

> **By the Way**
>
> In scientific notation, the number following the E represents the number's **magnitude**. The magnitude specifies the number of decimal places in the number. For example, 6.45E+8 is equal to 6.45 * 10^8, or 645,000,000, and 6.45E-8 is equal to 6.45 * 10^-8, or 0.0000000645. Therefore, 3.4028235E+38 is a *very big* number!

To create a variable of type `Single`, use the following syntax:

```
Dim variableName as Single
```

A more precise nonintegral numeric data type that also allows for larger numbers is `Double`, which can accept values ranging from –1.79769313486231570E+308 through –4.94065645841246544E–324 for negative values and from 4.94065645841246544E–324 through 1.79769313486231570E+308 for positive values. To create a variable of type `Double`, use the following syntax:

```
Dim variableName as Double
```

The third and final nonintegral numeric data type is `Decimal`, which scales the decimal place by powers of 10. `Decimals` can have from 0 to 28 decimal places. With zero decimal places, the largest number a `Decimal` can have is 79,228,162,514,264,337,593,543,950,335 (the smallest being –79,228,162,514,264,337,593,543,950,335). The `Decimal` can have, at most, 28 decimal digits. Hence, the largest number with 28 decimal digits is

7.9228162514264337593543950335. To create a variable of type `Decimal`, use the following syntax:

```
Dim variableName as Decimal
```

Boolean Data Types

A Boolean variable is a variable that can be assigned only one of two values: either `True` or `False`. To create a Boolean variable, use the `Boolean` variable type. The following syntax demonstrates how to create a variable of type `Boolean`:

```
Dim variableName as Boolean
```

String Types

A string is a sequence of characters. For example, `"ASP.NET is fun!"` is a string composed of 15 characters, the first being `A`, the second being `S`, and so on, with the 15th one being `!`. To create a variable that can store string values, use the type `String`. To create a variable of type `String`, use the following syntax:

```
Dim variableName as String
```

Date Types

To allow for a variable to store specific dates, specify the variable's data type as `Date` using the following syntax:

```
Dim variableName as Date
```

A `Date` variable can store dates between midnight on January 1, 0001, through 11:59:59 p.m. on December 31, 9999.

The `Object` Type

Visual Basic contains a catchall type, a data type that can be assigned *any* value. This base type is the `Object` type. The `Object` type is, by its nature, extremely flexible because you can assign a variable of any type to it. For example, as the following code shows, you can assign a string to an `Object` type, and then an integer, and then a nonintegral number:

```
Dim catchall as Object
catchall = "Jisun"
catchall = 4
catchall = 3.14159
```

Despite its flexibility, you should rarely, if ever, create a variable of type `Object`. The benefit of using more specific types like `Integer`, `String`, and `Double` is that if you accidentally try to assign an inappropriate value to one of these variables, an error message will be displayed.

Examining the `Dim` Statement

As we discussed earlier, before using a variable, you must declare the variable. When declaring a variable in a strongly typed programming language, you must specify not only the name of the variable, but also the variable's type. In Visual Basic, this is accomplished using the `Dim` statement.

In its simplest form, the `Dim` statement simply specifies the variable's name and type, as follows:

```
Dim variableName as type
```

If you want to declare three variables of type `Integer`, you can use three separate `Dim` statements, such as

```
Dim a as Integer
Dim b as Integer
Dim c as Integer
```

Or you can use one `Dim` statement, separating each variable name and type with a comma, such as

```
Dim a as Integer, b as Integer, c as Integer
```

You can also supply a comma-delimited list of variable names and just one type. In this instance, all of the variable names appearing before the one type will have the same type. That is, you can declare three variables, `a`, `b`, and `c`, all to be of type `Integer` using the following syntax:

```
Dim a, b, c as Integer
```

Performing Assignment When Declaring a Variable

As we've seen thus far, the `Dim` statement is used for declaring a variable but not for assigning the variable a value. That is, if you wanted to create a variable named a of type `Integer` and have it assigned the value 6, you'd use the following code:

```
Dim a as Integer
a = 6
```

The preceding syntax is fine as-is, but you can save yourself a line of code by combining the assignment with the variable declaration on one line. To do this, use the following syntax:

```
Dim a as Integer = 6
```

Or, more generally

```
Dim variableName as type = value
```

Performing an assignment when declaring a variable is purely optional. We will use this variant of the Dim statement in many examples in this book in the interest of saving space.

Examining Visual Basic's Operators

Simply having a variable with some value in it is not very interesting. Typically, we'd like to be able to perform some sort of operation on that variable, or on multiple variables in tandem. For example, in mathematics there are numbers and operators. Numbers are things like 4, 17.5, pi, and so on, whereas operators are things like negate, add, subtract, divide, and so on.

Many of the traditional mathematical operators are operators in Visual Basic. For example, to add together two numeric variables in Visual Basic, you use the + operator. To multiply two numeric variables, you use the * operator.

There are different classes of operators, the most important being arithmetic operators, comparison operators, the concatenation operator, and assignment operators. We'll examine these four classes of operators in the following four sections.

Arithmetic Operators

The four most-used arithmetic operators in Visual Basic are +, -, *, and /, which perform addition, subtraction, multiplication, and division, respectively. These operators are referred to as **binary operators** because they operate on two variables.

For example, to add together two integer variables and store the result in an integer variable, you could use the following code:

```
Dim a, b, c as Integer
b = 15
c = 20
a = b + c
```

Here, a will be assigned a value equal to the value of b plus the value of c, which is 35.

The - operator can be used both as a binary operator and as a **unary operator**. A unary operator is an operator that operates on just one variable. When the - operator is used as a unary operator, it performs the negation of a number. That is, if we had the code

```
Dim a, b, c as Integer
b = 15
c = 20
a = -(b + c)
```

a would be assigned the value –35. Here, the - operator is used as a unary operator on the expression b + c, thereby negating the value returned by b + c.

By the Way

Note that parentheses can be used to determine the order of operations. If, in the preceding code snippet, instead of

```
a = -(b + c)
```

we had used

```
a = -b + c
```

a would have been assigned the value 5 because negation has precedence over addition. That is, when the expression -b + c is evaluated, b is negated first, and then its negated value is added to c. With -(b + c), first b and c are summed, and then the resulting sum is negated.

The arithmetic precedence rules in Visual Basic mirror the standard precedence rules of mathematics. If you ever need to alter the order of operations, simply use parentheses to group those expressions that should be evaluated first.

The / operator always returns a nonintegral numeric value, even if the resulting quotient does not have a remainder. That is, the value returned by 4 / 2 is the nonintegral numeric value 2.0, not the integer value 2. Of course the / operator can also have a quotient with a decimal remainder; for example, the value returned by 3 / 4 is 0.75.

Exploring the Comparison Operators

Comparison operators are binary operators that compare the value of two variables. The six comparison operators are listed in Table 5.1. Comparison operators always return a Boolean value—True or False—depending on the value of the two variables being compared.

TABLE 5.1 Visual Basic .NET's Comparison Operators

Operator	Description
<	Less than
<=	Less than or equal
>	Greater than
>=	Greater than or equal
=	Equal
<>	Not equal

The following statements evaluate to `True`:

```
4 < 8

3.14159 >= 2

"Bob" <> "Sue"

(10/2) = (20/4)

4 <= 4
```

The following statements evaluate to `False`:

```
7 > 100

"Bob" = "Frank"

(10/2) = 7.5

4 < 4
```

By the Way

Usually, comparison operators are used in control structures, which we'll look at in detail in the next hour.

Understanding the Concatenation Operator

The concatenation operator **concatenates** two string variables. Concatenating two strings produces a string that consists of the content of the first string with the content of the second string appended. The string concatenation operator in Visual Basic is the ampersand, &.

Let's look at a quick code snippet to see how the concatenation operator works. Consider the following code:

```
Dim firstWord as String = "ASP.NET"
Dim secondWord as String = "is"
Dim thirdWord as String = "neat"

Dim sentence as String
sentence = firstWord & " " & secondWord & " " & thirdWord & "."
```

The variable `sentence` will end up with the value `"ASP.NET is neat."` Note that first three string variables—`firstWord`, `secondWord`, and `thirdWord`—are created, where each variable holds a word in a sentence. Next, the string variable `sentence` is declared. We want to assign to `sentence` the value of each of the three words concatenated together, with a space between each word and a period at the end.

To accomplish this, we use the & operator to join together six strings. First, the string `firstWord` and `" "` are concatenated, resulting in the temporary string `"ASP.NET "`. I use the word *temporary* here because this string is immediately concatenated with `secondWord`, resulting in `"ASP.NET is"`, which is then concatenated with `" "`, resulting in `"ASP.NET is "`. Next, this is concatenated with `thirdWord`, resulting in `"ASP.NET is neat"`, and finally this is concatenated with `"."`, resulting in `"ASP.NET is neat."`, which is then assigned to the variable `sentence`.

Inserting the Value of a Variable into a String

In many situations, we may want to insert the value of a string variable into another string. For example, imagine that we have a variable called `firstName` that contains the user's first name, and we want to display a message on the web page that reads `"Hello` *`FirstName`*`"`, where *`FirstName`* is the value of the variable `firstName`. That is, if the value of `firstName` is `Scott`, we want the message `"Hello Scott"` to appear.

First, we might want to create a string variable named `output` that would contain the final string that we want to display. To accomplish this, we would use code like

```
Dim output as String
output = "Hello, " & firstName
```

It is important to realize that after these two lines of code execute, the variable `output` will contain the value `"Hello,` *`FirstName`*`"`, where *`FirstName`* is the value of `firstName`. Note that we did *not* use

```
Dim output as String
output = "Hello, firstName"
```

Had we used this syntax, the value of `output` would be precisely as we indicated: `"Hello, firstName"`. To insert the value of `firstName` into the string `output`, we need to concatenate the string `"Hello, "` with the string value of `firstName`. This is done using the concatenation operator, *not* by simply inserting the variable name into the string.

Visual Basic's Assignment Operators

The most common assignment operator is the = operator, which takes the form

```
variableName = value
```

For example, to assign the value 5 to an integer variable, we can use the following code:

```
Dim age as Integer
age = 5
```

The *`value`* assigned to a variable can be things more complex than simple values like 5. The *`value`* can be an expression involving other operators. For example, we might want to add two numbers and store this sum in a variable. To accomplish this, we could use code like

```
'Create three integer variables
Dim sum, number1, number2 as Integer
number1 = 15
number2 = 20

'Assign the sum of number1 and number2 to sum
sum = number1 + number2
```

Shorthand Versions for Common Assignments

In many situations we might have a variable that is routinely updated in some fashion. We'll see some concrete examples of this in the next hour, but for now take my word for it that commonly we will be interested in incrementing an integer variable by one.

To accomplish this, we could use the following code:

```
Dim someIntegerVariable as Integer = 0

...
someIntegerVariable = someIntegerVariable + 1
...
```

Initially, `someIntegerVariable` is declared with an initial value of 0. Later, we want to increment the value of `someIntegerVariable`. To do this, we add one to the current value of `someIntegerVariable` and then store the new value back into `someIntegerVariable`. So, if `someIntegerVariable` equals 0,

```
someIntegerVariable = someIntegerVariable + 1
```

will take the value of `someIntegerVariable` (0), add 1 to it (yielding 1), and store 1 into `someIntegerVariable`. The next time the line

```
someIntegerVariable = someIntegerVariable + 1
```

is encountered, `someIntegerVariable` will equal 1. Hence, this line of code will first evaluate `someIntegerVariable + 1`, which is the value of `someIntegerVariable` (1) plus 1. It will then assign this value (2) back into `someIntegerVariable`. As you can see, this line of code increments the value of `someIntegerVariable` by 1 regardless of what the current value of `someIntegerVariable` is.

Because this is a very common line of code, Visual Basic provides an alternate assignment operator to reduce the amount of code we need to write. This shorthand operator, +=, has the form

```
variableName += value
```

and has the effect of adding *value* to the current value of *variableName* and then storing the resulting value of this addition back into *variableName*. The following two lines have exactly the same meaning and produce exactly the same results—incrementing someIntegerVariable by 1:

```
someIntegerVariable = someIntegerVariable + 1
```

and

```
someIntegerVariable += 1
```

In addition to +=, there are a number of other shorthand assignment operators, as shown in Table 5.2. Along with the shorthand arithmetic operators, you'll notice the shorthand concatenation operator, &=. This and the += operator are the two shorthand assignment operators we'll use most often.

TABLE 5.2 The Shorthand Assignment Operators

Operator	Description
+=	*variable* += *value* adds *value* to the value of *variable* and then stores this resulting value back into *variable*.
-=	*variable* -= *value* subtracts *value* from the value of *variable* and then stores this resulting value back into *variable*.
*=	*variable* *= *value* multiplies *value* to the value of *variable* and then stores this resulting value back into *variable*.
/=	*variable* /= *value* divides *value* into the value of *variable* and then stores this resulting value back into *variable*. Recall that the / operator returns a nonintegral value.
&=	*variable* &= *value* concatenates *value* to the value of *variable* and then stores this resulting value back into *variable*.

Learning Visual Basic's Type Rules

Recall that Visual Basic is a strongly typed language. This implies that all variables declared in a Visual Basic program must be given an explicit data type. Furthermore, the set of values that can be assigned to a variable are limited by the variable's type. That is, a variable that is of type Integer can be assigned only positive or negative whole number values that range between, approximately, positive two billion and negative two billion.

What happens, though, when you try to assign a nonintegral number to an integer variable, or when you try to assign an integer to a nonintegral numeric variable?

What about when you try to assign a string variable to a nonintegral numeric variable, or an integer variable to a string variable?

Because Visual Basic is strongly typed, a value of one type cannot be assigned to a variable of a different type. That means you should not be able to assign an integer value to a nonintegral numeric variable. However, the following code will work fine:

```
Dim fpVariable as Single
fpVariable = 5
```

Why does the preceding code snippet not produce an error? After all, doesn't it violate the typing rules of Visual Basic by assigning an integer value to a nonintegral numeric variable?

Such an assignment is legal because, behind the scenes, Visual Basic **casts** the integer value 5 into a nonintegral value (5.0) and *then* assigns it to the nonintegral numeric variable.

Understanding Casting

Casting is the process of changing the type of a variable or value from one type to another. There are two types of casting: implicit casting and explicit casting.

Implicit casting occurs when the casting occurs without any needed intervention by the programmer. In the code snippet we looked at last, implicit casting is utilized because the integer variable 5 is cast to a nonintegral representation of 5.0 without any extra code provided by us, the programmers.

> The documentation accompanying the .NET Framework SDK refers to implicit casting as **coercion**.

Explicit casting, on the other hand, requires that we, the programmers, explicitly indicate that a cast from one type to another should occur. To explicitly cast a variable from one type to another, we use Visual Basic's built-in `CType()` function, which has the following syntax:

```
CType(variableName, typeToCastTo)
```

The `CType()` function casts the variable *`variableName`* from its current type to the type specified by *`typeToCastTo`*. For example, imagine the code snippet we looked at earlier implicitly casting an integer to a `Single`. We can make this cast explicit by using the following code:

```
Dim fpVariable as Single
fpVariable = CType(5, Single)
```

Here, the `CType()` function is used to explicitly cast the integer value 5 to a `Single`, which is then assigned to the `Single` variable `fpVariable`.

In addition to Visual Basic's `CType` function, there is a `Convert` class in the .NET Framework that contains methods of the form `To`*`DataType`*`()`. For example, to explicitly cast the integer 5 to a `Single` type, you could use

```
fpVariable = Convert.ToSingle(5)
```

Widening and Narrowing Casts

Visual Basic can be run in one of two modes: strict and nonstrict. In the strict mode, implicit casting is allowed only for **widening casts**. In a widening cast, the set of legal values for one data type is a subset of the set of legal values for the data type the variable is being cast to. For example, a cast from an integer to a nonintegral number is a widening cast because every possible integer value can be expressed as a nonintegral value.

Another example of a widening cast is casting a variable of type `Integer` to a variable of type `Long`. This is a widening cast because any legal value for an `Integer` is included in the legal values for a `Long`.

The opposite of a widening cast is a **narrowing cast**. Consider casting a nonintegral numeric variable to an integer. If the nonintegral numeric variable has the value 5.0, we can safely cast this to the integer 5. But what if the variable has the value 3.14? There is no integer value that can represent 3.14 precisely. When we're casting 3.14 to an integer, the resulting integer value is 3; the remainder is dropped.

In a narrowing cast there is the potential for lost information. When we're casting 3.14 to an integer, the 0.14 portion of the number is lost in the narrowing cast.

Rules for Implicit Casting

Considering that narrowing casts can result in a loss of data, should Visual Basic allow for implicit narrow casts, or would it be prudent for the language to require that an explicit cast be used if a narrowing cast is required?

Truly strongly typed programming languages would require that all narrowing casts be explicit. In this case, if you tried to use code that would invoke an implicit narrowing cast, an error would result. That is, in a truly strongly typed programming language, the following code would produce an error:

```
Dim x as Integer
x = 8 / 4
```

The reason this would result in an error is that the / operator returns a nonintegral number (2.0), which must be cast to an integer in order to assign it to x. However, this cast is a narrowing cast. In a truly strongly typed language, you would have to provide an implicit cast, like so:

```
Dim x as Integer
x = CType(8 / 4, Integer)
```

or

```
Dim x as Integer
x = Convert.ToInteger(8 / 4)
```

The disadvantage of requiring explicit casting for narrowing casting is that older versions of Visual Basic allowed for implicit narrowing casts, meaning that old Visual Basic code could not be reused as-is in programs created with today's version of Visual Basic; rather, the programmer would have to alter the code to include explicit casting.

The designers of Visual Basic decided to take a middle-of-the-road approach. By default, implicit narrowing casts are permitted, meaning that the code

```
Dim x as Integer
x = 8 / 4
```

will run without error, assigning the integer value 2 to the variable x.

Watch Out!

Keep in mind that casting a nonintegral number to an integer drops the remainder portion of the nonintegral number. That is, after the following code is executed, the value of x will be 0:

```
Dim x as Integer
x = 3 / 4
```

To disallow implicit narrow casting on an ASP.NET page, open it by double-clicking on the file in the Solution Explorer. Next, in the Properties window go to the properties for the DOCUMENT (select the DOCUMENT item from the Properties window's drop-down list). In the ASP.NET section, you'll find an option titled Strict. Set this to True to disallow implicit narrow casting. Figure 5.2 shows the Properties window and the Strict option set to True.

When you set the Strict option to True, Visual Basic will not allow implicit narrowing casts. You will get a compile-time error message if you try to perform an implicit narrowing cast. For example, say you create an ASP.NET web page whose source code content contains the following code in the Page_Load event handler:

```
Dim a as Integer
a = 8/4    'An implicit narrowing cast will occur here!
```

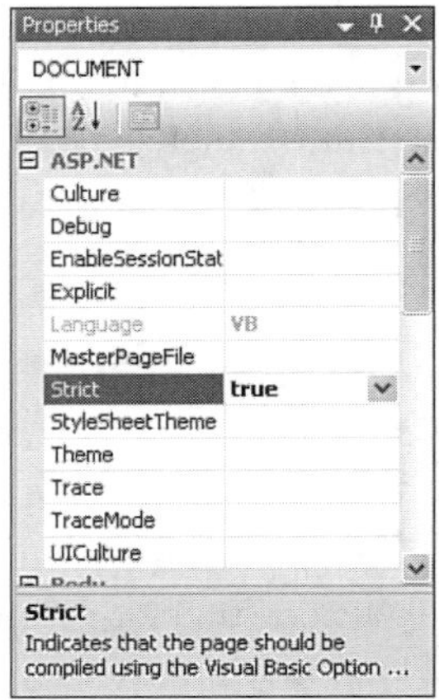

FIGURE 5.2 The Strict option can be found in the ASP.NET section of the Properties window for the DOCUMENT.

In this case, you will get the error shown in Figure 5.3 when viewing the ASP.NET page through a browser.

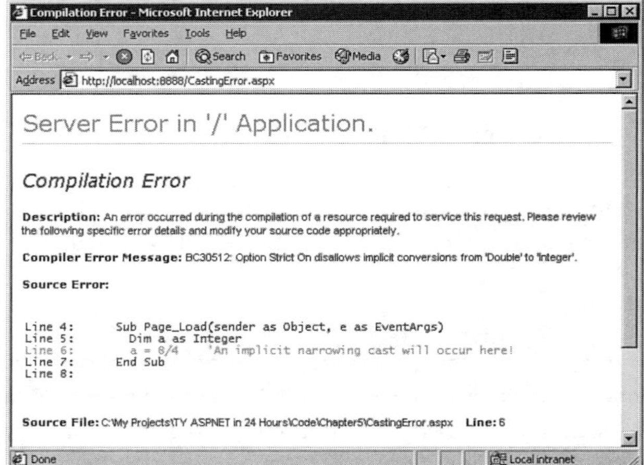

FIGURE 5.3 A compile-time error occurs if *`Strict="True"`* is set and an implicit narrowing cast is found.

For this book, I will *not* be adding `Strict="True"`. In some code examples there may be implicit narrow casting. If you choose to add `Strict="True"`, you will have to add the appropriate explicit casting for such code examples.

Summary

In this hour we examined the syntax and semantics for variables and operators in Visual Basic. Variables are defined by three properties: their name, their data type, and their value. The name and data type of a variable are specified when the variable is declared and are immutable. Variables are declared in Visual Basic via the `Dim` statement in the following fashion:

```
Dim variableName as type
```

The type of a variable dictates what values the variable can contain. Each type has a subset of legal values. For example, a variable of type `Integer` can store negative or positive whole numbers that range from –2,147,483,648 to 2,147,483,647.

A variable is assigned a value via an assignment statement, which is = in Visual Basic. Along with the assignment operator, there are a number of other operators in Visual Basic, including arithmetic operators, like +, -, *, and /; comparison operators, like <, <=, >, >=, =, and <>; and the string concatenation operator, &.

When you're assigning a value to a variable, it is vital that the type of the value matches the type of the variable. If the types do not match, Visual Basic may be able to implicitly cast the value's type into the needed type.

Casts can be implicit or explicit, narrowing or widening. An explicit cast can be declared by using Visual Basic .NET's built-in `CType()` function or by using the `Convert` class's methods. Visual Basic, by default, allows for implicit, narrowing casts. However, when you set the `Strict="True"` option in the `@Page` directive of your ASP.NET web page, implicit narrowing casts are not allowed.

In the next hour we will look at control structures in Visual Basic. Control structures allow for changes in the program's instruction execution. Commonly, this is translated into having specified portions of code executed repeatedly until some condition is met, or encapsulating a series of related instructions in a subroutine or function, which can then be invoked in a single line of code.

Q&A

Q. ***Are the shorthand assignment operators used often in practice?***

A. Visual Basic contains a number of shorthand assignment operators, such as `+=`, `-=`, `*=`, and so on. These operators first perform a mathematical computation (such as addition in the case of +=) and then an assignment. They are used in the following form:

```
variable += expression
```

They have the effect of adding the value of *`expression`* to the current value of *`variable`* and then storing this summation as the new value of *`variable`*.

These shorthand assignment operators were first introduced in Visual Basic 7, which was the version of Visual Basic released when Microsoft's .NET platform first came out. (The Visual Web Developer uses Visual Basic version 8.) Prior to .NET, the shorthand assignment operators did not exist. Therefore, if a developer wanted to increment a variable by one, she'd have to use the more verbose code:

```
variable = variable + 1
```

as opposed to the more succinct option that is available in VB.NET:

```
variable += 1
```

Shorthand assignment operators are used quite often in practice due to this succinctness. In fact, in a number of examples throughout this book, we'll see these shorthand assignment operators in use.

Q. ***Are there any advantages to setting*** `Strict` ***as*** `True` ***in an ASP.NET page?***

A. Recall that setting the `Strict` option to `True` in the Properties window configures Visual Basic so that implicit casting is not allowed. Setting it to `False` (or simply leaving it unspecified) allows implicit castings that are widening.

Personally, I prefer to enable implicit widening casts because I find that it leaves the code less cluttered. However, implicit casting is more error prone because a variable may be automatically cast from one type to another without your knowledge. For example, the / operator returns a nonintegral result. The following code, however, will not produce an error message unless `Strict` is set to `True`:

```
Dim x as Integer
x = 10/3
```

Here, the value of `10/3` will be `3.3333333`. However, because the result is assigned to `x`, an `Integer`, the value is implicitly cast to an `Integer`, meaning that the decimal portion is truncated.

To see why implicit casting can lead to potential errors, imagine that at some point later in your code, you display a particular message that `x` is greater than 3. This conditional code will never execute because `x` is equal to 3, not greater than 3. However, this may baffle you, since, in examining the code, you might mistakenly think that `x` has the value 3.3333333 and therefore the conditional code should execute.

Workshop

Quiz

1. What is the one mutable property of a variable, and how is it changed throughout the execution of the program?
2. If you wanted a variable to store whole numbers with values from 0 up to a value no greater than 10,000, what data type should you use?
3. Does the following code contain an implicit narrowing cast?

```
Dim a, b as Integer
b = 10
a = b / 2
```

4. Does the following statement evaluate to True or False?

```
(4 / 3) = 1
```

5. Does the following statement evaluate to True or False?

```
CType(4 / 3, Integer) = 1
```

Answers

1. The value of a variable is the only mutable property; the name and data type are immutable. The value of a variable is changed via the assignment statement, which assigns a new value to a variable.
2. You could use the `Short` data type, although in the examples throughout this book, the default integer data type used will be `Integer`.
3. Yes. The / operator always produces a nonintegral result, so `b / 2` will return the value 5.0. Because this value must be cast to an integer to be assigned to a, a narrowing cast must be performed. The cast is implicit because there is no `CType()` function call there explicitly indicating that a cast should occur.
4. It evaluates to `False`. The division `4 / 3` will produce the value 1.3333333333..., which is not equal to 1.
5. It evaluates to True. The division `4 / 3` will produce the value 1.3333333333..., but when this is cast to type `Integer`, the remainder will be truncated, resulting in the value 1. Because 1 = 1, this will return `True`.

Exercises

There are no exercises for this hour mainly because all that we know how to do in Visual Basic at this point is declare typed variables and assign the values of expressions to these variables.

In the next hour we will be covering Visual Basic control structures, which allows for code to be executed repeatedly or conditionally. After we have covered this material, we'll be able to examine a number of germane coding examples.

HOUR 6

Managing Program Flow with Visual Basic's Control Structures

In this hour, we will cover

- Using conditional statements
- Identifying the types of looping constructs Visual Basic supports
- Using `For` loops
- Using `Do` loops
- Understanding the differences between subroutines and functions
- Using subroutines and functions

In the preceding hour we looked at variables and operators in Visual Basic, two important concepts in any programming language. In this hour we will examine an equally important aspect of all programming languages: **control structures**.

Control structures are constructs that alter the control flow during a program's execution. Without control structures, programs are executed by running the first line of code, then the second, and so on, where each line of code is executed precisely once in the order in which it appears.

Control structures, however, alter the order of instruction execution and can allow for a group of instructions to execute more than once. The control structures that we'll be examining in this hour are conditionals, loops, subroutines, and functions.

Understanding Control Structures

A computer is good at doing one thing and one thing only—executing a series of instructions. From the computer's point of view, it is simply handed a sequence of instructions to execute, and it does so accurately and quickly.

The instructions executed by the computer are spelled out using a programming language, such as Visual Basic. For example, if you want the computer to create an integer variable, assign the value 4 to it, and then multiply the variable's value by 2, you could use the following code:

```
'Create a variable of type Integer and assign it the value 4
Dim someVariable as Integer = 4

'Multiply the value of someVariable by 2 and assign the product
'back to the variable someVariable (this is equivalent to using
'   someVariable = someVariable * 2)
someVariable *= 2
```

When this program is executed, the first line of code is executed (the `Dim` statement), which declares a variable of type `Integer` and assigns the value 4 to this variable. Next, the code `someVariable *= 2` is executed, which multiplies the value of `someVariable` by 2 and then assigns the result (8) to `someVariable`.

By the Way

> Note that the lines of code in this snippet executed exactly once, with the first line of code executing before the second. This style of code execution is known as **sequential flow**.

What if we don't necessarily want to have `someVariable` assigned twice its value? Perhaps we want to execute the `someVariable *= 2` line of code only if `someVariable` is less than 5. Or perhaps we want to continue to double the value of `someVariable` until the value is greater than 100.

To alter the flow of instructions, we use control structures. The three primary classes of control structures are

- The conditional control structure, which executes a set of instructions only if some condition is met
- Looping control structures, which repeatedly execute a set of instructions until some condition is met
- Modularizing control structures, which group sets of instructions into modules that can be invoked at various places in the program

In this hour we will examine the syntax and semantics of all three classes of control structures.

Exploring the Conditional Control Structure

The conditional control structure is used to conditionally execute a set of instructions. The syntax for the conditional control structure, in its simplest form, is given as

```
If condition Then
   Instruction1
   Instruction2
   ...
   InstructionN
End If
```

Here, *`condition`* is a Boolean expression, one that evaluates to either `True` or `False`. If *`condition`* evaluates to `True`, instructions *`Instruction1`* through *`InstructionN`* are executed. If *`condition`* evaluates to `False`, *`Instruction1`* through *`InstructionN`* are skipped and therefore are *not* executed.

By the Way

Conditional statements are commonly referred to as `If` statements.

Recall from the preceding hour that the comparison operators always return a Boolean value. These operators are commonly used to compare the values of two variables or the value of a variable with a literal. For example, with Visual Basic the current hour can be determined via the following code:

```
DateTime.Now.Hour
```

This returns an integer value between 0 and 23, where 0 is midnight, 9 is 9:00 in the morning, 13 is 1:00 in the afternoon, and so on. We could create a simple ASP.NET web page that uses a conditional statement to determine the current hour and display an appropriate message based on the hour of the day (good morning versus good afternoon versus good evening).

Let's create such an ASP.NET web page. To start, create a new ASP.NET website on your personal computer's file system. Next, add a new ASP.NET page named `TimeAppropriateMessage.aspx`.

By the Way

Remember, when adding a new ASP.NET page to a website in Visual Web Developer, select the Web Form item type from the Add New Item dialog box. Also, be sure that the Place Code in Separate File check box is checked and that the Language choice is set to Visual Basic.

First, let's add a Label Web control that will display the message. From the Toolbox, drag and drop the Label Web control onto the page. Next, from the Properties window, change the Label's `ID` property to `lblMessage` and clear out the Label's `Text` property. Your screen should look similar to Figure 6.1.

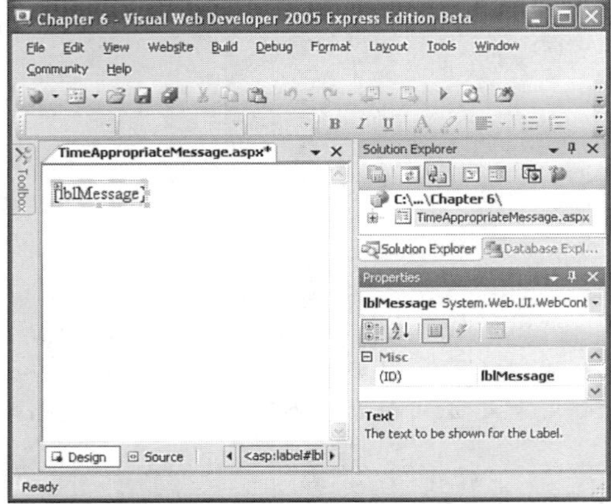

FIGURE 6.1
A Label control has been added.

We now want to create some code that will run every time the ASP.NET page is visited. To accomplish this, create an event handler for the page's `Load` event. You can accomplish this in one of two ways: either double-click the page in the Design view, or go to the ASP.NET page's source code portion and select Page Events from the left drop-down list and Load from the right one.

After you have created the `Page_Load` event handler, enter the code shown in Listing 6.1.

LISTING 6.1 A Different Message Is Displayed Based on the Current Hour

```
Partial Class TimeAppropriateMessage
    Inherits System.Web.UI.Page

    Protected Sub Page_Load(ByVal sender As Object, ByVal e As
➥System.EventArgs) Handles Me.Load
        If DateTime.Now.Hour >= 6 And DateTime.Now.Hour < 12 Then
            lblMessage.Text = "Good morning."
        End If

        If DateTime.Now.Hour >= 12 And DateTime.Now.Hour <= 17 Then
            lblMessage.Text = "Good afternoon."
        End If

        If DateTime.Now.Hour > 17 Or DateTime.Now.Hour < 6 Then
            lblMessage.Text = "Good evening."
        End If
    End Sub
End Class
```

After you enter the code in Listing 6.1 into your ASP.NET web page's source code portion, view it through a browser by going to the Debug menu and choosing Start Without Debugging. You should see the message `"Good morning"` if the current hour is after 6 a.m. but before noon, `"Good afternoon"` if it's past noon and before 5 p.m., and `"Good evening"` if it's after 5 p.m. and before 6 a.m.

By the Way

> Notice that the message displayed to you is based on the current time of the machine where the web server is running. This means that if your ASP.NET web page is being hosted by a web-hosting company that is another time zone, the output you see may not be reflective of the current time in your time zone.

The code in Listing 6.1 works by using three `If` statements. The first `If` statement (lines 5–7) checks to see whether the current hour is greater than or equal to 6 and less than 12.

Note that the condition on line 5 contains two conditional statements: `DateTime.Now.Hour >= 6` and `DateTime.Now.Hour < 12`. These two conditions are joined by the keyword `And`. Visual Basic contains two keywords for joining conditional statements: `And` and `Or`. The semantics of `And` and `Or` are just like their English counterparts. That is, the expression *`condition1`* `And` *`condition2`* will return `True` if and only if both *`condition1`* and *`condition2`* are true, whereas the expression *`condition1`* `Or` *`condition2`* will return `True` if either *`condition1`* is true or *`condition2`* is true (or if both *`condition1`* and *`condition2`* are true).

Did you Know?

> Parentheses can be used to specify order of operations and to help make compound conditionals more readable. For example, if we wanted to run a sequence of instructions if the hour was between 9 and 12, or if the hour was 17, then we could use a statement like this:
>
> ```
> If (DateTime.Now.Hour >= 9 AND DateTime.Now.Hour <= 12) OR (DateTime.Now.Hour
> ➥ = 17) then
>    ' ... Instructions ...
> End If
> ```

So, if the current hour is both greater than or equal to 6 and the current hour is less than 12, then the condition on line 2 is true, and line 3 will be executed, which causes the message `"Good morning"` to be displayed.

Another conditional statement is found on line 9. This one checks to see whether the current hour is between noon and 5 p.m. (Because the hour is returned as a value between 0 and 23, 5 p.m. is returned as 17.) If the hour is both greater than or equal to 12 and less than or equal to 17, then line 7 is executed and the message `"Good afternoon"` is displayed.

A third condition on line 13 checks to see whether the hour is greater than 17 or whether the hour is less than 6. If either of these conditions is true, then the code on line 11 is executed, which displays the message `"Good evening"`.

> Note that all three of these conditional statements are executed, but only one of the three conditionals will return `True`, meaning only one of the three messages will be displayed.

Executing Instructions If the Conditional Is False

As we have seen, the `If` statement executes a set of instructions if the supplied conditional is true. But what if we want to execute some instructions if the condition is false? For example, say that there is some string variable named `password` that contains the password for the user visiting our website. If the `password` variable is equal to the string `"shazaam"`, we want to display some sensitive information; if, however, the password is *not* `"shazaam"`, then the user has an incorrect password, and we want to display a warning message.

In this scenario we want to use an `If` statement because we want to execute one piece of code if the password is correct and another piece of code if the password is incorrect. We can accomplish this using the `If` statement as we saw earlier, like so:

```
If password = "shazaam" then
  'Display sensitive information
End If

If password <> "shazaam" then
  'Display message informing the user they've entered an
  'incorrect password
End If
```

However, there is an easier way to accomplish this. An `If` statement can contain an optional `Else` clause. The source code that appears within the `Else` portion is executed when the condition evaluates to `False`. The general form of an `If` statement with an `Else` clause is

```
If condition Then
   Instruction1
   Instruction2
   ...
   InstructionN
Else
   ElseInstruction1
   ElseInstruction2
   ...
   ElseInstructionN
End If
```

Here, if *condition* is true, then *Instruction1* through *InstructionN* are executed, and *ElseInstruction1* through *ElseInstructionN* are skipped. If, however, *condition* is false, then *ElseInstruction1* through *ElseInstructionN* are executed, and *Instruction1* through *InstructionN* are skipped.

Using the Else statement, we can rewrite the password-checking code from two conditionals to one, as in the following code:

```
If password = "shazaam" then
   'Display sensitive information
Else
   'Display message informing the user they've entered an
   'incorrect password
End If
```

> **Did you Know?**
> An If statement can have either no Else clause or precisely one Else clause. There cannot be multiple Else clauses for a single If statement.

Performing Another If Statement When the Condition Is False

In addition to the Else statement, If statements can have zero to many optional ElseIf statements. An ElseIf clause follows an If statement, much like the Else. The ElseIf clause has a condition statement like the If statement. The instructions directly following the ElseIf are executed only if the If statement's condition, as well as all of the preceding ElseIf conditions, are false and the condition of the ElseIf in question is true.

This description may sound a bit confusing. An example should help clear things up. First, note that the general form of an If statement with ElseIf clauses is as follows:

```
If condition Then
   Instruction1
   Instruction2
   ...
   InstructionN
ElseIf elseIf1Condition
   ElseIf1Instruction1
   ElseIf1Instruction2
   ...
   ElseIf1InstructionN
ElseIf elseIf2Condition
   ElseIf2Instruction1
   ElseIf2Instruction2
   ...
   ElseIf2InstructionN
...
```

```
ElseIf elseIfNCondition
   ElseIfNInstruction1
   ElseIfNInstruction2
   ...
   ElseIfNInstructionN
Else
   ElseInstruction1
   ElseInstruction2
   ...
   ElseInstructionN
End If
```

If the `condition` is true, then the instructions `Instruction1` through `InstructionN` are executed and the other instructions are skipped. If, however, `condition` is false, then the first `ElseIf` condition, `elseIf1Condition`, is evaluated. If this condition is true, then instructions `ElseIf1Instruction1` through `ElseIf1InstructionN` are executed. If, however, `elseIf1Condition` is false, then the second `ElseIf` condition, `elseIf2Condition`, is evaluated. Again, if it is true, then instructions `ElseIf2Instruction1` through `ElseIf2InstructionN` are executed. If, however, `elseIf2Condition` is false, then the third `ElseIf` condition is evaluated, and so on. If *all* `ElseIf` conditions are false, then the `Else`'s instructions (`ElseInstruction1` through `ElseInstructionN`) are executed.

Let's return to the `TimeAppropriateMessage.aspx` example, whose source code was displayed in Listing 6.1. Take a moment to look back over that code listing; notice that we used three conditions: one to check whether the time was between 6 a.m. and 11 a.m., one to check whether the time was between noon and 5 p.m., and one to check whether the time was after 5 p.m. or before 6 a.m.

We can accomplish this with a single `If` statement using either two `ElseIf`s or one `ElseIf` and an `Else`. The code for using two `ElseIf`s is as follows:

```
If DateTime.Now.Hour >= 6 And DateTime.Now.Hour < 12 then
  lblMessage.Text = "Good morning."
ElseIf DateTime.Now.Hour >= 12 And DateTime.Now.Hour <= 17 then
  lblMessage.Text = "Good afternoon."
ElseIf DateTime.Now.Hour > 17 Or DateTime.Now.Hour < 6 then
  lblMessage.Text = "Good evening."
End If
```

The code for using an `ElseIf` and an `Else` looks like this:

```
If DateTime.Now.Hour >= 6 And DateTime.Now.Hour < 12 then
  lblMessage.Text = "Good morning."
ElseIf DateTime.Now.Hour >= 12 And DateTime.Now.Hour <= 17 then
  lblMessage.Text = "Good afternoon."
Else
  lblMessage.Text = "Good evening."
End If
```

Working with Visual Basic's Looping Control Structures

Looping control structures allow for a set of instructions to be executed a repeated number of times. The number of times the code is repeated can be a fixed number of times, such as with `For ... Next` loops, or repeated until some condition is met, such as with `Do ... Loop` loops.

In the next three sections we'll be looking at two of Visual Basic's looping constructs: `For ... Next` loops and `Do ... Loop` loops. These two constructs are, at a high level, equivalent, though they have differing syntax. That is, they accomplish essentially the same task—repeating a set of instructions a certain number of times. In fact, either one of the two looping structures we'll be examining can be implemented with the other.

Using `For ... Next` Loops

`Next` looping control structure is likely the looping structure best suited for your needs. The `For ... Next` loop has the following syntax:

```
For integerVariable = start to stop
  Instruction1
  Instruction2
  ...
  InstructionN
Next integerVariable
```

Did you Know?

> `For ... Next` loops are often referred to as `For` loops.

The semantics of the `For` loop are as follows: The variable *`integerVariable`*, which should be an integer variable type (`Short`, `Integer`, or `Long`), is assigned the value *`start`*. This variable is often referred to as the **looping variable**.

By the Way

> The looping variable does not necessarily need to be an integer; it can be any numeric type. However, in practice the overwhelmingly vast majority of `For ... Next` loops use an integer looping variable because `For ... Next` loops are designed to iterate a sequence of instructions an integral number of times.

After the looping variable is initially assigned to the *`start`* value, instructions *`Instruction1`* through *`InstructionN`* are executed. After these instructions are executed, the value of the looping variable is incremented by one. If, at this point, the value of the looping variable is less than or equal to *`stop`*, instructions

`Instruction1` through *`InstructionN`* are executed again, the value of the looping variable is incremented by one, and again, the looping variable's value is checked against *`stop`*. The loop continues to execute, with the value of the looping variable being incremented at each loop iteration, until the value of the looping variable is greater than *`stop`*.

By the Way

> Instructions *`Instruction1`* through *`InstructionN`* are commonly referred to as the **body** of the loop.

So, to display the message `"Hello, World!"` in the user's browser three times, you could put the following `For ... Next` loop in the ASP.NET web page's `Page_Load` event handler:

```
Dim i as Integer
For i = 1 to 3
  LabelWebControl.Text &= "Hello, World!"
Next i
```

The first thing we do is create an integer variable named `i`. When the `For` loop executes, `i` is initially assigned the value 1. Then the body of the loop is executed, which concatenates the string `"Hello, World!"` to the current value of some Label Web control's `Text` property. (Recall that &= is an operator that takes the value of the variable on the left side and concatenates to it the value on the right side, saving the resulting concatenation back to the variable on the left side.

After the body finishes executing, the value of `i` is incremented by one. A check is then made to see whether `i`'s current value is less than or equal to 3. The reason is that, at this point, `i` equals 2. Therefore, the loop body is executed again, which will again concatenate `"Hello, World!"` to the Label's `Text` property. As before, `i` is incremented and compared to see whether it is less than or equal to 3. Being equal to 3, `i` is indeed less than or equal to 3, so the loop body executes again. After concatenating `"Hello, World!"` to the Label's `Text` property, `i` is (again) incremented, equaling 4. At this point, `i` is *not* less than or equal to 3, so the `For` loop body does not execute. Instead, the line of code immediately following the `Next i` executes.

Incrementing the Looping Variable by More Than One Each Loop Iteration

The standard `For` loop syntax increments the looping variable by one with each iteration of the loop body. But what if you want to increment the looping variable by more than one, or what if you want to decrement the looping variable?

To accommodate for different looping variable increments per loop iteration, Visual Basic's `For` loop can have an optional `Step` portion that indicates specifically the amount that the looping variable should be incremented per loop. The syntax of the For loop with a Step clause is as follows:

```
For integerVariable = start to stop Step stepAmount
  Instruction1
  Instruction2
  ...
  InstructionN
Next integerVariable
```

Imagine that you wanted to perform a loop that iterated through the even numbers between 0 and 10. You could accomplish this using a For ... Next loop that started at 0 and went to 10, incrementing by 2 at each iteration. The syntax for such a For loop would be

```
Dim evens as Integer
For evens = 0 to 10 Step 2
  LabelWebControl.Text &= evens & " is an even number.<br />"
Next evens
```

This For loop, if added to an ASP.NET web page's Page_Load event handler, will display in the specified Label:

```
0 is an even number.
2 is an even number.
4 is an even number.
...
10 is an even number.
```

Did you Know?

If you want a For loop that has its looping variable **decremented** at each iteration, you need to set the step amount to a negative value. For example, to display the even numbers between 0 and 10, but starting with 10 and working down to 0, you would need to use the following For loop:

```
Dim evens as Integer
For evens = 10 to 0 Step -2
  LabelWebControl.Text &= evens & " is an even number.<br />"
Next evens
```

Do ... Loop **Loops**

The Do ... Loop loop, often referred to simply as a Do loop, executes the loop body either while a condition holds or until a condition is met, depending on the syntax.

First, let's consider the Do loop that iterates while a condition holds. The syntax for such a loop is as follows:

```
Do While condition
  Instruction1
  Instruction2
  ...
  InstructionN
Loop
```

condition is an expression that evaluates to a Boolean value. When the Do loop is encountered, the *condition* is checked. If it evaluates to True, the loop body—instructions *Instruction1* through *InstructionN*—is executed. After the loop body has executed, the *condition* is checked again. If it is still True, the loop body is executed again. This process repeats until *condition* evaluates to False after the execution of the loop body.

A Do loop can also be constructed so that its loop body is executed repeatedly until a condition is met. The syntax for this form of the Do loop is

```
Do Until condition
  Instruction1
  Instruction2
  ...
  InstructionN
Loop
```

Here, the semantics of the Do loop are as follows: When the Do loop is encountered, the *condition* is checked. If it evaluates to False, the loop body—instructions *Instruction1* through *InstructionN*—is executed. After the loop body has executed, the *condition* is checked again. If it is still False, the loop body is executed again. This process repeats until *condition* evaluates to True after the execution of the loop body.

Like with the For loop, the Do loop can be used to display the even numbers between 0 and 10. To accomplish this, we could use the following syntax:

```
Dim number as Integer = 0
Do While number <= 10
  LabelWebControl.Text &= number & " is an even number.<br />"

  number += 2
Loop
```

Here, an Integer number is created and assigned the value 0. The Do loop then iterates while the value of number is less than or equal to 10. Because 0 (number's initial value) is less than or equal to 10, the loop body executes. In the loop body a message ("0 is an even number") is appended to a Label Web control's Text property and then the value of number is incremented by 2. This loop will continue to be executed until the end of the sixth iteration, after which number will have the value 12.

> The loop bodies of Do loops typically have a line of code that updates some variable that is used in the Do loop's *condition*. In such cases, if you forget to add this line of code, your loop will become an **infinite loop**, one that never ends. For example, imagine what would happen if we removed the number += 2 line of code from the previous Do loop example. Clearly, the value of number would remain 0, meaning that the loop body would continuously execute, never ending.

Exploring the Modularizing Control Structures: Subroutines and Functions

The code examples we looked at in this hour and the preceding one have all been a few simple lines of code designed to illustrate the concept being discussed. In examining the execution of these code samples, we discussed how Visual Basic interprets one line of code at a time, starting with the first line and working down. With control structures, however, this sequential flow of instructions can be altered, such as with loops or conditional statements.

In addition to altering the flow control with loops and conditionals, Visual Basic allows for **modularizing control structures**. A modularizing control structure is a control structure that can be used to create a module of source code. This module may contain many lines of source code, can accept zero to many input parameters, and can optionally return a value. Furthermore, these modules can then be called from any location in the Visual Basic source code.

There are two flavors of modularization control structures: **subroutines** and **functions**. Subroutines are modularization control structures that do *not* return any value, whereas functions always return a value. Subroutines and functions are handy for encapsulating programming logic.

To understand subroutines and functions, let's look at a somewhat contrived example that utilizes a subroutine to encapsulate the logic behind displaying a repeated text message. Start by creating a new ASP.NET web page named `SubroutineLesson1.aspx`. Add a Label Web control to the page's HTML portion, clearing out its `Text` property and settings its `ID` property to `output`. Next, create an event handler for the page's `Load` event. Now, we want this ASP.NET page to display the string `"Welcome to my Website"` precisely four times. To accomplish this, we can use a simple `For` loop that concatenates the string `"Welcome to my Website"` to the `output` Label's `Text` property in the loop body.

Listing 6.2 contains the source code that you should enter into the page's source code portion.

LISTING 6.2 The `Page_Load` Event Handler Displays a Message Four Times

```
Partial Class SubroutineLesson1
    Inherits System.Web.UI.Page

    Protected Sub Page_Load(ByVal sender As Object, ByVal e As
➥System.EventArgs) Handles Me.Load
        output.Text = String.Empty

```

LISTING 6.2 Continued

```
 7:         Dim i As Integer
 8:         For i = 1 To 4
 9:             output.Text &= "Welcome to my Website<br />"
10:         Next i
11:     End Sub
12: End Class
```

Notice that on line 5 we clear out the Label Web control's `Text` property programmatically. We accomplish this by setting the `Text` property to an empty string. An empty string can be denoted in one of two ways: using `String.Empty`, as on line 5, or using a string literal with no contents (`""`). That is, the code's output would be identical if we replaced line 5 with `output.Text = ""`.

After you have entered this code, view the page through a browser. Notice that this web page displays the message `"Welcome to my Website"` four times, as shown in Figure 6.2.

FIGURE 6.2 The `"Welcome to my Website"` message is displayed four times.

Now, imagine that we also wanted a Button Web control on the web page that, when clicked, would display the message `"Welcome to my Website"` four times as well.

To accomplish this, we first need to add a Button Web control. To do this, return to the HTML portion of the ASP.NET page and drag and drop a Button Web control from the Toolbox onto the page. At this point your screen should look similar to Figure 6.3.

To add an event handler for the Button's `Click` event, either double-click on the Button Web control from the Design view or go to the code portion and select the Button Web control from the left drop-down list and its Click event from the drop-down list on the right. Either of these approaches will automatically add the appropriate event handler syntax. Recall from our discussions in Hour 4, "Designing,

Creating, and Testing ASP.NET Web Pages," that when the Button is clicked, the Button's `Click` event handler is executed. Therefore, to have the message `"Welcome to my Website"` displayed four times when the Button is clicked, we want to place the same code that appears in the `Page_Load` event handler in the Button's `Click` event handler.

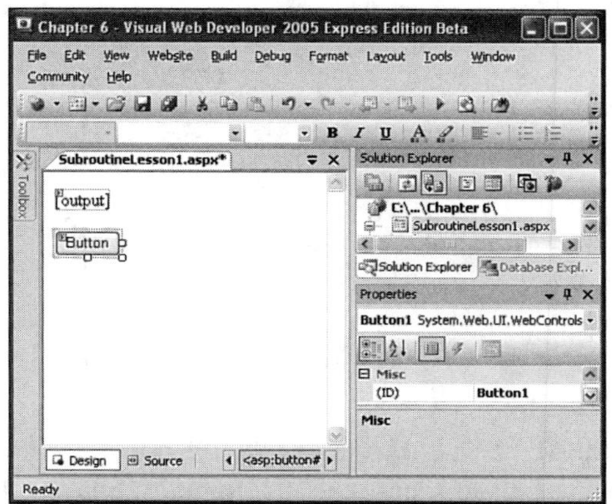

FIGURE 6.3
A Button Web control has been added.

Listing 6.3 contains the ASP.NET page's source code portion with the added `Click` event handler (lines 11 through 16), which you should enter.

LISTING 6.3 The Message Is Displayed Four Times When the Button Web Control Is Clicked

```
 1: Partial Class SubroutineLesson1
 2:     Inherits System.Web.UI.Page
 3:
 4:     Protected Sub Page_Load(ByVal sender As Object, ByVal e As
➥System.EventArgs) Handles Me.Load
 5:         output.Text = String.Empty
 6:
 7:         Dim i As Integer
 8:         For i = 1 To 4
 9:             output.Text &= "Welcome to my Website<br />"
10:         Next i
11:     End Sub
12:
13:     Protected Sub Button1_Click(ByVal sender As Object, ByVal e As
➥System.EventArgs) Handles Button1.Click
14:         Dim i As Integer
15:         For i = 1 To 4
16:             output.Text &= "Welcome to my Website<br />"
17:         Next i
18:     End Sub
19: End Class
```

With this addition to the ASP.NET web page, when you first visit the web page, the message `"Welcome to my Website"` is displayed four times (from the `Page_Load` event handler). Additionally, a Button is displayed. Figure 6.4 shows `SubroutineLesson1.aspx` after the code from both Listings 6.2 and 6.3 has been added to the source code portion.

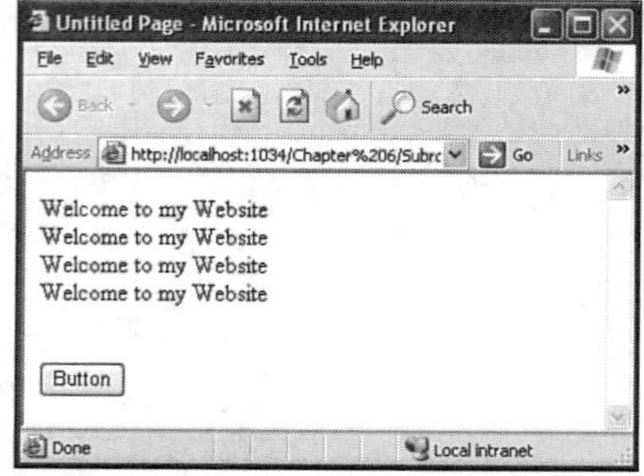

FIGURE 6.4 A Button Web control is displayed after the message.

When the Button Web control is clicked, the ASP.NET page is posted back, which causes the Button's `Click` event handler to fire. In addition to the Button's `Click` event handler being executed, the `Page_Load` event handler is executed as well because the page is being loaded again. This causes the message `"Welcome to my Website"` to be displayed *eight* times, as shown in Figure 6.5.

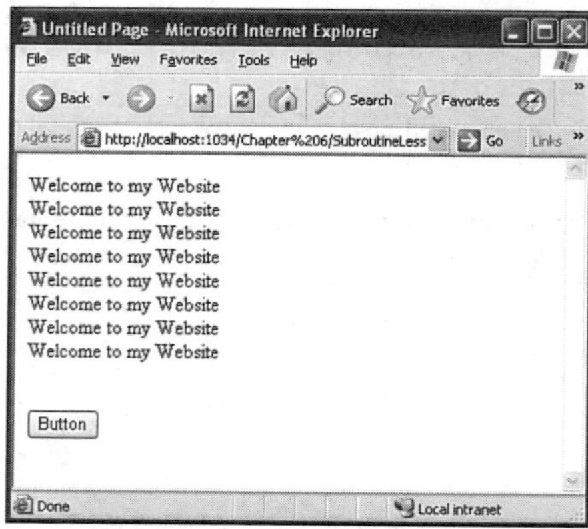

FIGURE 6.5 The `"Welcome to my Website"` message is displayed eight times after the button is clicked.

By the Way

> Recall that in Hour 4, we briefly discussed the series of actions that happen when a Button Web control is clicked. If you are still a bit confused or unclear, don't worry; we'll be covering this topic in much greater detail in Hour 9, "Web Form Basics."

Reducing Code Redundancy Using Subroutines and Functions

Although the code for our ASP.NET web page is fairly simple, it contains redundancies. The code to display the `"Welcome to my Website"` message is repeated twice: once in the `Page_Load` event handler and once in the Button's `Click` event handler. We can use a subroutine to reduce this redundancy.

We can create a subroutine using the following syntax:

```
Sub SubroutineName()
  Instruction1
  Instruction2
  ...
  InstructionN
End Sub
```

The code that appears between the `Sub` and `End Sub` lines is referred to as the **body** of the subroutine and is executed whenever the subroutine is **called**. A subroutine is called using the following syntax:

```
SubroutineName()
```

For our ASP.NET Web page, we can create a subroutine named `DisplayMessage()` that has as its body the code to display the `"Welcome to my Website"` message four times. Then, in the `Page_Load` and the Button's `Click` event handlers, we can replace the code that displays the message four times with a call to the `DisplayMessage()` subroutine.

To employ a subroutine to display the message, replace the source code contents entered from Listings 6.2 and 6.3 with the source code provided in Listing 6.4.

LISTING 6.4 The Code to Display the `"Welcome to my Website"` Message Is Moved to a Subroutine

```
Partial Class SubroutineLesson1
    Inherits System.Web.UI.Page

    Protected Sub Page_Load(ByVal sender As Object, ByVal e As
➥System.EventArgs) Handles Me.Load
        output.Text = String.Empty

        DisplayMessage()
    End Sub

    Protected Sub Button1_Click(ByVal sender As Object, ByVal e As
➥System.EventArgs) Handles Button1.Click
        DisplayMessage()
    End Sub

    Private Sub DisplayMessage()
```

LISTING 6.4 Continued

```
15:         Dim i As Integer
16:         For i = 1 To 4
17:             output.Text &= "Welcome to my Website<br />"
18:         Next i
19:     End Sub
20: End Class
```

Listing 6.4 has encapsulated the code to display the `"Welcome to my Website"` message four times in a subroutine (lines 14–19). The body of the subroutine can be invoked from anywhere else in the ASP.NET source code portion by calling the subroutine (see lines 7 and 11).

View it through a browser by going to the Debug menu and choosing Start Without Debugging. Upon first loading the page, you should see the same output shown in Figure 6.4: the message `"Welcome to my Website"` displayed four times, followed by a Button. By clicking on the Button, you should see the output shown in Figure 6.5: the message `"Welcome to my Website"` displayed eight times, followed by a Button.

> Strive to reduce code redundancy by modularizing repeated code into a subroutine or function. Redundant code has a number of disadvantages, such as making the code harder to read (due to its increased length), harder to update (because changes to the redundant code require updating the code in multiple places), and more prone to typos (because you have to reenter the code multiple times, the chances of making a mistake increase).

Passing in Parameters to a Subroutine or Function

In Listing 6.4 we used a subroutine to display a message four times. Specifically, the message `"Welcome to my Website"` was displayed in a Label Web control through a `For` loop. But what if we wanted to generalize the `DisplayMessage()` subroutine so that instead of always displaying the message `"Welcome to my Website"`, any message could be displayed four times?

Subroutines and functions can be generalized in this manner through the use of **parameters**. A parameter is a value that is passed into a subroutine or function when the subroutine or function is called. For a subroutine or function to utilize parameters, the syntax used differs in that a list of the parameters the subroutine or function accepts must be added, as in the following code:

```
Sub SubroutineName(Param1 as Type, Param2 as Type, ... ParamN as Type)
  Instruction1
  Instruction2
  ...
  InstructionN
End Sub
```

Param1 through *ParamN* are referred to as the subroutine's **parameters**. A subroutine may have zero to many parameters. Because Visual Basic is a strongly typed language, each parameter must have a type. The instructions in the subroutine's body can access these parameters just like they would any other variable.

Let's take a moment to rewrite the `DisplayMessage()` subroutine from Listing 6.4 so that any message can be displayed four times. To accomplish this, the `DisplayMessage()` subroutine needs to accept a string parameter that indicates the message to display. This updated version of the `DisplayMessage()` subroutine is as follows:

```
Private Sub DisplayMessage(ByVal message as String)
  'Display the message, "Welcome to my Website" 4 times
  Dim i as Integer
  For i = 1 to 4
    output.Text &= message
  Next i
End Sub
```

With this change, the `DisplayMessage()` subroutine accepts a parameter `message` of type `String`. In the subroutine's body, instead of using `output &= "Welcome to my Website<br />"`, which would display the message `"Welcome to my Website"`, we'll use `output &= message`, which emits the value of the `message` variable.

To call this updated version of the `DisplayMessage()` subroutine, we use the following code:

```
DisplayMessage(messageToDisplay)
```

So, if we want to display the message `"Welcome to my Website"`, we would call the subroutine like this:

```
DisplayMessage("Welcome to my Website<br>")
```

Let's use this updated version of the `DisplayMessage()` subroutine to create a page whose output is exactly identical to that of Listing 6.4. Start by creating a new ASP.NET web page named `SubroutineLesson2.aspx`. As with `SubroutineLesson1.aspx`, add a Label Web control with `ID output` and a Button Web control. Also, be sure to create the event handlers for the page's `Load` event and the Button's `Click` event. After you have done this, enter the source code in Listing 6.5.

LISTING 6.5 The `DisplayMessage()` Subroutine Accepts a Parameter

```
Partial Class SubroutineLesson2
    Inherits System.Web.UI.Page

    Protected Sub Page_Load(ByVal sender As Object, ByVal e As
➥System.EventArgs) Handles Me.Load
        output.Text = String.Empty

        DisplayMessage("Welcome to my Website<br />")
    End Sub

    Protected Sub Button1_Click(ByVal sender As Object, ByVal e As
➥System.EventArgs) Handles Button1.Click
        DisplayMessage("Welcome to my Website<br />")
    End Sub

    Private Sub DisplayMessage(ByVal message As String)
        Dim i As Integer
        For i = 1 To 4
            output.Text &= message
        Next i
    End Sub
End Class
```

When viewing this page through a browser, you should initially see the same output shown in Figure 6.4: the message `"Welcome to my Website"` displayed four times, followed by a Button. By clicking on the Button, you should see the output shown in Figure 6.5: the message `"Welcome to my Website"` displayed eight times, followed by a Button.

A subroutine or function may have more than one parameter. To create a subroutine with multiple parameters, simply list the parameters and their types using a comma to separate each parameter.

Each subroutine's or function's parameter has a keyword that specifies low-level details on how the parameter is sent from the caller to the subroutine or function. There are two possible values: `ByVal` and `ByRef`. A thorough discussion of these two keywords and the effects they have is beyond the scope of this book. For all examples in this book, we'll be using `ByVal`, which is the default. In fact, when typing in the subroutine or function parameters, you can omit the `ByVal` keyword; Visual Web Developer will add it automatically.

Returning Values with Functions

At this point we've looked only at subroutines, so you may be wondering what, exactly, the differences are between subroutines and functions. Subroutines and functions actually have quite a bit in common. Both are modularization control structures, and both can have zero to many parameters. Both are used to reduce code redundancy and to enhance encapsulation of programming logic.

The main difference between subroutines and functions is that a function returns a resulting value, whereas a subroutine does not. In Listing 6.5, we looked at creating a `DisplayMessage()` subroutine that used a `For` loop to display the passed-in string parameter four times. Because no resulting value is returned, we used a subroutine. But what if we wanted to modularize some programming logic that performed some sort of calculation.

In Hour 4 we created a financial calculator web page. This page accepted some inputs—the user's home loan amount, the interest rate, and so on—and determined the monthly cost. This was accomplished in a little less than 20 lines of code and was coded directly in the `Click` event handler for the Web page's Button Web control.

A more modular approach would be to place this logic in a function and then have the `Click` event handler call the function.

When creating a function, realize that a function's syntax differs from a subroutine's syntax in a few ways. First, instead of using the `Sub ... End Sub` keywords, we use `Function` and `End Function`. Second, because a function returns a value, we must specify the type of the value returned by the function. Finally, in the function body, we need to actually return some value. This is accomplished via the `Return` keyword.

The general syntax of a function is as follows:

```
Function FunctionName(Param1 as Type, ..., ParamN as Type) as ReturnType
  Instruction1
  Instruction2
  ...
  InstructionN
End Function
```

The *`ReturnType`* specifies the type of the value returned by the function. As with subroutines, functions can have zero to many input parameters. Functions are called in an identical fashion to subroutines, except that because functions return a value, often you will be using a function call in an expression, like the following:

```
Dim costPerMonth as Double
costPerMonth = ComputeCostPerMonth(P, r, t)
```

Here `ComputeCostPerMonth()` is a function that accepts three inputs and returns a `Double` value. Typically, you will assign the result of a function to a variable, although you can call a function and disregard its result, as in

```
ComputeCostPerMonth(P, r, t)  'disregards the return value
```

Let's create a function to compute the monthly cost of a mortgage. If you created the `FinancialCalculator.aspx` web page from Hour 4, you can cut and paste the source code from the `performCalc_Click` event handler into the new function, `ComputeCostPerMonth()`. The code for the new function is given in Listing 6.6.

LISTING 6.6 The `ComputeCostPerMonth()` Function Computes the Monthly Cost of a Mortgage

```
 1: Private Function ComputeMonthlyCost(P as Double, r as Double, t as
➥Double) as Double
 2:    'Specify constant values
 3:    Const INTEREST_CALCS_PER_YEAR as Integer = 12
 4:    Const PAYMENTS_PER_YEAR as Integer = 12
 5:
 6:    Dim ratePerPeriod as Double
 7:    ratePerPeriod = r/INTEREST_CALCS_PER_YEAR
 8:
 9:    Dim payPeriods as Integer
10:    payPeriods = t * PAYMENTS_PER_YEAR
11:
12:    Dim annualRate as Double
13:    annualRate = Math.Exp(INTEREST_CALCS_PER_YEAR *
➥Math.Log(1+ratePerPeriod)) - 1
14:
15:    Dim intPerPayment as Double
16:    intPerPayment = (Math.Exp(Math.Log(annualRate+1)/payPeriods) - 1)
➥ * payPeriods
17:
18:    'Now, compute the total cost of the loan
19:    Dim intPerMonth as Double = intPerPayment / PAYMENTS_PER_YEAR
20:
21:    Dim costPerMonth as Double
22:    costPerMonth = P * intPerMonth/(1-Math.Pow(intPerMonth+1,-payPeriods))
23:
24:    Return costPerMonth
25: End Function
```

The `ComputeMonthyCost()` function accepts three parameters, all of type `Double`, and returns a value of type `Double`. Recall from Hour 4 that to compute the monthly cost of a mortgage, we need three bits of information: the mortgage principal (`P`), the interest rate (`r`), and the duration of the mortgage (`t`). The `ComputeMonthyCost()` function receives these three values and uses them to compute the monthly mortgage cost. It then returns this final value using the `Return` statement (line 24).

The code in Listing 6.6 from lines 2 through 22 was taken directly from the `performCalc_Click` event handler in the `FinancialCalculator.aspx` page created in Hour 4.

Now that we have the ComputeMonthyCost() function written, we can call it from the performCalc_Click event handler, which is the event handler that fires whenever the page's Button Web control is clicked. The event handler's code replaces the computation with a call to ComputeMonthyCost(), as shown in Listing 6.7.

LISTING 6.7 The performCalc_Click Event Handler Calls the ComputeMonthyCost() Function

```
1: Protected Sub performCalc_Click(ByVal sender As Object, ByVal e As
➥System.EventArgs) Handles performCalc.Click
2:    'Create variables to hold the values entered by the user
3:    Dim P as Double = loanAmount.Text
4:    Dim r as Double = rate.Text / 100
5:    Dim t as Double = mortgageLength.Text
6:
7:    results.Text = "Your mortgage payment per month is $" &
➥ComputeMonthlyCost(P, r, t)
8: End Sub
```

On lines 3–5, the values entered by the user into the loan amount, interest rate, and mortgage length TextBox Web controls are read and stored into local variables P, r, and t. Then, on line 7, the Text property of the results Label is assigned the string "Your mortgage payment per month is $", concatenated with the Double value returned by ComputeMonthyCost().

Watch Out!

If you have the Strict="True" setting specified, the code in Listing 6.7 will generate an error because lines 3, 4, and 5 use implicit casting to cast a String (loanAmount.Text, rate.Text, and mortgageAmount.Text) into a Double. If you are using Strict="True", you will need to use the Convert.ToDouble() method to convert the Strings to Doubles, like so:

```
Dim P as Double = Convert.ToDouble(loanAmount.Text)
```

Where Do Event Handlers Fit In?

As we discussed in the "Exploring the Modularizing Control Structures: Subroutines and Functions" section, Visual Basic has two forms of modularization control structures: subroutines and functions. In this hour we looked at an example of using a subroutine in an ASP.NET web page, as well as an example using a function. However, one thing that we have been using in virtually all of our ASP.NET page examples throughout this entire book is an **event handler**. You may be wondering where, exactly, event handlers fit into the picture of subroutines and functions. To understand, let's first look at the form of the Page_Load event handler in the following code:

```
Protected Sub Page_Load(ByVal sender As Object, ByVal e As System.EventArgs)
➥ Handles Me.Load
   ...
End Sub
```

As you can tell by the syntax of the `Page_Load` event handler, an event handler is a subroutine. Event handlers were designed as subroutines because event handlers never return a value. In addition, the event handlers we have looked at thus far—the `Page_Load` event handler and the `Click` event handler for Button Web controls—accept two parameters: the first of type `Object` and the second of type `EventArgs`. The details of these parameters are unimportant for now; in later hours we'll examine their meaning in more depth.

Finally, note that an event handler's subroutine definition ends with `Handles` *`object.Event`*. *`object.Event`* is the event that is associated with this event handler. That is, when the specified event fires, the event handler will execute. It's the `Handles` keyword that wires up the specified event to this event handler.

The important information to grasp here is that an event handler is a subroutine. An event handler provides a modularized chunk of code that is executed whenever its corresponding event fires, and that corresponding event is spelled out in the `Handles` clause.

Summary

In this hour we looked at Visual Basic's control structures. Control structures alter the program flow from a sequential, one-line-after-the-other model, to one where lines of code can be conditionally executed and can be executed repeatedly until some specified set of criteria is met.

Visual Basic supports conditional control structures through the `If` statement. The `If` statement evaluates a condition and, if it is true, executes the instructions following the `Then`. In addition to the `If ... Then` portion of an `If` statement, `ElseIf` and `Else` clauses can be included.

Visual Basic has a number of looping constructs, the two most common ones being the `For` loop and the `Do` loop. The `For` loop works with an integer variable that it assigns an initial starting value to. It then executes the loop body, incrementing the looping variable at the end of each execution of the loop body. The `For` loop executes until the looping variable has surpassed the specified bounds.

The `Do` loop is more general. Rather than having a looping variable, it simply executes the loop body until a specified condition is met. There are two flavors of `Do` loop: a `Do` loop that executes the loop body *while* the condition is true and a `Do` loop that executes the loop body *until* a condition is true.

We also looked at modularization control structures: the subroutine and function. Both the subroutine and function allow for programming logic to be encapsulated, both can accept zero to many parameters, and both are called using the same syntax. The difference between the two is that a function always returns a value, whereas a subroutine never does.

The next hour, "Working with Objects in Visual Basic," will be our last hour focusing specifically on Visual Basic's syntax and semantics. After that, we'll turn our attention back to the HTML portion of ASP.NET web pages.

Q&A

Q. ***What is the difference between a subroutine and a function?***

A. Subroutines and functions both are modularization control structures that can accept zero or more input parameters. However, a function returns a value, whereas a subroutine does not.

Q. ***What is the purpose of the*** `Protected` ***or*** `Private` ***keywords found at the beginning of subroutine and function definitions? Are they necessary? When I'm creating a subroutine or function, what should I be using?***

A. In its simplest form, a subroutine merely spells out the subroutine's name and input parameters, whereas a function must include its name, input parameters, and return value. However, in addition to these bare minimum pieces of information, a number of additional keywords can, optionally, be included.

One such set of keywords is the **access modifier** keywords. These are the keywords that precede the keyword `Sub` or `Function`, and include these options: `Private`, `Protected`, `Public`, `Friend`, or `Protected Friend`. These access modifiers define how other classes and derived classes can use the subroutines and functions. The details aren't important for the code examples we'll be examining throughout this book. In fact, when entering your own methods, you can always use `Private`. You can opt to type in this access modifier explicitly or simply omit it because the default is `Private`. (Event handlers, however, *must* be `Protected`. Let Visual Web Developer create the event handlers for you and don't change their access modifiers.)

Q. ***When calling a function, must its return value be assigned to a variable?***

A. Recall that functions always return a value. Typically, the return value of a function is either used in an expression or stored in a variable. However, it is not required that the return value of a function be used at all. Imagine that we had a function called `SaveCustomerInformation(name, age)` that took as input parameters the name and age of the customer and saved this information in a database. The return value of this function might be a `DateTime` variable that indicated when the last time the customer's information was updated. In certain situations, we might not care about when the customer's information was last updated; all we want to do is update the customer's information. In such a case, we could call the function and just disregard its return value. This is accomplished by calling a function just like we would a subroutine, as follows:

```
SaveCustomerInformation("Scott", 24)
```

Workshop

Quiz

1. True or False: Conditional control structures alter the control flow of a program.

2. If we wanted to print out a message five times if the current hour was past 12, what control structures would we need to use?

3. Is the following `For ... Next` loop an example of an infinite loop?

```
Dim i as Integer
For i = 10 to 20 STEP -1
  ' Instructions
Next i
```

4. True or False: Functions and subroutines must always have at least one input parameter.

Answers

1. True. Computer programs execute sequentially by default; however, control structures allow for more flexible control flow scenarios.

2. We'd need to use two controls structures: a conditional control structure to evaluate if the hour is past 12 and a looping control structure to output the message five times. The code for this could look like so:

```
Dim i as Integer
If DateTime.Now.Hour = 12 then
  For i = 1 to 5
    LabelWebControl.Text &= "This is my message to you.<br>"
  Next i
End If
```

3. Yes. It is an infinite loop because, at each loop iteration, the looping variable is decreased by 1 (due to the `STEP -1`). Therefore, the looping variable, which starts at 10, will never reach the loop termination value, 20. This means that this loop is an infinite loop and will run forever.

4. False. Subroutines and functions can have zero or more input parameters. It is not required that they have more than zero.

Exercises

1. A common mathematical function is the *factorial function*. The factorial function takes an integer input *n* that is greater than or equal to 1, and computes `n * (n-1) * ... * 2 * 1`. In mathematical texts, factorial is denoted with an exclamation point, as in `n!`.

   For this exercise, write a function called `Factorial()` that takes a single `Integer` input and returns an `Integer` corresponding to the factorial of the inputted parameter. To help get you started, your function will look like this:

   ```
   Function Factorial(n as Integer) as Integer
     ' Write code here to compute n!
     ' Return the value n!
   End Function
   ```

   Note that:

   ```
   1! = 1
   2! = 2 * 1 = 2
   3! = 3 * 2 * 1 = 6
   4! = 4 * 3 * 2 * 1 = 24
   5! = 5 * 4 * 3 * 2 * 1 = 120
   ```

   After you have written this `Factorial()` function, add a `Page_Load` event handler that calls the function, displaying on the ASP.NET web page the values of 1! through 5!.

   Hint: The `Factorial()` function will need to contain a looping construct from 1 to *n*, where, at each iteration, a variable is multiplied by the value of the looping variable.

HOUR 7

Working with Objects in Visual Basic

In this hour, we will cover

- The difference between objects and classes
- Creating an object
- Setting an object's properties
- Calling an object's methods
- Handling an object's events
- Examples of creating objects from classes in the .NET Framework

In Hour 5, "Understanding Visual Basic's Variables and Operators," we looked at using variables and operators in Visual Basic. In Hour 6, "Managing Program Flow with Visual Basic's Control Structures," we looked at control structures, such as `If` statements, looping constructs, and subroutines and functions. There's one more important topic we need to discuss regarding Visual Basic before moving on to future topics. Specifically, we need to examine how to use objects in Visual Basic.

Recall from our discussion of object-oriented programming in Hour 2, "Understanding the ASP.NET Programming Model," that the key component of an object-oriented programming language is an **object**, which is an instance of a **class**. In this hour we'll reexamine the relationship between an object and a class and discuss the role of classes and objects in Visual Basic, the .NET Framework, and ASP.NET web pages.

Whether you realize it or not, you've already used an assortment of objects in the source code you've written in the previous chapters. Each ASP.NET Web control, for example, exists as an object in the source code portion. When setting the `Text` property of a Label control or handling the `Click` event of a Button Web control, you are working with objects. Objects are widely used in object-oriented programming languages, like Visual Basic, which is why the topic merits a thorough examination.

Reexamining the Role of Classes and Objects

In Hour 2 we discussed the ideas behind object-oriented programming. To refresh your memory, object-oriented programming is a programming paradigm in which the object is a key construct of the programming language. Objects contain methods, properties, and events. Properties define the state of the object, and methods perform some action. Events commonly represent state changes or indicate that some action has transpired.

By the Way

> Recall that in Hour 2 we described object-oriented programming using a car as an analogy. The properties of the car were such things as make, model, and color; its events were stepping on the brakes and turning on the windshield wipers; and its methods were drive, reverse, turn, and so on.
>
> The list of properties, methods, and events that describe a car is referred to as a **class**, whereas an actual, concrete instance of a car, such as a 2002 green Honda Accord, is referred to as an **object**.

Classes are the abstractions from which objects are created. To understand the relationship between a class and an object, think of a calculator. The calculator may have properties like current battery power, current value on the screen, last operation entered, and others. It might have methods like add, subtract, and so on. Its events might include clearing the last computation and turning off. If you were to sit down and list all of the properties, methods, and events that a calculator has, this list would be equivalent to a class. This list is an abstract idea of what a calculator is and what it does. It clearly is not a concrete representation of a calculator; you cannot use the list to compute the product of 19.34 and 78.

An object, on the other hand, is a concrete representation of the class. The actual calculator that supports the properties, methods, and events outlined by the class is an object and is said to be an **instance** of the class it represents.

> To summarize, a class is an abstract definition, a simple list of properties, methods, and events that are supported. An object, however, is an instance of the class, a concrete "thing" whose properties we can set, whose methods we can call, and whose events can fire.

The Role of Objects in an ASP.NET Web Application

Recall from our earlier discussions that the .NET Framework contains a plethora of classes that allow for a variety of functionality. For example, each and every Web control that can be used in an ASP.NET page is represented by a class in the .NET Framework.

There are also classes in the .NET Framework that allow for an email to be sent from a web page, for data to be retrieved from a database, for an image to be created, and so on. The source code portion of your ASP.NET web page can utilize the variety of functionality present in the .NET Framework.

To use a class in the .NET Framework, we first must create an object from the particular class whose functionality we are interested in. Once we have an object, we may need to set some of the object's properties and call some of the object's methods. Additionally, we may want to create event handlers for some of the object's events.

As we will see starting with Hour 13, "An Introduction to Databases," ASP.NET's DataSource Web controls make it possible to retrieve and work with databases without having to write a lick of code. However, sometimes you still may need to programmatically access database data. While we won't be examining how to programmatically access databases in this book, understand that there are a number of database-related classes in the .NET Framework, such as `SqlConnection`, `SqlCommand`, and `SqlDataReader`.

The Four Common Tasks Performed with Objects

When using objects, we'll perform four tasks again and again:

- **Instantiation**—To work with an object, we'll need to create an instance of the object from the desired class. This is a required step that we must always do once when working with an object.

- **Setting property values**—Not all objects have properties, and we do not always need to use the properties of those that do. However, most of the time we'll find ourselves setting the properties of an object. Remember that properties are values that describe the state of the object. For example, a class that sends an email message might have properties like body, subject, to, from, cc, and so on.

- **Calling methods**—When using objects, we will always call one or more of the object's methods. A class that sends email messages might have a method called `Send()`, which would send the email. Therefore, to send an email from an ASP.NET web page using this class, we would first create an instance of the class; then set its body, subject, to, from, and other pertinent properties; and then call its `Send()` method.

- **Creating event handlers**—As with properties, not all objects have events, and we do not always need to use the events of those that do. Sometimes, however, we'll want to run a set of instructions only when a particular event for a particular object fires. To accomplish this, we'll need to create an event handler that's wired up to the object's pertinent event. We've seen examples of this in previous hours in creating event handlers for a Button Web control's `Click` event, or an event handler for the ASP.NET page's `Load` event.

In the remainder of this hour, we will look at the Visual Basic syntax required to accomplish these four tasks.

Creating an Object

Recall that classes are an abstract definition, listing functionality that is provided. In addition to properties, methods, and events, classes contain **constructors**. A constructor is a special method that is used to create an instance of the class.

By the Way

> In a later section, "Calling an Object's Methods," we'll discuss what, exactly, methods are. For now, you can think of a method as a function or subroutine. Like functions and subroutines, methods are a means of encapsulating a number of program instructions, can have zero or more parameters, and may return a value.

Constructors always have the same name as the class. For example, one of the classes used to programmatically work with database data is the `SqlCommand` class. The constructor for this class is a method named `SqlCommand()`.

To create an instance of an object, we use the following syntax:

```
Variable = New Constructor()
```

The constructor *`Constructor`* returns an object of the class *`Constructor`*. Because Visual Basic is a strongly typed language, the type of *`Variable`* must be of the class whose constructor is being called. For example, to create an instance of the `SqlCommand` class, we would first create a variable whose type was of `SqlCommand` as follows:

```
Dim myCommand as SqlCommand
```

And then we would assign to this variable the object returned by the constructor:

```
myCommand = New SqlCommand()
```

The first line of code creates a variable named `myCommand` of type `SqlCommand`; the second line of code assigns to `myCommand` the object returned by the constructor `SqlCommand()`.

Did you Know?

Recall that to use an object, we must first create an instance of the object. This process is commonly called **instantiation**. We can instantiate an object like this:

```
Dim variable as type
variable = New Constructor()
```

Or we can also instantiate an object with the following line of code:

```
Dim variableName as type = New Constructor()
```

With the `SqlCommand` example we examined, we could have rewritten it as follows:

```
Dim myCommand as SqlCommand = New SqlCommand()
```

Constructors with Parameters

Constructors, like functions and subroutines, can have zero or more parameters. Additionally, classes may have more than one constructor. When constructors accept one or more parameters, typically the parameters are for initial values of various properties. For example, the `SqlCommand` class has a constructor that accepts zero parameters, as well as one that accepts a string parameter. The constructor that accepts zero parameters does not assign any initial value to any of its properties. The constructor that accepts a string parameter, however, assigns the passed-in parameter value to the object's `CommandText` property.

By the Way

In general, any class method (such as the constructor) can have multiple versions, each that accepts a different number of input parameters. Class methods that have versions that accept a different number of parameters are referred to as **overloaded.**

Constructors that accept more than one parameter are used frequently for reducing the amount of code that needs to be written. For example, to create an `SqlCommand` object and set its `CommandText` property, we would need to use the following two lines of code:

```
Dim myCommand as SqlCommand = New SqlCommand()
myCommand.CommandText = "some value"
```

However, by using the `SqlCommand()` constructor that accepts a string parameter, we can condense these two lines into one as follows:

```
Dim myCommand as SqlCommand = New SqlCommand("some value")
```

By the Way

> Most classes have more than one constructor—one that accepts zero parameters and also a myriad of others that accept one, two, three, four, or even more parameters. The constructor that accepts zero parameters is typically referred to as the **default constructor.**

Setting an Object's Properties

After we have created an object, often we want to set some of the object's properties. To reference an object's properties, we use the following syntax:

```
objectVariable.PropertyName
```

Here, *`objectVariable`* is the object variable. That is, in the code

```
Dim myCommand as SqlCommand
myCommand = New SqlCommand()
```

the *`objectVariable`* is `myCommand`. The *`PropertyName`* is the name of the property that you want to access. Properties are used just like variables; they can be assigned values, they have types, and they can be used in expressions just like variables.

Typically, you will assign a value to a property just once and then will call one of the object's methods, which uses the value of the property in some manner.

For example, to send an email message from an ASP.NET page, we use the `MailMessage` class. When an instance of this class is created, a number of properties need to be set, such as `From`, `To`, `Subject`, and others. The following code snippet demonstrates how to create an instance of this class and set its properties:

```
'Create an instance of the MailMesage class
Dim myMailMessage As MailMessage = New MailMessage()

'Set the From, To, Subject, and Body properties
myMailMessage.From = "someone@example.com"
myMailMessage.To = "someone@example.com"
myMailMessage.Subject = "Email Subject"
myMailMessage.Body = "Hello!"
```

> Not all properties can necessarily be written to and read from. Some classes mark certain properties as **read only** or **write only**. The vast majority of properties, however, are both readable and writeable. When examining a new class and its properties, I'll point out if any of those properties are read only or write only.

Calling an Object's Methods

An object's methods are called just like other subroutines and functions, except that the name of the object whose method you want to call must precede the method being called. That is, the syntax for calling an object's method is as follows:

```
objectVariable.MethodName(param1, param2, ..., paramN)
```

> **By the Way**
>
> Methods in classes are semantically just like subroutines and functions. That is, methods in classes can accept zero to many input parameters and can optionally provide a return value.

As we discussed earlier, the `SqlCommand` class is used for retrieving information from a database. In using the `SqlCommand` class, we must specify the database to retrieve the data from, as well as what data to retrieve. These two bits of information are specified via the `Connection` and `CommandText` properties. The `SqlCommand` class contains an `ExecuteReader()` method, which returns the data specified by the `CommandText` property from the database specified by the `Connection` property.

To call this method, we first must create an instance of the `SqlCommand` class and set its `Connection` and `CommandText` properties. After these two steps have been accomplished, we can call the `ExecuteReader()` method. The following code snippet demonstrates the syntax for calling a method:

```
'Create an instance of the SqlCommand class
Dim myCommand as SqlCommand = New SqlCommand()

'Set the Connection and CommandText properties
myCommand.Connection = ...
myCommand.CommandText = "..."

'Call the ExecuteReader() method
Dim myReader as SqlDataReader
myReader = myCommand.ExecuteReader()
```

As you can see in this code snippet, the `ExecuteReader()` method returns an object of type `SqlDataReader`.

> **By the Way**
>
> The `SqlDataReader` class is designed for holding data retrieved from a database.

Methods that return a value are similar to functions; some methods do not return a value, making them similar to subroutines. Also, methods—both ones that do and ones that do not return a value—can have zero to many input parameters.

Creating Event Handlers for an Object's Events

In addition to methods and properties, objects may also have events. Events typically represent a state change or indicate that some action has transpired. For example, the ASP.NET Button Web control has a `Click` event which indicates that the user has performed some action, namely she's clicked the button in her browser, resulting in a postback. A good example of an event representing a state change is the TextBox Web control's `TextChanged` event. This event fires on postback if the TextBox's text content has been changed.

Often we'll want to have some code we've written run in response to a particular event firing. To accomplish this, we must create an **event handler**. An event handler is simply a subroutine with a particular set of input parameters that is **wired** to a particular event. This wiring process, which we'll examine shortly, causes the event handler to be executed whenever the event is raised.

All event handlers in a .NET program must be created as a subroutine and must accept precisely two input parameters: the first one must be of type `Object`, while the second one must be of a type derived from `EventArgs`. For example, the event handler for a Button Web control's `Click` event (which Visual Web Developer can create for us automatically) has the following signature:

```
Protected Sub Button1_Click(ByVal sender As Object, ByVal e As
➥System.EventArgs) Handles Button1.Click
   ...
End Sub
```

This statement defines a subroutine named `Button1_Click` that serves as an event handler for `Button1`'s `Click` event.

As you can see, the first parameter passed into the event handler is an `Object`. This `Object` parameter is the object that raised the event being handled. The second parameter is of type `EventArgs`. This second parameter can contain additional event-related information. In this event handler, as well as the page's `Load` event handler, no additional information is passed in. However, in future hours we will see examples of event handlers that are sent additional information through this second input parameter.

In addition to the input parameters, the event handler's definition also includes the `Handles` keyword. This is responsible for wiring the event handler to a particular event. In the case of the `Button1_Click` event handler, the subroutine is wired up to `Button1`'s `Click` event. `Button1` is an object representing the Button Web control defined in the page's HTML portion with `ID Button1`.

By the Way

> You can create an event handler in Visual Basic by typing in the appropriate syntax by hand. However, Visual Web Developer removes this need because it can auto-generate event handler syntax. As we saw in previous hours, double-clicking a Web control in the Design view will create an event handler for the Web control's default event. Alternatively, you can always go to the source code portion and select the appropriate object and event from the drop-down lists at the top.

Summary

In this hour we reexamined the concepts behind objects and classes. To use an object, we first must create it. This is accomplished using the Visual Basic `New` keyword along with a constructor. As we saw, a constructor is a method that has the same name as the class and returns an instance of the class. For example, to create an instance of the `SqlCommand` class, we could use

```
Dim myCommand as SqlCommand
myCommand = New SqlCommand()
```

After an object has been created, we can set its properties, call its methods, and create event handlers. An object's property can be accessed by listing the object's name, followed by a period, followed by the property name. For example, to access the `CommandText` property of the `myCommand` object, we would use the following syntax:

```
myCommand.CommandText
```

Properties have the same semantics as ordinary variables; they have a type and can be used in expressions or assigned values.

An object's method is called by listing the object's name, followed by a period, followed by the method's name. Methods are like subroutines and functions in that they may accept zero or more input parameters and can optionally return a value.

Objects can also have a number of events that can fire at different times; when an event fires, we may want to execute some code. Event handlers are special subroutines that are wired up to a particular event and execute when that specified event fires. Event handlers must accept two input parameters and use the `Handles` keyword to indicate the particular event that they execute in response to. Although an event handler's syntax can be entered manually, Visual Web Developer will gladly create the appropriate event handler syntax: You just specify the object and event from the drop-down lists at the top of the source code portion of an ASP.NET page.

This hour concludes our in-depth examination of Visual Basic. In the next hour we will look at the two ASP.NET Web controls that are used for displaying text: the

Label and Literal Web controls. Following that, we will spend the next several hours examining how to collect and process user input.

Q&A

Q. ***This hour showed us how to use classes in the .NET Framework, but is it possible to create our own classes?***

A. With object-oriented programming languages like Visual Basic, you can create your own classes. However, this is far beyond the scope of this book. Although we'll be using a number of the .NET Framework classes throughout the course of this book, we'll not ever need to create our own classes.

Q. ***Will we be examining how to send email messages from an ASP.NET page in this book?***

A. No, I'm afraid we won't have the time to dissect sending an email message from an ASP.NET page. However, a plethora of online articles show how to accomplish this common task.

The two classes used in ASP.NET 2.0 for sending email messages are the `MailMessage` and `SmtpClient` classes. In the previous version of ASP.NET, the classes used were `MailMessage` and `SmtpMail`. If you search online for information on sending an email message from an ASP.NET 2.0 page, be sure to use the `SmtpClient` class in lieu of the deprecated `SmtpMail` class.

Workshop

Quiz

1. What are the four actions commonly performed on objects?
2. True or False: The .NET Framework contains classes that we will be using in our ASP.NET web pages.
3. In the past two hours, we examined a number of fundamental programming concepts. In this hour, we looked at objects, which have properties, methods, and events. What programming concept is analogous to an object's properties?
4. What programming concept is analogous to an object's methods?
5. In Visual Basic, what keyword in the subroutine definition indicates that the subroutine should be called when a specified event fires?

Answers

1. Before objects can be used, they must first be instantiated. Once an object instance exists, often the properties of the object are then set, followed by calling the object's methods. Additionally, event handlers may need to be created in order to have code executed in response to the firing of an object's event.
2. True. In fact, all ASP.NET Web controls are implemented as classes in the .NET Framework.
3. Properties are analogous to variables.
4. Methods are analogous to subroutines and functions.
5. The `Handles` keyword.

Exercises

There are no exercises for this hour.

HOUR 8

ASP.NET Web Controls for Displaying Text

In this hour, we will cover

- Displaying text using the Literal and Label Web controls
- Using the Literal Web control
- Using the Label Web control
- Understanding the differences between the Literal and Label Web controls
- Altering the appearance of the Label Web control

In the past three hours we examined the syntax and semantics for Visual Basic, the programming language we'll be using in the source code portion of our ASP.NET web pages. Prior to these three hours, we discussed ASP.NET fundamentals, such as how each ASP.NET web page comprises a source code portion and an HTML portion. Recall that the HTML portion can contain HTML markup as well as Web controls.

Web controls, like regular HTML markup, are placed in the HTML portion. When a browser requests an ASP.NET web page, the Web controls are converted into their associated HTML markup. However, Web controls can be accessed programmatically through the page's source code. In this manner, Web controls serve as an intermediary between the source code and HTML portions of an ASP.NET page.

In the financial calculator example in Hour 4, "Designing, Creating, and Testing ASP.NET Web Pages," our ASP.NET page had a number of Web controls. There were three TextBox Web controls, one for each of the inputs the user needed to enter; a Button Web control, which the user would click after he had entered the information and wanted the result; and a Label Web control, where the output of the calculation was displayed.

We'll be examining a variety of Web controls throughout this book. These various Web controls can be divided into a number of categories, such as Web controls that are used to display text, Web controls that are used to collect user input, Web controls that are used to display data from a database, and so on.

Examining the Web Controls Designed for Displaying Text

Two ASP.NET Web controls are designed for displaying text: the Literal Web control and the Label Web control.

These two controls differ in the HTML markup that is rendered by each control when the ASP.NET web page is executed. Recall from our discussions in Hour 4 that when an ASP.NET web page is visited through a browser, the ASP.NET engine executes the page, producing HTML markup that is then sent back to the web server. This HTML markup is then sent from the web server back to the user's browser.

The HTML markup produced by an ASP.NET web page can come from

- The static HTML markup in the HTML portion
- The HTML markup that is rendered by the Web controls

The static HTML markup in the HTML portion is passed on to the browser exactly as it's typed in. However, the HTML markup produced by Web controls depends on the various property values of each Web control.

The differences between the Literal and Label Web controls are in the HTML markup produced by each control. The Literal Web control HTML markup is simply the value of its `Text` property. The Label Web control, on the other hand, has a number of formatting properties, such as `BackColor`, `ForeColor`, `Font`, and so on, that specify how the Label's `Text` property should be displayed.

In this hour we'll examine how to use each of these two Web controls, including how to add these Web controls to an ASP.NET web page's HTML portion and how to set their properties.

Using the Literal Web Control

The Literal Web control is one of the simplest Web controls. The HTML markup rendered by the Literal Web control is precisely the value of the Web control's `Text` property.

To illustrate the Literal's behavior, let's create an ASP.NET page that has a Literal control. Start by creating a new ASP.NET web page named `LiteralControl.aspx`;

as always, make sure that the Language selected is Visual Basic and that the Place Code in a Separate File check box is checked. Next, drag the Literal control from the Toolbox onto the page. Figure 8.1 shows the Design view after the Literal control has been added.

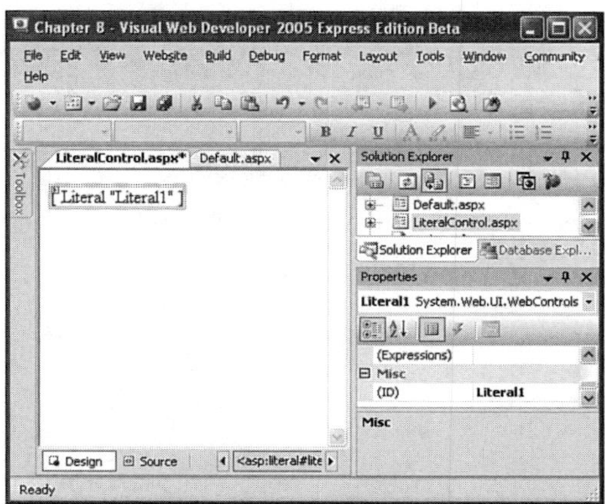

FIGURE 8.1
A Literal Web control has been added to the designer.

Make sure that the Literal Web control you just added is selected, and then examine the Properties window in the lower-right corner. Note that the Literal Web control has only six properties. These six properties, as displayed in the Properties window, are

- Text
- EnableViewState
- Mode
- Visible
- (Expressions)
- (ID)

The only two properties that we will be working with in this hour are the `ID` and `Text` properties. As with the financial calculator example we examined in Hour 4, the `ID` property uniquely names the Web control so that its properties can be referenced in the source code portion of the ASP.NET web page. The `Text` property of the Literal Web control is the value that is displayed in the ASP.NET web page when the Literal Web control is rendered.

When the Literal Web control's `Text` property is not set, the Literal Web control is shown in the designer as

```
[Literal "ID"]
```

where *ID* is the value of the Literal Web control's `ID` property. In Figure 8.1 the Literal control is displayed as `[Literal "Literal1"]` because the `ID` property value is `Literal1`, and the `Text` property is not set.

If the `Text` property is set to some value, though, the designer displays the Literal Web control as this property value. For example, take a moment to change the Literal Web control's `Text` property to `Hello, World!`. Figure 8.2 shows the designer after this change has been made. Note that the Literal Web control is displayed in the designer as the text `"Hello, World!"`.

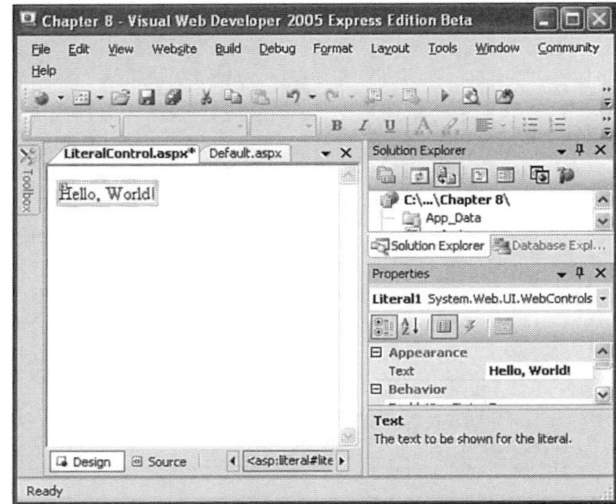

FIGURE 8.2 The Literal Web control is displayed as `"Hello, World!"` in the designer.

Now that we've added this Literal Web control and set its `Text` property, let's view this ASP.NET web page through a browser. Go to the Debug menu and choose Start Without Debugging. Figure 8.3 shows the `LiteralControl.aspx` web page when viewed through a browser. Note that the output is simply the value `"Hello, World!"`.

FIGURE 8.3 `LiteralControl.aspx`, when viewed through a web browser.

After you have loaded the web page in your web browser, view the HTML source code received by your browser. Listing 8.1 contains the HTML received by my browser when testing this page.

LISTING 8.1 The HTML Markup Produced by the `LiteralControl.aspx` Web Page

```
 1: <!DOCTYPE html PUBLIC "-//W3C//DTD XHTML 1.0 Transitional//EN"
➥ "http://www.w3.org/TR/xhtml1/DTD/xhtml1-transitional.dtd">
 2:
 3: <html xmlns="http://www.w3.org/1999/xhtml" >
 4: <head><title>
 5:     Untitled Page
 6: </title></head>
 7: <body>
 8:     <form name="form1" method="post" action="LiteralControl.aspx"
➥id="form1">
 9: <div>
10: <input type="hidden" name="__VIEWSTATE" id="__VIEWSTATE"
➥ value="/wEPDwUKMTYyNzcxNDY4NmRkXqmMGDevFsKo9Quh9HOipCp7Cro=" />
11: </div>
12:
13:     <div>
14:         Hello, World!</div>
15:     </form>
16: </body>
17: </html>
```

In Listing 8.1, line 14 contains the HTML markup produced by the Literal Web control. It is precisely the value of the Literal Web control's `Text` property. The remainder of the HTML markup is a byproduct of the HTML content added when creating a new ASP.NET web page with the Web Matrix Project.

Examining the Additional HTML Markup

In Listing 8.1, the `<html>`, `<head>`, and `<body>` tags on lines 3 through 7 and lines 16 through 17 were added by Visual Web Developer when we created `LiteralControl.aspx` as a new Web Form. Additionally, the `<div>` element on lines 13 and 14 was inserted by Visual Web Developer as well.

Lines 8–11 contain a `<form>` tag and an `<input>` tag that has its `type` set to `hidden`. This HTML content is the markup that is produced by the Web Form. Recall from our discussions in Hour 4 that a Web Form is rendered as an HTML form with some extra information stored in a hidden `<input>` tag. Our ASP.NET web page has a Web Form in it because Visual Web Developer adds one in by default when creating a new ASP.NET web page. We will discuss the details of Web Forms in the next hour, "Web Form Basics."

Regarding the `<div>` element starting on line 13 and ending on line 14, realize that this element was *not* added by the Literal Web control. I point this out because as we will see moving forward, most Web controls add additional HTML markup. For example, the Label Web control renders as a `<span>` element. The Literal control, however, does not render as an HTML element; it simply outputs the value of its `Text` property.

Setting the Literal Control's `Text` Property Programmatically

As we just saw, the `Text` property of the Literal Web control can be set through the Properties window. If you know what the `Text` property's value should be, there is nothing wrong with using this approach. However, if you want the value of the `Text` property to be dynamic, you will have to set the property value through the source code portion of your ASP.NET page.

For example, imagine that you wanted to use a Literal control to display the current date and time. Programmatically, the current date and time can be retrieved by the `DateTime.Now` property.

To set the Literal control's `Text` property programmatically, we can use the following syntax in our source code portion:

```
LiteralControlID.Text = value
```

`LiteralControlID` is the value of the Literal Web control's `ID` property, and *`value`* is a string value that we want to assign to the Label Web control's `Text` property.

Let's create an ASP.NET web page that uses a Label Web control to display the current date and time. Start by creating a new ASP.NET web page named `LiteralTime.aspx`, and then drag and drop a Literal Web control onto the designer. We don't need to set the `Text` property through the Properties window because we will be setting this property programmatically. We should, however, rename the Literal Web control's `ID` property from the ambiguous `Label1` to something more descriptive, such as `currentTime`.

After you have added the Label Web control and changed its `ID` property to `currentTime`, take a moment to compare what your screen looks like with Figure 8.4.

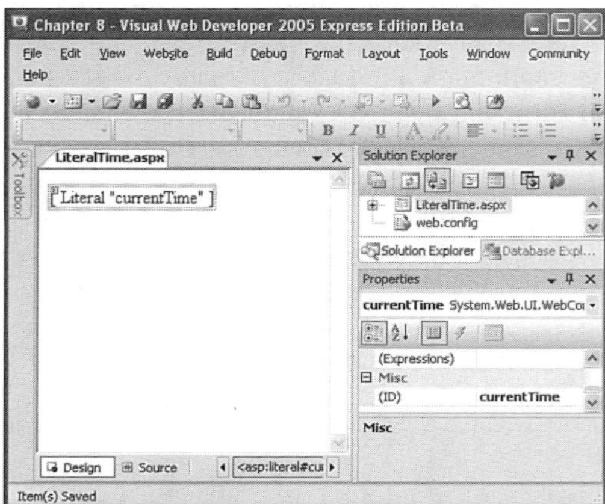

FIGURE 8.4
The designer after the Literal Web control has been added and its *ID* property set.

After we've added the Literal Web control and set its `ID` property to `currentTime`, we're ready to add the needed source code. Start by creating an event handler for the page's `Load` event by double-clicking in the Design view region or going to the source code portion and selecting (Page Events) from the left drop-down list and Load from the right. For this ASP.NET web page, we want to have the Literal Web control's `Text` property set to the current date and time whenever the page is visited. Therefore, we will do so in the `Page_Load` event handler.

Enter the following code into your `Page_Load` event handler:

```
currentTime.Text = DateTime.Now
```

After you have entered this source code content, save the ASP.NET web page and view it through a web browser. Figure 8.5 shows the `LiteralTime.aspx` web page when viewed through a browser.

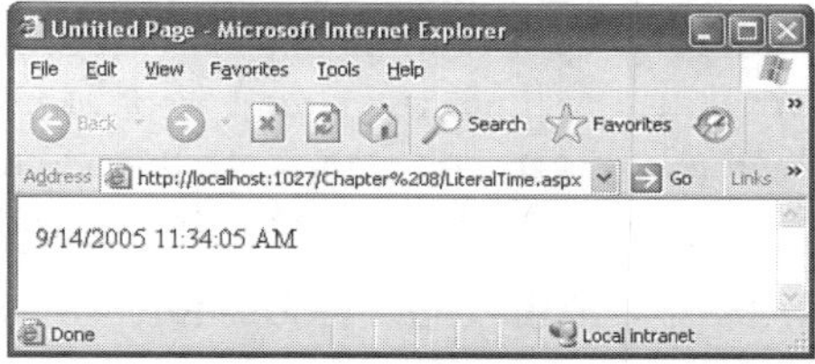

FIGURE 8.5
The current date and time are displayed.

Did you Know?

> To convince yourself that the current date and time are being shown, refresh your web browser every few seconds, noting that the time displayed is updated accordingly.

Let's take a moment to examine the HTML markup received by the web browser. Listing 8.2 contains this HTML content.

LISTING 8.2 The HTML Markup Produced by the `LiteralTime.aspx` Web Page

```
<!DOCTYPE html PUBLIC "-//W3C//DTD XHTML 1.0 Transitional//EN"
➥ "http://www.w3.org/TR/xhtml1/DTD/xhtml1-transitional.dtd">

<html xmlns="http://www.w3.org/1999/xhtml" >
<head><title>
    Untitled Page
</title></head>
<body>
    <form name="form1" method="post" action="LiteralTime.aspx" id="form1">
<div>
<input type="hidden" name="__VIEWSTATE" id="__VIEWSTATE"
➥value="/wEPDwUKMTYyNzcxNDY4Ng9kFgICAw9kFgICAQ8WAh4EVGV4dAUVOS8xNC8
➥yMDA1IDExOjM0OjA1IEFNZGTwwTq/1izzu6mHYaOGM9vvRW3s2A==" />
</div>
```

LISTING 8.2 Continued

```
12:
13:     <div>
14:         9/14/2005 11:34:05 AM
15:     </div>
16:     </form>
17: </body>
18: </html>
```

The important line to pay attention to is line 14, which is the HTML markup produced by the Literal Web control. When the browser requests the `LiteralTime.aspx` web page, the ASP.NET engine executes the page. The `Page_Load` event handler is fired, and the source code within that event handler is executed. This single line of code sets the `currentTime` Literal Web control's `Text` property to the current date and time.

After executing the `Page_Load` event handler, the ASP.NET engine renders the Web controls in the HTML portion. By this point, the Literal Web control has had its `Text` property set to the current date and time. The Literal Web control renders as this current date and time, and it is this HTML, along with the additional static HTML markup that was included by Visual Web Developer, that is sent to the web browser.

When refreshing your web browser, the entire process is repeated, and the HTML sent back to your browser has the updated date and time.

By the Way

> What do you think the output of the `LiteralTime.aspx` web page would be if we changed the code in the `Page_Load` event handler from
>
> ```
> currentTime.Text = DateTime.Now
> ```
>
> to
>
> ```
> currentTime.Text = "The current time is: " & DateTime.Now
> ```
>
> I encourage you to try this code change to see how the output changes.

The Literal Web control does not contain any properties to specify the format of the output. If you need to format the Literal control's output, you will have to insert the appropriate HTML markup in the control's `Text` property. For example, to display the current time in a bold font, you would need to explicitly include the HTML bold element (<b>):

```
currentTime.Text = "<b>" & DateTime.Now & "</b>"
```

Clearly, the Literal Web control is not well suited for displaying formatted text. The Label Web control, which we'll examine in the next section, has a host of properties that make formatting the Label control's output a breeze.

The Literal Web control is most useful in scenarios in which you need to precisely output specific markup. The Label control's emitted markup depends on both its `Text` property and its formatting property values. The Literal control, however, offers finer control over the output because it emits just the value of its `Text` property.

Using the Label Web Control

The Label Web control differs from the Literal Web control in that it contains a number of formatting properties that, when set, specify how the `Text` property should be displayed in the user's web browser.

For example, we can display the Label text in a bold font by setting the control's `Font` property's `Bold` subproperty to `True`. Let's create a new ASP.NET web page to demonstrate using a Label Web control.

Start by creating an ASP.NET page named `LabelControl.aspx`; then drag and drop a Label Web control onto the page. Select the Label Web control and note its list of properties in the Properties window. There are far more properties listed here than with the Literal Web control.

First, let's set the Label Web control's `Text` property to `Hello, World!`. After you have done this, your screen should look like Figure 8.6.

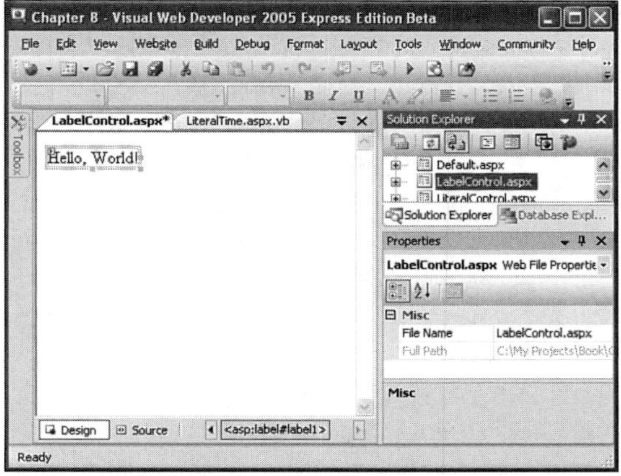

FIGURE 8.6 A Label Web control has been added and its `Text` property has been set.

After the `Text` property has been set, let's make it display its content in a bold font. To accomplish this, click the Label Web control, which will load the control's properties in the Properties window. One of the properties listed is `Font`. To the left of this property name, you'll find a plus, which indicates that this property has subproperties. Click the plus to expand these subproperties.

The subproperties of the `Font` property are listed in Table 8.1. One of these subproperties is `Bold`, which defaults to a value of `False`. Go ahead and select `True` from the drop-down list. This has the effect of making the Label Web control's text in the designer appear bold, as you can see in Figure 8.7, which shows how the control looks after the `Bold` subproperty has been set to `True`.

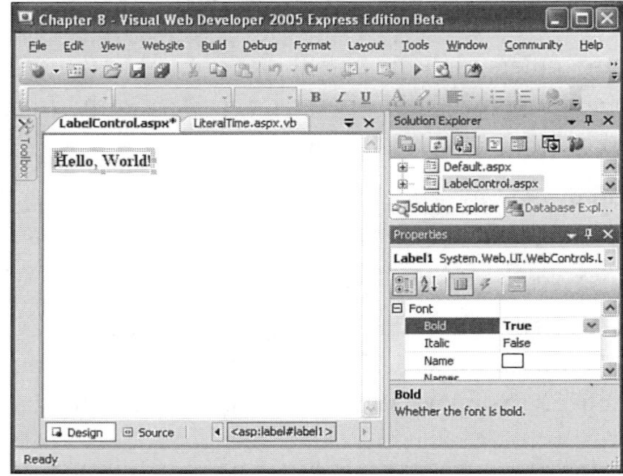

FIGURE 8.7 The Label Web control's **`Bold`** subproperty has been set to `True`.

TABLE 8.1 The Subproperties of the Label Web Control's `Font` Property

Subproperty Name	Description
`Bold`	A Boolean value indicating whether the `Text` property will be displayed in a bold font.
`Italic`	A Boolean value indicating whether the `Text` property will be displayed in an italic font.
`Name`	The preferred font to use when displaying the text. Common font choices include Arial, Helvetica, and Verdana.
`Names`	A sequence of font names. If the browser visiting the page does not support one of the fonts, it will try using the next listed one.
`Overline`	A Boolean value indicating whether the `Text` property will be displayed with an overline.
`Size`	The size that the `Text` property will be displayed in. You can choose settings such as Smaller, Medium, Larger, and so on. You can also enter a point value, like 14pt.
`Strikeout`	A Boolean value indicating whether the `Text` property will be displayed with a strikeout.
`Underline`	A Boolean value indicating whether the `Text` property will be displayed underlined.

Go ahead and view the ASP.NET page through a web browser. When viewing the `LabelControl.aspx` page through a browser, you should see the message `"Hello, World!"` in a bold font, just like we saw in the designer.

Examining the HTML Markup Generated by the Label Web Control

With the Literal Web control, the HTML markup sent to the web browser was the value of the Literal Web control's `Text` property. With the Label Web control, the `Text` property is sent in addition to extra HTML markup to provide the associated formatting.

But what HTML markup does the Label send to the browser? Interestingly, this depends on what browser visits the ASP.NET web page! Whenever a browser makes a request for a web page, it sends along a piece of information known as the **User-Agent header**. This bit of information specifies what browser is being used.

By the Way

> As we saw in the previous section, when we set the Literal Web control's `Mode` property to `Transform`, the nonsupported markup will be automatically stripped from the Literal's output. The ASP.NET engine can determine whether or not the requesting browser can support HTML or XHTML by inspecting the User-Agent header.

Recall from the "Examining the Web Controls Designed for Displaying Text" section that when the ASP.NET web page is being executed by the ASP.NET engine, the various Web controls are rendered and converted into HTML markup. When these controls are rendered, they take into account the User-Agent header and render HTML appropriate for the particular browser.

For example, Listing 8.3 contains the HTML markup received when visiting the `LabelControl.aspx` web page using an **uplevel** web browser. (ASP.NET classifies uplevel web browsers as those that include support for client-side script, cascading style sheets, and HTML 4.0. Some examples of uplevel browsers include versions of Internet Explorer 4.0 or higher, Mozilla FireFox, and versions of Netscape 6.0 or higher.)

LISTING 8.3 An Uplevel Browser Receives the Following HTML Markup from `LabelControl.aspx`

```
<!DOCTYPE html PUBLIC "-//W3C//DTD XHTML 1.0 Transitional//EN"
➥ "http://www.w3.org/TR/xhtml1/DTD/xhtml1-transitional.dtd">

<html xmlns="http://www.w3.org/1999/xhtml" >
<head><title>
    Untitled Page
```

LISTING 8.3 Continued

```
 6: </title></head>
 7: <body>
 8:     <form name="form1" method="post" action="LabelControl.aspx" id="form1">
 9: <div>
10: <input type="hidden" name="__VIEWSTATE" id="__VIEWSTATE"
➥ value="/wEPDwUJODExMDE5NzY5ZGR5Pm2YFjJUcWvsLSH4OZzhXFfAyQ==" />
11: </div>
12:
13:     <div>
14:         <span id="Label1" style="font-weight:bold;">Hello, World!
➥</span></div>
15:     </form>
16: </body>
17: </html>
```

Line 14 contains the HTML markup produced by the Label Web control. Note that it uses a <span> HTML tag whose `id` attribute is equal to the `ID` property of the Label Web control. Also note that for uplevel browsers, the text `"Hello, World!"` is made bold through the <span> tag's `style` attribute.

Listing 8.4 contains the HTML markup produced by `LabelControl.aspx` when visited by Netscape version 4, an antiquated web browser that does not have support for HTML version 4.0. Such browsers, like Netscape 4, that are not considered uplevel are said to be **downlevel**.

LISTING 8.4 Downlevel Browsers Receive the Following HTML Markup from `LabelControl.aspx`

```
 1: <!DOCTYPE html PUBLIC "-//W3C//DTD XHTML 1.0 Transitional//EN"
➥ "http://www.w3.org/TR/xhtml1/DTD/xhtml1-transitional.dtd">
 2:
 3: <html xmlns="http://www.w3.org/1999/xhtml" >
 4: <head><title>
 5:         Untitled Page
 6: </title></head>
 7: <body>
 8:     <form name="form1" method="post" action="LabelControl.aspx" id="form1">
 9: <input type="hidden" name="__VIEWSTATE" id="__VIEWSTATE"
➥ value="/wEPDwUJODExMDE5NzY5ZGR5Pm2YFjJUcWvsLSH4OZzhXFfAyQ==" />
10:
11:     <div>
12:         <span id="Label1"><b>Hello, World!</b></span></div>
13:     </form>
14: </body>
15: </html>
```

Line 12 in Listing 8.4 differs from line 14 in Listing 8.3. Instead of specifying that the text `"Hello, World!"` should be bold using the <span> tag's `style` attribute, the HTML markup produced for downlevel browsers uses a <b> tag to make the text bold.

By the Way

Despite the fact that an uplevel browser and a downlevel browser receive different HTML markup, both browsers display the same output—the message `"Hello, World!"` in a bold font. ASP.NET Web controls take care to make the rendered output as similar as possible between uplevel and downlevel browsers.

Examining the Formatting Properties of the Label Web Control

The Label Web control contains a number of formatting properties. We've already seen how to make the text of the Label Web control bold. There is a plethora of other Label Web control formatting properties worth examining. These formatting properties can be divided into the following classes: color properties, border properties, font properties, and miscellaneous properties. We'll examine each of these classes of properties in the next four sections.

Looking at the Color Properties

The Label Web control contains two properties for specifying the color of the outputted text: `ForeColor` and `BackColor`. If you couldn't guess, `ForeColor` specifies the text's foreground color, whereas `BackColor` specifies its background color.

Let's create a new ASP.NET web page to try out these two color properties. Start by creating an ASP.NET web page named `ColorLabel.aspx`, and drag and drop a Label Web control onto the page. After adding the Label Web control, change the `Text` property to `This is a test of the color properties.`

Now, let's set the `BackColor` to Navy and the `ForeColor` to White. To accomplish this, make sure that the Label Web control is selected so that its properties are displayed in the Properties window. Then find the `BackColor` property in the Properties window.

Selecting the `BackColor` property will display a palette with three tabs: Custom, Web, and System. As Figure 8.8 shows, the Custom tab contains 64 colors that you can choose from for setting the `BackColor` property.

By the Way

If you select the `BackColor` property from the Properties window while in the Source view, you won't see the palette shown in Figure 8.8. Instead, you'll see just a list of color names. To get the full palette listing, simply switch to the Design view.

If you see a color that you want to set the `BackColor` to, simply click the color. If you do not see the color you want, you can right-click one of the blank color boxes in the bottom two rows, which will open the Define Color dialog box (see Figure 8.9). From here, you can choose a particular color from the color palette. After you select a color and click the Add Color button, the color you right-clicked in the Custom tab will be replaced by the new color you defined. Additionally, the `BackColor` property will be set to this newly created color.

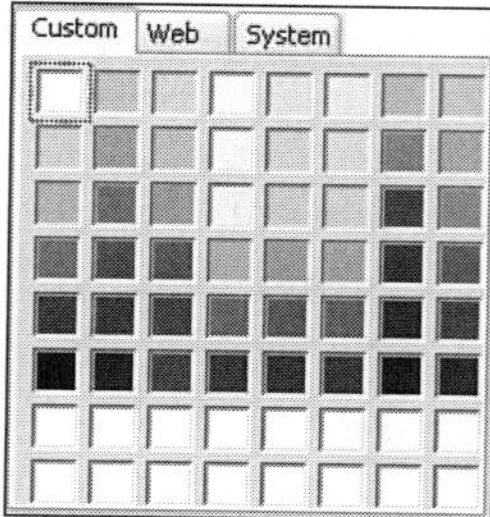

FIGURE 8.8
The Custom tab displays various colors.

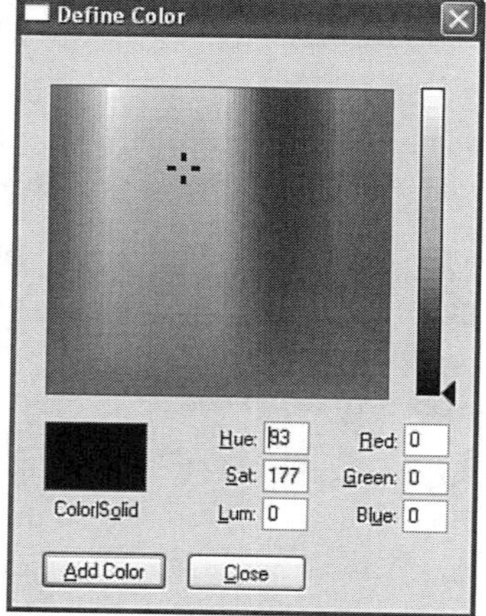

FIGURE 8.9
The Define Color dialog box allows you to create a custom color.

You can also choose a color by clicking on the Web tab. The Web tab lists a number of colors that you can select from.

Finally, the System tab contains a list of Windows-specific color properties, such as ActiveCaption, Desktop, and WindowText. These names refer to various user-definable color settings in the Windows operating system. For example, the Desktop color is the background color of your Windows Desktop. If you choose to use one of these color names, the color displayed in the user's browser will depend on the color settings she has specified in Windows.

> **Did you Know?**
>
> To change the color settings in Windows, right-click the Desktop and choose Properties. Then select the Appearances tab.

Let's go ahead and set the `BackColor` to Navy, which is a color listed in the Web tab.

The Label Web control's `ForeColor` property indicates the foreground color of the text displayed. When the `ForeColor` property is selected, the same three-tabbed palette appears. For this, select the White color from the Web tab.

At this point we've set three of the Label Web control's properties. We set the `Text` property to `This is a test of the color properties`, the `BackColor` to Navy, and the `ForeColor` to White. The designer should show the text `"This is a test of the color properties"` in a white foreground color with a navy background color, as shown in Figure 8.10.

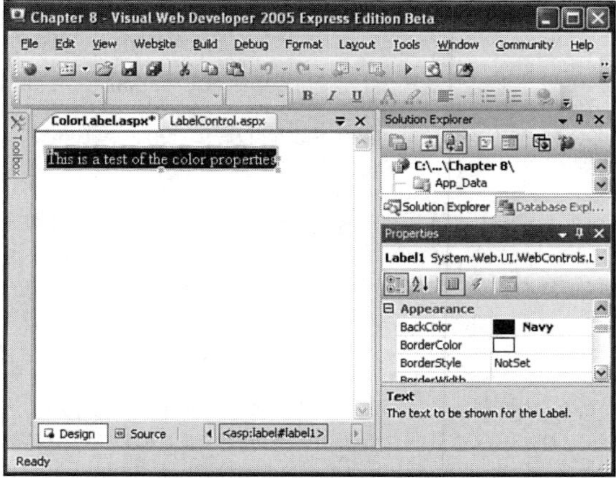

FIGURE 8.10 A Label with a white foreground and navy background is shown in the designer.

Now, take a moment to save the ASP.NET web page and view it through a browser. If you view the page through an uplevel browser, you will see the same output shown in the designer—the text `"This is a test of the color properties"` in a white foreground color with a navy background color.

However, if you view the web page through a downlevel browser, such as Netscape version 4.0, you will see...nothing! Figure 8.11 shows Netscape 4.0 when visiting `ColorLabel.aspx`.

To understand why we don't see anything, let's look at the HTML markup received by Netscape 4.0 (or any downlevel browser). Listing 8.5 contains this HTML.

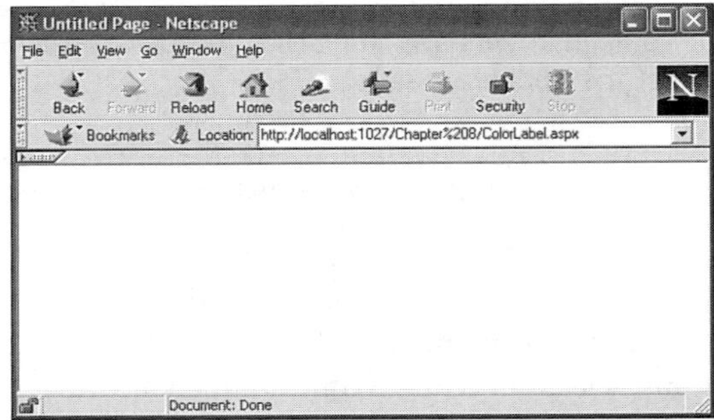

FIGURE 8.11 When we view the web page through a downlevel browser, no text appears on the screen.

LISTING 8.5 The HTML Markup Received by a Downlevel Browser

```
 1: !DOCTYPE html PUBLIC "-//W3C//DTD XHTML 1.0 Transitional//EN"
➥ "http://www.w3.org/TR/xhtml1/DTD/xhtml1-transitional.dtd">
 2:
 3: <html xmlns="http://www.w3.org/1999/xhtml" >
 4: <head><title>
 5:         Untitled Page
 6: </title></head>
 7: <body>
 8:     <form name="form1" method="post" action="ColorLabel.aspx" id="form1">
 9: <input type="hidden" name="__VIEWSTATE" id="__VIEWSTATE"
➥ value="/wEPDwUJODExMDE5NzY5ZGR5Pm2YFjJUcWvsLSH4OZzhXFfAyQ==" />
10:
11:     <div>
12:         <span id="Label1"><font color="White">This is a test of the
➥color properties</font></span>
13:     </div>
14:     </form>
15: </body>
16: </html>
```

As line 12 shows, the Label Web control's `ForeColor` property is rendered as a `<font>` tag with its `color` attribute set to White. But how is the `BackColor` property rendered? As you can see from Listing 8.5, it isn't; at least, it isn't for downlevel browsers. The reason is that without style sheets, the only way to give a background color to text is to place the text within an HTML `<table>` that has its `bgcolor` attribute set accordingly.

By the Way

> To set the background color of text using style sheets, we can use the `background-color` style sheet attribute. This is how the `BackColor` property is rendered in uplevel browsers.

The short of it is that the `BackColor` of the Label Web control is not displayed in downlevel browsers. Keep this in mind when setting color properties for a Label Web control.

Examining the Border Properties

In uplevel browsers, a border can be placed around the text displayed by a Label Web control. (In downlevel browsers, setting the border properties has no effect in the HTML markup rendered by the Label Web control.)

Let's create an ASP.NET web page that displays a border around the text displayed by a Label Web control. Start by creating a new ASP.NET page titled `BorderLabel.aspx`. Drag and drop a Label Web control onto the page and set the Label's `Text` property to `Testing the border properties`. Next, click the Label Web control's `BorderStyle` property. This should open a drop-down list that contains various options for the style of border to be placed around the Label Web control. These options are enumerated in Table 8.2.

TABLE 8.2 The `BorderStyle` Property Can Be Set to Any One of the Following Values

Border Style	Description
`NotSet`	The default option. The border around the Label Web control depends on external style sheet rules.
`None`	No border is displayed.
`Dotted`	A dotted border is displayed.
`Dashed`	A dashed border is displayed.
`Solid`	A solid border is displayed.
`Double`	A double border is displayed.
`Groove`	A grooved border is displayed.
`Ridge`	A ridged border is displayed.
`Inset`	An inset border is displayed.
`Outset`	An outset border is displayed.

Go ahead and select the `Solid` option for the `BorderStyle` property. In the designer you will see a solid border appear around the edges of the Label Web control. At this point your screen should look similar to Figure 8.12.

Note that the border displayed in Figure 8.12 is black. We can change the border's color via the `BorderColor` property. Selecting the color for the `BorderColor` property is identical to selecting a color for the `BackColor` or `ForeColor` properties. Go ahead and opt to have our Label Web control's `BorderColor` property set to Red, a color from the Web tab.

In addition to the `BorderStyle` and `BorderColor` properties, there's a `BorderWidth` property as well. Go ahead and enter a value of 2 as the `BorderWidth` property, which will create a border 2 pixels wide.

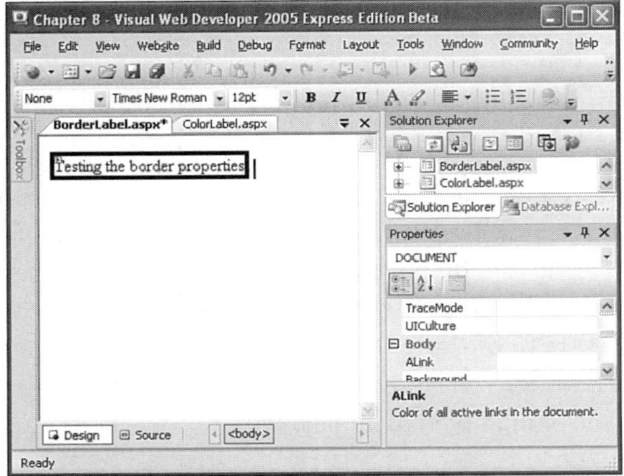

FIGURE 8.12 The Label Web control has a solid border.

Figure 8.13 shows the Design view with these property values set. Your screen should look similar.

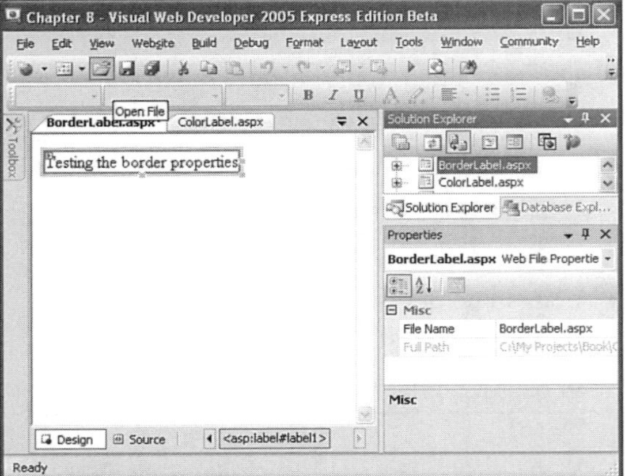

FIGURE 8.13 The designer shows a Label Web control with a solid red border 2 pixels thick.

Take a moment now to view this ASP.NET web page through a browser. If you view the page using an uplevel browser, the text `"Testing the border properties"` will be displayed with a red, solid border 2 pixels thick, just like in the designer. If you are viewing the page with a downlevel browser, just the text `"Testing the border properties"` will be displayed, without a border around it.

Delving into the Font Properties

As we saw earlier in this hour, the Label Web control has a `Font` property that contains a number of subproperties, such as `Bold`, `Italic`, `Underline`, `Name`, and others. We already examined how setting the `Bold` subproperty can make the text of a Label Web control appear in a bold font.

To further our examination of the other `Font` property's subproperties, create a new ASP.NET page named `LabelFont.aspx`, and drag and drop a Label Web control onto the designer. Set this Web control's `Text` property to `Working with the Font properties`. Next, expand the Label Web control's `Font` property by clicking on the plus to the left of the `Font` property name. This will expand the `Font` property, listing the subproperties. (You can find a complete list of the `Font` property's subproperties in Table 8.1.)

Let's set some of the `Font` property's subproperties. Start by setting the `Italic` subproperty to `True`, which should make the Label's text appear in an italic font in the designer. Next, under the `Name` property, choose the font name Arial. When selected, the Label Web control in the designer should be updated to show its text in the Arial font. Finally, set the `Size` subproperty to 22pt. This will cause the Label Web control's text in the designer to enlarge to a 22-point size.

Figure 8.14 shows Visual Web Developer at this point. If you're following along, your screen should look similar.

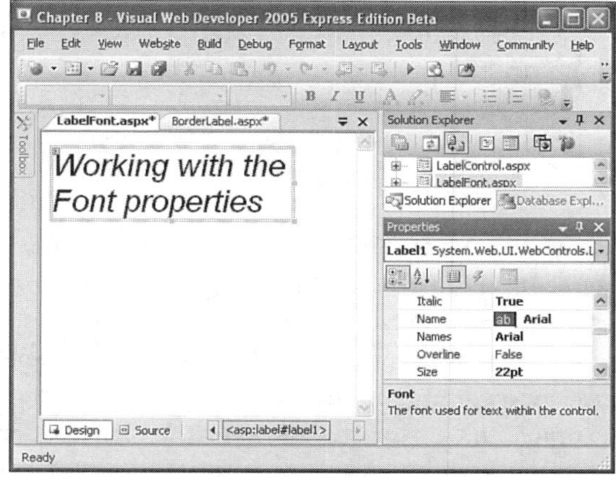

FIGURE 8.14 A Label Web control with some `Font` property subproperties set.

As with the previous examples, take a moment to view the page through a web browser, examining the HTML markup sent to the browser. If you visit the page with an uplevel browser, the Label Web control's rendered HTML markup will specify its style settings via the `style` attribute. For example, with the `Font` property settings we used, the following HTML will be rendered by the Label Web control in an uplevel browser:

```
<span id="Label1" style="font-family:Arial;font-size:22pt;font-style:italic;">
➥Working with the Font properties</span>
```

However, if you visit the web page in a downlevel browser, the HTML markup rendered by the Label Web control uses HTML tags to specify the style settings, as you can see here:

```
<span id="Label1"><i><font face="Arial" size="6">Working with the Font
➥ properties</font></i></span>
```

The Miscellaneous Properties

The remaining Label Web control properties can be grouped under miscellaneous properties. For example, there is a `Tooltip` property, which can be set to a string value. If you specify a `Tooltip`, whenever the user hovers his mouse pointer over the label's text in his browser, a floating light yellow box appears displaying the value of the `Tooltip` property. Figure 8.15 shows an ASP.NET web page that has its `Tooltip` property set to `This is a tooltip`.

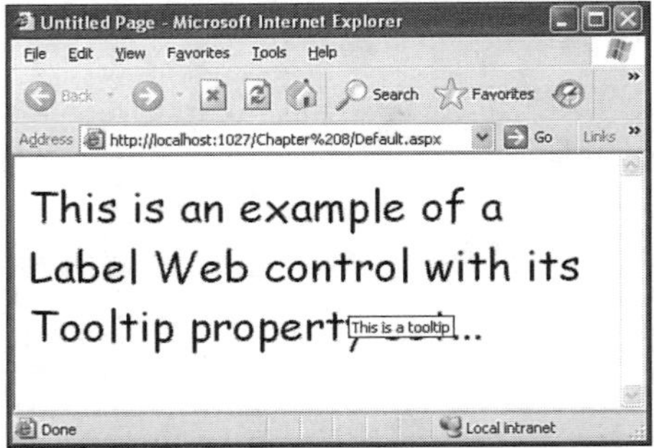

FIGURE 8.15
A tooltip is displayed when the mouse pointer hovers over the Label Web control.

Two other miscellaneous Label Web control properties are `Height` and `Width`. These two properties can be set to specific values through the Properties window. We can also set these values by resizing the Label Web control in the designer. To resize a Web control, simply select the Web control by left-clicking it. This will cause three small, empty squares to appear around the Web control—one along the bottom, one in the bottom-right corner, and one on the far right. Then left-click one of the boxes and, while holding down the mouse button, move the mouse. After you have resized the Web control appropriately, release the mouse button. The `Height` and `Width` properties will be updated accordingly.

The `Visible` property, a Boolean property, determines whether the Label Web control appears in the browser. If the `Visible` property is set to `True` (the default), the Label Web control's rendered HTML markup is sent to the browser. If, however, the `Visible` property is set to `False`, the Label Web control is not rendered, and therefore *no* HTML is sent to the browser for the Label Web control.

You may be wondering why in the world anyone would ever want to use this property. If someone didn't want to display the Label Web control, why create it and set its `Visible` property to `False` rather than simply not adding the Label Web control to an ASP.NET web page?

In the next few hours, when we examine using Web Forms to collect user input, we'll see scenarios in which we just might want to create a Label Web control and initially set its `Visible` property to `False`. For example, imagine that we have an ASP.NET web page that prompts the user for her username and password. If the user provides an incorrect username or password, we want to display an appropriate message. Therefore, we can place a Label Web control on the web page that has such a message and initially set its `Visible` property to `False`. Then, if the user enters an incorrect password, we can programmatically set the Label Web control's `Visible` property to `True`, thereby displaying the message.

By the Way

> The remaining Label Web control properties—`AccessKey`, `AssociatedControlID`, `CssClass`, `Enabled`, `EnableTheming`, `EnableViewState`, `(Expressions)`, `SkinID`, and `TabIndex`—are beyond the scope of this book. We will not be using these properties with Label Web controls in any of the examples in this book.

Summary

In this hour we looked at the two ASP.NET Web controls designed for displaying text output: the Literal Web control and the Label Web control. These two Web controls differ in the HTML markup they produce when being rendered.

When the Literal Web control is rendered, its `Text` property is returned as its HTML markup. No formatting is applied, and no extraneous HTML tags are added.

The Label Web control is useful for displaying formatted text—for example, if you want to display some text in a bold font or with a yellow background color. To accommodate this, the Label Web control has a number of display properties available, such as `BackColor`, `ForeColor`, `Font`, `BorderColor`, `BorderStyle`, and so on.

When a Label Web control is rendered, not only is the `Text` property displayed, but an additional HTML `<span>` element is emitted to provide the formatting specified by the various formatting property values.

Now that we've examined how to use the Literal and Label Web controls, we're ready to turn our attention to the Web controls that are designed to collect user input, such as the TextBox Web control, the DropDownList Web control, the RadioButton Web control, and others. Before we do, though, we need to examine how an ASP.NET web page collects data from a web visitor and returns that data to the web server. We'll tackle this subject in the next hour, "Web Form Basics."

Q&A

Q. ***Is there any difference in the HTML markup sent to the browser for a Literal and Label Web control?***

A. Recall from our discussions in this hour that when the ASP.NET engine executes an ASP.NET page, the Web controls are rendered into HTML markup. The precise HTML generated depends on the Web control's properties.

In this hour we discussed two different Web controls: the Literal Web control and the Label Web control. If you create an ASP.NET page with Literal and Label Web controls and set the `Text` property of both to `This is a test`, when you're visiting the ASP.NET web page through a browser, it may appear as if both Web controls produce the same HTML output. However, it is important to note that the Label Web control produces slightly different HTML markup than the Literal Web control.

In such a web page, the HTML markup produced by the Literal control is

```
This is a test
```

Note that the HTML markup produced by a Literal control is precisely the value of its `Text` property.

The Label Web control, however, actually uses a `<span>` HTML tag to display its `Text` property. That is, the HTML markup generated by the Label Web control in this example is

```
<span>This is a test</span>
```

The Label Web control wraps its `Text` property in a `<span>` HTML tag so that it can add formatting. For example, if the Label Web control's `Font` property's `Bold` subproperty is set to `True`, the following HTML markup is produced in an uplevel browser:

```
<span style="font-weight:bold;">This is a test</span>
```

Q. ***The ASP.NET engine renders Web controls differently if the page is visited by a downlevel browser versus an uplevel browser, but how common are downlevel browsers?***

A. Modern browsers, ones released in the past several years, are tagged as uplevel browsers by the ASP.NET engine. Downlevel browsers, on the other hand, encompass rather antiquated browsers—version 4 or earlier of Netscape and version 3 or earlier of Internet Explorer. As we saw in this hour, a Web control that appears correctly in an uplevel browser might not appear so in a downlevel browser. To ensure that your pages work well in both uplevel and downlevel browsers, you would need to test your pages in both classes of browsers.

Before you rush off and download Netscape 4, take a moment to consider whether your efforts are worth the reward. How many people are using these outdated browsers? Are there enough real-world users to justify spending additional time in perfecting your site's appearance for this minority?

Various sites online post browser usage. One such site is TheCounter.com, which has browser usage statistics available at http://www.thecounter.com/stats/. At the time of this writing (November 2005), TheCounter.com had counted more than 75 million web requests for the month, of which about 63,000 (or 0.08%) came from what would be dubbed a downlevel browser. Clearly, it's a tiny fraction of the total traffic. The vast bulk of requests came from Internet Explorer 5.0 and 6.0, FireFox, Safari, Netscape 7.0, and Opera.

Realistically, you probably don't need to concern yourself with the slightly downlevel browsers, unless your site is geared toward those who might be using antiquated computers, such as people in less technologically advanced countries.

Workshop

Quiz

1. What must you do to display formatted text with the Literal Web control?
2. What must you do to display formatted text with the Label Web control?
3. True or False: The Literal Web control contains only a single property, `Text`.
4. True or False: The Label Web control contains only a single property, `Text`.
5. Recall that when the ASP.NET engine executes an ASP.NET web page, it renders the Web controls into their corresponding HTML markup. What factor or factors determine the HTML markup generated by a particular Web control?
6. What purpose do the Literal and Label Web controls serve?

7. Why is it said that Web controls are an intermediary between an ASP.NET web page's HTML and source code portions?

8. True or False: The Label Web control's `ForeColor` property is ignored by downlevel browsers. (That is, all downlevel browsers display the `Text` of a Label control as black, regardless of the `ForeColor` property value.)

Answers

1. The Literal Web control does not have any formatting properties. Instead, its rendered HTML markup is precisely the value of its `Text` property. Therefore, if you want to display the Literal Web control with any kind of formatting, you must enter the appropriate HTML tags in the `Text` property.

2. The Label Web control contains a number of formatting properties that can be used to specify the resulting text's formatting. Therefore, you can display formatted text by simply setting the appropriate property values.

3. False. The Literal Web control contains, among others, an `ID` property.

4. False. In addition to its `Text` property, the Label Web control contains a plethora of formatting properties, an `ID` property, and several other less germane properties.

5. The HTML markup generated by a Web control depends on two factors: the value of the Web control's properties and the user's browser.

6. The Literal and Label Web controls are the two Web controls designed to display text.

7. Web controls are said to be an intermediary between the HTML portion and source code portions of an ASP.NET web page because they are placed in the HTML portion and generate HTML markup, but can be programmatically accessed in the source code portion.

8. False. It is the Label's `BackColor` property that is ignored by downlevel browsers.

Exercises

1. Create an ASP.NET web page that uses a Literal Web control to display the web page's URL. Rather than hard-coding the URL into the Literal's `Text` property, set the `Text` property programmatically in the `Page_Load` event handler. Note that you can obtain the current page's URL via `Request.Url.ToString()`.

That is, your ASP.NET web page should contain a Literal Web control with its `ID` property set to some value (say, `urlDisplay`). Then, in the page's `Page_Load` event handler, add the following code:

```
urlDisplay.Text = Request.Url.ToString()
```

2. Create an ASP.NET page and add a Label Web control. Set its `Text` property to `What pretty text!` and then set a number of its formatting properties. Feel free to specify whatever formatting property values you'd like, but be sure to set at least five formatting properties. Be sure to try out formatting properties that were not closely examined in this hour.

3. For this exercise, create an ASP.NET web page that uses a Label Web control to display the IP address of the visitor visiting the web page. (An IP address is a series of four numbers that identifies a computer on the Internet. If you are serving the ASP.NET web pages from your own computer, your IP address will be 127.0.0.1.)

   The visiting user's IP address can be obtained via `Request.UserHostAddress`. Therefore, to complete this exercise, you will need to create a Label Web control and set its `ID` property. Then you will need to create a `Page_Load` event handler in the ASP.NET web page's source code portion that contains the following code:

   ```
   LabelID.Text = Request.UserHostAddress
   ```

PART II

Collecting and Processing User Input

HOUR 9

Web Form Basics

In this hour, we will cover

- How user input is gathered through HTML
- What a Web Form is
- Using a Web Form in an ASP.NET web page
- Identifying properties of Web Forms
- Collecting user input in an ASP.NET web page
- Examining how the Web Form persists the state of its Web controls

To create a useful web application, we must be able to somehow collect user input and return to the user a web page customized to the input entered. For example, search engines like Google must be able to accept a user's search term and then display a web page with the results based on that search. Sites like Amazon.com must be able to read a shopper's credit card numbers so that they can correctly bill the shopper for purchases.

HTML was designed with these needs in mind, as evidenced by the various HTML elements designed to aid in collecting user input. The HTML `<input>` element, for example, can be used to display a text box, check box, radio button, or drop-down list. After the user enters information, the HTML `<form>` element specifies which web page the input should be sent to.

With ASP.NET we do not need to enter such HTML elements. Rather, we use various Web controls, which, when rendered, produce the appropriate HTML elements. That is, if we want to have a text box on our web page, instead of adding an `<input>` HTML element, we add a TextBox Web control. Similarly, instead of using the HTML `<form>` element, our ASP.NET web pages need to use Web Forms. We'll discuss what Web Forms are and their semantics in this hour.

If you have worked with HTML forms and collecting user input in dynamic web page technologies like ASP, PHP, or JSP, you'll find ASP.NET's model for collecting user input quite a bit different. By the end of this hour, though, you will likely find ASP.NET's way of collecting user input through Web Forms to be much more intuitive and sensible than the techniques required for user input collection in older, dynamic web page technologies.

Gathering User Input in an HTML Web Page

Imagine that we wanted to create a web page that calculated a user's Body Mass Index, or BMI.

By the Way

> The Body Mass Index, or BMI, is a ratio of a person's height to weight. BMI is commonly used as a quick determination of whether one is underweight, at a healthy weight, overweight, or obese. For more information about BMI, see http://www.cdc.gov/nccdphp/dnpa/bmi/.

To determine someone's BMI, we need to know his height and weight. For the time being, imagine that we want to create this web page without using ASP.NET, using HTML markup instead to generate the two text boxes needed for the user's inputted height and weight.

When HTML was designed, two elements were created to facilitate collecting user input. These two HTML elements are the `<form>` element and the `<input>` element. Although a thorough understanding of these elements is not needed for collecting user input in an ASP.NET web page, having a strong grasp on the concepts of how user input is collected from a web page is important. Therefore, let's briefly examine the `<input>` and `<form>` elements, as well as how they work in conjunction to allow a web page to collect user input.

Examining the `<input>` Element

The `<input>` tag can be used to create a text box, radio button, check box, or button. The `<input>` element's `type` attribute specifies what type of user input control is displayed in the user's web browser. For example, if you wanted to create an HTML web page that contained a text box, you could use the following HTML:

```
<input type="text">
```

To display a check box, you would use

```
<input type="checkbox">
```

We will not delve into the HTML specifics for collecting user input in this book. For more information on this topic, check out http://www.w3schools.com/html/html_forms.asp, or consider picking up *Sams Teach Yourself HTML and XHTML in 24 Hours* (ISBN: 0672320762).

Because our web page will need two text boxes—one for the person's height in inches and one for the person's weight in pounds—we will use two `<input>` elements, both with `type="text"`.

Listing 9.1 contains the preliminary HTML web page for our BMI calculator. Keep in mind that this page is far from complete!

LISTING 9.1 Our First Draft of the BMI Calculator

```
1: <html>
2: <body>
3:   <h1>BMI Calculator</h1>
4:   <p>Your Height (in inches): <input type="text" name="height" /></p>
5:
6:   <p>Your Weight (in pounds): <input type="text" name="weight" /></p>
7: </body>
8: </html>
```

Listing 9.1 simply displays two text boxes, one for the user's height and one for weight. As you can see in lines 4 and 6, the `<input>` elements of Listing 9.1 each contain a `name` property. The `name` property is needed to uniquely identify each `<input>` element. As we will see in the next section, "Passing the Input Back to the Web Server Using the `<form>` Element," the `<input>` element's `name` attribute is used when sending the contents of the various `<input>` elements back to the web server.

Figure 9.1 shows the code in Listing 9.1 when viewed through a browser.

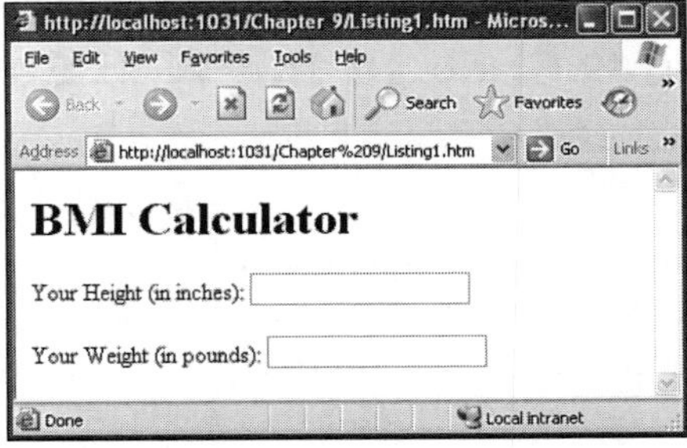

FIGURE 9.1
The user is presented with two text boxes.

In addition to the two text boxes, we need some way for the user to indicate to the web browser that she has completed entering her data. To accomplish this, a **submit**

button is used. A submit button is a button that, when clicked by the user, indicates to the web browser that the user has finished entering her input. The HTML markup for a submit button is as follows:

```
<input type="submit" value="Text to Appear on Submit Button">
```

Listing 9.2 contains the HTML from Listing 9.1, but augmented with the submit button. Figure 9.2 shows the HTML from Listing 9.2 when viewed through a browser.

LISTING 9.2 Our Second Draft of the BMI Calculator

```
<html>
<body>
  <h1>BMI Calculator</h1>
  <p>Your Height (in inches): <input type="text" name="height" /></p>

  <p>Your Weight (in pounds): <input type="text" name="weight" /></p>

  <p><input type="submit" value="Calculate BMI" /></p>
</body>
</html>
```

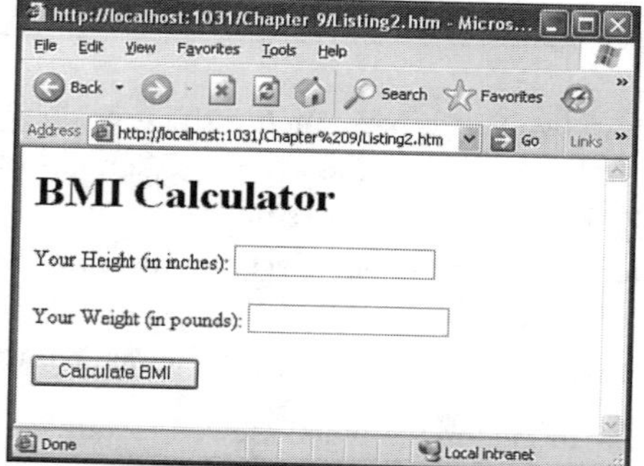

FIGURE 9.2
A submit button has been added.

Passing the Input Back to the Web Server Using the `<form>` Element

Recall from our discussions in Hour 1, "Getting Started with ASP.NET 2.0," that when a user requests a web page from a web server, the web server sends the web page's HTML to the user's browser. This HTML is then rendered graphically in the user's browser. For the browser to receive this HTML, the web browser and web server must communicate with one another, but after the web browser has received the HTML, the communication ends.

The important point to take away from this discussion is that there is a physical, logical, and temporal disconnect between the web server and the web browser. That is, the web server has no idea what the user is entering into his browser. All the web server ever does is wait for incoming web requests and then return the appropriate HTML.

Due to this disconnect between the web browser and the web server, the web browser needs some way to be able to let the web server know the input the user entered. This is accomplished via the HTML `<form>` element.

The `<form>` element must have contained within it the `<input>` elements used to collect the user input, as well as the submit button. When the `<form>` element's submit button is clicked, the form is said to have been **submitted**. When a form is submitted, a specified web page is requested by the browser, and the data entered into the various `<input>` elements within the `<form>` element are sent to this web page.

This description of the `<form>` element leaves two questions unanswered:

- When the `<form>` is submitted, how does it know what web page to send the contents of its `<input>` elements to?
- How, exactly, are the contents of the `<input>` elements sent to this web page?

We can answer these two questions by examining the `action` and `method` attributes of the `<form>` element. The `action` attribute specifies a URL that the browser is directed to after the `<form>`'s submit button is clicked. Therefore, it is the value of the `action` attribute that indicates the web page that is visited after the `<form>` is submitted.

The contents of the `<input>` elements are compacted into a single string and are sent in a specific format. Precisely, the format used is as follows:

```
InputName1=InputValue1&InputName2=InputValue2&...&InputNameN=InputValueN
```

Here, *`InputName1`* is the value of the first `<input>` element's `name` attribute, and *`InputValue1`* is the value of the first `<input>` element. *`InputName2`* is the value of the second `<input>` element's `name` attribute, and *`InputValue2`* is the value of the second `<input>` element, and so on. Note that each `<input>` element's name and value are separated by an equals sign (=), and each pair of names and values is separated by an ampersand (&).

The `method` attribute determines how this string of `<input>` element names and values is sent to the web server. The `method` attribute can have one of two possible values: `GET` or `POST`. If `method` is set to `GET`, the contents of the `<input>` elements are sent through the **querystring**. The querystring is an optional string that can be tacked on to the end of a web page's URL. Specifically, if a website URL has a question mark in it (?), everything after the question mark is considered the querystring.

You have probably seen web pages whose URL looks like

```
http://www.someserver.com/somePage.htm?Name=Scott&Age=21
```

Here, the contents after the question mark are considered the querystring.

If `method` is set to `POST`, the `<input>` elements' contents are sent through the **HTTP headers**, meaning there is no querystring tacked onto the end of the URL.

By the Way

> Whenever a web browser requests a web page, it sends HTTP headers in addition to the requested URL. These are simple strings of text. One such HTTP header, as we discussed in the preceding hour, is the User-Agent header, which sends information on the type of browser making the web request.
>
> When the `method` attribute is set to `POST`, the Post HTTP header is used to send along the contents of the `<input>` elements. When we place this information in an HTTP header, the querystring is left uncluttered.

Let's augment Listing 9.2 to include a `<form>` element that contains `action` and `method` attributes. Listing 9.3 is this augmented HTML page.

LISTING 9.3 A `<form>` Element Has Been Added

```
 1: <html>
 2: <body>
 3:
 4:   <form method="GET" action="SomePage.htm">
 5:     <h1>BMI Calculator</h1>
 6:     <p>Your Height (in inches): <input type="text" name="height" /></p>
 7:
 8:     <p>Your Weight (in pounds): <input type="text" name="weight" /></p>
 9:
10:     <p><input type="submit" value="Calculate BMI" /></p>
11:   </form>
12:
13: </body>
14: </html>
```

The `<form>` element—spanning from line 4 to line 11—encloses the two `<input>` elements that generate the two text boxes as well as the submit button `<input>` element. The `<form>`'s `action` attribute is set to `SomePage.htm`, and the `method` attribute is set to `GET`.

When the user visits the HTML page shown in Listing 9.3, he will be presented with two text boxes and a submit button, as was shown in Figure 9.2. After the user enters his height and weight and clicks the submit button, the web browser will request the web page, as follows:

```
SomePage.htm?height=heightEnteredByUser&weight=weightEnteredByUser
```

Figure 9.3 shows the web browser's Address bar after the user has visited the HTML page generated by Listing 9.3 and has entered the value 72 for height and 155 for weight.

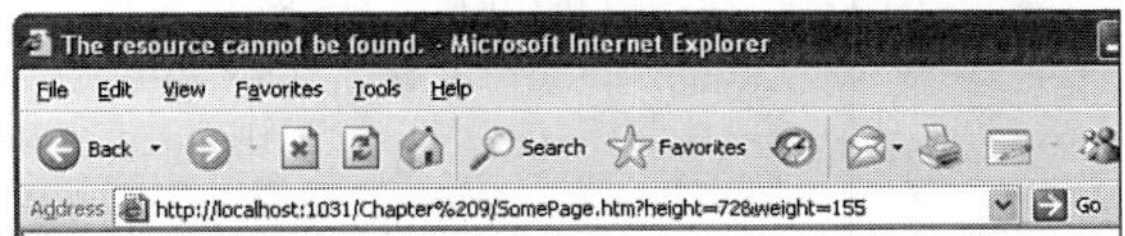

FIGURE 9.3
The querystring contains the values entered into the height and weight text boxes.

> `SomePage.htm` would likely read in the values passed in through the querystring, perform some calculation on these values, and then display the results to the user. Starting in the "Dissecting ASP.NET Web Forms" section, we'll see how to programmatically process user input in an ASP.NET page.

Comparing Postback Forms and Redirect Forms

If the `<form>`'s `method` attribute on line 4 in Listing 9.3 is changed to `POST`, when the user submits the form, she is still directed to `SomePage.htm`. This time, though, no information will be passed through the querystring. Rather, this data will be hidden from sight from the user, passed through the HTTP headers instead.

As we saw, the `<form>`'s `action` attribute specifies the web page that the browser requests after the `<form>` is submitted. In Listing 9.3, this web page was `SomePage.htm`. Such forms are typically called **redirect forms** because, when submitted, they redirect the user to a different web page.

Imagine, though, what would happen if the `action` property were set to the same URL as the page that contains the `<form>` element. That is, say we create an ASP.NET web page called `PostbackFormExample.htm` that has the following HTML:

```
<html>
<body>
  <form method="POST" action="PostbackFormExample.htm">
    <p>What is your age? <input type="text" name="age" /></p>
    <p><input type="submit" value="Click to Continue" /></p>
  </form>
</body>
</html>
```

When the user first visits `PostbackFormExample.htm`, she will be shown a text box labeled "What is your age?" Underneath this text box, she will see a submit button titled Click to Continue. After the user enters some information into the text box and submits the `<form>`, what will happen? Because the `method` attribute is set to `POST`, the `<input>` text box's data will be sent via the HTTP Post header. Because the `action` attribute is set to `PostbackFormExample.htm`, the user will be sent *back* to `PostbackFormExample.htm` (but this time with information passed in through the HTTP Post header).

Such `<form>`s are called **postback forms** because they use the POST method and because when the `<form>` is submitted, the user is sent back to the same page. That is, the `<form>`'s `<input>` element's data is posted back to the same web page.

Figure 9.4 shows a pictorial representation of both a redirect form and a postback form. Note how the postback form sends the contents of its `<input>` elements back to itself, whereas a standard form forwards the contents to a different web page.

FIGURE 9.4 Postback forms differ from redirect forms.

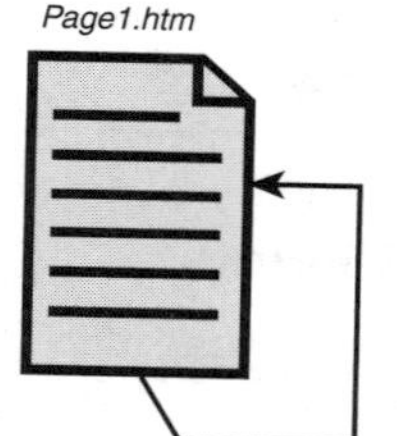

Postback Web Form Example
Page1.htm
A postback form is one whose ACTION properly is set to the URL of the page the form appears on (i.e., Page1.htm). When the form is submitted, the user's browser requests the same page (Page1.htm), passing the form field inputs through either the querystring or HTTP Post headers.

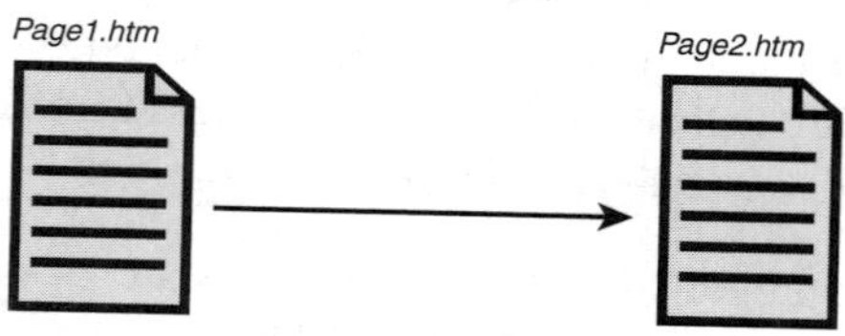

Dissecting ASP.NET Web Forms

In an ASP.NET page, collecting user input is much simpler than the techniques discussed in the preceding section. To collect user input, the ASP.NET web page must contain a **Web Form**. A Web Form is a Web control that has the following syntax:

```
<form runat="server">
  ...
</form>
```

When you create a new ASP.NET web page in Visual Web Developer, a Web Form is automatically added. To demonstrate that this is the case, let's create a new ASP.NET page, one that we'll build on throughout the remainder of this hour. Name this new ASP.NET web page `BMICalculator.aspx`. As always, be sure to have Visual Basic selected as the Language choice and check the Place Code in Separate File check box.

After the new file is created, go to the Source view if you are not already there and inspect the HTML markup automatically injected into this new ASP.NET page. As Figure 9.5 shows, the HTML portion already contains a Web Form (the `<form runat="server">` on line 10).

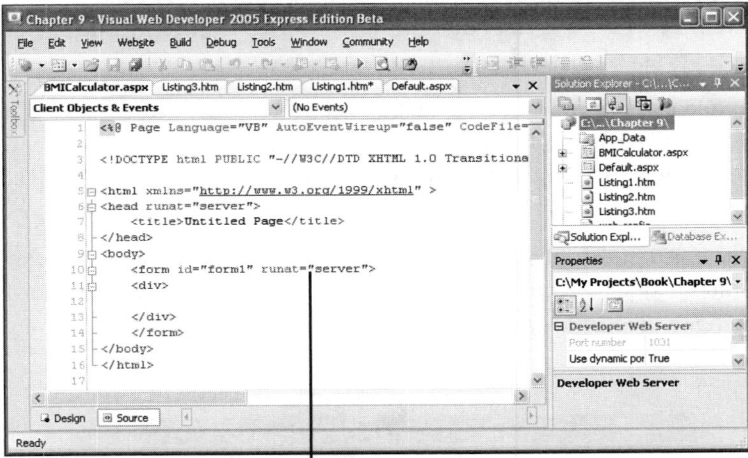

FIGURE 9.5 A Web form is automatically included in new ASP.NET web pages created by Visual Web Developer.

Now, view the page through the Design view. You should see an empty designer because we've yet to add any Web controls to our ASP.NET page. By default, the designer is a WYSIWYG editor, meaning that it displays only those Web controls and static HTML markup that you would see when viewing the ASP.NET page through a browser. Because Web Forms do not have any visual impact on a web page, the designer does not show the Web Form.

Adding Web Controls to Collect User Input

In an HTML web page, user input is collected using a number of `<input>` elements, which can provide a variety of input media, such as text boxes, check boxes, radio buttons, and so on. Additionally, a `<form>` must be placed around these `<input>` elements and have its `method` and `action` properties specified.

With an ASP.NET page, collecting user input is much simpler. As we've seen already, we need to have a Web Form, which Visual Web Developer has already kindly added for us. In addition to this Web Form, we need to have a number of input Web controls into which the user will enter his input.

For example, if we want to provide the user with a text box to enter his input, we would use a TextBox Web control. If we want to have the user enter his input via a radio button, we would use a RadioButton Web control. These various Web controls must be placed within the Web Form.

Earlier in this hour we looked at creating an HTML web page to collect user input for a BMI calculator. The BMI calculator needs to collect two bits of information from the user: height and weight. These two pieces of information can be provided via two text boxes. Therefore, let's add two TextBox Web controls to our `BMICalculator.aspx` ASP.NET page.

Before you add the first TextBox Web control, though, first type in the title to precede the TextBox Web control: `Your height (in inches):`. To enter this text into the designer, simply place the cursor in the designer and start typing. If needed, you can create a space by pressing the Enter key.

After you've typed in the label, next drag and drop a TextBox Web control from the Toolbox onto the designer, placing it immediately after the text you just added. Figure 9.6 shows the Visual Web Developer after adding this first TextBox Web control.

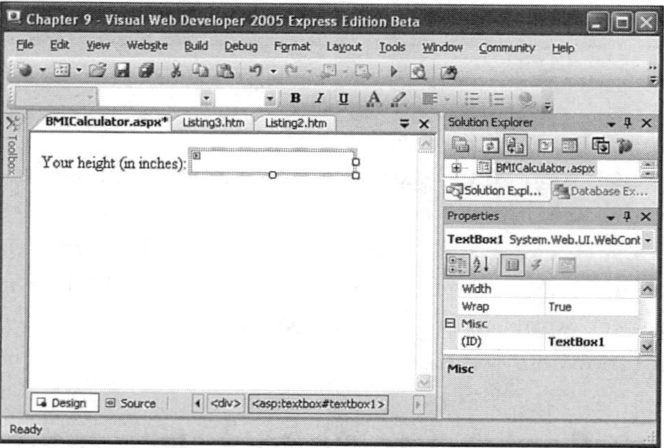

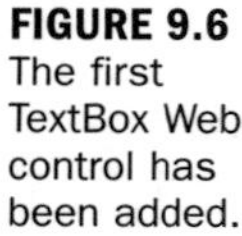
FIGURE 9.6
The first TextBox Web control has been added.

Now let's add the second TextBox Web control. Start by moving your mouse cursor after the TextBox Web control we just added and left-click. This will show the cursor in the designer. You can then type in the title for the TextBox Web control that we are about to enter. Specifically, enter the text `Weight (in pounds):`. As before, after entering this text, drag and drop a TextBox Web control from the Toolbox onto the designer, placing it immediately after the newly entered text. Take a moment to ensure that your screen looks similar to Figure 9.7.

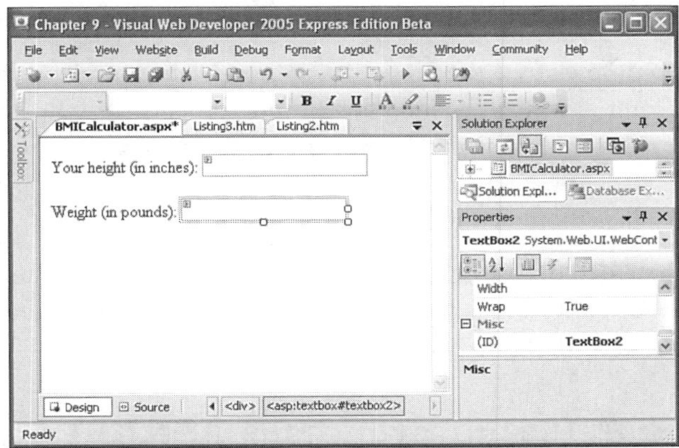

FIGURE 9.7
The second TextBox Web control has been added.

At this point we have added two TextBox Web controls to the ASP.NET page. We are still missing one Web control, though. Recall from our earlier discussion that the browser needs to know when the user has completed entering his input. This was accomplished in the HTML web page in Listing 9.2 by adding a submit button.

We need to add a submit button to our ASP.NET web page as well. To accomplish this, drag and drop the Button Web control from the Toolbox to the designer, placing it beneath the two TextBox Web controls.

Figure 9.8 shows the designer after the Button Web control has been added.

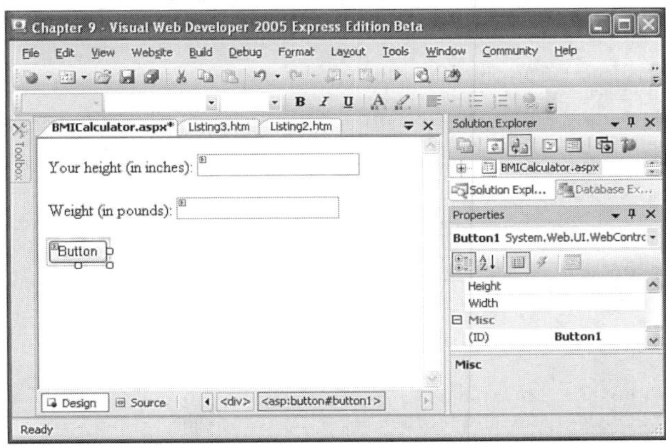

FIGURE 9.8
The final Web control—the Button Web control—has been added.

We have now added all of the Web controls that are needed to collect the user's input. The next step is to set the properties of these various Web controls. The Button Web control, for example, is currently displaying the text `"Button"`, which we can change to a more descriptive message by changing the Button Web control's `Text` property. Also, the `ID` properties of the three Web controls are still set to their default values, which are not very descriptive, either.

Let's take a moment to change the properties of these Web controls. First, click on the Button Web control, which will load the Button's properties in the Properties pane. Take a moment to change the `ID` property to `btnSubmit` and the `Text` property to `Calculate BMI`. After you change the `Text` property, the text appearing on the Button in the designer should change as well.

Next, click the first TextBox Web control, the one appearing after the text `"Your height (in inches):"`. Change the `ID` property to `height`. Finally, click on the second TextBox Web control and change its `ID` property to `weight`.

Testing the `BMICalculator.aspx` ASP.NET Page

Now that we have added the needed Web controls, let's visit `BMICalculator.aspx` through a browser. Go to the Debug menu and choose Start Without Debugging. This will launch a web browser and direct it to `BMICalculator.aspx`. The output you see should be identical to that shown in the designer in Figure 9.8.

After you have visited the ASP.NET web page through your browser of choice, take a moment to view the HTML source code that was sent to your browser. Listing 9.4 shows the source code received when visiting `BMICalculator.aspx` through a browser.

LISTING 9.4 The Browser Receives `<form>` and `<input>` Elements

```
<!DOCTYPE html PUBLIC "-//W3C//DTD XHTML 1.0 Transitional//EN"
➥ "http://www.w3.org/TR/xhtml1/DTD/xhtml1-transitional.dtd">

<html xmlns="http://www.w3.org/1999/xhtml" >
<head><title>
    Untitled Page
</title></head>
<body>
    <form name="form1" method="post" action="BMICalculator.aspx"
➥id="form1">
<div>
<input type="hidden" name="__VIEWSTATE" id="__VIEWSTATE"
➥ value="/wEPDwULLTExNTc2NTI3OTlkZJoJNpBsnkPdr0ZWq2RT3RHUWCu3" />
</div>

    <div>
        Your height (in inches):
        <input name="height" type="text" id="height" /><br />
```

LISTING 9.4 Continued

```
16:         <br />
17:         Weight (in pounds):
18:         <input name="weight" type="text" id="weight" /><br />
19:         <br />
20:         <input type="submit" name="btnSubmit" value="Calculate BMI"
➥id="btnSubmit" /></div>
21:
22: <div>
23:
24:     <input type="hidden" name="__EVENTVALIDATION" id="__EVENTVALIDATION"
➥ value="/wEWBALMiLCKDgKTiPDXAQL0h/DXAQLCi9reA4sPc44od9PA4VnJV6x4fFH0CRNB" />
25: </div></form>
26: </body>
27: </html>
```

The first thing to notice from Listing 9.4 is that the Web Form and Web controls produce roughly the same HTML markup that we crafted by hand in Listing 9.3. This is a powerful concept because it pleases both us, the ASP.NET developers, and the web browser requesting the ASP.NET page. It allows us not to have to worry about HTML specifics. Rather, we can just drag and drop the Web controls needed onto our ASP.NET page. When the page is visited, the ASP.NET engine will convert the Web controls into the appropriate HTML markup, which is what the browser expects.

> ASP.NET's Web control model relieves developers from having to know HTML details. Rather, ASP.NET developers can focus on creating the user interface as they see fit (by dragging and dropping controls onto the designer), and working on the source code portion of the ASP.NET web page.

You should take note of three more important things in Listing 9.4 before we move on. First, notice that the Button Web control is rendered as a submit button (line 20). That means when this button is clicked, the `<form>` element contained within will be submitted.

Next, note that the Web Form in our ASP.NET web page is rendered as a postback `<form>` element (line 8). (Recall that a postback form is one that has its `method` set to `POST` and its `action` set to its own URL.) This means that when the user clicks the Button Web control, the `<form>` will submit, causing the page to be reloaded.

Finally, take note of the `<input>` elements on lines 10 and 24. They are hidden `<input>` elements (note that the `type` attributes are set to `hidden`), meaning that they are not displayed in the browser. These hidden `<input>` elements are produced when the Web Form is rendered and provide information used by the ASP.NET engine when handling a postback. A thorough discussion of what, exactly, these hidden `<input>` elements accomplish is beyond the scope of this book.

Web Forms Remember the Values the Users Enter

While you have `BMICalculator.aspx` loaded into your browser, take a moment to fill some values into the two text boxes and then click the Calculate BMI button. What happens? Upon first glance, it may appear that nothing happened. The same web page is shown, and the text boxes contain the values you entered.

However, something has happened. Specifically, when you clicked the submit button, the `<form>` was submitted. Because this `<form>` is a postback form, the same web page was reloaded, which is why you still see the same web page in your browser. In fact, the HTML markup sent to your web browser has changed, but ever so slightly. If you view the HTML received by your browser *after* entering some data into the text boxes and submitting the form, you'll see that the TextBox Web controls' rendered `<input>` elements now contain a `value` attribute with the value equal to the value you entered into the text box.

To better understand what has just happened, take a look at Figure 9.9. This figure shows `BMICalculator.aspx` after the values 70 and 155 have been entered into the height and weight text boxes and the submit button has been clicked.

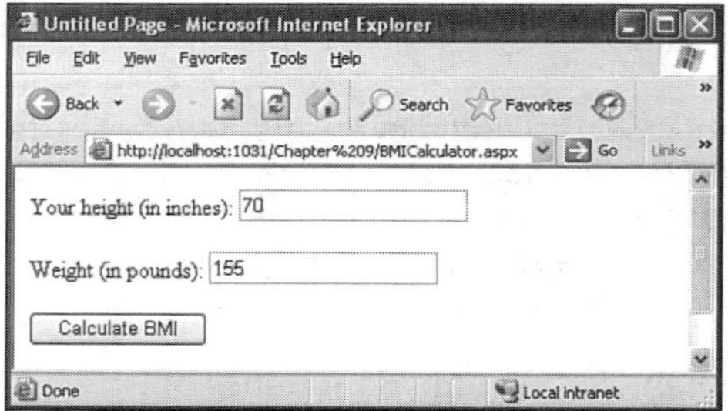

FIGURE 9.9 The text boxes have had values entered into them, and the form has been submitted.

The HTML sent to the browser in Figure 9.9 is shown in Listing 9.5. Note that the HTML markup in Listings 9.4 and 9.5 is nearly identical, the only exception being that the `<input>` elements on lines 15 and 18 of Listing 9.5 differ from lines 15 and 18 of Listing 9.4. Specifically, the `<input>` elements in Listing 9.5 have a `value` attribute set to the value entered into each respective text box (see Figure 9.9). The HTML markup rendered by the TextBox Web controls is different in Listing 9.5 than it was in Listing 9.4.

LISTING 9.5 The HTML Received by the Browser After the Form Has Been Submitted

```
<!DOCTYPE html PUBLIC "-//W3C//DTD XHTML 1.0 Transitional//EN"
➥ "http://www.w3.org/TR/xhtml1/DTD/xhtml1-transitional.dtd">

<html xmlns="http://www.w3.org/1999/xhtml" >
<head><title>
    Untitled Page
</title></head>
<body>
    <form name="form1" method="post" action="BMICalculator.aspx"
➥id="form1">
<div>
<input type="hidden" name="__VIEWSTATE" id="__VIEWSTATE"
➥value="/wEPDwULLTExNTc2NTI3OTlkZJoJNpBsnkPdr0ZWq2RT3RHUWCu3" />
</div>

    <div>
        Your height (in inches):
        <input name="height" type="text" value="70" id="height" /><br />
        <br />
        Weight (in pounds):
        <input name="weight" type="text" value="155" id="weight" /><br />
        <br />
        <input type="submit" name="btnSubmit" value="Calculate BMI"
➥id="btnSubmit" /></div>

<div>

    <input type="hidden" name="__EVENTVALIDATION" id="__EVENTVALIDATION"
➥value="/wEWBALMiLCKDgKTiPDXAQL0h/DXAQLCi9reA4sPc44od9PA4VnJV6x4fFH0CRNB" />
</div></form>
</body>
</html>
```

To understand why the TextBox Web controls rendered different HTML markup after the form was submitted (Listing 9.5) than before (Listing 9.4), let's step through this process in detail.

First, realize that the TextBox Web control has a `Text` property. If this property is set to some value, the HTML markup rendered by the TextBox Web control is different than if this property is not set at all. That is, if this property is not set, the HTML rendered by the TextBox Web control is simply

```
<input name="ValueOfIDProperty" type="text" id="ValueOfIDProperty" />
```

For example, on line 15 in Listing 9.4 you can see that the first TextBox Web control, whose `ID` property is set to `height`, produces the following HTML markup:

```
<input name="height" type="text" id="height" />
```

If, however, the `Text` property is set to some value, the `value` attribute is included in the rendering of the TextBox Web control like so:

```
<input name="ValueOfIDProperty" type="text" value="ValueOfTextProperty"
➥id="ValueOfIDProperty" />
```

So, when the `BMICalculator.aspx` page was first visited, the `Text` property of the TextBox Web controls was not set, as evidenced by the HTML markup produced (see lines 15 and 18 in Listing 9.4). When the user enters some values into these two text boxes, such as 70 in the height text box and 155 in the weight text box, and then submits the form, the `Text` properties of the TextBox Web controls are set to the values the user entered. Then, when the TextBox Web controls are rendered, they include the `value` attribute set to the value the user entered (see lines 15 and 18 in Listing 9.5).

Writing the Source Code Portion for `BMICalculator.aspx`

Note that when we enter values into the text boxes and submit the form, the web page is reloaded (because we're using a postback form) and the values entered into the text boxes are persisted across the postback. Although this is fine and good, we still need to provide code to actually perform the Body Mass Index calculation. The BMI calculation is quite simple and is shown in Figure 9.10.

FIGURE 9.10 The BMI is a ratio of weight to height.

English Formula:

$$BMI = \left(\frac{WeightInPounds}{HeightInInches^2}\right) \cdot 703$$

Metric Formula:

$$BMI = \frac{WeightInKi\log rams}{HeightInMeters^2}$$

The code required for this calculation is fairly straightforward and is shown in Listing 9.6.

LISTING 9.6 The Code for the BMI Calculation

```
'Find out the person's height and weight
Dim h as Integer = height.Text
Dim w as Integer = weight.Text

'Calculate the person's BMI
Dim BMI as Double
BMI = (w / (h * h)) * 703

'Output the BMI value
LabelWebID.Text = "Your BMI is " & BMI
```

On line 2 an `Integer` variable named `h` is declared and assigned the value of the `height` TextBox Web control's `Text` property. On line 3 an `Integer` variable named `w` is declared and assigned the value of the `weight` TextBox Web control's `Text` property. Next, on line 6 a `Double` variable named `BMI` is created. On line 7 it is assigned the person's weight divided by the person's height squared; that quantity is then multiplied by 703.

By the Way

> The code in Listing 9.6 outputs the BMI to a Label Web control, which we've yet to add to our ASP.NET page. Take a moment to add a Label Web control with an appropriate `ID` value and have the BMI calculation displayed in this Label. Refer to the preceding hour for more information on the Label Web control.

Clearly, this code must appear in our ASP.NET web page's source code portion, but where? One option would be to place the code in Listing 9.6 in the `Page_Load` event handler. Recall that the `Page_Load` event handler is executed every time the page is visited. This is not what we want, though. If we were to place the code in the `Page_Load` event handler, the code would execute every time the page is loaded, even when a user first visits the web page, before she had a chance to enter in her height and weight.

Watch Out!

> In fact, if you place the code in Listing 9.6 in the `Page_Load` event handler, you will get an `"Input string was not in a correct format"` error when visiting the page. This error results from line 2 of Listing 9.6. When the page is first loaded, the `Text` property of the `height` and `weight` TextBox Web controls is a blank string. Visual Basic cannot convert a blank string into an Integer, hence the error.

The `Page_Load` event handler is not a suitable place for the code in Listing 9.6 because we want this code to run whenever the user submits the form, not whenever the page is loaded. Fortunately, the Button Web control contains a `Click` event, which fires whenever the Web Form is submitted. When we add this event handler to our ASP.NET page's source code section and place the code in Listing 9.6 in this event handler, the code will execute whenever the Web Form is submitted.

To add a `Click` event handler for the button, simply double-click the Button Web control in the Design view. This will take you to the page's source code portion with the appropriate event handler created. Now simply add the code from Listing 9.6 inside the `Click` event handler.

After you have added this code, view the ASP.NET page through a browser. When you first visit the page, you should see two empty text boxes and a button labeled Calculate BMI; Figure 9.11 shows the browser when the page is first visited.

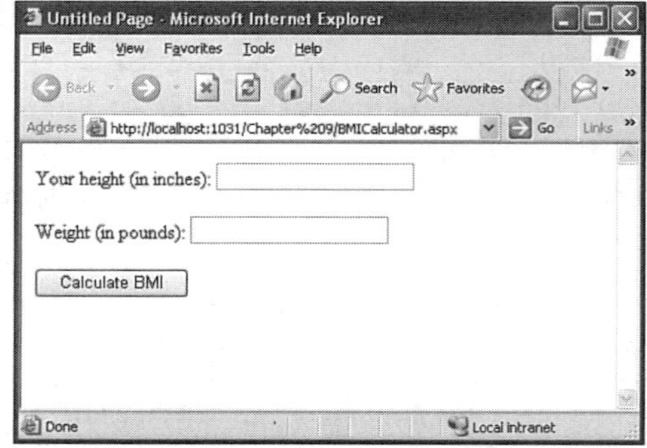

FIGURE 9.11 The final `BMICalculator.aspx` ASP.NET web page when first visited.

Now enter some appropriate values into the two text boxes and then click the Calculate BMI button. If you enter my height and weight—70 and 155—you should see the output shown in Figure 9.12.

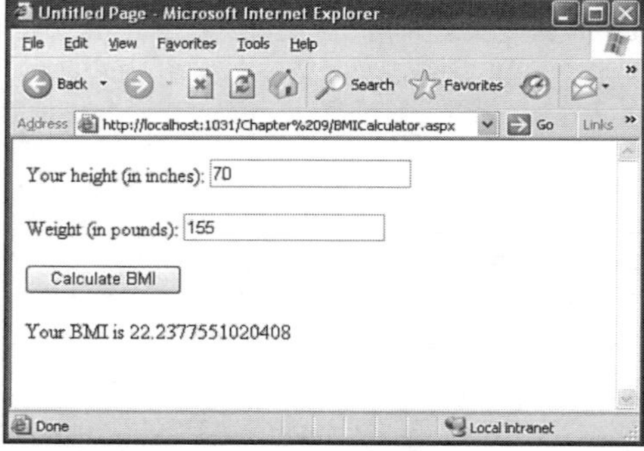

FIGURE 9.12 The user's BMI is displayed.

Did you Know?

To determine what the various BMI ratings mean, visit http://nhlbisupport.com/bmi/bmicalc.htm. Briefly, a healthy BMI range is between 18.5 and 24.9. Persons with a BMI of 25.0 to 29.9 are considered overweight, whereas a BMI over 30 indicates obesity. (BMI conclusions can be inaccurate for athletes and the elderly.)

Watch Out!

If you enter noninteger values into the text boxes in `BMICalculator.aspx`, you will get an error when submitting the page. Similarly, if you enter negative values for your height or weight, the computed BMI might be a negative number itself.

In Hour 12, "Validating User Input with Validation Controls," we'll examine how to use a special kind of Web control that ensures a user's input is in an acceptable form and within acceptable boundaries.

Summary

In this hour we examined how user input can be collected in an ASP.NET web page. We started by examining the HTML elements needed to collect user input, which include a number of `<input>` elements for each text box, check box, radio button, or drop-down list; and a `<form>` element, inside which the `<input>` elements must be enclosed. Additionally, a submit button is needed.

With ASP.NET web pages, we do not need to worry about creating these HTML elements by hand. Rather, we can simply use appropriate Web controls, such as the TextBox Web control for displaying a text box, a CheckBox Web control for displaying a check box, and so on. To collect a user's input, these Web controls must be placed inside a Web Form. A Web Form, as we saw, is a Web control of the form, as follows:

```
<form runat="server">
  ...
</form>
```

Visual Web Developer automatically enters a Web Form when creating a new ASP.NET page.

In addition to the Web controls needed to collect the user's input, a Button Web control should be added in the Web Form. The Button Web control is rendered as a submit button that, when clicked, submits the form, performing a postback. If you have source code that you want to execute whenever the Web Form is submitted, you can place it in the Button Web control's `Click` event handler. To add a `Click` event handler to your ASP.NET web page, simply double-click the Button Web control from the Design view.

Now that we have seen how an ASP.NET page can collect user input and perform calculations on this input, we're ready to examine the Web controls for collecting user input in much finer detail. In the next hour we'll focus on examining the TextBox Web control. Following that hour, we'll look at collecting a user's input using the DropDownList, RadioButton, and CheckBox Web controls.

Q&A

Q. ***Sometimes when I refresh my browser on a web page with a form, I receive the message*** `"This page cannot be refreshed without resending the form information"` ***or*** `"The page contains POSTDATA. Do you want to refresh?"` ***What does this mean?***

A. Recall that there are two ways an HTML form can submit its values: through the querystring or through the HTTP Post headers. When a postback form is used, the HTML form uses the HTTP Post headers and submits the form to the same URL. (Refer to Figure 9.4 for more on postback forms.)

When you ask your browser to refresh the web page after you have submitted a postback form, the browser doesn't know whether you want to repost the web page resubmitting the HTTP Post headers. Therefore, it asks if you want to resend the form information.

You may also notice this behavior when clicking the Back button to return to a page that has been requested via a postback.

Q. *Why do ASP.NET Web Forms use postback? Why not direct the user to another page or pass the information along in the querystring?*

A. ASP.NET Web Forms use postback forms over alternative methods for a number of reasons. The most important being that postback forms allow the ASP.NET Web controls to maintain their state across postbacks. Recall that when a user enters a value into a TextBox Web control and submits the form, the ASP.NET page is posted back and the TextBox Web control's `Text` property is updated to the value the user entered. For the TextBox Web control's `Text` property to be updated with the value the user entered, the Web Form must submit back to the same page that contains the TextBox Web control. (A lengthy discussion on *why* this is the case is far beyond the scope of this book.)

Additionally, the HTTP Post headers are used as opposed to the QueryString because often a large amount of data is being passed back in the Post headers. Some older browsers have a limit on the amount of information that can be passed through the querystring. Furthermore, it would be unsightly to have such a mangled querystring.

Workshop

Quiz

1. What are the germane differences between a form with its `method` attribute set to `GET` versus a form with its `method` attribute set to `POST`?

2. Imagine that you saw the following querystring:

```
SomePage.aspx?SSN=123-45-6789&age=24&gender=M
```

What does this tell you about the form that the user filled out?

3. What are the differences between postback forms and redirect forms?
4. What types of forms do ASP.NET Web Forms use?

Answers

1. A form with its `method` property set to `GET` passes its form values through the querystring. A form with its `method` property set to `POST` passes its form values through the HTTP Post headers. When passing information through the querystring, it appears in the browser's Address bar (see Figure 9.3). With the HTTP Post headers, however, the information is hidden from sight. Realize that ASP.NET Web forms use the HTTP Post header to pass form value information.
2. Because the information is passed in the querystring, it is obvious that the form's `action` property was set to `GET`. Also, based on the values in the querystring, it can be determined that there were three form fields with the names `SSN`, `age`, and `gender`, and that the user entered the values `123-45-6789`, `24`, and `M` for the three form fields.
3. Postback forms are forms whose `method` property is set to `POST` *and* whose `action` property is set to the same URL that the form exists on. That is, if the web page `Page1.aspx` has a postback form, its form's `action` property will be set to `Page1.aspx`.

   Redirect forms are ones whose `action` property is set to a URL other than the URL the form exists on. That is, if the web page `Page1.aspx` has a redirect form, its form's `action` property is set to some other web page's URL, such as `Page2.aspx`.

   (Refer to Figure 9.4 for more on the differences between postback forms and redirect forms.)
4. ASP.NET Web Forms use postback forms.

Exercises

There are no exercises for this hour. Web forms, by themselves, are quite useless. To make Web forms useful, we need to add Web controls designed for collecting a user's input. In the next hour, "Using Text Boxes to Collect Input," we'll see how to use the TextBox Web control to collect user input. At the end of this next hour, we'll work on a number of exercises that examine the use of Web forms.

HOUR 10

Using Text Boxes to Collect Input

In this hour, we will cover

- Creating multiline text boxes
- Creating password text boxes
- Specifying the number of columns in a text box
- Indicating the maximum number of characters that can be entered into a text box
- Changing the look and feel of the text box by changing the font size, font name, and color of the text box

In Hour 9, "Web Form Basics," we examined how to collect user input through an ASP.NET web page. To summarize, we saw that in order to retrieve user input, we need to use a Web Form. Inside the Web Form, Web controls are placed to allow user input.

For example, in the preceding hour we looked at a BMI Calculator ASP.NET page. For this web page, users needed to enter two pieces of information: their height and weight. So that users could enter this information, we used two TextBox Web controls.

The TextBox Web control contains a number of properties that can be set to specify the appearance of the resulting text box. For example, the `TextMode` property of the TextBox Web control can be set to `MultiLine`, which will create a text box with multiple lines; or it can be set to `Password` to show a series of asterisks when the user types in a value. The `Columns` property can be adjusted to specify how many columns wide the text box should be.

Now we will look at the various TextBox Web control properties and the visual effects they have.

Learning About the TextBox Web Control Basics

As you already know, when an ASP.NET page is visited, its Web controls are rendered into HTML markup. The Label Web control, for example, is rendered as a `<span>` tag whose content is the Label's `Text` property. The TextBox Web control, as we saw in the preceding hour, is rendered into an `<input>` tag whose `type` attribute is set to `text`.

TextBox Web controls are used when user input is needed. Text boxes are ideal for collecting user input that is general text, such as a person's name, mailing address, or credit card number.

> For certain types of user input, a text box might not be ideal. In the next hour we will examine other Web controls designed for collecting user input and why they are better suited than the TextBox Web control for some situations.

In this hour we will examine the various types of text boxes—such as password text boxes and multiline text boxes—as well as how to alter their aesthetics. Before we begin this exploration, though, let's practice adding a TextBox Web control to an ASP.NET web page and displaying the value the user entered.

To do this, start by creating a new ASP.NET page named `TextBoxPractice.aspx`. In this page we will add two TextBox Web controls to collect two bits of information from the user: name and age.

Start by entering the following title for the first TextBox Web control into the designer: `Your name:`. After entering this text, drag and drop a TextBox Web control from the Toolbox onto the page. Next, enter the text `Your age:` and, after this text, add another TextBox Web control. Finally, as with all Web forms, we will need a Button Web control. Add this below the two TextBox Web controls.

Figure 10.1 shows the Design view in Visual Web Developer after these three Web controls have been added. Take a moment to make sure that your screen looks similar.

Now let's set the properties of our three Web controls. For the two TextBox Web controls, we'll specify only their `ID` properties at this time. (Later in the hour we will look at the other TextBox Web control properties.) The Button Web control will have both its `ID` property and its `Text` property set. Recall that the Button's `Text` property indicates the text that appears on the button.

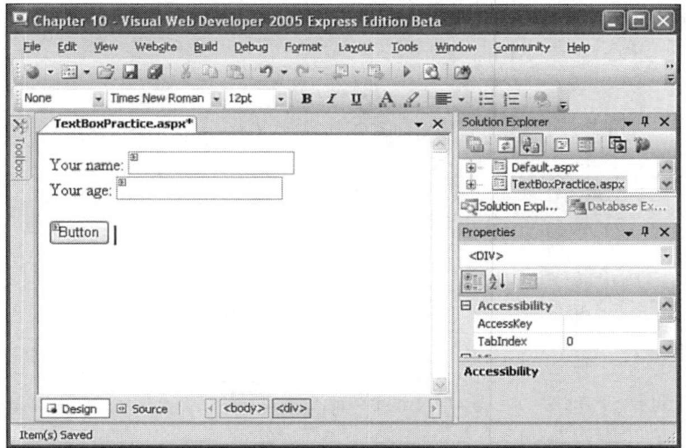

FIGURE 10.1 Two TextBox Web controls and a Button Web control have been added to the page.

Start with the first TextBox Web control. Because this Web control is used to collect the user's name, let's set its `ID` property to `name`. To accomplish this, follow these steps:

1. Click the TextBox Web control, which will load its properties into the Properties window.
2. Change its `ID` property to `name`.

Repeat the same process for the second TextBox Web control, but set its `ID` property to `age`.

Finally, click the Button Web control to set its properties. Start by setting the `ID` property to `btnSubmit` and its `Text` property to `"Click Me"`.

Let's take a moment to test this ASP.NET page so that we can observe the HTML markup generated by the TextBox Web controls. Visit the ASP.NET page via your web browser by going to the Debug menu and choosing Start Without Debugging. Figure 10.2 shows the web page when visited through a browser. Note that the two TextBox Web controls and the Button Web control we added through the web designer are present.

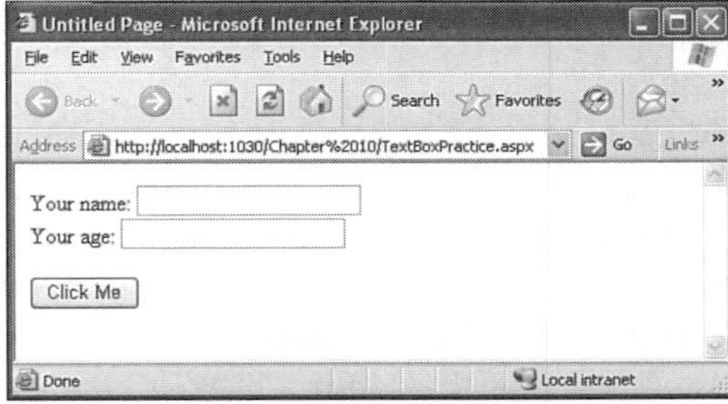

FIGURE 10.2 The ASP.NET page, when visited through a browser, displays two text boxes and a button.

Listing 10.1 contains the HTML markup received by the web browser when visiting the ASP.NET web page.

LISTING 10.1 The TextBox Web Controls Are Rendered as <input> Tags

```
 1: <!DOCTYPE html PUBLIC "-//W3C//DTD XHTML 1.0 Transitional//EN"
➥"http://www.w3.org/TR/xhtml1/DTD/xhtml1-transitional.dtd">
 2:
 3: <html xmlns="http://www.w3.org/1999/xhtml" >
 4: <head><title>
 5:     Untitled Page
 6: </title></head>
 7: <body>
 8:     <form name="form1" method="post" action="TextBoxPractice.aspx"
➥id="form1">
 9: <div>
10: <input type="hidden" name="__VIEWSTATE" id="__VIEWSTATE"
➥value="/wEPDwULLTExNTc2NTI3OTlkZMRJuARZnpdkaYvVsuCrgXkFBPiT" />
11: </div>
12:
13:     <div>
14:         Your name:
15:         <input name="name" type="text" id="name" />
16:         <br />
17:         Your age:
18:         <input name="age" type="text" id="age" />
19:         <br /><br />
20:         <input type="submit" name="btnSubmit" value="Click Me"
➥id="btnSubmit" />
21:     </div>
22:
23: <div>
24:
25:     <input type="hidden" name="__EVENTVALIDATION" id="__EVENTVALIDATION"
➥ value="/wEWBAKu6rmqBAL7uPQdAtCCr6oGAsKL2t4D39d7pTImtC5ICq4saMTgctPugho=" />
26: </div></form>
27: </body>
28: </html>
```

As you can see on lines 15 and 18, the TextBox Web controls are rendered as `<input>` tags with their `type` attribute set to `text`.

Performing an Action When the User Submits the Form

Currently, the `TextBoxPractice.aspx` ASP.NET page does nothing when the form is submitted. Typically, though, when the user submits information, you want to do something with it. Perhaps you want to perform a calculation on the data entered and present some computed value to the user. As we will see in later hours, you may want to display data from a database that matches the input provided by the user. In either case, the input provided by the user is utilized in some fashion.

To access the values entered into the two text boxes, we need to add an event handler for the Button Web control's `Click` event. By doing so, we can provide source code that will run after the user has submitted the form (by clicking the button).

As we saw in the preceding hour, adding an event handler for the Button's `Click` event is easy. Simply double-click the Button Web control in the Design view, or go to the source code portion and select the Button Web control and the `Click` event from the left and right drop-down lists at the top. Either of these actions will automatically insert the necessary syntax for the event handler, into which you can add the needed code. Now we have to decide what, specifically, we want to do with the user's input once he submits the form. For this ASP.NET page, let's simply display the user's input in the browser. Specifically, we'll use a Label Web control to display the output.

Start by adding a Label Web control to the `TextBoxPractice.aspx` ASP.NET page. You can add this anywhere in the HTML portion; if you want to follow along with my example, add it after the Button Web control.

Remember from Hour 8, "ASP.NET Web Controls for Displaying Text," that to add a Label Web control, you simply need to drag and drop it from the Toolbox onto the page. After you have done this, set the Label Web control's `ID` property to `results` and clear out the `Text` property. Figure 10.3 shows the Design view after this Label Web control has been added and its properties set.

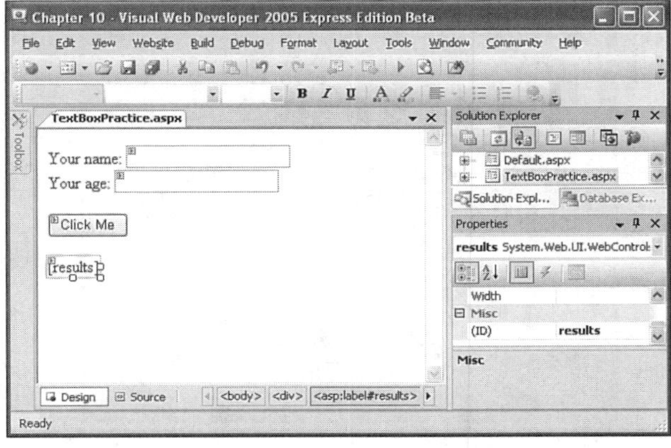

FIGURE 10.3 A Label Web control has been added to `TextBoxPractice.aspx`.

By the Way

> If you want to set some of the aesthetic properties of the `results` Label Web control at this time, feel free to do so. (Recall that the aesthetic properties of the Label Web control include properties such as `Font`, `BackColor`, `ForeColor`, and so on.

Now that you have added the Label Web control, let's go ahead and add the source code for the Button Web control's `Click` event handler. Listing 10.2 shows what the ASP.NET page's source code portion should look like after you have added the necessary code to the Button Web control's `Click` event handler. Note that you will need to manually type in only lines 5 and 6; all of the other lines of code should already be there, courtesy of Visual Web Developer.

LISTING 10.2 The `Click` Event Handler Displays the User's Name and Age in the `results` Label Web Control

```
1: Partial Class TextBoxPractice
2:     Inherits System.Web.UI.Page
3:
4:     Protected Sub btnSubmit_Click(ByVal sender As Object, ByVal e As
➥System.EventArgs) Handles btnSubmit.Click
5:         results.Text = "Hello, " & name.Text
6:         results.Text &= ". You are " & age.Text & " years old."
7:     End Sub
8: End Class
```

The code in the event handler sets the `results` Label's `Text` property so that it displays the user's entered name and age. Recall that the `ID` of the TextBox Web control into which the user's name is entered is `name`, and the `ID` of the TextBox Web control into which the user's age is entered is `age`.

Figure 10.4 shows `TextBoxPractice.aspx` when visited through a browser. The screenshot was taken after a user entered his name and age and submitted the form by clicking the Click Me button.

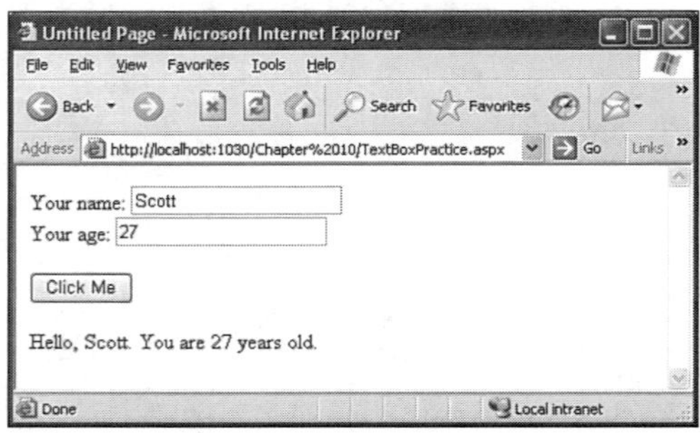

FIGURE 10.4 The user's supplied name and age are displayed.

`TextBoxPractice.aspx` demonstrates the basics of using TextBox Web controls in an ASP.NET web page. For the remainder of this hour, we will focus on the various properties of the TextBox Web control and how these properties alter the appearance of the resulting text box in the user's web browser.

Creating Multiline and Password Text Boxes

Take a moment to examine the text boxes in Figure 10.4. Note that these text boxes allow for a single line of text. As you likely know from your Internet surfing experience, text boxes come in other forms. The two variants of the text box are multiline and password.

A multiline text box contains more than one row of text. This type of text box is commonly used when the user needs to input a large amount of text. For example, online messageboard sites are discussion websites where web visitors can post questions or comments and reply to other comments. Typically, multiline text boxes are used when the user enters a comment. (See Figure 10.5 for an example of a multiline text box.) Password text boxes are text boxes whose input is masked by asterisks (*). Password text boxes are used to collect sensitive input from the user, such as her password or personal identification number (PIN). The masked input prevents an onlooker from being able to glance over the web user's shoulder to determine the user's password or other sensitive information. (Consult Figure 10.6 to see an example of a password text box.)

The TextBox Web control contains a `TextMode` property that specifies how the resulting text box is displayed: as a normal text box, as a multiline text box, or as a password text box. As we have seen, the TextBox Web control displays a normal text box by default. In the next two sections, we will examine how to get the TextBox Web control to render as a multiline text box and then as a password text box.

Using Multiline Text Boxes

Creating a multiline text box involves the following simple steps:

1. Add a TextBox Web control to the ASP.NET web page.
2. Set the TextBox Web control's `TextMode` property to `MultiLine`.
3. Set the TextBox Web control's `Columns` and `Rows` properties to specify the number of columns and rows the multiline TextBox should have.

Let's create an ASP.NET page with a multiline text box. Start by creating a new ASP.NET web page named `MultiLineTextBox.aspx`. Start by typing the following text into the designer inside the Web form: `Share your Thoughts:`.

The first step in adding a multiline text box is to add the TextBox Web control to the web page. So, drag and drop a TextBox Web control from the Toolbox onto the page after the `"Share your Thoughts:"` text.

Next, we need to set the TextBox Web control's `TextMode` property. To accomplish this, first click the TextBox Web control so that its properties are loaded in the Properties window. Next, scroll down through the list of properties until you reach the `TextMode` property.

By the Way

> By default, the `TextMode` property is set to the value `SingleLine`, which creates a standard, single-line text box like the ones shown in Figure 10.4.

Clicking on the `TextMode` property drops down a list of three options: `SingleLine`, `MultiLine`, and `Password`. Select the `MultiLine` option. When you choose the `MultiLine` option, the TextBox Web control in the designer will automatically be displayed as a multiline text box.

At this point, we can adjust the number of columns and rows in the multiline text box by setting the TextBox Web control's `Columns` and `Rows` properties. Go ahead and set these two properties to values of 25 and 5, respectively. The columns and rows displayed by the TextBox Web control in the designer will be updated accordingly.

Figure 10.5 shows the Visual Web Developer after these steps have been completed.

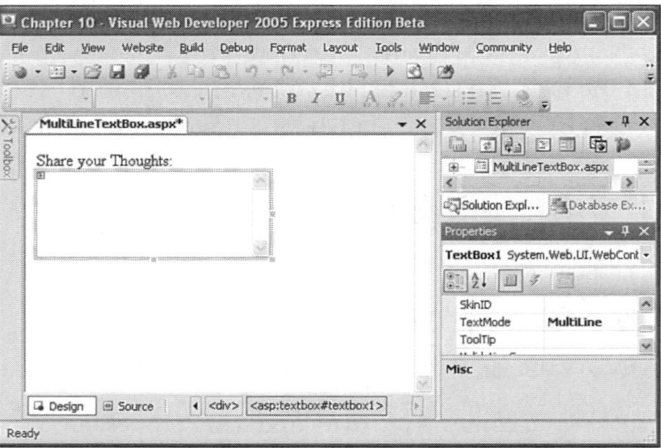

FIGURE 10.5 A multiline text box is displayed.

> For practice, you are encouraged to complete the `MultiLineTextBox.aspx` web page by adding a Button Web control and providing source code in the Button's `Click` event handler. For now, simply have the source code display the text the user entered.

In addition to using the `Columns` and `Rows` properties to specify the size of the multiline TextBox Web control, you can also resize the TextBox Web control directly by clicking on the TextBox and selecting one of the resize icons on the bottom, right, or bottom-right corner. Resizing a TextBox in this way adjusts the TextBox Web control's `Height` and `Width` properties rather than its `Columns` and `Rows` properties.

The difference between these two methods is that if you set the `Height` and `Width` properties, the text box displayed in the user's browser will have the exact size specified by these properties, regardless of the font used within the text box. That is, regardless of whether a small-sized or large-sized font is used, the text box will be the same dimensions. However, if you specify the size through the `Columns` and `Rows` properties, the rendered text box's dimensions will depend on the size of the font being used for the text box. That is, there will *always* be the specified number of columns and rows, so if a large font size is used, the absolute size of the text box will be larger than if a smaller font size is used.

Using Password Text Boxes

Many Web applications require users to create an account before they can enjoy the services of the site. For example, to check your email at Hotmail.com, you must first sign in by providing your username and password.

The password text box is a variant of the standard text box created for hiding the text a user entered. With a password text box, each character entered by the user is displayed as an asterisk in the text box. Figure 10.6 shows a password text box that has had the text `"This is a password"` typed into it.

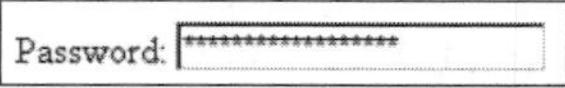

FIGURE 10.6
A password text box masks the text entered by the user.

To create a password text box in an ASP.NET web page, we simply need to add a TextBox Web control and set its `TextMode` property to `Password`. Create an ASP.NET page named `PasswordTextBox.aspx` to try out creating a password text box.

Start by typing the text `Username:` into the page. After this, add a TextBox Web control. On the next line, type in the text `Password:` and, after this, add another TextBox Web control. Set the second TextBox Web control's `TextMode` property to `Password`.

Setting the TextBox Web control's `TextMode` property to `Password` will not change the display in the Design view. (Recall that setting the `TextMode` property to `MultiLine` had the effect of displaying a multiline text box in the designer.)

After these two TextBox Web controls, add a Button Web control. Set the Button Web control's `Text` property to `Login`.

After you perform these steps, your screen should look similar to Figure 10.7.

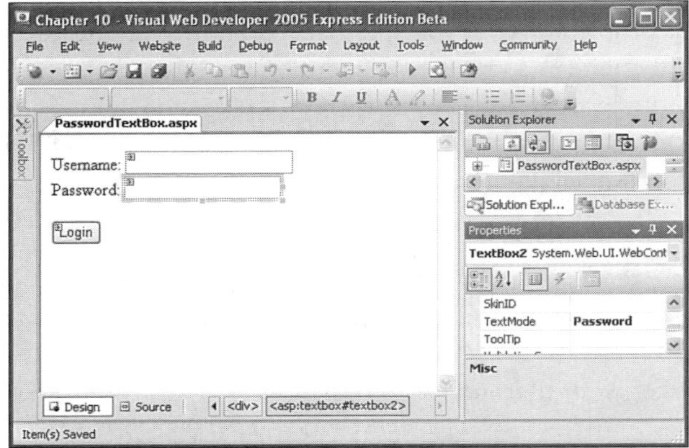

FIGURE 10.7 The ASP.NET web page has two TextBox Web controls and a Button Web control.

Password Text Box Values Are Not Continued Across Postbacks

The password text box has some potentially unexpected behavior when viewed through a web page. To illustrate these subtleties, let's view the `PasswordTextBox.aspx` through a browser. When you first visit the page, take a moment to enter some text into the username and password text boxes. Note that the username text box behaves like a normal text box, but the password text box has its input masked by asterisks. Figure 10.8 shows the `PasswordTextBox.aspx` ASP.NET web page through a browser and with values entered into both text boxes.

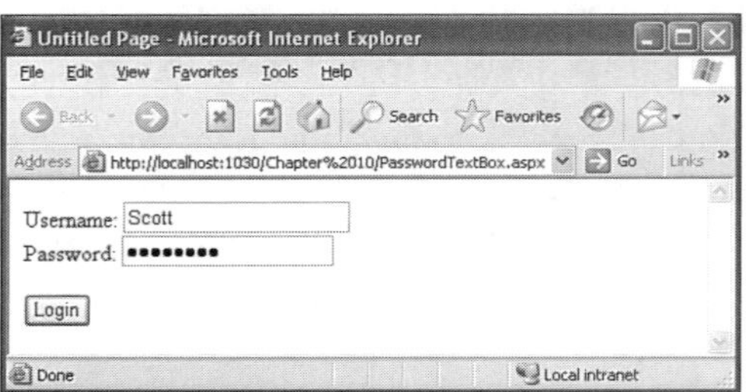

FIGURE 10.8 The text in the password text box is masked by asterisks.

After you have entered information into the two text boxes, submit the form by clicking the Login button. Clicking the button will cause the form to be submitted. Because Web Forms, as we discussed in the preceding hour, are postback forms, the web page will be reloaded.

Upon the page's reloading, though, the text entered into the password text box will disappear, as Figure 10.9 illustrates. (Note that the text in the username text box still remains.)

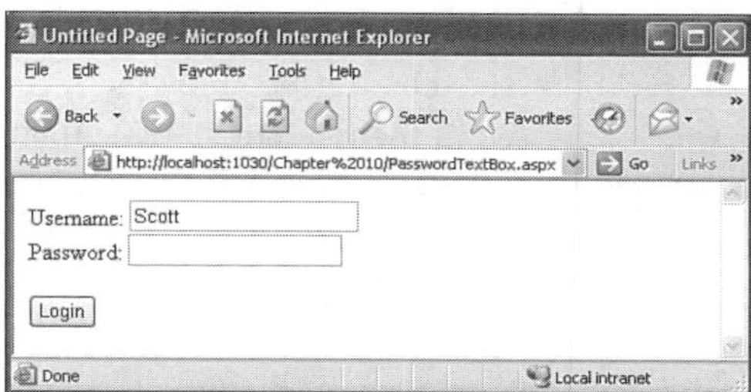

FIGURE 10.9
When the Web Form is posted back, the text in the password text box is not redisplayed.

Why did the text in the username text box remain, but the text in the password text box disappear? Recall that when the button is clicked, the Web Form is submitted and the data the user entered into the text boxes is sent back to the `PasswordTextBox.aspx` ASP.NET web page.

When the request for the `PasswordTextBox.aspx` ASP.NET page arrives at the web server, the ASP.NET engine is invoked to produce the proper HTML output for the page. The ASP.NET page can determine that the page has been posted back and sets the `Text` properties of the two TextBox Web controls to the values the user entered.

With TextBox Web controls whose `TextMode` property is set to `SingleLine` or `MultiLine`, the value of the `Text` property is expressed in the HTML markup generated by the TextBox Web control when it is rendered. For example, a TextBox Web control whose `Text` property equals `Scott` and whose `ID` property equals `TextBox1` will render the following HTML markup:

```
<input name="TextBox1" type="text" value="Scott" id="TextBox1" />
```

However, when a password text box is rendered, the `Text` property is not expressed in the resulting HTML markup. Security reasons prevent the `Text` property from being expressed in the TextBox Web control's resulting HTML markup.

Imagine that a TextBox Web control with its `TextMode` property set to `Password` had its `Text` property set to `password123` and its `ID` property set to `TextBox2`. Now, if the

Text property were expressed in the resulting HTML markup, the TextBox Web control would produce the following HTML markup when rendered:

```
<input name="TextBox2" type="text" value="password123" id="TextBox2" />
```

Now imagine that a user visits a web page where he is prompted for his username and password, and imagine that after he enters his correct username and password, the ASP.NET web page displays some information specific to his user account in a Label Web control on the same web page.

If the user gets up from his computer to get a quick drink of water, an unscrupulous co-worker could view the HTML received by the web browser. If the Text property of the password text box were expressed in the rendered HTML, the HTML received by the browser, which the nefarious coworker is viewing, would contain the following HTML markup:

```
<input name="TextBox2" type="text" value="password123" id="TextBox2" />
```

(This assumes password123 was the person's password.)

At this point the co-worker could learn the user's password. To help prevent this, Text properties for a TextBox Web control whose TextMode property is set to Password are not displayed.

By the Way

> Once a month or so, a person will ask the following question on one of the ASP.NET newsgroups: "Why is it that when I set a password TextBox Web control's Text property, it does not appear when I visit the ASP.NET web page through a browser?" Now you can answer this type of question!

Examining the TextBox Web Control's Properties

So far in this hour, we have looked at one property in particular—the TextMode property—which is used to specify if the TextBox Web control should be rendered as a standard text box, a multiline text box, or a password text box. In addition to this property, we will examine a number of other TextBox Web control properties for the remainder of this hour.

Specifying the Length of a Text Box

Sometimes you may need to use the TextBox Web control to collect information from users such as their age or the two-letter abbreviation of the state they live in.

In such cases, the users' input will be only a few characters long. However, as you can see with the age text box in Figure 10.4, the text box displayed in the web browser is much larger than it has to be for such cases.

Fortunately, you can specify how many columns wide the text box should be by setting the TextBox Web control's `Columns` property. To demonstrate this property, open the ASP.NET web page `TextBoxPractice.aspx`. Recall that this is the ASP.NET page we created in the first example in this hour (see Figure 10.4).

Now let's adjust the age TextBox Web control's `Columns` property so that the text box into which the user enters his age is more appropriately sized. To accomplish this, click the age TextBox Web control so that its properties are loaded in the Properties pane. Then set this TextBox's `Columns` property to a value of 3.

After you set the `Columns` property to 3, the text box in the designer will shrink from its default width to a width of three columns. Refer to Figure 10.10 for a screenshot of Visual Web Developer after this property has been set.

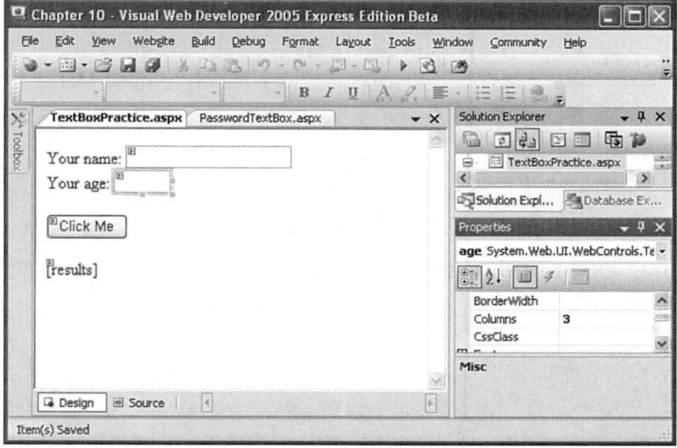

FIGURE 10.10 The age text box is three columns wide.

This shorter text box is more appropriate for this situation than the longer one displayed in Figure 10.4.

By the Way

> You can also resize the TextBox by dragging it to a wider width in the Design view. This sets the TextBox's `Height` and `Width` properties. As discussed at the end of the "Using Multiline Text Boxes" section, the `Height` and `Width` properties specify the absolute size of the resulting text box, whereas the `Columns` property dictates the number of columns to display, making the size of the rendered text box relative to the text box's font size.

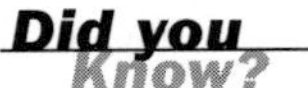

Be sure to have your TextBox Web controls properly sized for the input you are expecting users to enter. Properly sized text boxes help ensure that users enter the data in the correct format. For example, if you want users to enter a *short* description about themselves, they will be more apt to enter a shorter description if you provide them with a single-line text box than if you provide them with a multiline text box.

Limiting the Number of Characters a User Can Enter into a Text Box

Adjusting the size of the text box by setting the TextBox Web control's `Columns` property does not regulate how much text the user can enter. Even if you create a TextBox Web control three columns wide, the user can still enter hundreds of characters of text.

Sometimes, however, you may want to limit the amount of text a user may enter into a particular text box. For example, sites like eBay allow only 80 characters to be entered when providing feedback about another buyer or seller.

Websites typically limit the number of characters that can be entered into a text box for two reasons. First, and most importantly, it is usually easier to format data for display at a later time by limiting the number of characters that can be supplied by the user. For example, the feedback a user enters at eBay about a buyer or a seller can be viewed by other eBay users in a feedback summary page. This summary page is clean and concise because no one user can enter more than 80 characters of feedback at a time. Due to this restriction in feedback input, the feedback summary page can be formatted so that it doesn't contain any lengthy blocks of feedback.

Second, sites like eBay use databases to store the information their users enter. When you're setting up a database, you must specify the maximum number of characters for text fields in advance. Therefore, this feedback limit is in place because of the limit imposed by those who designed eBay's database tables. (We'll be examining how to create and use databases later in this book, starting with Hour 13, "An Introduction to Databases.")

To set a limit to the number of characters that can be entered into a TextBox Web control, set the `MaxLength` property accordingly. In our `TextBoxPractice.aspx` example, we may want to limit the age text box to a maximum of three characters (because it would be impossible for a visitor to have an age greater than 999).

To do so, click the age TextBox Web control and set its `MaxLength` property to 3. Note that this change will not have any visual effect on the designer. After you have made this change, take a moment to view the `TextBoxPractice.aspx` ASP.NET web page through a browser. Try to type more than three characters into the age text box—you can't!

By the Way

Although you might think that a `MaxLength` value of 0 would not permit users to enter information into the text box at all, it means quite the opposite. A `MaxLength` value of 0 means that there are no restrictions on the amount of information users can enter into the text box.

Watch Out!

Advanced users can circumvent the text box restrictions imposed by the `MaxLength` property. Therefore, the `MaxLength` property does not guarantee that a user's supplied value will indeed be less than `MaxLength` setting. In Hour 12, "Validating User Input with Validation Controls," we will see how to ensure that a user has entered no more than a specified number of characters into a particular text box.

Furthermore, the `MaxLength` property works only with `SingleLine` and `Password` text boxes. If you set your TextBox Web control's `TextMode` property to `MultiLine`, the `MaxLength` property is ignored. There is a workaround for limiting the number of characters that can be entered into a `MultiLine` text box, but it involves the use of the ASP.NET validation controls. We'll examine how to accomplish this in Hour 12.

Aesthetic Properties—Changing the Text Box's Font and Color

The Label Web control has a number of aesthetic properties, such as `BackColor`, `ForeColor`, `Font`, and so on. In Hour 8 we examined these various properties and looked at how to specify them and the visual effect they had on the text displayed by the Label Web control.

The TextBox Web control has the exact same aesthetic properties as the Label Web control, which are summarized in Table 10.1.

TABLE 10.1 The Aesthetic Properties of the TextBox Web Control

Property	Description
`BackColor`	Specifies the background color of the text box.
`BorderColor`	Specifies the color of the text box's border.
`BorderStyle`	Specifies the style of the text box's border.
`BorderWidth`	Specifies the width of the text box's border.
`Font`	Specifies the font properties for the text entered by the user into the text box. Recall that the `Font` property has a number of subproperties, such as `Name`, `Size`, `Bold`, and so on.
`ForeColor`	Specifies the color of the text entered into the text box by the user.

Let's create a new ASP.NET web page called `PrettyTextBox.aspx`, in which we'll create a number of TextBox Web controls to determine the effects of various aesthetic properties. After you create the ASP.NET page, add two TextBox Web controls to the designer by dragging and dropping them from the Toolbox.

Now let's set some aesthetic properties for these two TextBox Web controls. Let's first specify a `BackColor` property for the first TextBox. Recall that when you're selecting a color property, Visual Web Developer provides three tabs: Custom, Web, and System. Click the Web tab and set its `BackColor` property to Linen. Next, choose the `BorderColor` property, click the Web tab, and select the color Maroon. Choose the `Dashed` option from the `BorderStyle` property and, finally, enter a value of `5px` for the `BorderWidth` property.

For the second TextBox Web control, set the `Font` property's `Bold` subproperty to `True`, the `Name` subproperty to `Comic Sans MS`, and the `Size` subproperty to `Large`. Then, for the `ForeColor` property, select the Web tab and choose the color Red.

Figure 10.11 shows Visual Web Developer after these properties have been set. (Some of the color differences may not be noticeable in the figure.)

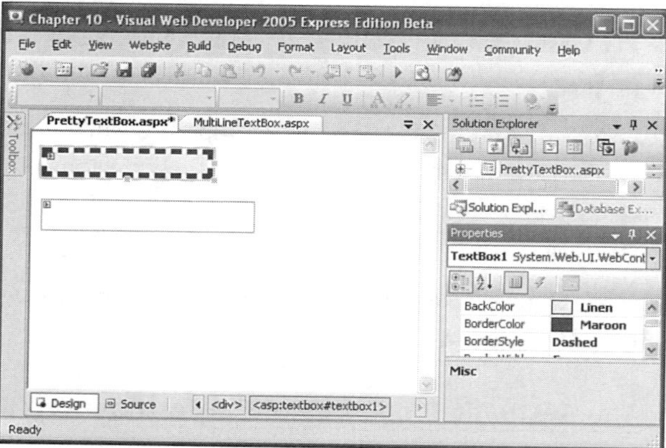

FIGURE 10.11 Both TextBox Web controls have had a number of their aesthetic properties set.

Take a moment to view the `PrettyTextBox.aspx` ASP.NET page through a browser. When viewing the page, type some text into the second text box and note that it is red, large, and in the Comic Sans MS font. Figure 10.12 shows `PrettyTextBox.aspx` when viewed through Internet Explorer.

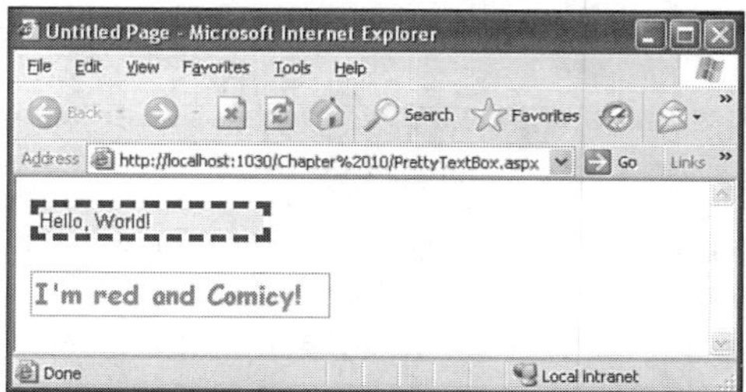

FIGURE 10.12 The `PrettyTextBox.aspx` ASP.NET page, viewed through an uplevel browser.

Unfortunately, the aesthetic properties of the TextBox Web control are reflected only in uplevel browsers. That means that if you view the `PrettyTextBox.aspx` ASP.NET page using a downlevel browser, you will be shown two plain text boxes, as shown in Figure 10.13.

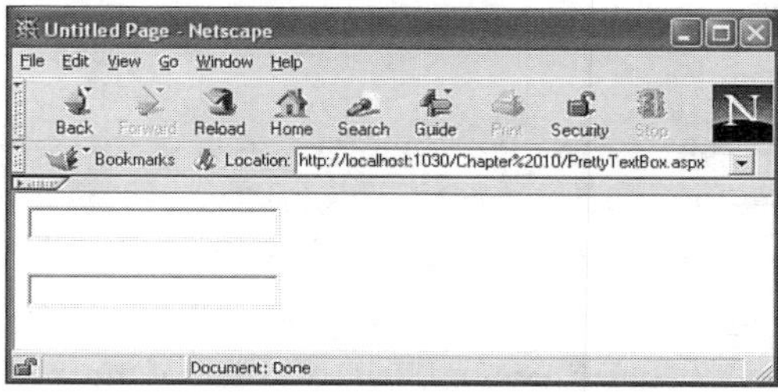

FIGURE 10.13 The `PrettyTextBox.aspx` ASP.NET web page, viewed via Netscape 4.0.

Summary

In this hour we looked at one of the most commonly used Web controls for collecting user input: the TextBox Web control. The TextBox Web control can be used to create three types of text boxes: a single-line text box, a multiline text box, or a password text box. To specify what kind of text box should be rendered by the TextBox Web control, you use the `TextMode` property.

In addition to the `TextMode` property, the TextBox Web control contains a number of other properties. The `Columns` property, for example, specifies how wide the text box is. The `MaxLength` property can be used to indicate the maximum number of characters a user is allowed to enter into a text box. Like the Label Web control, the TextBox Web control also contains a number of aesthetic properties, such as `BackColor`, `ForeColor`, `Font`, and so on.

In addition to the TextBox Web control, a number of other Web controls can be used to collect user input, which is our topic for the next hour.

Q&A

Q. ***I want to create a text box that allows the user to enter only a certain type of input, such as numbers. How can I do this?***

A. In the BMI calculator example we examined in the preceding hour, the user was prompted for his weight and height. Clearly, these inputs must be numeric ones. As we saw, if the user enters some input like `Fred` as his weight, it breaks the BMI calculator.

Therefore, you might think that an ideal solution would be to create a text box into which the user can enter *only* numbers. Such *masked text boxes*, as they are called, are rarely, if ever, used on web pages for a number of reasons.

First, while a masked text box would prevent the user from entering something like `Fred` as his weight, it would not prevent the user from entering nothing into the weight text box. Entering nothing will also break the BMI calculator.

Second, creating masked text boxes requires a bit of tricky client-side JavaScript programming. Users who have JavaScript disabled in their browser would therefore be able to enter any values into a masked text box.

Finally, and perhaps most importantly, users are not accustomed to masked text boxes on web pages. Therefore, the inclusion of masked text boxes would likely irritate users and lead them to conclude that your website was fundamentally different from the plethora of other websites they're used to.

As we will see in Hour 12, it is quite easy to ensure that a user's text box input conforms to a certain format. This is accomplished through validation Web controls, which we'll discuss in detail two hours from now.

(There are, however, masked input ASP.NET controls you can purchase. The nice thing about these third-party controls is that they take care of the tricky client-side JavaScript needed. You just drag and drop them onto your ASP.NET page, much like you would a regular TextBox. I've used and have been pleased with the masked input controls available at http://www.peterblum.com/.)

Q. ***Why does the*** `MaxLength` ***property not work with a*** `MultiLine` ***TextBox Web control?***

A. Whereas a `SingleLine` or `Password` TextBox Web control is rendered as an `<input>` HTML element, `MultiLine` TextBoxes are rendered as the `<textarea>` HTML element. The HTML specification defines a `maxlength` attribute for `<input>` elements, but not for `<textarea>`.

Despite this limitation, it is still possible to restrict the number of characters entered into a `MultiLine` TextBox. In Hour 12 we'll examine one such workaround.

Workshop

Quiz

1. What are the possible values of the TextBox Web control's `TextMode` property?
2. If you wanted to create a multiline text box with 40 columns and 5 rows, what TextBox Web control properties would you need to set?
3. True or False: Aesthetic settings for text boxes will display the same in all web browsers.
4. What TextBox Web control property contains the text that was entered by the user?
5. What Web control that we've examined in previous hours shares a number of properties with the TextBox Web control?
6. If you set the `Text` property of a TextBox Web control whose `TextMode` is set to `Password`, no text will appear in the text box when viewed through a web browser. Why is this the case?

Answers

1. The TextBox Web control supports three possible values for its `TextMode` property. They are `MultiLine`, `Password`, and `SingleLine`. The default property value is `SingleLine`.
2. To create such a text box, you would need to set the TextBox Web control's `TextMode` property to `MultiLine`, its `Columns` property to 40, and its `Rows` property to 5.
3. False. ASP.NET web controls are rendered differently depending on whether the page is visited by an uplevel or downlevel browser. Downlevel browsers will not render many of the aesthetic settings of the TextBox Web control.
4. The `Text` property.
5. The Label Web control shares a number of properties with the TextBox Web control. For example, both have a `Text` property, the same set of aesthetic

properties, the `ID` property, and so on. In fact, as we'll see throughout the remainder of the book, *all* Web controls share a base set of properties.

6. Password text boxes cannot have their `Text` property programmatically set, nor do they continue their values across postbacks. The reason is that doing so would serve as a security risk because a nefarious user could simply examine the HTML received by the browser to determine the user's password.

Exercises

1. For this exercise we'll create an ASP.NET web page that prompts the user for two integers and then computes and displays the integers' greatest common divisor. (The greatest common divisor of two integers `a` and `b`, commonly denoted `gcd(a,b)`, is the largest number that divides both `a` and `b` without a remainder. For example, `gcd(49, 21)` is 7.)

Because the user will need to provide two integers, you'll need two TextBox Web controls. Set the `ID` property of the first Web control to `a`, and the second to `b`. You'll also need to add a Button Web control, as well as a Label Web control. Set the `ID` property of the Label Web control to `results`.

As with the BMI calculator example from the preceding hour, you'll need to create an event handler for the Button Web control's `Click` event. This event handler will need to compute the greatest common divisor of the values entered into the `a` and `b` TextBox Web controls.

The greatest common divisor of two integers can be quickly computed using the Euclidean Algorithm. If you are not familiar with the details of this algorithm, don't worry, the needed source code is as follows:

```
'Assign the maximum of a and b to x and the minimum to y
If a.Text < b.Text then
  x = b.Text
  y = a.Text
Else
  x = a.Text
  y = b.Text
End If

'Compute the remainder of x / y
z = x mod y
While z <> 0
  x = y
  y = z

  z = x mod y
End While

gcd = y
```

For more information on the Euclidean Algorithm, check out http://en.wikipedia.org/wiki/Euclidean_algorithm.

2. Given two integers a and b, their least common multiple, commonly denoted `lcm(a,b)`, is the smallest integer that is a multiple of both a and b. For example, the least common multiple of 6 and 4 is 12 because 12 is both a multiple of 6 (6 times 2) and 4 (4 times 3) and is the smallest such multiple. For this exercise, create an ASP.NET web page that accepts two integer inputs from the user and computes the least common multiple.

   Fortunately, computing the least common multiple of two numbers is quite simple after you compute the greatest common divisor of the two numbers. Specifically,

   ```
   lcm(a,b) = (a * b) / gcd(a,b)
   ```

   Therefore, for this exercise you should create a function named `GCD` that takes in two integer inputs and returns an integer value. You can cut and paste the greatest common divisor code that you entered in for exercise 1.

   As with the previous exercise, be sure to include two TextBox Web controls, a Button Web control, and a Label Web control. The Button Web control's `Click` event handler should compute the least common multiple of the two integers entered by the user using the `GCD()` function.

HOUR 11

Collecting Input Using Drop-down Lists, Radio Buttons, and Check Boxes

In this hour, we will cover

- Ideal times for using Web controls other than the TextBox Web control
- Adding DropDownList Web controls to an ASP.NET web page
- Programmatically accessing a selected value and text from a DropDownList Web control
- Using the RadioButton Web control
- Grouping related RadioButton Web controls
- Using the CheckBox Web control
- Programmatically determining whether a particular CheckBox Web control is checked

In the preceding hour we saw how to collect user information through the TextBox Web control. Often, though, the text box is not the most suitable means for collecting a particular piece of input. For example, imagine that you wanted to create a web page where the user answered a bunch of yes/no questions. Would it make sense to use a TextBox Web control for these yes/no questions, making the user type in the words "Yes" or "No"?

Fortunately, there are alternative Web controls for collecting user input, such as the DropDownList Web control, the RadioButton Web control, and the CheckBox Web control. We will examine these three Web controls in this hour.

Examining the Different Types of User Input Classifications

So far we have seen only one Web control that is used to gather user input, the TextBox Web control. As we have seen in the examples thus far in the book, the TextBox Web control presents users with a text box into which they can type their input. For example, in the monthly mortgage cost calculator in Hour 4, "Designing, Creating, and Testing ASP.NET Pages," the user inputted the amount, duration, and interest rate of a mortgage to determine its monthly cost. In the BMI Calculator in Hour 9, "Web Form Basics," the user supplied his height and weight in text boxes. Additionally, there was a plethora of TextBox Web control examples in the preceding hour.

Text boxes, however, are not the only means by which user input can be collected. As we will see in this hour, other input collection Web controls include the DropDownList Web control, the CheckBox Web control, and the RadioButton Web control. The DropDownList Web control presents users with a list of options, from which they may choose one. The CheckBox Web control presents users with a box that can be ticked or cleared to indicate a yes or no type answer. The RadioButton Web control presents users with a single, selectable option. Typically, a series of RadioButton controls are used, each displaying a single option from which the visitor can select only one of the available choices.

Given that there are a number of Web controls designed to collect user input, you may be wondering when you should use a TextBox Web control versus an alternative Web control. The type of Web control should be determined by the kind of input that is being collected.

The input collected from users can be classified into various types. The following classifications group input in terms of their restrictiveness, from the most restrictive form of input, to the least:

1. Yes/No input
2. Input selected from a finite list of acceptable choices
3. General text input

The first classification, Yes/No input, is input that can be inputted in only one of two ways. For example, an online survey may ask you for your gender, which can be only one of two values, Male or Female.

A slightly more general input classification is input selected from a list of acceptable choices. If you live in the United States and are filling out your address on an online form, the state you live in can be selected from a finite list of the 50 states. Another example of input that falls into this category is a list of shipping options that an eCommerce site might provide for you to select from.

General text input is the most lax of the three categories. Input that falls into this category includes filling in your name and address on an online form or entering your message on an online messageboard site.

Using an Appropriate Web Control

When collecting user input, you must decide what Web control to use. For example, if you are asking users to specify their gender, you could use a TextBox Web control, asking users to type in whether they are Male or Female. However, this approach lends itself to user error. A visitor may misspell `Female` or type in `Woman` instead. A less error-prone approach would be to use a DropDownList Web control with two options: Male or Female.

Other Yes/No inputs work well with check boxes. For example, many websites require you to create an account to access certain portions of the site. When filling in the account information, you will typically find a check box labeled something like Send Me the Site Newsletter or Keep Me Abreast of New Products from Your Company.

In this same account creation page, users may be prompted to specify how they learned about the website. Rather than requiring users to type in an explanation, many websites will provide a drop-down list that contains a number of potential choices, such as Read About It in Print, Heard About It from a Friend, and so on. A series of radio buttons would also work here.

Did you Know?

When you're prompting the user to select one choice from a series of acceptable answers, either a drop-down list or a series of radio buttons will suffice. If there are many available options to pick from, however, a list of radio buttons can become cumbersome and take up valuable screen real estate. A good rule of thumb is to stick with the drop-down list when presenting more than five options. For five or fewer options, either a series of radio buttons or a drop-down list will get the job done.

Input that falls into the general text input category, such as a person's name or mailing address, must be entered via TextBox Web controls.

The point of this discussion is to highlight that there are different classes of user input, and different Web controls work best with different classes of user input. Keep this in mind while you're learning about the DropDownList, CheckBox, and RadioButton Web controls in this hour.

Table 11.1 summarizes the classifications of user input and what types of Web controls work best.

TABLE 11.1 Choose an Appropriate Web Control Based on the Data Being Collected

Class of User Input	Description	Web Control(s) to Use
Yes/No	The user can select only one of two potential values.	DropDownList, CheckBox, or two RadioButtons
One selection from a list of acceptable answers	The user must select one option from a finite list of acceptable options.	DropDownList or a series of RadioButtons
General text	The user can provide text input in any form.	TextBox

Examining the DropDownList Web Control

For certain forms of input, users must select precisely one option from a list of suitable choices. For example, a software company might want to create a support site where users can find answers to common questions about the company's various software products. When a user is searching for an answer to his question, it would be helpful if, along with searching for certain keywords, he could select what particular software product he was having trouble with.

In such a scenario, a suitable Web control for collecting this bit of input would be a DropDownList Web control. The DropDownList Web control creates a drop-down list of one to many options from which the user can choose.

Figure 11.1 shows an example of a drop-down list in an HTML web page.

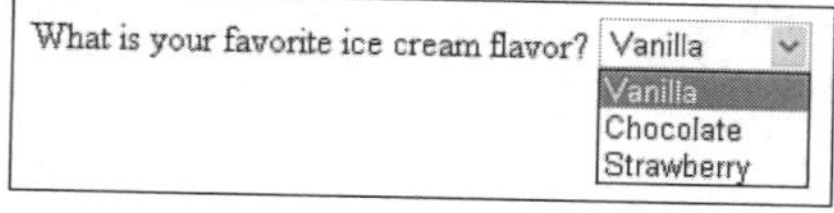

FIGURE 11.1 With a drop-down list, the user can select one option from a list of options.

Adding Options to the DropDownList Web Control

When using the DropDownList Web control, you must specify the drop-down list's various **list items**. The list items are the legal choices that the user can select from. Each individual option in the list of choices is a list item. There are two ways to specify a DropDownList Web control's list items. This first method, which we'll be examining in this hour, is to enter the list items by typing them in, one after another. This approach works well if you know in advance what list items the user should be presented with. For example, if you are using a DropDownList Web control to present the user with a list of the 50 states in the United States, this method is sufficient.

Imagine, however, that you wanted to populate the choices shown in the DropDownList Web control based on some external input. An online banking website, for example, might allow customers to have more than one account, such as a savings account, a checking account, a money market account, and so on. Some customers may have just a checking account, whereas others may have checking and savings accounts.

When the user first logs on to the website, you might want to have the user select which of her accounts (assuming she has multiple accounts) she wants to start working with. These options could be presented in a DropDownList Web control. However, the accounts shown depend on what accounts the customer has opened with the bank. So the list items in the DropDownList Web control will depend on the user's accounts with the bank. Therefore, the list items shown in the DropDownList Web control depend on external input—namely, the accounts that the user has opened with the bank.

To handle situations like this, you can store the list items in a database. Then, when using the DropDownList Web control, you can indicate that the list items to be displayed in the drop-down list should come from the database. We'll examine this mode of specifying list items in Hour 17, "Working with Data-Bound DropDownLists, RadioButtons, and CheckBoxes."

Adding a DropDownList Web Control to an ASP.NET Web Page

To demonstrate using a DropDownList Web control and adding list items to it, let's create a new ASP.NET page named `DropDownList.aspx`. Within the Web Form, type in the text `What is your favorite ice cream flavor?`. After this text, drag and drop a DropDownList Web control from the Toolbox.

> Be certain that you add a DropDownList Web control to the ASP.NET web page, not a ListBox Web control. The DropDownList Web control allows the user to select precisely one list item from a list of acceptable ones. The ListBox Web control, on the other hand, allows the user to select zero or more list items. (We will not cover the ListBox Web control in this book.)

Next, add a Button Web control beneath the DropDownList Web control. After you have typed in the text prior to the DropDownList Web control and have added both the DropDownList and Button Web controls, your screen should look similar to Figure 11.2.

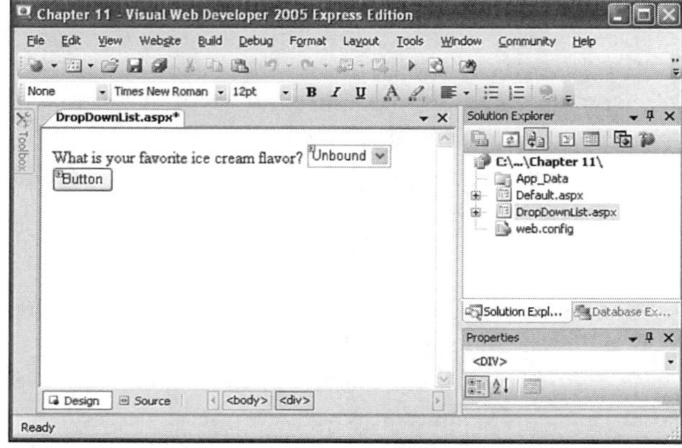

FIGURE 11.2 A DropDownList Web control and Button Web control have been added to the designer.

At this point we've yet to add any list items to the DropDownList Web control. If you view the ASP.NET web page through a browser at this point, you'll be presented with an empty drop-down list, as shown in Figure 11.3.

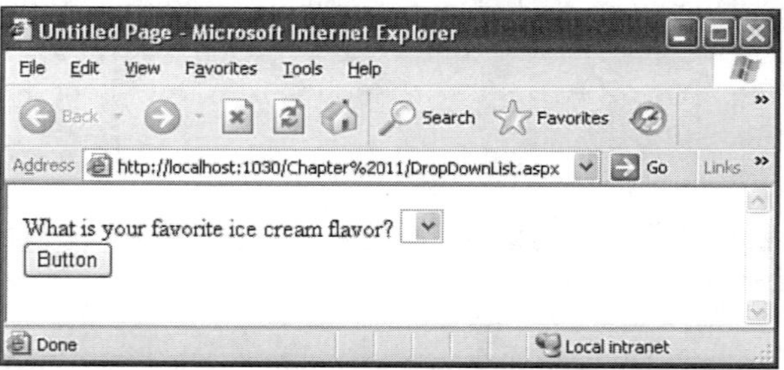

FIGURE 11.3 The drop-down list is empty; it contains no items for the user to choose from.

The `Items` property of the DropDownList Web control contains the list items that appear in the DropDownList Web control. So, to add list items to the DropDownList Web control, we will need to edit this property. Start by clicking on the DropDownList Web control so that its properties are loaded in the Properties window. Next, scroll down to the `Items` property. You should see that the property value currently reads `(Collection)`. If you click this property value, a button with a pair of ellipses will appear to the right of `(Collection)` (see Figure 11.4).

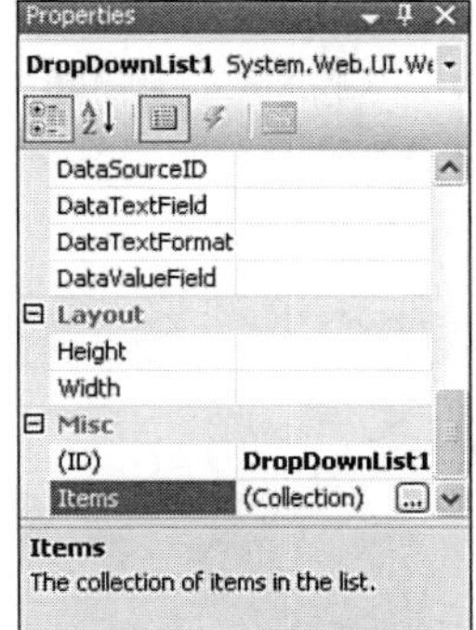

FIGURE 11.4 Clicking on the `Items` property reveals a button with a pair of ellipses.

Go ahead and click this button; when you do so, a ListItem Collection Editor dialog box will appear. This dialog box, shown in Figure 11.5, allows you to add and remove list items from the DropDownList Web control.

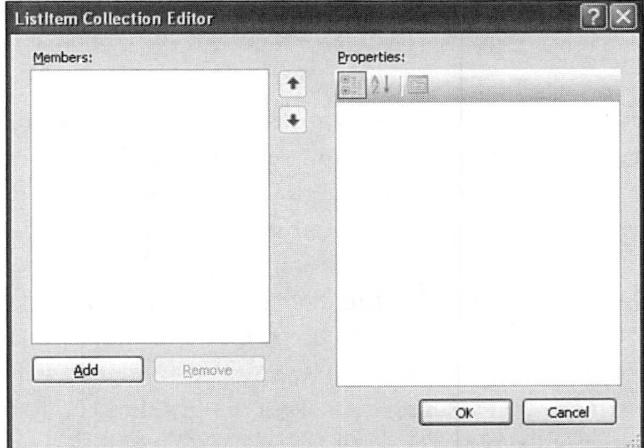

FIGURE 11.5 The ListItem Collection Editor dialog box allows you to manage the options for a DropDownList Web control.

Because users will be using our web page to specify their favorite ice cream flavor, let's add a couple of ice cream flavors as list items. To add a new list item, click the Add button.

After you click the Add button, a new entry is added to the left text box in the ListItem Collection Editor dialog box. On the right side, the properties of the newly added list item are displayed. As Figure 11.6 shows, list items have four properties: `Enabled`, `Selected`, `Text`, and `Value`.

The first property, `Enabled`, expects a Boolean value (either `True` or `False`). `Enabled` indicates whether the particular list item is present in the rendered drop-down list.

That is, if you have a DropDownList Web control with three list items—Vanilla, Chocolate, and Strawberry—and set Chocolate's `Enabled` property to `False`, the drop-down list in the user's browser would have only two items—Vanilla and Strawberry.

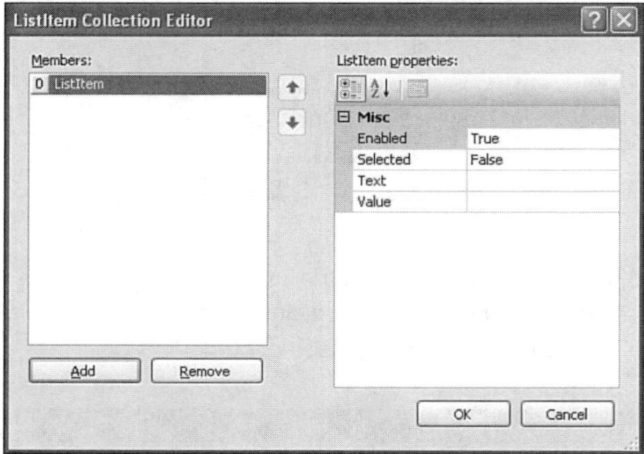

FIGURE 11.6 After you have added a new list item, you can specify its properties.

The second property, `Selected`, also expects a Boolean value, and indicates if the list item is the item that is selected by default when the web page loads. To elaborate, realize that there may be many list items in a drop-down list, and because only one item is shown at a time, the `Selected` property specifies what list item is selected when the web page is first loaded. For example, when we're visiting the ASP.NET page with our DropDownList Web control that contains the list items Vanilla, Chocolate, and Strawberry, the drop-down list will, by default, show the first option—Vanilla. However, what if you want the Strawberry option to be the selected item, by default? One option is simply to make it the first list item. Another option is to set its `Selected` property to `True`.

The `Text` and `Value` properties expect string values. The `Text` property is the text that is displayed to the user in the drop-down list. For our flavors of ice cream, we'd want the `Text` property to be Vanilla for the first list item, Chocolate for the second, and Strawberry for the third. The `Value` property, on the other hand, is not seen by the user. It serves as a means to pass along additional information with each list item that you may not want the user to see.

By the Way

> The `Value` property is typically used when displaying list items from a database. In this hour we won't examine the `Value` property further; instead, we will be setting only the `Text` property.

Now that you understand the roles of the three list item properties, go ahead and set the `Text` property for the list item just added to `Vanilla`. Next, add another list item and set its `Text` property to `Chocolate`. Finally, add a third list item and set its `Text` property to `Strawberry`.

By the Way

For the three list items added, you don't need to set the `Value` properties. If you don't specify a `Value` property for the list item, the ListItem Collection Editor will automatically set the `Value` property to the same value as the `Text` property.

After you have added the three list items, the ListItem Collection Editor should look similar to the one shown in Figure 11.7.

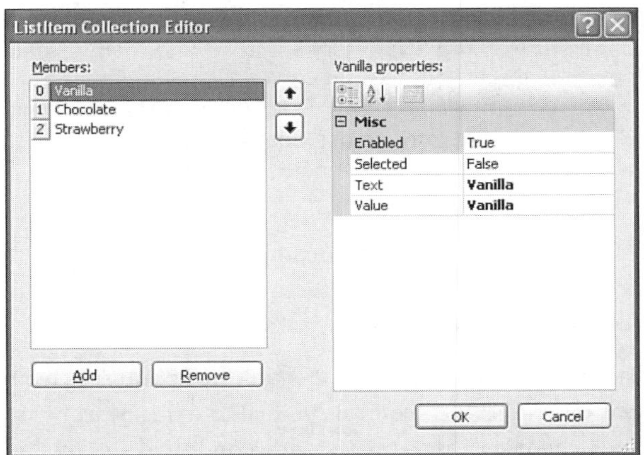

FIGURE 11.7 Three list items have been added.

Did you Know?

You can rearrange the order of the list items through the ListItem Collection Editor. To do so, click the list item in the left text box whose position you want to alter. Then click the up and down arrows in the middle of the ListItem Collection Editor dialog box to move that particular list item up or down with respect to the other list items.

Finally, click OK on the ListItem Collection Editor dialog box. Note that the DropDownList Web control in the designer has changed such that it shows the word `Vanilla` as its selected list item.

Now let's take a moment to check out our progress by visiting `DropDownList.aspx` through a browser (see Figure 11.8). Note that all three ice cream flavors, which weren't present before we added the three list items via the ListItem Collection Editor, are now listed. (Refer to Figure 11.3 to see the output prior to adding list items.)

FIGURE 11.8 The web page presents the user with the three ice cream flavor options.

By the Way

When you're visiting the `DropDownList.aspx` web page, if you choose a list item from the drop-down list (say the Strawberry list item) and then submit the form by clicking on the button, the ASP.NET web page will be posted back and the Strawberry item will remain selected. This indicates that the DropDownList Web control continues the selected item across postbacks, just like the TextBox Web control continues its `Text` property value across postbacks.

To have the ASP.NET web page take some action when the form is submitted, we need to provide code in the ASP.NET page's source code portion. Specifically, we must add some code to the Button Web control's `Click` event handler.

For now, let's just have the web page output equal the option selected by the user, placing the output in a Label Web control. To facilitate this, start by adding a Label Web control to the `DropDownList.aspx` web page and then specify the Label Web control's `ID` property as `results`. Also, clear out the `Text` property.

Let's also take a moment to specify some properties for our other Web controls. Set the Button Web control's `ID` property to `btnSubmit` and its `Text` property to `Click Me`. Then set the DropDownList Web control's `ID` property to `flavors`.

Next, double-click the Button Web control. This will, as you know, add an event handler for the Button's `Click` event. In this event handler we need to provide code that will set the `results` Label Web control's `Text` property to some message that indicates what option the user just selected. This can be accomplished with the following line of code:

```
results.Text = "You like " & flavors.SelectedItem.Text
```

As this source code illustrates, the DropDownList Web control's selected list item can be accessed using

```
DropDownListID.SelectedItem
```

Recall that each list item has the properties `Enabled`, `Selected`, `Text`, and `Value`. So, to retrieve the `Text` property, we use

```
DropDownListID.SelectedItem.Text
```

If we wanted to get the `Value` property, we could use

```
DropDownListID.SelectedItem.Value
```

By the Way

> In addition to the `Enabled`, `Selected`, `Text`, and `Value` properties of the DropDownList Web control's `SelectedItem` property, you may have noticed a fifth, additional property: `Attributes`. You can use this property, which is not accessible through the ListItem Collection Editor dialog box, to set HTML attributes in the markup rendered by the DropDownList Web control. This property is rarely needed in practice, so we won't invest any more time discussing it.

After you have added the needed source code to the Button Web control's `Click` event handler, go ahead and view the ASP.NET web page through a browser. When the page loads up, select a particular flavor and click the Click Me button. This will cause the form to be posted back. Upon the ASP.NET web page's reloading, you should see the message `"You like` *`flavor`*`"` (where *`flavor`* is the ice cream flavor you selected from the drop-down list).

Figure 11.9 shows `DropDownList.aspx` after the Strawberry flavor has been selected and the Click Me button has been clicked.

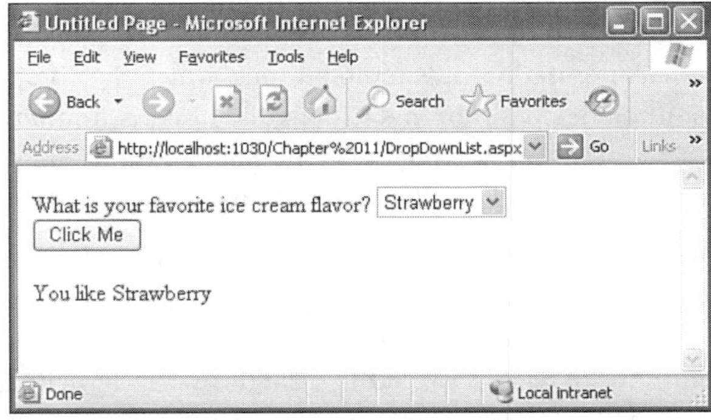

FIGURE 11.9 The web page presents the user with the three ice cream flavor options.

The DropDownList Web Control's Aesthetic Properties

Along with the `Items` property, the DropDownList Web control has a number of aesthetic properties. These aesthetic properties are the same as the aesthetic properties for the Label and TextBox Web controls and are listed in Table 11.2 for reference. As with the Label and TextBox Web controls, these aesthetic properties are specified in the same manner.

TABLE 11.2 The Aesthetic Properties of the DropDownList Web Control

Property	Description
`BackColor`	Specifies the background color of the drop-down list.
`Font`	Specifies the font properties for the text entered by the user into the drop-down list. Recall that the `Font` property has a number of subproperties, such as `Name`, `Size`, `Bold`, and so on.
`ForeColor`	Specifies the color of the text in the drop-down list.

You may have noticed that Table 11.2 is missing some of the aesthetic properties examined in earlier chapters, namely the border-related properties. Although these are, technically, properties of the DropDownList Web control, you won't find them in the Properties window in Visual Web Developer.

Most browsers do not render border-related CSS settings for drop-downs.

Selecting One Option from a List of Suitable Choices with RadioButton Web Controls

Another way of collecting user input is radio buttons, which, like drop-down lists, are suited for choosing one option from a list of valid options. You have probably seen and used radio buttons on web pages before. Radio buttons are small circles that, when selected, have a black circle displayed within them. See Figure 11.10.

Radio buttons can be grouped into a series of related radio buttons. Given a related group of radio buttons, only one of the radio buttons from the group can be selected at a time. That means, if there are three related radio buttons and the first one is selected, the second cannot be selected; if the second is selected, neither the first nor third one can be selected; and so on. Another way to put it is that related radio buttons are **mutually exclusive**.

To create a radio button in an ASP.NET web page, we use the RadioButton Web control. The RadioButton Web control, when rendered, produces the HTML for creating a single radio button. Therefore, if we want the user to select one option from a list of, say, three, we must use three RadioButton Web controls.

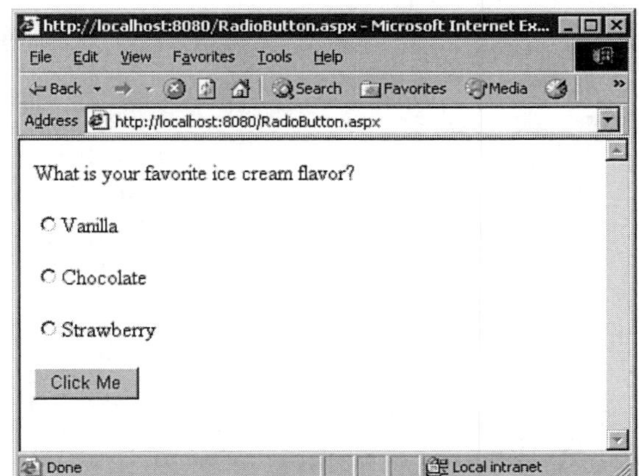

FIGURE 11.10
Radio buttons allow the user to select one option from a list of options.

Let's create a new ASP.NET web page named `RadioButton.aspx` and examine how to use the RadioButton Web control. The `RadioButton.aspx` page will be similar in functionality to the `DropDownList.aspx` page; that is, the users will be asked to provide their favorite ice cream flavor.

After you create the new ASP.NET web page, go ahead and type into the designer the text `What is your favorite ice cream flavor?`. Beneath this text, drag and drop a RadioButton Web control onto the designer. A radio button and the RadioButton Web control's `ID` property (in brackets) will be displayed in the designer.

By the Way

> In the Toolbox you may have noticed that beneath the RadioButton Web control there is a RadioButtonList Web control. The RadioButtonList Web control is used when the options for the radio buttons are stored in a database. We'll examine using the RadioButtonList Web control in Hour 17.

Figure 11.11 shows the designer after the first RadioButton Web control has been added.

Now change the `ID` property of the RadioButton Web control just added from the default `RadioButton1` to `vanilla`. Next, add two more RadioButton Web controls, each one beneath the other, and set their `ID` properties to `chocolate` and `strawberry`, respectively. Finally, add a Button Web control after all three RadioButton Web controls. Set the Button Web control's `ID` property to `btnSubmit` and its `Text` property to `Click Me`.

Figure 11.12 shows the Visual Web Developer after these additional two RadioButton Web controls and the Button Web control have been added.

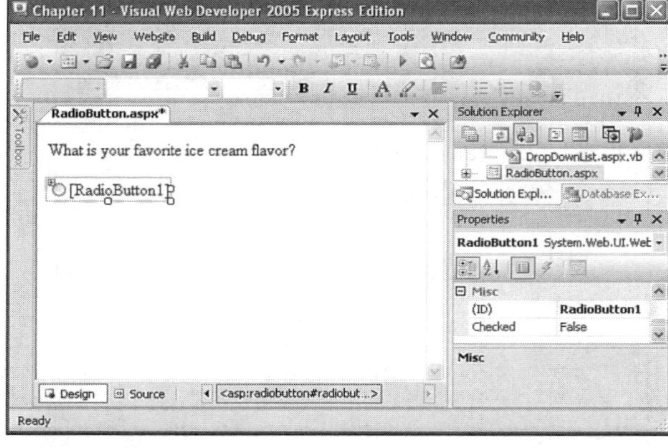

FIGURE 11.11 A RadioButton Web control has been added to `RadioButton.aspx`.

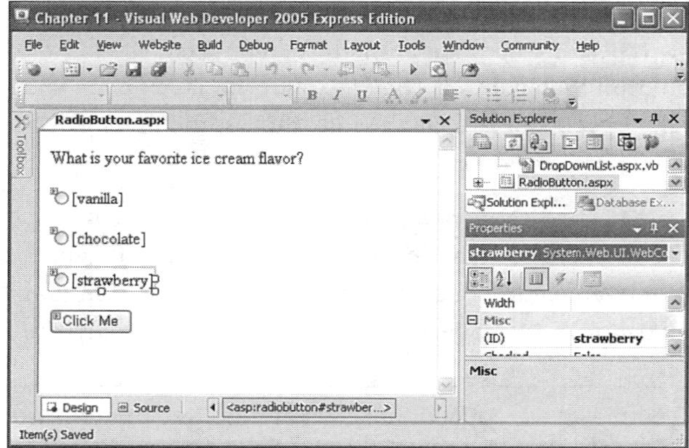

FIGURE 11.12 The `RadioButton.aspx` page now contains three RadioButton Web controls and a Button Web control.

Take a moment to view the `RadioButton.aspx` ASP.NET web page through a browser. As you do this, take note of two things. First, there are only three radio buttons and no text explaining what each radio button represents. Second, you can select more than one radio button. (To see this, click the first radio button and then click the second—*both* radio buttons will be selected.) Figure 11.13 shows the `RadioButton.aspx` web page when viewed through a browser, highlighting these two issues.

Using the `Text` and `GroupName` Properties

Notice that for each RadioButton Web control, you must add some text explaining what choice the resulting radio button represents. To accomplish this, simply set the RadioButton Web control's `Text` property to the appropriate text. For the

RadioButton.aspx web page, set the first RadioButton Web control's Text property to Vanilla, the second's to Chocolate, and the third's to Strawberry. When you do this, your screen should look similar to Figure 11.14.

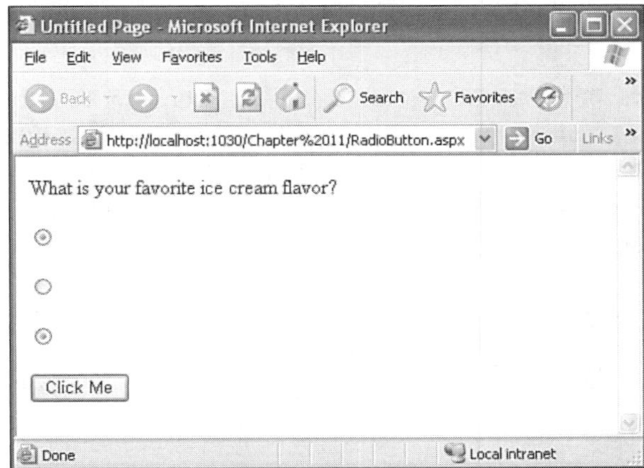

FIGURE 11.13 There is no text explaining what each radio button represents, and multiple radio buttons can be selected.

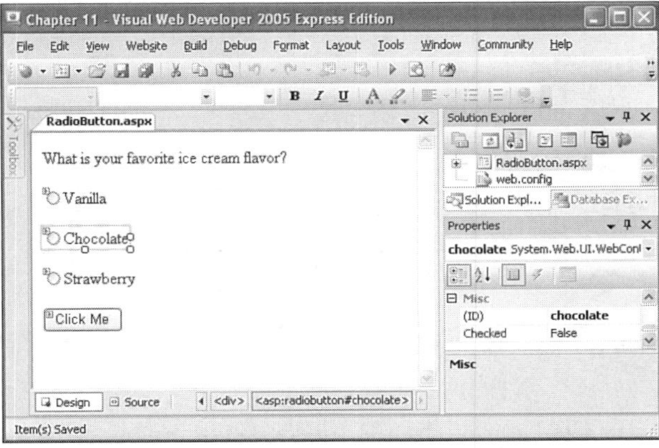

FIGURE 11.14 Text has been added next to each RadioButton Web control.

Now we need to be able to group the three RadioButton Web controls so that the user can select *only one* option from the three. The RadioButton Web control contains a string property named GroupName. Those RadioButton Web controls on a web page that have the same value for their GroupName properties are considered to be related. Therefore, to make the three RadioButton Web controls related (so that the user can select only one flavor of the three), set the GroupName property for the three RadioButton Web controls to the value flavors.

What value you set the GroupName property to doesn't matter; what is important is that all related RadioButton Web controls have the same GroupName value. That is, we could have set the GroupName property of all three RadioButton Web controls to ScottMitchell, and the result—the user now being able to select only one of the three radio buttons—would be the same.

Let's view the RadioButton.aspx web page through a browser now that we've specified the Text and GroupName properties for each of the three RadioButton Web controls. Figure 11.15 shows the web page when visited through a browser. Note that the three radio buttons are mutually exclusive; that is, only one radio button from the three can be selected at a time.

FIGURE 11.15 The radio buttons have text explaining what they represent now.

Determining What RadioButton Web Control Was Selected

Allowing the user to select a radio button from a list of radio button options is only half of the battle in collecting user input. The other half is determining what option the user selected in our ASP.NET web page's source code portion. Each RadioButton Web control has a Checked property, which returns True if the RadioButton Web control's resulting radio button is selected, and False if not.

Therefore, to determine if the vanilla RadioButton Web control was selected, we can use an If statement like this:

```
If vanilla.Checked then
  'The vanilla radio button was selected.
End If
```

Imagine that we simply wanted to display the flavor the user chose using a Label Web control, much like we did with the DropDownList Web control example earlier in this hour. The first step would be to add a Label Web control after the Button Web control. After adding the Label Web control, clear out its `Text` property and set its `ID` property to `results`.

The code for setting the `results` Label Web control's `Text` property needs to appear in the Button Web control's `Click` event handler. Add the code shown in Listing 11.1 to the `Click` event handler.

LISTING 11.1 **The Code for the Button's `Click` Event Handler**

```
1:  If vanilla.Checked then
2:    results.Text = "You like Vanilla"
3:  ElseIf chocolate.Checked Then
4:    results.Text = "You like Chocolate"
5:  ElseIf strawberry.Checked Then
6:    results.Text = "You like Strawberry"
7:  End If
```

The code in Listing 11.1 starts by checking to see if the first RadioButton Web control, `vanilla`, was selected (line 1). If it was (that is, if `vanilla.Checked` is `True`), then the `results` Label Web control has its `Text` property set to `You like Vanilla` on line 2. Similarly, if `chocolate` was the selected RadioButton Web control, then the `results` Label Web control's `Text` property is set to `You like Chocolate` (lines 3 and 4). Finally, if the `strawberry` RadioButton Web control is checked, `You like Strawberry` is displayed (lines 5 and 6).

Realize that all three conditionals—`vanilla.Checked`, `chocolate.Checked`, and `strawberry.Checked`—may be `False`. This case occurs if the user does not select a radio button before clicking the Click Me button.

A Look at the Aesthetic Properties

Just like the DropDownList, TextBox, and Label Web controls, the RadioButton Web control has the same aesthetic properties. As you may have already guessed, *all* Web controls contain these aesthetic properties. (For this reason I won't mention those aesthetic properties in Table 11.2 when discussing future Web controls.)

By the Way

Recall that the DropDownList Web control lacks the border-related aesthetic properties. The RadioButton, on the other hand, does have these border-related properties (`BorderColor`, `BorderStyle`, and `BorderWidth`).

Using the CheckBox Web Control

In the "Examining the Different Types of User Input Classifications" section at the beginning of this hour, we examined three different classes of user input. The most restrictive class of user input was the Yes/No input class, which is Boolean input. That is, input in the Yes/No input classification is input that can be answered in only one of two ways. The check box is an ideal candidate for collecting user input that falls into this category. The check box, as you've no doubt seen in use before, is a square box that can be checked or unchecked.

Check boxes can also be used for presenting a list of options from which the user can select multiple choices. For example, in our previous two examples—`DropDownList.aspx` and `RadioButton.aspx`—users can select only one flavor of ice cream as their favorite. If we use three check boxes, however, users can select zero, one, two, or three of the options.

The CheckBox Web control is used to add a check box to an ASP.NET web page. Like the RadioButton Web control, a single CheckBox Web control displays a single check box, so to create a page with three check boxes, for example, we must add three CheckBox Web controls.

Let's create an ASP.NET page to demonstrate using the CheckBox Web control. Start by creating a new page named `CheckBox.aspx`. This web page will be similar to the previous two examples in that we will be prompting the users for their favorite ice cream flavors. With the check boxes, however, the users will be able to choose more than one flavor, if they so desire.

After you have created the new ASP.NET page, type in the text `What are your favorite ice cream flavors?`. After this text, drag and drop three CheckBox Web controls from the Toolbox onto the designer, one after another. After the three CheckBox Web controls, place a Button Web control. Let's go ahead and also add a Label Web control after the button.

By the Way

> In the Toolbox you may have noticed that, beneath the CheckBox Web control, there is a CheckBoxList Web control. The CheckBoxList Web control produces a list of check boxes from data found in a database. We'll examine using the CheckBoxList in Hour 17.

Now let's set the properties for the Web controls we just added. First, clear the Label Web control's `Text` property and set its `ID` to `results`. Next, click the Button Web control and set its `Text` property to `Click Me` and its `ID` property to `btnSubmit`. For the three CheckBox Web controls, specify their `Text` and `ID` properties just like we did for the three RadioButton Web controls in our previous example. That is, set the first CheckBox Web control's `Text` property to `Vanilla` and its `ID` to `vanilla`; set the second CheckBox Web control's `Text` property to `Chocolate`; and so on.

After you have set these Web controls' properties, your screen should look similar to Figure 11.16.

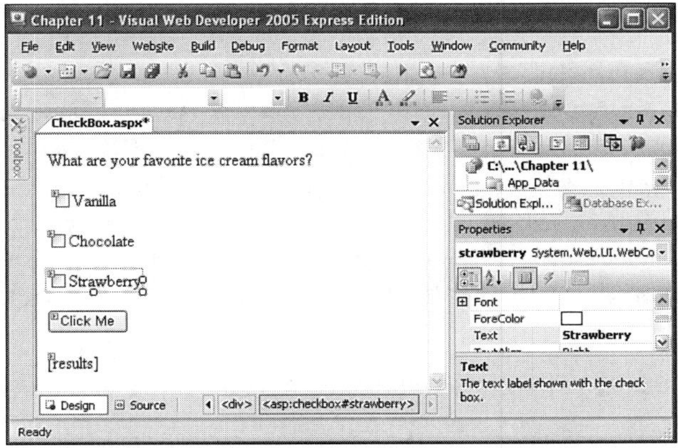

FIGURE 11.16 The ASP.NET web page has three CheckBox Web controls.

Take a moment to view the `CheckBox.aspx` web page through a browser. In Figure 11.17 you can see that the page lists three check boxes and that more than one of the three check boxes can be checked.

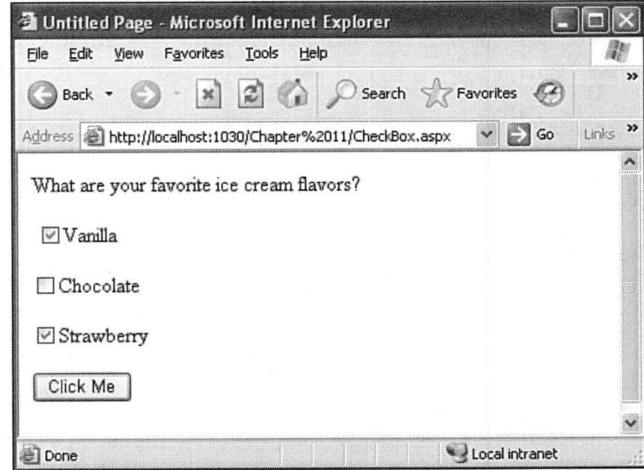

FIGURE 11.17 The user can select zero to three ice cream flavors.

Determining What Check Boxes Have Been Checked

To determine what CheckBox Web controls have been checked, we use the same syntax as with the RadioButton Web controls, which returns either a `True` or `False` value, namely:

```
CheckBoxID.Checked
```

So, to determine if the `vanilla` check box is checked, the following code will suffice:

```
If vanilla.Checked then
  'The vanilla CheckBox is checked
End If
```

Let's add an event handler for the Button Web control's `Click` event, in which we'll add code that lists what check boxes the user checked. You may be tempted to use the same code that was used in Listing 11.1 for the RadioButton Web controls example. However, if you look back over Listing 11.1, you will see that on lines 3 and 5 `ElseIf` statements are used, which means the conditional statements following them will be evaluated only if the previous conditional statement was `False`. To put it another way, line 3 in Listing 11.1 will be evaluated only if the condition on line 1—`vanilla.Checked`—is `False`.

Therefore, the code in Listing 11.1 will display only the name of the ice cream flavor that it first finds selected. This is not a problem for the RadioButton Web control example because the user can select only one of the three radio buttons. However, with this CheckBox Web control example, we'll need to allow for multiple ice cream flavors to be listed in the Label Web control because multiple ice cream flavors may be selected.

Listing 11.2 contains the source code needed.

LISTING 11.2 The User's Ice Cream Preferences Are Displayed

```
 1:   'Clear out the value of the results Text property
 2:   results.Text = ""
 3:
 4:   If vanilla.Checked then
 5:     results.Text &= "You like Vanilla."
 6:   End If
 7:
 8:   If chocolate.Checked then
 9:     results.Text &= "You like Chocolate."
10:   End If
11:
12:   If strawberry.Checked then
13:     results.Text &= "You like Strawberry."
14:   End If
```

The first thing that happens in Listing 11.2 is that the `Text` value of the `results` Label Web control is cleared out (line 2). Next, on lines 4, 8, and 12, the `Checked` property is examined for each of the three CheckBox Web controls. If the check box is checked, an appropriate message is concatenated with the current value of the `results` Label Web control's `Text` property.

For example, on line 8, the `chocolate.Checked` property is examined. If this property returns `True`, this means that the Chocolate check box has been selected, and line 9 is executed. On line 9, the `results` Label Web control's `Text` property has its current value concatenated with the string `"You like Chocolate."`.

By the Way

Recall from Hour 5, "Understanding Visual Basic's Variables and Operators," that the &= operator takes the value of the variable on its left side, concatenates it with the expression on the right side, and then assigns the resulting concatenated value to the left-side variable. That is, the following two statements are equivalent:

```
Variable = Variable & "Some string"
```

and

```
Variable &= "Some string"
```

We concatenate the current value of the Label Web control's `Text` property with our message instead of just assigning our message to the Label Web control's `Text` property because we do not want to overwrite the Label Web control's property. Why? Because if the Vanilla check box is checked, it will add the message `You like Vanilla.` to the Label Web control.

Figure 11.18 shows the `CheckBox.aspx` web page when visited through a browser and after the user has selected multiple check box choices and submitted the form. Note that all of the user's checked choices are listed in the Label Web control at the bottom of the web page.

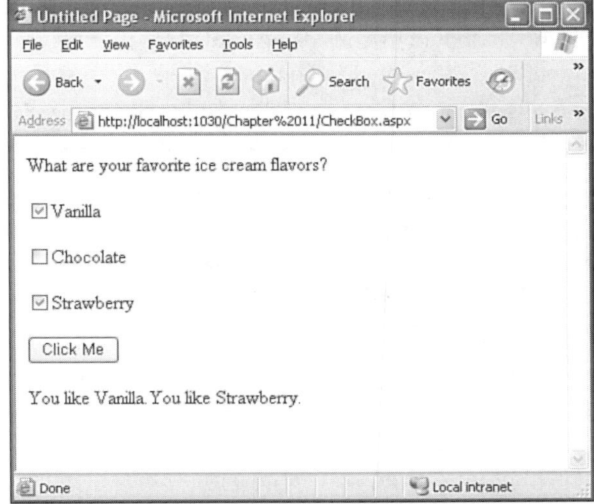

FIGURE 11.18
Users can select multiple ice cream flavors as their favorites.

Summary

In this hour we examined three Web controls commonly used to collect user input: the DropDownList, RadioButton, and CheckBox Web controls. These Web controls are typically used when the user's input is restricted to either a subset of available options or just one of two options.

For example, if the user is asked to specify the time zone he lives in, a DropDownList Web control could be used that contains the various time zones in the world, from which the user can choose one. Another example is when a user is asked a yes/no question, which is common in online surveys. For such a question, a CheckBox Web control can be used.

In examining the DropDownList Web control, we saw that it has a number of list items, which are the options from which the user can select one. When adding a DropDownList Web control to an ASP.NET web page, we need to explicitly specify those list items that should appear in the drop-down list. Fortunately, this is a simple task through Visual Web Developer's ListItem Collection Editor dialog box (refer to Figure 11.5). In the ASP.NET source code portion, the list item that was selected can be determined by the DropDownList Web control's `SelectedItem` property.

Like drop-down lists, radio buttons allow the user to select one option from a series of options. Specifically, a radio button is needed for each option, and these radio buttons must be made mutually exclusive with one another so that the user can select only one radio button from the group of related radio buttons.

The RadioButton Web control creates a single radio button. To denote that multiple RadioButton Web controls should be considered related (so that the user can select only one radio button from the related radio buttons), we use the `GroupName` property. We can use the RadioButton Web control's `Checked` property to determine whether the user selected a particular RadioButton Web control's corresponding radio button.

With radio buttons and drop-down lists, the user can choose only one option from a list of options. A list of check boxes, however, permits the user to choose multiple options. To create a check box, we use the CheckBox Web control. Like the RadioButton, the CheckBox Web control has a `Checked` property that indicates whether the check box was selected.

Now that we've examined the Web controls for collecting user input, we're ready to learn how to ensure that the input entered is valid. Typically, when we're collecting user input, the input must be of a certain format or within certain constraints. For example, if users are prompted to enter their age, the value entered should be numeric and within an acceptable range (say 0 to 110). In the next hour we'll examine ASP.NET's validation Web controls, which are Web controls designed to validate input data.

Q&A

Q. ***If I use a DropDownList or series of RadioButton Web controls to let the user choose one option from, say, 50 legal choices, does this mean I have to enter in all 50 choices by hand?***

A. With what you know now, the answer is yes. In Hour 17, "Working with Data-Bound DropDownLists, RadioButtons, and CheckBoxes," we will examine how to populate the DropDownList Web control with data from a database. Furthermore, we will see how to create a series of radio buttons or check boxes from database data using the RadioButtonList and CheckBoxList Web control.

Q. ***I have created a DropDownList with 10 list items on an ASP.NET web page. Now, I want to provide this exact same DropDownList Web control on a different ASP.NET web page. Obviously, I can accomplish this by creating a new DropDownList web control on the second page and reentering the 10 options by hand. Is there any easier or quicker way?***

A. If you want to copy a DropDownList Web control and all of its list items from one ASP.NET web page to another, start by loading up both ASP.NET web pages. On the ASP.NET page that contains the DropDownList Web control, go to the Source view and find the DropDownList Web control in the ASP.NET page's HTML section. This will contain Web control markup like

```
<asp:DropDownList id="DropDownListID" runat="server">
    <asp:ListItem Value="Value1">Text1</asp:ListItem>
    <asp:ListItem Value="Value2">Text2</asp:ListItem>
    ...
    <asp:ListItem Value="ValueN">TextN</asp:ListItem>
</asp:DropDownList>
```

Note that for each list item in the DropDownList, there will be an `<asp:ListItem>`. Copy all of the DropDownList Web control syntax and then paste it into the Source view of the ASP.NET page that you want to add the same DropDownList to.

Using this technique, you will not have to reenter all of the DropDownList options by hand in the second ASP.NET page.

Q. ***When I'm displaying a series of radio buttons, none of the radio buttons are selected by default. This means that a user can simply not pick one of the options. What if I want to require that a user select one of the radio buttons?***

A. When a radio button in a group of radio buttons is selected, the end user cannot unselect a choice. However, when a user first visits a page, none of the radio buttons are selected. This means a user can simply not choose one of the options in the group by virtue of not clicking on any radio button in the group.

Typically, you want the user to have to select one of the options. To accomplish this, you need to have one of the radio buttons in the group selected by default. To accomplish this, in Visual Web Developer, click on the RadioButton Web control that you want selected by default. This will load its properties in the Properties window. From there, set the RadioButton control's `Checked` property to `True`.

Keep in mind that only *one* of the radio buttons in the group can be selected by default. If you set the `Checked` property to `True` for multiple RadioButton Web controls in the group, the user's browser will select only one such radio button.

Workshop

Quiz

1. Imagine that you wanted to create an online multiple-choice quiz that presented the users with a question that had one correct answer. The users would be asked to choose the correct answer from a list of five. What user input Web control would be best suited for this web page?
2. Imagine that you wanted to have the users specify what time zone they live in. What user input Web controls could be used for this task, and what ones could not be used? What user input Web control would be the *best* option?
3. True or False: The DropDownList Web control can be used to allow the users to select multiple items from a list of available options.
4. Imagine that you wanted to create a web page where users could specify how many countries they've visited from a list of 100 countries. Why would using a series of CheckBox Web control make sense here?
5. For the example in Question 4, precisely how many CheckBox Web controls would you need to add to the ASP.NET page?
6. What CheckBox Web control property specifies whether a check box was checked?
7. What is the major difference between a series of RadioButton Web controls and a series of CheckBox Web controls?
8. If you wanted to add five RadioButton Web controls to an ASP.NET web page such that users could select only one of the five resulting radio buttons, what property of each of the RadioButtons would you need to set?

Answers

1. Because users can select precisely one option from a list of options, either a DropDownList Web control or a series of RadioButton Web controls would suffice. The best choice would likely be a series of RadioButton controls because virtually all existing online quizzes use radio buttons for the quiz user interface.

2. This information could be provided via a text box, a series of radio buttons, or a drop-down list. A series of check boxes would not be suitable since a single user cannot live in multiple time zones. The best user input Web control for the job, though, would likely be either a series of RadioButtons or the DropDownList because the user is restricted to choosing one option from a list of possible options.

3. False. The DropDownList Web control allows users to select only *one* item from a list of items.

4. A series of CheckBox Web controls would allow users to select more than one option. Had we opted to use, say, RadioButton Web controls, the users would be able to select only *one* country from the list of 100.

5. A CheckBox Web control would need to be added for each option. Because there are 100 countries from which the users can select, there would need to be 100 CheckBox Web controls on the ASP.NET page.

6. The `Checked` property indicates whether a CheckBox Web control has been checked.

7. The RadioButton Web control is designed to allow users to choose precisely one option from a list of available options. The CheckBox Web control, on the other hand, is designed so that users can choose zero or more options. Therefore, a series of RadioButton Web controls would restrict users to selecting just one option from the array of options, whereas a series of CheckBox Web controls would allow users the flexibility to choose many of the available options.

8. RadioButton Web controls are grouped via the `GroupName` property. That is, each RadioButton Web control that has the same value for its `GroupName` is considered "grouped," and users can select only *one* radio button from the group. Therefore, to have five grouped radio buttons, each of the five RadioButton Web controls would need to have its `GroupName` property set to the same value.

Exercises

1. The book you have in your hands is my sixth book on ASP and ASP.NET. As a shameless plug for my other books, please create an ASP.NET page that allows the user to indicate what other books of mine she has read. That is, create five CheckBox Web controls, each with its `Text` property set to the title of one of my five other books. In case for some odd reason you are not familiar with my other books, the five titles are (1) *Sams Teach Yourself Active Server Pages 3.0 in 21 Days;* (2) *Designing Active Server Pages;* (3) *ASP.NET: Tips, Tutorials, and Code;* (4) *ASP.NET Data Web Controls;* and (5) *Sams Teach Yourself ASP.NET in 24 Hours.*

   In addition to creating the five CheckBox Web controls, create a Button Web control and a Label Web control. In the Button Web control's `Click` event handler, count the number of books that the reader has read and emit an appropriate message. If I may so humbly suggest, if the user has read, say, four or more of my books, you might display the message `"You are indeed a wonderful person"`, whereas if the user has yet to read any of my other books, you could emit a message like `"It is absolutely imperative that you go to your nearest bookstore without delay and pick up one (or more) of Scott's books"`.

2. For this exercise, create a short online quiz. Make sure the quiz has at least three questions and that each question has at least three options. Each question should have exactly one correct answer.

   After the questions, there should be a Button Web control that, when clicked, will display the user's score. If you are interested in a more difficult challenge, in addition to displaying the user's score, list next to each *incorrect* question the correct answer.

HOUR 12

Validating User Input with Validation Controls

In this hour, we will cover

- The various classes of input validation
- How to use the RequiredFieldValidator to ensure that the user has provided input
- How to use the CompareValidator
- How to ensure that the user's input falls between a range of values by using the RangeValidator
- How to use the RegularExpressionValidator
- The aesthetic properties of the validation Web controls

As we have examined in previous hours, collecting user input through an ASP.NET page is a relatively easy task. Unfortunately, when we're collecting a user's input, there is no guarantee that he has provided the desired input in an acceptable format. That is, imagine that you are asking the user to specify his weight, much like we did with the BMI calculator a few hours ago. What should happen if, for weight, the user enters something like "Far too much"?

Ensuring that user input is in a proper format is a technique known as **input validation** and is the topic for this hour. If you have had experience with other dynamic web page creation technologies, such as ASP, PHP, or JSP, you likely are more than familiar with input validation. Performing input validation in these older technologies was a real headache.

Fortunately, ASP.NET makes input validation a breeze with the help of **validation controls**, which are Web controls designed to do nothing else but perform input validation. We will examine how to use four validation controls in this hour: the RequiredFieldValidator, the CompareValidator, the RangeValidator, and the RegularExpressionValidator.

Examining the Need for User Input Validation

In the past two hours, we've examined a number of ways to collect user input. In Hour 10, "Using Text Boxes to Collect Input," we saw how to use the TextBox Web control to collect text input; in Hour 11, "Collecting Input Using Drop-Down Lists, Radio Buttons, and Check Boxes," we saw how to use DropDownList, RadioButton, and CheckBox Web controls to collect user input that was restricted to one or more items from a predefined list of items.

Typically, when collecting user input, we want the input to be in a certain format or to conform to some set of guidelines. **Input validation** is the process of ensuring that the data entered by a user is in the proper format and/or meets certain constraints.

For example, imagine that you wanted to collect the following information from a user:

- Name
- Age
- ZIP code

To collect this input, you would probably want to use three TextBox Web controls, one for each of the three inputs. When presented with a text box, clearly users can enter any value they choose. Or users may enter no input at all. That is, when asked to input his age, a user could choose not to enter any value. On the other hand, the user may choose to enter `24`. Or, instead of entering `24`, the user may use an alternative representation for 24, like `twenty-four`. Or, the user might enter something nonsensical, like `I am a Jisun`.

More likely than not, we would want the age entered as a number because a number is less ambiguous than a string. (That is, 24 is unambiguous, because it's the only numerical way to specify the value 24; with text, however, 24 can be written as `twenty-four`, `twenty four`, `Twentyfour`, `Twenty Four`, and so on.) Furthermore, a number can be used in mathematical calculations, whereas a string like `"twenty-four"` cannot.

Even if we can ensure that users will enter their age as a number, users can still enter bad input. For example, values like –3,456,354.14159, 750, and 0.576 are valid numbers, but not valid ages.

Types of Input Validation

The validation requirements for age input show that there are different classes of input validation. For example, ensuring that users enter a value for the age input and ensuring that the age is entered as a number are both considered forms of input validation, but they differ in that the former simply checks to see whether a value is entered, and the latter ensures that the entered data is in a predefined format.

Input validation can be broken down into five distinct classes. Let's take a moment to examine these five classes.

Required Field Input Validation

The first type of input validation is **required field validation**. Required field validation is used to ensure that the user has entered a value for a particular input. For example, when users are filling out shipping information at an eCommerce website, required fields would include the street address, city, state, and ZIP code the package was being shipped to; optional fields might include special shipping instructions.

By the Way

Many websites that allow visitors to sign up to create an account have many required fields that the users must fill out in order to create their account. Typically, these required fields include email address, age, gender, and other such information.

Data Type Validation

For numeric inputs it is often important that the input be entered as a number, not a string. That is, when users are prompted for the year they were born, it is important that they enter the year as four digits, like `1978`, as opposed to a string, like `"Nineteen seventy eight"`.

Humans think in terms of language, whereas computer programs work in terms of data. Data type validation helps ensure that the text entered by the user can be converted into a suitable data format the computer program expects.

Range Input Validation

For certain numeric inputs, it is important that the resulting input fall within a certain range of values. For example, if a user is prompted for her age, we might want to ensure that it's between the values 0 and 150.

Comparison Validation

Another typical input validation for numeric inputs is a comparison validation. For example, if users are asked to enter their salary, we might want to make sure that the number entered is greater than or equal to 0.

Alternatively, we may want to compare the value of one user input with the value of another user input. An example here might be if users are asked to enter their total income for a particular year and then are later asked to enter how much their income tax was for that same year. Clearly, a person's income taxes can't amount to more than her total income. Therefore, we may want to ensure that the number the user entered for a particular year's income tax is less than the number entered for that same year's total income.

Pattern Validation

Certain types of string input must conform to a particular format. For example, if users are asked to enter their phone number, you might want to ensure that they enter it in the following format, where each X is a digit:

```
(XXX) XXX-XXXX
```

Did you Know?

Clearly, there are alternative ways to provide a phone number, such as

```
XXX-XXX-XXXX
```

Typically, though, data that has numerous legal formats should always be recorded in one specific format. This makes it easier to search the data. For example, imagine that you are storing the phone numbers entered by your web visitors. If all phone numbers are required to be entered in the format `(XXX) XXX-XXXX`, it is much easier to search for all phone numbers in, say, a certain area code, than it would be if phone numbers could be entered in a myriad of formats. (The area code is the first three digits of the phone number.)

Validating User Input in an ASP.NET Web Page

In ASP.NET input, validation is performed through the use of—you guessed it—Web controls. The Web controls that perform input validation are commonly called **validation Web controls**, or just **validation controls**.

We'll be examining four kinds of validation controls in this hour, which are summarized in Table 12.1. Each of these Web controls is geared for providing one or more of the input validation classes discussed in the preceding sections.

TABLE 12.1 The ASP.NET Validation Web Controls

Validation Control	Type of Validation	Description
RequiredFieldValidator	Required Field validation	Ensures that data has been entered into a specific input.
CompareValidator	Data type validation and comparison validation	Ensures that a value in one input is less than, less than or equal, equal, greater than, greater than or equal, or not equal to some constant value or some user-inputted value. Can also be used to perform data-type validation.
RangeValidator	Range validation	Ensures that a numeric value in an input is between two constant numeric values.
RegularExpressionValidator	Pattern validation	Ensures that a string value matches some specified pattern.

In the following sections, we will examine each of these validation Web controls in detail. Specifically, we will look at how to add these Web controls to an ASP.NET page, how to specify what user input they are to validate, and how to determine whether the user's input meets the required validation.

After examining each of these four Web controls individually, we will see how to use multiple validation controls on a single ASP.NET page.

An ASP.NET Web Page for Examining the Validation Controls

Before examining how to use these validation controls, let's first create an ASP.NET web page that we can use throughout all of these exercises. Specifically, we will create an ASP.NET page that collects the following information from users:

- **Name**, which is a required field
- **Age**, which is a numeric field that must be between 0 and 150
- **Social Security number (ssn)**, which is a string input with the format `NNN-NN-NNNN`, where `N` is a digit
- **Number of children**, which must be greater than or equal to 0
- **Number of male children**, which must be greater than or equal to 0 and less than or equal to the number of total children the person has

Start by creating a new ASP.NET page named `ValidationControlTestBed.aspx`. Now, let's add five TextBox Web controls for the five user inputs. Before each TextBox, enter a descriptive title, such as `Your name:`, `Your age:`, and `Social-security number:`. Figure 12.1 shows the Visual Web Developer after these five TextBox Web controls and label text have been added.

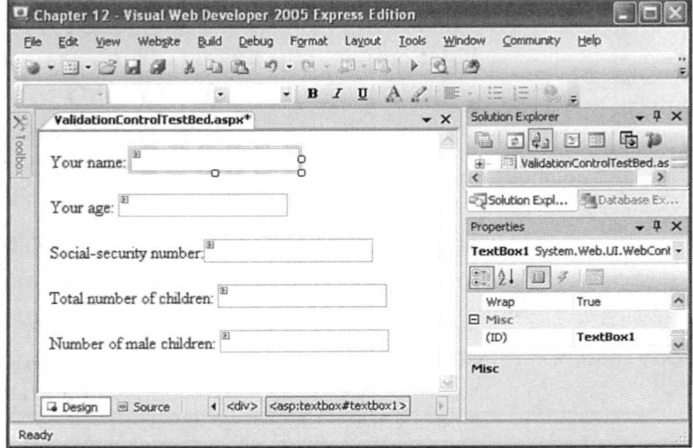

FIGURE 12.1 Five TextBox Web controls have been added, along with a title for each.

Now that we've added the needed TextBox Web controls, let's set the `ID` properties for these TextBox Web controls. Set the first TextBox Web control's `ID` property to `name`; the second's to `age`; the third's to `ssn`; the fourth's to `totalChildren`; and the fifth's to `maleChildren`. For the `age`, `totalChildren`, and `maleChildren` TextBox Web controls, also set the `Columns` property to 4.

Next, add a Button Web control after the five TextBox Web controls. Set this Web control's `ID` property to `btnSubmit` and its `Text` property to `Click Me`. Finally, add a Label Web control with `ID` `results` below the Button Web control.

Your screen should now look similar to Figure 12.2.

At this point, you may want to test the `ValidationControlTestBed.aspx` ASP.NET page (you can see this page in Figure 12.7). When you visit the ASP.NET page via a browser, go ahead and enter some test information into the various text boxes. Naturally, there is no input validation, meaning you can enter nonsensical text into any of these text boxes.

As we will see shortly, with the ASP.NET validation controls, if you enter data that violates the validation control that is assigned to that particular input, a warning will immediately appear.

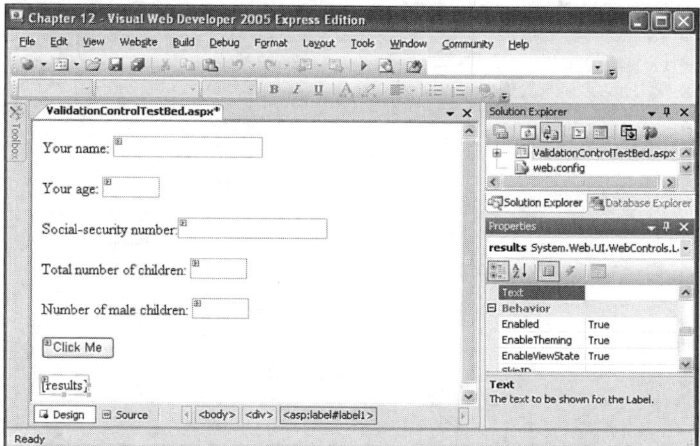

FIGURE 12.2
The TextBox Web controls have had their properties set, and a Button Web control has been added.

Now that we have created the ASP.NET web page to which we will add the various ASP.NET validation controls, we are ready to begin our examination of these controls, starting with the RequiredFieldValidator Web control.

Examining the RequiredFieldValidator Validation Control

When we're prompting a user for input, the input can be divided into two categories: required input and optional input. Required input is the set of input that the user *must* provide, whereas optional input is the set of input that the user may choose to provide or not to provide. To ensure that the user provides a response for a particular input, we can use a RequiredFieldValidator Web control.

To add a RequiredFieldValidator validation Web control to an ASP.NET web page, all that we have to do is drag and drop the control from the Toolbox onto the page, just like we do with any other Web control. Go ahead and drag the RequiredFieldValidator Web control from the Toolbox onto the designer; specifically, place the Web control immediately to the right of the first TextBox Web control.

By the Way

> All of the validation controls are grouped within the Validation section of the Toolbox.

When you drag and drop the RequiredFieldValidator validation control onto the designer, your screen should look similar to Figure 12.3. Although the image in this book doesn't show it, the text `"RequiredFieldValidator"` appears in a red font.

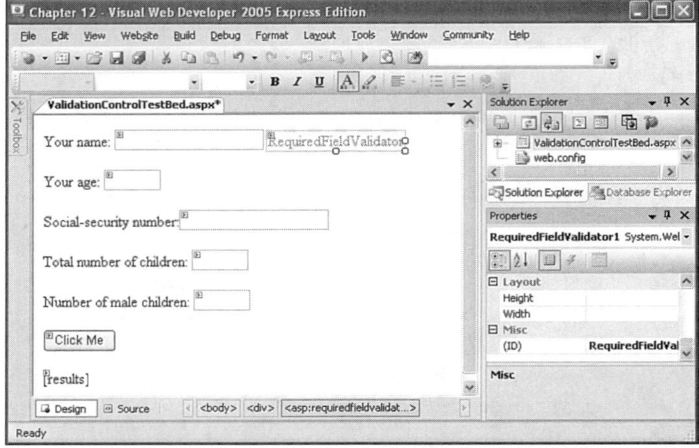

FIGURE 12.3
A RequiredField Validator has been added to the ASP.NET web page.

Specifying What Web Control the Validation Web Control Is Validating

Realize that the validation Web controls are designed to validate input for a particular **input Web control**. By input Web control, I mean a Web control that is used to collect user input, such as the TextBox Web control.

All validation Web controls contain a `ControlToValidate` property, which specifies what input Web control the validation Web control is validating. For example, because we want to require users to provide their name in the `ValidationControlTestBed.aspx` ASP.NET page, we need to add a RequiredFieldValidator and set the RequiredFieldValidator's `ControlToValidate` property to `name`, the `ID` of the Web control that has a required field.

Note that each validation Web control that you add to your ASP.NET page can validate only a single input Web control. Therefore, if in our `ValidationControlTestBed.aspx` ASP.NET web page, we had three required input fields (say name, age, and Social Security number), we would need three RequiredFieldValidator validation controls on the page.

For now, let's assume that the only required field is the `name` input. Therefore, we need to set the `ControlToValidate` property of the RequiredFieldValidator that we just added to the page to `name`. To do this, click on the RequiredFieldValidator, which will load its properties in the Properties window.

Next, click on the `ControlToValidate` property, which will show a drop-down list of the various Web controls on the page (see Figure 12.4). Go ahead and select the `name` option from the list.

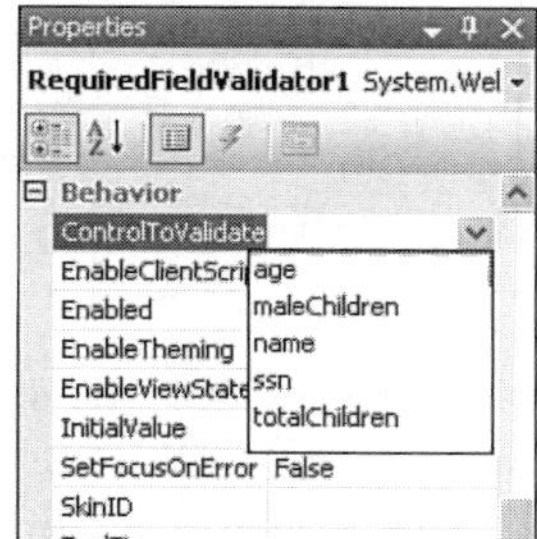

FIGURE 12.4 Select the Web control you want the RequiredFieldValidator to validate.

One important word of warning: If you set the `ControlToValidate` property to a specific Web control and then change that Web control's `ID` property, you will get an error when visiting the ASP.NET page through a browser (see Figure 12.5). The reason is that the validation Web control's `ControlToValidate` property is not automatically updated when the Web control it is to validate has its `ID` property changed. Therefore, if you change a Web control's `ID` property after you have added validation controls to the page, make sure to double-check that the `ControlToValidate` properties for your validation controls map to the correct, current value of the `ID` property of the Web control it is set to validate.

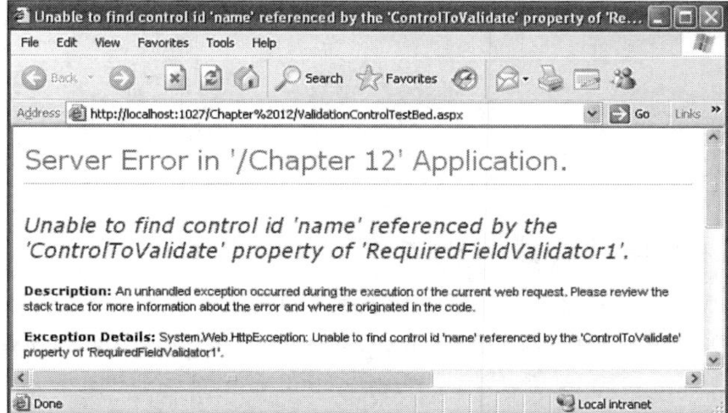

FIGURE 12.5 An error will occur if the validation Web control's `ControlToValidate` property is incorrectly set.

Specifying What Error Message to Display for Invalid Input

Along with a `ControlToValidate` property, all validation Web controls contain an `ErrorMessage` property. This string property contains the text that is displayed when the user's input fails to meet the validation requirements. Typically, this text should provide a brief explanation as to the problem with the user's input and what she needs to do to fix it.

For example, for a RequiredFieldValidator, you might want to set the `ErrorMessage` to `"You must provide a value for input"`, where *`input`* is the name of the input that the user is required to provide. Another common `ErrorMessage` value for RequiredFieldValidators is an asterisk. As you probably know from first-hand experience, many websites place asterisks next to required form fields.

For the `ValidationControlTestBed.aspx` ASP.NET page, go ahead and set the RequiredFieldValidator's `ErrorMessage` to `You must provide your name`. After you enter this value, the text for the RequiredFieldValidator in the designer will change to the new `ErrorMessage` value (see Figure 12.6).

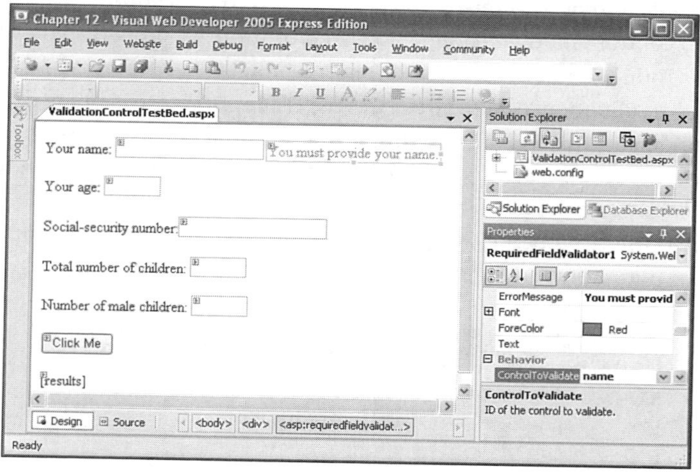

FIGURE 12.6
The designer, after the RequiredField Validator's `ErrorMessage` property has been set.

Testing the ASP.NET Page

Now that we have specified the `ControlToValidate` and `ErrorMessage` properties, the RequiredFieldValidator will inform users if they forget to provide a value for the name text box. To test this, view the `ValidationControlTestBed.aspx` page through a browser. Figure 12.7 shows this web page when first visited.

Note that there is a slight difference in the appearance of the web page when viewed through a browser and when shown in the Design view. Namely, the RequiredFieldValidator is not displayed.

Now, go ahead and click on the Click Me button *without* entering any text into the name text box. What happened? If you are using a browser that supports client-side script (virtually all modern web browsers), clicking the button did not cause the form to be submitted, but instead caused the message `"You must provide your name"` to appear next to the name text box. If you are using a browser that does not support these features (or has them disabled), clicking the button caused the form to submit, but, upon postback, the message `"You must provide your name"` was displayed next to the name text box.

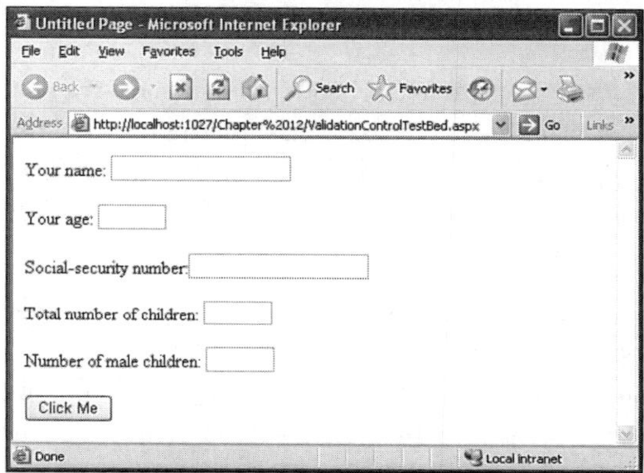

FIGURE 12.7
The `ValidationControlTestBed.aspx` web page, when first visited.

Figure 12.8 shows the `ValidationControlTestBed.aspx` page after the Click Me button has been clicked when there was no input entered into the name text box.

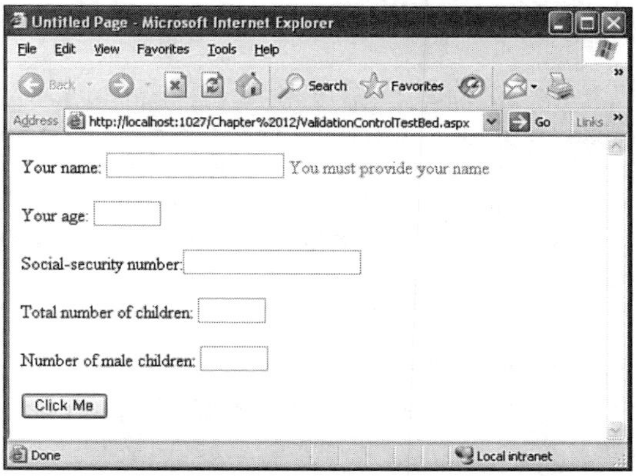

FIGURE 12.8
The message `"You must provide your name"` appears next to the name text box.

Now, enter some text into the name text box. After you have done this, click on a different text box so that some other text box receives the focus. If you are using a browser that supports it, clicking out of the name text box after entering text into the name text box will cause the `"You must provide your name"` message to magically disappear! If you are using a browser that does not support such features, the message will still be present; however, if you submit the form by clicking the Click Me button, upon postback the message will have disappeared.

Client-side and Server-side Validation

What's going on here? Why does the validation error message behave differently depending on what browser is being used? The difference arises due to the fact that validation Web controls include **client-side validation** for browsers that have such capabilities.

Client-side validation involves JavaScript code that runs on the user's web browser. When the user tabs or clicks out of a text box, a piece of JavaScript code that determines whether the input provided is valid is run on the user's web browser; if the data is invalid, the client-side script automatically displays the validation Web control's `ErrorMessage` property value.

Browsers that do not have client-side scripting features or have them disabled, on the other hand, employ just **server-side validation**. Server-side validation, as the name implies, is validation that occurs in code that is executed on the web server. This is the reason why with such a browser the `"You must provide your name"` message does not disappear, even after text has been entered into the name text box, until the user submits the form. For the message to disappear, the ASP.NET page must be posted back, which, as you already know, causes the ASP.NET page to be fetched from the web server again. When this page is requested from the web server, the user's input can be checked there, and it can be determined whether the user's input meets the validation criteria.

By the Way

All validation controls, regardless of what browser is being used, perform server-side validation checks. That means that, for *both* the client-side and server-side, checks are performed for browsers that can support client-side script. Server-side validation is included even when client-side validation is present because client-side validation can be circumvented by simply disabling JavaScript in an uplevel browser.

Client-side validation's main advantage over server-side validation is that it provides immediate feedback to the user without requiring a postback to the web server. This has the advantage of saving the user time, especially if he is on a slow connection, because it does not require a roundtrip to the web server.

By the Way

To learn more about client-side validation, check out the article "Form Validation on the Client Side," at http://www.sitepoint.com/article/form-validation-client-side.

Programmatically Determining Whether the User's Input Is Valid

As we have seen, by simply setting the `ControlToValidate` and `ErrorMessage` properties of the validation Web controls, these controls will automatically alert the user if her input is in an improper format. But how can we determine whether all of the user's input is valid programmatically?

Typically, we will want to process the user's input in some fashion; for example, in previous hours we have seen how to create a mortgage cost calculator and a BMI calculator. In both examples we needed to perform some mathematical computations on the user's input. Of course, we don't want to perform these calculations unless the data entered by the user is valid.

To determine programmatically whether the user's input is valid, we can check the `Page.IsValid` property. The `Page.IsValid` property returns `True` only if *all* validation Web controls on the ASP.NET page have indicated that the input entered into its respective input Web control has been entered in the proper format. Put another way, if any one user's input is not valid, `Page.IsValid` will be `False`.

To demonstrate using this property, let's create an event handler for the Button Web control's `Click` event. Recall that when we create an event handler for the `Click` event, the event handler's code will be executed every time the Web form is posted back. To create an event handler for the `Click` event, simply double-click on the button in the Design view.

Next, enter the following code into the generated `Click` event handler:

```
If Page.IsValid then
  'User input is valid
  results.Text = "Input is valid..."
Else
  'There is at least some invalid input
  results.Text = "Input is <b>not</b> valid..."
End If
```

A quick examination of the code reveals that if the `Page.IsValid` property is `True`, then the string `"Input is valid..."` will be displayed; if there is any invalid input, however, the string `"Input is not valid..."` will be displayed.

This behavior can be seen in Figures 12.9 and 12.10. Figure 12.9 shows the `ValidationControlTestBed.aspx` ASP.NET page when no input has been entered into the name text box and the form has been submitted. Note that the message `"Input is not valid..."` is displayed at the top of the web page. Figure 12.10 shows the same ASP.NET page after the user has entered some value into the name text box and has submitted the form. Here, the message `"Input is valid..."` is displayed.

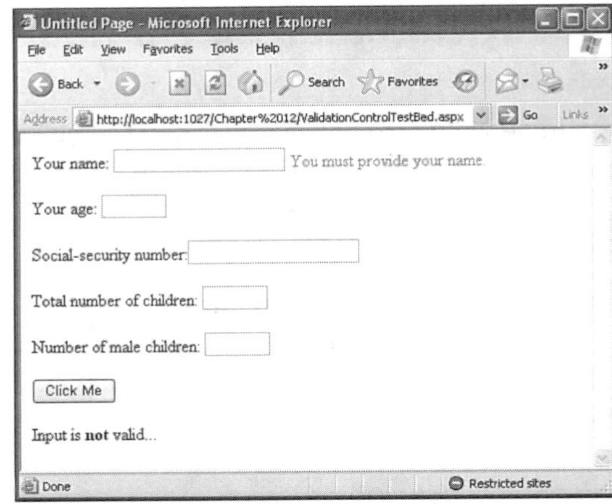

FIGURE 12.9
The form has been submitted with invalid user input.

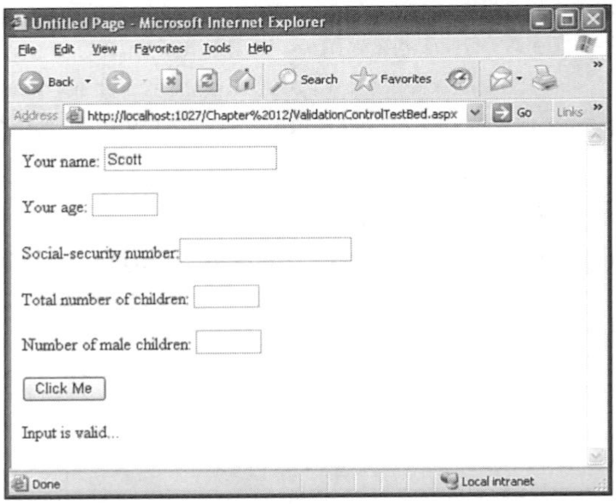

FIGURE 12.10
The form has been submitted, and all of the user input is valid.

If you are visiting the page with a browser that supports client-side script, you will likely not be able to submit the form without entering a value into the name text box. The reason is that the validation controls render client-side validation logic that prevents a postback until the data is valid. Therefore, in browsers that support client-side script, the server-side `Click` event handler won't run until the user enters valid data.

Given the very small percentage of users with browsers that don't support client-side script, you might reason that you need not bother with checking the `Page.IsValid` property in the Button's `Click` event handler. However, you should *always* check to ensure that the page is valid before working with the user-submitted data. A nefarious user can easily circumvent the client-side validation checks. (In creating Figure 12.9, I configured Internet Explorer to treat http://localhost as a Restricted Site;

therefore, it automatically prevented JavaScript from running, allowing me to cause a postback even when I had failed to provide a name.)

To summarize, you should *always* check the results of the server-side validation. Client-side validation, which is provided free in browsers that support it, is simply an added bonus. Regardless of whether your users are visiting with such browsers, be sure to always check the `Page.IsValid` property before working with the data submitted.

Summarizing the Basic Validation Control Features

We started with a discussion of the RequiredFieldValidator and quickly turned to the common properties, features, and semantics of the validation Web controls in general. Before we move on to examining the other validation Web controls, let's take a moment to summarize the common features of validation controls.

First, all validation Web controls are designed to validate a single input Web control. The input Web control a given validation Web control validates is specified via the validation control's `ControlToValidate` property.

All validation controls also contain an `ErrorMessage` property, which specifies the text that is displayed if the input is invalid. The actual validation behaves differently depending on the browser being used by the visitor. If the user has a capable browser, the user's experience is enhanced through the use of client-side validation, as well as server-side validation. For nonsupporting browsers, however, only server-side validation occurs.

Finally, to determine programmatically whether the input entered by a user is valid, we can refer to the `Page.IsValid` property.

Examining the CompareValidator

The CompareValidator validation control is useful for comparing the value of a user's input to a constant value or to the value of a different user input. For example, on the `ValidationControlTestBed.aspx` ASP.NET web page, the last two inputs, which ask users for the total number of children they have and the number of male children, are prime candidates for the CompareValidator.

The input that prompts users for their total number of children, for example, must be a value that is greater than or equal to 0. The input for the number of male children must be both greater than or equal to 0 and less than or equal to the value the user entered into the total number of children text box.

Let's first provide this validation check for the total number of children input. Start by dragging and dropping a CompareValidator from the Toolbox onto the designer, placing the CompareValidator immediately after the `totalChildren` TextBox Web control, as shown in Figure 12.11.

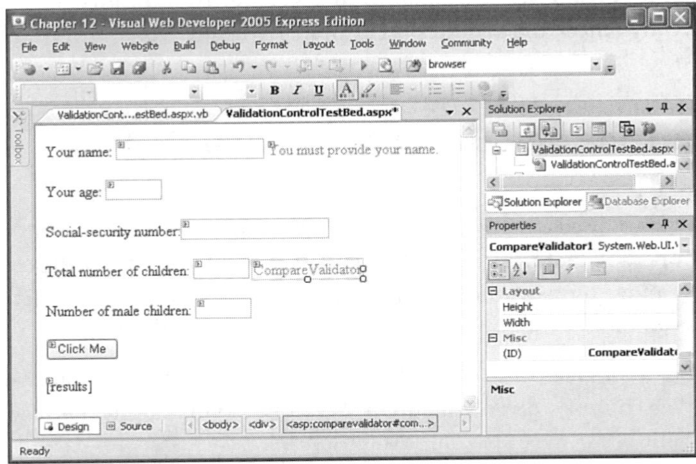

FIGURE 12.11 A Compare Validator Web control has been added.

The CompareValidator is capable of performing a number of comparisons. For example, the CompareValidator can compare an input to ensure that it's less than some value, greater than or equal to a value, or not equal to some value. The `Operator` property specifies what comparison the CompareValidator should perform.

To set the `Operator` property, click on the CompareValidator whose property you want to set; this will load the CompareValidator's properties in the Properties pane. Scroll down to the `Operator` property. When you click on this property, a drop-down list box will appear that shows the valid settings for this property. Specifically, the `Operator` property can be set to one of the following comparisons:

- `Equal`
- `NotEqual`
- `GreaterThan`
- `GreaterThanEqual`
- `LessThan`
- `LessThanEqual`
- `DataTypeCheck`

Because we want to ensure that the number of total children entered by users is greater than or equal to 0, we will set the `Operator` property to `GreaterThanEqual`.

By the Way

If you select the `Operator` choice `DataTypeCheck`, the CompareValidator will be considered valid only if the associated input Web control's contents are of the specified data type. The `DataTypeCheck Operator` is useful when you want to ensure a value of the right data type, such as a Date, but you don't care about the value especially (such as requiring that the Date be after January 1, 2005).

In addition to the `Operator` property, we need to set the `Type` property. The `Type` property indicates what data type users' input should be provided in. The `Type` property, which can be accessed via the Properties pane just like the `Operator` property, can be set to one of the following data types:

- `String`
- `Integer`
- `Double`
- `Date`
- `Currency`

Because we want the user to enter the total number of children input as a numeric value without a decimal, set the `Type` property to `Integer`.

At this point we have specified what comparison should be performed and what data type the user's input should appear as. We must now specify the value we want to compare the user's input to. The value to compare the user's input to can be either a constant value or the value entered by the user in some other input.

Because we want to ensure that the user's input is greater than or equal to 0, the comparison is being performed against a constant value, namely 0. To specify this, set the CompareValidator's `ValueToCompare` property to 0.

After we set this property, all that remains is to set the `ControlToValidate` and `ErrorMessage` properties. Because the CompareValidator is validating the user's input for the `totalChildren` TextBox Web control, set the `ControlToValidate` property to `totalChildren`. Then set the `ErrorMessage` property to a descriptive message, such as `The total number of children must be a whole number greater than or equal to 0`.

After you have set all of these properties, your screen should look similar to Figure 12.12.

At this point we can test the functionality of the CompareValidator by visiting the `ValidationControlTestBed.aspx` page through a browser. If you enter invalid input into the total number of children text box, you will get the error message `"The total number of children must be a whole number greater than or equal to 0"`, as in Figure 12.13.

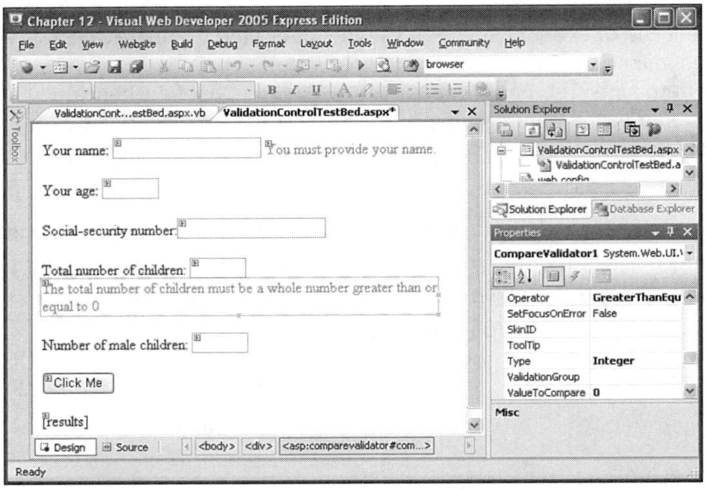

FIGURE 12.12
The Compare Validator will ensure that the input is greater than or equal to 0.

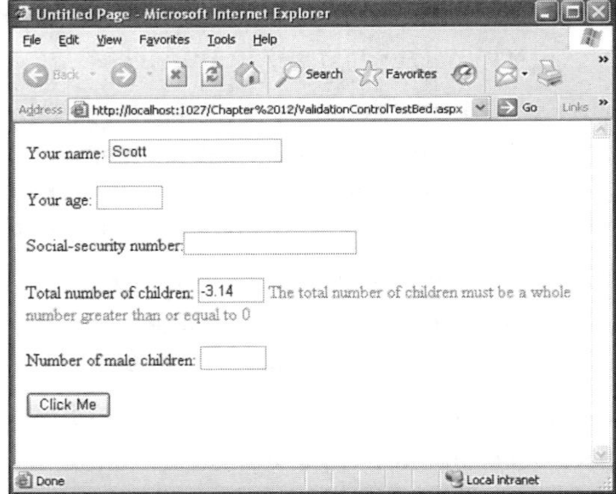

FIGURE 12.13
Invalid input produces an appropriate error message.

Invalid input is input that is not an integer and not greater than or equal to 0. Some examples of invalid input are

- Scott
- –4
- 3,456 (the presence of the comma makes this an illegal input)
- 3.14159

Some examples of legal input include

- 0
- 2
- 3456
- 45533

Did you Know?

> Putting an upper bound on the total number of children input might make sense. For example, we can safely assume that no one will have more than 50 children. To place such an upper bound, we could add an additional CompareValidator and set its `Operator` property to `LessThanEqual` and its `ValueToCompare` property to 50.
>
> Alternatively, instead of having to use two CompareValidators, we could use a single RangeValidator. In the next section we will examine the RangeValidator Web control.

One very important point is that the end user can omit a value for the total number of children input. That is, if the user enters a value into the name text box but enters no value into the total number of children text box and clicks the Click Me button, the ASP.NET page will post back and display the `"Input is valid..."` message.

The lesson to take away from this is that only the RequiredFieldValidator ensures that input is provided. That is, if you also want to require that the user enter a value into the total number of children input, you must add a RequiredFieldValidator for this input as well as a CompareValidator. (In the next section we will see how to have multiple validation controls validating a single input Web control.)

Using the CompareValidator to Compare One Input to Another

In the preceding example we used a CompareValidator to compare the total number of children input with a constant value—0. In addition to comparing the value of a user input with a constant value, CompareValidators can also be used to compare the value of a user input with the value of another user input. For example, the value entered into the number of male children input must be less than or equal to the value the user entered into the total number of children input.

The only difference between a CompareValidator that performs a comparison against a constant value and one that performs a comparison against the value in another input is that in the former case the CompareValidator's `ValueToCompare` property is set to the constant value to compare the user's input to. In the latter case, instead of setting the `ValueToCompare` property, we set the `ControlToCompare` property, specifying the `ID` property of the input Web control whose value we want to compare.

To add a CompareValidator that ensures that the value entered into the number of male children input is less than or equal to the total number of children input, start by dragging and dropping a CompareValidator from the Toolbox onto the designer, placing the CompareValidator after the `maleChildren` TextBox Web control. Next, set the CompareValidator's `ControlToValidate` property to `maleChildren`, its `Operator` to `LessThanEqual`, its `Type` to `Integer`, its `ErrorMessage` to `The number of male children must be less than or equal to the number of total children`, and its `ControlToCompare` property to `totalChildren`.

After you have set these five properties, your screen should look similar to Figure 12.14.

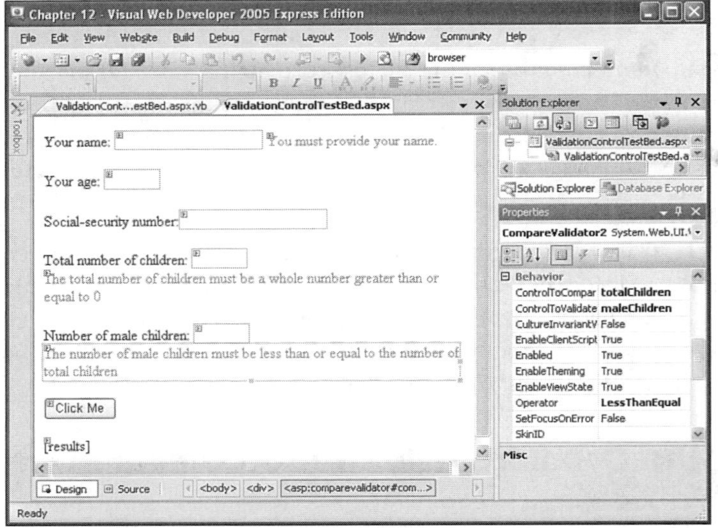

FIGURE 12.14 A Compare Validator has been added after the `totalChildren` TextBox Web control.

Now take a moment to visit the ASP.NET page through a browser. If you enter a value of, say, 4 into the total number of children text box and a value of 8 into the number of male children text box, you will be shown the error message `"The number of male children must be less than or equal to the number of total children"`. Similarly, if you enter a noninteger value into the number of male children text box (such as `"Scott"` or 4.5), you will get the same error message.

What, though, will happen if you enter a value of 5 into the total number of children text box and a value of –2 into the number of male children text box? No error message is displayed because –2 is less than 5, and –2 is an integer.

To protect against this, we must do what we did for the total number of children input: add a CompareValidator that checks to ensure that the value entered into the number of male children input is greater than or equal to 0.

To provide this additional validation, we need to add an additional CompareValidator. To accomplish this, drag and drop another CompareValidator, placing it after the `maleChildren` TextBox Web control's existing CompareValidator. Next, set this CompareValidator's `ControlToValidate` property to `maleChildren`, its `Type` property to `Integer`, its `Operator` property to `GreaterThanEqual`, its `ErrorMessage` property to `The number of male children must be greater than or equal to 0`, and its `ValueToCompare` property to `0`.

Figure 12.15 shows the Visual Web Developer after this CompareValidator has been added and its properties have been set.

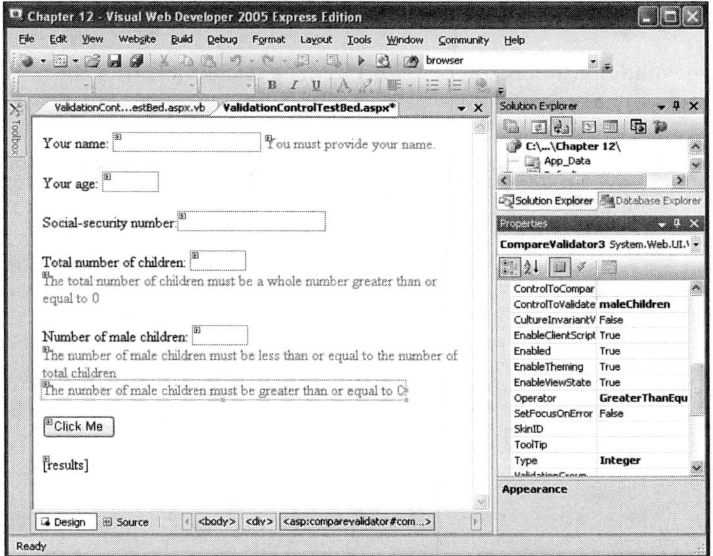

FIGURE 12.15 An additional CompareValidator has been added to help validate the number of male children input.

With this additional CompareValidator, an error message is displayed on the ASP.NET page if the user enters a negative value for the number of male children input.

Using the RangeValidator

As we saw in the preceding section, the CompareValidator can be used to ensure that an input maintains some relation with either a constant value or the value in another user input. However, what if we wanted to ensure that an input was between a range of values? If we were to use the CompareValidator, we'd need to use two CompareValidators, one that did a `GreaterThanEqual` comparison on the lower bound of the range and one that did a `LessThanEqual` comparison on the upper bound of the range.

If the upper and lower bound of the range are constant values, we can use a single RangeValidator instead of using two CompareValidators. For the `ValidationControlTestBed.aspx` ASP.NET page, the age input is a suitable candidate for a RangeValidator because the input must fall within a sensible range (such as 0–150).

By the Way

> The RangeValidator can be used only when *both* the upper and lower bounds of the range are constant values. Therefore, a RangeValidator could not be used for the number of male children input because the upper bound of the range is the value the user entered in the total number of children text box.

Add a RangeValidator immediately following the `age` TextBox Web control, as shown in Figure 12.16.

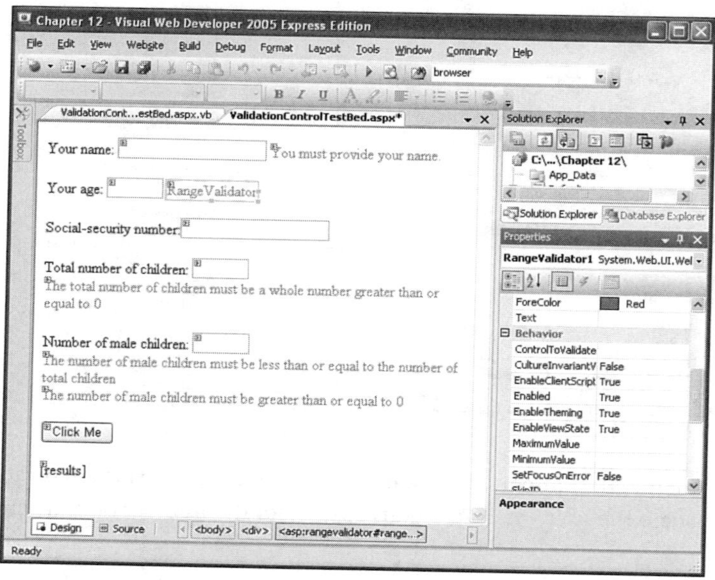

FIGURE 12.16 A Range Validator has been added to the ASP.NET page.

As with all validation controls, we need to set the `ControlToValidate` and `ErrorMessage` properties. Because we want to validate the input from the `age` TextBox Web control, set the `ControlToValidate` property to `age`. Set the `ErrorMessage` property to `Age must be between 0 and 150`.

The RangeValidator, like the CompareValidator, has a `Type` property that specifies the data type the input must be provided in. Because we want the user to enter his age as a number without decimals, set the `Type` property to `Integer`.

All that remains is to specify the upper and lower bound of the acceptable range of values for the age input. The RangeValidator's `MaximumValue` and `MinimumValue` properties specify the upper and lower bound, respectively. Because we want to enforce that the user enters an age between 0 and 150, set the `MaximumValue` property to 150 and the `MinimumValue` property to 0.

After you have set these properties, your screen should look similar to Figure 12.17.

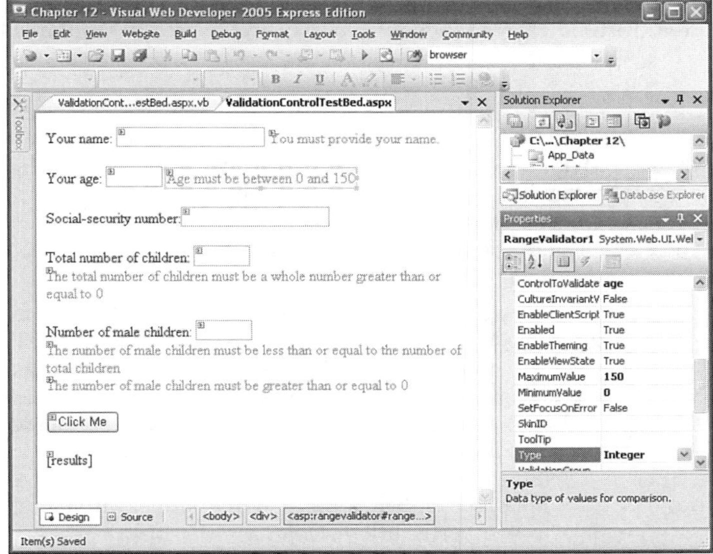

FIGURE 12.17 The properties of the Range Validator have been set.

If you take a moment to view the `ValidationControlTestBed.aspx` ASP.NET page through a browser, you can see that an error message is displayed unless either no input is provided into the age text box or the input provided is an integer value between 0 and 150.

Validating Input with the RegularExpressionValidator

Many forms of user input must be entered in a certain format. For example, when we're asking a user for her email address, the provided email address must follow this particular format: one to many alphanumeric characters; the at symbol (`@`);

one to many alphanumeric characters; period; top-level domain name, such as com, net, org, edu, us, uk, fr, and so on.

For the `ValidationControlTestBed.aspx` ASP.NET web page, users are asked for their Social Security number. In the United States, all citizens are given a Social Security number, which contains nine digits and is typically written in the form

```
XXX-XX-XXXX
```

To ensure that a string input meets some specified format, we can use a RegularExpressionValidator. The RegularExpressionValidator uses **regular expressions** to determine whether the user's input matches the accepted pattern. A regular expression is a string that contains characters and special symbols and specifies a general pattern. Fortunately, you do not need to be well versed in regular expression syntax to be able to use the RegularExpressionValidator.

By the Way

> Regular expressions are commonly used in a number of program domains and are definitely worth learning. However, an extensive examination of the topic is far beyond the scope of this book, especially because Visual Web Developer provides a number of built-in regular expression patterns that you can use in the RegularExpressionValidator without knowing a thing about regular expression syntax.
>
> If you are interested in learning about regular expressions, I encourage you to read "An Introduction to Regular Expressions" at http://www.4guysfromrolla.com/webtech/090199-1.shtml and "Common Applications of Regular Expressions" at http://www.4guysfromrolla.com/webtech/120400-1.shtml. There's also an extensive regular expression repository and community at http://www.regexlib.com/.

To ensure that the Social Security number is inputted in a proper format, let's add a RegularExpressionValidator Web control to the ASP.NET page. Drag and drop this Web control from the Toolbox onto the designer, placing it immediately after the `ssn` TextBox Web control, as shown in Figure 12.18.

Set the RegularExpressionValidator's `ControlToValidate` property to `ssn` and its `ErrorMessage` property to `Your social security number must be in the format XXX-XX-XXXX`. After you set these two properties, the only other property you need to specify is the `ValidationExpression` property, which specifies the regular expression pattern that the user's input must conform to.

To edit this property, click on the `ValidationExpression` property; to the right you will see a pair of ellipses. Clicking on these ellipses will display the Regular Expression Editor dialog box (see Figure 12.19).

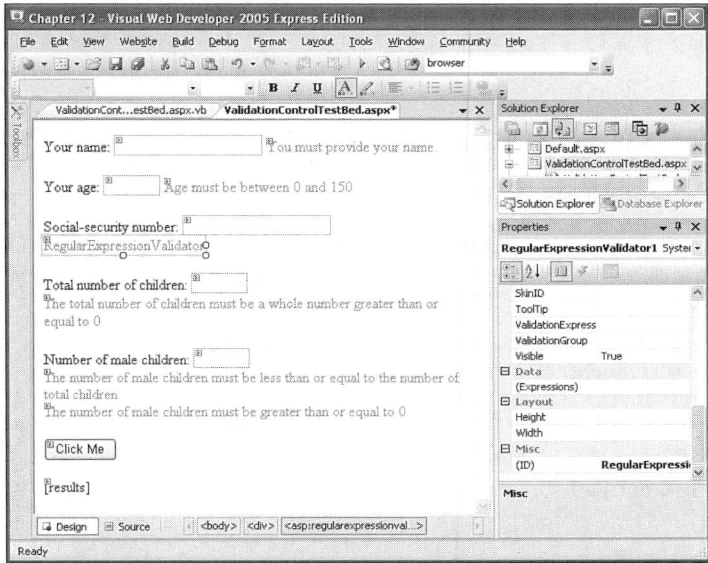

FIGURE 12.18 A Regular Expression Validator has been added to the ASP.NET web page.

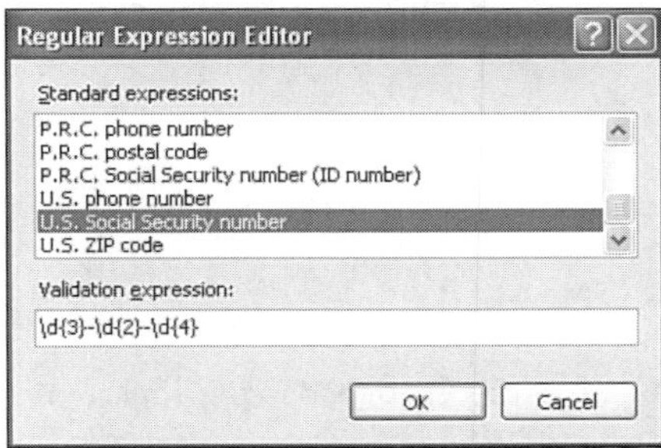

FIGURE 12.19 The Regular Expression Editor dialog box allows you to choose a predefined regular expression pattern.

The Regular Expression Editor dialog box contains a list of standard regular expression patterns that you can choose from. Alternatively, you can type a custom regular expression pattern into the Validation Expression text box. Because we need validation for a Social Security number, scroll down to the U.S. Social Security Number option.

After you have selected the U.S. Social Security Number option, the regular expression pattern will be displayed in the Validation Expression text box. Click the OK button to set the RegularExpressionValidator's `ValidationExpression`.

After you have done this, take a moment to view the `ValidationControlTestBed.aspx` ASP.NET page through a browser. Note that an error message is displayed if you provide a Social Security number that doesn't follow the correct format: three digits, hyphen, two digits, hyphen, four digits. For example, a legal social security number would follow this format: 123-45-6789.

Aesthetic Properties for the Validation Web Controls

As we have seen numerous times in this hour, when a user enters invalid input, the appropriate validation control's ErrorMessage is displayed. In all of the examples, this error message has been displayed in a red font. However, the look and feel of the error message can be specified by setting the various aesthetic properties of the validation Web controls.

As with all Web controls, the validation Web controls contain the typical aesthetic properties—BackColor, BorderColor, BorderStyle, Font, and so on. In addition to these standard aesthetic properties, the validation controls also contain a Display property.

The Display property specifies how the ErrorMessage property is displayed when the user provides invalid input. Specifically, the Display property can accept one of three values:

- None
- Static (the default)
- Dynamic

Setting Display to None causes the ErrorMessage property not to be displayed ever, even if a user's input is invalid. When Display is set to Static, the error message takes up the same amount of space on the web page when it isn't displayed as when it is displayed. On the other hand, when Display is set to Dynamic, the validation control's error message does not take up space when not being displayed.

To illustrate the difference between the Static and Dynamic settings, create a new ASP.NET page named DynamicVsStatic.aspx. In the web page, add two TextBox Web controls, one right beneath the other. After each TextBox Web control, type in the text This text appears right after a text box. Figure 12.20 shows the Visual Web Developer designer at this point.

Next, between each of the TextBox Web controls and the entered text, drop a RequiredFieldValidator control. Set the RequiredFieldValidator control's ControlToValidate properties to the ID values of the two TextBox Web controls. Set the ErrorMessage property to the value This demonstrates the differences between Static and Dynamic Display. Finally, set one of the two RequiredFieldValidator's Display properties to Dynamic, leaving the other's as Static.

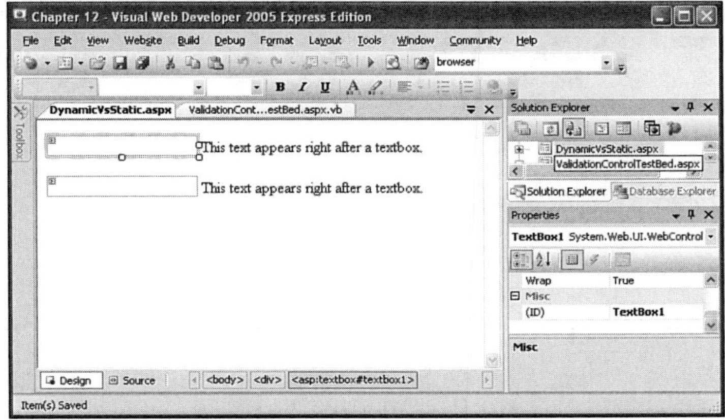

FIGURE 12.20
Two TextBox Web controls have been added to the designer.

Finally, add a Button Web control beneath both TextBox Web controls. Take a moment to make sure your screen looks similar to Figure 12.21.

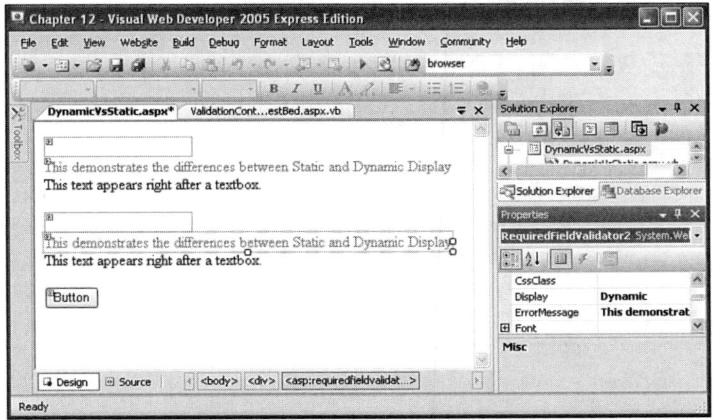

FIGURE 12.21
Two Required FieldValidators have been added to the mix.

Now, view the DynamicVsStatic.aspx ASP.NET page through a browser. Notice that for the RequiredFieldValidator whose Display property was left as Static, the text "This appears right after a text box" is far from the right side of the text box. This gap represents the space where the RequiredFieldValidator's error message will be displayed.

For the RequiredFieldValidator whose `Display` property was set to `Dynamic`, however, the text `"This appears right after a text box"` appears immediately after the text box. Figure 12.22 shows the `DynamicVsStatic.aspx` when viewed through a browser.

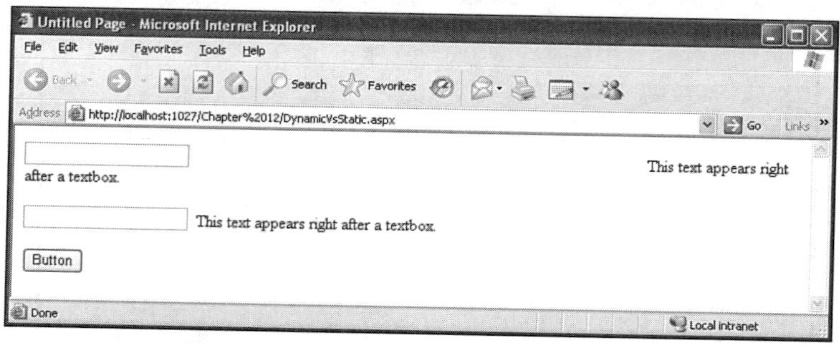

FIGURE 12.22 The apparent gap is due to the RequiredFieldValidator whose `Display` property is set to `Static`.

Now, click the button on the web page without entering any input into either of the text boxes. This will cause the error message to display for each of the RequiredFieldValidators. Figure 12.23 shows the page after both error messages are displayed. For the RequiredFieldValidator whose `Display` property was set to `Dynamic`, the text `"This appears right after a text box"` was dynamically moved to the right to accommodate the error message.

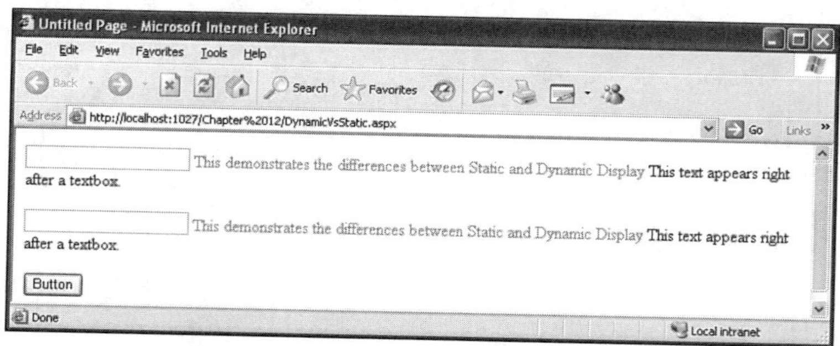

FIGURE 12.23 The page after the button has been clicked.

Table 12.2 contains a summary of the validation Web controls' aesthetic properties.

TABLE 12.2 The Aesthetic Properties of the Validation Web Controls

Property	Description
`BackColor`	Specifies the background color of the error message.
`BorderColor`	Specifies the color of the error message's border.
`BorderStyle`	Specifies the style of the error message's border.

TABLE 12.2 Continued

Property	Description
`BorderWidth`	Specifies the width of the error message's border.
`Display`	Specifies how the error message should be displayed.
`Font`	Specifies the font properties for the error message. Recall that the `Font` property has a number of subproperties, such as `Name`, `Size`, `Bold`, and so on.
`ForeColor`	Specifies the color of the error message. (Defaults to red.)

A Look at the Remaining Validation Controls

In addition to the four validation controls we examined in this hour, there are two additional validation controls. The first is the CustomValidator, which is, as its name implies, a validation control that is customizable. The CustomValidator can be used to validate user input in a way that is not handled by one of the four validation controls we've looked at.

However, in my experience, rarely will you find that you need to use a CustomValidator. More often than not, one of the main four validation controls will suffice. If, however, you find that you do need the power of a CustomValidator, I encourage you to read "Using the CustomValidator Control" at http://aspnet.4guysfromrolla.com/articles/073102-1.aspx.

The other validation control is the ValidationSummary control. The ValidationSummary control lists the `ErrorMessage` properties for all of the validation controls on a web page that have indicated invalid user input data.

To learn more about the ValidationSummary control, refer to http://www.w3schools.com/aspnet/control_validationsummary.asp.

Summary

Typically, when we're collecting user input, it is important that the user input conform to some set of guidelines. Perhaps certain input is required or must be numeric. Maybe the input needs to be less than a certain value or between two constant values. Or perhaps the input needs to conform to some pattern, such as a United States ZIP code, which needs to be in the form `XXXXX` or `XXXXX-XXXX`, where each `X` is a digit.

The process of ensuring that a user's input is in the correct format is referred to as input validation. In previous technologies, such as ASP and PHP, input validation was a real bear, requiring developers to write code to validate user input. With ASP.NET, however, input validation is a breeze because of its various validation Web controls. In this hour we examined four such controls: the RequiredFieldValidator, the CompareValidator, the RangeValidator, and the RegularExpressionValidator.

This hour concludes our examination of collecting user input. Starting with the next hour we'll be turning our attention to working with databases. Although there are no more hours dedicated to collecting user input, a number of the examples throughout the remainder of the book will require user input, so be certain that you have a firm grasp on this material before continuing.

Q&A

Q. ***I noticed that the*** `Display` ***property can have one of three settings:*** `None`, `Static`, ***and*** `Dynamic`. ***I understand the*** `Static` ***and*** `Dynamic` ***settings, but why on earth would anyone want to ever use the None setting?***

A. When a validation Web control's `Display` property is set to `None`, the `ErrorMessage` property is *never* displayed, regardless of whether the data being validated is valid. It may seem confounding as to why anyone would ever want to do this.

One of the validation Web controls that we didn't discuss at length in this hour is the ValidationSummary control. This Web control lists all of the validation errors on a web page. If each validation Web control displays its error message and the ValidationSummary Web control displays each error message, each error message is displayed twice on the page. For this reason, when using the ValidationSummary Web control, some developers prefer to set the various validation Web controls' `Display` properties to `None` so that the `ErrorMessage` property is displayed only once—in the ValidationSummary control.

Alternatively, you can specify what message should appear in the validation control's location and what message should appear in the ValidationSummary using the `ErrorMessage` and `Text` properties of the validation controls. If a validation control has values for both its `Text` and `ErrorMessage` properties, the `Text` value is displayed at the validation Web control's location, while the `ErrorMessage` property is displayed in the ValidationSummary control (if present). So another option is to have your validation controls include a detailed error explanation in the `ErrorMessage` property and an abbreviated message—perhaps just an asterisk (*)—for the `Text` property value.

Q. ***Whenever a user clicks a button, the validation controls' perform their validation logic. What if I want a Cancel button on the page or some other button that, when clicked, doesn't invoke the validation logic?***

A. Button, LinkButton, and ImageButton Web controls all contain a `CausesValidation` property, which defaults to `True`. If you set this property to `False`, however, the button, when clicked, won't invoke the validation controls' validation logic.

Workshop

Quiz

1. To have a validation Web control display a particular error message when the data is invalid, what property would you set?
2. How does the `Display` property affect the display of the validation Web control's error message?
3. Many websites allow users to create accounts. When creating an account, the user often must choose a password. When choosing a password, she must enter her desired password twice, to ensure that there were no typos. Now, imagine that you are asked to create such a web page. What validation Web control would you use to ensure that the text entered into these two text boxes was identical?
4. True or False: A CompareValidator can be used to ensure that a user's input is a certain data type.
5. What are regular expressions, and why is it worthwhile to have a RegularExpressionValidator validation Web control?
6. True or False: Each user input Web control can have at most one validation Web control associated with it.

Answers

1. The `ErrorMessage` property.
2. The `Display` property can be set to one of three values: `None`, `Static`, and `Dynamic`. If `Display` is set to `None`, then the `ErrorMessage` property is never shown, regardless of whether the input data is valid. A value of `Static` allocates space on the web page for the validation Web control's error message,

regardless of whether the error message is displayed. A value of `Dynamic` does *not* preallocate space for the error message. See Figures 12.22 and 12.23.

3. You would use a CompareValidator with its `ControlToValidate` and `ControlToCompare` properties being set to the two TextBox Web controls. The CompareValidator's `Operator` property should be set to `Equal`. (Exercise 3 asks you to implement this scenario.)

4. True.

5. A regular expression is a string that contains characters and special symbols and specifies a general pattern. A RegularExpressionValidator is a validation Web control that validates user input using a regular expression. Such a validation control is worthwhile because it can be used to validate that a user's input is in a certain pattern. For example, you may want to ensure that the user provides his phone number as three digits, followed by a hyphen, followed by three digits, followed by a hyphen, followed by four digits. This can be easily accomplished with a RegularExpressionValidator, but could not be accomplished by any of the other validation Web controls.

6. False. Web controls may have an arbitrary number of associated validation Web controls. For example, if you had a TextBox Web control where the user needed to enter her Social Security number, you'd want to use both a RegularExpressionValidator, to ensure that the data was entered in the proper format, and a RequiredFieldValidator, to ensure that the user supplied a value and did not leave the text box blank.

Exercises

1. Build a simple ASP.NET page that uses a CompareValidator and two RequiredFieldValidators. Specifically, create an ASP.NET web page that prompts the user for his two favorite ice cream flavors. There should be two TextBox Web controls, one for each of the user's two favorite flavors. Add the needed validation Web controls to ensure that the user provides input for both of these TextBoxes and that the values for the two TextBoxes are different from one another.

2. Create an ASP.NET page that prompts the user to provide her email address and the URL to her home page. Add the necessary validation Web controls to ensure that the user supplies an email address and that both the email address and home page URL are in the proper format. (Hint: The RegularExpressionValidator Regular Expression Editor contains predefined regular expressions for both Internet E-mail Addresses and Internet URLs.)

3. Many websites allow users to create an account. The account creation process usually prompts the user, at minimum, to provide a desired username, a password, and an email address. Create an ASP.NET page that has a TextBox Web control for the user's desired username, two TextBox Web controls for the user's password, and one TextBox Web control for the user's email address.

   For the user input to be valid, all TextBoxes must have a value entered. The user's email address must conform to the standard email address format, and the values entered into the two password TextBoxes must be equal. (Be sure to set the password TextBox Web controls' `TextMode` property to `Password`.)

   (As we will see in Hour 20, "Managing Your Site's Users," ASP.NET includes a number of Login controls that provide the user interface for many common user-related tasks, including creating a user account. Regardless, this exercise is still worthwhile because it gives you valuable practice with working with input and validation Web controls.)

PART III

Working with Databases

HOUR 13

An Introduction to Databases

In this chapter, we will cover

- What databases are
- How data is stored in a database
- What database tables, columns, and records are, and how they pertain to storing data
- The types of data that can be stored in a table column
- Some of the popular, commercially available database systems, as well as some of the free database systems
- How to create a new database and new database tables with Microsoft SQL Server 2005 Express Edition

One of the most powerful and useful features of ASP.NET is the ability for ASP.NET web pages to interact seamlessly with database systems. Databases, as we'll discuss in detail in this chapter, are software applications designed to serve as efficient and powerful repositories of data.

In this chapter we will look at what databases are and how data is stored in them. We'll also quickly examine a number of popular commercial and free database systems, focusing specifically on Microsoft SQL Server 2005 Express Edition, a free database system from Microsoft that you installed along with Visual Web Developer back in Hour 1, "Getting Started with ASP.NET 2.0."

By the end of this hour, you will have an understanding of database fundamentals, have created a database, and have populated this database with some data.

Examining Database Fundamentals

You may have heard the term **database** used before but might not be completely clear about what a database is or what it is used for. In the simplest terms, a database is a collection of structured information that can be efficiently accessed and modified.

Databases contain data and allow four operations to be performed on that data: retrieval, insertion, modification, and deletion. Most commonly, databases are used as a means to retrieve already inserted data. Therefore, we will spend the bulk of our study of databases examining how to retrieve the database's data.

Before you can insert, update, delete, or query a database, you must first install the database software, create the database file, and define the structure of the data the database will hold. In this hour we will first examine the basic concepts of a database; after this, we will look at using Microsoft SQL Server 2005 Express Edition, a free database system that you installed along with Visual Web Developer back in Hour 1.

By the Way

> We can access a database in a number of ways. Typically, database systems provide some sort of application to create databases and insert, delete, update, and access the database's data.
>
> More interestingly from our perspective, we can access databases through an ASP.NET web page. This means that we can create an ASP.NET page that reads data from a database and displays its contents to the visitor. This approach is common in a vast number of real-world websites. For example, when you search for a book at Amazon.com, the search query web page retrieves matching records from a database and then displays these matching records in a resulting web page.
>
> Over the next several hours we will examine how to display data from a database in an ASP.NET page.

After we've examined the fundamental properties and aspects of a database , we'll turn our attention to the syntax databases use for inserting, updating, deleting, and retrieving data. This language, referred to as **Structured Query Language**, or **SQL**, is the topic for the next hour.

Following this hour and the next, we'll focus on using various ASP.NET Web controls that are designed to access and display database data. For example, in Hour 14, "Accessing Data with the Data Source Web Controls," we'll examine ASP.NET's DataSource Web controls, which are a set of Web controls used for accessing, updating, inserting, and deleting database data. In Hours 15, "Displaying Data with the Data Web Controls," and 16, "Deleting, Inserting, and Editing Data," we'll see how easy it is to display and modify data using the GridView and DetailsView Web controls. In Hour 17, "Working with Data-Bound DropDownLists, RadioButtons, and CheckBoxes," we'll look at how to populate the contents of DropDownList, RadioButton, and CheckBox Web controls from data residing in a database. (Recall from Hour 11, "Collecting Input Using Drop-Down Lists, Radio Buttons, and Check Boxes," that the DropDownList, RadioButton, and CheckBox Web controls, along with the TextBox Web control, are Web controls designed for collecting user input.)

A Look at Current Database Systems

A slew of commercial and free database systems are available that will run on a variety of platforms. Some of the more popular commercial database systems include

- **Microsoft SQL Server**—http://www.microsoft.com/sql/
- **Oracle**—http://www.oracle.com/
- **IBM's DB2**—http://www-3.ibm.com/software/data/db2/
- **Microsoft Access**—http://www.microsoft.com/office/access/
- **IBM's Informix**—http://www-3.ibm.com/software/data/informix/

These commercial database products are industrial-strength, suited for large companies with demanding data needs. Because these are such high-grade database systems, the costs can be quite high, in the tens of thousands of dollars.

Fortunately for us amateur developers, there are also a number of free database systems. These database systems are still impressive software accomplishments, but they lack the features and high performance that the commercial-grade database systems have. However, because we are just using these databases to test our ASP.NET pages, they more than meet our needs. Some of the more popular free databases include

- **PostgreSQL**—http://www.postgresql.com/
- **MySQL**—http://www.mysql.com/
- **Microsoft SQL Server 2005 Express Edition (MSDE)**—
  http://www.microsoft.com/sql/express/

Microsoft SQL Server 2005 Express Edition ships with Visual Web Developer; at this point you have already installed SQL Server 2005 Express Edition.

While we'll be using Microsoft SQL Server 2005 Express Edition for all of our database examples through the remainder of this book, don't think that ASP.NET pages can communicate only with Microsoft's own database software products. On the contrary, virtually any database system can be accessed through an ASP.NET page. So, if you or your company is already using a database system other than SQL Server 2005 Express Edition, don't worry—you can still work with that particular system. For the book's examples, though, I encourage you to follow along using SQL Server 2005 Express Edition.

Storing Structured Data

Recall from our earlier definition that a database is a collection of **structured** information that can be efficiently accessed and modified. Databases structure their data by storing it into **tables**. A table is a combination of columns and rows in the form of a two-dimensional grid. (Sometimes a table's columns are referred to as **fields**; in this book, we'll use the word **columns** exclusively; we'll also refer to a table's rows as **records**.) Each column corresponds to an attribute of the data, whereas each row corresponds to an actual data item. Furthermore, each table is assigned a unique name to differentiate it from other tables in the database.

To clarify this concept, imagine that we wanted to use a database to store information about customers. Because we plan to store customer information in this database table, let's name the table `Customers`. To decide how to store the customer information, we must first decide what information, specifically, describes a customer. For this example, assume that we need to store the customer's name, phone number, and ZIP code, as well as the date the customer made his first purchase from our fictitious company.

These customer attributes make up the columns of the `Customers` table. Figure 13.1 shows a graphical representation of a table designed to store information about customers.

FIGURE 13.1 The `Customers` table's columns represent attributes of the customer.

The Customers Database Table

Name	Phone	Zip Code	DateBecameCustomer

Now, imagine that our company has five customers (it's amazing that it stays in business!). These five customers and their associated data might be

- Jisun Lee, 858-321-1234, 92109, January 27, 2001.
- Dave Yates, 619-123-4321, 92101, October 10, 2000.
- Todd Callister, 630-555-9898, 60126, August 27, 1989.
- Marie Vogan, 314-555-1111, 65401, September 8, 1997.
- Kate Wiseman, 858-555-4343, 92108, November 24, 2000.

Each of these five customers would be represented by one record in the `Customers` table. Figure 13.2 graphically represents the `Customers` table after these five records have been added to the table.

Name	Phone	ZipCode	DateBecameCustomer
Jisun Lee	858-321-1234	92109	January 27, 2001
Dave Yates	619-123-4321	92101	October 10, 2000
Todd Callister	630-555-9898	60126	August 27, 1989
Marie Vogan	314-555-1111	65401	September 8, 1997
Kate Wiseman	858-555-4343	92108	November 24, 2000

FIGURE 13.2
The `Customers` table contains five records, one row for each customer record.

Examining a Table's Columns

The columns of a database table, like variables in Visual Basic, have a name and a type. In our `Customers` table example, the names of the four database columns might be `Name`, `Phone`, `ZipCode`, and `DateBecameCustomer`. In addition to their names, these columns each have a type, which specifies the type of data that can be stored in the column.

For example, the `Name` column would likely have a type of `nvarchar(50)`; the `Phone` column, a type of `nvarchar(12)`; the `ZipCode` column, a type of `nvarchar(5)`; and the `DateBecameCustomer` column, a type of `datetime`. Despite the type name differences, table columns can have types quite similar to the types that Visual Basic variables can have. That is, the type `nvarchar(50)` is akin to a `String` type in Visual Basic, where the string can have, at most, 50 characters. The `datetime` table column type is synonymous with Visual Basic's `DateTime` type.

In addition to the `nvarchar(`*n*`)` and `datetime` types, there are a number of other types. Table 13.1 summarizes some of the more common table column types and their Visual Basic parallels.

TABLE 13.1 Commonly Used Table Column Types

Table Column Type	Description	Visual Basic Parallel
`nvarchar(`*n*`)`	A string of up to *n* characters in length	`String`
`int`	An integer	`Integer`
`bit`	Can be 0 or 1—a Boolean	`Boolean`
`datetime`	A date and time	`DateTime`
`money`	A monetary value	`Decimal`
`float`	A floating-point number	`Single`

When we create a database table later in this hour, you will see that there are many more column types than those listed in Table 13.1. However, the types presented in Table 13.1 are the ones you'll find yourself using the most of the time. You can find a complete list of SQL Server 2005's data types at http://msdn.microsoft.com/library/en-us/tsqlref/ts_da-db_7msw.asp.

By the Way

> When you are creating a database table, you may notice that in addition to the `nvarchar` data type, there are similarly named data types `nchar`, `varchar`, and `char`.
>
> The difference between `nvarchar` and `nchar` and `varchar` and `char` is that the types with `var` in the name are *variable* length character columns. That is, a `nvarchar(50)` column can have up to 50 characters but will take up only as many as are used. A `nchar(50)` or `char(50)` typed column, on the other hand, will always take up 50 characters, regardless of whether the value stored there is one character long or 50.
>
> The difference between the data types beginning with `n` (`nvarchar` and `nchar`) and those that don't (`varchar` and `char`) is that those prefixed with `n` store **Unicode** characters. Unicode is a character set that allows for a greater range of characters to be stored, enabling columns of this flavor to be able to store characters in any alphabet. `Varchar` and `char` data types, on the other hand, have a much smaller character set and are limited to the standard English alphabet.
>
> Although each of the string data types has a time and place, the `nvarchar` data type is the one most universally used and is what we'll be using throughout this book to store string data in a table.

Regardless of the data type being used, database columns can store a special value referred to as **Null**. The Null value indicates an "unknown" value. For example, imagine that you had a database table that captured information about customers, such as their name, payment information, shipping address, and so on. If, when entering the customer's information, you didn't know her phone number, you could use a value of Null.

When defining a column, in addition to its name and data type, you can also specify whether the column can be set to the Null value. In some circumstances you might not want to allow an "unknown" value to be entered, in which case you can mark the column to not allow Nulls.

Primary Key Columns

In addition to the various table columns that store pertinent data, database tables often contain a **primary key column** in addition to their other columns. A primary key column is typically a column of type `int` that has some special flags set. (We'll see how, specifically, to add a primary key column to a database table in the

"Creating Database Tables" section.) A column that is marked as a primary key requires that each record in the table have a *unique* value for that column. For this reason, primary key columns are often given the name `TableNameID`.

Primary key columns of type `int` can be marked as **Auto-increment** columns. An Auto-increment primary key column automatically assigns each record in the table with an increasing integer value. That is, when you add a new record to the table, you can't specify the value for the Auto-incrementing column; it will automatically be given the next sequentially increasing number.

To make sense of this information, let's return to our `Customers` table example and add a primary key. Because primary key columns are usually named `TableNameID`, let's call the `Customers` primary key `CustomerID`. With the addition of this new column, the `Customers` table would have the structure shown in Figure 13.3.

The Customers Database Table with a primary key field added

CustomerID	Name	Phone	ZipCode	DateBecameCustomer

FIGURE 13.3 A primary key column has been added to the `Customers` table.

Now, if we were to insert the five records examined earlier, the table's rows would have the data shown in Figure 13.4. Note that the value in the Auto-increment primary key column is unique and increasing for each row in the `Customers` table. Furthermore, realize that when inserting data, we would not specify the value for the `CustomerID` column; rather, the database system would automatically do this for us.

with a primary key field added

The Customers Database Table

CustomerID	Name	Phone	ZipCode	DateBecameCustomer
1	Jisun Lee	858-321-1234	92109	January 27, 2001
2	Dave Yates	619-123-4321	92101	October 10, 2000
3	Todd Callister	630-555-9898	60126	August 27, 1989
4	Marie Vogan	314-555-1111	65401	September 8, 1997
5	Kate Wiseman	858-555-4343	92108	November 24, 2000

FIGURE 13.4 Each row contains a unique `CustomerID` value.

Creating a New Database

Before you can start using a database system like SQL Server 2005 Express Edition, the first thing you will need to do is create a new database. Each database contains a group of one or more database tables.

Each SQL Server 2005 Express Edition database is physically implemented as a separate file. ASP.NET provides a special directory, `App_Data`, where you can place these database files for use in your ASP.NET web application. Creating a new database, then, is as simple as adding the appropriate database file to the `App_Data` folder.

By the Way

> Modeling databases as files in the `App_Data` folder makes it very easy to move your data-driven ASP.NET application from your local computer to a web-hosting company. All you need to do is upload your `App_Data` folder and related database file(s) along with your ASP.NET web pages!

To create a new database with Visual Web Developer, start by creating a new website using the ASP.NET Web Site template. Recall that the ASP.NET Web Site template, among other things, adds an `App_Data` folder to your website. (If you do not have an `App_Data` folder in your website, go to the Website menu, select the Add ASP.NET Folder menu option, and then pick the `App_Data` option.)

To add a database to your website, right-click on the `App_Data` folder in the Solution Explorer and choose Add a New Item. This will bring up the Add New Item dialog box, which contains three choices, one of which is to add a new SQL Database (see Figure 13.5).

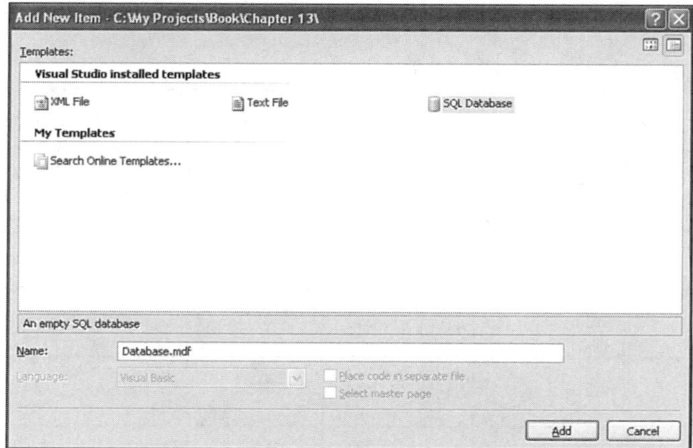

FIGURE 13.5 To add a database to your website, add a new SQL Database item.

Select the SQL Database option and change the name of your database file in the Name text box from `Database.mdf` to `MyFirstDatabase.mdf`. After you click the OK button, Visual Web Developer will start to create your new SQL Server database file. When it has completed, the Solution Explorer will be updated to show the new database file in the `App_Data` folder (see Figure 13.6).

FIGURE 13.6 The new database is listed in the `App_Data` folder.

In addition to adding the database file to the `App_Data` folder, you should now also see the newly added database within the Data Connections section of the Database Explorer window. By default, the Database Explorer window shares a pane with the Solution Explorer. If you don't see the Database Explorer on your screen, go to the View menu and select the Database Explorer option.

The Database Explorer provides a more detailed listing of a database's elements than the Solution Explorer. As Figure 13.7 shows, many database elements can be manipulated through Visual Web Developer, such as database diagrams, tables, views, stored procedures, and so on.

FIGURE 13.7 The Database Explorer lists the elements of the database.

For the data-driven examples we'll be exploring in this book, the only database element we'll need to use are the tables. The next section, "Creating Database Tables," examines how to create and define database tables; the section after that looks at how to populate tables with data through Visual Web Developer.

More advanced data-driven web applications commonly use views and stored procedures; however, an exploration of these topics is beyond the scope of this book. For more information on these topics, I invite you to check out "SQL Server Views," at http://odetocode.com/Articles/299.aspx, and "Writing a Stored Procedure," at http://www.4guysfromrolla.com/webtech/111499-1.shtml.

Creating Database Tables

Now that we have created a database, we're ready to create our first database table. When creating a database table, we do not specify any of the data; rather, we simply specify the table's structure—its columns. When creating a new table, we specify the name of the table as well as the name and type of each of the table's columns.

Creating database tables through Visual Web Developer is quite easy. The Database Explorer (shown in Figure 13.7) has a Tables folder for each database. Simply right-click on the Tables folder and choose the Add a New Table option. This will bring up the database table editor, where you can specify the column names and types for the new table. After you opt to add a new table, your screen should look similar to the one in Figure 13.8.

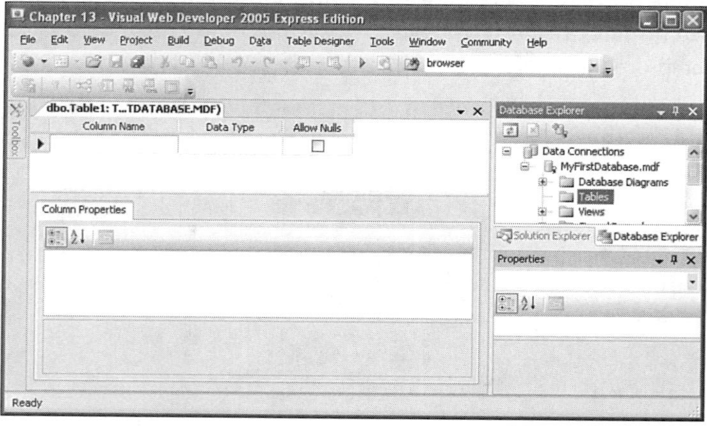

FIGURE 13.8
When creating a new database table, you will need to specify the column names and data types.

To illustrate the steps needed to define the structure of a new database table, let's build a simple database table that could be used to store information about a book collection. When you're crafting a database table, it's important to first spend adequate time defining the attributes you want to have expressed in the database; these typically translate to columns in a table. For our book collection example, imagine that we want to capture the following information:

- The book's title
- The book's author
- The year the book was published
- The cost of the book
- The last date we read the book
- The number of pages in the book

Now that we have defined the information to capture, the next step is to translate this into columns in a database table. We'll use a single table, called `Books`, that has an appropriately typed column for each of the six bits of information required.

Start by adding a new column named `Title` that's of type `nvarchar(150)` and does not allow Nulls. To accomplish this, type into the Column Name text box the name of the new column, `Title`. Then, in the Data Type drop-down list, type in `nvarchar(150)`. Last, uncheck the Allow Nulls check box. After you perform these steps, your screen should look similar to Figure 13.9.

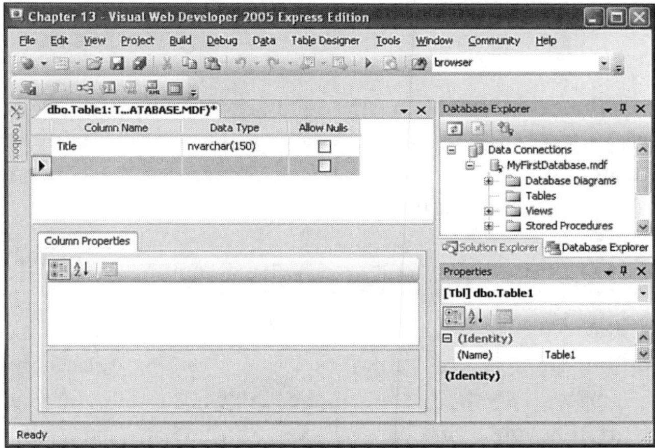

FIGURE 13.9 The `Title` column has been added to the table's definition.

Using the same technique, create the following columns:

- `Author`, of type `nvarchar(150)`, do not allow Nulls
- `YearPublished`, of type `int`, do not allow Nulls
- `Price`, of type `money`, do not allow Nulls
- `LastReadOn`, of type `datetime`, allow Nulls
- `PageCount`, of type `int`, do not allow Nulls

After adding these five additional columns, take a moment to ensure that your screen matches Figure 13.10.

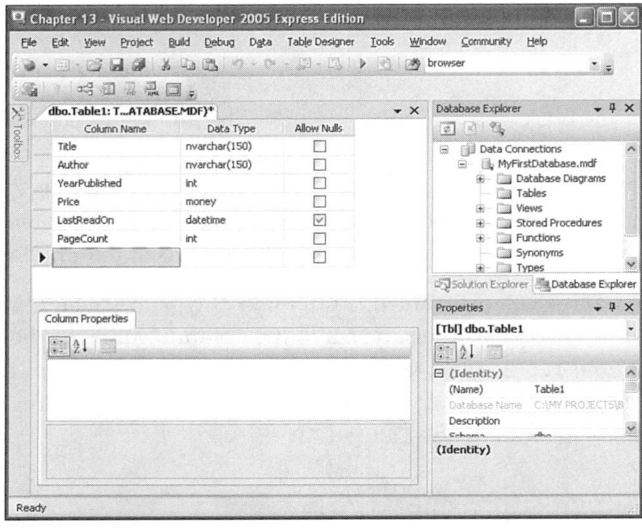

FIGURE 13.10
The table now contains six columns.

At this point, go ahead and save your new table by clicking on the Save icon in the Toolbar or by going to the File menu and choosing the Save Table1 option. You will be prompted to give your table a name. Choose the name `Books`. Congratulations, at this point you have created your first database table!

A Discussion on Database Design

When you're building a data-driven application, the application's **database design** is of paramount importance. The database's design is the set of decisions made in structuring the database; it's the process of deciding what tables you need, what columns make up these tables, and what relationships, if any, exist among the tables. If you start building your application using a poorly designed database, you'll likely run into unseen shortfalls or limitations further in the development process. The later you find a shortcoming, the more energy, time, and effort it will take to correct. Therefore, it behooves you to invest the time to properly model the data.

Unfortunately, we do not have the time or space to embark on a lengthy discussion of database design techniques, methodologies, and theories; entire books have been written on this subject. There are, however, a few quick concepts that I'd like to take a moment to highlight.

Uniquely Identifying Each Record

Because we'll often be interested in accessing, updating, or deleting a particular record in a particular database table, each record should be uniquely identifiable.

This can be accomplished in a number of ways, but most often is done through an Auto-increment primary key column. When you make a column a primary key column, the database will automatically enforce that each value is unique. A primary key column alone, though, still requires that you provide the unique values. When you also make the column Auto-increment, the database system will automatically provide a value for that column for each added record.

In our `Books` database table, we do not currently have a column that is guaranteed to be unique. The `Title` column might be a unique identifier if you are certain no two books in your collection will ever have the same title. If you wanted to indicate that a book's title could be used to uniquely identify each record, you'd need to make the `Title` column the table's primary key. To accomplish this, select the `Title` column in the table editor in Visual Web Developer and then click the primary key icon in the toolbar (see Figure 13.11).

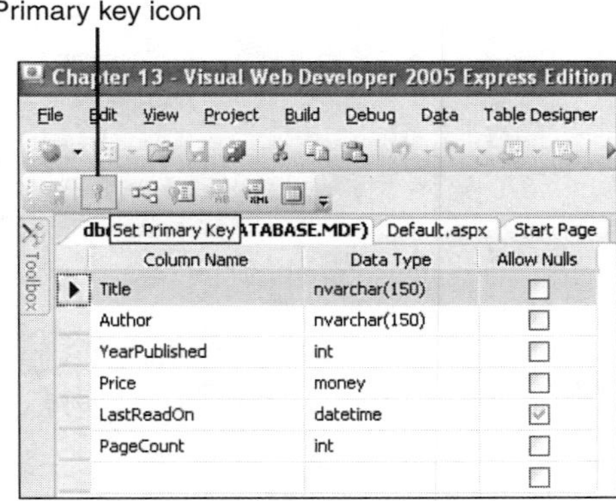

FIGURE 13.11 Select a column and click the primary key icon to mark it as the table's primary key.

What if a book's title, however, is not guaranteed to be unique? What if we might have two books in our collection with the same title? In that case we need to create a new column in our table, one whose explicit purpose is to uniquely identify each record. Typically, these types of columns are named *`TableName`*`ID`, where *`TableName`* is the name of the table the column is being added to. Furthermore, these columns are not only marked as primary key columns, but also marked as Auto-increment columns.

For practice, let's add an Auto-increment, primary key column to the `Books` table. Call this new column `BookID`, set its data type to `int`, configure it to *not* allow Nulls, and mark the column as a primary key by selecting the column and clicking on the primary key icon in the toolbar.

Did you Know?

You can add a new table column anywhere in the list of columns in the table editor: Just right-click the column in the editor and select the Insert Column option. For example, if you want to add `BookID` as the first column in the table, right-click on the `Title` column (which is the first one listed) and choose Insert Column. This will add a blank row at the top of the column list into which you can enter the information for the new `BookID` column.

Next, we need to mark the column as an Auto-increment column. To accomplish this, select the `BookID` column; this will load up the column's properties in the Column Properties pane at the bottom of the screen. Scroll down through the various properties until you reach the Identify Specification property, which will have a value of No. Change this value to Yes (see Figure 13.12).

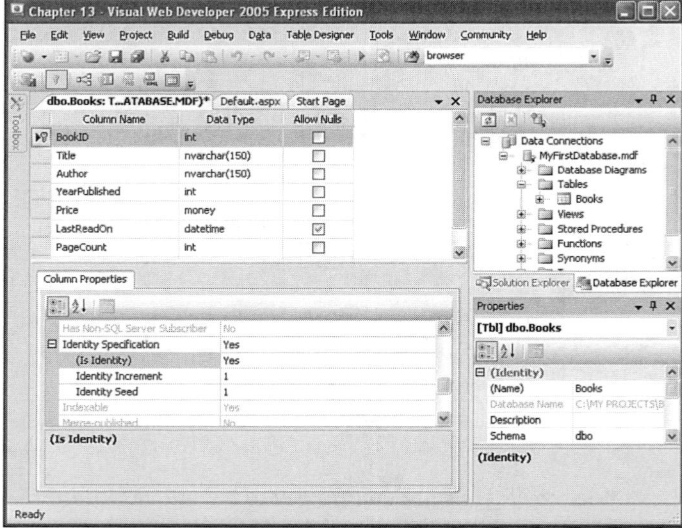

FIGURE 13.12 The `BookID` column is an Auto-increment, primary key column.

At this point `BookID` is now an Auto-increment, primary key column. Click the Save icon in the toolbar to save the table's changes.

Modeling a System's Logical Entities as Related Tables

When deciding what tables your database should contain, typically you'll want each table to represent a **logical entity** in your proposed system. For example, if you were creating an application to record the books in your collection, the logical entities in your system could include

- Books
- Authors
- Genres
- Publishers

For a system that tracked information about the book's authors, genres, and publishers, we'd most likely want four tables in our database, one to represent each logical entity. In addition to having these four tables, we'd also want to indicate that they were related in a certain manner. Database systems include various techniques to indicate that a given table is related to another. For example, we would want to indicate that each record in the `Books` table could have one to many related records in the `Authors` table. This relationship would indicate who wrote the book. Similarly, we might indicate that each record in the `Books` table must be related to precisely one record in the `Publishers` table, indicating the book's publisher.

While database models should ideally have a table for each logical entity and explicit relationships among the tables, most of the examples in this book will use a single-table design. This approach is not a recommended design approach; however, it makes creating, accessing, inserting, updating, and deleting the data much simpler.

By the Way

If you are interested in learning about good database design in greater detail, pick up a copy of Michael Hernandez's book *Database Design for Mere Mortals* (ISBN: 0201752840).

Adding Data to the Books Table

At this point we have created a database and created a `Books` table. However, there is currently no information stored in our table! The next step, then, is to add data to the `Books` table. This can be accomplished either through Visual Web Developer or from an ASP.NET page. In this hour we'll add database records using Visual Web Developer; in Hour 16, "Deleting, Inserting, and Editing Data," we'll see how to add data to a database table from an ASP.NET page.

To edit, delete, or add data to a database table via Visual Web Developer, go to the Database Explorer and expand the Tables folder, which will list the tables of the database. Next, right-click on the table whose data you want to edit and select the Show Table Data option. This action will display the contents of the selected table, as shown in Figure 13.13.

As Figure 13.13 shows, currently there are no records in the `Books` table. To add a new record to the table, simply click on the text box beneath the `BookID` column. You can now use the Tab key to move from one field to another, using the keyboard to enter the text you want in the table.

When entering data into these cells, keep in mind that the values you enter must correspond to the particular column's properties. That is, the `PageCount` column is an `int` type, meaning that you must enter a number. If you try to enter a value like

Scott or one hundred pages, you will get an error message. Similarly, some columns can accept Null values, whereas others are not. Those columns that *cannot* accept Null values must have a value entered, whereas the ones that can accept Nulls may optionally be left as Null.

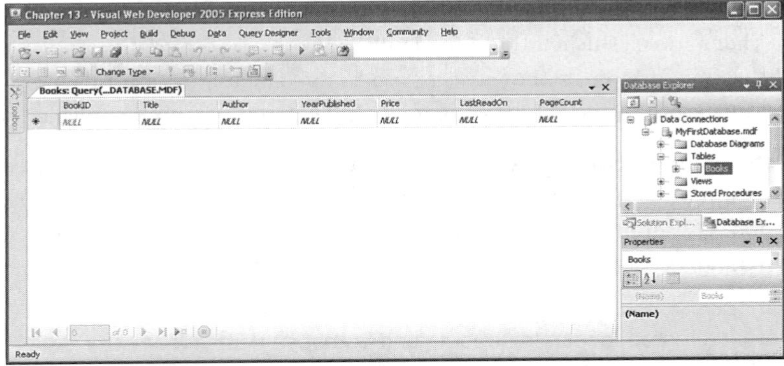

FIGURE 13.13 The contents of the Books table are shown.

Similarly, for certain data types, the format you enter the data is important. For example, the Price column, which is of type money, accepts only numeric values, like 14.95. If you try entering currency signs, you will get an error. Furthermore, when you enter dates, the date format depends on your computer's date/time settings. In the United States, you can enter the date as month/day/year, like 11/19/2005 for November 19, 2005. In many European countries, the format is day/month/year, like 19/11/2005. To circumvent any cultural date/time intricacies, you can always enter a date using the universal format, which is year-month-day, like 2005-11-19 for November 19, 2005.

By the Way

Don't worry if you happen to enter invalid data when trying to create a new record. You won't lose your database's data. Rather, you'll be presented with a helpful error message explaining the problem.

Add a new record to the table by entering Visual Studio Hacks in the Title cell, James Avery in the Author cell, 2005 for YearPublished, 24.95 for Price, and 478 for PageCount. Leave the BookID and LastReadOn cells with their default values, Null. At this point your screen should look similar to Figure 13.14.

Note that when you first start entering data in the row's cells, a new, blank row appears below the row you're typing in. Also, whenever you change a cell value and move to the next cell, a little red exclamation point icon appears. This indicates that the value of the cell has changed. If your cursor is still sitting in the PageCount cell and you still see the red exclamation point icons (as is the case in Figure 13.13), the new record has yet to be created. To commit the new record to the database, simply click in the next row (or press the Tab key to move the cursor down to the next row).

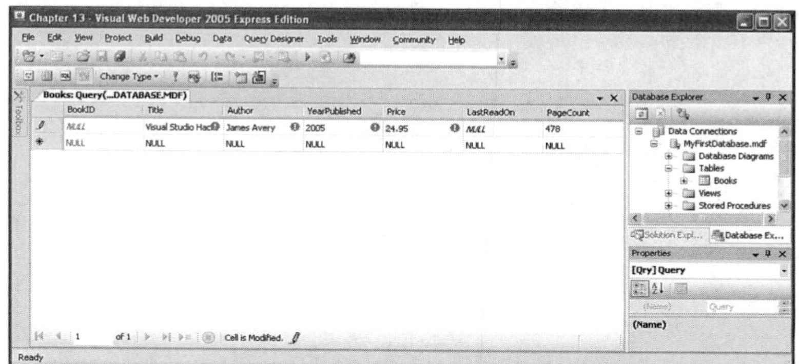

FIGURE 13.14
Our first book in the Books table is James Avery's *Visual Studio Hacks*.

Watch Out!

> The BookID column is an Auto-increment column, meaning that you cannot specify its value. Rather, you need to let the database system decide what value to use. Therefore, when adding a new record to the Books table, you *must* leave BookID as Null. If you attempt to enter a value, you will receive an error.
>
> If you left BookID as Null and, when trying to save the record, were told that you needed to provide a value for BookID, then you did not correctly mark the column as Auto-increment. Return to the "Uniquely Identifying Each Record" section and make sure to mark BookID as Auto-increment.

After you have done this, the red exclamation point icons will disappear, and a value will be automatically inserted into the BookID cell (see Figure 13.15). Remember that BookID is an Auto-increment column, meaning its value is automatically inserted by the database. For example, if you add another record to this table, the next record will have a BookID value of 2.

Let's practice by adding a few more records to the Books table. Go ahead and add the following four records:

- The book *Create Your Own Website* written by Scott Mitchell in 2005. The cost of this book is $19.99 and is 195 pages long. Assume that you last read this book on August 1, 2005.
- The book *The Number*, by Alex Berenson. This book was published in 2003 at a cost of $24.95, totaling 274 pages in length. Assume that you last read this book on November 14, 2005.

- The book *The Catcher in the Rye* by J.D. Salinger. Your copy of this book was published in 1991 and costs $6.95. There are 224 pages. Assume you last read this book on June 12, 2004.
- The book *Fight Club*, by Chuck Palahniuk. This book was published in 1999 and costs $16.95. There are 187 pages. Assume that you have yet to read this book (that means to leave `LastReadOn` as Null).

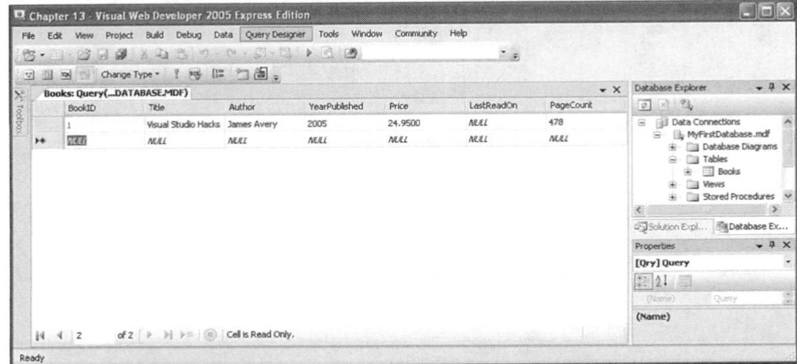

FIGURE 13.15 A new record has been added to the `Books` table.

After you have entered these four additional rows into the `Books` table, your screen should look similar to Figure 13.16. Notice that the `BookID` value, which we never entered, has automatically increased with each new record added.

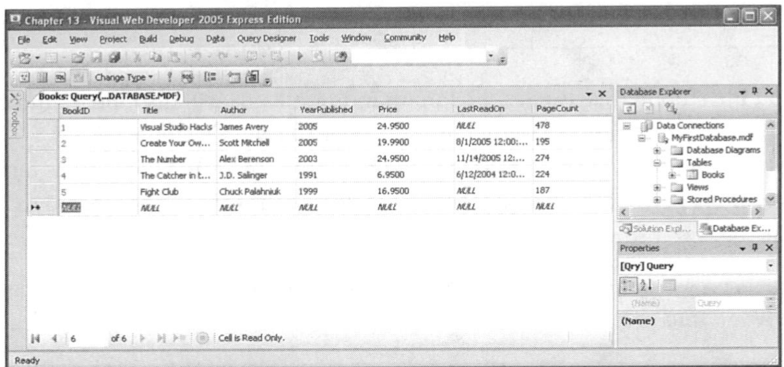

FIGURE 13.16 The `Books` table now contains five rows.

In addition to your being able to add new records to the `Books` table, Visual Web Developer also makes it easy to edit a table's existing data through the same interface. To change an existing record's contents, simply click in the appropriate row's area and make any changes needed.

Recall from the beginning of this hour that a database is a collection of structured information that can be efficiently accessed and modified. We've seen how to create the structures to hold information (database tables) and we've looked at how to add data to a table, but we've yet to examine the most useful aspect of databases: efficiently accessing the data stored within. This topic, though, will have to wait until the next hour.

Summary

In this hour we learned that databases are software systems designed for storing structured data that can be efficiently accessed and modified. Data in a database is structured by means of tables. A table is described by its columns, which have a name and type.

In addition to columns, database tables contain rows. The rows of a table make up the table's data. For example, in Figure 13.16, the `Books` table has five rows, which indicates that there is information about five books. To view, add, and edit the content of a database table in Visual Web Developer, right-click on the Table name and choose the Show Table Data option.

Now that we've examined the structure of databases, how to create databases and database tables, and how to add data to a database table, we're ready to read the data from a table. In the next hour we will examine a query language specifically designed for accessing database data.

Q&A

Q. ***Can I add new columns or remove existing columns from a database table after I've already created and saved the table? What if the table contains rows?***

A. You most definitely can alter a table's structure after it has been saved—even if it has existing rows. There are no rules when it comes to removing columns from an existing database table. Simply edit the table and remove a row. (Of course, you will lose the data expressed in those columns for all existing rows.)

Adding new columns to an existing database table without any rows is just as simple: Go into the table editor, add the new column(s), and save the results. This process is a little trickier if the table has existing rows because the database table must decide what values to place into the new column(s) for the existing rows. Here, you have two options: You can either have the new column(s) allow Nulls, or you can specify a default value for the column. (You can set the default value through the Column Properties pane.) If you specify a default value for the new column(s), all existing rows will have the default value inserted for the new column(s). If you do not specify a default value, but instead elect to allow Nulls, then the new column(s) for the existing rows will have a value of Null.

Workshop

Quiz

1. How are columns, tables, and databases related to one another?
2. A particular column for a particular row in a database table is a lot like a variable in a programming language in that it can be completely described by what three attributes?
3. What does a Null value represent?
4. How does an Auto-increment primary key column guarantee that it will uniquely identify each row?
5. True or False: When you create a database table, the table must have a primary key column.

Answers

1. A table contains one or more columns. A database contains one or more tables.
2. The column name, the column data type, and the value of the column for the specific row.
3. A Null value represents *unknown* or *no value*. For example, in the `Books` database, the `LastReadOn` column accepts Null values because we might not have read the book yet, in which case there is no value for this column.
4. When you insert a new row into a column with an Auto-increment primary key column, the database server decides the value of the Auto-increment primary key column. Because the database server gets to determine this value, it can ensure that the value is unique from all other rows. This is accomplished by incrementing the Auto-increment primary key column value from the last-inserted row.
5. False. The vast majority of the time you will want your tables to include a primary key, Auto-increment column, but you can create tables without a primary key.

Exercises

1. To familiarize yourself with Visual Web Developer and SQL Server 2005 Express Edition, create a new database named TestDB. After creating the database, create a new database table called `Albums`. Imagine that you want to use this database table to hold information about the albums you own. Add columns with appropriate types and names. Some suggested columns include: an Auto-increment primary key column named `AlbumID`; an `nvarchar(50)` column titled `Name`; an `nvarchar(75)` column titled `Artist`; and a `date/time` column titled `DatePurchased`. (Take the time to add additional pertinent columns.)

2. In the "Storing Structured Data" section, we talked about a `Customers` table that captured information about potential customers, such as their name, phone number, ZIP code, and so on (refer to Figure 13.1). Take a moment to create this database table with the appropriate schema. Next, add the five records detailed in Figure 13.2.

HOUR 14

Accessing Data with the Data Source Web Controls

In this hour, we will cover

- Working with data source controls
- Understanding SQL, the language of databases
- Retrieving specific columns from a database table
- Returning database data that meets certain criteria
- Ordering the results of a database query

In the preceding hour we examined, from a high-level perspective, what databases are, their internal structure, and their purpose. We looked at creating a database with SQL Server 2005 Express Edition through Visual Web Developer. We also saw how to create database tables and populate them with data.

Often we will want to retrieve information from a database and display it on an ASP.NET web page. To be able to do this, we need to learn how to retrieve data from a database. ASP.NET provides a set of Web controls—called **data source controls**—that are designed specifically to access data from an underlying database. With the data source controls, retrieving database data is as simple as dropping a control onto your ASP.NET page and stepping through a wizard, indicating the database data you want to grab.

Underneath the covers, the data source controls are simply sending commands to the database using a language called **Structured Query Language**, or **SQL** (pronounced either *S-Q-L* or *Seequell*). SQL is the language used by all modern database systems for retrieving data. In addition to examining the ASP.NET data source controls, we'll also spend a bit of time in this hour learning the general syntax of SQL.

Examining the Data Source Controls

ASP.NET contains a myriad of Web controls, which we grouped into various categories in earlier hours. For example, in Hour 8, "ASP.NET Web Controls for Displaying Text," we looked at those Web controls designed for displaying text content on an ASP.NET page; in Hours 10, "Using Text Boxes to Collect Input," and 11, "Collecting Input Using Drop-Down Lists, Radio Buttons, and Check Boxes," we looked at Web controls designed to collect user input. In this hour we'll examine a new class of Web controls—ones designed for accessing database data. This class of Web controls, referred to as **data source controls**, can be found in the Toolbox in the Data section (see Figure 14.1).

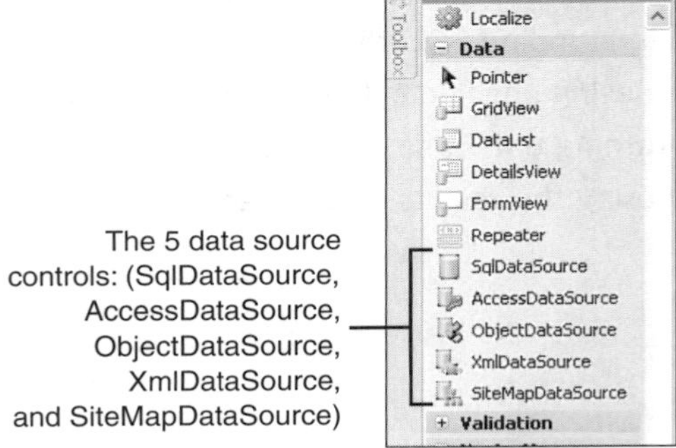

FIGURE 14.1 The Visual Web Developer Toolbox contains a number of data source controls.

With the data source controls, you can access database data by simply dragging and dropping the appropriate data source control onto an ASP.NET page. You will then be prompted to specify what database you want to connect to and, from that database, what data you want to retrieve. All of this configuration can be accomplished through the ASP.NET page's Design view without having to write a single line of code.

By the Way

> Data source controls just serve as a bridge between the ASP.NET page and the database. That is, a data source control only retrieves database data and does *not* have any capabilities for displaying the retrieved data on the page. To display the data, you'll need to use an additional Web control, such as the DropDownList, GridView, DetailsList, CheckBoxList, and so on. This chapter focuses on retrieving data using the data source controls. In the next hour, "Displaying Data with the Data Web Controls," we'll see how to display the data retrieved by a data source control in an ASP.NET page.

Five data source controls ship with ASP.NET. Each data source control, shown in Figure 14.1, has a name that ends in DataSource, like SqlDataSource, AccessDataSource, and so on. Each data source Web control is designed for working with data from a different type of source. For example, SqlDataSource is designed to retrieve data from databases; XmlDataSource can be used to access data from an **XML file**; SiteMapDataSource is used to query a **site map** and return the website's navigational structure so that it can be displayed in a TreeView or Menu Web control.

By the Way

> An **XML file** is a text file that contains data encoded in a special syntax. A thorough discussion of XML is beyond the scope of this book; for more information, refer to www.XMLFiles.com or pick up a copy of *Sams Teach Yourself XML in 24 Hours* (ISBN: 0672322137).
>
> A **site map** is an XML file that is formatted in a particular way and contains information about a website's navigational structure. This information can then be displayed in the form of navigational breadcrumbs, menus, or hierarchical trees. We'll examine ASP.NET's site map features and SiteMapDataSource in detail in Hour 19, "Defining a Site's Structure and Providing Site Navigation."

In this hour we are interested only in accessing data from a database, namely the SQL Server 2005 Express Edition database created in Hour 13, "An Introduction to Databases." Therefore, we will be using only one data source control in this hour, SqlDataSource.

Working with the SqlDataSource Control

To practice using the SqlDataSource control, we'll need an ASP.NET website with a database. To save time in creating a new website and database, let's just use the website and database from Hour 13.

Start by creating a new ASP.NET web page named `AccessingData.aspx`. Next, go to the Design view and, from the Toolbox, drag on a SqlDataSource control. Each data source control, when on the Design view, is rendered as a gray box with the data source control type followed by its `ID` value. As Figure 14.2 shows, after we add a SqlDataSource control to the page, the gray box says `SqlDataSource - SqlDataSource1`. Here, `SqlDataSource1` is the `ID` of the control.

In addition to this gray box, there's also a **smart tag**. A smart tag is a list of common tasks that can be performed from the Web control. For the data source controls, the smart tag contains a single option, at first: Configure Data Source. Clicking on this link starts the Configure Data Source Wizard, from which we'll specify what data we want to retrieve from the database.

FIGURE 14.2
A SqlDataSource control has been added to the ASP.NET page.

To be able to work with a database's data, the SqlDataSource control needs to know two bits of information:

- How to connect to the database
- What query to issue to the database

The SqlDataSource control's wizard prompts you to provide these two vital pieces of information and does so in a very intuitive and developer-friendly manner.

Let's start examining the SqlDataSource control's wizard! Go ahead and click the Configure Data Source link.

Step 1: Choose Your Data Connection

The first step of the Configure Data Source Wizard is to select what database you want to work with. A drop-down list contains those databases listed in your Database Explorer and should include the `MyFirstDatabase.mdf` database we created in the preceding hour. Go ahead and select this database from the drop-down list (see Figure 14.3).

Beneath the drop-down list of available databases is a Connection string label with a plus next to it. If you click this plus, it will display the **connection string** used to access the database data. A connection string is low-level information required by ASP.NET that provides the specific details for connecting to the database. In previous versions of ASP.NET, you'd have to craft this connection string yourself; with Visual Web Developer, however, the connection string is automatically generated for you based on the database you select from the drop-down list.

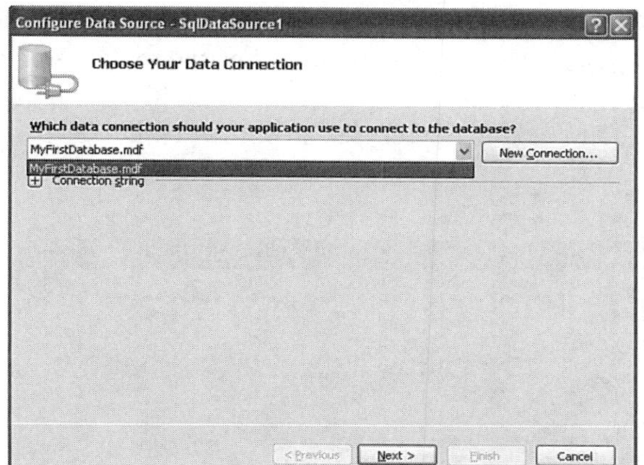

FIGURE 14.3
Select the `MyFirstDatabase.mdf` database from the drop-down list.

By the Way

If you need to connect to a database other than the one created in the preceding hour, you can click the New Connection button. This will bring up a dialog box that asks you what type of database you want to connect to, along with another dialog box prompting you for the specific connection information.

If this is the first time you've used a data source control to connect to this database, you'll be prompted to save the connection information in the web application's configuration file (see Figure 14.4). Because ASP.NET needs the database connection string to communicate with the database, this information must be present in the ASP.NET page in one form or another. If you choose to save the connection string information in the web application's configuration file, which I heartily recommend, a new setting will automatically be inserted into the `web.config` file that associates the name provided with the connection string. Then, in your ASP.NET pages that use this database, rather than specifying the connection string, there will simply be a reference to the connection string's name in the `web.config` file.

The benefit of saving the connection string information in the web application's configuration file is that it adds a level of indirection in your application, which makes responding to changes easier. For example, imagine that you are using the `MyFirstDatabase.mdf` file and have created a dozen ASP.NET pages that work with this database's data. Furthermore, assume that you have decided *not* to save this information in `web.config`. That implies that in each of these 12 ASP.NET pages, the database's connection string is present. Now the gotcha: Imagine that your database's connection string changes. Perhaps you've renamed the file, or your boss has created a new database file that he wants you to use instead. With the connection string hard-coded into each of the dozen ASP.NET pages, you'll have to go into those pages and update the connection information through the data source controls' wizards. Had you stored the connection string information in `web.config`, however, you would have had to modify the connection string in only one place—the `web.config` file.

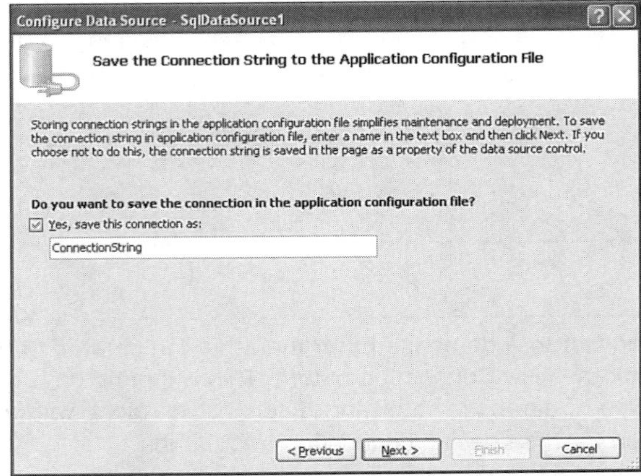

FIGURE 14.4 You can save the connection string in your website's configuration file.

Because the data source control's wizard will handle adding the connection string setting in `web.config` automatically, there's no reason *not* to store the connection string there. Therefore, leave the check box in Figure 14.4 checked and click Next to proceed to the next step.

Step 2: Configure the Select Statement

After you specify the database to use and, if needed, store the connection string information in the web application's configuration file, the next step is to specify what data you want to retrieve from the database. With the SqlDataSource Wizard, you can select data in one of two ways:

- By specifying a database table, along with the columns to return
- By providing a **SQL** `SELECT` **query**

Regardless of what approach you use, the result is the same: the SqlDataSource control concocts some SQL statement that is sent to the database to retrieve the data. Recall that SQL is the language used by modern database systems used for running queries.

With the first option, you can pick the table and specify the columns to retrieve through the wizard. With the second option, you'll need to spell out the precise SQL query to use. We'll examine the basics of SQL later in this hour in the "A Look at SQL, the Language of Databases" section. For now, let's practice with using the first option.

In the Configure the Select Statement step of the wizard, you can choose whether you want to select a database table or specify your own SQL query. You make this decision by choosing the appropriate radio button. To pick a table, select the Specify Columns from a Table or View radio button (see Figure 14.5).

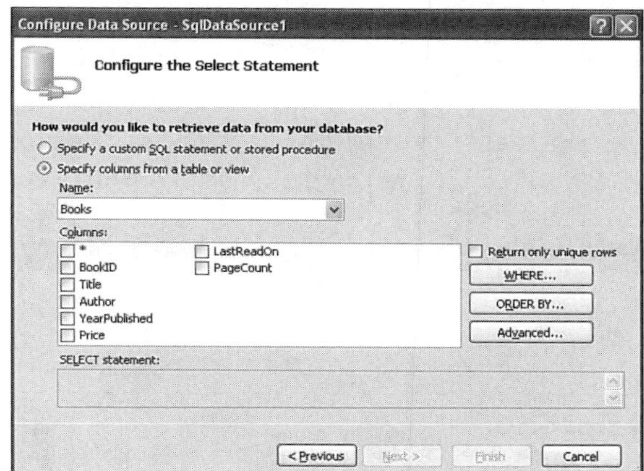

FIGURE 14.5
Pick the table whose data you want to retrieve.

The tables in the database are listed in the drop-down list, with the selected table's columns listed underneath. Because there is only one database table in our database—`Books`—it's the only option in the drop-down list. The area beneath lists the columns—`BookID`, `Title`, `Author`, `YearPublished`, `Price`, `LastReadOn`, and `PageCount`. There's also a `*` option list. This represents *all* columns.

We need to check those columns that we want returned from the `Books` table. If you want to retrieve all column values, select the `*` option, or check each of the individual columns. Sometimes, however, you may need only a subset of the columns. For example, we might have an ASP.NET page that lists just the titles of the books, omitting other information. For this page we could have the database query return only the results from the `Title` column. For this example, though, let's return all columns.

Check the `*` check box, which indicates that you want to retrieve all columns from the `Books` table. After you check this, a `SELECT` query appears at the bottom of this dialog box. Specifically, you'll see the query syntax:

```
SELECT * FROM [Books]
```

This statement is called a `SELECT` query, and is the syntax used in SQL to retrieve information. There are many parts to the `SELECT` query, some of which we'll examine further in this chapter. For now, don't worry about the intricacies of the SQL syntax. Instead, focus on how the table data is selected through the SqlDataSource control's wizard.

Now that we've specified the data we want returned from the `Books` table, click the Next button to proceed to the final wizard step.

Step 3: Test the Query

The final step in the SqlDataSource control's wizard is the Test Query screen. The Test Query screen allows you to run the query to see what data, exactly, is returned. As Figure 14.6 shows, the `SELECT * FROM [Books]` SQL query returns *all* records from the `Books` table, with each record containing *all* of the table's columns.

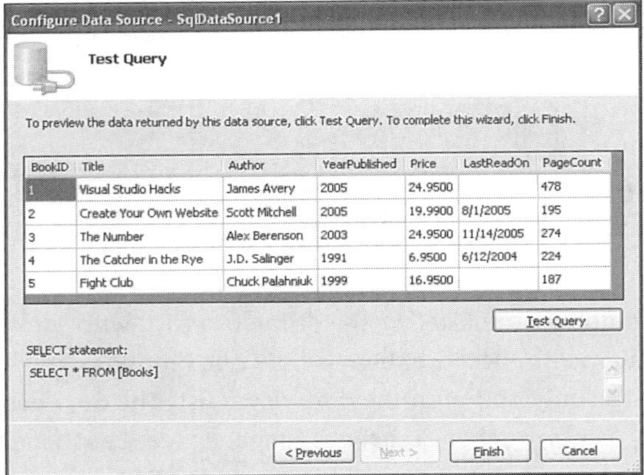

FIGURE 14.6 All columns from all rows are returned from the query.

If you received the database results you expected, click the Finish button to complete the wizard. If something is awry, you can click the Previous button and adjust the query as needed.

By the Way

> Notice that when you select a table to display, *all* records from the table are returned. Furthermore, the results are ordered by the `BookID` values. The SQL `SELECT` statement makes it easy to limit the records returned—such as retrieving only those books with a price less than $20.00—and order the results on some column. We'll examine the SQL syntax for filtering and sorting results in the "A Look at SQL, the Language of Databases" section and will see how to apply these settings through the SqlDataSource's wizard later in this hour.

Examining the SqlDataSource Control's Markup

While Visual Web Developer makes it easy to add Web controls and static content through a page's Design view, there is always a corresponding markup presented in the Source view. Let's take a moment to examine the markup generated in the Source view by the SqlDataSource control's wizard. After clicking the Finish button in the wizard, click on the Source tab to view the HTML content of the ASP.NET page. You should find a SqlDataSource control declaration like so:

```
<asp:SqlDataSource ID="SqlDataSource1" runat="server"
   ConnectionString="<%$ ConnectionStrings:ConnectionString %>"
   SelectCommand="SELECT * FROM [Books]">
</asp:SqlDataSource>
```

As you can see, the SqlDataSource control has three property values at this point:

- `ID`—This property uniquely identifies the data source control from all other Web controls on the page. Feel free to rename this to something more descriptive, like `BooksData`, rather than the nondescript `SqlDataSource1`.
- `ConnectionString`—This property indicates the connection string to connect to the database. If you opted to place the connection string information in the web application's configuration file, the value will be the name of the connection string setting in `web.config`. The syntax `<%$ connectionStringName %>` tells the data source control to look at the application's connection strings information to retrieve the appropriate information. If you decided against putting the connection string in `web.config`, then the full connection string will be here in place of `<%$ connectionStringName %>`.
- `SelectCommand`—This property specifies the `SELECT` query issued to the database. Note that this property's value is identical to the `SELECT` command listed in the wizard.

At this point, the SqlDataSource's declarative markup is pretty simple; it's just three property values, after all. However, as we get into more involved examples that include interactive user filtering and updating, inserting, and deleting database data, the declarative markup generated by the SqlDataSource will quickly balloon. The lesson to take away from this discussion is that the SqlDataSource control's wizard is helpful in two ways: First, it helps us construct the appropriate SQL statements, rather than having to enter them ourselves by hand; and second, it saves a lot of tedious and cryptic typing of markup in the Source view.

A Look at SQL, the Language of Databases

For the SqlDataSource control to be able to retrieve database data, two pieces of information were required: the database's connection string and the query to issue to the database. As we discussed in the preceding section, the query issued to the database must be in a dialect that the database understands. The common dialect among all modern database systems is **SQL**, or the **Structured Query Language**.

To retrieve data from a database, we use a **SQL `SELECT` statement**. The `SELECT` statement, in its simplest form, specifies what database table to retrieve data from, along with what columns of data to return. For example, to return the title of each book in the `Books` table, we would use the following SQL statement:

```
SELECT Title
FROM Books
```

We will examine the SQL `SELECT` clause in great detail in the next section.

Although SQL is used primarily for retrieving database data, it can also be used to insert new data and update or delete existing data. These data modification capabilities are expressed using `INSERT`, `UPDATE`, and `DELETE` statements.

By the Way

> In this hour we will focus strictly on using SQL to retrieve data. However, starting in Hour 16, " Deleting, Inserting, and Editing Data," we will examine how to delete and edit database data.

Delving into the SQL `SELECT` Statement

We use the SQL `SELECT` statement to retrieve the values of a particular database table's columns via the following syntax:

```
SELECT Column1, Column2, ..., ColumnN
FROM TableName
```

`Column1 ... ColumnN` are columns from the database table *`TableName`*. For example, to retrieve the values from the `Title` and `Author` columns from the `Books` table, we would use the following SQL statement:

```
SELECT Title, Author
FROM Books
```

Note that this `SELECT` statement contains two **clauses**: the `SELECT` clause and the `FROM` clause. Clauses are keywords in the SQL `SELECT` statement that precede the data they operate on. The two required clauses in a `SELECT` statement are the

SELECT and FROM clauses. As you have probably already ascertained, the SELECT clause specifies the columns whose values are to be returned and the FROM clause specifies what database table to retrieve data from.

By the Way

A number of optional clauses can be found in the SELECT statement, many of which we will examine in this section. For example, you can use the WHERE clause to return only those rows that meet certain criteria. You can use the ORDER BY clause to sort the results of the SELECT statement by a particular column.

Did you Know?

The SELECT clause contains a comma-delimited list of the columns whose values you are interested in. If you want to retrieve the values of *all* columns for a specific table, you can use the asterisk (*) instead of having to enter each column name.

Viewing SQL Queries Results in Visual Web Developer

When you're learning SQL, it helps to be able to run a SQL query against a database so that you can see the specific results returned by the SQL query. Fortunately, Visual Web Developer makes this task quite simple. In fact, Visual Web Developer even can assist with building the SQL query itself!

As we saw in the preceding hour, the Database Explorer window lists the databases used in the current ASP.NET website. Take a moment to go to the Database Explorer, right-click on the database name, and choose the New Query option from the context menu. This will display the query window, which first prompts you to select what tables you'd like to query. Because our database has only one table—Books—this is the only option you'll see listed (see Figure 14.7).

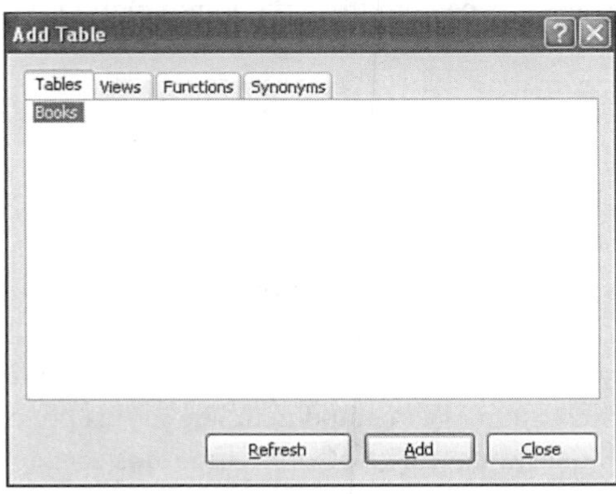

FIGURE 14.7 Select what table(s) you want to query.

Select the Books table and click the Add button; this will add the table to the query window. After adding the Books table, click the Close button in the dialog box. At this point your screen should look similar to Figure 14.8.

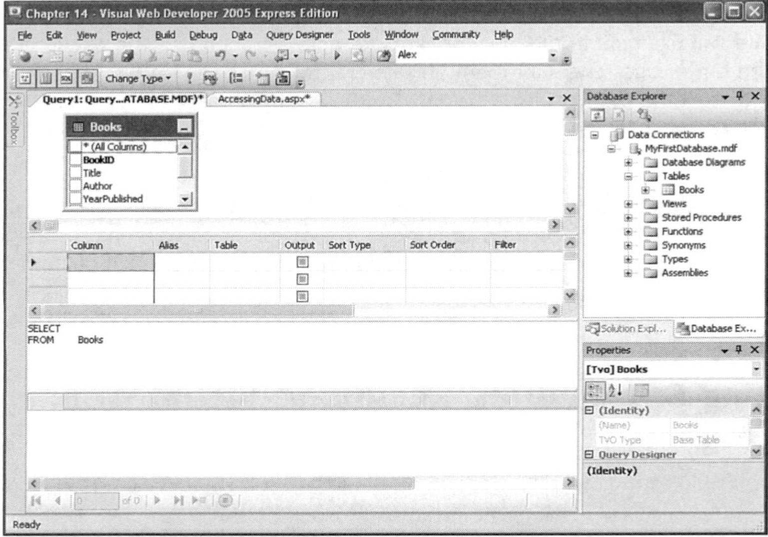

FIGURE 14.8 Create and run a query from the query window.

By default, the query window contains four regions:

- **Diagram Pane**—This pane lists the tables added, along with their columns at the top of the query window.
- **Criteria Pane**—This grid comes beneath the diagram pane and lists the columns that are returned by the query, along with any conditions (whether they're sorted, whether a filter applies, and so on).
- **SQL Pane**—This pane is beneath the criteria pane and lists the SQL query that will be executed.
- **Results Pane**—This final, bottommost pane lists the results after the query has been executed.

The first three panes work together, in a sense. For example, if you check a subset of columns in the Books table representation in the diagram pane and then execute the query, the criteria pane and SQL pane will be updated accordingly. Likewise, if you write a SQL query by hand in the SQL pane and then execute the query, the diagram pane and criteria pane will be updated. The results pane merely shows the results of the executed query, regardless of what pane was used to express the query.

Along the top of the query window are a series of icons that are especially useful (see Figure 14.9). Starting from the left, the first four icons toggle what panes are displayed. You can show or hide the panes you don't use. (Personally, I like to enter my SQL queries by hand, so I turn off the diagram and criteria panes.) Next is the Change Type icon, from where you can specify what type of SQL query you are interested in running (SELECT, INSERT, UPDATE, or DELETE). Next to that is the red exclamation point icon. This icon, when clicked, executes the query and displays the results in the results pane. The next icon, when clicked, validates the SQL query syntax, informing you of any syntax errors in your SQL query. The remaining icons are for functionality that's beyond the scope of this book.

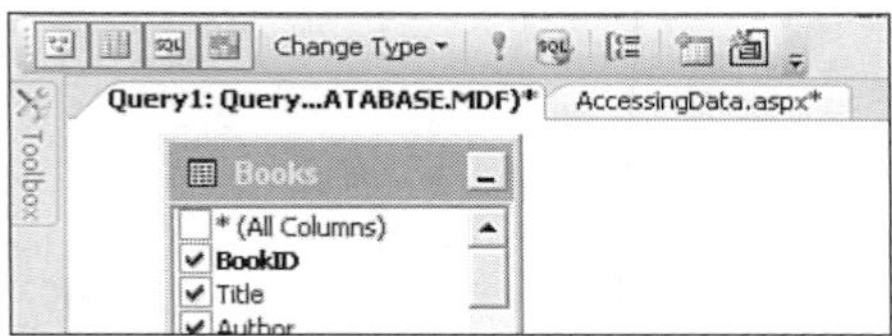

FIGURE 14.9
The Toolbar icons can be used to customize the query window.

Let's practice using the query window. Go ahead and type into the SQL pane the following query:

```
SELECT * FROM Books
```

Next, click the red exclamation point icon in the Toolbar to execute the query. At this point the diagram and criteria panes should update to reflect the SQL query entered in the SQL pane, and the results should be shown in the results pane. Figure 14.10 shows the query window after this SELECT statement was executed.

In addition to clicking the red exclamation point icon, you can also execute the query by going to the Query Designer menu and choosing the Execute SQL menu options. If you prefer executing the query using keyboard shortcuts, either Ctrl+R or Alt+X will work.

One thing to note is that at times the query engine will rewrite your SQL queries. I typed in SELECT * FROM Books as my query, but the query was rewritten to

```
SELECT     BookID, Title, Author, YearPublished, Price, LastReadOn, PageCount
FROM         Books
```

Of course, this query and my query are identical in their results. Also, note that the results in the results pane are identical to the results we saw in the Test Query step of the SqlDataSource control's wizard in Figure 14.6.

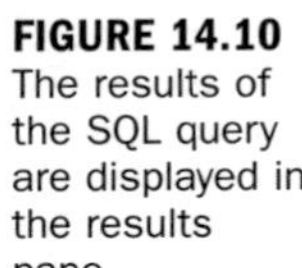

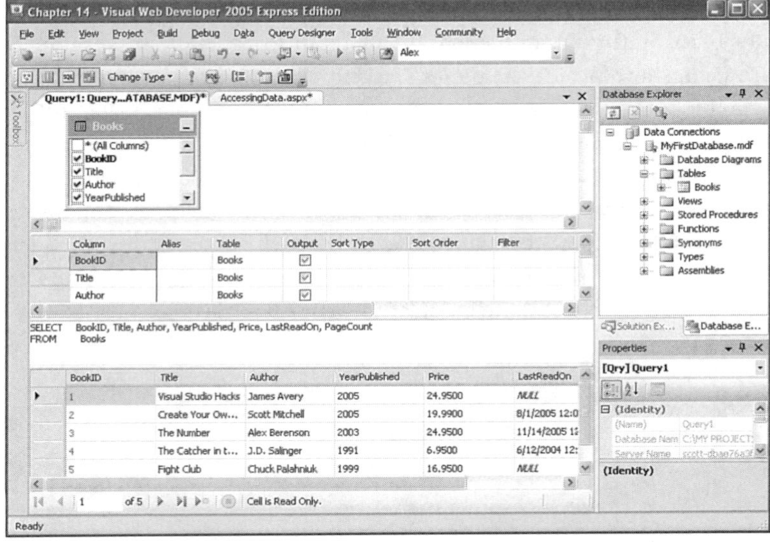

FIGURE 14.10
The results of the SQL query are displayed in the results pane.

Let's try executing another `SELECT` statement. Change the SQL query in the SQL pane from `SELECT * FROM Books` to

```
SELECT Title, Author
FROM Books
```

This SQL query will return all of the rows from the `Books` table, displaying the values for the `Title` and `Author` columns. After you have entered this query into the text box, execute the query; the results are shown in Figure 14.11. Notice how the diagram and criteria panes have been updated to reflect the new SQL query and how the results pane has only two columns returned instead of seven.

Restricting Returned Rows Using the `WHERE` Clause

The `SELECT` statement, when composed of just the `SELECT` and `FROM` clauses, returns *all* of the rows of the specified database table. For example, the SQL query results shown in Figures 14.10 and 14.11 display all of the rows in the `Books` table, the only difference between the two results being the columns whose values are returned.

Often, when querying database data, we are not interested in all of the data in a table, but only a subset. For example, when you are searching Amazon.com for books on ASP.NET, the search results page lists only those books that match your search criteria rather than all of the books in Amazon.com's database.

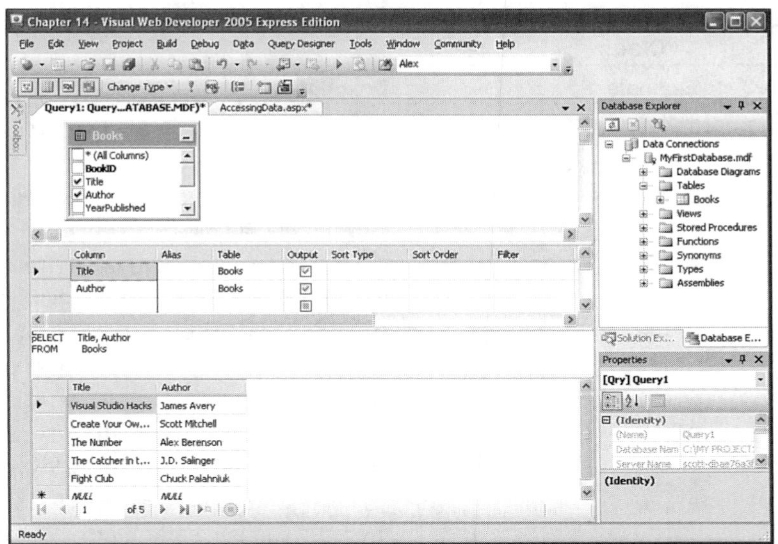

FIGURE 14.11 The SQL query returns the values for two columns.

To limit the rows returned by the SELECT statement, we use the WHERE clause. The WHERE clause specifies conditions that a row must match in order to be returned by the SELECT statement. For example, the following SQL SELECT statement returns only those rows in which the Title column's value equals The Number:

```
SELECT *
FROM Books
WHERE Title = 'The Number'
```

Go ahead and enter this query into the text box of the Test Query dialog box and click the Test Query button. The results should show all of the columns of the Books table, but only one row—the book *The Number*.

> Note that there are single quotation marks around the string The Number in the WHERE clause. If you accidentally enter double quotation marks instead of single quotation marks, you will get the following error message when you click the Test Query button: `Invalid Query: Invalid column name 'The Number'.`

As you can see, the WHERE clause has a Boolean condition preceding it: `Title = 'The Number'`. The = operator here is synonymous with the = operator in Visual Basic, which we examined in Hour 5, "Understanding Visual Basic's Variables and Operators." In addition to the = operator, other comparison operators, such as <, <=, >, and >=, can be used as well. Table 14.1 summarizes these other comparison operators.

TABLE 14.1 Comparison Operators That Can Be Used in the `WHERE` Clause

Operator	Example	Description
=	`Title = 'The Number'`	Compares two values, returning `True` if they are equal.
<>	`Title <> 'The Number'`	Compares two values, returning `True` if they are *not* equal.
<	`Price < 14.95`	Compares two values, returning `True` if the left value is less than the right value.
<=	`Price <= 14.95`	Compares two values, returning `True` if the left value is less than or equal to the right value.
>	`Price > 14.95`	Compares two values, returning `True` if the left value is greater than the right value.
>=	`Price >= 14.95`	Compares two values, returning `True` if the left value is greater than or equal to the right value.

In addition to the comparison operators, a number of Boolean operators can be used to string together multiple Boolean expressions. These Boolean operators are `AND` and `OR`, and are synonymous with the Visual Basic `And` and `Or` keywords. For example, the following SQL `SELECT` statement returns the `Title`, `Author`, and `Price` columns of books whose `YearPublished` equals `2004` or whose `Price` is less than or equal to `20.00`:

```
SELECT Title, Author, Price
FROM Books
WHERE YearPublished = 2004 OR Price <= 20.00
```

This query returns the `Title`, `Author`, and `Price` columns for three books: *Create Your Own Website, The Catcher in the Rye,* and *Fight Club.*

When comparing a column's value to a string or date/time constant, such as `WHERE Title = 'Fight Club'` or `WHERE LastReadOn < '2005-01-01'`, you must enclose the string or date/time constants (`Fight Club` and `2005-01-01`, in this example) in single quotation marks. If, however, you are comparing a numeric column to a numeric constant, the numeric constant does not need to be surrounded by single quotation marks.

Fortunately, we need to worry about this esoteric rule only when crafting SQL statements by hand in the query window. When we build `SELECT` statements through the SqlDataSource control's wizard, this minutia is handled for us automatically by the data source control.

Understanding What Happens When a WHERE Clause Is Present

When a WHERE clause is used, the following sequence of steps happens behind the scenes. Each record in the queried table is enumerated. The condition in the WHERE clause is checked for each record. If the condition returns the value True, the record is included in the output; otherwise, it is discarded.

For example, consider the following query:

```
SELECT Title, Author
FROM Books
WHERE Title <> 'The Number' AND BookID <= 3
```

For each row in the Books table that is visited, the WHERE clause's condition is analyzed. Starting with the first book, *Visual Studio Hacks*, we see that this book's title doesn't equal The Number and its BookID is indeed less than or equal to 3; therefore, the book *Visual Studio Hacks* will be returned by the SELECT statement. The next book is *Create Your Own Website*. Again, this book's title does not equal The Number and its BookID is less than or equal to 3, so it's returned in the results as well.

The third book, however, is *The Number*. Clearly, this book *won't* be returned because the Title <> 'The Number' condition will return False. The next book evaluated is *The Catcher in the Rye*; this book, however, won't be in the resultset. Yes, the book's title is not The Number, but its BookID is equal to 4, which is *not* less than or equal to 3. Similarly, the final book, *Fight Club*, will also be omitted from the results because its BookID value is greater than 3.

Therefore, the aforementioned SQL statement will return the Title and Author columns for two books: *Visual Studio Hacks* and *Create Your Own Website*.

Ordering the Results Using the ORDER BY Clause

You may have noticed that the results returned by the SQL queries we have examined so far have all been ordered by the BookID value. To see this point illustrated, refer to Figure 14.10, which shows the results of the query SELECT * FROM Books. What if we want the results ordered by some other column value, though? Perhaps we want to list the books and have the list ordered alphabetically by the books' titles.

The SELECT statement can include an optional ORDER BY clause, which specifies the column to sort the results by. To retrieve books sorted alphabetically by title, we could use the following SELECT query:

```
SELECT *
FROM Books
ORDER BY Title
```

Figure 14.12 shows the query window when this SQL query is used. Note that the books are ordered by the values in the `Title` column, instead of by the values in the `BookID` column.

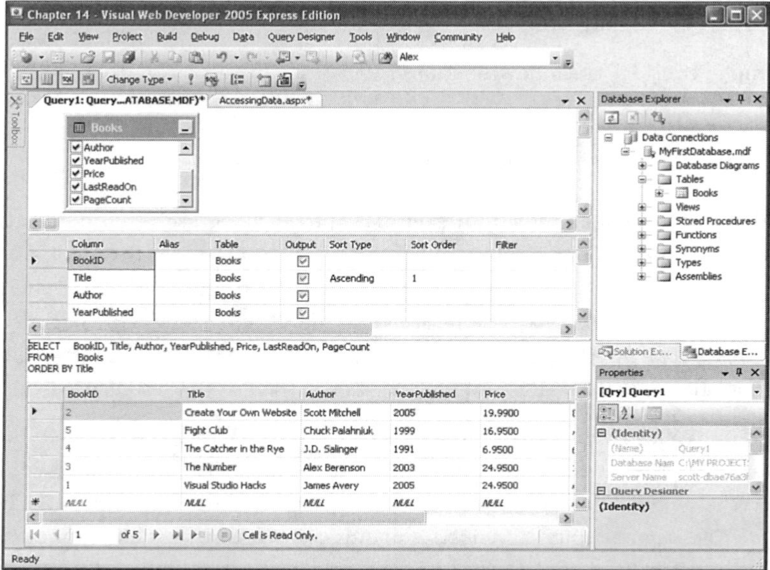

FIGURE 14.12 The books are ordered alphabetically by their `Title` column value.

Did you Know?

If you want to construct a query that has both a `WHERE` clause *and* an `ORDER BY` clause, it is vital that the `ORDER BY` clause appear *after* the `WHERE` clause. The following is a legal SQL query:

```
SELECT *
FROM Books
WHERE Title <> 'Fight Club'
ORDER BY Author
```

The following is not:

```
SELECT *
FROM Books
ORDER BY Author
WHERE Name <> 'Fight Club'
```

Sorting in Ascending and Descending Order

By default, the `ORDER BY` clause sorts the results of a query by a specified column in ascending order. You can specify that the sort ordering should be in descending order by adding the `DESC` modifier in the following fashion:

```
ORDER BY ColumnName DESC
```

Notice that sorting the results by a column that contains alphabetic characters in ascending order, such as the `Title` column, has the effect of sorting the results in alphabetical order. If you want to sort the results in reverse alphabetical order, use the `DESC` keyword.

Filtering and Sorting Data from the SqlDataSource Control's Wizard

In the "Working with the SqlDataSource Control" section, we looked at how to use the SqlDataSource control's wizard to return all records from a specific table. However, we didn't examine how to filter or sort the results. Now that we have a bit more experience with the SQL `SELECT` statement, let's return to examining the SqlDataSource control's wizard and see how to filter and sort the results.

Start by returning to the `AccessingData.aspx` page we created earlier in this hour. Add another SqlDataSource control to your page's Design view and click the Configure Data Source link from the control's smart tag. Because we've already created and stored a connection string for the `MyFirstDatabase.mdf` file in our web application's `web.config` file, the drop-down list in step 1 of the wizard lists this connection string. Pick this connection string value and click the Next button.

From the Configure the Select Statement screen, go ahead and select the `Books` table from the drop-down list and click the `*` option (refer to Figure 14.5). As we saw earlier in this hour, this will issue a `SELECT * FROM [Books]` query to the database, which will return *all* records from the `Books` table ordered by the `BookID` values.

At this point we are ready to filter and sort the data as needed. Note the WHERE and ORDER BY buttons on the right of the Configure the Select Statement screen. These buttons will bring up dialog boxes that we'll use to configure the `WHERE` and `ORDER BY` clauses of our `SELECT` statement.

Filtering the SqlDataSource Control's Data

As things stand now, all of the records from the `Books` table will be returned. Imagine, however, that we want to return only those records that have a `BookID` value of 3 or less and were published in 2005. We can add these `WHERE` clause filters via the SqlDataSource's wizard by clicking the WHERE button. This will display the Add `WHERE` Clause dialog box, shown in Figure 14.13.

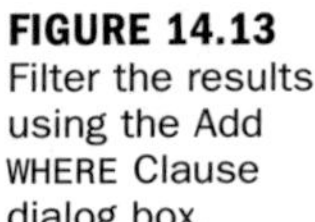
FIGURE 14.13
Filter the results using the Add WHERE Clause dialog box.

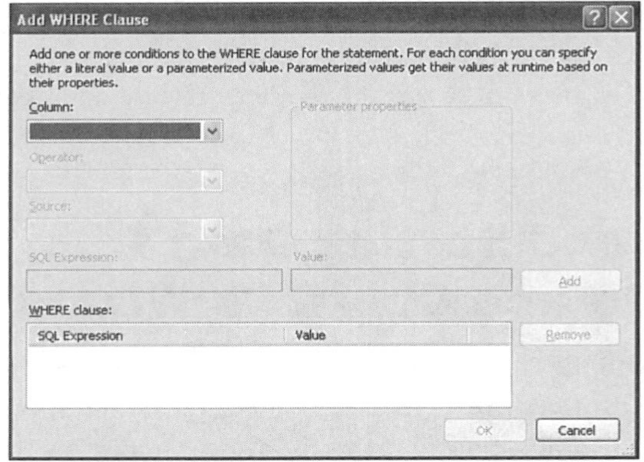

Adding a filter through the Add WHERE Clause dialog box involves a number of steps, such as choosing what column to filter on, the operator to filter with, and what value to use in filtering. To add the filter expression on the BookID column, perform the following steps:

1. Choose a column to filter. Because we want to filter on BookID, select the BookID value from the Column drop-down list.
2. Select the filtering operator from the Operator drop-down list. Because we want books with a BookID value less than or equal to 3, choose the <= operator from the list.
3. Specify the source of the filter value. The Source drop-down list contains the potential places where the filter value can be read from. For example, you may want to let the user visiting the web page provide the BookID value. In that case you'd set the Source to the Control option. However, we want to enter a hard-coded value as our filter value (3, for this example). Therefore, choose None for the Source.
4. After you choose None, the Parameter Properties section will display a Value text box. Here, you can enter the hard-coded filter value. Enter **3**. (Figure 14.14 shows the Add WHERE Clause dialog box at the end of this step.)
5. To add the filter expression to the WHERE clause, click the Add button.

Congratulations, you have added your first WHERE clause expression using the SqlDataSource wizard!

Because we want our query to have *two* WHERE clause expressions, our work is only halfway done. Repeat the preceding steps, this time adding an expression that filters on the `YearPublished` column for results with values of 2005. After adding both filter expressions, click the OK button to return to the Configure the Select Statement screen. At the bottom of this screen, you will see the SQL query the wizard has constructed thus far:

```
SELECT * FROM [Books] WHERE (([BookID] <= @BookID) AND
➥([YearPublished] = @YearPublished))
```

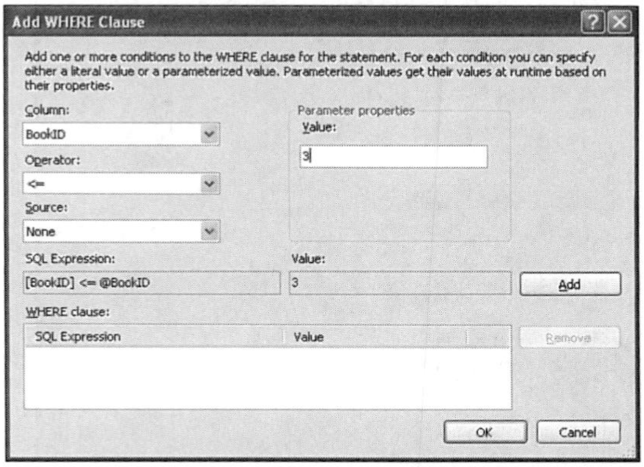

FIGURE 14.14 A less than or equal filter on `BookID` has been defined for the hard-coded value 3.

The Add `WHERE` Clause dialog box works great if you want to add only one filter expression or if all of the filter expressions are joined by `AND` logical operators. However, if you want to have multiple filter expressions joined by `OR` operators, such as filtering on books with a `BookID` less than or equal to 3 *or* `YearPublished` equaling 2005, then you'll need to craft the SQL statement yourself. That is, from the Configure Select Statement screen, you'll need to select the Specify a Custom SQL Statement or Stored Procedure radio button and then provide the precise SQL query.

Sorting the SqlDataSource Control's Data

At this point we have added two filter expressions to the `WHERE` clause. However, the results will still be returned ordered by `BookID`. Let's instead have the books ordered by `Price` in **descending** order (from most expensive to least). If there are any ties in `Price`, let's break them by alphabetically sorting on the `Title`.

To accomplish this, click on the ORDER BY button, which is beneath the WHERE button in the Configure Select Statement screen. This will bring up the Add `ORDER BY` Clause dialog box, from which you can specify up to three columns to order the results. The second and third columns specified in this dialog box dictate how ties are to be broken. That is, the results are sorted by the column specified in the first drop-down list. If there are any ties in the results, the second column is consulted; finally, if there are any ties there, the third column specified is used to break those ties.

Figure 14.15 shows the Add `ORDER BY` Clause dialog box after it has been configured to sort first by `Price` in descending order, with ties being broken based on the alphabetical ordering of the `Title`.

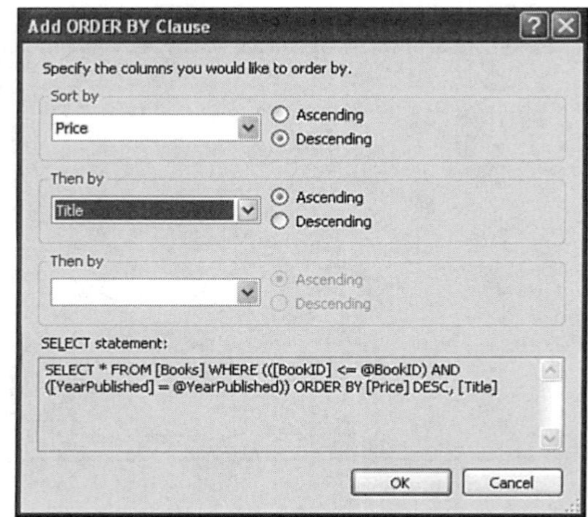

FIGURE 14.15 The results will be ordered by `Price` in descending order, with ties being broken by `Title`.

As Figure 14.15 shows, after we add the `ORDER BY` clause, the final SQL statement for our SqlDataSource control is

```
SELECT * FROM [Books] WHERE (([BookID] <= @BookID) AND
➥([YearPublished] = @YearPublished)) ORDER BY [Price] DESC, [Title]
```

Testing Queries with `WHERE` Clauses

After you've entered the `ORDER BY` clause, click the OK button to return to the Configure Select Statement screen. At this point, our SQL query is complete; it returns all columns from the `Books` table, sorting by `Price` in descending order, breaking ties by sorting on `Title` alphabetically, where only records that have a `BookID` less than or equal to 3 and were published in 2005 are returned. Click the Next button to advance to the Test Query screen.

When you have a query that involves a `WHERE` clause, clicking the Test Query button will prompt you to supply values for the `WHERE` clause filter expressions. For this example, we are prompted to enter values for `BookID` and `YearPublished` (see

Figure 14.16). You can either leave in the default values—3 and 2005, respectively—or you can enter different numbers.

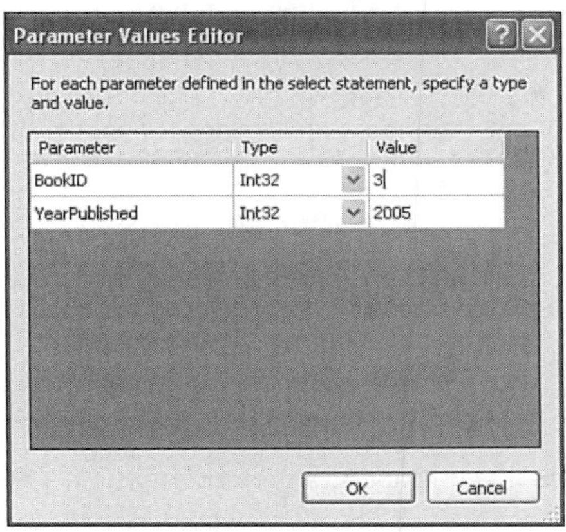

FIGURE 14.16
Specify the values for the `WHERE` clause filter expressions.

If you leave in the values of 3 and 2005 for the `BookID` and `YearPublished` filter expressions, you should see two books in the results—*Visual Studio Hacks* and *Create Your Own Website* (see Figure 14.17). These are the only two books that have a `BookID` value of less than or equal to 3 *and* were published in 2005. *Visual Studio Hacks* is listed before *Create Your Own Website* because it has a higher price.

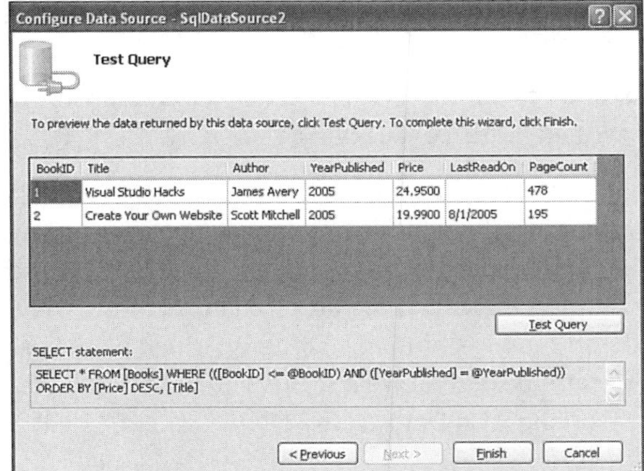

FIGURE 14.17
The query returns two records from the `Books` table.

To complete the SqlDataSource control's wizard, click the Finish button. If you want to practice with the Add `WHERE` Clause and Add `ORDER BY` Clause dialog boxes, click the Previous button to return to the Configure Select Statement screen.

A Look at the SqlDataSource Control's Markup

After you have configured the SqlDataSource control to have both `WHERE` and `ORDER BY` clauses, take a moment to go to the page's Source view to examine the markup generated by the control:

```
<asp:SqlDataSource ID="SqlDataSource2" runat="server"
   ConnectionString="<%$ ConnectionStrings:ConnectionString %>"
   SelectCommand="SELECT * FROM [Books] WHERE (([BookID] <= @BookID)
➥ AND ([YearPublished] = @YearPublished)) ORDER BY [Price] DESC,
[Title]">
  <SelectParameters>
    <asp:Parameter DefaultValue="3" Name="BookID" Type="Int32" />
    <asp:Parameter DefaultValue="2005" Name="YearPublished"
Type="Int32" />
  </SelectParameters>
</asp:SqlDataSource>
```

The `ID` and `ConnectionString` properties are nothing new; we examined them back in the "Examining the Data Source Controls" section at the start of this hour. The `SelectCommand` has been made more intricate, though, now including both a `WHERE` clause and an `ORDER BY` clause. Notice that no values are supplied for the filter expression values, even though we provided hard-coded values in the Add `WHERE` Clause dialog box. Instead, a **parameterized query** is used.

A **parameter** is a placeholder in a SQL statement that has the form `@`*`ParameterName`*. It serves as a location where a value will be inserted right before the actual SQL statement is sent off to the database. The SqlDataSource control lists the parameters for the `SelectCommand` in the `<SelectParameters>` element. There are two `<asp:Parameter>` elements within `<SelectParameters>`: one for the `@BookID` parameter and one for the `@YearPublished` parameter. Here, their hard-coded values are specified in the `DefaultValue` property.

When a user visits the ASP.NET page, the SqlDataSource control will take those parameter values and squirt them into the appropriate places within the `SELECT` query before sending off the query to the database. Although this may seem like a bit of overkill now because the values are hard-coded, its utility will become more apparent when we start having parameter values specified by the user visiting the page or from other external sources. We'll see how to base parameter values on user input in Hour 17, "Working with Data-Bound DropDownLists, RadioButtons, and CheckBoxes."

Summary

In this hour we discussed the ASP.NET data source controls, focusing specifically on the SqlDataSource control, which is designed to retrieve data from a database. The SqlDataSource control needs two bits of information to be able to grab data from a database: information on how to connect to the database and the SQL query to execute. As we saw in the "Working with the SqlDataSource Control" section, the SqlDataSource control contains a wizard that makes specifying this information a breeze.

The SqlDataSource control's wizard eventually generates a SQL `SELECT` statement that specifies what data to retrieve from the underlying database. This query is written using the Structured Query Language, or SQL, which is the language used by all modern databases for retrieving, inserting, updating, and deleting data.

To retrieve rows from a database table, a `SELECT` statement is used, which has the syntax

```
SELECT Column1, Column2, ..., ColumnN
FROM TableName
WHERE whereConditions
ORDER BY ColumnName
```

where the `WHERE` and `ORDER BY` clauses are optional.

Fortunately, we do not have to be SQL aficionados to retrieve database data in an ASP.NET web page. The SqlDataSource control's wizard allows us to construct our queries through an easy-to-use graphical interface.

Now that we have examined how to retrieve data from a database using the ASP.NET SqlDataSource control, the next step is to display that data in an ASP.NET page. This is accomplished through the use of data Web controls, which are examined in depth in the next hour.

Q&A

Q. ***Can SQL be used to retrieve data from multiple database tables?***

A. Yes. Although in this book we will be studying only examples that involve a single database table, commonly database tables share relationships. For example, imagine that we were working on a website for an eCommerce site, like Amazon.com. There might be a database table called `Orders`, which would contain a row for each order. Each order, of course, could have one or more items. Therefore, we might also have a table called `OrderItems`, which would contain a row for each item placed in each order.

These two tables obviously share a relationship with one another. That is, each row in the `OrderItems` table "belongs" to a particular row in the `Orders` table. This relationship can be expressed using **foreign keys**, which are special column types that relate a row in one table to a row in another. The topic of foreign keys is beyond the scope of this book.

After a relationship has been established between two tables, often you will want to retrieve results from both tables. For example, using the `Orders` and `OrderItems` example, we might want to issue a query that returns the list of orders placed in the past 24 hours. Along with each order, we might want to also retrieve its particular items. Such multitable SQL queries are beyond the scope of this book, but realize they are quite common in practice.

For more information on multitable relationships and more advanced SQL queries, consider picking up a copy of *Sams Teach Yourself SQL in 24 Hours* (ISBN: 0672324423).

Workshop

Quiz

1. Imagine that you had a database table named `Albums` that contained the following columns: `AlbumID`, `Name`, `Artist`, and `DatePurchased`. Write a SQL query to retrieve the name of the albums, ordered alphabetically.
2. Write a SQL query to retrieve, in this order, the artist, name, and date the album was purchased, ordered alphabetically by the artist.
3. Write a SQL query that retrieves the names of all of the albums by the artist Nirvana, ordered by the date the album was purchased, starting with the most recently purchased.
4. True or False: The following two SQL queries would return the exact same data:

```
SELECT AlbumID, Name, Artist, DatePurchased
FROM Albums
```

   And:

```
SELECT *
FROM Albums
```

5. Describe the steps you would take to add a data source control that returned the name and purchase date of albums whose `AlbumID` is greater than 5 that were recorded by the artist Pavement.

Answers

1. The following SQL query would suffice:

```
SELECT Name
FROM Albums
ORDER BY Name
```

2. The following SQL query would suffice:

```
SELECT Artist, Name, DatePurchased
FROM Albums
ORDER BY Artist
```

3. The following SQL query would suffice:

```
SELECT Name
FROM Albums
WHERE Artist = "Nirvana"
ORDER BY DatePurchased DESC
```

4. True.

5. Start by dragging a SqlDataSource control onto the Design view of an ASP.NET page and click the Configure Data Source link. Next, specify the database's connection information. From the Configure Select Statement screen, choose the `Albums` table from the drop-down list and select the `Name` and `DatePurchased` columns. Next, click the WHERE button to bring up the Add `WHERE` Clause dialog box.

   In that dialog box, add two filter expressions. For the first, on `AlbumID` use the > operator with a Source of None and a Value of 5. The second filter expression would be on the `Artist` column, using the = operator, with a Source of None and a Value of `Pavement`.

Exercises

1. This exercise is intended to improve your proficiency with SQL. Open the query window by right-clicking on the database in the Database Explorer and choosing New Query.

   In the query window craft the SQL query to retrieve those books whose `BookID` is less than or equal to 3. (You can enter the SQL directly into the SQL pane or use the diagram or criteria panes if you prefer.) Note the list of books you see when testing the query. Now, run another query, this time retrieving those books that have a price greater than $10.00. (You are encouraged to experiment with the query window further.)

HOUR 15

Displaying Data with the Data Web Controls

In this hour, we will cover

- Associating data Web controls with data source controls
- Using the GridView and DetailsView controls
- Customizing the appearance of the GridView and DetailsView controls
- Displaying only a subset of data source columns in a data Web control

Displaying data in an ASP.NET page requires using two classes of Web controls. First, a data source control is used to access the data; next, a data Web control is employed to display the data retrieved by the data source control. In the preceding hour we discussed what data source controls are, focusing in on the SqlDataSource control. In this hour we'll turn our attention to the data Web controls, which are a suite of controls that display the data from a data source control.

Just like the data source controls have a single job—to retrieve data from some data source—the data Web controls, too, have a single function—to display data. Therefore, the data Web controls do not provide any functionality to actually retrieve data. Instead, they simply take data from a data source and render it in an ASP.NET page. The data Web controls' differences lie in how they render the underlying data. For example, the GridView control displays data in a grid, with one row for each record in the data source control. There are also controls for displaying one record from the data source control at a time.

An Overview of Data Web Controls

ASP.NET contains a number of Web controls whose sole purpose is to display data from a data source control. These controls, which I call **data Web controls**, can be found in the

Data region of the Toolbox above the data source controls. As Figure 15.1 shows, there are five data Web controls: GridView, DataList, DetailsView, FormView, and Repeater. In this hour we will be examining only two of these data Web controls—the GridView and the DetailsView.

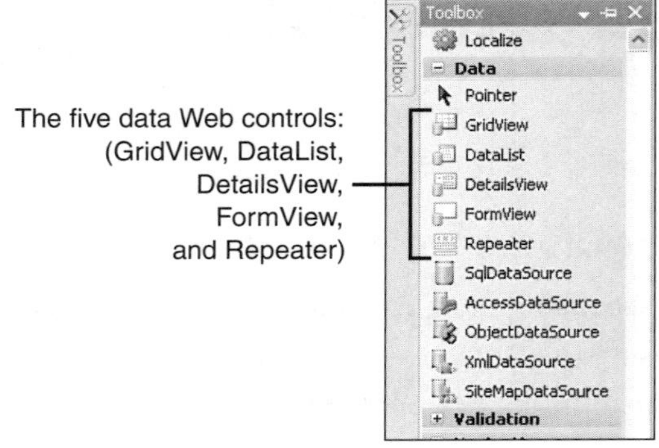

FIGURE 15.1 The Visual Web Developer Toolbox contains a number of data Web controls.

By the Way

The DropDownList, CheckBoxList, and RadioButtonList, which we examined in Hour 11, "Collecting Input Using Drop-Down Lists, Radio Buttons, and Check Boxes," can also be bound to data source controls. We'll look at binding data source controls to the DropDownList, CheckBoxList, and RadioButtonList controls in Hour 17, "Working with Data-Bound DropDownLists, RadioButtons, and CheckBoxes."

To display data with a data Web control, we need a populated data source control, such as the SqlDataSource control. After this data source control has been added to the page and configured, displaying its data through a data Web control is a cinch: Simply drag the appropriate data Web control onto the ASP.NET page and, through its smart tag, specify the data source control to use. That's it!

To illustrate the simplicity in displaying data in an ASP.NET page, let's take the `AccessingData.aspx` page from the preceding hour and enhance it by adding a GridView control. (Recall that the `AccessingData.aspx` page has two SqlDataSource controls: one that returns *all* records and columns in the `Books` table and one that returns only those books whose `BookID` is less than or equal to 3 and was published in 2005.)

Start by bringing up this page and going to the Design view. Next, drag on a GridView control from the Toolbox's Data section. The GridView, which we'll be examining in much greater detail later in this hour as well as next hour, displays the data in the data source control in a grid. After you add the GridView to your page's Design view, your screen should look similar to Figure 15.2.

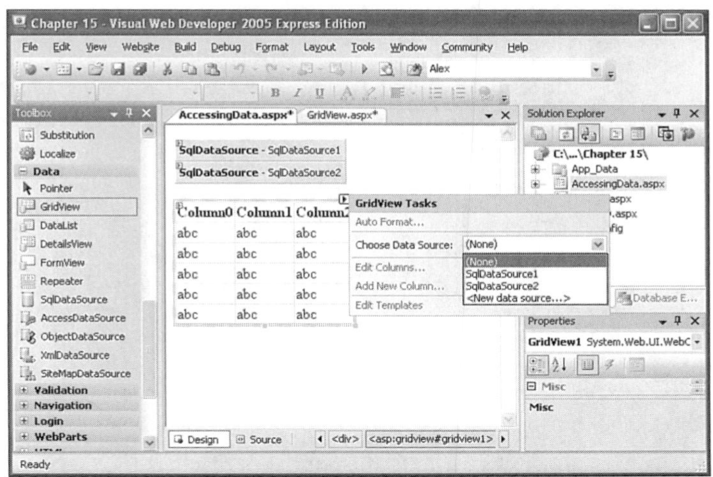

FIGURE 15.2
A GridView has been added to the page.

By default, the GridView shows up as a five-row grid in the Design view with generic field names Column0, Column1, and Column2. This is how the GridView appears in Visual Web Developer when there is no data source associated with it.

By the Way

There can be some confusion when using the word *column* when talking about database tables and GridViews. Both have columns, after all, thereby making it easy to confuse the context. To help remedy this, I will use the word *field* to refer to a GridView's columns and *column* to refer to the columns of a database table.

Assigning a data source control to the GridView is easy. In the smart tag there's a Choose Data Source task with a drop-down list that contains the data source controls on the page. Simply select the data source control whose contents you want to display in the GridView. After you make a selection, the GridView's field structure will be updated to mirror the columns in the data source control.

Go ahead and select `SqlDataSource1` as the GridView's data source. When you make this selection, the GridView's appearance in the Design view will be updated to reflect the columns returned by `SqlDataSource1`, as Figure 15.3 shows.

Did you Know?

If selecting a data source merely changes the GridView's field headers from Column0, Column1, and Column2 to Databound Col0, Databound Col1, and Databound Col2, click the Refresh Schema link in the smart tag. This will update the GridView's display with the columns returned by the data source control.

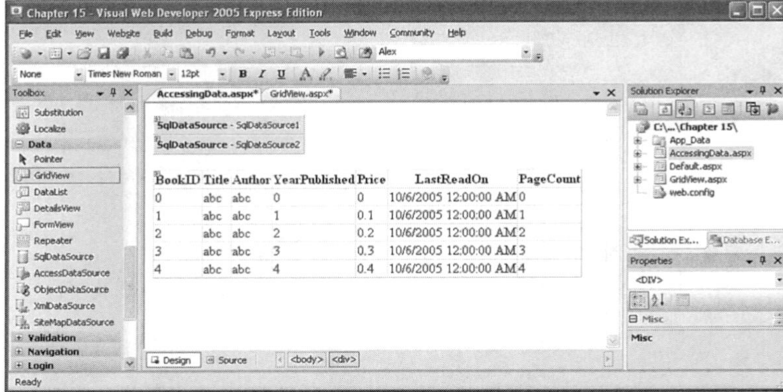

FIGURE 15.3 `SqlDataSource1` has been assigned as the GridView's data source control.

Congratulations, you now have an ASP.NET page that displays the contents of the query executed by `SqlDataSource1`. Take a moment to view the ASP.NET page in a browser (go to the Debug menu and choose Start Without Debugging). You should see a grid in your browser with a row for each of the five books in the `Books` table (see Figure 15.4).

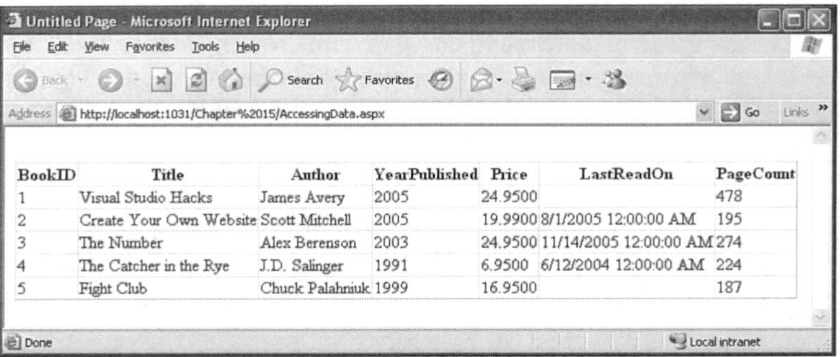

FIGURE 15.4 The contents of the `Books` table are displayed through an ASP.NET page.

By the Way

> If you visit the ASP.NET page *before* specifying the GridView's data source, you'll see only a blank page. Similarly, if the GridView is assigned a data source control, but the data source control does not return any records (perhaps the underlying database table has no records, or the `WHERE` condition suppresses all records), then you'll also see a blank page.
>
> The GridView renders a grid only if it is assigned a data source control and if the data source control returns one or more records.

The output in Figure 15.4 is hardly ideal; it lacks any attractive fonts or colors, displays the columns in the order in which they were returned from the data source control, and applies no cell-level formatting. (For example, the `LastReadOn` value unnecessarily includes the time; the `Price` value does not include a currency symbol and has four decimal places rather than the typical two.) Don't worry, though, we'll look at how to customize the GridView later in this hour.

For now, take note of the process for displaying data on an ASP.NET page. The first step is to add the data source control that retrieves the appropriate subset of data. Following that, we'll add a data Web control and, through its smart tag, specify what data source to use. Although our example in this section used the GridView, the process for associating a data source control with other data Web controls is identical.

Displaying Data with the GridView Control

When we're displaying data on a web page, more often than not we want to display all records from a particular query. The query might be a static query, such as `SELECT * FROM [Books]`, or it may be a more dynamic one whose filter expressions are based on the visitor's input. Regardless of the type of query, if you want to display all of the results at once, then consider using the GridView.

In addition to showing each of the records retrieved by the data source control, the GridView, by default, shows an additional **header row**, which lists the names of the displayed fields. By default, the GridView contains a field for each of the data source control's columns, although this can be customized as we'll see shortly.

In this hour we already examined adding a GridView to an ASP.NET page and associating it with a data source control. There are but two steps:

1. Add a data source control to the page and configure it to retrieve the data you are interested in displaying.
2. Add a GridView to the page and configure it to use the data source control added in step 1.

The result of these two simple steps is an ASP.NET page that displays the retrieved data in a grid.

A Look at the GridView's Declarative Markup

When adding the GridView control to our ASP.NET page, we did everything through the Design view. Like any other Web control, the GridView can also be configured declaratively, through the Source view. However, the tools available through the

Design view can save you a great deal of typing. Figure 15.2 showed the Design view immediately after adding a GridView to the page. The declarative markup added to the Source view is very concise:

```
<asp:GridView ID="GridView1" runat="server">
</asp:GridView>
```

However, after you set the GridView's data source through the smart tag, the declarative markup explodes. Listing 15.1 contains the declarative markup after the GridView has been bound to `SqlDataSource1`. Figure 15.3 shows what the GridView looks like in the Design view after making this setting.

LISTING 15.1 The GridView's Markup, After It's Been Bound to a Data Source Control

```
 1: <asp:GridView ID="GridView1" runat="server" AutoGenerateColumns="False"
➥DataKeyNames="BookID"
 2:     DataSourceID="SqlDataSource1">
 3:     <Columns>
 4:         <asp:BoundField DataField="BookID" HeaderText="BookID"
➥InsertVisible="False" ReadOnly="True"
 5:             SortExpression="BookID" />
 6:         <asp:BoundField DataField="Title" HeaderText="Title"
➥SortExpression="Title" />
 7:         <asp:BoundField DataField="Author" HeaderText="Author"
➥SortExpression="Author" />
 8:         <asp:BoundField DataField="YearPublished"
➥HeaderText="YearPublished" SortExpression="YearPublished" />
 9:         <asp:BoundField DataField="Price" HeaderText="Price"
➥SortExpression="Price" />
10:         <asp:BoundField DataField="LastReadOn" HeaderText="LastReadOn"
➥ SortExpression="LastReadOn" />
11:         <asp:BoundField DataField="PageCount" HeaderText="PageCount"
➥ SortExpression="PageCount" />
12:     </Columns>
13: </asp:GridView>
```

The `<asp:GridView>` tag (lines 1 and 2) has three new properties:

- `AutoGenerateColumns`—This property indicates whether the GridView bases its fields on the data source's columns or on the columns explicitly defined in the `<Columns>` tag. With `AutoGenerateColumns="False"`, the fields rendered are those specified in the `<Columns>` tag.
- `DataKeyNames`—This property specifies the column name(s) that uniquely identify each row being bound to the GridView. This is, by default, the primary key column(s). The smart tag was able to determine the primary key of the data source control and assigned this property accordingly.
- `DataSourceID`—This property specifies the `ID` of the GridView's data source control.

Starting on line 3 is the <Columns> element, which defines the fields of the GridView (lines 4 through 11). Each <asp:BoundField> element represents a field rendered in the GridView. As you can see from Listing 15.1, there are seven fields in the GridView, one for each of the columns returned by the data source control. Each <asp:BoundField> element contains an assortment of properties, specifying the name of the database column whose data is to be displayed (`DataField`) and the text shown in the column's header (`HeaderText`), among others. This tag can also contain column-specific formatting information, as we'll see shortly.

The purpose of Listing 15.1 is to highlight the benefit of the Design view in Visual Web Developer. Without the Design view, we would have to enter in the GridView's declarative markup by hand. Thanks to the Design view and the GridView's smart tag, this declarative markup was automatically generated for us the moment we specified the GridView's data source control.

By the Way

In an upcoming section, "Customizing the Appearance of the GridView," we'll see how to tweak the aesthetic properties of the GridView through the Design view. Keep in mind, however, that you can always make the same changes through the declarative syntax, if needed. Granted, this approach might not be as easy or quick, but do keep in mind that there is a one-to-one correspondence between everything we do in the Design view and the resulting declarative markup of the control being edited.

Examining the GridView's Rendered Markup

When an ASP.NET page is requested through a browser, the page is rendered into HTML. This requires that the Web controls on the page be converted from the declarative markup to HTML. The GridView is translated into an HTML <table> with a table row (<tr>) for each row in the data source control and a table cell (<td>) for each column and for each row. The header row's columns are rendered as table headers (<th>).

Listing 15.2 shows the HTML generated by the GridView. When the browser receives this HTML, it will display the output shown in Figure 15.4.

LISTING 15.2 A GridView Is Rendered as an HTML <table>

```
<table cellspacing="0" rules="all" border="1" id="GridView1"
➥style="border-collapse:collapse;">
  <tr>
    <th scope="col">BookID</th><th scope="col">Title</th><th scope="col">
➥Author</th><th scope="col">YearPublished</th><th scope="col">Price</th>
➥<th scope="col">LastReadOn</th><th scope="col">PageCount</th>
  </tr><tr>
    <td>1</td><td>Visual Studio Hacks</td><td>James Avery</td>
➥<td>2005</td><td>24.9500</td><td> </td><td>478</td>
```

LISTING 15.2 Continued

```
    </tr><tr>
        <td>2</td><td>Create Your Own Website</td><td>Scott Mitchell</td>
➥<td>2005</td><td>19.9900</td><td>8/1/2005 12:00:00 AM</td><td>195</td>
    </tr><tr>
        <td>3</td><td>The Number</td><td>Alex Berenson</td>
➥<td>2003</td><td>24.9500</td><td>11/14/2005 12:00:00 AM</td><td>274</td>
    </tr><tr>
        <td>4</td><td>The Catcher in the Rye</td><td>J.D. Salinger</td>
➥<td>1991</td><td>6.9500</td><td>6/12/2004 12:00:00 AM</td><td>224</td>
    </tr><tr>
        <td>5</td><td>Fight Club</td><td>Chuck Palahniuk</td>
➥<td>1999</td><td>16.9500</td><td> </td><td>187</td>
    </tr>
</table>
```

Customizing the Appearance of the GridView

The GridView shown in Figure 15.4 is rather unattractive. It lacks any color; uses the default system font; displays, perhaps, fields that don't concern the user (such as `BookID`); and lacks any sort of formatting for currency and date values. Also, all values are left-aligned and look alike. Perhaps we want the `PageCount` right-aligned and want to emphasize the title of the book by displaying it in *italics*. Finally, the field names displayed in the grid's header are the precise names of the database columns—`BookID`, `YearPublished`, `LastReadOn`, `PageCount`, and so on. Ideally, we would want these to be more readable names, like ID, Published, Last Read, and Pages.

All of these customizations can be easily accomplished with the GridView. The GridView allows customization of its appearance on a number of levels:

- **The GridView-level**—Changes specified at this level affect *all* of the data in the GridView.
- **The Field-level**—You can use this level to format a particular field in the GridView.
- **The Row-level**—You can specify customized formatting for various classes of rows. For example, you can make alternating rows have a different background color, or you can have the header row displayed in a larger font size.

These various levels of settings can be set through the Auto Format dialog box, the Fields dialog box, or the Properties window. Let's examine how to tailor the GridView's appearance at each of the levels using each of the tools available.

Formatting from the Properties Window

GridView-level and row-level formatting can be accomplished directly through the Properties window. Take a moment to click on the GridView in the Design view, which will load the GridView's properties in the Properties window. In the Appearances section (see Figure 15.5), you can set a number of GridView-level properties.

Table 15.1 lists these Appearance properties along with a brief description. Realize that these properties affect the entire GridView's formatting. That is, if you set, say, the `BackColor` property to Green, all of the rows and all of the fields in the GridView will have a Green background color.

TABLE 15.1 The Appearance Properties Affect the Entire GridView's Formatting

Property	Description
`BackColor`	Specifies the GridView's background color.
`BackImageUrl`	Specifies an image to display in the GridView's background.
`BorderColor`	Specifies the color of the GridView's border.
`BorderStyle`	Specifies the GridView's border's style. Can be `NotSet`, `None`, `Dotted`, `Dashed`, and `Solid`, among others.
`BorderWidth`	Specifies the width of the border.
`CssClass`	Specifies the class name if you want to apply an external cascading style sheet (CSS) class to the GridView.
`EmptyDataText`	Specifies whether you want a message to be displayed in the event that there are no records. Recall that a GridView is rendered only if there are records returned by its data source control.
`Font`	Specifies the font settings for the GridView. Refer to Table 8.1 for a listing of the `Font` property's subproperties.
`ForeColor`	Specifies the GridView's foreground color.
`GridLines`	Specifies how lines are drawn between the cells of the grid. Can be `None`, `Vertical`, `Horizontal`, or `Both` (the default).
`ShowFooter`	Specifies a Boolean value that indicates whether the footer row is shown; `False` by default.
`ShowHeader`	Specifies a Boolean value indicating whether the header row is shown; `True` by default.

Take a moment to try out some of these Appearance properties. Figure 15.5 shows Visual Web Developer after I set a number of properties. While making changes to these properties, notice how the GridView's appearance in the Design view is automatically updated to reflect the new formatting choices. Furthermore, note how the Appearance property settings affect the *entire* GridView.

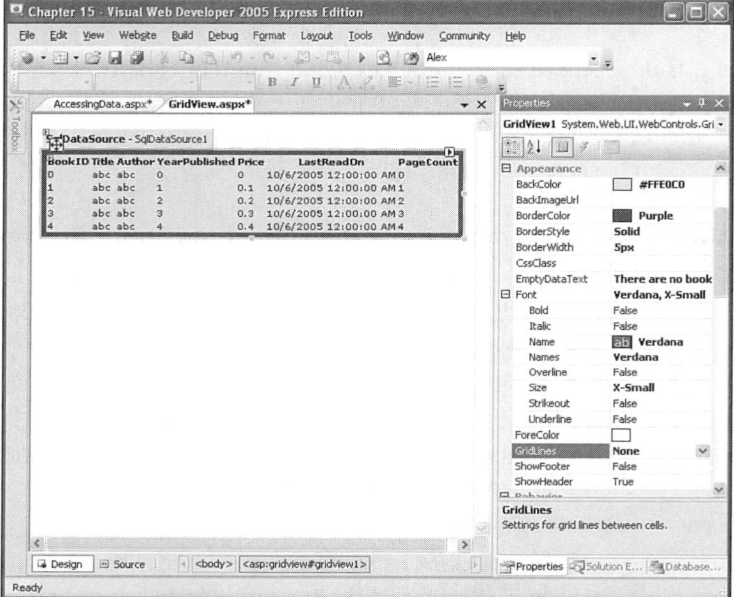

FIGURE 15.5 Customize the formatting of the entire GridView using the Appearance properties.

The Properties window also includes properties that you can set to specify the formatting at the row-level. In the Styles section of the Properties window, you'll find a suite of properties that apply to various classes of rows. Table 15.2 lists these row-level style properties.

TABLE 15.2 The Styles Properties Affect Various Classes of Rows

Property	Description
`AlternatingRowStyle`	Specifies style information for alternating rows.
`EditRowStyle`	Specifies the formatting for an editable row. When you're working with an editable GridView—a topic for Hour 16, "Deleting, Inserting, and Editing Data"—you will have a particular row being edited.
`EmptyDataRowStyle`	Specifies the style for a row if there are no records in the GridView's data source and you have set the `EmptyDataText` property in the Appearance settings.
`FooterStyle`	Specifies the style of the footer row.

TABLE 15.2 Continued

Property	Description
`HeaderStyle`	Specifies the header row style.
`PagerStyle`	Specifies the style for the GridView's paging controls. When you're creating pageable GridViews—again, a topic for Hour 16—a pager row is included.
`RowStyle`	Specifies the style for a GridView row.
`SelectedRowStyle`	Specifies the style for a selected row. Unfortunately, we won't have time to examine how to make a GridView row "selected."

Each of these properties has a number of subproperties: `BackColor`, `ForeColor`, `Font`, `CssClass`, `HorizontalAlign`, and the like. Take a moment to set some of the subproperties for `RowStyle`, `AlternatingRowStyle`, and `HeaderStyle`. Figure 15.6 shows Visual Web Developer after I customized my GridView's formatting a bit.

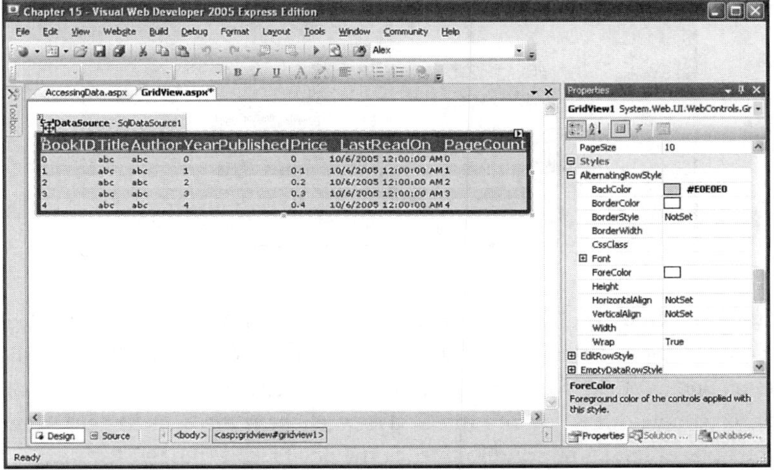

FIGURE 15.6
The Styles properties allow you to customize various classes of rows.

Formatting the GridView's Fields

At this point we've seen how to perform GridView-level formatting as well as row-level formatting. The only level we've yet to examine is field-level. You cannot edit the fields of the GridView through the Properties window; instead, go to the GridView's smart tag and click the Edit Columns link. This will display the Fields dialog box (see Figure 15.7).

The Fields dialog box lists the fields in the GridView in the bottom-left corner. Selecting a field from this list will load that field's properties in the list on the right. At the upper-left portion of the Fields dialog box is the list of types of fields that can be added to a GridView. Currently, all of the fields used by the GridView are **BoundFields**. A BoundField simply displays the value from a particular column in the corresponding data source control. Other types of fields enable other functionality. For example, the HyperLinkField displays a hyperlink in each row; the ButtonField displays a button in each row. We'll examine some of these additional field types in more detail in Hour 16.

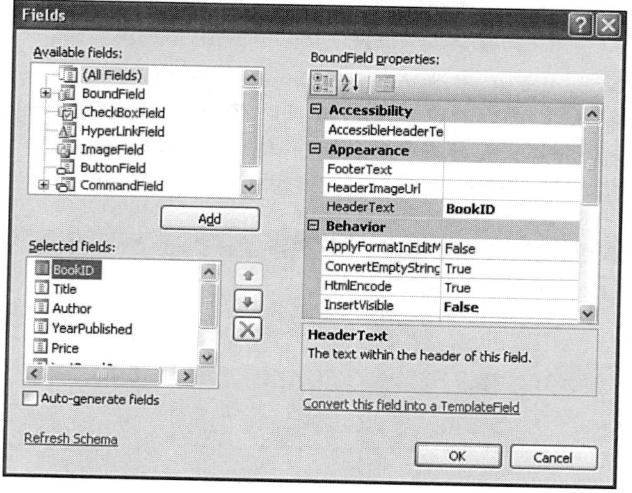

FIGURE 15.7 Customize the columns of the GridView through the Fields dialog box.

In addition to listing all of the fields currently in the GridView, the Selected Fields list allows you to remove fields and reorder the fields in the GridView. For example, let's remove the `BookID` field from the GridView because end users don't need this information. To remove this field from the GridView, click on the `BookID` field from the list in the bottom-left corner and then click the delete icon (the red X). Next, let's have the `PageCount` field displayed after the `Author` field. To accomplish this, click on the `PageCount` field and then click the up-arrow icon until `PageCount` is the third field in the list.

To customize a particular field, first click on the field in the list. This will load its properties in the right side of the dialog box. Table 15.3 lists some of the more germane field-level properties.

TABLE 15.3 A Field Can Be Customized Through the Fields Dialog Box

Property	Description
`HeaderText`	Specifies the text that is displayed in the field's header row.
`DataFormatString`	Indicates how the values for this field are formatted.
`HtmlEncode`	Specifies a Boolean value that indicates whether the value is HTML encoded before being bound to the grid (the default is `True`). HTML encoding is recommended because it removes `<script>` elements and other HTML that might not render properly in the grid. However, to have the `DataFormatString` property work, you must set `HtmlEncode` to `False`.
`HeaderStyle`	Specifies the field's header row style. You can customize the header row style on a field-by-field basis using this property.
`ItemStyle`	Indicates the style for the rows of the field. For example, you could have all of the book titles displayed in italics by setting this property for the `Title` field.

Change the `HeaderText` properties of the `PageCount`, `YearPublished`, and `LastReadOn` fields to `Pages`, `Published` and `Last Read`, respectively. Next, go to the `Title` field's `ItemStyle` property and expand it, locating the `Font` property. Expand the `Font` property and set the `Italic` subproperty to `True`.

Let's also configure the `Price` and `LastReadOn` fields to format their values more appropriately. To format a field, we need to set two properties: `HtmlEncode` must be set to `False`, and `DataFormatString` should be set to the **format string** of the form `{0:`*`format specifier`*`}`. The format specifier indicates how the data is to be formatted. A number of built-in format specifiers are designed to format specific data types. For example, `c` formats a number into a currency; `d` formats a date/time value into just a date. You can find a complete list of format specifiers by searching the Visual Web Developer help for "formatting."

To format the `Price` field as a currency and the `LastReadOn` field as just a date, set the `HtmlEncode` property to `False` for both fields and then set the `DataFormatString` properties of the `Price` field to `{0:c}` and the `LastReadOn` field to `{0:d}`.

Click OK to close the Fields dialog box. When you return to the Design view, the GridView should be updated to show the new changes: The `BookID` field has been removed, the `Pages` field now comes after the `Author` field, the `Title` field is displayed in *italics*, and so on. Figure 15.8 shows Internet Explorer when viewing the GridView after making these field-level formatting settings.

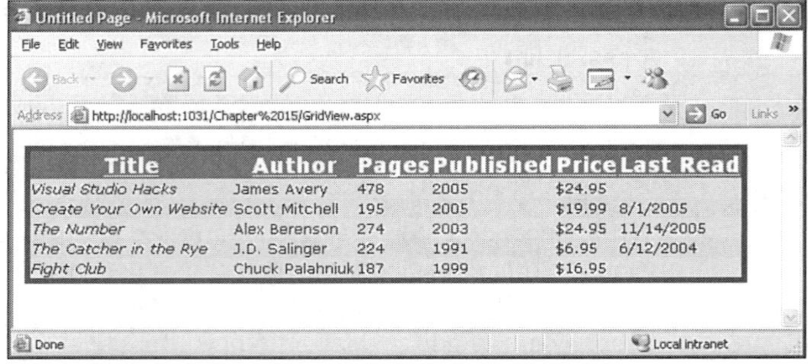

FIGURE 15.8
The fields of the GridView have been customized.

Formatting with the Auto Format Dialog Box

As you may have gathered from the formatting I've applied to the GridView, its rows, and its fields, I am hardly one to be trusted with choosing the GridView's formatting. I have about as much artistic skill as a vegetable. We can be thankful that the GridView includes an Auto Format option. From the smart tag, click the Auto Format link, which shows the Auto Format dialog box (see Figure 15.9). From this dialog box, you can pick one of a number of predefined styles.

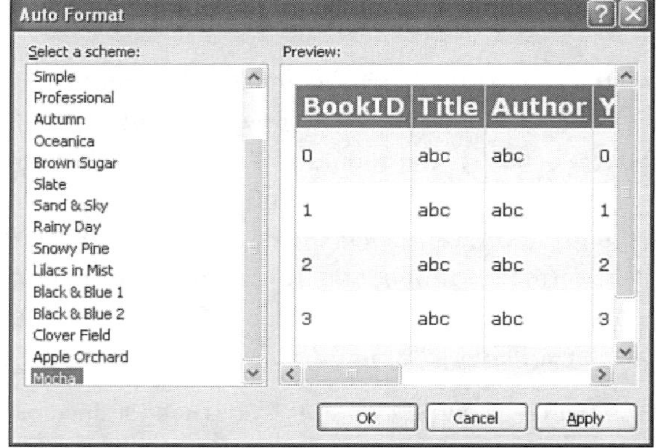

FIGURE 15.9
The Mocha style looks so much nicer than anything I could craft.

Selecting one of the Auto Format styles will cause a number of Appearance and Styles properties to be automatically set in order to display the chosen format. If you are an artistic individual, you might rather just define these formatting settings yourself. However, if you're like me, the Auto Format feature will quickly become your best friend!

Showing One Record at a Time with the DetailsView

The GridView control shows all of the records from its data source control at once. Sometimes, however, we may want to show just one record at a time. The DetailsView control provides this functionality. Like the GridView control, the DetailsView control is bound to a data source control in the same manner. Drag the DetailsView onto a page with a data source control and then, from the smart tag, associate the DetailsView with the data source control. After you assign the data source control, the DetailsView presents a vertical list of the columns in the data source control.

To familiarize ourselves with the DetailsView control, let's create a new ASP.NET page called `DetailsView.aspx`. As in the preceding hour, add a SqlDataSource control to the page, configuring it to select all records and columns from the `Books` table. Next, add a DetailsView to the page and associate it with the SqlDataSource control. After you have completed these steps, your screen should look similar to Figure 15.10.

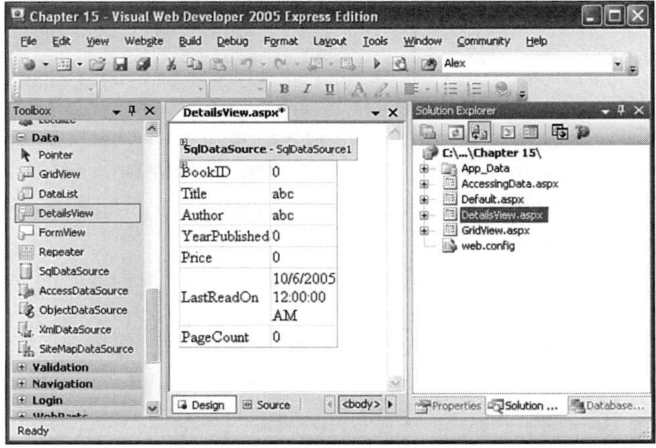

FIGURE 15.10
A DetailsView control has been added to the page and assigned a data source control.

Take a moment to view the DetailsView in a web browser by going to the Debug menu and choosing Start Without Debugging. Figure 15.11 shows Internet Explorer when viewing `DetailsView.aspx`. Note that the first record returned by the SqlDataSource control is displayed.

You may have noticed that the DetailsView, by default, doesn't provide any mechanism by which to view the next record in the data source. That is, with the

DetailsView we see one record at a time, but there's no way to move to the next record. To provide a means to step through the records, check the Enable Paging check box in the DetailsView's smart tag. This will add a **pager row** to the bottom of the DetailsView. The pager row contains the user interface for stepping through the records of the corresponding data source control. By default, the paging interface uses **page numbers** to allow the user to jump to a particular record.

FIGURE 15.11
A single record from the data source control is displayed.

After checking the Enable Paging check box, take a moment to view the ASP.NET page in a browser. Note that now there are five links at the bottom of the DetailsView, allowing you to navigate to any of the five records in the `Books` table by clicking on the appropriately numbered link.

> The GridView control makes it easy to allow the user to page through and sort the displayed data. We'll look at how to implement paging and sorting with the GridView later in this hour, in the "Paging and Sorting with the GridView" section.

Customizing the Paging Interface

The DetailsView control's pager row can be customized through the Properties window. First, click on the DetailsView in the Design view to load the properties. Next, scroll down to the Paging section of the Properties window. There, you'll see two properties:

- `AllowPaging`—This property indicates whether paging is supported (it defaults to `False`). When you checked the Enable Paging check box in the smart tag, this property was set to `True`.

- `PagerSettings`—This property contains a number of subproperties that customize the appearance of the pager row. For example, instead of having page number links, you can use Next/Previous links.

Let's change the `PagerSettings` property so that instead of the page number links, we use next, previous, first, and last links. Expand the `PagerSettings` property and go to the `Mode` subproperty. Here, you'll find a drop-down list with the various choices. By default, the `Numeric` option is selected; change this to the `NextPreviousFirstLast` option. Note how the DetailsView changes in the Design view in Visual Web Developer to include the next, previous, first, and last links. Figure 15.12 shows this pageable DetailsView when viewed through a browser.

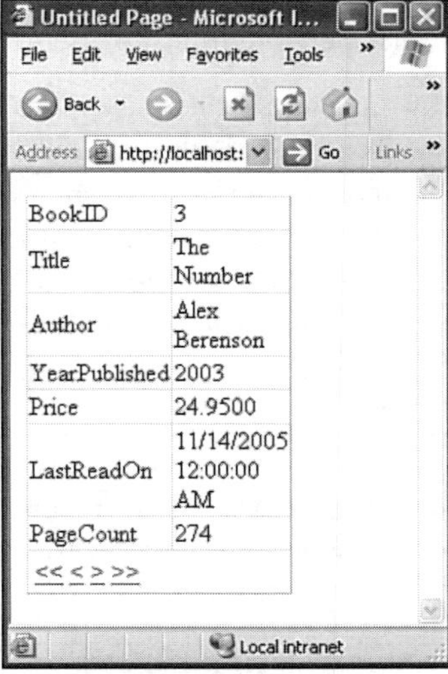

FIGURE 15.12 The DetailsView now supports paging and is showing information for the book *The Number*.

Did you Know?

By default, the next, previous, first, and last links are displayed as >, <, <<, and >>, respectively. You can change these, if you like, via the `PagerStyle`'s `NextPageText`, `PreviousPageText`, `FirstPageText`, and `LastPageText` properties. One important note—if you want to display a < or >, you need to use the escaped HTML equivalent: `<` or `>`.

By the Way

The GridView also supports pagination. With the GridView, however, you typically page through 10 or 20 records at a time, as opposed to one record at a time. In the next hour we'll examine how to implement and customize the paging features of the GridView control.

Customizing the Appearance of the DetailsView

The DetailsView's appearance can be customized just like the GridView's. There are DetailsView-level, row-level, and field-level formatting properties. The DetailsView-level and row-level properties can be configured through the Properties window in the Appearance and Styles sections, and the field-level properties are accessible through the smart tag's Edit Fields link, which displays the—you guessed it—Fields dialog box. The DetailsView also has an Auto Format option in its smart tag, just like the GridView.

While the process of customizing the formatting of the GridView and DetailsView is identical, there are some differences between the two controls' formatting properties. For example, the DetailsView does not have the notion of a "selected" row, so there's no `SelectedRowStyle`. As we'll see in the next hour, the DetailsView can be used to insert data into a database, and therefore it has an `InsertRowStyle` property.

For practice, take a moment to customize the appearance of the DetailsView. Go ahead and customize its fields like we did with the GridView. Add some color and font settings to liven up the web page. Figure 15.13 shows the DetailsView in a browser after gussying up the appearance. Note that I applied the same field-level customizations that we did with the GridView (renaming the header rows, moving the `Price` field to come after the `Authors` field, formatting the `Price` as a currency, and so on).

When setting the `DataFormatString` for the `Price` and `LastReadOn` fields, don't forget that you also need to set the `HtmlEncode` property to `False`. If you forget to do this, the formatting won't be applied to the field.

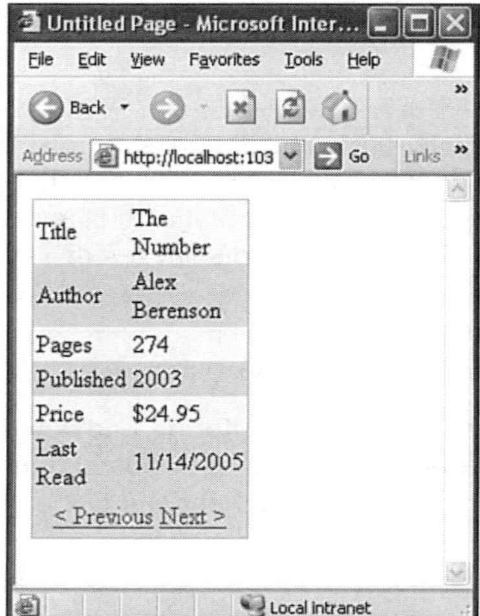

FIGURE 15.13 With some formatting, the DetailsView is much easier on the eyes.

A Look at the DetailsView's Markup

When examining the GridView earlier in this hour, we took time to examine both the GridView's declarative markup in the Source view through Visual Web Developer and the rendered HTML that is sent to the web browser. Whenever you are working with a new Web control, I encourage you to explore both the control's declarative and HTML markup because doing so helps foster a better understanding as to how these controls are represented in the ASP.NET page and in the browser.

We're not going to spend the time to explore the DetailsView's markup in earnest here; that is a task that you can handle on your own. However, I do want to point out that the DetailsView is rendered as an HTML `<table>`. Instead of having a table row for each record in the associated data source control and a table cell for each column of each row, the DetailsView has a table row for each column of the data source control with two table cells per table row: one for the data source control's column's name and one for its value. The result is a two-columned HTML `<table>` that has one row for each database table column returned by the data source control.

Listing 15.3 shows the HTML emitted by the DetailsView shown in Figure 15.11.

LISTING 15.3 The DetailsView Control Is Rendered as an HTML `<table>`

```
<table cellspacing="0" rules="all" border="1" id="DetailsView1"
➥ style="height:50px;width:125px;border-collapse:collapse;">
    <tr>
        <td>BookID</td><td>1</td>
    </tr><tr>
        <td>Title</td><td>Visual Studio Hacks</td>
    </tr><tr>
        <td>Author</td><td>James Avery</td>
    </tr><tr>
        <td>YearPublished</td><td>2005</td>
    </tr><tr>
        <td>Price</td><td>24.9500</td>
    </tr><tr>
        <td>LastReadOn</td><td> </td>
    </tr><tr>
        <td>PageCount</td><td>478</td>
    </tr>
</table>
```

Paging and Sorting with the GridView

By default, the DetailsView shows a *single* record from its data source control. To allow the user to view *all* records, stepping through them one at a time, we needed to configure the DetailsView to allow paging. This, of course, was as simple as checking the Enable Paging check box in the DetailsView's smart tag and then customizing the paging interface through the Properties window. (Refer back to the "Customizing the Paging Interface" section for more information on this process.)

The GridView, by default, shows *all* of the records in its data source control. Showing all of the records, however, can lead to information overload if hundreds or thousands of records are being retrieved by the data source control. For example, in Figure 15.8 all five records of the `Books` table are displayed. However, imagine that instead of five records in this table there were five *hundred*. Such a page would be unwieldy and would likely intimidate any users who were interested in what books we were reading. (Although they'd likely be impressed with the breadth of our library!) To help make the information more digestible, we can implement paging with a GridView, showing only a small subset of the records at a time.

In addition to paging, another feature that helps improve the usefulness of data that users are familiar with is sorting. When you go to a travel planning site to book a flight, the results are usually sorted by price, from the least expensive tickets to the most expensive. However, you may be interested in some other criteria, such as departure time or airline. Many sites offer users the ability to sort the results by these other features. ASP.NET makes it easy to add similar functionality to your site. The GridView provides a means for the user to sort the results by a particular field.

In the next two sections we'll see how to implement and customize the paging and sorting capabilities in the GridView.

A Look at Paging

Enabling paging in the GridView is similar to enabling paging in the DetailsView: Simply go to the GridView's smart tag and check the Enable Paging check box. To customize the paging interface, go to the Properties window and locate the Paging section. The GridView's Paging section contains four properties:

- `AllowPaging`—This property indicates whether paging is supported (it defaults to `False`). When you checked the Enable Paging check box in the smart tag, this property was set to `True`.
- `PageIndex`—This property indicates the index of the page of data displayed. (The value is indexed starting at 0; to display the first page of data by default, leave this set at 0.)
- `PagerSettings`—This property contains a number of subproperties that customize the appearance of the pager row. For example, instead of having page number links, you can use Next/Previous links.
- `PageSize`—This property indicates the number of records to show per page.

The `AllowPaging` and `PagerSettings` properties should look familiar because they were the two properties in the Pager section of the DetailsView's properties. You probably won't ever need to set `PageIndex` through the Properties window; its default value of 0 ensures that the first page of data is displayed when the web page is first loaded in the user's browser. The final property, `PageSize`, specifies how many records to show per page. By default, 10 records will be shown per page. If you want to display more or fewer records per page, change this property value appropriately.

Testing the Paging Functionality

Because our `Books` table has only five records in total, leaving the `PageSize` at 10 would be uninteresting since there would be only one page of data. Instead, let's set this property value to 2. After you have done that, take a moment to view the ASP.NET page through a browser. Figure 15.14 shows my browser when first visiting this page. Note that I'm using the Numeric mode for the paging interface (the default). There are three pages in total, of which I am viewing page 1. Click the 3 hyperlink in the paging interface. This will reload the page, showing the third page of data (see Figure 15.15).

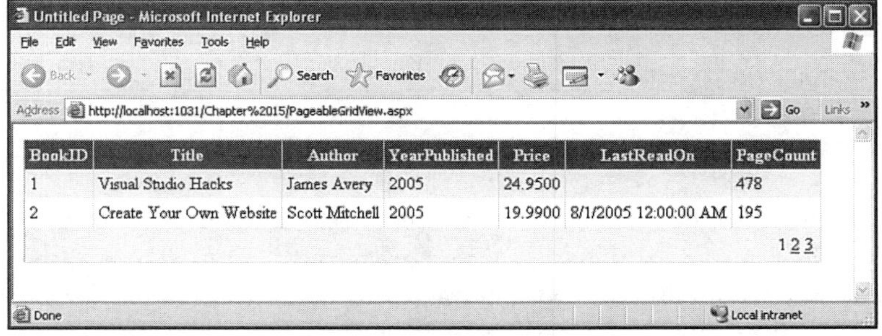

BookID	Title	Author	YearPublished	Price	LastReadOn	PageCount
1	Visual Studio Hacks	James Avery	2005	24.9500		478
2	Create Your Own Website	Scott Mitchell	2005	19.9900	8/1/2005 12:00:00 AM	195
						1 2 3

FIGURE 15.14 The first page of data is shown, displaying the first two books from the `Books` table.

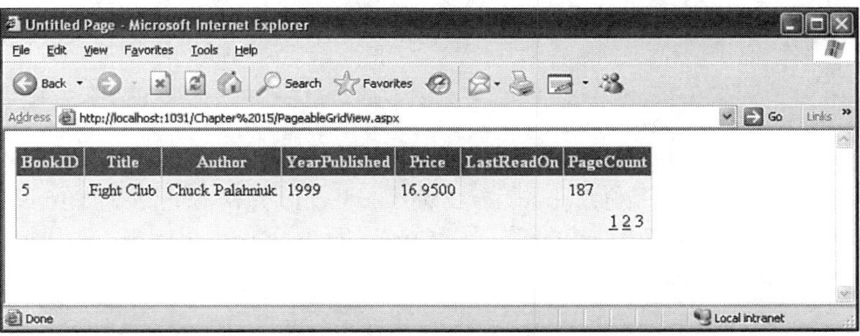

BookID	Title	Author	YearPublished	Price	LastReadOn	PageCount
5	Fight Club	Chuck Palahniuk	1999	16.9500		187
						1 2 3

FIGURE 15.15 The third page of data is shown, displaying the fifth and final book.

For you to be able to page through the results of a SqlDataSource, the SqlDataSource control's `DataSourceMode` property must be set to `DataSet`. `DataSet` is the default value, so paging should "just work" with the SqlDataSource you have added to the page.

However, if you have changed this property to `DataReader` and attempt to page through its records with a GridView (or DetailsView), you will get an exception. Simply change this property back to `DataSet` to get things working.

This caution also applies to sorting a GridView's data, which we'll be examining shortly.

What's Happening When Moving from One Page to Another?

Regardless of whether the GridView is configured to page through the data, the associated data source control always grabs *all* of the records from its specified SQL query. When a pageable GridView is used, the GridView uses only a subset of its data source control's records. Specifically, the GridView grabs records based on two parameters:

- The number of records to show per page (`PageSize`)
- The current page being displayed (`PageIndex`)

It uses the following formula:

```
StartRecordIndex = PageSize * PageIndex
EndRecordIndex = PageSize + (PageSize * PageIndex) - 1
```

Here, `StartRecordIndex` and `EndRecordIndex` specify the starting and ending indexes of the range of the data source control's records that need to be displayed. The data source control indexes each of the records returned from the database, starting the indexing at 0. Therefore, if the GridView needs to get the first five records, it can ask the data source control for those records whose index lies between 0 and 4. To get the next five, it can ask for those whose index lies between 5 and 9, and so on.

Back in our earlier example, we set `PageSize` to 2 through the Properties window; when the page is first loaded, `PageIndex` will equal 0. This means that the values of `StartRecordIndex` and `EndRecordIndex` will be 0 and 1, respectively. Therefore, the GridView will be given the first two records from its data source control, which it will display (see Figure 15.14).

When the user clicks the 3 link to jump to the third page of data, the ASP.NET page is posted back. The GridView notes that the user has requested to see the third page of data and internally updates the value of its `PageIndex` property to 2. Next, the values for `StartRecordIndex` and `EndRecordIndex` are recomputed, this time returning the values 4 and 5, respectively. The data source control, again, grabs *all* of the records from the database. Because the data source control's records are indexed only up to 4 (remember, there are only five records in the `Books` table), the data source control returns just the record with index 4 (see Figure 15.15).

Did you Know?

> Even though a GridView may be configured to show only, say, two records per page, the data source control will still grab *all* records from the database each time the user pages through a page of data. This is inefficient, especially if you're paging through large amounts of data.
>
> To alleviate grabbing all of the redundant records, you'll need to look into using the ObjectDataSource control. For more information on this technique, refer to my article series on the GridView, available online at http://msdn.microsoft.com/library/default.asp?url=/library/en-us/dnaspp/html/GridViewEx.asp.

A Look at the Pagination Events

When the user clicks on one of the paging interface links—a page number or one of the first/next/previous/last links—the ASP.NET page is posted back and the GridView's `PageIndex` property is automatically updated. When this postback occurs, the GridView raises two events related to paging that you can create event handlers for, if needed. The events are

- `PageIndexChanging`—This event fires before the `PageIndex` property is updated.
- `PageIndexChanged`—This event fires after the `PageIndex` property has been updated to the new value.

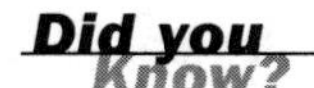

> Recall that to create an event handler in Visual Basic, you need to go to the ASP.NET page's code file and select the control and the event from the left and right drop-down lists at the top of the screen. For a refresher on creating event handlers, refer to Hour 7, "Working with Objects in Visual Basic."

Providing Sortable Data

In addition to allowing for its data to be paged, the GridView also makes it easy to make the data sortable. To indicate that a GridView's data should be sortable, simply click the Enable Sorting check box in the smart tag. That's all there is to it!

Enabling sorting will make the text in the header of each of the GridView's fields a link that, when clicked, will cause the ASP.NET page to be posted back. Upon postback, the GridView re-queries the data from its data source control and applies the appropriate sort command.

Take a moment to check the Enable Sorting check box on your GridView and then view the ASP.NET page through a browser. As Figure 15.16 shows, with sorting enabled, the header of each field is rendered as a link. When one of these links is clicked, the data is sorted in ascending order by the field whose header link was clicked. The GridView even supports bidirectional sorting; that is, if the user clicks the same field header again, the sort order will be reversed, ordering the results in *descending* order! Figure 15.17 shows the web page after the Price field's header link has been clicked.

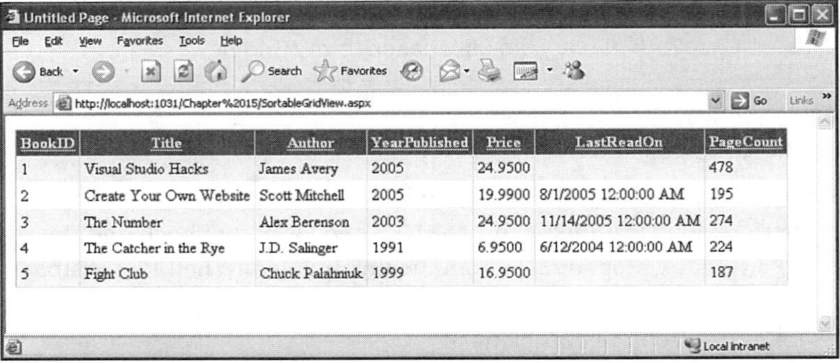

FIGURE 15.16 The data is initially sorted by `BookID`; each field's header is rendered as a link.

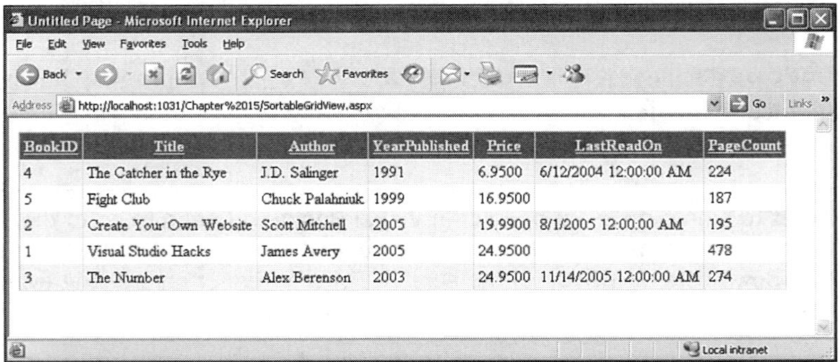

FIGURE 15.17 The Price field's header link has been clicked, sorting the books by price.

When the GridView is sorted, any default ordering of the retrieved data specified by an `ORDER BY` clause is overridden. That is, if your SqlDataSource retrieves the contents of the `Books` table ordered by the `Price` column, and the user opts to sort by author, the GridView's sorting preferences will trump the data source control's.

That doesn't mean that, when you're using a sortable GridView, the data source control's `ORDER BY` clause isn't useful. You can use the `ORDER BY` clause to specify the **default** sort order; this is how the records will be sorted when the user first visits the page. The user, then, can override the sort order by clicking on a particular column's header link.

Customizing the Sorting Interface

The GridView's sorting interface can be customized to the extent that you can indicate what fields should be sortable. (By default, all fields of a GridView are made sortable.) To indicate that a particular field should not be sortable, open the Fields dialog box by going to the GridView's smart tag and selecting the Edit Columns link.

In the Fields dialog box, the fields in the GridView are listed in the bottom-left corner. Select the field that you want to be unsortable. This will load the field's properties on the right. Scroll down until you find the property named `SortExpression` and then clear out this value (see Figure 15.18). When you remove the `SortExpression` property, the field will become unsortable.

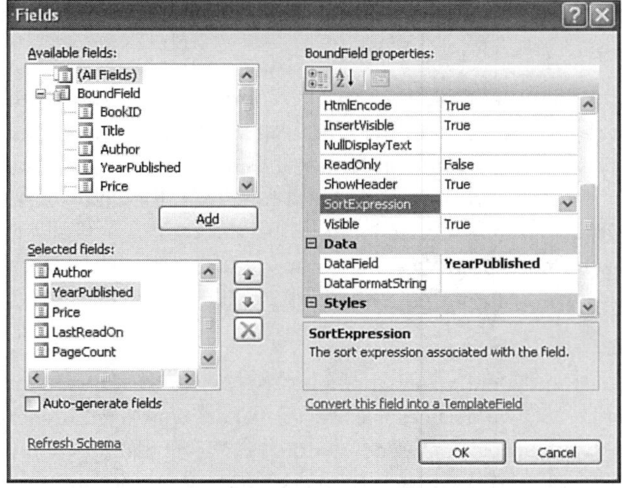

FIGURE 15.18
The `YearPublished` field's `SortExpression` property has been cleared out.

Closing Comments on Sorting

At this point we've examined both paging and sorting in the GridView, but what about creating a pageable, sortable GridView? Although we've not looked at an example of such a GridView, providing such functionality involves simply checking Enable Paging *and* Enable Sorting.

Like paging, when a user clicks on a sortable column's header link, a postback ensues. During the postback, the GridView fires two events:

- `Sorting`—This event fires before the GridView is sorted.
- `Sorted`—This event fires after the GridView has been sorted.

The GridView maintains a read-only property named `SortExpression` that indicates the field by which the data is sorted. Just like with the paging events, you can create event handlers for these events.

Summary

In the preceding hour we saw how to retrieve data from a database in an ASP.NET page through the SqlDataSource control. In this hour, we saw how to take that data and display it in the page using a data Web control. All data Web controls essentially work the same: They are added to the page and assigned a data source control. When a user visits the ASP.NET page, the data source control grabs the data from the database, and the data Web control renders its content based on the data in its data source control. There are five data Web controls, with the two most commonly used ones being the GridView and DetailsView.

The GridView displays all of the records in its corresponding data source control in an HTML `<table>`. Each record in the data source control is rendered as a table row, with each column in each row being rendered as a table cell. The DetailsView, on the other hand, displays only one record at a time from the data source control. This record is also displayed in a `<table>`, but unlike the GridView, the DetailsView renders a table row for each of the columns in its data source control, with each row having two columns containing the name and value of the corresponding database table column.

Both the GridView and DetailsView make it very easy to customize the appearance at a number of levels. The numerous control-level and row-level properties can be accessed through the Properties window, while field-level changes can be made through the Fields dialog box, which is accessible through the smart tag. Best of all, both controls sport an Auto Format dialog box for artistically challenged individuals like myself.

This hour focused on displaying data. In the next hour we'll see how to use the data source controls and the data Web controls in tandem to edit, update, insert, and delete data.

Q&A

Q. ***The GridView and DetailsView look neat, but how can I customize the appearance further? I want to be able to have, say, three records displayed per table row rather than having one record per row as with the GridView.***

A. The GridView and DetailsView both render their contents as an HTML `<table>` according to the rules discussed in this hour. So that means the GridView is always going to display exactly one record per table row, and the DetailsView is going to use a two-column `<table>` to display the columns of a particular database table record. Of course, both the GridView and DetailsView allow for a high degree of customization of the colors, fonts, borders, and so on.

If you need to customize the output more radically, you'll need to use one of the other data Web controls. The other three controls—the DataList, the Repeater, and the FormView—use **templates**. A template allows you to specify a mix of HTML markup and Web controls, thereby allowing a greater degree of customizability. As we'll see in the next hour, both the GridView and DetailsView do have some support for templates, but the support is only at the field-level. With the DataList, Repeater, or FormView, you can have row-level templates.

Q. ***The GridView seems to have a lot of functionality. Where can I learn more about the GridView control?***

A. You're right, the GridView is a rather complex and feature-rich control, easily the most feature-heavy control in all of ASP.NET. In the next hour we'll examine many useful features of the GridView, including editing, deleting, paging, and sorting of the data. However, in this book we are only able to scratch the surface of the GridView. For more in-depth information on the GridView, check out "GridView Examples for ASP.NET 2.0" at http://msdn.microsoft.com/library/default.asp?url=/library/en-us/dnaspp/html/GridViewEx.asp. It's an online article I authored with downloadable source code that includes more than 120 pages of GridView examples and lessons.

Workshop

Quiz

1. How do you associate a data source control with a data Web control?
2. True or False: A data source control can be used to display data.

3. True or False: A data Web control can be used to retrieve data from a database.

4. How can a DetailsView control be configured to allow the user to step through the records of its data source control?

5. What are the formatting specifiers for formatting a numeric field as a currency? What about for formatting a date/time field as just a date?

Answers

1. Add the data Web control to the page. In the data Web control's smart tag, a Choose Data Source drop-down list will list the data source controls on the page. Simply select the data source control that you want to bind to the data Web control.

2. False. A data source control simply retrieves data from a database. It's up to a data Web control to display it.

3. False. A data Web control merely displays data. It's the data source control that must get the data from the underlying data source. In this way, data source controls and data Web controls work in tandem.

4. By default, the DetailsView control does *not* support paging. That means when visiting the page through a browser, the user will see just the first record in the data source control. To allow the user to step through all of the records in the associated data source control, you need to enable paging. You can do this by checking the Enable Paging check box in the DetailsView's smart tab or by setting the `AllowPaging` property to `True` in the Properties window.

5. The format specifier for a currency is `c`. To display just the date portion of a date/time field, use `d`. To use these format specifiers in a GridView or DetailsView field, you need to set the `HtmlEncode` property to `False` and set the `DataFormatString` to `{0:`*`format specifier`*`}`.

Exercises

1. Create a new ASP.NET page named `MyBookTitles.aspx`. Add a SqlDataSource control to the page and configure it to return only the `Title` column from the `Books` table, ordering the results alphabetically by `Title`. Next, add a GridView to the page and bind it to the SqlDataSource. Take a moment to format the GridView using the Auto Format dialog box.

   Test this page by visiting it through a web browser.

2. Create another ASP.NET page, this one named `MostRecentlyReadBook.aspx`. Add a SqlDataSource that returns all columns from the `Books` table but orders them by `LastReadDate` in descending order. Next, add a DetailsView to the page and bind it to the data source control. Do not enable paging in the DetailsView.

   Customize the fields-level properties so that only the `Title`, `Author`, and `LastReadOn` fields are displayed, where the `Title` field is displayed in *italics* and the `LastReadOn` field is displayed in **bold**. Change the `LastReadOn` field's `HeaderText` property to `Finished Reading On` and have it formatted so only the date is displayed.

   Test this page by visiting it through a web browser.

HOUR 16

Deleting, Inserting, and Editing Data

In this hour, we will cover

- Configuring the SqlDataSource for updating, inserting, and deleting
- Learning the basics of the `UPDATE`, `INSERT`, and `DELETE` statements, which are SQL statements for modifying database data
- Editing and deleting data with the GridView
- Inserting data with the DetailsView

As we saw in Hour 15, "Displaying Data with the Data Web Controls," the ASP.NET data Web controls make displaying data a breeze. We simply drag a GridView or DetailsView onto an ASP.NET page and bind it to a configured data source control. Although displaying database information on a web page is handy, sometimes we might want to let a user *modify* the database's contents. For example, in the preceding hour we saw how to show the list of books in the `Books` database. It might be nice to allow visitors to add their own books to the table or leave comments about a particular book.

In addition to displaying data, the GridView and DetailsView controls can also be used to insert new records and delete and edit the existing data being displayed. Best of all, this can all be accomplished without having to write a single line of source code! These code-free insert, update, and delete capabilities are possible thanks to the power of the data source controls. Just like the data source controls are used to retrieve data, they also can be used to modify data.

We have a lot to cover in this hour. But after you've worked through this hour, you'll be able to display, edit, update, and delete data from a database through an ASP.NET page.

Updating, Deleting, and Inserting Data with the SqlDataSource

In Hour 14, "Accessing Data with the Data Source Web Controls," we saw how to use the SqlDataSource control to retrieve data from a SQL Server 2005 Express Edition database. Then, in the preceding hour, we saw how to use ASP.NET's data Web controls to display that data. The data source control and data Web control architecture provides a clean separation between accessing data and working with it.

In addition to being able to retrieve data, the data source controls can also be used to modify the underlying data. The SqlDataSource control can be configured to insert new records into the database and delete or modify existing records. After the SqlDataSource has been configured to support inserting, updating, and deleting, this functionality can be utilized by the GridView and DetailsView controls, allowing users not only to view, but also update, insert, and delete data from a database via a web page.

Adding support for inserts, updates, and deletions with the SqlDataSource control is as easy as checking a check box. To illustrate this process, take a moment to create a new ASP.NET web page called `RichDataSourceEx.aspx`. Next, drag on a SqlDataSource control and configure the data source. As before, select the appropriate database or the connection string in the first step and proceed to the Configure the Select Statement screen.

Make sure the `Books` table is selected in the drop-down list and then check the * option to retrieve all columns from the table. At this point you have configured the SqlDataSource control to retrieve all records and columns from the `Books` table using the query `SELECT * FROM [Books]`, just like we did in Hour 14. To set up the SqlDataSource to support updating, deleting, and inserting, click the Advanced button, which will bring up the Advanced SQL Generation Options dialog box (see Figure 16.1).

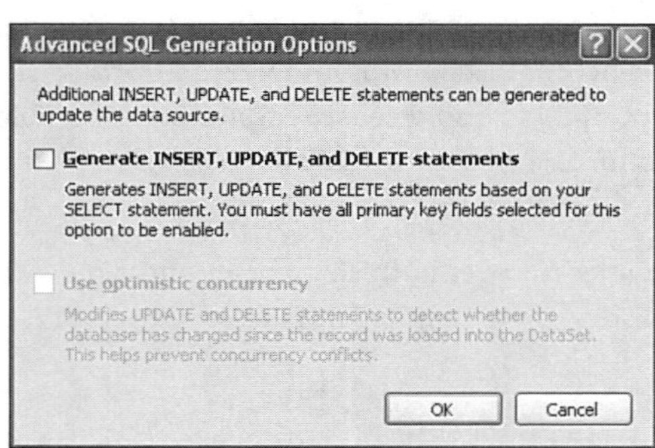

FIGURE 16.1 Add inserting, updating, and deleting support from the Advanced SQL Generation Options dialog box.

This dialog box has two check boxes: Generate INSERT, UPDATE, and DELETE Statements and Use Optimistic Concurrency. To enable the SqlDataSource's capabilities for inserting, updating, and deleting data, simply check the first check box. As we'll see in the section "Looking at the Data Modification SQL Statements," in addition to the `SELECT` statement, SQL includes `INSERT`, `UPDATE`, and `DELETE` statements for inserting, updating, and deleting data. When we check the Generate INSERT, UPDATE, and DELETE Statements check box, the SqlDataSource automatically creates these data modification SQL statements in addition to the `SELECT` statement.

By the Way

> The Generate INSERT, UPDATE, and DELETE Statements check box will be selectable only if the database table you selected in the Configure the Select Statement screen returns the table's primary key. The SqlDataSource wizard can automatically generate `INSERT`, `UPDATE`, and `DELETE` statements only when the `SELECT` statement provides a means to uniquely identify each row. For our example, you must include `BookID` in the column list, either by selecting * (which will return all columns) or checking the `BookID` column name.
>
> If you forgot to make the `BookID` column in the `Books` table a primary key column, take a moment to review the discussion on the creation of the `Books` table and the role of primary key columns in Hour 13, "An Introduction to Databases."

The second check box, Use Optimistic Concurrency, is selectable only if the first check box is checked. If checked, it allows updates and deletions to occur only if the data being updated or deleted has not changed since the data was last accessed from the database. That probably doesn't make a whole lot of sense at this point, but don't fret; it's a topic we'll return to later in this hour after we've actually built an ASP.NET page that provides support for modifying data.

For now, just check the first check box, Generate INSERT, UPDATE, and DELETE Statements, leaving the Use Optimistic Concurrency check box unchecked. Click the OK button to return to the Configure the Select Statement screen. Click Next to go to the Test Query screen and then Finish to complete the SqlDataSource wizard.

Looking at the SqlDataSource Control's Declarative Markup

After you've completed the SqlDataSource control's wizard, take a minute to view the declarative markup generated by the wizard. Go to the Source view; you should see markup identical to that shown in Listing 16.1.

LISTING 16.1 The SqlDataSource Control's Markup Contains Commands for Deleting, Inserting, and Updating

```
 1: <asp:SqlDataSource ID="SqlDataSource1" runat="server"
➥ConnectionString="<%$ ConnectionStrings:ConnectionString %>"
 2:     DeleteCommand="DELETE FROM [Books] WHERE [BookID] = @BookID"
➥InsertCommand="INSERT INTO [Books] ([Title], [Author], [YearPublished],
➥ [Price], [LastReadOn], [PageCount]) VALUES (@Title, @Author, @YearPublished,
➥@Price, @LastReadOn, @PageCount)"
 3:     SelectCommand="SELECT * FROM [Books]" UpdateCommand="UPDATE [Books]
➥SET [Title] = @Title, [Author] = @Author, [YearPublished] = @YearPublished,
➥ [Price] = @Price, [LastReadOn] = @LastReadOn, [PageCount] = @PageCount
➥WHERE [BookID] = @BookID">
 4:     <DeleteParameters>
 5:         <asp:Parameter Name="BookID" Type="Int32" />
 6:     </DeleteParameters>
 7:     <UpdateParameters>
 8:         <asp:Parameter Name="Title" Type="String" />
 9:         <asp:Parameter Name="Author" Type="String" />
10:         <asp:Parameter Name="YearPublished" Type="Int32" />
11:         <asp:Parameter Name="Price" Type="Decimal" />
12:         <asp:Parameter Name="LastReadOn" Type="DateTime" />
13:         <asp:Parameter Name="PageCount" Type="Int32" />
14:         <asp:Parameter Name="BookID" Type="Int32" />
15:     </UpdateParameters>
16:     <InsertParameters>
17:         <asp:Parameter Name="Title" Type="String" />
18:         <asp:Parameter Name="Author" Type="String" />
19:         <asp:Parameter Name="YearPublished" Type="Int32" />
20:         <asp:Parameter Name="Price" Type="Decimal" />
21:         <asp:Parameter Name="LastReadOn" Type="DateTime" />
22:         <asp:Parameter Name="PageCount" Type="Int32" />
23:     </InsertParameters>
24: </asp:SqlDataSource>
```

In Hour 14 we saw the declarative markup of the SqlDataSource when it was configured to issue just a `SELECT` statement, and it was much simpler than the 24 lines of markup shown in Listing 16.1. However, the simplicity from Hour 14 was possible because we were only retrieving data from a database; here, we need to include markup that specifies how to also insert, update, and delete that data.

In addition to the `SelectCommand` on line 3, there are three additional command statements on lines 2 and 3: `DeleteCommand`, `InsertCommand` (both on line 2), and `UpdateCommand` (line 3). These command statements specify the SQL statements that will be passed to the underlying database when inserting, updating, or deleting the data. In addition to these command statements, there are a number of related parameters, spanning from line 4 through line 23. Recall that the SQL statements in a SqlDataSource control can use **parameters**, which are placeholders for values to be inserted at a later point in time. The parameters are denoted in the command statement using `@`*`ParameterName`*.

The parameters are further defined in the `<DeleteParameters>`, `<UpdateParameters>`, and `<InsertParameters>` sections. For example, in the `DeleteCommand` statement, a single parameter, `@BookID`, is used to uniquely identify the row that's to be deleted. Then, in the `<DeleteParameters>` section (lines 4—6), a single `<asp:Parameter>` element identifies that the `BookID` parameter is an integer. Notice, however, that no *value* is specified for this parameter. If you'll remember back to Hour 14 when we used the SqlDataSource wizard's capabilities to add filter expressions, we provided a hard-coded value for the `WHERE` clause. This hard-coded value then appeared in the associated `<asp:Parameter>` element.

The `<asp:Parameter>`s in the `<DeleteParameters>`, `<UpdateParameters>`, and `<InsertParameters>` sections, however, lack any hard-coded values. The reason is that their values will be determined at runtime. That is, the value of the `@BookID` parameter for the `DeleteCommand` will depend on what row the user has decided to delete; that particular row's `BookID` will be used as the value for the `@BookID` parameter.

Later in this hour we'll be looking at how to work with the GridView and DetailsView controls to insert, update, and delete data. At that point it will become clearer how visitors will indicate what record they want to delete or update and how the data Web control plugs that information into the data source control. For now, though, just understand that checking the Generate INSERT, UPDATE, and DELETE Statements check box in the Advanced SQL Generation Options dialog box causes the data source control to provide commands and parameters for inserting, updating, and deleting the data specified in the Configure the Select Statement screen of the wizard.

Looking at the Data Modification SQL Statements

As we discussed in Hour 14, SQL is the language used by all modern databases to retrieve and modify data. We've already examined the `SELECT` statement, which is used to retrieve data. Let's now turn our attention to three other SQL statements: `INSERT`, `UPDATE`, and `DELETE`. These three statements are automatically generated by the SqlDataSource control when appropriately configured and, as you can probably guess, are instrumental in modifying a database's content.

A thorough understanding of the `INSERT`, `UPDATE`, and `DELETE` statements is not required. After all, the SqlDataSource will merrily create the necessary statements for you; all you need to do is check the appropriate check box! However, I do think it is worthwhile to have at least a cursory understanding of the syntax and semantics of these statements.

If you are already familiar with the basics of these three SQL statements, feel free to skip this section because it is intended for readers who are new to SQL. In the section "Editing and Deleting Data with the GridView," we'll begin our examination of modifying data through an ASP.NET page.

Examining the `INSERT` Statement

The `INSERT` statement, as its name implies, inserts a new record into a database table. The general syntax is as follows:

```
INSERT INTO TableName(Column1, Column2, ..., ColumnN)
VALUES(Column1Value, Column2Value, ..., ColumnNValue)
```

Here *`Column1, Column2, ..., ColumnN`* is a comma-delimited list of the column names of the table whose values you are providing in the `VALUES` portion. You do *not* want to include column names for any Auto-increment columns; furthermore, you may optionally leave off a column if it either has a default value specified or accepts Nulls, in which case the default value will be used if it exists; otherwise, a Null value will be inserted. The *`Column1Value, Column2Value, ..., ColumnNValue`* is the place where you specify the values for the columns listed.

By the Way

> These rules for when to supply a column value for the `INSERT` statement should sound familiar. In Hour 13 we looked at adding records to an existing database table through Visual Web Developer. In that example, we did not specify values for the Auto-increment column (`BookID`) or those records where we wanted to insert a Null value. Similarly, we had to provide a value for those columns that did not allow Nulls.

Now that we've discussed the general form of the `INSERT` statement, let's look at a more concrete example. The following `INSERT` statement was generated by the SqlDataSource control's wizard (refer to Listing 16.1, line 2):

```
INSERT INTO [Books] ([Title], [Author], [YearPublished], [Price],
➥[LastReadOn], [PageCount])
VALUES (@Title, @Author, @YearPublished, @Price, @LastReadOn, @PageCount)
```

Note that the `INSERT` statement adds a new record to the `Books` table and provides values for all fields except for `BookID`. `BookID` is omitted from the column list because it is an Auto-increment column, which means that the database system will supply the value. (Providing a value for `BookID` will result in an error when the code is executed.)

Rather than providing specific values, the `InsertCommand` uses parameters—`@Title`, `@Author`, `@YearPublished`, and so on. As we will see later in this hour, the

DetailsView can be used to collect the visitor's input and use that input to insert a new record into the underlying database table. Specifically, when the visitor provides the data, the DetailsView control assigns it to the appropriate parameters of its data source control and then invokes the data source control's `InsertCommand`.

Deleting Data with the DELETE Statement

The general form of the `DELETE` statement is as follows:

```
DELETE FROM TableName
WHERE whereCondition
```

The `WHERE` condition is optional, but you'll almost always want to include it because the `DELETE` statement deletes *all* records from the table *`TableName`* that match the `WHERE` condition. Therefore, if you omit the `WHERE` clause, *all* records from the table *`TableName`* will vanish into thin air!

Most commonly, the `DELETE` statement is used to delete one record at a time. For example, the `DeleteCommand` used by the SqlDataSource has a `WHERE` clause that's based on the `Books` table's primary key column, `BookID`. (Remember that the primary key column is what uniquely identifies each row in the table.)

```
DELETE FROM [Books]
WHERE [BookID] = @BookID
```

In some circumstances you might want to relax the `WHERE` condition in the `DELETE` statement to delete multiple records. For example, if you wanted to delete all books that were published in 2005, you could use this statement:

```
DELETE FROM [Books]
WHERE YearPublished = 2005
```

This might delete zero books, one, three, ... maybe all of them. The result would depend on the values of the `YearPublished` column.

Editing Data with UPDATE

The `UPDATE` statement is used to change the values of existing rows. With `UPDATE` you can specify what columns to change to what values; like the `DELETE` statement, the `UPDATE` statement contains a `WHERE` clause that specifies the scope of the update. That is, the `UPDATE` statement can be used to update a single row (which is how it is most commonly used), or it can be used to update a batch of records.

The general form of the `UPDATE` statement is as follows:

```
UPDATE TableName SET
  Column1 = Column1Value,
```

```
  Column2 = Column2Value,
  ...
  ColumnN = ColumnNValue,
WHERE whereCondition
```

The column/value list after the `UPDATE TableName SET` portion indicates what columns' values are being changed and to what values. The *whereCondition* indicates what rows this update applies to; as with the `DELETE` statement, if you omit the `WHERE` clause, the update applies to *all* records in the table.

The `UpdateCommand` in Listing 16.1 (line 3) updates a single record in the `Books` table and updates the value of all columns *except* for the Auto-increment column:

```
UPDATE [Books] SET
  [Title] = @Title,
  [Author] = @Author,
  [YearPublished] = @YearPublished,
  [Price] = @Price,
  [LastReadOn] = @LastReadOn,
  [PageCount] = @PageCount
WHERE [BookID] = @BookID
```

The `WHERE` clause is based on the primary key column, so only one record from the database table will be updated with this statement.

At this point we have examined how to configure a SqlDataSource to generate the `INSERT`, `UPDATE`, and `DELETE` commands through its wizard and have taken a cursory look at the related SQL statements. We're now ready to turn our attention to configuring the data Web controls to insert, update, and delete data. In the next section, "Editing and Deleting Data with the GridView," we'll see how to use the GridView to edit and delete data. Further on, in the "Inserting Data with the DetailsView" section, we'll see how to insert data using the DetailsView.

Editing and Deleting Data with the GridView

In addition to just displaying data, the GridView can be used to edit and delete the displayed data as well. To edit or delete data, the GridView must be bound to a data source control that has an `UpdateCommand` and `DeleteCommand`. Fortunately, these command statements can be automatically generated for us by the SqlDataSource control's wizard when retrieving data from a database table with a primary key.

Like adding sorting and paging support to a GridView, enabling a user to delete or edit the GridView's underlying data is as simple as checking a check box in the GridView's smart tag. With deleting, it really is as simple as checking a check box. With editing, however, the GridView leaves a bit to be desired in how to render the row being edited. As we'll see, if you have anything but the most trivial data entry requirements, you'll likely need to instruct the GridView on how to create the editable row. We'll see how to accomplish this in the "Customizing the Editing Interface and Updating Rules" section later in this hour.

In this hour we are going to examine editing and deleting as two separate tasks. However, there's no reason why you can't create a GridView whose data can both be edited and deleted. Just follow the steps from the editing and deleting sections on a single GridView.

Allowing Users to Delete Data

The GridView can be configured to provide the user with the ability to delete the GridView's underlying data, one record at a time. A deletable GridView adds a field of Delete buttons or links; to delete a particular row, the user visiting the page simply clicks the applicable row's Delete button. After the Delete button is clicked, the ASP.NET page is posted back. The GridView then populates the appropriate data source control parameters with the appropriate values and invokes its data source control's `DeleteCommand`. After it issues this command, the GridView re-retrieves and redisplays its data from its data source control. From the user's perspective, he clicks a particular row's Delete button and that row disappears.

This interaction that occurs automatically is not trivial and deserves a bit of exploration. Before we worry about the intricacies, however, let's first create a working, deletable GridView. Start by creating a new ASP.NET page called `DeleteBook.aspx`. As you may have guessed, this page will list all of the books in the `Books` table, providing a Delete button for each. The visitor to this page can then delete a book from the table by clicking the book's corresponding Delete button.

After the page is created, go to the Design view and drag on a SqlDataSource control. Configure the data source so that the query returns all records and all columns from the `Books` table, and have the wizard generate the `INSERT`, `UPDATE`, and `DELETE` statements (but don't check the Use Optimistic Concurrency check box).

After the data source has been configured, add a GridView to the page and specify its data source as the SqlDataSource you just added. If you configured the data source control correctly, in the GridView's smart tag there will be an Enable Deleting check box. Check this.

Checking the Enable Deleting check box will update the Design view to show a field of Delete links (see Figure 16.2). Congratulations, you've created a deletable GridView! Take a moment to test your page by going to the Debug menu and choosing Start Without Debugging. In the browser, if you click a particular row's Delete link—poof!—that record disappears because it has been deleted.

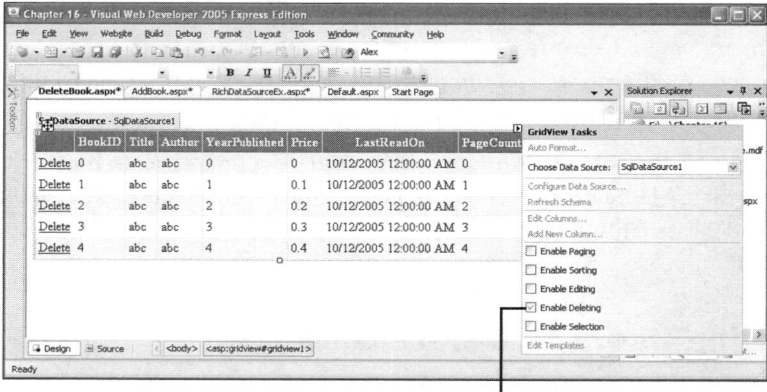

FIGURE 16.2 The GridView has been configured to support deleting.

Customizing the Delete Field

By default, the Delete field displays as a column of links with the word "Delete" as the text for each link. You can customize this field if needed, changing the link text or having the link displayed as a button or image. To accomplish this, go to the GridView's smart tag and click the Edit Columns link, which will display the Fields dialog box (see Figure 16.3).

In the bottom-left corner are the fields displayed in the GridView. In addition to the BoundFields for displaying the `BookID`, `Title`, `Author`, and other columns, there's also a CommandField called Delete. This CommandField was automatically added when the Enable Deleting check box was checked in the GridView's smart tag.

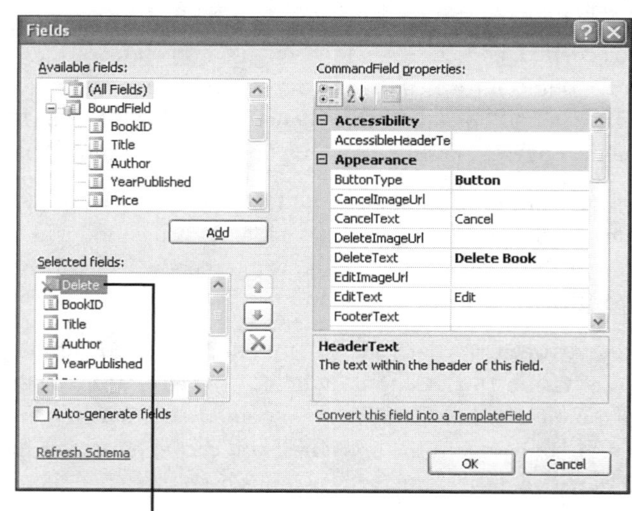

FIGURE 16.3 A CommandField named Delete was added when the Enable Deleting check box was checked.

Selecting the Delete CommandField in the lower-left corner displays its properties on the right. The first property in the Appearance section is `ButtonType`, which dictates how the Delete field is displayed. Currently, it is set to its default value, `Link`, which causes the Delete field to render as a series of links. You can change the field's appearance by setting this property to `Button` or `Image`.

If you have `ButtonType` set to `Link` or `Button`, you can customize the text displayed in the button or link using the `DeleteText` property. If you are using a `ButtonType` value of `Image`, set the `DeleteImageUrl` property to the URL of the image you want displayed.

Figure 16.4 shows the GridView in the Visual Web Developer Design tab after the Delete field has been customized to render as a button with the `DeleteText` `"Delete Book"`.

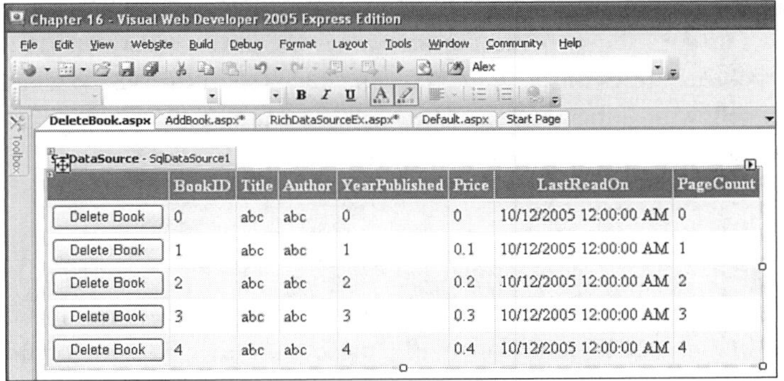

FIGURE 16.4 Each row in the GridView includes a Delete Book button.

Did you Know?

> The Delete field's aesthetic appearance—its background color, font, alignment, and so on—can be customized through the various properties in the Style section of the Fields dialog box. Refer to Hour 15 for a more in-depth look at customizing the GridView's fields.

Looking at the Inner Workings of Deleting

What, exactly, happens when the end user clicks a Delete button? From the end user's perspective, the page flashes and the record whose Delete button she clicked vanishes. But what happens behind the scenes?

When a user clicks the Delete button, a postback ensues. On postback, the GridView notes that a particular row's Delete button has been clicked and in response raises its `RowDeleting` event. The GridView then takes the value that uniquely identifies the row (the `BookID` value), assigns that to its data source control's `<DeleteParameters> @BookID` parameter, and invokes the `DeleteCommand`. The data source control, then, issues the DELETE statement to the database, substituting in the value of the @BookID parameter. After it deletes the record via its data source control, the GridView raises its RowDeleted event.

If you need to programmatically tap into the deleting life cycle, you can do so by creating an event handler for the RowDeleting or RowDeleted events. The RowDeleting event handler can be used to programmatically abort the delete. For example, if the user attempts to delete a book authored by Scott Mitchell, you might want to cancel the delete. Check out the exercises at the end of this hour for some practice with programmatically canceling a deletion.

For example, imagine that the user visits DeleteBook.aspx and clicks the Delete button for the book *The Number*. This causes a postback, and the GridView control is notified that the Delete button was clicked for its third row. The GridView then determines that the BookID value for the third row is 3, assigns this to the @BookID parameter of its data source control, and invokes the DeleteCommand. The data source control substitutes in the value 3 for the @BookID in the DELETE statement, sending the following statement to the underlying database:

```
DELETE FROM [Books]
WHERE [BookID] = 3
```

This, of course, would delete *The Number* from the database.

After this statement is executed, the GridView re-retrieves its data from its data source control. Because there are now only four books, the GridView is rendered with only four rows. The result is that the user visiting the page now sees the four remaining books in the Books table.

At this point you may be wondering how, exactly, the GridView knows that the third row is uniquely identified with the value 3. This GridView has a property called DataKeyNames that can be set to the name(s) of the primary key columns(s) of the data being bound to the GridView. If this property is set, the GridView automatically keeps track of each of the primary key column value(s) of each of its rows. When you bind a data source control to a GridView, this property is automatically set to the primary key column(s) returned by the data source control. (Take a moment to check out the Properties window for the GridView; you'll see that the DataKeyNames property is set to BookID.)

It is essential that the underlying database table's primary key column or columns are specified in the GridView's DataKeyNames property. If this property value is missing, clicking the Delete button will cause the page to post back but won't delete the record. If clicking the Delete button leaves the page unchanged, take a moment to make sure that the DataKeyNames property is set.

Creating an Editable GridView

In addition to providing deleting support, the GridView also offers functionality that allows the end user to edit the GridView's underlying data. Specifically, when the GridView is configured to support editing, an Edit button is added to each row. When the end user clicks the Edit button, the row becomes **editable**, which means, by default, that its various editable fields turn into text boxes. Also, the Edit button is replaced by two new buttons: Update and Cancel. The user can then enter the new values for the record into these text boxes and click the Update button to save his changes, or he can click the Cancel button to return to the pre-editing GridView without saving any changes. Figure 16.6 shows a browser displaying an editable GridView where the user has clicked on the second row's Edit button.

The steps for creating an editable GridView are quite similar to those for creating a GridView that supports deleting:

1. Add a SqlDataSource to the ASP.NET page that is configured to include the `INSERT`, `UPDATE`, and `DELETE` commands.
2. Add a GridView to the page, binding it to the data source control added in step 1.
3. From the GridView's smart tag, check the Enable Editing check box.

In other words, the only difference is that instead of checking the Enable Deleting check box, you check the Enable Editing check box instead. (Actually, you can check *both* check boxes to create an editable GridView that supports deleting.)

Although enabling editing support is fairly straightforward, often we'll want to tailor the GridView's default editing interface. Fortunately, this is relatively easy and, like many of the other GridView's features, can typically be accomplished without having to write any code.

Before we delve into customizing the GridView's editing interface, let's first practice creating an editable GridView. Start by creating a new page named `EditBooks.aspx` and follow the three steps outlined at the beginning of this section. After you check the Enable Editing check box in the GridView's smart tag, the Visual Web Developer Design view should display an Edit field, as shown in Figure 16.5.

At this point you have created an editable GridView. Take a moment to try out this GridView in a browser. Each GridView row has an Edit link that, when clicked, makes the row editable. The end user can enter new values for the editable fields and click the Update link to save his changes (see Figure 16.6).

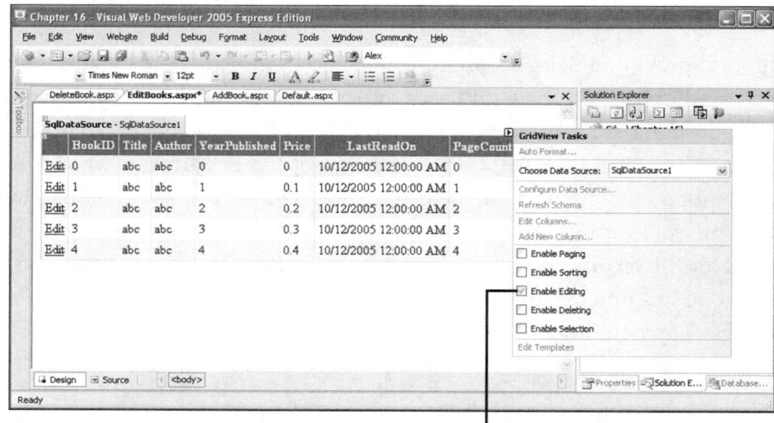

FIGURE 16.5 A CommandField named Edit was added when the Enable Editing check box was checked.

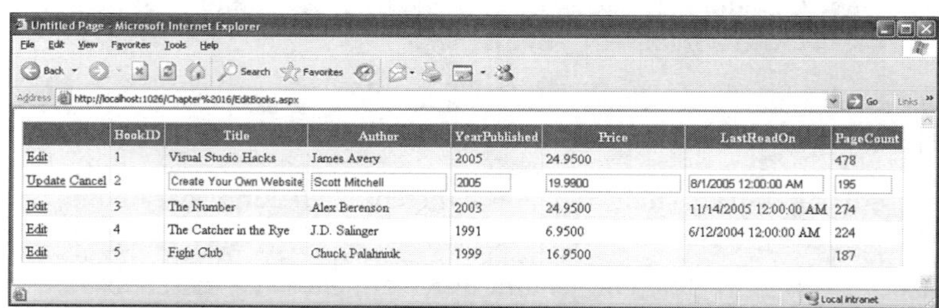

FIGURE 16.6 The user has opted to edit the second row of this editable GridView.

As with deleting, editing data through a GridView requires that the underlying database table's primary key column or columns be specified in the GridView's `DataKeyNames` property. If this property value is reset, any changes specified to the editable record in a GridView won't be saved back to the underlying data. If you experience this when testing the GridView through a browser, ensure that the `DataKeyNames` property is set accordingly.

The format of the values entered into the editable row's text boxes is sensitive to the underlying database table's data type. For example, the `LastReadOn` field's underlying database table column's data type is a `datetime` field. Therefore, if you attempt to edit a row and enter an invalid `datetime` value—like `"Yesterday"`—you'll get an exception when you click the Update button.

Similarly, if a field does not accept Null values or have a default value defined, you must provide a value. In our example, if you clear out the `Title` field value and try to save the changes, you'll get an exception.

In the "Customizing the Editing Interface and Updating Rules" section, we'll see how to change the interface for each field in the editable row, including how to add validation controls to ensure that a value was entered or conforms to a particular data type.

The GridView's Edit field's appearance can be customized just like the Delete field. That is, you can turn the Edit link into a button or image, and change the text displayed in the Edit link or button. As with the Delete field, the Edit field's settings can be modified through the Fields dialog box, which you can reach by clicking the Edit Columns link in the GridView's smart tag.

Customizing the Editing Interface and Updating Rules

Take a moment to try out the editable GridView. Try entering different values for different fields or omitting values and see what happens. As you likely will discover, it is fairly easy to end up with an exception when saving an editable GridView. Simply omit the value for a required field (like `Title` or `Author`) or put in a improperly formatted value (such as `"Long"` for the `PageCount` field). Figure 16.7 shows the resulting page in Internet Explorer when attempting to update the book *Visual Studio Hacks* with the `LastReadOn` value of `"Yesterday"`.

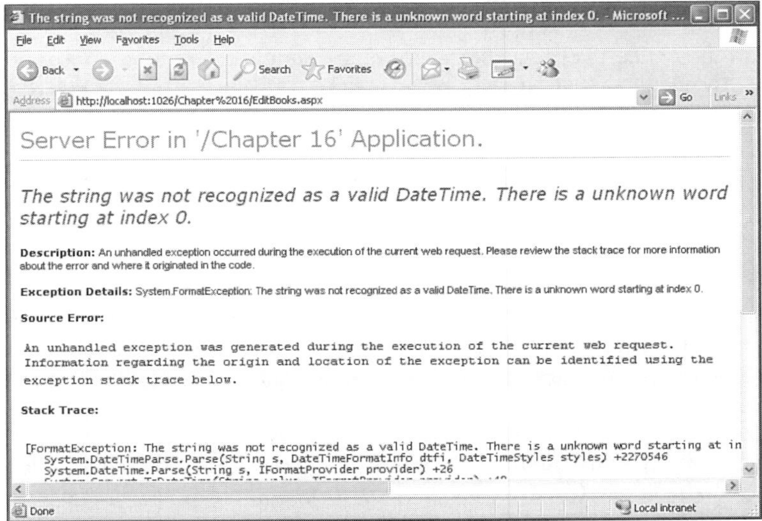

FIGURE 16.7
Attempting to input an improperly formatted string into the `LastReadOn` field results in an exception.

These exceptions arise because the GridView blindly passes back to its data source control whatever values the end user provides. When the data source control attempts to issue an `UPDATE` statement to the database with improperly formatted or missing values, the database raises an exception, which is what you see in Figure 16.7.

To prevent these types of errors, we want to customize the editing interface generated by the GridView. The GridView allows you to customize the markup used for each field. For example, for the `Title`, `Author`, `YearPublished`, `Price`, and `PageCount` fields, we want to include a RequiredFieldValidator control, to ensure that the user has entered a value. For `Price`, `LastReadOn`, `YearPublished`, and `PageCount`, we want to use a `CompareValidator` to ensure that the values are of the proper data type and, perhaps, bounded by some value or values. (We might want to ensure that the value entered for `Price` is always greater than or equal to 0, for example.)

In addition to customizing the interface for an editable field, we might want to indicate that a particular field should *not* be editable. When the GridView row in Figure 16.6 is edited, notice that the `BookID` field remains as text, disallowing the end user from modifying the value of a row's `BookID`. The GridView automatically makes the primary key column or columns *read-only* because those columns uniquely identify the row that's being edited. We can easily indicate that other fields should be read-only as well. For example, we might not want to let a user change the title of a book.

Finally, the GridView provides options that can be set to indicate how the user-entered data should be sent to the database. If the user omits entering a value for a string data type (like `Title`, `Author`, and so on), should the database record be updated using Null or a blank string? These settings can be managed through the Fields dialog box.

Over the next few sections we'll examine each of these methods of customizing the editing interface and specifying database-related update rules.

Marking Fields as Read-Only

By default, any fields in the GridView that map to primary key columns in the underlying database table are made read-only. When the visitor clicks the Edit button for a GridView row, the read-only fields are simply displayed as text. See the `BookID` field in Figure 16.6 for an example of how a read-only field is rendered.

You can optionally mark additional fields as read-only. Go to the Fields dialog box and select the field you want to make read-only, loading its properties on the right. One of the properties in the Behavior section is named `ReadOnly`. Set this property to `True` to make the field uneditable (see Figure 16.8).

That's all there is to it. When we mark a field as read-only, it will be displayed as text when a row's Edit button is clicked.

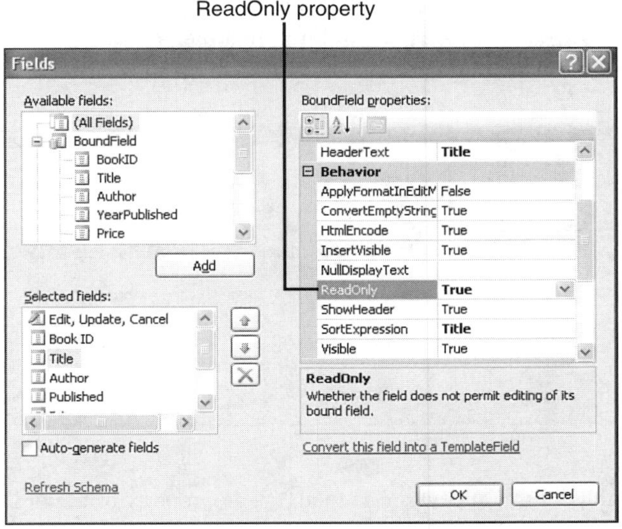

FIGURE 16.8
Set the `ReadOnly` property to `True` to make a field uneditable.

Editing and Formatted Fields

In the preceding hour we looked at how to format the values of the GridView fields, such as formatting the `Price` field as a currency and the `LastReadOn` field to display just the date and omit the time. By default, the formatting applied to a GridView field is *not* carried over to the default editing interface. To highlight this, take a moment to format the `Price` and `LastReadOn` fields using the currency and date-only format strings. To accomplish this, perform the following steps:

1. Open the Fields dialog box by clicking on the Edit Columns link in the GridView's smart tag.
2. Click on the appropriate field in the list of fields in the lower-left corner.
3. Set the `HtmlEncode` property to `False` for both the `Price` and `LastReadOn` fields, and set the `DataFormatString` property to `{0:c}` and `{0:d}`, respectively.

After you make these settings, the Design view in Visual Web Developer should show the fields formatted as specified. Next, view the page in a browser and click on the Edit button for a row (see Figure 16.9). As you can see, the values for the `Price` and `LastReadOn` fields are properly formatted for the noneditable rows. For the row being edited, however, the text box shows the values in their unformatted state.

You can indicate that the formatted values should apply for the editable view through the field's `ApplyFormatInEditMode` property, which is accessible through the Fields dialog box. By default, this value is `False`; if you set it to `True`, however, the formatting will apply to the row being edited. Because we are interested only in the date of the LastReadOn date field and not the time, it makes sense to set the ApplyFormatInEditMode property of the LastReadOn field to True.

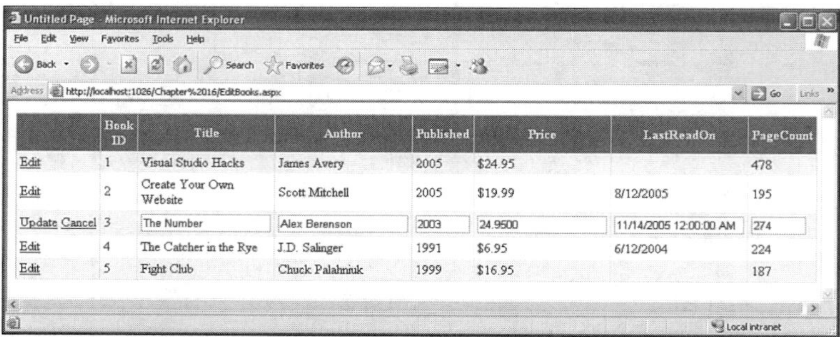

FIGURE 16.9 The formatting for the Price and LastReadOn columns isn't applied to the editable row.

Before you blindly set the ApplyFormatInEditMode property of the Price field to True, realize that doing so will cause problems because the currency formatting introduces illegal characters. The Price field is tied to a database table column of type money, which expects a numeric value. If you apply the currency formatting, however, the formatted expression includes a currency symbol (such as a dollar sign). If the user edits a row and doesn't remove the currency symbol from the Price text box, when she saves the changes, the ASP.NET page will raise an exception. (There's no problem with formatting the LastReadOn field because the database will happily work with a date value that lacks a time portion.)

Using Nulls or Blank Strings

Some fields in the GridView map to database table columns that allow Nulls. For example, the LastReadOn column does not require a value; if we've yet to read the book, we can simply put a Null in this column. By default, if the user omits a value for a field, the GridView will attempt to place a Null value in the corresponding database table column. To illustrate this concept, edit a row that has a LastReadOn date value and clear out this value from the text box. After saving this change, check out the database table's data; you'll see that a Null value has been placed in the book's LastReadOn column.

Sometimes, however, you may want to have the GridView use a blank string as opposed to a Null value. For example, imagine that you had a GridView field that mapped to a database table column that was of type nvarchar that did *not* allow Nulls. (Recall that nvarchar fields hold strings.) Now, if a user editing a GridView leaves off the value for this field, the GridView will use a Null value; this will cause an exception, however, because the database table column was configured to not allow Nulls.

To remedy this, you would need to have the GridView's field opt to use a **blank string** instead of a Null value. (A blank string is a string with no characters.) To accomplish this, set the field's `ConvertEmptyStringToNull` property to `False` through the Fields dialog box.

Replacing the Auto-Generated TextBox with a Custom Editing Interface

When you click the Edit button in a GridView, by default all of the editable fields are converted into text boxes. Sometimes, though, you might not want to use a text box as the editing interface, or you might want to augment the editing interface by tweaking the text box's aesthetic appearance or including validation controls. For example, it would be prudent to include RequiredFieldValidators for those GridView fields that map to database columns that do not allow Nulls and for which we do not want to allow a blank string to be present. Furthermore, we should add CompareValidators to the numeric and date/time fields to ensure that the data format entered by the user conforms to the corresponding data type.

To customize the editing interface for a field, we'll need to convert it from a BoundField into a **TemplateField**. The BoundField—which is added by default after associating a GridView with a data source control—displays the associated data source control column values as text for the noneditable rows and as a text box for the editable row. A TemplateField, on the other hand, allows us, the page developers, to specify precisely the Web controls that will be used in displaying the column values for both the editable and noneditable rows.

A TemplateField is defined as a collection of **templates**, where a template is a mix of Web controls and static HTML markup. There are five possible templates, all of which are optional:

- ItemTemplate
- AlternatingItemTemplate
- EditItemTemplate
- HeaderTemplate
- FooterTemplate

As the GridView is rendered row-by-row, a TemplateField is rendered depending on the row's type and the templates available. For example, if the TemplateField has a HeaderTemplate specified, when the field's header row is rendered, the HeaderTemplates markup is used. For noneditable items, the ItemTemplates or AlternatingItemTemplates are used, depending on whether the AlternatingItemTemplate is defined and, if so, if the row is a normal row or alternating row. For the editable row, the EditItemTemplate is used, if provided.

This may, understandably, sound a bit confusing at this point. I hope things will become clearer after you see an example. To illustrate using a TemplateField, we first need to create one. You can add a brand new TemplateField to the GridView if you like, but because we want to customize the editing interface of an existing BoundField template, we can simply turn those BoundFields into TemplateFields. To accomplish this, simply open the Fields dialog box, select the BoundField to turn into a TemplateField, and click the `Convert this field into a TemplateField` link at the bottom of the properties on the right (see Figure 16.10).

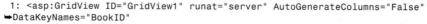

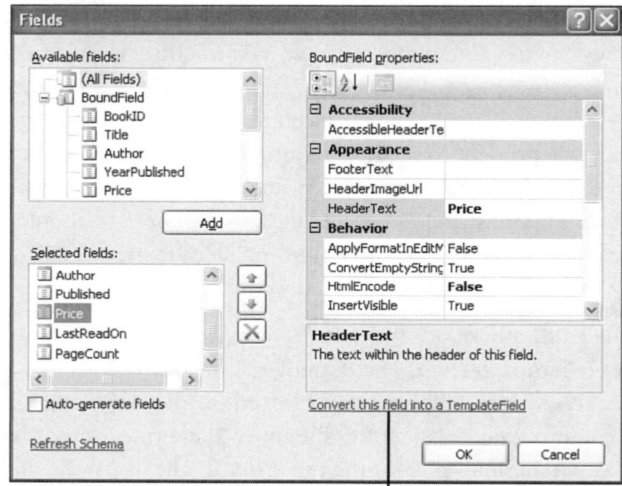

FIGURE 16.10
To customize the editing interface, turn the BoundField into a TemplateField.

Take a moment to convert the `Price` field into a TemplateField and then close the Fields dialog box by clicking the OK button. You won't notice anything different in the Design view. In fact, if you test the page through a browser, it will behave just as it did before converting the field to a TemplateField. The reason is that converting the BoundField into a TemplateField creates a TemplateField with two templates: an ItemTemplate that contains a Label Web control and an EditItemTemplate that contains a TextBox Web control. Listing 16.2 shows the GridView's declarative markup after converting the `Price` field into a TemplateField (pay particular attention to lines 10 through 17).

LISTING 16.2 The TemplateField Has an ItemTemplate and EditItemTemplate

```
 1: <asp:GridView ID="GridView1" runat="server" AutoGenerateColumns="False"
➥DataKeyNames="BookID"
 2:      DataSourceID="SqlDataSource1" BackColor="White" BorderColor="#DEDFDE"
➥ BorderStyle="None" BorderWidth="1px" CellPadding="4" ForeColor="Black"
➥GridLines="Vertical">
 3:      <Columns>
```

LISTING 16.2 Continued

```
 4:         <asp:CommandField ShowEditButton="True" />
 5:         <asp:BoundField DataField="BookID" HeaderText="Book ID"
➥InsertVisible="False" ReadOnly="True"
 6:             SortExpression="BookID" />
 7:         <asp:BoundField DataField="Title" HeaderText="Title"
➥SortExpression="Title" />
 8:         <asp:BoundField DataField="Author" HeaderText="Author"
➥SortExpression="Author" />
 9:         <asp:BoundField DataField="YearPublished" HeaderText="Published"
➥ SortExpression="YearPublished" />
10:         <asp:TemplateField HeaderText="Price" SortExpression="Price">
11:             <EditItemTemplate>
12:                 <asp:TextBox ID="TextBox2" runat="server"
➥Text='<%# Bind("Price") %>'></asp:TextBox>
13:             </EditItemTemplate>
14:             <ItemTemplate>
15:                 <asp:Label ID="Label2" runat="server"
➥Text='<%# Bind("Price", "{0:c}") %>'></asp:Label>
16:             </ItemTemplate>
17:         </asp:TemplateField>
18:         <asp:BoundField DataField="LastReadOn" HeaderText="LastReadOn"
➥SortExpression="Last Read" ApplyFormatInEditMode="True"
➥DataFormatString="{0:d}" HtmlEncode="False" />
19:         <asp:BoundField DataField="PageCount" HeaderText="PageCount"
➥SortExpression="Pages" />
20:     </Columns>
21:     <FooterStyle BackColor="#CCCC99" />
22:     <RowStyle BackColor="#F7F7DE" />
23:     <SelectedRowStyle BackColor="#CE5D5A" Font-Bold="True"
➥ForeColor="White" />
24:     <PagerStyle BackColor="#F7F7DE" ForeColor="Black"
➥HorizontalAlign="Right" />
25:     <HeaderStyle BackColor="#6B696B" Font-Bold="True" ForeColor="White" />
26:     <AlternatingRowStyle BackColor="White" />
27: </asp:GridView>
```

Note that the `<EditItemTemplate>` (lines 11—13) and `<ItemTemplate>` (lines 14—16) sections contain a single Web control. Furthermore, the Web control's `Text` property is assigned a value using **data binding syntax**. Data binding syntax has the form `<%# Bind(`*`columnName`*`, `*`optionalFormatSpecifier`*`) %>` and grabs a particular column value from the data source control. In the `<ItemTemplate>` a Label Web control is configured to display the value of the `Price` column formatted as a currency (`{0:c}`); in the `<EditItemTemplate>`, a TextBox Web control's `Text` property is assigned the value of the `Price` column.

A TemplateField's templates can also be edited through the Design view. From the GridView's smart tag, click on the Edit Templates link. This will show the ItemTemplate for the `Price` field. You can click to edit other templates from the drop-down list. Figure 16.11 shows the Design view when editing the ItemTemplate of the `Price` field.

Did you Know?

To exit the template-editing interface and return to the GridView in the Design view, click the End Template Editing link in the smart tag (see Figure 16.11).

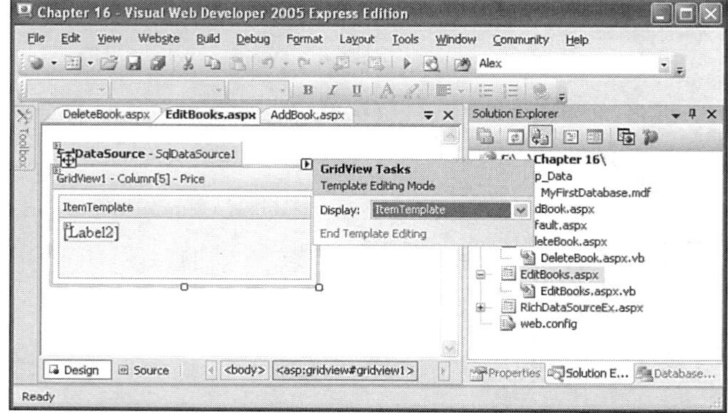

FIGURE 16.11 A TemplateField's templates can also be edited through the Design view.

Note that the ItemTemplate contains a Label Web control with `ID Label2`. This is the Label control whose declarative markup appeared on line 15 of Listing 16.2. Click on the Label Web control and examine the Properties window. Note that the `Text` property has a little disc icon next to it; this indicates that the `Text` property is assigned using a data binding expression.

Did you Know?

You can edit the data binding expression for a Web control through the DataBindings dialog box, which is accessible by clicking on the Edit DataBindings link in the Web control's smart tag.

By the Way

We'll be examining data binding syntax in much greater detail in Hour 18, "Exploring Data Binding and Other Data-Related Topics."

Next, change the template being viewed from the ItemTemplate to the EditItemTemplate. You should now see a TextBox Web control whose `Text` property in the Properties window also has a disc icon. To customize the `Price` field's editing interface, make whatever modifications necessary to the EditItemTemplate. For our page, let's do the following:

1. Put a currency symbol in front of the TextBox Web control to indicate to the user that she doesn't need to enter a currency symbol. To accomplish this, click in the EditItemTemplate before the TextBox Web control and then type in the appropriate currency symbol.

2. Set the TextBox Web control's `Columns` property to 10, shortening the length of the TextBox.

3. Add a RequiredFieldValidator control to the EditItemTemplate by dragging it from the Toolbox into the EditItemTemplate. Set its `ControlToValidate` property to the `ID` of the TextBox in the EditItemTemplate, its `Display` property to `Dynamic`, and its `ErrorMessage` property to `"You must enter a price"`.

4. Add a CompareValidator control to the EditItemTemplate and configure it to require that the user enter a currency value greater than or equal to 0. (That is, set the `Type` property to `Double`, the `Operator` property to `GreaterThanEqual`, and the `ValueToCompare` property to `0`.)

By the Way

> If you need to refresh your memory on using the ASP.NET validation controls, consult Hour 12, "Validating User Input with Validation Controls."

After you have completed these four steps, view the page through a browser and attempt to edit the `Price` field. Note that if you omit the price or attempt to enter a noncurrency value or a currency value less than zero, you will receive a descriptive error message, and the value will not be saved to the database (see Figures 16.12 and 16.13).

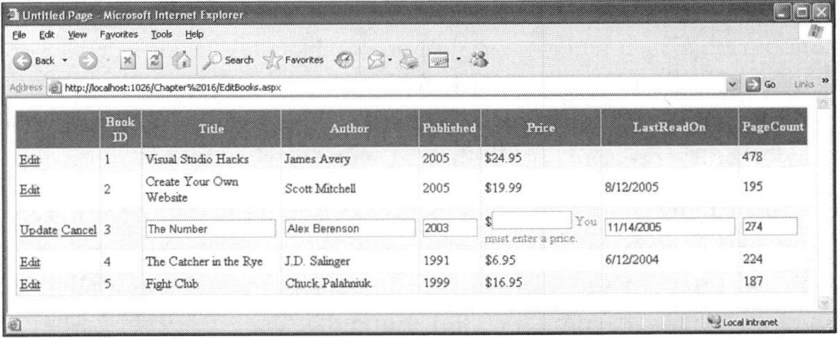

FIGURE 16.12
An error message is displayed if the `Price` field value is omitted.

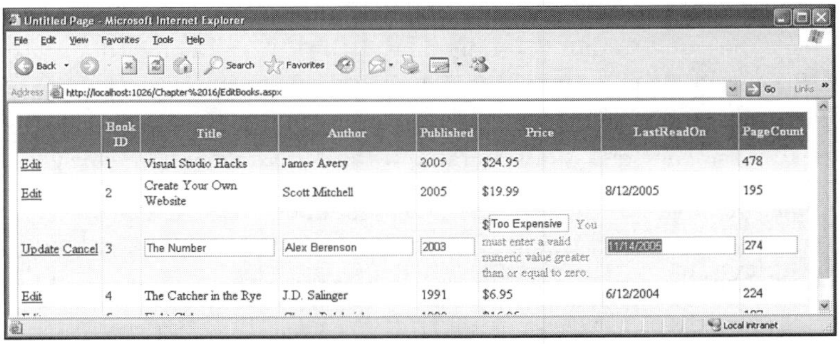

FIGURE 16.13
The GridView won't post back until a valid currency value is provided for the `Price` field.

In addition to being able to add validation controls and tweak the TextBox Web control's aesthetic properties, when customizing the editing interface, you can replace the TextBox Web control with a more appropriate Web control, if needed. For example, if a GridView field displayed the gender of the book's author, we might want to have a drop-down list of genders rather than requiring the user to type in Male or Female. The exercises in this chapter include a task that involves customizing the editing interface by replacing the TextBox with an alternate input Web control.

By the Way

> We set the CompareToValidator's `Type` property to `Double` instead of `Currency` because the default format of the data returned by the database leaves the price with *four* decimal places. However, the `Currency` data type used by the CompareValidator requires that the value have at most *two* decimal places. Therefore, if we used a type of `Currency`, the validator would complain whenever we edited a row and did not manually pare down the value from four decimal places to two (or less).
>
> A better workaround would be to adjust the data binding expression used in the `Text` property of the `Price` field's TextBox Web control. Ideally, we would have the result formatted to two decimal places, which could be accomplished using the following format specifier: `{0:0.00}`. Interested readers are encouraged to try to tweak the data binding expression to format the data like so; if you succeed, feel free to change the CompareValidator's `Type` to `Currency`.

Understanding Optimistic Concurrency

When configuring a SqlDataSource to support `INSERT`, `UPDATE`, and `DELETE` commands, we are given the option of whether to use optimistic concurrency. This applies specifically to editing and deleting data, so let's examine this concept briefly before moving on to inserting data with the DetailsView control.

With web applications there may be many users visiting the website at the same time. If you have a web page that allows users to edit or delete the same database data, some concurrency issues can arise due to the fact that there is a physical and temporal disconnect between the web server and the client (the web browsers visiting the site). In English, if you let multiple users visit a page and edit or delete data from the same database table, there's a chance that two people may be trying to edit or delete the same data at the same time. There's no technological problem with allowing multiple people to work with the same database data concurrently, but there can be confusion among those working with the data because they would not know that someone else is also working with that data simultaneously.

For example, we have built an ASP.NET page that allows users to edit the contents of the books in the `Books` table. Imagine that two users—Jisun and Sam—both visit this page at about the same time. When they visit this page, both Jisun and Sam will be sent the same data, so they both see that the book *Visual Studio Hacks* was authored by James Avery in 2005. Now, imagine that Jisun wants to change the data, instead recording that the book was authored by Dave Yates, so she clicks the Edit button and the values are displayed in text boxes; at the same time, Sam wants to change the year the book was published from 2005 to 2002, so she clicks the Edit button as well, loading the values into the text boxes.

Now, Jisun makes her change of the author and clicks the Update button. The Books table is updated successfully, changing the author of *Visual Studio Hacks* to Dave Yates. A few moments later Sam clicks the Update button. Because Sam clicked the Edit button *before* Jisun's change to the author, the author for *Visual Studio Hacks* in Sam's screen still says James Avery, so when Sam commits her changes, Jisun's change to the author will be overwritten. Figure 16.14 illustrates this problem graphically.

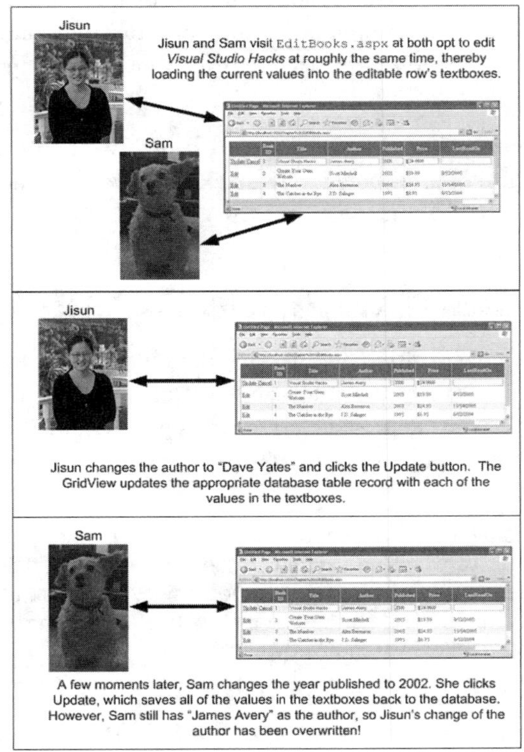

Jisun
Jisun and Sam visit EditBooks.aspx at both opt to edit Visual Studio Hacks at roughly the same time, thereby loading the current values into the editable row's textboxes.
Sam
Jisun
Jisun changes the author to "Dave Yates" and clicks the Update button. The GridView updates the appropriate database table record with each of the values in the textboxes.
Sam
A few moments later, Sam changes the year published to 2002. She clicks Update, which saves all of the values in the textboxes back to the database. However, Sam still has "James Avery" as the author, so Jisun's change of the author has been overwritten!

FIGURE 16.14
Two users working with the same data around the same time can lead to overwriting one another's changes.

To avoid this problem, you can check the Use Optimistic Concurrency check box in the SqlDataSource control's wizard. Without optimistic concurrency, the WHERE clause in the DELETE and UPDATE statements is based solely on the primary key column(s)—BookID in our example. However, with optimistic concurrency, the WHERE clause is updated to include *all* of the columns and their original values. That is, with optimistic concurrency the SqlDataSource control's UPDATE statement looks something like

```
UPDATE [Books] SET
  [Title] = @Title,
  ...
WHERE [BookID] = @BookID AND [Title] = @orig_Title AND
➥[Author] = @orig_Author AND ...
```

where @orig_*ColumnName* is a parameter that holds the value of the column when the user clicks the Edit button. That way, an UPDATE is saved only if there have been no changes in any of the other columns in the table since the user clicked the UPDATE button. With optimistic concurrency enabled, when Sam updates *Visual Studio Hacks* with the new YearPublished value, the UPDATE would apply to any rows because the WHERE clause would be looking for a row that, among other things, had an Author value of "James Avery"—however, that was changed by Jisun's edit moments before.

Optimistic concurrency is a nice feature, but it is really useful only if you expect to have multiple, concurrent users potentially updating or deleting the same data. If you do expect this, go ahead and check the Use Optimistic Concurrency check box.

Inserting Data with the DetailsView

While the GridView makes editing and deleting data a breeze, it doesn't provide a way to insert a new record into the database. The DetailsView, however, does, and configuring the DetailsView to provide inserting support is quite similar to adding editing and deleting support to a GridView.

In addition to providing inserting support, the DetailsView also offers editing and deleting capabilities. We won't be examining the DetailsViews editing and deleting support; I leave that as an exercise for you. You'll find, though, that enabling and configuring editing and deleting support in the DetailsView is nearly identical to providing such functionality with the GridView.

As with the GridView, the first step in creating a DetailsView that supports inserting is to add a SqlDataSource control to the page that has been configured to include the INSERT, UPDATE, and DELETE statements. Take a moment to create a new ASP.NET page and add and configure the SqlDataSource control as we've done throughout this chapter.

Next, add a DetailsView to the Design view and bind it to the SqlDataSource control. In the DetailsView control's smart tag, you'll find an Enable Inserting check box. Check this. Doing so adds a New button beneath the other DetailsView fields, as shown in Figure 16.15. (Also take a moment to check the Enable Paging check box so that we can scroll through the records rather than just sitting at the first record.)

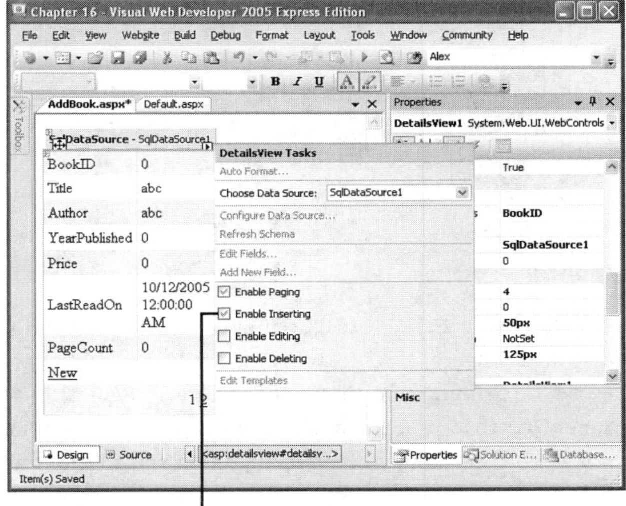

FIGURE 16.15 The DetailsView has been configured to support inserting.

When you view the ASP.NET page through a browser, you'll see that the first book, *Visual Studio Hacks*, is displayed, with links to page through the results. Additionally, there's a New link that, when clicked, will display the DetailsView in an insertable mode (see Figure 16.16). When the DetailsView is in insertable mode, the user can enter values for the various editable fields, creating the new record by clicking the Insert button.

Customizing the Insertable DetailsView

Like the GridView, the insertable DetailsView is highly customizable. Enabling inserting in a DetailsView adds an Insert field to the DetailsView, which can be examined through the Fields dialog box. Like the Edit or Delete fields in an editable or deletable GridView, the Insert field's appearance can be customized. By default, it displays the text `"Insert"` in a link, but these aesthetic settings can be changed via the field's `ButtonType` and `InsertText` properties. Just like with the GridView, you can make the DetailsView's Insert field a link, button, or image, and for buttons or links, you can specify the text displayed.

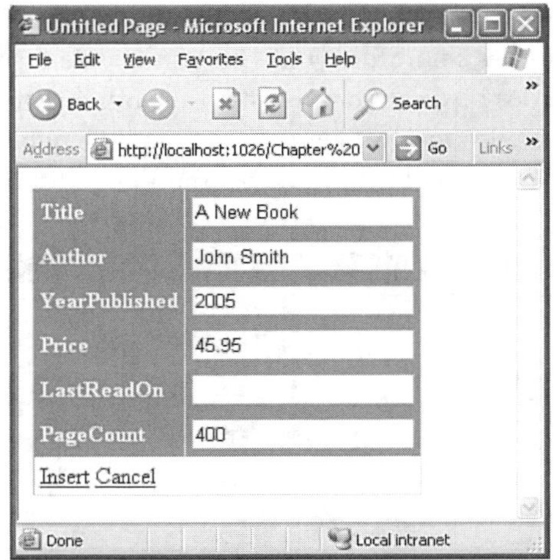

FIGURE 16.16 Clicking the New button displays the DetailsView in insertable mode.

Each DetailsView field has an `InsertVisible` property that can be set through the Fields dialog box. If this property is set to `False`, the field does not appear when adding a new record. By default, all primary key columns—`BookID` in our example—have this `InsertVisible` property set to `False`. As Figure 16.16 shows, the `BookID` field is nowhere to be seen when inserting a new record into the `Books` table.

By the Way

> The DetailsView fields also have a `ReadOnly` property; however, the `ReadOnly` property value is ignored when we're working with an insertable DetailsView. It is used, however, when we're working with an editable DetailsView control.

Like an editable GridView, an insertable DetailsView emits a default inserting interface, which results in a TextBox Web control for each field displayed in the insertable view. If you need to customize this inserting interface, convert the BoundFields into TemplateFields and edit the InsertItemTemplate accordingly.

As you can see, working with an insertable DetailsView is very similar to working with an editable GridView. The same issues and customization options exist with both data Web controls.

Summary

In this hour we looked at how to edit, delete, and insert data into a database through an ASP.NET page. Like displaying data, modifying a database's content through a web page involves both a data source control and a data Web control. To insert, update, or delete data, we need to configure the SqlDataSource control to generate the appropriate INSERT, UPDATE, and DELETE statements, which can be accomplished by checking the appropriate check box in the wizard.

When the SqlDataSource has been configured correctly, adding, editing, and deleting support with the GridView is as simple as binding the GridView to the data source control and checking the Enable Deleting and Enable Editing check boxes in the smart tag. At a bare minimum, this is all that is needed to implement deleting and editing of the GridView's underlying data. However, often we'll want to customize the Edit or Delete field or tweak the editing interface. These tasks, though, are not difficult, require zero source code, and can be accomplished through Visual Web Developer's Design view. If more advanced logic is required when updating or deleting a GridView's data, a number of related events are fired during the updating and deleting processes. (See the exercises section for practice on one of these GridView events.)

This hour concluded with a look at using the DetailsView to insert new records into the underlying database table. Creating an insertable DetailsView involved the same steps as creating an editable or deletable GridView. Additionally, the DetailsView provides similar mechanisms for customizing the insertable interface as the GridView does for customizing the editable interface.

In this hour and the preceding one, we examined how to display and modify database data using the GridView and DetailsView controls. In the next hour we'll look at binding database data to DropDownList, RadioButtonList, and CheckBoxList controls, and we'll also illustrate how to use the DropDownList and GridView Web controls in conjunction to provide filtering of data.

Q&A

Q. ***When I'm working with a GridView that supports deleting, is there any way to include a confirmation message when a user clicks the Delete button?***

A. You can configure the GridView to display a client-side confirmation message box when the user clicks a Delete button, asking her if she's certain she wants to delete the record (see Figure 16.17). This prompt is displayed *before* the page is posted back. If the user clicks OK, the page is posted back, and the Delete proceeds exactly as it would have had you omitted the client-side confirmation message box. If, however, the user clicks the Cancel button, the postback is canceled, and therefore the record is not deleted.

To learn how to add a client-side confirmation message box to each Delete button in a GridView, refer to the "Utilizing Client-Side Script to Confirm Deletions" section of the article online at http://msdn.microsoft.com/library/default.asp?url=/library/en-us/dnaspp/html/GridViewEx10.asp.

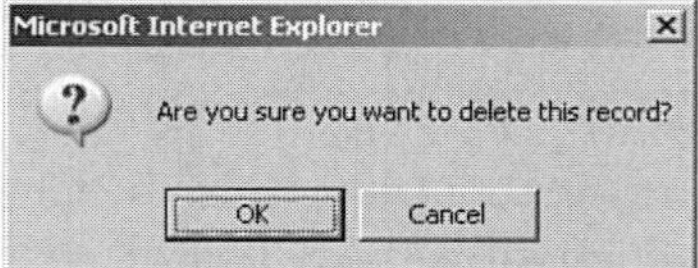

FIGURE 16.17 A client-side confirmation message box prompts the user as to whether she wants to delete the record.

Q. ***With optimistic concurrency, if a user's update or delete is not applied due to the record being changed, how can I alert the user that this was the case?***

A. The optimistic concurrency feature simply acts as a safeguard against multiple, concurrent users overwriting each other's changes. It does *not* provide a means for alerting the user that his update or deletion was not propagated to the database due to the fact that the underlying data has since changed. That is, in our Jisun and Sam scenario in Figure 16.14, had optimistic concurrency been used, when Sam clicked the Update button, his changes wouldn't be submitted. By default, he'd receive no feedback; when the page refreshed, it would be back to its pre-editing state, but instead of seeing the year published as 2002, it would be set to 2005, with the author as Dave Yates.

Ideally, it would be nice to alert Sam that his change was not saved because it would have overwritten another user's recent modifications. This can be accomplished by creating an event handler for the GridView's `RowUpdated` event. The `RowUpdated` event fires after the user has clicked the Update button and the GridView has submitted the update request to its data source control.

The `RowUpdated` event handler is passed in as its second parameter an object of type `GridViewUpdatedEventArgs`, which includes a property called `AffectedRows`. This property, as you may have guessed, specifies how many rows were affected by the `UPDATE` statement issued to the database. If this value is 0, then the user's `UPDATE` did not succeed in finding any matches, either because the row has since been deleted, or optimistic concurrency is being used and another user has since modified the contents. In either case, we can display a message to the user when this scenario unfolds by using the following code in the ASP.NET page's source code portion:

```
Protected Sub GridView1_RowUpdated(ByVal sender As Object,
➥ByVal e As System.Web.UI.WebControls.GridViewUpdatedEventArgs)
➥Handles GridView1.RowUpdated
    If e.AffectedRows = 0 Then
        LabelID.Text = "Your update was not committed either because the
➥record no longer exists or another user recently made a change
➥to this record and your update
➥would have overwritten these changes."
    End If
End Sub
```

To create the event handler for the GridView's `RowUpdated` event, go to the source code portion and select the GridView from the left drop-down list at the top of the screen and the `RowUpdated` event from the right drop-down list.

Workshop

Quiz

1. True or False: Optimistic concurrency, if enabled, applies to inserting, updating, and deleting data.
2. What conditions must be true in order for the SqlDataSource control's wizard to be able to automatically generate `INSERT`, `UPDATE`, and `DELETE` commands?
3. How do we customize the editing interface of an editable GridView?
4. When a web page visitor clicks on the Delete, Edit, or Insert buttons for the GridView or DetailsView, what sequence of events takes place?
5. What two GridView events fire during the deletion process?

Answers

1. False. Optimistic concurrency applies only to updating and deleting data. With inserting new records, there's no possibility that one user's insert will overwrite another's because both users are creating new data.
2. The table being queried must have a primary key, and the `SELECT` statement specified must, at minimum, return this primary key.
3. By default a GridView renders each BoundField as a TextBox Web control. To customize this editing interface, we need to convert the BoundField into a TemplateField. Then, we can edit the field's EditItemTemplate, making whatever changes are necessary.
4. When the user clicks on one of these buttons, the ASP.NET page is posted back. Upon postback, the GridView or DetailsView notes that the Edit, Delete, or Insert button was clicked and raises the first of two events: for the GridView, `RowDeleting` for deleting, and `RowUpdating` for updating; for the DetailsView, `ItemDeleting` for deleting, `ItemUpdating` for updating, and `ItemInserting` for inserting.

   Next, the data Web control's associated data source control has the appropriate `InsertCommand`, `UpdateCommand`, or `DeleteCommand` command invoked, which sends a SQL statement to the database, inserting, updating, or deleting the record. Finally, the data Web control signals that the data modification has completed, raising the `RowDeleted` or `RowUpdated` event for the GridView and `ItemDeleted`, `ItemUpdated`, or `ItemInserted` for the DetailsView.

5. `RowDeleting` and `RowDeleted`.

Exercises

1. In the "Allowing Users to Delete Data" section, we examined how to use the GridView to allow users to delete a record from the GridView. In that section I mentioned that when the user clicks the Delete button, a postback ensues and the GridView, before instructing its data source control to delete the data, raises the `RowDeleting` event. If we want the delete to be canceled if some condition is met, we can create an event handler for this event and determine whether to cancel the delete.

   Your task for this exercise is to create an ASP.NET page that lists the books from the `Books` database table in a GridView that supports deleting. In addition to this GridView control, add a Label Web control on the page with the `ID` `deleteFailed`, the `Visible` property set to `False`, and the `Text` property value `"Why oh why would you want to delete this book?"`. (When we set the `Visible` property to `False`, this control won't be rendered, so it won't appear in the user's browser until, on a postback, we set this property to `True`.)

   Next, create an event handler for the GridView's `RowDeleting` event. This event handler will be passed as its second parameter an object of type `GridViewDeleteEventArgs`, which has a property named `Cancel`. We can stop the user-initiated delete by simply setting this `Cancel` property to `True`. Additionally, this class has a property of type `Values`, which we can use as follows to grab a value from the row that the user is attempting to delete:

   ```
   e.Values(columnName)
   ```

   Your task is to cancel the delete and have the `deleteFailed` Label displayed if the user attempts to delete a book authored by yours truly (Scott Mitchell). If the user is deleting some other author's book, hide the `deleteFailed` Label and let the delete continue unabated.

   Here's a snippet of code to get you started; this will go inside the `RowDeleting` event handler:

   ```
   If e.Values("Author") = "Scott Mitchell" Then
     ...
   Else
     ...
   End If
   ```

2. In the "Customizing the Editing Interface and Updating Rules" section, we saw how to use TemplateFields to customize a particular field's editing interface. In this hour we looked at customizing the `Price` field to include both a RequiredFieldValidator and a CompareValidator. These two validation controls ensured that the user provided a currency value for the `Price` that was greater than or equal to zero.

   Please complete what we started here, adding RequiredFieldValidators to the `Title`, `Author`, `YearPublished`, and `PageCount` fields. Also add CompareValidator controls to the `YearPublished` and `PageCount` fields. The CompareValidator controls should ensure that both fields are integers that are greater than zero.

3. In addition to adding validation controls to a TemplateField's EditItemTemplate, we can also replace the TextBox Web control with a different Web control. For this exercise, customize the editable interface for the `LastReadOn` field, replacing the TextBox with the Calendar Web control.

   To accomplish this, convert the `LastReadOn` field to a TemplateField. Next, delete the TextBox control from the EditItemTemplate and drag a Calendar control from the Toolbox into the EditItemTemplate. At this point test the functionality in the browser. You'll see that when the user tries to edit a row, a calendar is displayed in the editable row's `LastReadOn` field. However, no date is selected in the calendar (even if there's a `LastReadOn` value), and if you select a date from the calendar and click Update, the value is not saved.

   To have the current value displayed in the Calendar Web control and to have the user's selected value persisted back to the database, we need to use a data binding expression that assigns the `LastReadOn` field to the Calendar control's `SelectedDate` property. We can accomplish this through the Design tab by going to the Calendar control's smart tag and clicking on the Edit DataBindings link. This will bring up the DataBindings dialog box. Simply select the appropriate Web control property from the list on the left (`SelectedDate`) and then select the data source control field to bind to this value from the drop-down list on the right (`LastReadOn`). Make sure the Two-way Databinding check box is checked.

   After making this change, take a moment to test the page in a browser. If you edit a book that has a `LastReadOn` value, the Calendar control's `SelectedDate` property will be assigned to the Calendar. Furthermore, whatever date is selected in the Calendar control is what is saved as the `LastReadOn` value when the Update button is clicked. However, as you may have noticed, when the row is made editable, the Calendar control shows the month and year of the value of its `VisibleDate` property (which defaults to the current date). So if the `LastReadOn` value of the editable row is November 11, 2005, but the current date is March 13, 2006, you'll have to click back through the months to November to be able to see the selected date. Obviously, we want the month and year of the `LastReadOn` date to be shown when a row is first made editable. To accomplish this, go back to the Calendar's DataBindings dialog box and bind the `VisibleDate` property to the `LastReadOn` field value, but this time make sure Two-way Databinding is unchecked.

At this point the editable GridView should work as desired with rows that have a `LastReadOn` value; however, for those rows where this value is Null, you will get an exception when trying to edit. Why this happens, as well as why we had the Calendar's `SelectedDate` property use two-way databinding versus the one-way databinding used by the `VisibleDate` property, are topics we'll discuss in Hour 19, "Defining a Site's Structure and Providing Site Navigation."

HOUR 17

Working with Data-Bound DropDownLists, RadioButtons, and CheckBoxes

In this hour, we will cover

- Populating the items of a drop-down list with the results from a database query
- Creating check boxes and radio buttons based on the results of a database query
- Using the DropDownList control to filter the contents displayed in a GridView
- The benefits of using database information versus hard-coding drop-down list, check box, and radio button values

As we've seen over the past three hours, the data source controls enable us to easily work with database data. We simply specify what table and columns we want to work with and whether we need corresponding `INSERT`, `UPDATE`, and `DELETE` statements. When a data source control has been properly configured, one of a number of data Web controls can be used to allow the end user to interact with that data through an ASP.NET page. In addition to the GridView, DetailsView, FormView, Repeater, and DataList controls, ASP.NET includes a number of list controls that can also be bound to data source controls: the DropDownList, CheckBoxList, and RadioButtonList controls.

In Hour 11, "Collecting Input Using Drop-Down Lists, Radio Buttons, and Check Boxes," we looked at using the DropDownList, RadioButton, and CheckBox controls in an ASP.NET page, but we had to explicitly provide the values for the drop-down list items, radio buttons, and check boxes. That is, if we wanted a drop-down list from which users could choose their favorite ice cream flavor, we had to manually add the available flavors to the drop-down list. Now that we know how to work with databases, we can re-examine these controls from Hour 11.

An Overview of the List Web Controls

ASP.NET includes a bevy of Web controls designed for collecting user input, many of which we examined in Hours 10 and 11. The **list Web controls**, a special class of input collection Web controls, present the user with a list of options. The DropDownList, which we examined in Hour 11, falls into this category of Web controls because it presents users with a series of options from which they must pick one. While the CheckBox and RadioButton controls represent a single check box or radio button and, therefore, aren't list controls, often multiple radio buttons or check boxes are used in tandem to provide users with a list of check boxes or radio buttons to select among. ASP.NET does provide two Web controls designed to present a list of check boxes or radio buttons. These two Web controls—the CheckBoxList and RadioButtonList—are list Web controls.

The list Web controls share a number of features. Conceptually, they are all a collection of items of one sort or another. The DropDownList is a collection of drop-down list items; the CheckBoxList, a collection of check boxes; and the RadioButtonList, a collection of radio buttons. More concretely, they share a number of programmatic traits, such as

- Each list Web control provides programmatic access to its items through the `Items` property.
- Each item in a list Web control is an instance of the `ListItem` class. When the list Web control is rendered, it turns each `ListItem` instance into the appropriate markup.
- Each list Web control can optionally be configured to induce a postback when an end user makes a change in the selected state of the control. (This is discussed in the "Automatically Posting Back When a List Web Control Changes" section later in this hour.)
- If a list Web control's selected item or items are changed across postbacks, the `SelectedIndexChanged` event is raised.
- The list Web controls' `Items` collection can be propagated statically, programmatically, or through a data source control.

In Hour 11 we saw how to assign the items of a DropDownList control statically. Recall that the DropDownList's smart tag has an Edit Items link that, when clicked, displays the ListItem Collection Editor dialog box. This dialog box permits us to statically specify the items of a list control. The CheckBoxList and RadioButtonList also have a smart tag with an Edit Items option that likewise brings up the ListItem Collection Editor dialog box.

In addition to specifying a list Web control's items statically, we can also assign the values through a data source control. That is, we can add a SqlDataSource control to our page, configure it to grab a set of records from a database table, and then bind that data to the list Web control. For each record returned by the SqlDataSource, the list Web control adds an item to its list.

Binding Data to a List Web Control

Binding data to a list Web control is very similar to binding data to a GridView or DetailsView. The only difference is that while a GridView or DetailsView can be bound to a variable number of database table columns, list Web controls can be bound to, at most, two columns. The reason is that each item in a list control has two properties, `Text` and `Value`. The `Text` property is the value displayed onscreen—the text shown in the drop-down list item or the text of the radio button or check box—whereas the `Value` property is not displayed, but provides an additional bit of information about each item.

Let's not get bogged down with the differences between the `Text` and `Value` properties at this point; if the distinction is not clear now, it will be as we work through some examples. For now, let's practice binding database results to the various list Web controls.

Start by creating a new ASP.NET page named `ListControls.aspx`. Next, add a SqlDataSource control to the page and configure it to return all columns and all rows of the `Books` table. You don't need to configure the SqlDataSource control to include the `INSERT`, `UPDATE`, and `DELETE` statements. After you have finished this, drag a DropDownList, CheckBoxList, and RadioButtonList onto the page, preceding each with text that shows the name of the control. After you have added the SqlDataSource control and the three list Web controls, your screen should look similar to Figure 17.1.

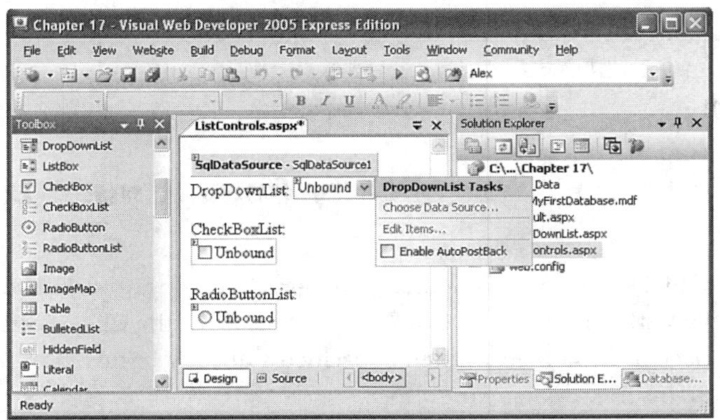

FIGURE 17.1
A SqlDataSource and the three list Web controls have been added to the page.

Each of these list Web controls has a smart tag with a Choose Data Source link. Clicking this link displays the Data Source Configuration Wizard, which prompts for the data source control to use and the column(s) to bind to the `Text` and `Value` properties of each list Web control. Take a moment to configure the data source for each of the three list Web controls, having each one display the `Title` column and use the `BookID` column as the value. Figure 17.2 shows this dialog box when configuring the DropDownList control's data source.

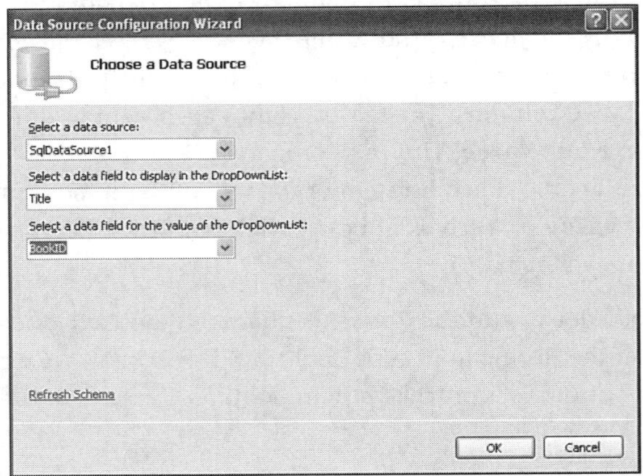

FIGURE 17.2 Choose the data source control and the columns to bind to the list Web control.

After you specify a data source for the list Web control, the Design view in Visual Web Developer will change slightly; instead of using the word `"Unbound"` for the DropDownList, RadioButtonList, or CheckBoxList (see Figure 17.1), the word `"Databound"` will be used instead. To see the actual values displayed in the drop-down list, check boxes, or radio buttons, you'll need to view the ASP.NET page through a browser. Take a moment to do this and ensure that your screen looks similar to Figure 17.3.

Note that each list Web control has five items, one for each record returned by its SqlDataSource. The difference among the three list Web controls is the way they render their items.

The Benefits of Dynamically Populating a List Control

In Hour 11 we looked at how to populate the items in a DropDownList control statically, using the ListItem Collection Editor dialog box. Both the CheckBoxList and RadioButtonList can have their list items specified statically in this manner. Simply click the Edit Items link in their smart tags.

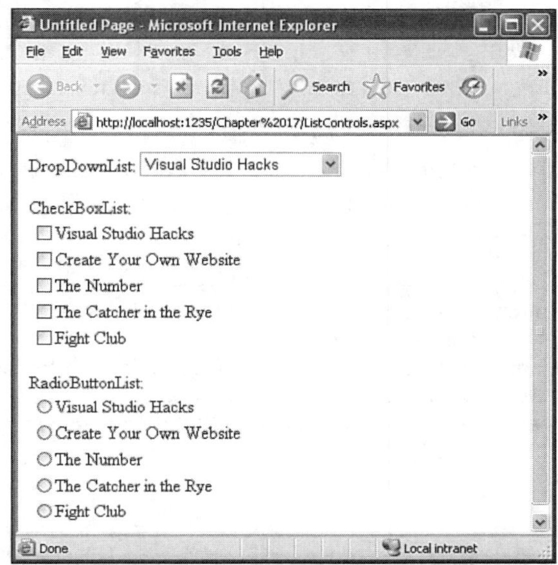

FIGURE 17.3
The list Web controls have five items, one for each book in the `Books` table.

While the list Web controls do support having their items set statically, it's often advantageous to do so dynamically, through binding the control to a data source. The problem with statically assigning the items to a list control is that if there are changes to the items to be displayed in the future, you must visit each and every page that uses this data and update the list control appropriately. If you dynamically bind your items, though, if there are any changes, you can just update the database table from which the items are retrieved and you're done!

For example, in Hour 11 we looked at using a DropDownList that was statically populated with a list of ice cream flavors, from which we asked visitors to choose their favorite. These values were entered statically but could have been entered dynamically. That is, we could have created a table in our database called `IceCreamFlavors` that had two columns:

- `IceCreamFlavorID`, a primary key, Auto-increment field of type `int` that uniquely identifies each ice cream flavor
- `Flavor`, an `nvarchar(100)` column that contains the name of the flavor (Chocolate, Vanilla, and so on)

Then, in our ASP.NET page, we could use a SqlDataSource control to grab the contents of this table and bind it to the DropDownList. This may sound like a lot of work to just display some ice cream flavors, and this approach obviously isn't as quick as just typing in a handful of flavors in the DropDownList's ListItem

Collection Editor dialog box. However, it will save you time if you need to replicate this functionality on other pages, if you expect the list of ice cream flavors to change in the future, or if you need to provide some association in the database between, say, users and their favorite ice cream flavors.

I encourage you to use dynamic list Web controls for all but the most trivial scenarios that are guaranteed not to change in the future, such as a drop-down list with gender options, Yes/No options, hours of the day, and so on.

By the Way

> In Hour 13, "An Introduction to Databases," we briefly discussed how many real-world databases are composed of multiple, related tables. With such relational database models, there are often scenarios in which you need to populate related data using a list Web control. For such scenarios it is of the utmost importance to grab the data dynamically from the database, rather than hard-coding in the related options statically.

Programmatically Responding to a Changed Selection

When using list Web controls on a web page, we are often interested in knowing when a list control's selected item has changed. Each of the list controls contains a `SelectedIndexChanged` event that fires upon postback if the list control's selection has changed. Returning to our earlier example, `ListControls.aspx`, let's add a Button Web control and a Label Web control to the page. Set the Button's `Text` property to `"Click Me"` and the Label's `ID` and `Text` properties to `status` and a blank string, respectively.

Next, create a `SelectedIndexChanged` event handler for the DropDownList. You can accomplish this by simply double-clicking the DropDownList in the Design view, or by going to the code view and choosing the DropDownList's `ID` and the `SelectedIndexChanged` event from the drop-down lists at the top of the screen. After you have added this event handler, your ASP.NET page's source code portion should look like this:

```
Partial Class ListControls
    Inherits System.Web.UI.Page

    Protected Sub DropDownList1_SelectedIndexChanged(ByVal sender As Object,
➥ ByVal e As System.EventArgs) Handles DropDownList1.SelectedIndexChanged

    End Sub
End Class
```

This event handler—`DropDownList1_SelectedIndexChanged`—will execute whenever the page is posted back and there's been a change in the selected item of the

DropDownList. To test this, add the following line of code in the event handler:

```
status.Text = "The drop-down list value is now " & DropDownList1.SelectedValue
```

Set a breakpoint at this line by positioning your cursor on the line and pressing F9, or by clicking in the margin; next, start the debugger by going to the Debug menu and choosing Start. This will load the ASP.NET page in a browser. Notice that on the initial page load, the `SelectedIndexChanged` event doesn't fire because there's been no change to the selected state of the DropDownList. At this point your screen should look similar to Figure 17.3, except with the addition of a button.

By the Way

> The basics of debugging an ASP.NET web page were discussed in Hour 4, "Designing, Creating, and Testing ASP.NET Pages." Feel free to return to Hour 4 to refresh your memory, if needed.

Without changing the value of the DropDownList, click the button, posting back the ASP.NET page. Again, the `SelectedIndexChanged` event does not fire because the selected DropDownList item—*Visual Studio Hacks*—has yet to change. This time, however, select a different book from the DropDownList and click the button. Upon postback, the `SelectedIndexChanged` event will fire, and the debugger will break on the breakpoint we set. Continue debugging by pressing F5. The browser window should now refresh, displaying a message in the `status` Label indicating the `BookID` value of the selected book (see Figure 17.4).

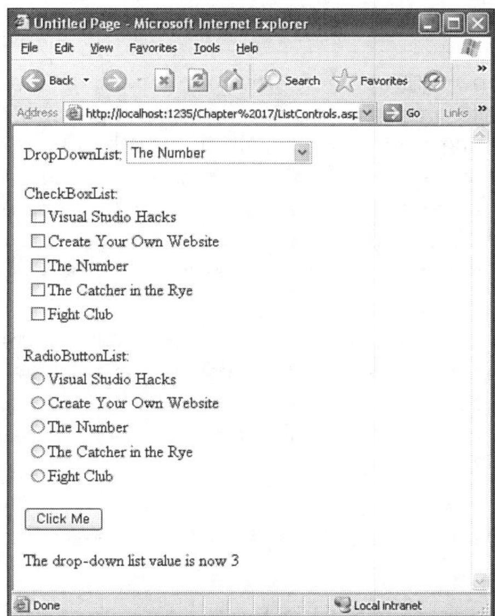

FIGURE 17.4 The Label displays the `BookID` of the last selected book.

Note that if you click the button again without changing the book selection, the `SelectedIndexChanged` event does not fire. As we've seen, it fires only on the postback immediately following a change in the list Web control's selection state.

As we discussed in Hour 9, "Web Form Basics," server-side events and code, such as a list control's `SelectedIndexChanged` event and its associated event handler, can fire and execute on the web server only when the browser explicitly re-requests the page (a postback). By default, changing the selection of a list control does *not* cause a postback. Therefore, the control's `SelectedIndexChanged` event does not fire immediately after the user changes the selection state of a list control, but only when a postback ensues. For instance, in our previous example, you can change the drop-down list from *The Number* to *Visual Studio Hacks*, but the DropDownList Web control's `SelectedIndexChanged` event doesn't fire until the Click Me button is clicked, thereby causing a postback.

If the drop-down list's selection was changed from *The Number* to *Visual Studio Hacks* to *Fight Club*, and then the Click Me button was clicked, the `SelectedIndexChanged` event would fire only once, because from the web server's perspective, the drop-down list's selection has only changed once, from *The Number* to *Fight Club*. Similarly, if the drop-down list is changed from *The Number* to *Visual Studio Hacks*, and then back to *The Number*, and then the Click Me button is clicked, the `SelectedIndexChanged` event *won't* fire, because from the web server's perspective, no selection change has been made. That is, when the web server initially rendered the page, the DropDownList Web control's initial selection was *The Number* and on postback the selection was still *The Number*.

By the Way

In some scenarios you might be interested to immediately know when a list Web control's selection state has changed. For example, a page might have a "Quick Links" DropDownList that contains some of the popular pages on your website. In this case you might want to have a `SelectedIndexChanged` event handler that redirects the user to the appropriate page whenever the DropDownList value is changed. In such scenarios you want the page to be posted back as soon as the user changes her selection; the next section discusses how to add such behavior to the list controls.

Other times, though, you may not really care when a list control's selection changes, but are rather just interested in what values are selected on postback. In this case, you can put your programmatic login in the Button Web control's `Click` event handler, which will run when the page is posted back.

Automatically Posting Back When a List Web Control Changes

In the smart tags for the list Web controls, you may have noticed a check box labeled Enable AutoPostBack. This check box indicates the value of the control's

AutoPostBack property, which indicates whether the list Web control induces a postback upon having its selected state changed. As we've seen, by default the list controls don't cause postbacks on their own; rather, a postback is typically caused by the user clicking a Button Web control. Therefore, when working with list Web controls, the end user can make any sort of change to the list control—checking or unchecking the check boxes of a CheckBoxList, selecting different radio buttons from the RadioButtonList, or choosing different options in the DropDownList—and our server-side code won't know of these changes until the form is posted back.

However, we might want to be immediately alerted whenever a user changes the selection state of a list Web control. That is, if the user chooses a different DropDownList item, checks or unchecks a check box in a CheckBoxList, or picks a different radio button in a RadioButtonList, we might want to be notified right away, rather than having to wait for the user to click a button. We can implement this behavior by checking the Enable AutoPostBack check box in the list Web control's smart tag. With this check box checked, the list control is rendered with additional client-side JavaScript that causes a postback as soon as the user alters the selection state. On postback the list control's SelectedIndexChanged event fires.

The remainder of this hour focuses on using these three list Web controls in real-world situations. In the next section we'll see an example of using a DropDownList to filter the results displayed in a GridView. In this example, the DropDownList's AutoPostBack property will be set to True so that the data is automatically refreshed as soon as the DropDownList is changed. We'll also examine using the RadioButtonList and CheckBoxList to collect and process user input.

Filtering Results Using the DropDownList

In the past three chapters we've been working with the Books database table and have seen how to use a GridView to display all of the books in this table. In Hour 14, "Accessing Data with the Data Source Web Controls," we saw how to add hard-coded filtering expressions with the SqlDataSource to limit the books returned by the data source control; specifically, we added two expressions that limited the returned books to those whose BookID was less than or equal to 3 and that were published in 2005.

Specifying hard-coded filtering expressions is one way to limit the data returned by a data source control, but we might rather allow the user visiting the web page to be able to specify how, exactly, the data is filtered. When specifying the values for a filter expression through the SqlDataSource control's wizard, we can specify that the value be based on another Web control on the page, rather than a hard-coded value. That is, we can craft a SqlDataSouce control such that its `WHERE` clause is based on, say, the selected value of a DropDownList control.

To illustrate this, let's first add an additional column to the `Books` table by which we can easily filter the records. Take a moment to add a `Genre` column of type `nvarchar(50)` to the `Books` table. Because there are existing records in the `Books` table, you'll either need to give this column a default value or configure it to allow Nulls. For now, let the `Genre` column allow Nulls.

By the Way

> If you need to review how to specify the definition of a SQL Server 2005 database table in Visual Web Developer, consult Hour 13.
>
> Those with a database background know that rather than adding an `nvarchar(50)` `Genre` column, we should ideally create a new `Genre` lookup table, adding a foreign key `GenreID` to the `Books` table. Feel free to go this route, if this makes sense to you; if what I just said is Greek to you, don't worry; just create the `Genre` column as discussed.

After you've added this new table column, show the table data in Visual Web Developer and enter values for the genres for each of the books. I used the genre Technology for *Visual Studio Hacks* and *Create Your Own Website*, the genre Business for *The Number* and the genre Fiction for *The Catcher in the Rye* and *Fight Club*.

Next, create a new ASP.NET page named `DropDownList.aspx`. When we're done, this page will contain a DropDownList control that lists all of the available genres and a GridView control that displays those books that match the genre selected in the DropDownList. This will require two SqlDataSource controls: one to retrieve the list of genres for the DropDownList and the other to grab those books that are of the selected genre for the GridView.

Listing the Genres in a DropDownList

Let's first concentrate on adding the DropDownList of genres. The DropDownList of genres will list each of the genres defined in the `Books` table. The user visiting the page can then filter the GridView results depending on the selected genre from the DropDownList. To create a DropDownList control listing the available genre choices, perform the following steps:

1. Add a SqlDataSource control that is configured to return just the `Genre` column from the `Books` table. Have the results ordered by the value of the `Genre` column in ascending order.
2. After completing the wizard, change this control's `ID` property from `SqlDataSource1` to a more descriptive `genresDataSource`.

3. Enter the text **`Choose a genre:`** and then add a DropDownList control to the page. Bind the DropDownList control to the `genresDataSource` SqlDataSource, using the `Genre` column as both the text and values of the DropDownList's items.

4. Change the DropDownList control's `ID` from `DropDownList1` to a more descriptive `genres`.

At this point, test your ASP.NET page through a browser (see Figure 17.5). Notice that the drop-down list contains *five* items—one for each record in the `Books` table—even though the table contains only three unique genre values.

FIGURE 17.5
A drop-down list item is available for each record in the `Books` table, rather than one for each unique genre.

To remedy this, we need to configure the SqlDataSource to return only the *unique* genres in the `Books` table. To accomplish this, reopen the SqlDataSource control's wizard, and in the Configure the Select Statement screen, check the Return Only Unique Rows check box, as shown in Figure 17.6.

Watch Out!

For this solution to work as needed, it is important that the `SELECT` statement return only a single column, `Genre`.

The Return Only Unique Rows check box looks at *all* columns in the `SELECT` clause and considers a row a duplicate only if *every* value in the column list is equal to some other row's. That is, if you have the `SELECT` statement return, say, `Title` and `Genre`, currently all five records will be returned. If there were two books in the database with the same title and genre, then, and only then, would only one of these records be returned.

After making this change, view the page through a browser again. This time the drop-down list will have only three items: Business, Fiction, and Technology.

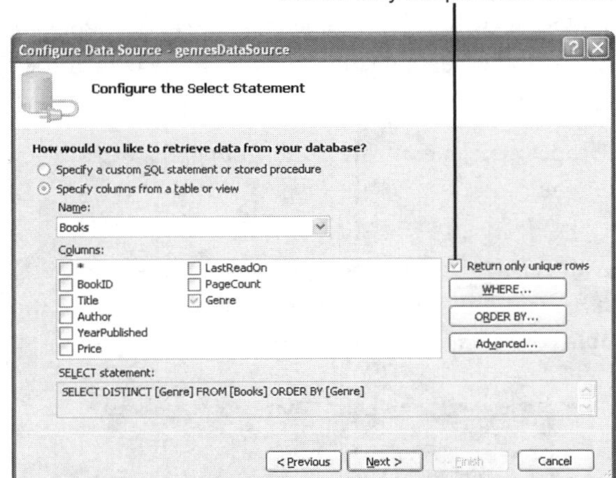

FIGURE 17.6
Only the unique genres will be returned.

Filtering the Data Based on the Selected Genre

Our next step is to add a GridView control that displays only those books that belong to the selected genre. Let's first just add a GridView that displays *all* books from the `Books` table. We've done this many times in the past two hours, so this should be an easy task. Just drag on a SqlDataSource and configure it to return all columns and all records from the `Books` table. As we did with the genre-returning SqlDataSource, change this SqlDataSource control's `ID` from `SqlDataSource1` to a more descriptive `booksDataSource`. Next, add a GridView to the ASP.NET page, binding it to the `booksDataSource` data source control. Rename the GridView's `ID` to `books`.

Take a moment to test the page in a browser. Because the `booksDataSource` SqlDataSource isn't filtering the books based on the genre yet, the GridView shows all of the books, regardless of what genre is selected from the drop-down list. Our next step, then, is to implement filtering within the `booksDataSource` SqlDataSource. To accomplish this, return to the data source control's wizard and, from the Configure Select Statement screen, click the WHERE button to bring up the Add WHERE Clause dialog box.

We want to add a `WHERE` clause to the `SELECT` statement that looks like:

```
SELECT *
FROM [Books]
WHERE [Genre] = Genre selected in the DropDownList
```

Because we want this `WHERE` clause to operate on the `Genre` column, choose this column from the Column drop-down list. Select the = operator from the Operator drop-down list and then, from the Source drop-down list, choose Control because we want the filter expression to be based on the value of a Web control on the page. Choosing the Control option updates the Parameter Properties box in the upper-right corner to provide a drop-down list titled Control ID and a text box titled Default Value. From the Control ID drop-down list, select the `genres` control (our DropDownList); you don't need to pick a default value, so you can leave this text box blank.

Make sure your screen looks similar to Figure 17.7 and then click the Add button to add the parameter to the SqlDataSource. Click OK to return to the Configure the Select Statement screen and then complete the wizard.

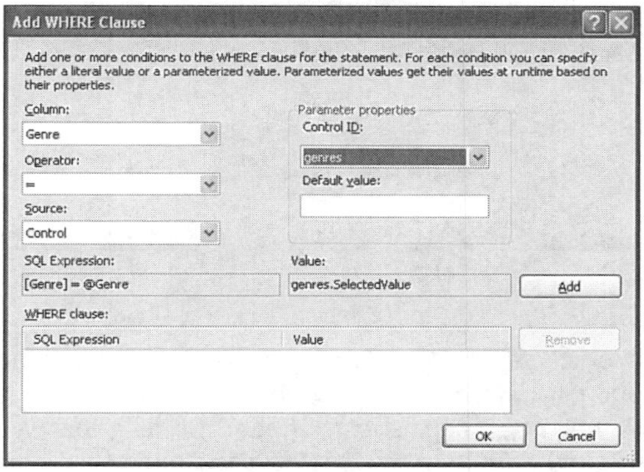

FIGURE 17.7
Add a `WHERE` clause parameter whose value is the selected value of the `genres` DropDownList.

View the ASP.NET page through a browser again. This time, when the page first loads, the GridView should display only one book, *The Number*, because that's the only book that falls within the Business genre (see Figure 17.8). Go ahead and try changing the drop-down list to another genre. Nothing happens! We still see the GridView with one record, listing *The Number*. The reason is that we've yet to enable AutoPostBack in the DropDownList control. Simply changing the DropDownList doesn't cause a postback unless the DropDownList's `AutoPostBack` property is set to `True`. Take a moment to fix this and then revisit the page. Now selecting a different genre from the drop-down list invokes a postback and causes the GridView to be updated (see Figure 17.9).

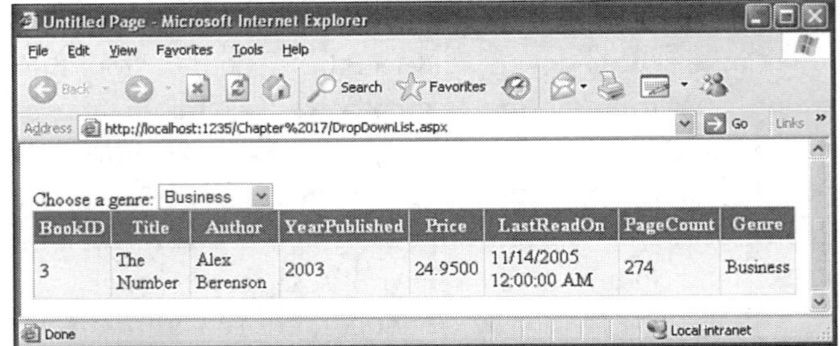

FIGURE 17.8 The `DropDownList.aspx` page, when first visited.

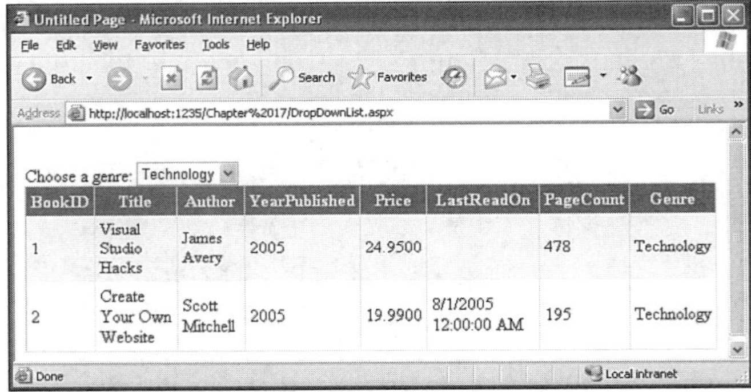

FIGURE 17.9 The page after the user has changed the drop-down list's selection from Business to Technology.

By the Way

Setting the DropDownList's `AutoPostBack` property to `True` was not necessary. We could have optionally added a Button Web control to the page after the DropDownList with a `Text` property like "Refresh." Clicking this would have induced a postback and refreshed the GridView based on the user's drop-down list selection. In essence, we need a postback to refresh the GridView's display, which can be accomplished either through setting the `AutoPostBack` property to `True` or by adding a Button that the user can click to instigate the postback.

Collecting User Input with CheckBoxLists and RadioButtonLists

In Hour 11 we saw how to use the CheckBox and RadioButton controls to collect user input. When using these individual controls, we had to manually add one CheckBox or one RadioButton control for each check box or radio button needed. Rather than using a series of single CheckBox or RadioButton controls, we can use, instead, the CheckBoxList or RadioButtonList.

By the Way

> Recall that a series of check boxes allows the user to select zero to many items from the list of choices. With radio buttons, however, the user is restricted to selecting *one* of the available choices.

The CheckBoxList and RadioButtonList's items can be specified statically via the ListItem Collection Editor dialog box, which you can reach by clicking the Edit Items link in the control's smart tag. The process for adding items to a CheckBoxList or RadioButtonList using the ListItem Collection Editor dialog box is identical to adding items this way for a DropDownList. These steps were covered in detail in Hour 11.

The CheckBoxList and RadioButtonList can also be bound to a data source control as we saw in the "Binding Data to a List Web Control" section earlier in this hour. What we didn't look at earlier, though, was how to determine what item or items, in the case of a CheckBoxList, were selected by the user. There are a couple ways to accomplish this:

- Enumerate the list control's items, checking each item to see if it has been selected.
- Use the `SelectedItem` property to get a reference to the item that was selected.

Let's examine both of these techniques. First, let's create a new ASP.NET page named `CheckAndRadio.aspx` that has on it a SqlDataSource control, a CheckBoxList, and a RadioButtonList. Configure the SqlDataSource to return all columns and all records of the `Books` table. Bind this SqlDataSource to both the CheckBoxList and RadioButtonList, having the list controls display the `Title` column with their values set to the `BookID` column.

Finally, add a Button Web control and a Label Web control. Create a `Click` event handler for the Button Web control. Then clear out the `Text` property of the Label control and assign it an `ID` property value of `results`.

Take a moment to view the page through a browser. You should see a series of check boxes listing each of the five books in the table, followed by a series of radio buttons listing the same books.

Enumerating the List Web Control's List Items

As discussed earlier in this hour, all three list Web controls have an `Items` property that is a collection of list items. This collection can be programmatically enumerated using the following code:

```
'Enumerate the list of items in the CheckBoxList
For Each li As ListItem In listWebControlID.Items
  ' Work with the list item, li
Next
```

Within the `For Each` loop, you can access the properties of the current list item (`li`), with the germane ones being

- `Selected`—A Boolean value indicating whether the list item has been selected by the user
- `Text`—The displayed text of the list item
- `Value`—The value assigned to the list item

If we wanted to display a list of the selected items in the `results` Label Web control, we could use the following code:

```
results.Text = String.Empty

'Enumerate the list of items in the CheckBoxList
For Each li As ListItem In CheckBoxList1.Items
    If li.Selected Then
        results.Text &= li.Text & " was selected!<br />"
    End If
Next
```

This code starts by clearing out the `Text` property of the Label control and then enumerates the list items of the CheckBoxList `CheckBoxList1`. If an item is selected—that is, if `li.Selected` is `True`—then the Label's `Text` property has appended a string indicating that the particular list item was selected. (The `<br />` in the string is an HTML tag that adds a breaking line; it's used to help improve the readability of the output in the page.)

Figure 17.10 shows this ASP.NET page. Note that for each selected check box a corresponding message is displayed in the Label. (This approach works equally well for RadioButtonLists.)

Using `SelectedItem` and `SelectedValue`

In Hour 11 we saw how to programmatically determine the selected item or value of the DropDownList using the `SelectedItem` and `SelectedValue` properties. The `SelectedItem` property returns the `ListItem` instance of the selected item; `SelectedValue` returns the value of the selected item. Both the RadioButtonList and CheckBoxList have these two properties as well; however, more care must be taken when using these properties with either of these two controls.

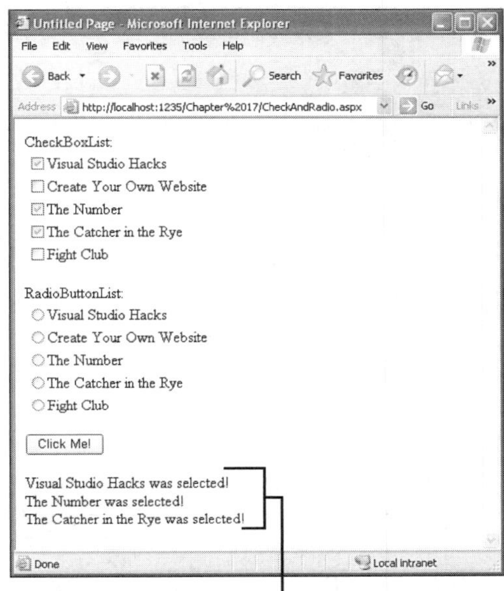

Three lines of text at the bottom of the web page

FIGURE 17.10
The Label's output is dictated by what check boxes were selected.

When you're using a RadioButtonList or CheckBoxList, understand that the user may not choose *any* item. With either of these controls, the user can simply avoid selecting a check box or radio button. (This concern doesn't exist with the DropDownList control.) Before using these properties, then, you must first ensure that a value was selected. The simplest way to ensure that a value has been selected is to test to see whether the `SelectedItem` property is equivalent to `Nothing`; if it is, then that means an item was *not* selected.

We can use the following code to proceed within the conditional only if an item has been selected. That is, we test to see whether `SelectedItem` is *not* `Nothing` and, if so, we can then work with the `SelectedItem` or `SelectedValue` properties (see Figure 17.11):

```
'See what item was selected in the RadioButtonList
If RadioButtonList1.SelectedItem IsNot Nothing Then
    results.Text &= "From the RadioButtonList you selected " &
➥RadioButtonList1.SelectedItem.Text
End If
```

If you do not use a conditional statement to ensure that `SelectedItem` is not `Nothing`, you will get an exception if the user has not selected any item and you try to access the `SelectedValue` property or one of the properties of `SelectedItem` (such as `SelectedItem.Text`).

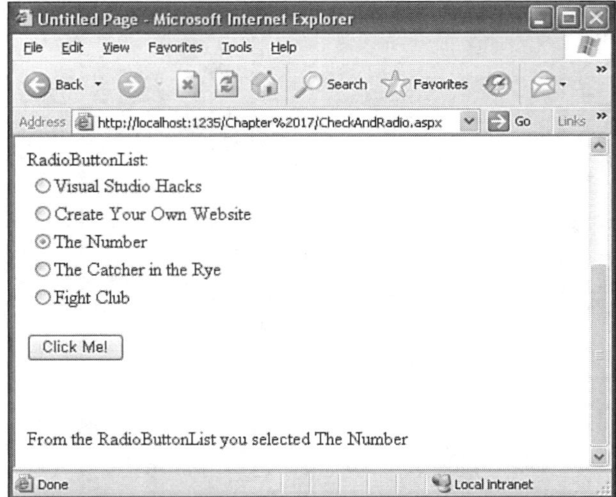

FIGURE 17.11 The selected radio button's text is displayed in the `results` Label.

Another concern with `SelectedItem` and `SelectedValue` is that they return a single `ListItem` instance or value. How does this work with the CheckBoxList, which might have multiple selected items? `SelectedItem` and `SelectedValue` return the *first* selected item from the list. Therefore, we typically use `SelectedItem` or `SelectedValue` only with DropDownLists or RadioButtonLists. For determining the selected items in a CheckBoxList, stick with enumerating the CheckBoxList's `Items` collection, as we saw in the previous section.

Customizing the Appearance of the RadioButtonList and CheckBoxList Controls

Like the other ASP.NET Web controls we've examined throughout this book, the RadioButtonList and CheckBoxList controls have `Font`, `ForeColor`, `BackColor`, and other common properties we've seen before. As with other Web controls, these properties can be found in the Appearance section within the Properties window.

In addition to these properties, the RadioButtonList and CheckBoxList also have some additional properties worth noting in the Layout section of the Properties window. By default, both the RadioButtonList and CheckBoxList are rendered as one-column HTML `<table>` elements, with each item of the control displayed as a row in the `<table>`. Listing 17.1 shows the HTML rendered by a CheckBoxList that's bound to the contents of the `Books` table with its Layout settings left as the default values.

LISTING 17.1 The HTML Produced by a CheckBoxList with the Default Layout Settings

```
<table id="CheckBoxList1" border="0">
    <tr>
        <td><input id="CheckBoxList1_0" type="checkbox"
➥name="CheckBoxList1$0" /><label for="CheckBoxList1_0">Visual Studio Hacks
➥</label></td>
    </tr><tr>
        <td><input id="CheckBoxList1_1" type="checkbox"
➥name="CheckBoxList1$1" /><label for="CheckBoxList1_1">Create Your Own Website
➥</label></td>
    </tr><tr>
        <td><input id="CheckBoxList1_2" type="checkbox"
➥name="CheckBoxList1$2" /><label for="CheckBoxList1_2">The Number
➥</label></td>
    </tr><tr>
        <td><input id="CheckBoxList1_3" type="checkbox"
➥name="CheckBoxList1$3" /><label for="CheckBoxList1_3">The Catcher in the Rye
➥</label></td>
    </tr><tr>
        <td><input id="CheckBoxList1_4" type="checkbox"
➥name="CheckBoxList1$4" /><label for="CheckBoxList1_4">Fight Club
➥</label></td>
    </tr>
</table>
```

As you can see, the CheckBoxList renders as a one-column HTML `<table>` element, with one table row for each check box. The result in the end user's browser is a vertical column of check boxes, as we saw in Figure 17.3.

Although the default Layout properties will likely suffice for CheckBoxLists or RadioButtonLists with a small number of items, displaying dozens of check boxes or radio buttons in this vertical, single-column manner could easily chew up a lot of screen real estate. Rather than confining the items to a single column, we might want to have the check boxes or radio buttons span multiple columns. The Layout properties allow you to customize the layout direction along with other facets dictating how these two Web controls are rendered; the germane properties are listed in Table 17.1.

TABLE 17.1 The RadioButtonList and CheckBoxList's Layout Properties

Property Name	Description
`CellPadding`	Specifies the padding between the edge of each table cell and its inner content for the rendered `<table>`.
`CellSpacing`	Specifies the spacing between each cell in the `<table>`.
`RepeatColumns`	Specifies how many columns of radio buttons or check boxes should be used. A value of 0 (the default) indicates that one column should be used.

TABLE 17.1 Continued

Property Name	Description
`RepeatDirection`	Indicates how the items are laid out. Can be either `Horizontal` or `Vertical` (the default).
`RepeatLayout`	Dictates the HTML markup used when rendering the RadioButtonList or CheckBoxList control. Can be one of two values: `Table` (the default) or `Flow`. When set to `Table`, an HTML `<table>` is used to render the assorted check boxes or radio buttons; with `Flow`, `<span>` elements are used instead.

The `RepeatLayout` property determines the HTML elements used when rendering the controls' radio buttons or check boxes. The default value is `Table`, indicating that an HTML `<table>` should be used, as was shown in Listing 17.1. If you set this property to `Flow`, `<span>` elements are used in place of the `<table>`. Listing 17.2 shows the HTML produced by a CheckBoxList whose `RepeatLayout` property is set to `Flow`.

LISTING 17.2 The HTML Produced by a `Flow` CheckBoxList

```
<span id="CheckBoxList1">
  <input id="CheckBoxList1_0" type="checkbox" name="CheckBoxList1$0" />
  <label for="CheckBoxList1_0">Visual Studio Hacks</label>
  <br />

  <input id="CheckBoxList1_1" type="checkbox" name="CheckBoxList1$1" />
  <label for="CheckBoxList1_1">Create Your Own Website</label>
  <br />

  <input id="CheckBoxList1_2" type="checkbox" name="CheckBoxList1$2" />
  <label for="CheckBoxList1_2">The Number</label>
  <br />

  <input id="CheckBoxList1_3" type="checkbox" name="CheckBoxList1$3" />
  <label for="CheckBoxList1_3">The Catcher in the Rye</label>
  <br />

  <input id="CheckBoxList1_4" type="checkbox" name="CheckBoxList1$4" />
  <label for="CheckBoxList1_4">Fight Club</label>
</span>
```

In place of the `<table>` element, a `<span>` element is used. Furthermore, after each check box there's a `<br />` element, which adds a breaking line in the user's browser. The HTML in Listing 17.2 will render in a browser almost exactly like the `<table>` markup in Listing 17.1.

The `CellPadding` and `CellSpacing` properties specify how much space to pad the cells and their contents when using the `Table` layout. If you set the `RepeatLayout` property to `Flow`, these property values are ignored.

Laying Out Items Horizontally

By default the CheckBoxList and RadioButtonList controls display their items vertically, using one column. For lengthy CheckBoxLists or RadioButtonLists, you may want to have the items laid out using multiple columns. To accomplish this, use the `RepeatColumns`, which specifies how many columns to display and can be assigned any non-negative integer value. The `RepeatDirection` property indicates the direction the items are laid out, and can be either `Horizontal` or `Vertical` (the default).

Figure 17.12 shows a CheckBoxList and RadioButtonList with three columns. The figure also illustrates the effects of the `RepeatDirection` property: The CheckBoxList has its `RepeatDirection` property set to `Vertical`, whereas the RadioButtonList's is set to `Horizontal`. The results here are ordered by `BookID`, so *Visual Studio Hacks* is the first book, then *Create Your Own Website*, followed by *The Number,* and so on. As you can see, with the CheckBoxList, the first two books are in the first column, the second two in the second column, and so on. In essence, the output is grouped by row. With the RadioButtonList's `Horizontal` `RepeatDirection` value, the output is grouped by column, with the first three books in the first column and last two books in the second column.

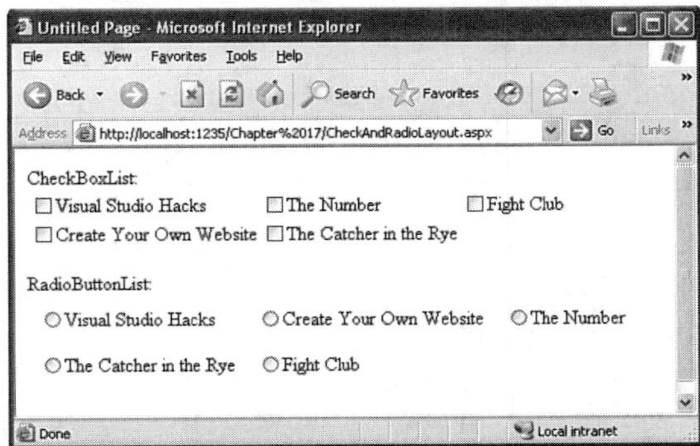

FIGURE 17.12
A RadioButtonList and CheckBoxList, with `RepeatColumns` set to 3.

Also notice that there is more padding within each cell in the RadioButtonList than in the CheckBoxList. The reason is that I've set the `CellPadding` property of the RadioButtonList to `8`.

Summary

In this hour we examined the ASP.NET list Web controls: the DropDownList, CheckBoxList, and RadioButtonList. These three controls are composed of a series of list items that can be specified statically, programmatically, or through data binding. The manner by which these three controls differ is in how they render their list items. A DropDownList control renders as a drop-down list, with each item an option in the list. A CheckBoxList renders each of its items as a check box, and the RadioButtonList renders its items as radio buttons.

A common use of the list controls is to list a particular column from a database table, enabling a visitor to easily filter displayed results. We saw an example of this in the "Filtering Results Using the DropDownList" section. In our example, a DropDownList contained the various genres, while a GridView displayed only those books of the selected genre.

Next hour will be our last hour that focuses on working with data and databases in an ASP.NET page. We'll touch on a variety of common data-related tasks that will be of particular use in the final three hours, when we build a photo album web application from the ground up.

Q&A

Q. ***Earlier in this chapter we worked on an example of filtering a GridView's data using a DropDownList. Would it have been possible to use a RadioButtonList in place of the DropDownList?***

A. Sure, a RadioButtonList would have worked equally as well; in fact, exercise 1 asks you to build an ASP.NET page that filters the data displayed using a RadioButtonList.

When using a RadioButtonList to filter results, however, there is one point to keep in mind: by default, a RadioButtonList doesn't have a selected item. Therefore, when the page first loads the parameter used to filter, the SqlDataSource will be missing and an exception will be raised. To circumvent this problem, you'll need to add a default value to the parameter when constructing your `WHERE` clause parameter in the SqlDataSource control's wizard. Simply use as a default value one of the values of the `Genre` column, like Business, or a blank string if you don't want any results returned initially.

Workshop

Quiz

1. Name some of the ways in which the three list Web controls examined in this hour are similar to one another.
2. Name some ways in which the list Web controls differ from one another.
3. What is the name of the event that is raised when a list Web control's selected state is changed across postbacks?
4. What properties must you set in order to have the RadioButtonList or CheckBoxList controls render their items laid out horizontally using multiple columns?
5. The DropDownList, RadioButtonList, and CheckBoxList controls all have an `AutoPostBack` property. What happens when this property is set to `True`?

Answers

1. All are composed of list items and contain a similar set of base properties—`Items`, `SelectedItem`, `SelectedValue`, and so on. They all have a `SelectedIndexChanged` event that fires on postback if the selected state of the control has changed. Additionally, they all can have their list items specified in one of three ways: statically, through the ListItem Collection Editor dialog box; programmatically; and through a data source control.
2. Each list Web control renders its list items differently. The DropDownList will always have one selected item, whereas the RadioButtonList can have zero or one, and the CheckBoxList can have zero to many selected items.
3. `SelectedIndexChanged`.
4. The `RepeatColumns` property specifies how many columns the RadioButtonList or CheckBoxList's items will use; the `RepeatDirection` property indicates whether the items are laid out vertically or horizontally.
5. When `AutoPostBack` is set to `True`, any client-side change in the control's selection state causes a postback. For example, with a DropDownList whose `AutoPostBack` property is set to `True`, when the user chooses a new option from the list, the page automatically posts back and the DropDownList's `SelectedIndexChanged` event is fired.

Exercises

1. Using the same techniques discussed in the "Filtering Results Using the DropDownList" section, create an ASP.NET page that uses a GridView to display the books from the `Books` table and a RadioButtonList of all of the authors to allow the user to filter the books displayed. (Be sure to set the RadioButtonList's `AutoPostBack` property to `True`.)

   Like in our earlier example, make sure that the RadioButtonList displays only *unique* author names. Also, because on the initial page load, the RadioButtonList will not have any item selected, you'll need to set a default value for the parameter you create in the GridView's SqlDataSource wizard. Set the default parameter value to a blank string. With this setting, when the page first loads, before a user selects an author from the list of radio buttons, the GridView should not be shown because there should be no authors with a blank string. Upon selecting a new author, the page will post back and the books that the selected author has written will be displayed.

   When testing this, be sure to edit the `Books` table so that there are at least two books written by the same author. Also, take a moment to set the GridView's `EmptyDataText` property to an applicable message. Recall that the value of this property is displayed when binding a GridView to a data source control that returns no records, as is the case with this exercise when the user first visits the page, before selecting an author.

HOUR 18

Exploring Data Binding and Other Data-Related Topics

In this hour, we will cover

- The different fields available for the GridView and DetailsView controls
- Displaying hyperlinks, check boxes, and images in the GridView and DetailsView controls
- Using wildcards in the SQL WHERE clause
- Understanding data binding and the data-binding syntax

Over the past five hours we've covered a number of data-related topics. In Hour 13, "An Introduction to Databases," we talked about the structure and purpose of databases, and looked at how to create a SQL Server 2005 Express Edition database using Visual Web Developer. Next, in Hour 14, "Accessing Data with the Data Source Web Controls," we saw how to get data from the database to an ASP.NET web page through ASP.NET's data source controls. In particular, we focused on the SqlDataSource control, which is designed for accessing data from a database.

In the preceding three hours we examined a variety of ASP.NET controls designed to display and to allow the end user to interact with the data retrieved from a data source control. In the preceding hour we looked at the DropDownList, RadioButtonList, and CheckBoxList controls; the two hours preceding that examined the GridView and DetailsView controls.

At this point we've covered the most important and commonly used data-related concepts of ASP.NET. Before we move on to our next topic, however, I want to take one more hour to touch on a number of data-related topics that didn't fit naturally into any of the previous hours.

Looking at the GridView's and DetailsView's Fields

Hours 15, "Displaying Data with the Data Web Controls," and 16, "Deleting, Inserting, and Editing Data," concentrated on displaying and modifying database data using the GridView and DetailsView controls. To work with data on an ASP.NET page, we first added a SqlDataSource control and configured it to retrieve the appropriate data. Next, we added the needed data Web control and specified that it should use the data source control just added.

Both the GridView and DetailsView are composed of **fields**. The fields in a GridView or DetailsView can serve one of two purposes:

- They can be used to display data from the control's associated data source control in some fashion.
- They can provide an interface for the end user to exact some functionality from the control.

When a GridView or DetailsView control is initially bound to a data source control through its smart tag, for each column in the data source control a BoundField is automatically added to the GridView or DetailsView. The BoundField is one type of field that falls into the first category of fields; it simply displays the value of the associated column as plain text when the data Web control is not being edited or inserted. When data is being edited or inserted, the BoundField renders as a TextBox Web control whose `Text` property is set to the value of the column.

The CommandField, which we've seen in the past few hours, is a field designed for providing an interface for the end user into the GridView's or DetailsView's functionality. Enabling inserting, editing, selecting, or deleting adds a CommandField to the data Web control. The CommandField can show any combination of insert, edit, select, and delete buttons; you can indicate which of these you want present through the `ShowInsertButton`, `ShowEditButton`, `ShowSelectButton`, and `ShowDeleteButton` properties. When you use the GridView or DetailsView's smart tag to turn on support for inserting, editing, selecting, or deleting, a CommandField is automatically added with the appropriate properties' values set accordingly.

In total the GridView and DetailsView have seven fields that we can use. We can view and edit the fields that make up these controls by going to the controls' smart tags and clicking the Edit Columns link. As we have seen in past hours, this brings up the Fields dialog box (see Figure 18.1). The bottom-left corner of the Fields dialog box lists the current fields of the control; the upper-left corner lists the field types that can be added. Table 18.1 lists the seven field types along with a brief description of each.

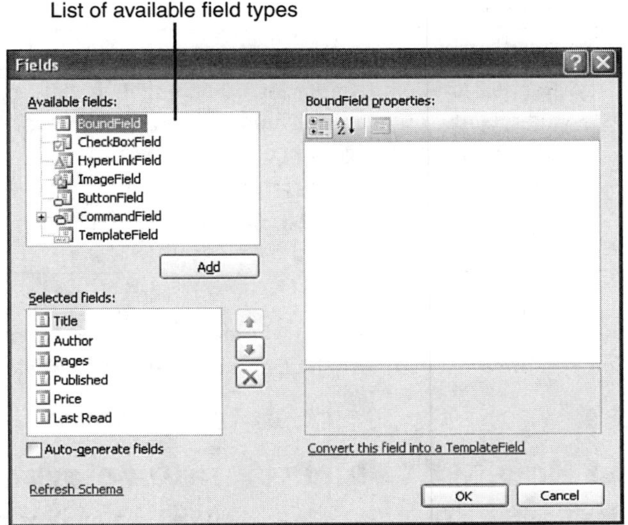

FIGURE 18.1 The Fields dialog box lists the fields in the data Web control, along with the field types that can be added.

TABLE 18.1 The GridView and DetailsView Can Be Composed of a Number of Fields of Differing Types

Field	Description
BoundField	Displays a corresponding data source control column's value as text or in a text box, when being edited or when inserting a new value. When binding a GridView or DetailsView control to a data source control through the smart tag, a BoundField is automatically created for each column in the associated data source control.
CheckBoxField	Renders a check box, whose checked state depends on the value in a specified data source control column. Useful for displaying the value of a `bit` database column. (Recall that a `bit` database column is a Yes/No-type column, one that can have a value of either 0 or 1.)
HyperLinkField	Creates a HyperLink control, whose `Text` and `NavigateUrl` property values can be either hard-coded or based on values from columns in the data source control.
ImageField	Renders an Image Web control whose `ImageUrl` property is based on some database column value.
ButtonField	Renders a Button Web control. Useful if you have some action you want the user to be able to initiate on a record-by-record basis other than editing, deleting, or selecting. (Those functions are already provided by the CommandField.)

TABLE 18.1 Continued

Field	Description
CommandField	Renders the interface for inserting, updating, deleting, or selecting records. Automatically added when enabling any of those functionalities through the control's smart tag.
TemplateField	Allows for a mix of static HTML markup, Web controls, and data binding syntax. In Hour 16, we used TemplateFields to customize the editing interface for the GridView.

We've already looked at using the BoundField, CommandField, and TemplateField. Over the next few sections we'll examine the CheckBoxField, HyperLinkField, and ImageField.

Looking at How `Bit` Columns Are Displayed

As we discussed in Hour 13, a database table is composed of a number of columns, each of which has a data type. The data type of a column indicates what types of values can be stored in the column. The `Title` column in the `Books` table, for example, has an `nvarchar(150)` data type, meaning that it can store strings with up to 150 characters; the `LastReadOn` column has a `datetime` data type, meaning it can store date and time values. One database column data type that we've yet to use in the `Books` table is the `bit` data type. A column that has a data type of `bit` can store one of two values: 0 or 1. Typically, a `bit` column is used to store a Yes/No or True/False type value.

Let's take a minute to add a `bit` column to our `Books` table. Go to the Database Explorer in Visual Web Developer, drill down to the `Books` table, right-click on the `Books` table name, and choose the Open Table Definition option. This will bring up the list of columns that make up the table. Next, add a new column named `Recommended` and choose a Data Type value of `bit`. Because the table contains existing data, this column either must allow Nulls or we must provide a default value. Let's use the latter approach.

First, uncheck the Allow Nulls check box. Next, we need to specify a default value for this column. In the Column Properties pane, search for the property titled Default Value or Binding in the General section. Then put in the default value there. Let's use a default of 0. Take a minute to ensure that your screen looks similar to Figure 18.2 and then save the table changes.

Now that we've added this new column, take a minute to create an ASP.NET page that displays all rows and all columns in an editable GridView. As soon as you bind the GridView to the SqlDataSource control through the GridView's smart tag, the

Recommended field in the GridView is shown as a series of check boxes. That is, the smart tag is smart enough to note that a particular column being bound to the GridView is a bit column. For such columns, the smart tag automatically uses a CheckBoxField instead of the standard BoundField (see Figure 18.3).

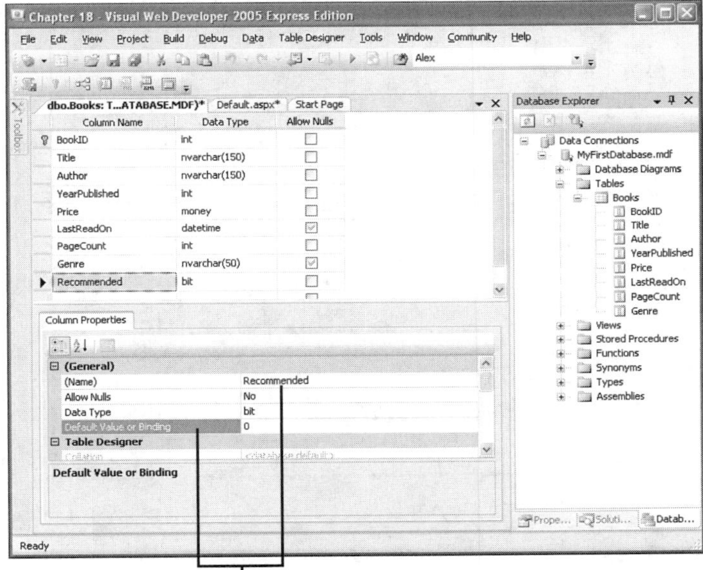

FIGURE 18.2 The Recommended column has been added; it's a bit column with a default value of 0.

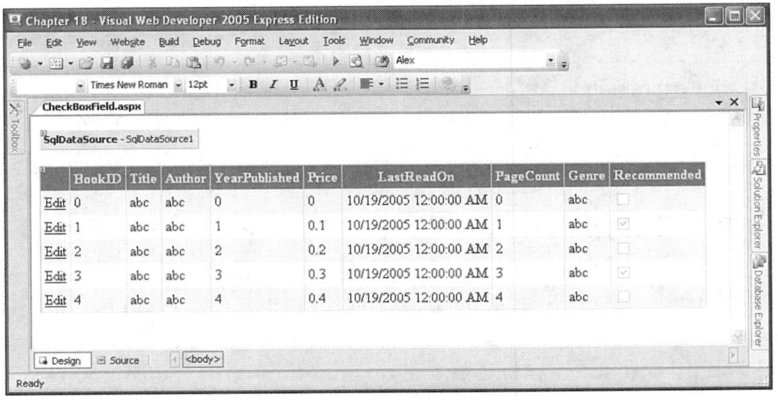

FIGURE 18.3 The Recommended field is displayed as a series of check boxes.

To see that the Recommended field is indeed a CheckBoxField, go to the GridView's smart tag and click on the Edit Columns link, bringing up the Fields dialog box. As

Figure 18.4 shows, from the bottom-left corner listing of the fields in the GridView, the `Recommended` field is a CheckBoxField. Selecting the `Recommended` field loads its properties on the right. As with the BoundField, you can customize the CheckBoxField's appearance through the properties in the Styles section.

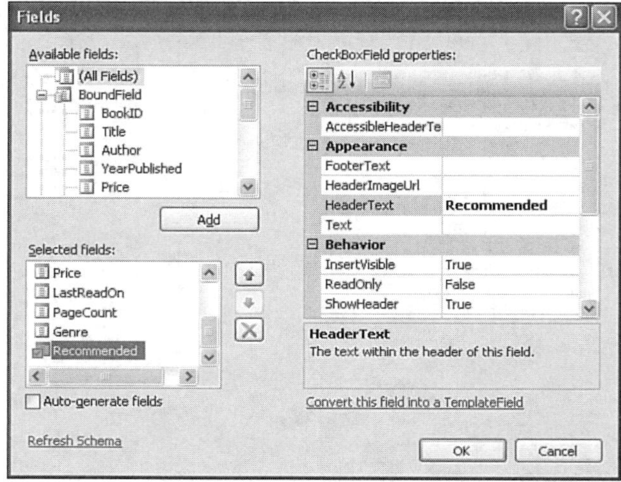

FIGURE 18.4 The GridView automatically uses a CheckBoxField for the `Recommended` field.

Take a moment to test this ASP.NET page through a browser. When you visit the page, each row in the `Recommended` field is displayed as a disabled check box. When a particular row is edited, the editable row's check box is enabled, allowing the end user to change the check box's value. This functionality is made possible thanks to the CheckBoxField.

By the Way

> Although our examination of CheckBoxFields has centered around the GridView, the functionality and behavior are the same with the DetailsView control.

Displaying Hyperlinks with the HyperLinkField

With the addition of a `Recommended` field to the `Books` table, users visiting your site can see both what books are in your bookshelf and what books you heartily recommend. A visitor who notes that the books you read and like are similar to the books he reads and likes might be interesting in buying some of the books you recommend that he has yet to read. To help streamline this process, you could add a link titled `"Buy"` in each book row that, when clicked, would whisk the user to some online bookstore, displaying the details of that particular book.

Adding such functionality through the GridView (or DetailsView) is possible and quite simple thanks to the HyperLinkField. As its name implies, the HyperLinkField displays a field of HyperLink Web controls, which render as the standard hyperlinks that, when clicked, take the visitor to some specified URL. With the HyperLinkField field, we can set the `Text` and `NavigateUrl` properties of the HyperLink control based on database values. That is, the text and URL of the rendered link for each row in the GridView can be based on the values of the columns of the database record that was bound to that row.

If this isn't yet clear, don't worry; an example should help. Because we want to add a `"Buy"` link to each row in a GridView that, when clicked, sends the visitor to an online bookstore, our first order of business is to determine what online bookstore to use and what the URL for viewing the details for a particular book on that site looks like. For this exercise, let's use Amazon.com as the online bookstore. With Amazon.com, the URL http://www.amazon.com/exec/obidos/ASIN/*ISBN*/ displays the details for the book with the specified *ISBN* value.

By the Way

The **ISBN** of a book is a 10- or 13-digit long number that uniquely identifies the book. Typically, the ISBN can be found on the back cover of a book.

To provide such a link, we need to store the ISBN for each of the books in the `Books` table; therefore, we need to add an `ISBN` column to the table. Because a book's ISBN can be up to 13 characters, create the `ISBN` column using the `nvarchar(13)` data type. We don't want to allow Nulls, but since there's already data in the `Books` table, we'll initially need to allow Nulls for this new column until we have a chance to provide values for the `ISBN` column for the existing rows. Take a moment to add this new column.

After adding the `ISBN` column, edit the table's data (right-click on the `Books` table in the Database Explorer and choose Show Table Data). Enter an ISBN for each of the books, omitting any hyphens (see Figure 18.5). The ISBN for the five books in the `Books` table are as follows:

- *Visual Studio Hacks*—0596008473
- *Create Your Own Website*—0672328267
- *The Number*—0375508805
- *The Catcher In The Rye*—0316769487
- *Fight Club*—0805076476

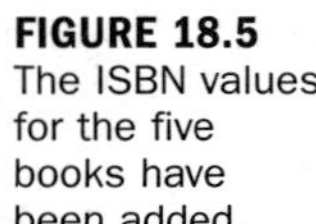

FIGURE 18.5
The ISBN values for the five books have been added.

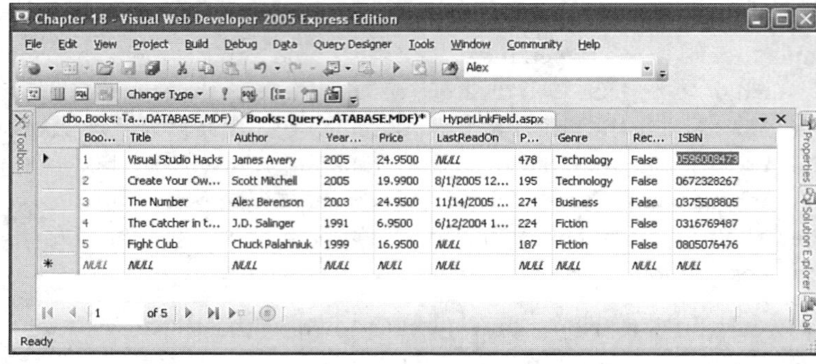

After you've supplied the ISBN values for all of the records in the `Books` table, return to editing the table's definition and uncheck the Allow Nulls check box for the `ISBN` column.

Create an ASP.NET page with a SqlDataSource that retrieves all of the columns and rows from the `Books` table. Next, add a GridView control and bind it to the SqlDataSource. At this point the GridView will be displaying the value of the ISBN column using a BoundField, showing the text of the ISBN. We want to replace this BoundField with a HyperLinkField. To accomplish this, go to the Fields dialog box by bringing up the GridView's smart tag and clicking on the Edit Columns link.

The lower-left corner of the Fields dialog box lists the fields currently being used by the GridView, one of which is an `ISBN` BoundField. Remove this field from the GridView by selecting it and clicking the Delete icon to the immediate right of this list, as shown in Figure 18.6.

FIGURE 18.6
Select the `ISBN` BoundField and delete it.

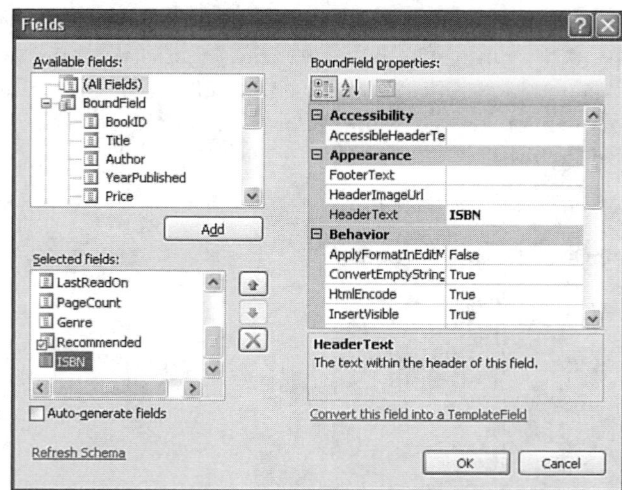

You can also delete any other BoundFields that you aren't interested in displaying. For this ASP.NET page, let's not bother showing the BookID, YearPublished, or LastReadOn BoundFields.

> **Watch Out!**
>
> If you are working with an editable GridView or editable or insertable DetailsView, you cannot blindly remove BoundFields from the data Web control because the SqlDataSource control is configured to save these values as well.
>
> If you do not want certain fields displayed when editing or inserting data, be sure to configure the data source control not to return those column values.

We're now ready to add the "Buy" HyperLinkField. From the Available Fields list in the upper-left corner, scroll down and select the HyperLinkField option and then click the Add button. This will add a HyperLinkField to bottom of the list of fields in the lower-left corner. Take a moment to move this HyperLinkField to the top of the list so that it's displayed in the far left of the GridView. We now need to set the HyperLinkField's properties, indicating what the rendered link's text and URL values should be.

The HyperLinkField's text and URL values can be static or dynamic. A dynamic value differs for each row in the GridView based on the data bound to that particular row; a static value is the same among all GridView rows. For our task we want a static text value—"Buy"—and a dynamic URL value, varying on each book's ISBN.

If you want to set the text or URL values to static values, use the Text or NavigateUrl properties. The Text property can be found in the Appearance section of the properties list; NavigateUrl is located in the Behavior section. Because we want the link's text to be "Buy" for all rows, set the Text property of the HyperLinkColumn to Buy.

To specify a dynamic value for the text or URL values, we need to use two properties. For the text, there are the DataTextField and DataTextFormatString properties; for the URL, there are the DataNavigateUrlFields and DataNavigateUrlFormatString properties. These four properties are found in the Data section of the HyperLinkField's properties. The properties work in tandem in the following manner: the DataTextField or DataNavigateUrlFields properties specify what database column values are used in the text or URL of the rendered link; the DataTextFormatString or DataNavigateUrlFormatString properties can be used to surround the database value with static text. With the DataTextFormatString and DataNavigateUrlFormatString properties, the string {0} is used to inject the dynamic value.

For our example, we want the URL to be dynamic based on the book's ISBN; therefore, set the DataNavigateUrlFields property to ISBN. Because we want the URL to be http://www.amazon.com/exec/obidos/ASIN/*ISBN*/, use the value `http://www.amazon.com/exec/obidos/ASIN/{0}/` as the value for the `DataNavigateUrlFormatString` property. This value instructs the HyperLinkColumn to inject the current row's `ISBN` value at the `{0}` position, resulting in a properly formatted hyperlink.

After you set these properties and click the OK button in the Fields dialog box, your screen should look similar to Figure 18.7. Note that the GridView now has a `"Buy"` HyperLinkField at its far left and that the `BookID`, `YearPublished`, and `LastReadOn` BoundFields have been removed.

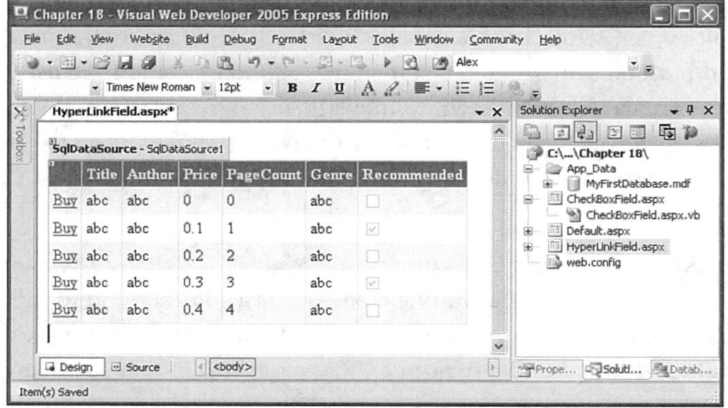

FIGURE 18.7
A HyperLinkField has been added to the GridView.

View the ASP.NET page in a browser. Each row in the rendered GridView will contain a `"Buy"` link that, when clicked, will whisk you to Amazon.com. For example, clicking the `"Buy"` link for *Create Your Own Website* will take you to http://www.amazon.com/exec/obidos/ASIN/0672328267/. Notice how the `ISBN` value for this book—0672328267—is injected into the URL of the link precisely where the `{0}` string was placed in the HyperLinkField's `DataNavigateUrlFormatString` property.

Did you Know?

You can have the URL value of the HyperLinkField include multiple values from database columns. Simply specify each database column name you need in the `DataNavigateUrlFields`, separated by commas. Then, in the `DataNavigateUrlFormatString`, use `{0}` to inject the value of the first column in the column list, `{1}` to inject the second column's value, `{2}` to inject the third's, and so on.

Displaying Images with the ImageField

In the last three hours of this book, we will be building, from the ground up, a photo album web application that allows a visitor to upload her pictures to the website. After these pictures have been uploaded, other visitors can come by and check them out and leave comments on a picture-by-picture basis. For this application, when a user uploads an image to the website, the image will be saved on the web server's file system in a particular directory. There will also be a database table called `Pictures` that has a record for each photo in the system. This table will have columns that capture the title of the photograph, a description, the user who uploaded the photo, and the path to the photo, among others. Because the uploaded pictures are stored on the web server's file system and only a path to the file is stored in the database, if we use a BoundField in a GridView to display the contents of the `Pictures` table, the path to the photo will just appear as text.

To make this concept more clear, imagine that a user uploads a picture of her dog, and the system stores the picture on the web server's file system as `Pictures/MyDog.jpg`. Adding this picture will add a new record to the database table that has a `Title` column value of, say, "My Dog," a `Description` value of "This is a picture of my dog; he's so cute!" and a `PhotoPath` value of `Pictures/MyDog.jpg`. If we display a GridView with a BoundField for each of the `Picture` columns, we'll see in the `PhotoPath` field the text `Pictures/MyDog.jpg`. What we want to see, though, is the image stored in the path `Pictures/MyDog.jpg`. The BoundField, whose sole purpose is to display the corresponding database column's value as text, is not suited for displaying an image based on a text path.

By the Way

> The `Pictures` table in the actual photo album application that we'll be building does not include a `PhotoPath` column. We'll use a slightly different approach, but the core concepts are the same.

The ImageField is designed to display an image whose URL is based on a database value. The ImageField injects an Image Web control, which renders as an HTML `<img>` element. Like the HyperLinkField, the ImageField has a pair of properties that can be used to specify a database column and a format string: `DataImageUrlField` and `DataImageUrlFieldString`. The URL of the image can either be a local image—one that's stored on the web server—or on a remote web server. Amazon.com has thumbnails of all of the books it sells at the URL http://images.amazon.com/images/P/*ISBN*.01.THUMBZZZ.jpg, where *ISBN* is the ISBN of the book. Therefore, we can use an ImageField whose `DataImageUrlField` property is set to `ISBN` and whose `DataImageUrlFieldString` property is set to `http://images.amazon.com/images/P/{0}.01.THUMBZZZ.jpg`.

As we did with the CheckBoxField example in the previous section, add an ImageField using the following steps:

1. Create a new ASP.NET page, adding a SqlDataSource that returns all of the records and columns from the `Books` table.
2. Drag a GridView onto the page and bind it to the SqlDataSource.
3. From the GridView's smart tag, click the Edit Columns link to open the Fields dialog box.
4. Remove the `BookID`, `YearPublished`, `LastReadOn`, and `ISBN` BoundFields.
5. Add a new ImageField to the GridView and move it to the top of the field list.
6. Click on the ImageField to load its properties. Set the `DataImageUrlField` property to `ISBN` and the `DataImageUrlFieldString` property to `http://images.amazon.com/images/P/{0}.01.THUMBZZZ.jpg`.

After step 6, your Fields dialog box should look similar to the one in Figure 18.8. After verifying this, click the OK button and then view the ASP.NET page through a browser. You should see the thumbnail images for each of the book's covers, as shown in Figure 18.9.

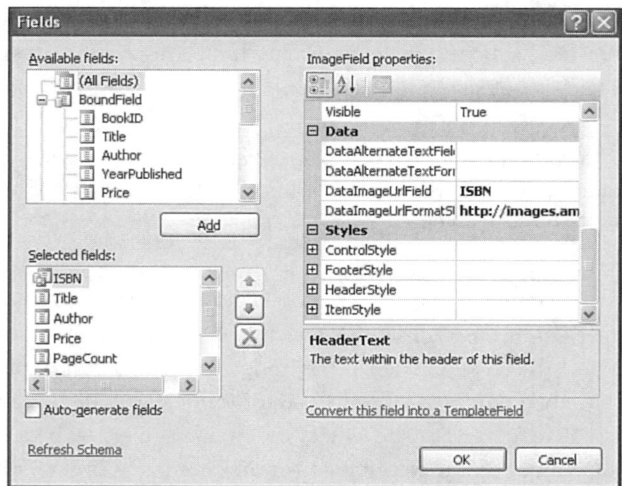

FIGURE 18.8
Set the properties of the ImageField through the Fields dialog box.

Because the images are being retrieved directly from Amazon.com's web servers, you will need to be connected to the Internet to be able to see the images. If you are developing your ASP.NET pages locally and are not online, you will see broken images along the left of the rendered GridView.

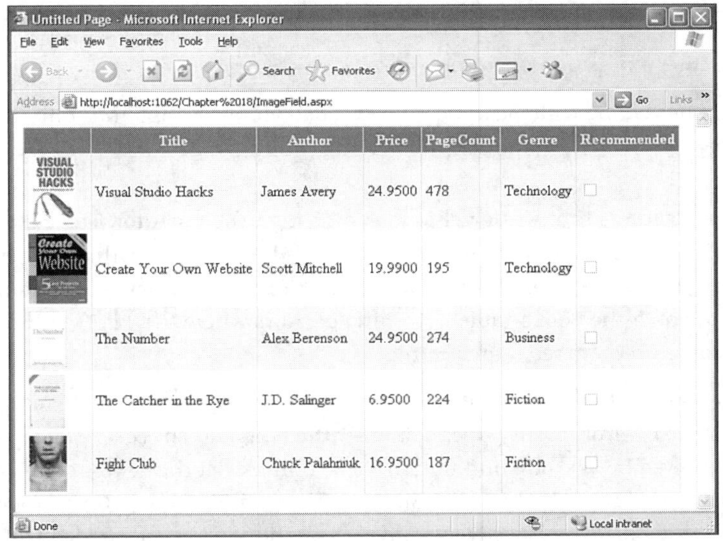

	Title	Author	Price	PageCount	Genre	Recommended
	Visual Studio Hacks	James Avery	24.9500	478	Technology	☐
	Create Your Own Website	Scott Mitchell	19.9900	195	Technology	☐
	The Number	Alex Berenson	24.9500	274	Business	☐
	The Catcher in the Rye	J.D. Salinger	6.9500	224	Fiction	☐
	Fight Club	Chuck Palahniuk	16.9500	187	Fiction	☐

FIGURE 18.9
A thumbnail image of the cover is shown for each book.

By the Way

When you are creating an editable GridView or editable or insertable DetailsView, the ImageField behaves like a BoundField when it's being edited or inserted. That is, the image will be replaced by a TextBox Web control with the value of the `DataImageUrlField` property. To make the image uneditable or not specifiable when inserting, set the ImageField's `ReadOnly` property to `True` and `InsertVisible` property to `False`.

As discussed in Hour 16, if you do make a field read-only or not visible on inserts, be sure to remove the column from the SqlDataSource control's `UpdateCommand` and `InsertCommands`.

Using Wildcards in a WHERE Filter Expression

In previous hours we saw how to use the SqlDataSource's wizard to add `WHERE` filter expressions to limit the results returned by the database. In Hour 17, "Working with Data-Bound DropDownLists, RadioButtons, and CheckBoxes," we saw how to use a DropDownList's selected value as the value for the filter expression, thereby allowing the user to display only those books that belonged to a particular genre.

When we're creating a filter expression through the SqlDataSource control's wizard, recall that we must specify three things:

- The database column the filter expression applies to
- The filter expression operator— =, <>, <, <=, >, and so on
- The filter value, which can be a hard-coded value or based on some external value, such as the value of a Web control on the page

One of the operators that we've yet to look at is the `LIKE` operator. The `LIKE` operator uses wildcards around the parameter value and works only with string or date/time database columns. We can use the `LIKE` operator to build an interface for the user to search the `Books` table, returning all rows where the `Title` column value contains some user-entered search term.

Let's create a page to demonstrate this filter expression operator. Before adding a SqlDataSource control to this page, first enter the text `Search for books by title:`, followed by TextBox and Button Web controls. Set the TextBox Web control's `ID` property to `titleSearch` and the Button Web control's `ID` and `Text` properties to `btnSearch` and `Search`, respectively. The user interface we've just added will allow the user visiting our page to enter a search term into the text box. After you do so and click the Search button, the page will post back and the GridView will display those books with matching titles.

Now that we have the user interface implemented, the next step is to add the SqlDataSource and GridView controls. Configure the SqlDataSource control to return all columns from the `Books` table. Add a `WHERE` clause filter expression on the `Title` column using the `LIKE` operator based on the `titleSearch` control (see Figure 18.10).

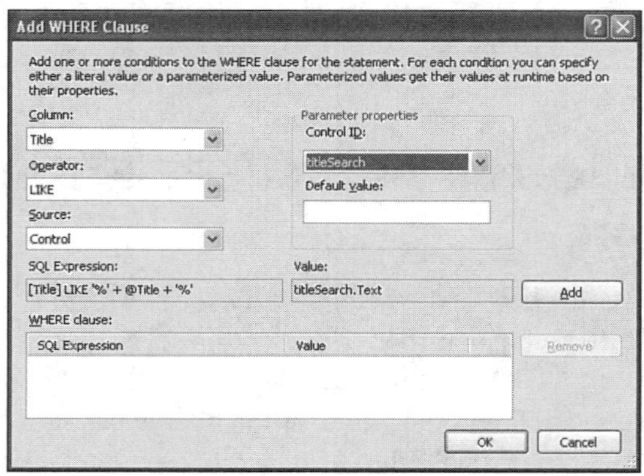

FIGURE 18.10
Add a `LIKE` filter expression on the `Title` column.

Watch Out!

> The `LIKE` operator can be applied only to string (`nvarchar`, `nchar`, `char`, or `varchar`) or date/time columns.

After you add this filter expression and return to the wizard's Configure the Select Statement screen, the wizard's proposed `SELECT` statement should look like `SELECT * FROM [Books] WHERE ([Title] LIKE '%' + @Title + '%')`. Note that the `WHERE` clause uses the `LIKE` operator and the wildcard characters (%) to return all records whose `Title` column value contains the value of the `@Title` parameter. This `@Title` parameter value will be set to the value in the `titleSearch` TextBox control.

Complete this page by adding the GridView control and binding it to the SqlDataSource. When the page is first visited through a browser, no records will be shown because the user hasn't entered a value into the text box. Similarly, if the user enters a search term that does not appear in any of the books' titles, no books will be returned by the SqlDataSource. These two scenarios may confuse the end user because he may be wondering why no books are being shown. To help alleviate any confusion, enter a helpful message into the GridView's `EmptyDataText` property. As we've discussed before, this value of the `EmptyDataText` property is displayed when no records are returned by the GridView's associated data source control. Also feel free to tailor the GridView's columns as you see fit; I used the column configuration from our HyperLinkField discussion earlier in this hour.

After setting the `EmptyDataText` property, take a moment to test this page in a browser. Figure 18.11 shows the page the user searches on the term `"the"`. This produces two results: *The Number* and *The Catcher in the Rye*. When a user enters a search term that is not in any title, such as `"Rolla"`, no results will be returned by the SqlDataSource control, and the GridView will display the value of its `EmptyDataText` property (see Figure 18.12).

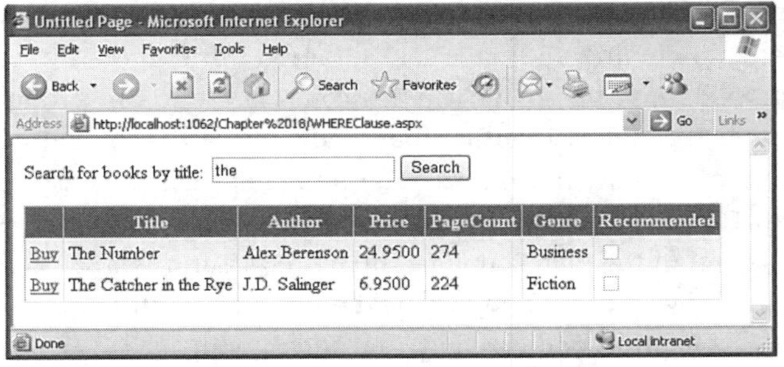

FIGURE 18.11
Two books match when searching on `"the"`.

FIGURE 18.12
The GridView's `EmptyDataText` property value is displayed when no matching book titles are found.

An Examination of Data Binding

Data binding is the process of tying a property of a Web control to the value of a database column; this process happens automatically all the time with the data Web controls. When we're using BoundFields, CheckBoxFields, or ImageFields, the GridView or DetailsView control handles all of the data binding for us. For example, the BoundField uses a Label Web control and automatically binds the Label's `Text` property to the corresponding database column; with a CheckBoxField, a CheckBox Web control is used, and its `Checked` property is data-bound to the corresponding database column.

In Hour 16 we saw how, when creating an editable GridView or DetailsView, the BoundFields defaulted to a TextBox Web control with the TextBox's `Text` property set to the value of the field's corresponding database column. However, sometimes we may want to customize the editing interface. This may include adding validation controls, changing the properties of the TextBox Web control, or replacing the TextBox control with other Web controls altogether.

To accomplish this, we need to use a TemplateField, which we can do in one of two ways: by adding a new TemplateField to the GridView or DetailsView, just like we added a HyperLinkField and an ImageField earlier in this hour; or by converting an existing BoundField into a TemplateField. I encourage you to convert an existing BoundField into a TemplateField rather than adding a new TemplateField because the conversion process automatically does a number of steps for you. Specifically, it creates the ItemTemplate and EditItemTemplates for the TemplateField, with a data-bound Label control in the ItemTemplate and a data-bound TextBox control in the EditItemTemplate. If you add a TemplateField manually, you'll need to add the Label and TextBox controls and configure the data binding.

The Difference Between One-Way and Two-Way Data Binding

ASP.NET supports two flavors of data binding: one-way and two-way. One-way data binding simply takes a specified database column's value and binds it to a specified Web control property. Two-way data binding can not only assign a database column's value to a Web control property, but can also do the inverse: It can take the value of a property and assign it to the value of a data source control parameter.

One-way data binding is used when working with a nonmodifiable data Web control. When we're using a data Web control that supports editing, inserting, or deleting, two-way data binding is used instead.

When working with BoundFields, CheckBoxFields, HyperLinkFields, or ImageFields, you do not need to concern yourself with the differences between one-way and two-way data binding; all the intricacies are automatically handled by the various fields. However, when adding data-bound Web controls to a TemplateField, you need to specify whether the data binding should be one-way or two-way. If the Web control is used to just display the information, use one-way data binding; if the Web control is also used to collect user input and save those values back to the database, use two-way data binding.

Specifying the Data Bindings for a Web Control

If you add a TemplateField manually or want to replace a converted TemplateField's Label or TextBox Web control with a different control, you'll need to specify the data bindings for the new controls you add to the TemplateField (including whether the data bindings are one-way or two-way). The data binding simply ties a particular property of the Web control to the field's corresponding database column.

To practice working with data bindings and custom TemplateColumns, let's create an editable GridView with a customized editing interface. Specifically, we'll create a GridView that lists the `BookID`, `Title`, and `Genre` columns from the database. By default, the `BookID` field will be read-only, and the `Title` and `Genre` fields will have a TextBox Web control for their editing interface. However, when editing a GridView row, we might want to instead have the `Genre` field displayed as a DropDownList with all of the existing genres. To accomplish this, we'll need to convert the `Genre` BoundField into a TemplateField and replace the TextBox Web control in the EditItemTemplate with SqlDataSource and DropDownList controls. In doing so, we'll need to use data binding to tie the DropDownList control's `SelectedValue` property to the value of the edited book's `Genre` column.

Let's not get too far ahead of ourselves here. Before we worry about creating a customized, data-bound editing interface for the `Genre` field, let's first just create an editable GridView that uses the default editing interface. Recall from Hour 16 that this involves first adding a SqlDataSource control configured to support updating. Because we want to allow the user to edit only the `Title` and `Genre` fields, in the SqlDataSource's wizard, be sure to bring back only the `BookID`, `Title`, and `Genre` columns, as shown in Figure 18.13. Also, be sure to click the Advanced button and check the Generate INSERT, UPDATE, and DELETE Statements check box.

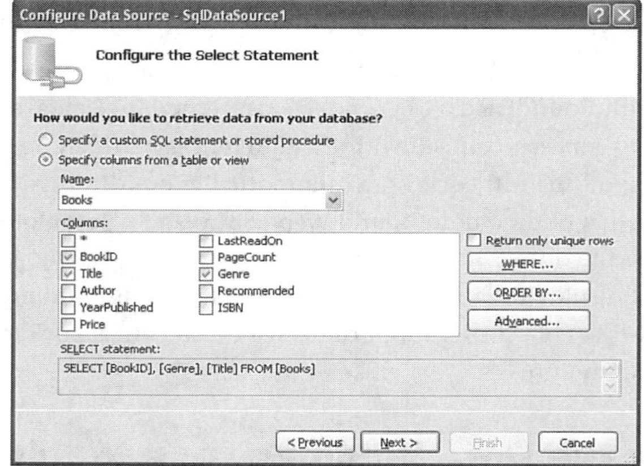

FIGURE 18.13 From the Configure the Select Statement screen, check the `BookID`, `Title`, and `Genre` columns.

Next, add a GridView to the page and bind it to the SqlDataSource control. Also, check the Enable Editing check box in the GridView's smart tag. Take a moment to view the page through a browser, editing the value for a particular book. Note that when you click the Edit button, the editing interface shows a text box for both the `Title` and `Genre` fields (see Figure 18.14).

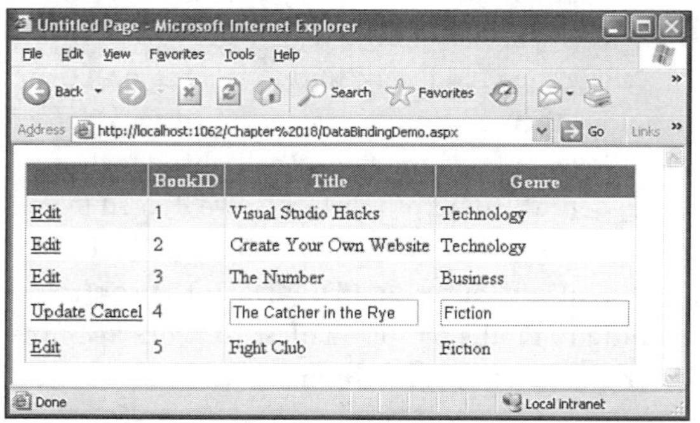

FIGURE 18.14 Both the `Title` and `Genre` fields use the default editing interface.

Let's now look at how to customize the Genre field so that it displays a DropDownList of the current genre values in the table, rather than using a TextBox control. To start, go to the Fields dialog box and convert the Genre BoundField into a TemplateField. This will automatically create an ItemTemplate with a data-bound Label Web control and an EditItemTemplate with a data-bound TextBox. In fact, if at this point you retest your page through a browser, there will be no discernable difference from the editable interface in Figure 18.14.

To change the Genre field's EditItemTemplate, go to the GridView's smart tag and click the Edit Templates link. This will take you to the template editing view of the GridView, with the smart tag listing the available templates. Choose the EditItemTemplate. You should see a TextBox Web control in the EditItemTemplate; this is the data-bound TextBox control that was added automatically when we converted the Genre BoundField to a TemplateField. Because we no longer want to use a TextBox in the editing interface, delete this Web control.

We now need to add a DropDownList to the EditItemTemplate that lists the genres in the Books table. To accomplish this, we need to first create a SqlDataSource control that retrieves the unique list of genres. This can be added directly to the Genre field's EditItemTemplate. After adding the SqlDataSource to the EditItemTemplate, set its ID property to genreDataSource. Next, run through the wizard, returning just the Genre column and checking the Return Only Unique Rows check box, just like we did in the preceding hour when using a DropDownList to filter the GridView results by genre.

After configuring the genreDataSource SqlDataSource control, add a DropDownList to the EditItemTemplate. Click the Choose Data Source link in the DropDownList's smart tag and bind it to the genreDataSource control, with the Genre column serving as both the field to display and the value field. After you've added both the SqlDataSource control and the DropDownList to the EditItemTemplate, and configured both, your screen should look similar to Figure 18.15.

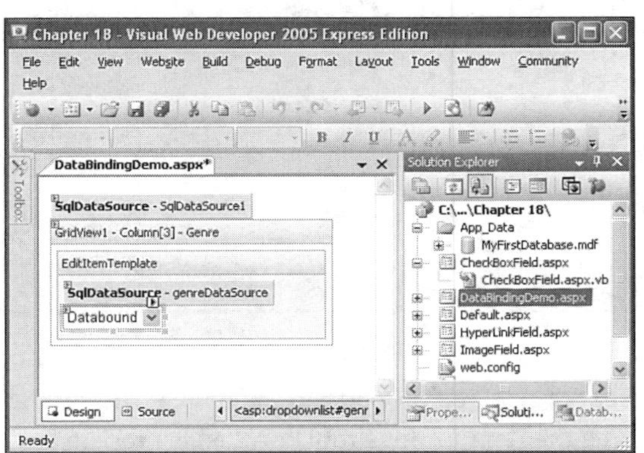

FIGURE 18.15
A SqlDataSource and DropDownList have been added to the Genre TemplateField's EditItemTemplate.

At this point, test the ASP.NET page through a web browser. When you edit a particular row, the `Genre` field is displayed as a drop-down list with the various genre values in the `Books` table (Business, Fiction, and Technology), as shown in Figure 18.17. However, notice that the *first* item of the DropDownList is selected, regardless of the edited book's actual `Genre` value. That is, if you edit *Visual Studio Hacks*, which has the genre Technology, the drop-down list has the Business genre selected. Furthermore, if you save the edits, by clicking the Update button, a value of Null is saved for the book's genre, regardless of what option you've selected from the drop-down list.

What's going on here? What we've yet to do is implement data binding on the DropDownList control in the EditItemTemplate. Right now the DropDownList doesn't know the value of the row's `Genre` column, nor does it provide its selected value to the GridView's SqlDataSource control when the data is updated. We need to have the DropDownList properly data-bound to have this interaction occur correctly.

Return to Visual Web Developer and go back to the `Genre` field's EditItemTemplate. Open the DropDownList's smart tag and click on the Edit DataBindings link. This will display the `genres` DataBindings dialog box, from which you can tie together the DropDownList's properties and the column values returned by the GridView's SqlDataSource control. Because we want the DropDownList's selection to be based on the `Genre` column value, select the `SelectedValue` property from the list on the left and pick the `Genre` field from the drop-down list on the right, as shown in Figure 18.16. Since the `SelectedValue` value also dictates the value of the edited book's `Genre` value, make sure that the Two-way Databinding check box is checked.

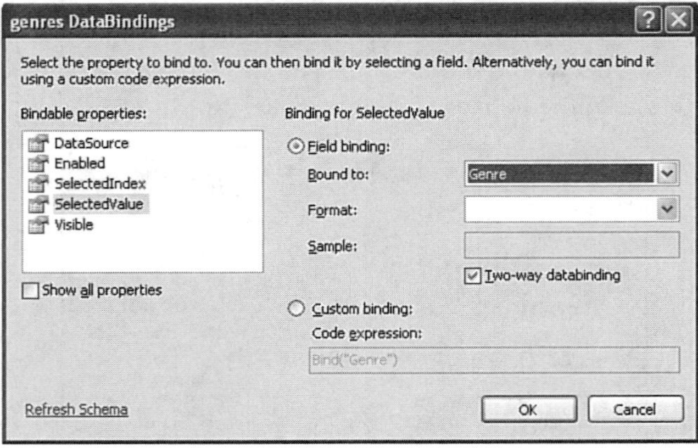

FIGURE 18.16 Bind the `SelectedValue` property to the `Genre` column value using two-way data binding.

After binding the `SelectedValue` property to the `Genre` column, revisit the page in the browser. This time the item in the DropDownList is properly set to the book's

Genre value, and when you save the edits, the selected DropDownList value is saved. Figure 18.17 shows the ASP.NET page in action.

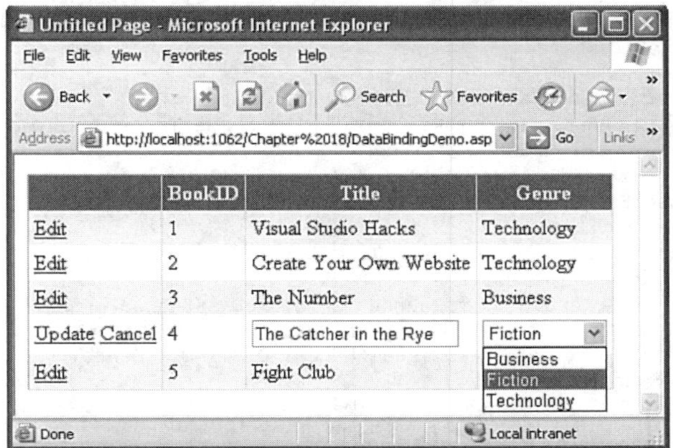

FIGURE 18.17
The Genre field provides a customized, data-bound editing interface.

Watch Out!

Because the DropDownList in the Genre EditItemTemplate lists the unique genres that already exist in the Books table, you can lose options from the DropDownList. For example, *The Number* is the only book that is in the Business genre. If we edit this book and change its genre to Fiction, the next time we edit a row, the genre drop-down list will have only two options: Fiction and Technology.

As discussed in previous hours, ideally we would implement the concept of genres as a separate table in the database, giving the Books table a foreign key to this genre table. With that approach, we'd have a well-defined set of available genres and not lose existing genre choices based on a user's actions.

In the photo album application we'll be building starting in Hour 22, "Devising a Plan for the Photo Album Application," we'll actually be using a multitable database model that will highlight the recommended way of modeling things like a book's genre.

A Look at the Declarative Markup

Visual Web Developer makes it very easy to specify the data bindings for a Web control. As Figure 18.16 showed, the DataBindings dialog box allows us to simply pick one of the Web control's properties, specify the database column to bind it to, and indicate whether to use one-way or two-way data binding. These steps, while done through the Design view, can also be performed through the Source view.

It's always worthwhile to see how actions in the Design view affect the underlying Source view, so let's take a moment to peruse the Source view. Listing 18.1 shows the GridView's declarative markup.

LISTING 18.1 The GridView's HTML Markup

```
 1: <asp:GridView ID="GridView1" runat="server" AutoGenerateColumns="False"
➥DataKeyNames="BookID"
 2:     DataSourceID="SqlDataSource1" BackColor="White" BorderColor="#DEDFDE"
➥ BorderStyle="None" BorderWidth="1px" CellPadding="4" ForeColor="Black"
➥GridLines="Vertical">
 3:     <Columns>
 4:         <asp:CommandField ShowEditButton="True" />
 5:         <asp:BoundField DataField="BookID" HeaderText="BookID"
➥InsertVisible="False" ReadOnly="True"
 6:             SortExpression="BookID" />
 7:         <asp:BoundField DataField="Title" HeaderText="Title"
➥SortExpression="Title" />
 8:         <asp:TemplateField HeaderText="Genre" SortExpression="Genre">
 9:             <EditItemTemplate>
10:                 <asp:SqlDataSource ID="genreDataSource" runat="server"
➥ConnectionString="<%$ ConnectionStrings:ConnectionString %>"
11:                     SelectCommand="SELECT DISTINCT [Genre] FROM [Books]">
➥</asp:SqlDataSource>
12:                 <asp:DropDownList ID="genres" runat="server"
➥DataSourceID="genreDataSource" DataTextField="Genre"
➥DataValueField="Genre" SelectedValue='<%# Bind("Genre") %>'>
13:                 </asp:DropDownList>
14:             </EditItemTemplate>
15:             <ItemTemplate>
16:                 <asp:Label ID="Label1" runat="server"
➥Text='<%# Bind("Genre") %>'></asp:Label>
17:             </ItemTemplate>
18:         </asp:TemplateField>
19:     </Columns>
20:     <FooterStyle BackColor="#CCCC99" />
21:     <RowStyle BackColor="#F7F7DE" />
22:     <SelectedRowStyle BackColor="#CE5D5A" Font-Bold="True"
➥ForeColor="White" />
23:     <PagerStyle BackColor="#F7F7DE" ForeColor="Black"
➥HorizontalAlign="Right" />
24:     <HeaderStyle BackColor="#6B696B" Font-Bold="True" ForeColor="White" />
25:     <AlternatingRowStyle BackColor="White" />
26: </asp:GridView>
```

Lines 8—18 show the `Genre` TemplateField. The ItemTemplate is defined on lines 15 through 17; the EditItemTemplate, on lines 9 through 14. The EditItemTemplate contains two Web controls: a SqlDataSource with `ID` `genreDataSource` on lines 10 and 11 and a DropDownList control on lines 12 and 13. The effects of the data binding performed in Figure 18.16 are shown on line 12: The DropDownList's `SelectedValue` property has been bound to the `Genre` column using `SelectedValue='<%# Bind("Genre") %>'`.

I find it a lot quicker and easier to use the Design view to specify the data bindings for controls in TemplateFields, but do realize that these data bindings can be expressed through the Source view if you prefer.

> The two-way data binding uses the `Bind(columnName)` syntax; one-way data binding uses `Eval(columnName)`.

By the Way

Summary

In this hour we looked at a hodgepodge of data-related topics, starting with an examination of the fields available for use with the data Web controls. The three fields we looked at were the CheckBoxField, HyperLinkField, and ImageField. The CheckBoxField is automatically used when binding a `bit` column to a GridView or DetailsView. The HyperLinkField renders a link; and the ImageField, an image. Both the HyperLinkField and ImageField have pairs of properties that allow us to associate a database field value with the properties of the fields' corresponding HyperLink or Image controls. Specifically, we saw how to add a `"Buy"` link to each book that, when clicked, would whisk the user to Amazon.com, as well as how to display a picture of the book's cover in each row of a GridView.

We also looked at how to use `WHERE` clause filter expressions with wildcards. This technique is useful if you want to allow the user to search for a particular substring within a database field. This hour concluded with an examination of data binding. Although the data Web controls natively handle data binding for us most of the time, if we add a TemplateField or want to use a Web control other than the TextBox in the editing or inserting interface, we need to be able to bind the appropriate database column values to the appropriate Web control properties. We can accomplish this by clicking on the Edit DataBindings link in the smart tag of a Web control in a TemplateField.

This hour wraps up our look at accessing and modifying database data through an ASP.NET web page. Working with data through a web page is a very common task, so it's important that you're comfortable with the processes examined. Before you continue, it behooves you to spend adequate time practicing creating data-driven ASP.NET pages. I strongly encourage that you work through all the exercises from Hour 13 through Hour 18 before moving onward in your studies.

Q&A

Q. ***In the "Displaying Hyperlinks with the HyperLinkField" section, we learned that the HyperLinkField's URL value can be constructed using multiple database values by setting the*** `DataNavigateUrlFields` ***property to a comma-delimited list of database column names. Does this also apply to the text value (***`DataTextUrlField`***)?***

A. No, the HyperLinkField supports multiple column names only in its URL portion. The `DataTextUrlField` property can accept only one column name. Similarly, the ImageField's `DataAlternateTextField` and `DataImageUrlField` properties can be assigned only to a single column name.

Q. ***In the "Using Wildcards in a*** `WHERE` ***Filter Expression" section, we saw how to display all books where the title contained a search term entered by the user. Would it be possible to make a more general search engine, one that would return a book whose title, author, or genre matched the search term entered by the user?***

A. Yes, this would be possible. You would need to add multiple `WHERE` clause conditions, using the same pattern for each. However, when you specify the `SELECT` clause through the Specify a Selected Statement screen of the SqlDataSource wizard, the `WHERE` clause filter expressions specified are joined by `AND`s. That is, if you followed the steps outlined earlier in this hour and added three filter expressions to the `Title`, `Author`, and `Genre` columns using the `LIKE` operator with a parameter value based on the `titleSearch` TextBox, the resulting `SELECT` query would be

```
SELECT *
FROM [Books]
WHERE ([Title] LIKE '%' + @Title + '%') AND
      ([Author] LIKE '%' + @Author + '%') AND
      ([Genre] LIKE '%' + @Genre + '%')
```

Note that the three conditions in the `WHERE` clause are joined by an `AND`. That means the only rows that will be returned will be those whose `Title` column value contains the user's search term *and* whose `Author` column value contains the user's search term *and* whose `Genre` column value contains the user's search term. What we want, though, is to have all books returned where *any* of those columns contain the search term.

To accomplish this, you'll have to craft the `SELECT` statement yourself through the SqlDataSource wizard's Define Custom Statements or Stored Procedures screen. (This screen was first discussed in Hour 14.)

Q. ***What if I want to display an image (or hyperlink), but I need more control over the way the image or hyperlink is rendered than the ImageField or HyperLinkField grants? For example, what if I want to have two images in the field, or I want some nonlinked text to appear after the hyperlink?***

A. For simple links and images, the HyperLinkField and ImageField work wonderfully. However, if you need greater flexibility in the appearance of these fields, you'll need to use a TemplateField instead. You can simply convert the

HyperLinkField or ImageField into a TemplateField and then customize the ItemTemplate as needed. If you add new Web controls, be sure to configure their data bindings as needed.

Workshop

Quiz

1. What HyperLinkField properties would you set to what values if you wanted to display a hyperlink with the text `"Buy *Title*"` that whisked the user to the URL http://www.buybooks.com/Buy.aspx?ISBN=*ISBN*, where *`Title`* was the title of the book and *ISBN* is the ISBN.
2. If you set the `DataNavigateUrlFields` property to multiple column names—like `BookID,ISBN`—what would you set the `DataNavigateUrlFormatString` property to in order to have a URL generated with the form http://www.books.com/Details.aspx?BookID=*BookID*&ISBN=*ISBN*?
3. True or False: The `LIKE` operator in the `WHERE` clause can be used with columns of any data type.
4. What are the seven types of fields that can be added to GridView or DetailsView controls?
5. How do one-way and two-way data binding differ?

Answers

1. To configure the URL portion of the hyperlink, you would set the `DataNavigateUrlFields` property to `ISBN` and the `DataNavigateUrlFormatString` property to `http://www.buybooks.com/Buy.aspx?ISBN={0}`. To configure the text portion, you would set the `DataTextField` property to `Title` and the `DataTextFormatString` property to `Buy {0}`.
2. You would use `{0}` to inject the value of the first database column (`BookID`) and `{1}` to inject the value of the second (`ISBN`). Therefore, you would use `http://www.books.com/Details.aspx?BookID={0}&ISBN={1}`
3. False. The `LIKE` operator must be used with string or date/time column types.
4. The seven fields are: BoundField, CheckBoxField, HyperLinkField, ImageField, ButtonField, CommandField, and TemplateField.

5. One-way data binding simply takes a specified database column's value and binds it to a specified Web control property. Two-way data binding can not only assign a database column's value to a Web control property, but can also do the inverse: It can take the value of a property and assign it to the value of a data source control parameter.

Exercises

1. In this hour we looked at one example that used a HyperLinkField to display a `"Buy"` link and another that displayed the book's cover image. Create a new page that displays all of the books from the `Books` table in a GridView and has both a `"Buy"` HyperLinkField and an ImageField showing the book's cover. Also change the HyperLinkField's text to `"Buy` *`Title`*`"`, where *`Title`* is the title of the book, and center the book cover image. (Hint: To center the book cover image, use the `ItemStyle` property of the ImageField.)

2. In this hour we added a `Recommended` field to the `Books` table. Because users might be interested in seeing only books that are recommended, create a page that has a DropDownList with two options—Recommended and Not Recommended—with values of 1 and 0, respectively. Next, add a SqlDataSource control that has a `WHERE` clause filter expression on the `Recommended` field based on the value of the DropDownList. Finally, add a GridView to the page, bind it to the SqlDataSource, and test the page in a browser.

3. In the "Specifying the Data Bindings for a Web Control" section this hour, we created an editable GridView that used a DropDownList for the `Genre` field's editing interface. Re-create this page, but this time use a RadioButtonList in place of the DropDownList.

PART IV

Site Navigation, User Management, and Page Layout

HOUR 19

Defining a Site's Structure and Providing Site Navigation

In this hour, we will cover

- ▶ The basics of site navigation with ASP.NET
- ▶ Creating and defining your website's structure
- ▶ Showing the user's current location in the site's structure with the breadcrumb control
- ▶ Displaying the site's structure using the TreeView Web control
- ▶ Using the Menu control

At its most granular level, a website is nothing more than a collection of discrete web pages. However, typically these pages are logically related and categorized in some manner. For example, Amazon.com has its site broken down into product categories, such as books, music, DVDs, and so on. Each of these sections is further categorized by genre. The classification of a website's pages into logical categories is referred to as the **site's structure**.

After a site's structure has been defined, most web developers will create the **site's navigation**. A site's navigation is the collection of user interface elements used to assist users in browsing the site. Common navigation elements include menus, treeviews, and breadcrumbs. These user interface elements serve two tasks: They let the users know where in the site they are currently visiting, and they make it easy for the users to quickly jump to another part of the site.

An Overview of ASP.NET's Site Navigation Features

Prior to ASP.NET 2.0, a very common and very time-consuming task for developers was defining their website's structure and implementing the site's navigation. Some developers simply hard-coded their site's structure within the navigational elements; others created database tables or used files to store the site's structure. Developers were left on their own for turning the site's structure into a coherent navigation. Although a number of third-party navigation components were available—menus, treeviews, breadcrumbs, and the like—there were no built-in ASP.NET Web controls.

Fortunately, these are concerns of the past. ASP.NET now provides a means to specify site structure by creating a **site map**. The site map is an **XML file** that defines the logical sections of the site and optionally ties each section to a particular URL. After the site map has been defined, a number of new ASP.NET Web controls can be used to turn the site's structure into a navigation user interface.

By the Way

> **XML**, which stands for **eXtensible Markup Language**, is a technology for expressing data in a text-based format using elements that can contain attributes and text content, much like the static HTML and Web controls are expressed through the HTML portion of an ASP.NET page. XML documents, however, are more flexible than HTML's syntax, allowing the creator of the XML document to define the document's markup. The ASP.NET site map file defines a special set of elements to express a site's structure.

ASP.NET version 2.0 provides three new navigation Web controls:

- **SiteMapPath**—This Web control provides a **breadcrumb**, which is a single line of text showing the user her location in the website's structure. For example, at an online bookstore, if a user had drilled down to *Visual Studio Hacks*, the breadcrumb might look like Home -> Computers -> Programming -> Visual Studio Hacks, with each section—Home, Computers, and so on—rendered as links back to the previous section. A breadcrumb allows the user to quickly see where she is in the site and to navigate back up the logical hierarchy. (Figure 19.7 shows the SiteMapPath control when viewed through a browser.)
- **TreeView**—This Web control provides a hierarchical view of the site's structure. For an online bookstore, the top level would contain the main categories—Computers, Fiction, History, and so on—while each of those main categories could be expanded to show subcategories. (Figure 19.8 shows the TreeView control when viewed through a browser.)
- **Menu**—A menu offers the same data as in the treeview, the only difference being in how the data is displayed. The treeview renders as an expandable/collapsible tree, whereas the menu is composed of menu items and submenus. (Consult Figure 19.11 to see the Menu control in action.)

Because the navigation Web controls' contents are rendered based on the page being visited and the site structure defined in the site map, updating the site map immediately updates the navigation controls used throughout the site. That is, if you want to add a new section to your website, simply create the appropriate ASP.NET pages and then tie those new pages into the site map. As soon as these changes are made and saved, the navigation Web controls used throughout the site—the breadcrumbs, treeviews, and menus—will automatically be updated to include this new section.

Before we can start using the navigation Web controls, we'll first need to define our website's structure using a site map. In the next section we'll create the site map file. In the sections after that, we'll examine each of ASP.NET's three navigation Web controls.

Defining the Website's Structure Using a Site Map

While a very small and trivial website composed of only a handful of pages might not have an easily identifiable site structure, all sufficiently large websites possess a logical structure that is typically easy to identify. The contents of the site, whether items for sale, discussions in online forums, or informational articles, can all be classified in some manner. These classifications usually define the structure of a site.

Because we've yet to create any multipage websites, let's take a minute to build a website with a number of related web pages. These pages won't do anything interesting; rather, we'll use them simply to create a mock website structure. For this example, imagine that we are building an online bookstore.

Start by creating a new ASP.NET website project in Visual Web Developer. This new project should already include one ASP.NET page, `Default.aspx`. (If you used a project type that does not include `Default.aspx`, add it now, please.) Next, add four new ASP.NET web pages: `OnSale.aspx`, `Legal.aspx`, `Privacy.aspx`, and `About.aspx`. Next, add a folder for each of the genres of books our store will be selling. Specifically, add three folders: `Business`, `Fiction`, and `Technology`. In each of these folders, add a single ASP.NET page, `Default.aspx`. Finally, in the `Technology` folder, add two subfolders, `Computers` and `Electronics`, adding a `Default.aspx` page to each of these subfolders.

Did you Know?

> To add a new folder, right-click on the project name in the Solution Explorer and choose the New Folder menu option. To add a web page to a particular folder, right-click on that folder in the Solution Explorer and choose Add Item.

After you have added these web pages and folders, your Solution Explorer should look similar to the one in Figure 19.1.

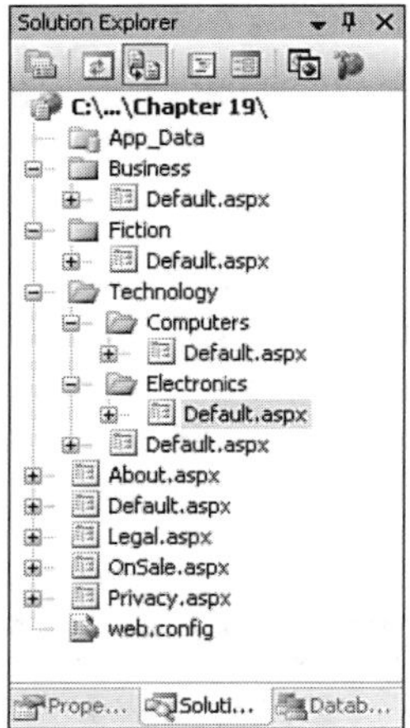

FIGURE 19.1
A number of new folders and web pages have been added to the project.

In each of these pages, add a short bit of text in the page providing a summary of the page's functionality. For example, in the root directory's `Default.aspx`, I put `"Welcome to my online book store!"`; in `OnSale.aspx`, I used `"This lists the books currently on sale."`; in the `Business` folder's `Default.aspx`, I added `"This lists the books in the Business genre."`. Add such a brief summary for each web page in the site.

Adding the Site Map

Now that we have created the pages for our mock site, we're ready to add the site map. To create the site map, follow the same steps as you normally would to add an ASP.NET web page to the project. That is, right-click on the project name in the Solution Explorer and choose the Add Item menu option. From the Add Item dialog box, choose the Site Map option (see Figure 19.2) and click the Add button. This will add a site map named `Web.sitemap` to your project.

When adding a site map to your project, put the site map in the root directory and leave the name of the file as `Web.sitemap`. If you place this file in another folder or choose a different name, the navigation Web controls won't be able to find the site's structure because, by default, they look for a file named `Web.sitemap` in the root directory.

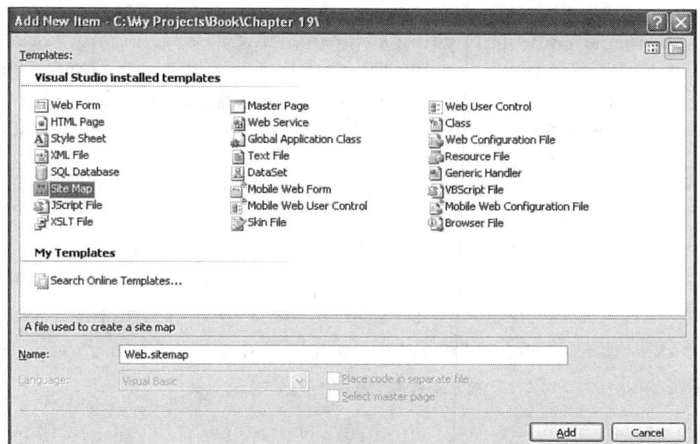

FIGURE 19.2
Add a new site map to the website.

After you have added the site map, open it by double-clicking on the `Web.sitemap` file in the Solution Explorer. Listing 19.1 shows the markup in the site map, by default.

LISTING 19.1 The Default Content of the Site Map

```
1: <?xml version="1.0" encoding="utf-8" ?>
2: <siteMap xmlns="http://schemas.microsoft.com/AspNet/SiteMap-File-1.0" >
3:     <siteMapNode url="" title=""  description="">
4:         <siteMapNode url="" title=""  description="" />
5:         <siteMapNode url="" title=""  description="" />
6:     </siteMapNode>
7: </siteMap>
```

The site map file is an XML file, just like the `web.config` file. This XML file contains the logical structure of the website. To define your site's structure, you need to edit this file manually. Don't forget that XML documents impose strict formatting rules. One such rule is that XML is case sensitive. If you try to add a `<siteMapNode>` using improper casing, like `<SITEMapNode>`, you'll get an exception when attempting to use the navigation Web controls. Another rule of note is that all elements must have opening and closing tags. Notice how the `<siteMap>` element has an opening tag on line 2 and a closing tag on line 7. The `<siteMapNode>` element on line 3 has its opening tag there and its closing tag on line 6. The two `<siteMapNode>` elements on lines 4 and 5 don't have an explicit closing tag because they use the shorthand notation, `/>`.

By the Way

An XML element with no inner content can have its closing tag expressed in one of two ways: verbosely, like *`<myTag attribute1="value1" ...></myTag>`*, or more tersely, using `/>` like so: *`<myTag attribute1="value1" ... />`*.

Visual Web Developer will notify you if you enter invalid XML when creating the site map. If you enter an element that the site map does not know about, either because of a misspelling or improper use of case, Visual Web Developer will underline the suspect tag in blue. If you forget to close an element, Visual Web Developer will underline the element in red.

The site map begins with a `<siteMap>` element (line 2), which contains a number of `<siteMapNode>` elements within. The `url`, `title`, and `description` attributes provide information about a particular section of the website's structure, while the location of the `<siteMapNode>` element relative to the other `<siteMapNode>` elements determines the position of the section relative to other sections.

If this isn't yet clear, don't worry; a more concrete example ought to help.

Building the Site Map from the Site's Structure

Given the mock website we've created, let's define a structure that exhibits the logical hierarchy shown in Figure 19.3. Each node in the hierarchy shows the title and URL for the section along with the section's place in the hierarchy.

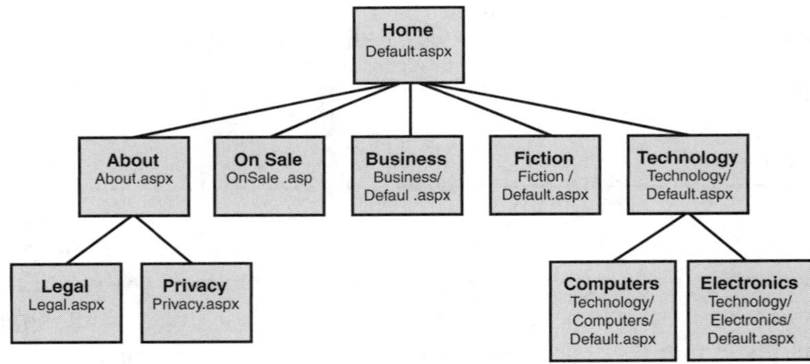

FIGURE 19.3 The site's structure categorizes books by their genre.

To implement this site structure in an ASP.NET site map, start by clearing out the `<siteMapNode>` elements from the default site map (remove lines 3 through 6 in Listing 19.1). Next, begin at the top section and work your way down the hierarchy, adding a `<siteMapNode>` for each section. Those sections that appear beneath a given section in the hierarchy will be nested within a `<siteMapNode>` element.

To put these concepts into practice, add a `<siteMapNode>` element for the Home section like so:

```
<siteMapNode url="Default.aspx" title="Home"  description="" />
```

Notice that I used the section URL in Figure 19.3 as the value for the `url` attribute and the section title as the `title` attribute value. I am going to leave the `description` attribute blank, but feel free to enter a meaningful value here if you like. Also, note that for the Home `<siteMapNode>` element I used the terse closing tag syntax, `/>`. After you add this element, your site map should look like this:

```
<?xml version="1.0" encoding="utf-8" ?>
<siteMap xmlns="http://schemas.microsoft.com/AspNet/SiteMap-File-1.0" >
   <siteMapNode url="Default.aspx" title="Home"  description="" />
</siteMap>
```

Because the next sections in the hierarchy exist as descendents of the Home section, the corresponding `<siteMapNode>` elements will be nested within the Home `<siteMapNode>` element. There are five such sections, requiring five `<siteMapNode>` elements:

```
<siteMapNode url="About.aspx" title="About" description="" />
<siteMapNode url="OnSale.aspx" title="On Sale" description="" />
<siteMapNode url="Business/Default.aspx" title="Business" description="" />
<siteMapNode url="Fiction/Default.aspx" title="Fiction" description="" />
<siteMapNode url="Technology/Default.aspx" title="Technology" description="" />
```

Watch Out!

> XML's formatting rules prohibit the characters <, >, &, and " from appearing within an element's text content and as the value for an attribute. If you want to include any of these characters in the `title` or `description` attributes, you will instead need to use the `<`, `>`, `&`, or `"`, respectively. For example, if you wanted to have the `title` attribute for a site map node be `"Business & Investing"` you would need to use the text `Business & Investing`.

These five `<siteMapNode>` elements should be nested within the Home `<siteMapNode>` element, resulting in the following site map:

```
<?xml version="1.0" encoding="utf-8" ?>
<siteMap xmlns="http://schemas.microsoft.com/AspNet/SiteMap-File-1.0" >
   <siteMapNode url="Default.aspx" title="Home"  description="">
      <siteMapNode url="About.aspx" title="About"  description="" />
      <siteMapNode url="OnSale.aspx" title="On Sale"  description="" />
      <siteMapNode url="Business/Default.aspx" title="Business"
➥description="" />
      <siteMapNode url="Fiction/Default.aspx" title="Fiction"
➥description="" />
      <siteMapNode url="Technology/Default.aspx" title="Technology"
➥description="" />
   </siteMapNode>
</siteMap>
```

Notice how the Home `<siteMapNode>`'s closing tag was changed from the terse dialect (`/>`) to the more verbose form (`</siteMapNode>`). The reason is that the verbose form is needed when an element contains inner content; since the Home

`<siteMapNode>` element now contains children elements, we have no choice but to use the verbose syntax.

If you continue this process through the remainder of the sections in Figure 19.3, you'll eventually wind up with the site map shown in Listing 19.2.

LISTING 19.2 The Completed Site Map Contents

```
<?xml version="1.0" encoding="utf-8" ?>
<siteMap xmlns="http://schemas.microsoft.com/AspNet/SiteMap-File-1.0" >
    <siteMapNode url="Default.aspx" title="Home" description="">
      <siteMapNode url="About.aspx" title="About" description="">
        <siteMapNode url="Legal.aspx" title="Legal" description="" />
        <siteMapNode url="Privacy.aspx" title="Privacy" description="" />
      </siteMapNode>
      <siteMapNode url="OnSale.aspx" title="On Sale" description="" />
      <siteMapNode url="Business/Default.aspx" title="Business"
➥description="" />
      <siteMapNode url="Fiction/Default.aspx" title="Fiction"
➥description="" />
      <siteMapNode url="Technology/Default.aspx" title="Technology"
➥description="">
        <siteMapNode url="Technology/Computers/Default.aspx"
➥title="Computers" description="" />
        <siteMapNode url="Technology/Electronics/Default.aspx"
➥title="Electronics" description="" />
      </siteMapNode>
    </siteMapNode>
</siteMap>
```

By the Way

Although a page developer can use folders to help organize the files in his website, the site's structure as defined in the site map need not model this folder hierarchy. For example, in the site map hierarchy shown in Figure 19.3, the Privacy and Legal sections are subsections of the About section, even though `About.aspx`, `Privacy.aspx`, and `Legal.aspx` all exist in the same folder.

Often, though, there is a correlation between the site's folder structure and site map. The book genre sections illustrate this: Technology is one section with a subsection for Computers and Electronics, and there's a `Technology` folder in the website with `Computers` and `Electronics` subfolders.

Displaying a Breadcrumb with the SiteMapPath Control

ASP.NET provides three navigation Web controls for displaying a navigation user interface based on the site's structure defined in a site map: the SiteMapPath, the TreeView, and the Menu. The SiteMapPath control, which is the focus of discussion in this section, displays a breadcrumb, showing the user where in the site he is currently visiting. All three of these controls are available from the Navigation section of the Toolbox (see Figure 19.4).

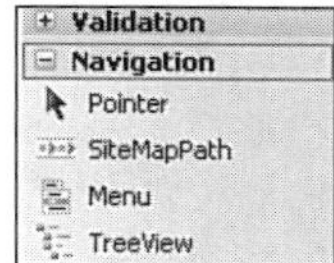

FIGURE 19.4 The navigation Web controls can be found in the Toolbox under the Navigation label.

Watch Out!

If you want to work with the SiteMapPath—or any of the other navigation Web controls, for that matter—it's imperative that a legally formatted site map exist in the root directory and be named `Web.sitemap`. If you followed along with the steps in the previous section, you should have, at this point, a valid `Web.sitemap` file in your root directory containing the contents in Listing 19.2.

Did you Know?

Breadcrumbs are especially useful for sites that have a particularly deep structural hierarchy. As users drill down through the levels of hierarchy in a site, they can easily become disoriented. A breadcrumb control shows them where in the hierarchy they are currently visiting and provides a means to quickly move back to a higher level, if necessary.

To add the SiteMapPath control to an ASP.NET page, simply drag it from the Toolbox onto the page. Take a moment to add the SiteMapPath control to the `Default.aspx` pages in the root directory, in the `Technology` folder, and the `Computers` subfolder. When we view the SiteMapPath in the pages' Design views, the SiteMapPath control shows the layout based on the values in the site map. Figure 19.5 shows the Visual Web Developer Design view for `Technology/Computers/Default.aspx`.

By the Way

If you do not see the SiteMapPath rendered in the Visual Web Developer Design view, as shown in Figure 19.5, one of several things could be awry. If you see a gray box with a warning message, the `Web.sitemap` file contains invalid XML. Returning to the site map and fixing the specified problems should remedy this situation.

If you see Root Node > Current Node > Parent Node in the Design view, you likely have not created a site map (or you have not named it `Web.sitemap` and placed it in the root directory). If you have a properly named and placed site map file, go to the View menu and choose Refresh.

FIGURE 19.5
The SiteMapPath shows the breadcrumb relative to the current page.

At this point we've successfully added three SiteMapPath controls to our ASP.NET website! That sure was easy. Take a minute to try out these three pages in a browser. The SiteMapPath renders just like in the Design view; clicking the links in the breadcrumb whisks you back to the appropriate section. (Refer to Figure 19.7 to see the SiteMapPath control on `Technology/Computers/Default.aspx`.)

Customizing the SiteMapPath's Appearance

Like most Web controls we've examined throughout this book, the SiteMapPath control has a number of properties that can be used to customize its appearance. These properties can be set manually through the SiteMapPath's properties listed in the Appearances and Styles sections of the Properties window.

To understand how these properties affect the rendered appearance of the SiteMapPath, we first need to discuss the components of the SiteMapPath. The SiteMapPath builds up a list of **nodes** and **path separators**. A node is a section in the hierarchy, and the path separator is what separates each node. For example, the SiteMapPath in the `Technology/Computers/Default.aspx` page has three nodes: Home, Technology, and Computers. Each node is separated by a path separator: >, by default. There are three possible types of nodes:

- **Root Node**—A SiteMapPath contains a single Root Node; it's the node that contains the section at the top of the site map hierarchy. In all pages that use the site map in Listing 19.2, the Root Node is Home.
- **Current Node**—A SiteMapPath contains a single Current Node. The Current Node is the section that corresponds to the page the user is visiting. In the SiteMapPath in the `Technology/Computers/Default.aspx` page, the Current Node is Computers.

- **General Nodes**—A SiteMapPath contains zero to many General Nodes, depending on the depth of the Current Node in the site map hierarchy. In the `Technology/Computers/Default.aspx` page, there's a single General Node, Technology.

Table 19.1 lists the SiteMapPath's appearance-related properties, along with a brief description of each one. Some of these properties affect the look and feel of the entire SiteMapPath, whereas others affect particular components of the SiteMapPath, such as just the Current Node or just the path separators.

TABLE 19.1 The SiteMapPath's Appearance Properties

Property Name	Description
`BackColor` `ForeColor`	Specify the background and foreground colors for the entire SiteMapPath.

`BorderColor`
`BorderStyle`
`BorderWidth`
	Indicate the border settings for the SiteMapPath.

`CssClass`	Specifies the name of the cascading style sheet (CSS) class to be applied to the SiteMapPath's rendered HTML element.
`Font`	Specifies the font-related settings for the entire SiteMapPath.
`PathDirection`	Can be one of two values: `RootToCurrent` (the default) or `CurrentToRoot`. With `RootToCurrent`, the breadcrumb is rendered as Root > ... > Current; with `CurrentToRoot`, it's rendered as Current > ... > Root.
`PathSeparator`	Specifies the string that separates each node. Defaults to >
`RenderCurrentNodeAsLink`	Specifies a Boolean value that indicates whether the Current Node is rendered as a link. Defaults to `False`.
`NodeStyle`	Specifies the default style for *all* of the nodes in the breadcrumb. Applies to the Root Node, Current Node, and General Nodes. This and the other style properties have subproperties such as `BackColor`, `ForeColor`, `Font`, and so on.
`CurrentNodeStyle`	Indicates the appearance settings applied to the Current Node. Any settings here override the `NodeStyle` settings for the Current Node.

TABLE 19.1 Continued

Property Name	Description
`RootNodeStyle`	Specifies the appearance settings applied to the Root Node. Any settings here override the `NodeStyle` settings for the Root Node.
`PathSeparatorStyle`	Indicates the appearance settings applied to the path separator.

Take a moment to tinker with these properties and note the results in the Design view.

If you don't trust your artistic skills, the SiteMapPath contains an Auto Format option, just like the GridView and DetailsView controls we examined back in Hour 15, "Displaying Data with the Data Web Controls." For some assistance in formatting the SiteMapPath, simply click the Auto Format link in the control's smart tag. Figure 19.6 shows the SiteMapPath's Auto Format dialog box, and Figure 19.7 shows the SiteMapPath control in `Technology/Computers/Default.aspx` after the Colorful Auto Format setting has been applied.

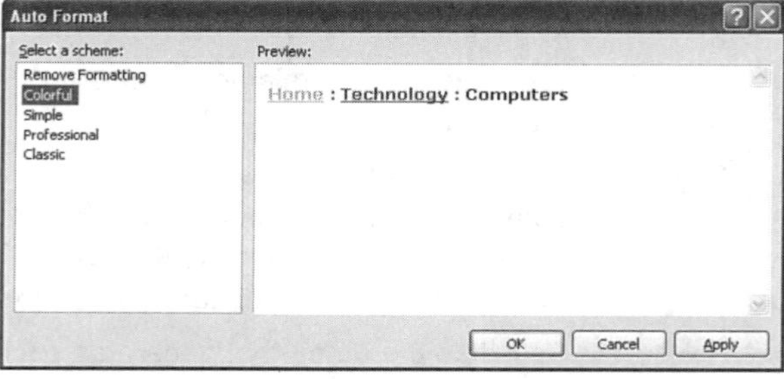

FIGURE 19.6 Let the Auto Format dialog box aid you in specifying the SiteMapPath's appearance.

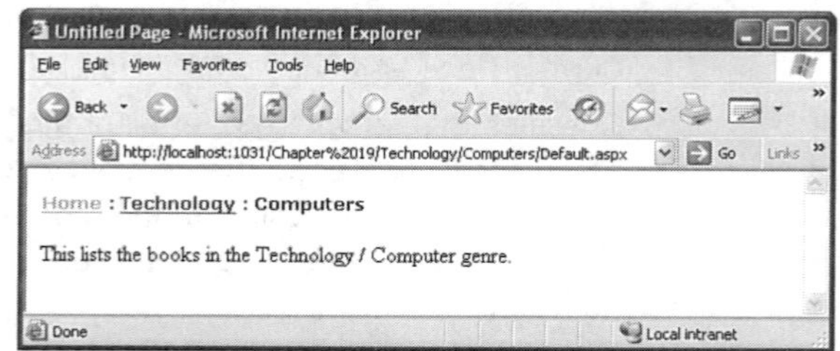

FIGURE 19.7 The SiteMapPath control when visiting `Technology/Computers/Default.aspx`.

Showing the Entire Site Structure

As Figure 19.7 shows, the SiteMapPath control displays only the current section based on the page where the user is visiting and those immediate ancestor sections.

Although the breadcrumb interface provided by the SiteMapPath makes it easy for a visitor to pinpoint his location in the site's navigational hierarchy and navigate further up the hierarchy quickly, it does not enable him to easily jump to any section of the site.

For example, imagine that a visitor comes to our online bookstore's home page. While there's only text right now, imagine that the page has links to the various genre pages titled Business Books, Fiction Books, and Technology Books. Our imaginary visitor might click on Technology Books, which would take her to `Technology/Default.aspx`, where there might be some technology books listed as well as links to drill down into the subcategories, Computer Books and Electronics Books. Say that our user clicks on the Computer Books link. On this page the SiteMapPath shows Home > Technology > Computers and would list the computer books for sale. However, at this point if the user decides that she wants to look at books on electronics instead, or if she realizes technology books aren't her thing and she'd rather browse the fiction titles, the user has to click her browser's Back button or go back via the breadcrumb to the appropriate parent level, and then drill down into whatever category she's interested in. The point is, the user can't jump directly from the computer books page to the electronics books or fiction books pages.

To allow a visitor to quickly hop to any section from any page, we need to use a navigation user interface element that lists the entire site structure. The final two ASP.NET navigation Web controls—the TreeView control and the Menu control—provide this functionality.

The Menu and TreeView controls are similar to the GridView and DetailsView controls examined in Hour 15 in that they require a data source control that contains the data to display. ASP.NET provides a SiteMapDataSource control that automatically retrieves the data from the site map and provides it in a manner that the TreeView and Menu controls can work with. Unlike the SqlDataSource control we used when working with the GridView and DetailsView, the SiteMapDataSource control doesn't have any wizard or require any configuration on our part.

Displaying the Site's Structure in a TreeView

The TreeView control lists the sections of the website as defined in the site map in a collapsible tree. A visitor can quickly see all of the sections of the site and his position in the site structure hierarchy. Each node in the tree is rendered as a hyperlink that whisks the user to the appropriate section when clicked.

Let's add a TreeView to the Home section (`Default.aspx` in the root directory). To do so, we must first add a SiteMapDataSource control to the page; this control can be found in the Data section of the Toolbox. Next, add the TreeView control to the page and, from its smart tag, specify the data source as the SiteMapDataSource we just added to the page. After we specify the TreeView's data source, the TreeView's appearance in the Design view will be updated, mirroring the hierarchy expressed in site map.

Take a moment to visit this page through a browser (see Figure 19.8). When trying out this control, notice that you can jump to any section in the site by clicking the appropriate section title in the TreeView. Furthermore, you can expand or collapse the TreeView's nodes by clicking on the + or - icons on the left of those nodes that have children nodes. Also, note that the SiteMapDataSource control does not cause any visual effect in the browser. The SiteMapDataSource, just like the SqlDataSourceControl examined in previous hours, simply retrieves data from a source—in particular, the site map—and does *not* render into HTML markup.

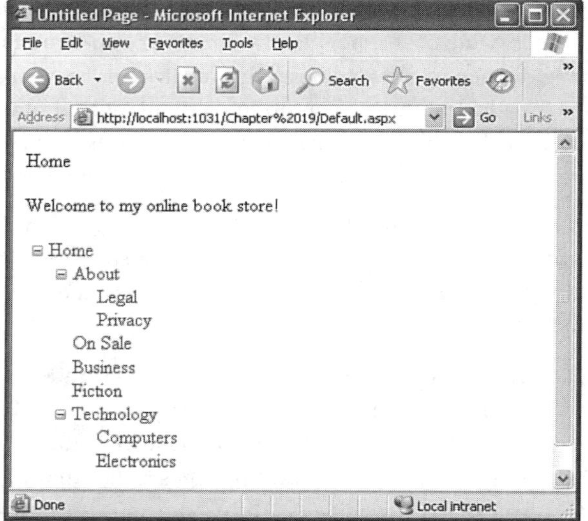

FIGURE 19.8 The TreeView's structure mirrors the site map.

Customizing the TreeView's Appearance

Like the SiteMapPath control, the TreeView contains a number of appearance-related properties, as well as an Auto Format option, that we can use to highly customize the look and feel of the TreeView. The TreeView is made up of a number of **nodes**, with each node representing a section defined in the site map. Each node has zero or one parent nodes and zero to many children nodes. For example, in the TreeView shown in Figure 19.8, the Home node has no parent and five children—About, On Sale, Business, Fiction, and Technology. The About node has one parent—Home—and two children—Legal and Privacy. The Business node has one parent—Home—and no children.

The four types of nodes in a TreeView are

- **Root Nodes**—These nodes have no parent (Home).
- **Parent Nodes**—These are nodes other than the Root Nodes that have children nodes (About and Technology).
- **Leaf Nodes**—These nodes have a parent but no children nodes (Legal, Privacy, Business, Fiction, Computers, and Technology).
- **Selected Node**—The selected node is the one that corresponds to the current page being visited. So when we're visiting the Home section, the Home node is the Selected Node; when we're visiting the Business books section, Business is the Selected Node.

Each of these types of nodes has style properties, which can be found in the Styles section of the Properties window. These style properties, which have subproperties like `BackColor`, `BorderColor`, `BorderWidth`, `BorderStyle`, `Font`, and so on, affect the appearance of these classes of nodes. For example, setting the `LeafNodeStyle` property's `BackColor` subproperty to Red will cause all Leaf Nodes to have a red background color.

In addition to the `RootNodeStyle`, `ParentNodeStyle`, `LeafNodeStyle`, and `SelectedNodeStyle` style properties, there are two additional node-related style properties: `NodeStyle` and `HoverNodeStyle`. `NodeStyle` specifies the default style applied to all nodes in the TreeView. `HoverNodeStyle` indicates the style settings to be applied when the user hovers his mouse pointer over a particular node.

Did you Know?

> Using the `HoverNodeStyle` property helps to provide feedback to the visitor, showing him what node he's currently hovered over. Personally, I like to set the `HoverNodeStyle`'s `ForeColor` and `BackColor` properties to complementary values, both of which stand out from the default node style.

The Styles section in the Properties window also includes a `LevelStyles` property. This property allows you to specify style information for particular levels of the TreeView, with the first level being the set of Root Nodes, the second level being those nodes that are children of the first-level nodes, the third level being the children of the second-level nodes, and so on. To specify a unique style for each level, go to the `LevelStyles` property in the Properties window and click the ellipses icon to the right of the property name. This will bring up the TreeNodeStyle Collection Editor dialog box, from which you can define the style for each level.

Click the Add button to add a new level to the list of levels on the left. For each level, you can specify its appearance-related properties from the list on the right.

Note that the topmost level in the list on the left corresponds to the first level (the set of Root Nodes), while the second level from the top corresponds to the second level (the children of the Root Nodes), and so on. Figure 19.9 shows the TreeNodeStyle Collection Editor dialog box for a TreeView control that has the style settings made for the first two levels.

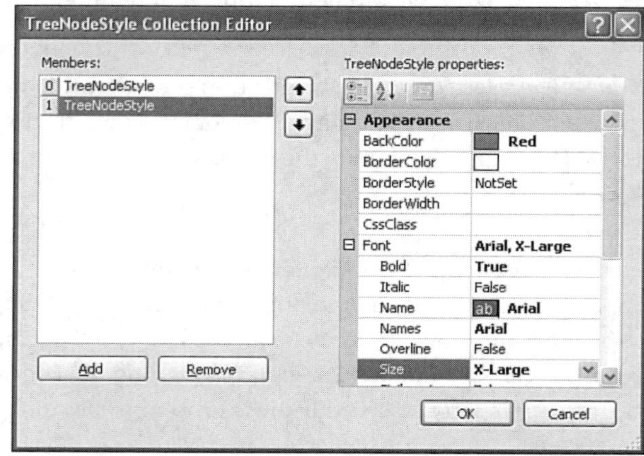

FIGURE 19.9 The styles for the TreeView's first two levels have been specified.

In addition to the properties in the Styles section of the Properties window, the TreeView contains a number of styles in the Appearances section worth noting. Of course, there are the usual properties—`BackColor`, `CssClass`, `Font`, and so on—but there are also a number of TreeView-specific properties. These appearance-related TreeView-specific properties are listed in Table 19.2.

TABLE 19.2 The TreeView-specific Appearance Properties

Property Name	Description
`CollapseImageTooltip` `ExpandImageTooltip`	Indicate the tooltip shown to the end user when she hovers the mouse pointer over the collapse or expand icons for a node. Any instances of `{0}` in the property value are replaced with the node's text. For example, an `ExpandImageTooltip` value of `Expand {0}` would display `"Expand Home"` when the user hovers her mouse pointer over the Home node's expand icon. (A **tooltip** is a small yellow box with a brief explanation or help message that appears when the user's mouse pointer hovers over a particular region on the web page.)

TABLE 19.2 Continued

Property Name	Description

`CollapseImageUrl`
`ExpandImageUrl`
`NoExpandImageUrl`
	Specify the image URLs to use for the collapse and expand icons for non-Leaf Nodes (those that can be expanded or collapsed), as well as the image to use for Leaf nodes (those nodes that cannot be expanded or collapsed because they have no children). You can also use the `ImageSet` property to indicate the collapse and expand icons.

`ImageSet`	Allows the TreeView's images to be custom defined or based on a packaged set of predefined images. Set this property to `Custom` to choose your own images or pick one of the numerous options to use predefined images. Defaults to `Custom`.
`NodeIndent`	Specifies the number of pixels to indent each level of the TreeView. Defaults to 20.
`NodeWrap`	Specifies a Boolean property that indicates whether a node's text should be wrapped. Defaults to `False`.
`ShowExpandCollapse`	Specifies a Boolean property that indicates whether the expand and collapse icons are shown. Defaults to `True`.
`ShowLines`	Specifies a Boolean property that indicates whether lines are drawn between each node and level in the TreeView. This property can also be turned on or off from the TreeView's smart tag.

The `ImageSet` property provides a list of packaged images to display next to each icon. This list includes choices like `WindowsHelp`, `BulletedList`, `Events`, and `Contacts`, each providing a different set of images for expand and collapse icons for non-Leaf Nodes, as well as images for the nonexpandable, noncollapsible Leaf Nodes. (Figure 19.10 shows the icons used when the `ImageSet` property is set to `Contacts`.) If you want to provide your own images, set `ImageSet` to `Custom` and then provide the URLs to your custom images in the `CollapseImageUrl`, `ExpandImageUrl`, and `NoExpandImageUrl` properties.

If you would rather let Visual Web Developer choose the appearance-related property settings, you can always use the Auto Format option, which is available through the TreeView's smart tag. Figure 19.10 shows the TreeView's Auto Format dialog box when choosing the Contacts Auto Format option.

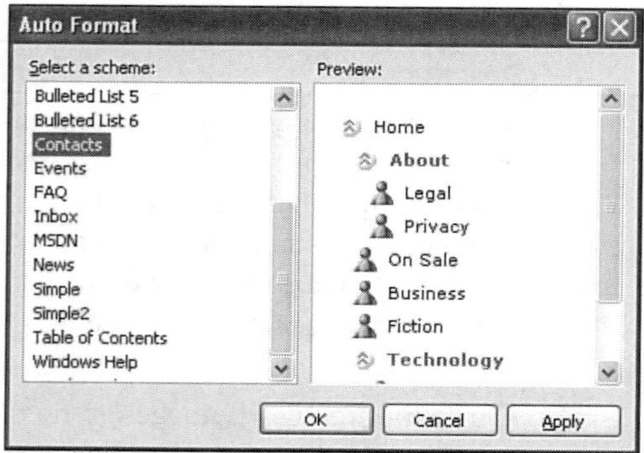

FIGURE 19.10 Let the Auto Format dialog box help you improve the appearance of the TreeView.

Using Menus to Show the Site's Structure

Like the TreeView control, the Menu control displays the entire contents of the site map. Rather than displaying the contents of the site map as a tree, however, the Menu control displays the items using a menu interface. By default, each section defined in the site map is rendered as an item in the menu with submenus used to reflect the hierarchy. To display navigation using a Menu control, we must first add a SiteMapDataSource control to the page that will contain the menu.

Let's add a Menu control to the `Default.aspx` page in the `Fiction` folder. Open this page in Visual Web Developer and start by adding a SiteMapDataSource control; next, add the Menu control, setting its data source to the SiteMapDataSource control just added. After you specify the Menu control's data source, the Menu will be updated in the Design view to reflect the structure of the site map. By default, the menu will show all top-level elements in the site structure hierarchy—Home, for our site map.

After setting the data source, take a minute to view this page in a browser. On the page the menu contains just a single displayed menu item, Home. If you move your mouse pointer over the Home item, though, a submenu appears, listing About, On Sale, Business, Fiction, and Technology. If you move your mouse pointer over About or Technology, another submenu appears, listing the appropriate items (see Figure 19.11). Clicking on a menu item will whisk you to the corresponding section in the site.

Configuring the Menu's Static and Dynamic Portions

A Menu control is composed of both a static and dynamic portion. The static portion of the menu is always shown when viewing the page, whereas the dynamic portion is shown only when the user interacts with the menu. By default, only the top-level sections in the site map are static; all other site map sections are placed in the dynamic portion. In Figure 19.11, only the Home menu item is shown when the page loads; the other sections are displayed only when the user interacts with the menu, hovering the mouse pointer over the Home menu item.

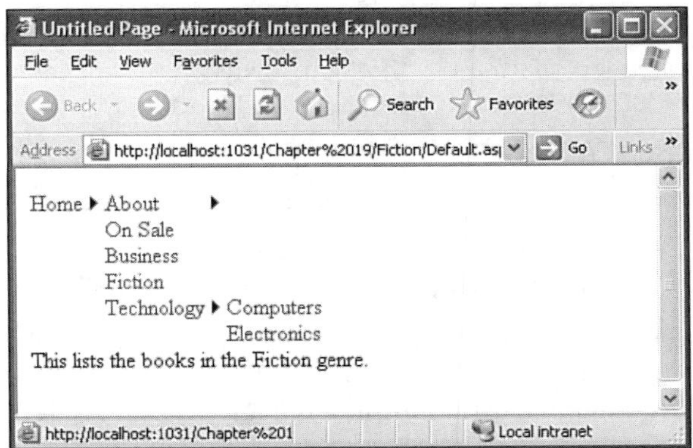

FIGURE 19.11 The menu's Home and Technology options have been selected.

The number of levels in the site map hierarchy that make up the static portion of the menu can be specified by the menu control's `StaticDisplayLevels` property. The default value for this property is 1. If we change this to 2, however, all of the sections in the first or second levels of the site map hierarchy—Home, About, On Sale, Business, Fiction, and Technology—will be shown as static menu items. Figure 19.12 shows the Menu control in the Visual Web Developer Design view after the `StaticDisplayLevels` property has been set to 2.

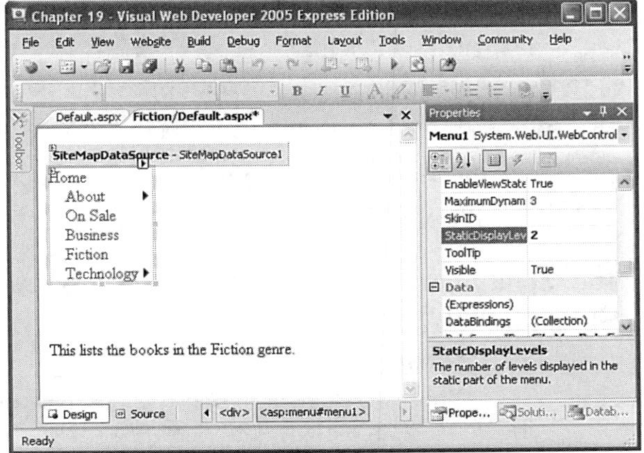

FIGURE 19.12 The menu shows the first two levels of the site map hierarchy statically.

Now instead of just the Home menu item showing when the page loads, Home, About, On Sale, Business, Fiction, and Technology will be displayed. The third level, which includes Legal, Privacy, Computers, and Electronics, will still be displayed in the dynamic portion. That is, the user will have to hover her mouse pointer over the About menu item to be able to see the Privacy or Legal menu items.

When the user's mouse pointer leaves a dynamically displayed submenu, the submenu stays for a period specified by the Menu control's `DisappearAfter` property. This value defaults to 500 milliseconds, which leaves a dynamic menu displayed for 0.5 seconds after the user's mouse pointer leaves the submenu. You can increase or decrease this time as needed.

Customizing the Menu's Appearance

The Menu control contains a wide array of appearance-related properties, far too many to cover them all in this hour. Rather than enumerate all of these properties, we'll instead look at the more germane ones and focus on the concepts as opposed to the specifics.

As always, I encourage you to tinker around with all of the Menu control's properties, not just those that we cover here. Try changing them and observe the effects; review the description of the properties using the MSDN Library. (We discussed using the MSDN Library in Hour 3, "Using Visual Web Developer.")

You should not be surprised that the Menu control has the base set of appearance-related properties: `BackColor`, `ForeColor`, `Font`, and the like. In addition to these properties, it has appearance-related properties for the dynamic and static portions of the Menu. The names of these properties start with either `Static` or `Dynamic`, such as `StaticItemFormatString` and `DynamicItemFormatString`. The prefix indicates whether the property value applies to the dynamic or static portion of the Menu control.

Table 19.3 lists a number of the Menu control's appearance-related properties. Figure 19.13 shows a Menu control after a number of these properties have been set.

TABLE 19.3 The Menu Control Contains Properties That Apply to Its Dynamic and Static Portions

Property Name	Description
`DynamicEnableDefaultPopOutImage` `StaticEnableDefaultPopOutImage`	Specify a Boolean property that indicates whether an image is displayed to show that an item has a submenu. Defaults to `True`. In Figure 19.11, the arrow icon next to Home was present because `StaticEnableDefaultPopOutImage` was set to `True`, and the arrow image next to About and Technology was present because `DynamicEnableDefaultPopOutImage` was set to `True`.

TABLE 19.3 Continued

Property Name	Description
`DynamicItemFormatString` `StaticItemFormatString`	Specify the text displayed in the menu item. Use `{0}` to inject the title of the menu item's corresponding site map section. That is, using `Visit {0}` would display `"Visit Business"` (instead of `"Business"`) for the Business menu item.
`DynamicPopOutImageTextFormatString` `StaticPopOutImageTextFormatString`	Specify the tooltip text displayed for the pop out image. Include a `{0}` to inject the current site map section's title.
`DynamicPopOutImageUrl` `StaticPopOutImageUrl`	Specify the URL to your own image if you want to use a pop-out image other than the default arrow.
`StaticSubMenuIndent`	Specifies the indentation between a static menu item and its static submenu. As Figure 19.12 shows, when displaying multiple levels in the static portion, there's an indentation between levels. Use this property to tailor the amount of indentation. (Defaults to 16 pixels.)
`Orientation`	Specifies whether the menu is laid out horizontally or vertically. Can be either `Vertical` or `Horizontal`; defaults to `Vertical`..
`DynamicHorizontalOffset` `DynamicVerticalOffset`	Specify the offset in pixels between the right border of a menu item and the left border of its submenu item (or of the bottom border of a menu item and the top border of its submenu item). Both properties default to 0.
`ItemWrap`	Specifies a Boolean property that indicates whether the text in a menu item should be wrapped. Defaults to `False`.

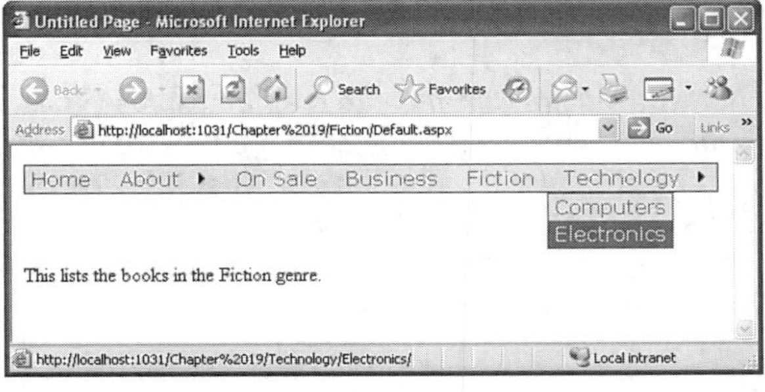

FIGURE 19.13 This menu has a `Horizontal Orientation` and was further customized with Auto Format.

Did you Know?

Like the SiteMapPath and TreeView controls examined earlier in this hour, the Menu control also offers an Auto Format option, which is available through its smart tag.

Furthermore, the Menu control has a number of properties in the Styles section of its Properties window that you can use to customize the appearance of the static and dynamic submenus and menu items.

Summary

In this hour we saw how to create a site structure and navigation using ASP.NET's new site map and navigation Web controls. The site map is an XML-formatted file that expresses the structural hierarchy of a website. Often it helps to first sketch out the proposed site structure (as we did in Figure 19.3) and then convert the items in the sketch into the appropriate XML elements in the site map file.

After the site map file has been created, the three ASP.NET navigation Web controls can be used. The SiteMapPath displays a breadcrumb, showing the user the current page he is visiting and its location in the site structure hierarchy. The TreeView and Menu controls display the entire site map, either in a tree or in a menu. To use either of these controls, you need to first add a SiteMapDataSource control to the page.

All three of these controls offer a high degree of customization, making it easy to tailor the appearance of the navigation controls to fit your site's look and feel. Furthermore, there is a clean separation between the navigation controls and the site map, making updating the site's structure a breeze. If you wanted to add a new section to your site or remove some existing sections, you would need to update only the site map file. The navigation controls throughout the site would automatically reflect these changes.

Q&A

Q. ***Why does ASP.NET require that the site map be expressed as a particularly formatted XML file? What if I already have a database or my own custom XML file with site structure information? Or what if I want the site map to be based on my website's folder structure and don't want to have to bother with mirroring the folder structure in the site map file? Does that mean I can't use the ASP.NET navigation controls?***

A. Actually, ASP.NET allows for developers to specify their own site map formats. You can create your own **site map provider** that would allow for a different mechanism for storing the site map information. A site map provider is a class that you would write to instruct ASP.NET on how to retrieve site map information. The default site map provider uses an XML file with the format we examined in this hour; however, there's no reason why you couldn't create your own provider.

A discussion on creating and working with custom providers is beyond the scope of this book. If you are interested in learning more, though, be sure to check out the articles at http://msdn.microsoft.com/library/en-us/dnaspp/html/extndsitenv.asp and http://msdn.microsoft.com/library/en-us/dnaspp/html/custsitemap.asp.

Q. ***In this chapter we added various navigation controls to various pages. If I want the Menu or SiteMapPath control to exist on all pages in my site, must I manually go to each page and add the appropriate controls, or is there a better way?***

A. When creating a website, typically we want all pages to have a similar look and feel, such as all pages having a menu across the top. A naïve way to accomplish this is to simply repeat the desired look and feel on each page. This approach, though, is asking for trouble, because if we decide to update our site's look, we then need to make changes to each and every page in the site!

A better approach is to use **master pages**. Master pages allow us to create a single page that specifies a standard look and feel. For example, the master page may contain a menu along the top and a list of common links at the bottom of the page. Then, when creating a new page, we can specify that it use the master page. The result is that all pages that use the master page will have a consistent look and feel. Furthermore, any changes to the master page are immediately reflected on those pages that use that master page, thereby making updating the site's appearance as easy as editing the master page.

We'll examine master pages in depth in Hour 21, "Using Master Pages to Provide Sitewide Page Templates."

Workshop

Quiz

1. What name must you give the site map file?
2. True or False: The site map file can appear in any folder in the web project.
3. What attributes can be found in the `<siteMapNode>` element?

4. What control must be added to the page to have the TreeView or Menu controls display the site's structure?

5. What is the difference between the static and dynamic portions of the Menu control?

Answers

1. `Web.sitemap`.

2. False. The site map file must appear in the web project's root directory.

3. The `<siteMapNode>` can contain the `url`, `title`, and `description` attributes.

4. The SiteMapDataSource control.

5. The static portion of a Menu control is always shown in the user's browser. The dynamic portion is shown only when the user interacts with the menu in some manner.

Exercises

1. Alter the site map created during this hour so that a new section titled Books is created. When specifying the Books section in the site map file, do *not* provide a value for the `url` attribute.

   Move the Business, Fiction, and Technology sections (and their subsections) to reside underneath this new Books section. Additionally, move the On Sale section here as well. Figure 19.14 shows the new site structure hierarchy.

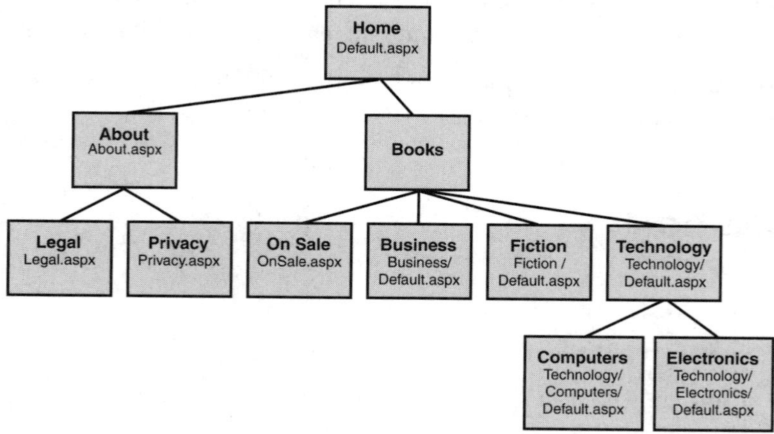

FIGURE 19.14
The Books section has been added.

2. In this hour we looked at only a handful of the Menu control's appearance-related properties. In particular, we didn't examine any of the properties in the Styles section of the Properties window.

Add a Menu control (and, of course, a SiteMapDataSource control) to the `Legal.aspx` page and practice with these Styles properties, noting the effects in the Design view and when visiting the page through a browser. Finally, be sure to try out the level-related style properties—`LevelMenuItemStyles`, `LevelSelectedStyles`, and `LevelSubMenuStyles`. These level-related style properties are similar to the `LevelStyles` property of the TreeView control.

HOUR 20

Managing Your Site's Users

In this hour, we will cover

- How to configure a website to support user accounts
- How and where user account information is stored
- Creating and managing user accounts and roles through the ASP.NET Website Administration Tool
- Granting and denying access to folders based on users, user type, or role
- Logging users on to the site using the Login control
- Recovering a user's forgotten password with the PasswordRecovery control

Starting in Hour 22, "Devising a Plan for the Photo Album Application," we will begin looking at how to create a website that allows users to upload and share their digital pictures. Such an application requires **user accounts**, which store information about a particular user. When a user wants to upload an image to his photo album, he'll first need to **log on** to the site by providing a username and password. This logon process identifies the user so that we can associate him with his account.

If you bank online or have ever purchased an item from an online retailer, then you're already familiar with the process of creating an account and logging on to a website from the end user's perspective. But what steps are required from the web developer's perspective to add support for user accounts? How and where does a web developer store user account information? What steps need to be taken to create a new user? How does a user log on to the site or log off?

Because user accounts are an increasingly common requirement for websites, the ASP.NET team has included a plethora of features designed to make supporting user accounts as easy as possible. As we'll see in this hour, we can configure our website to support user accounts with just a few clicks of the mouse. When the website has been configured properly, the login Web controls provide the user interface necessary for performing user account-related tasks, including logging in and out of the site, creating a new user account, sending a forgotten password, and so on.

An Overview of User Accounts in ASP.NET

When you make a purchase from an online retailer for the first time, you are prompted to create a **user account**. When creating a user account, you are prompted to enter information that uniquely identifies you, along with some bit of information known only to you. This identification information is referred to as **credentials**. Typically, the credentials for a site are your username and password, although some websites use an email address and password, or require not only a password, but also a personal identification number (PIN).

In addition to credentials a user account can also store additional user-specific information. An online retailer would likely collect billing information and a shipping address, while an online banking site might require that you provide your account numbers, Social Security number, and so on. After a user account has been created, you can log in to the site by providing your credentials.

A site that supports user accounts must store the user account information somewhere; most often, this information is stored in a database. Commonly, websites that need to provide such support will add a database table called `Users` (or something similar) that has one record for each user account in the system. The columns for this table would have names like `Username`, `Password`, `Email`, and so on. Once this database table has been defined, the process of creating a user account becomes trivial because it simply involves creating an ASP.NET page that prompts the user for the required inputs—username, password, and so on—and stores this information in a database. (We saw how to insert records into a database table in Hour 16, "Deleting, Inserting, and Editing Data.")

Fortunately, with ASP.NET version 2.0, you do not need to create your own user account database tables because ASP.NET now provides built-in support for user accounts through a feature called **membership**. To take advantage of this feature, we first must configure our website to support membership.

Configuring an ASP.NET Website to Support Membership

To configure our website to support membership, we must launch the ASP.NET Website Administration Tool. To accomplish this, either click the ASP.NET

Configuration icon at the top of the Solution Explorer or click the Website menu's ASP.NET Configuration option. Either way will open a web browser pointed to a page through which the ASP.NET site can be configured. Figure 20.1 shows the ASP.NET Website Administration Tool.

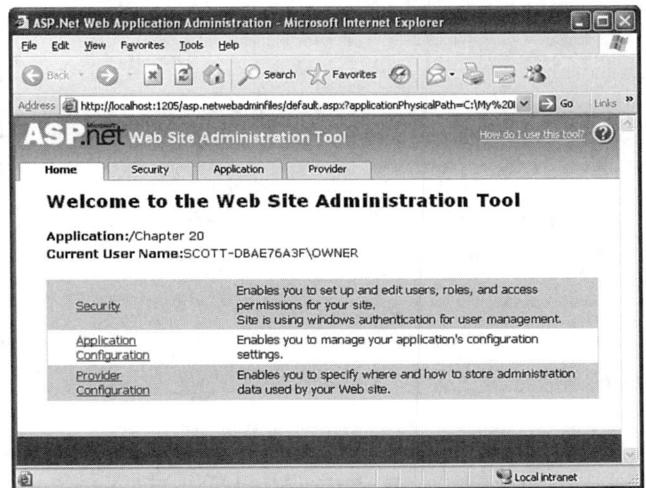

FIGURE 20.1
Configure your website through the ASP.NET Website Administration Tool.

Did you Know?

For help on using the ASP.NET Website Administration Tool, click the `"How do I use this tool?"` link in the upper-right corner of the web page.

To add user account support, click the `Security` link. This will take you to the Security screen shown in Figure 20.2. From this screen, you can specify the user accounts in your system, what roles for users exist, and the access rules for users.

By default, an ASP.NET website is set up to use **Windows authentication**. **Authentication** is the process of identifying the authenticity of a user. For Internet sites that support user accounts, typically authentication is achieved by prompting users for their credentials in a logon page. This style of authentication is commonly referred to as **forms-based authentication** because users are prompted for their credentials through a form. Windows authentication, on the other hand, is useful if you are building a website that is used on an **intranet**. An intranet is a local, private network within a company or organization. In such a setting, users typically log on to the network from their desktop computers. They can then visit the intranet and, because they've already logged on to their workstations, this logon information can be detected automatically by the intranet web server.

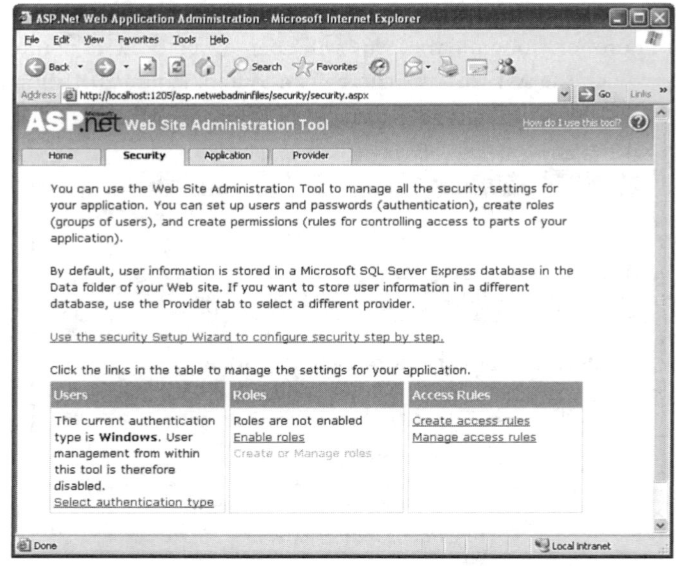

FIGURE 20.2
Configure your website's security-related settings from the Security screen.

By the Way

In this book we will be examining only **forms-based authentication**. If you are developing an application on an intranet, you'll likely want to explore Windows authentication.

To change the current authentication model from Windows authentication to forms-based authentication, click on the link titled `Select authentication type` at the bottom of the Users box. This will load the screen shown in Figure 20.3, where you can select how users will access your site:

- **From the Internet**—This option configures the website to use forms-based authentication and creates the necessary database tables to support membership.
- **From a local network**—This option configures the website to use Windows authentication.

Select the From the Internet radio button and click the Done button. Doing so will not only configure your application to use forms-based authentication, but will also automatically create a SQL Server 2005 Express Edition database named `ASPNETDB` with predesigned tables to support user accounts.

When you return to the Security screen, the Users box should now list the number of existing users—0—along with links titled `Create user` and `Manage users`.

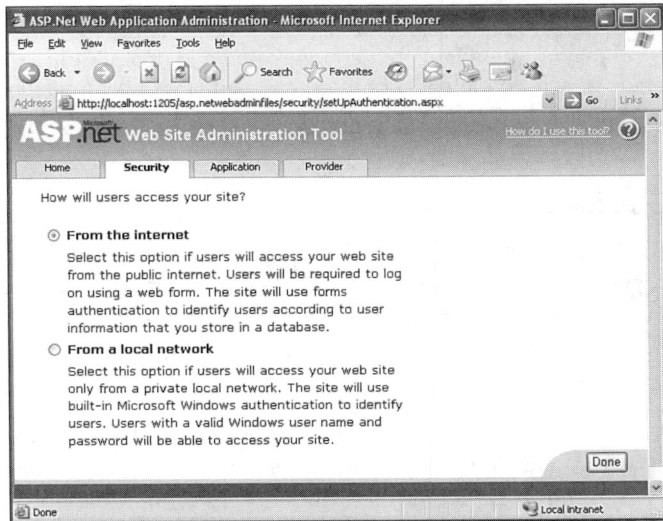

FIGURE 20.3
Indicate that users will connect to your site from the Internet.

Let's examine the `ASPNETDB` database that was created for us. Close the ASP.NET Website Administration Tool, returning to Visual Web Developer. From the Solution Explorer, right-click on the `App_Data` folder and choose Refresh Folder. You should now see the `ASPNETDB.MDF` file listed in this folder. Go to the Database Explorer and drill down into the tables of the `ASPNETDB` database. There are 11 tables in total, providing functionality that extends beyond simple user accounts.

For now, concentrate on just the `aspnet_Users` and `aspnet_Membership` tables. These database tables store user account information. That is, for each user account in the website, there will be a corresponding record in these two tables. The `aspnet_Users` table contains the base set of columns to identify a user, essentially his username. The `aspnet_Membership` table has columns that provide information required for a user account, such as his email address, password, last login date, date the account was created, security question and answer (in case the user forgets his password), and so on.

By the Way

The `aspnet_Users` and `aspnet_Membership` tables illustrate two related database tables, a common database concept mentioned in previous hours. A record in either table is uniquely identified by the `UserId` field (in database vernacular, the `UserId` column in the primary key column). Furthermore, a **foreign-key constraint** ensures that for each `UserId` in `aspnet_Membership` there is a matching `UserId` in `aspnet_Users`, thereby cementing the relationship between these two tables.

A foreign-key constraint is a special database rule that ensures that one column in one table contains a value from some other column in another table. These constraints help ensure the integrity of the data used to establish relationships between tables.

Creating and Managing Users

To accompany the user account database, ASP.NET ships with a number of login Web controls, one of which allows a user to create a new account. However, as the site administrator, you can also add new users through the ASP.NET Website Administration Tool. In addition to creating new user accounts, you can also manage existing user accounts.

To create a new user account through the ASP.NET Website Administration Tool, go to the Security screen and click on the `Create user` link in the Users box. This will bring up the screen shown in Figure 20.4, which is very similar to the screen users will see when creating a new account themselves.

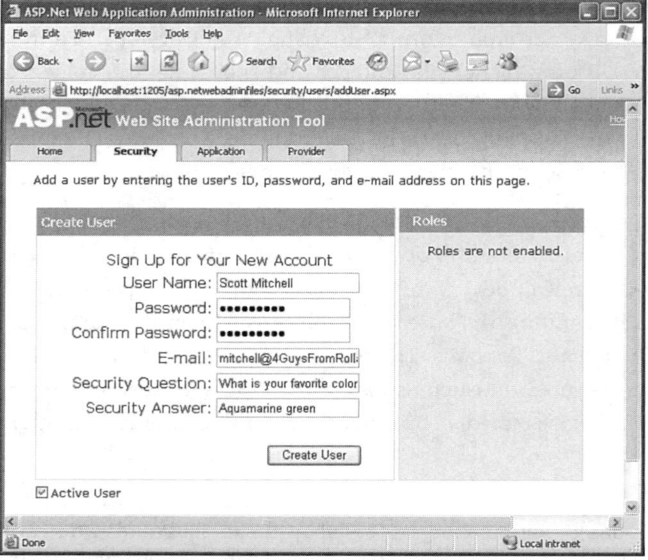

FIGURE 20.4 Create a new user account.

To create a new user account, simply provide the username, password, email, and security question for the new user and then click the Create User button. The security question is asked if the user forgets her password and wants to be reminded. The security answer is the answer the user must provide to be able to see her password.

When we're creating a new user account—either here, through the ASP.NET Website Administration Tool, or through the website using the CreateUserWizard control as we'll see in the "Allowing Visitors to Create New User Accounts" section—a number of validation checks are automatically made. You must provide values for the username, password, confirm password, and security question and answer text boxes. Furthermore, the username must be unique, the password must meet a certain password "strength" (by default, be seven characters long with at least one nonalphanumeric character), and the email address must in the proper format.

If you enter invalid data when creating a new user, a validation error message will be displayed, prohibiting the new user account from being created until the errors are corrected.

To manage the set of existing users, click on the `Manage users` link in the Security screen. This will take you to the screen shown in Figure 20.5, which lists all user accounts in the system. You can edit or delete users, or mark them as active or inactive.

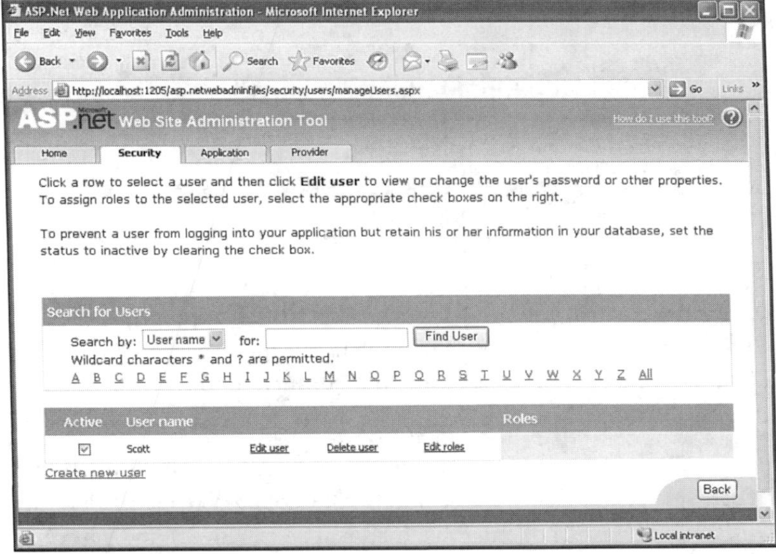

FIGURE 20.5
Edit and delete users from the "Manage users" screen.

Classifying Users by Role

You may have noticed the Roles functionality from the Security screen and the screens for managing and creating users. With roles, you can categorize users and then allow or deny functionality based on users' roles. For example, you may have a site that requires user accounts, with users divided into two groups: administrators and nonadministrators. Those users added to the administrator role might be able to access web pages in a certain folder that were off-limits to nonadministrators.

If you need to classify users by roles, click the `Enable roles` link in the Roles box of the Security screen. This will turn on role support, after which you can create and manage the roles in the system by clicking the `Create or Manage roles` link. Figure 20.6 shows the Create or Manage Roles screen, into which I've added two roles: Administrator and Non-Administrator.

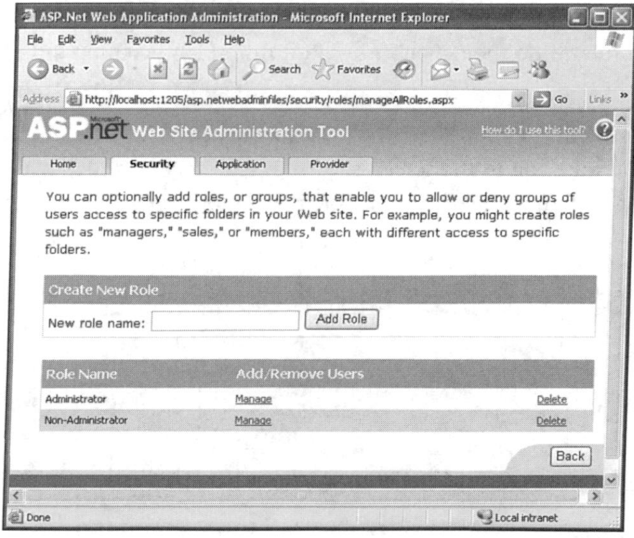

FIGURE 20.6 Two roles have been added to the system: Administrators and Non-Administrators.

After the roles are created, you need to assign users to the appropriate roles. Clicking the `Manage` link shows a listing of the users who belong to the selected role. You can add new users to the role by searching for them and then checking the User Is in Role check box (see Figure 20.7).

Rather than adding users to a role, you can assign roles to a user through the Manage Users screen (see Figure 20.5). Simply click the `Edit roles` link for the particular user. A check box list of available roles will be displayed, and you can select which roles, if any, the user belongs to.

By the Way

Role information is stored in the `ASPNETDB` database's `aspnet_Roles` table. The association between users and roles is captured by the `aspnet_UsersInRoles` table.

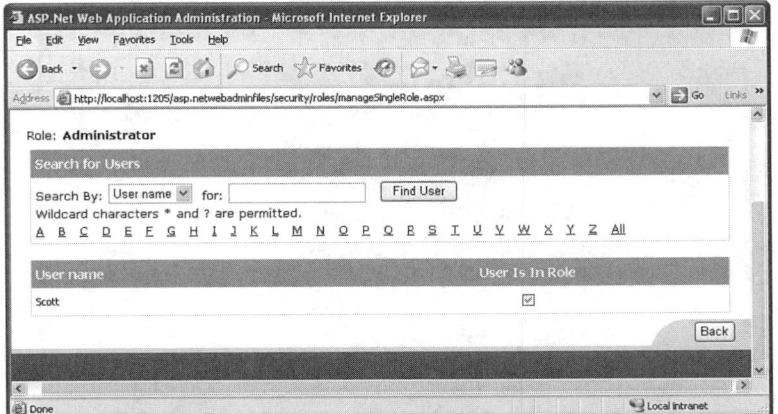

FIGURE 20.7
User Scott has been added to the Administrators role.

Creating and Managing Access Rules

Once you have users or roles defined in the system, you can, optionally, specify access rules. Access rules dictate what rights particular users or roles have to particular folders in the website. As discussed earlier, you might want to allow only users in the Administrators role to access web pages in a particular folder. Or you might want to require that only logged-in users can visit a certain folder in the website.

To create an access rule, go to the Security screen and click on the `Create access rules` link in the Access Rules box in the lower-right corner. This will take you to the screen shown in Figure 20.8. From here, you can select what folder the access rule applies to; whether the access rule applies to a role, a particular user, all users, or anonymous users; and whether the rule is to allow or deny access.

By the Way

> An anonymous user is one who has yet to log in to the site—that is, a user who has yet to be authenticated.

Because our website currently lacks any folders other than the default `App_Data` folder, we really can't define meaningful access rules unless we want them to apply to the whole site. Take a minute to add two folders to the project: `Admin` and `Users`. Don't bother adding any ASP.NET pages to either of these folders, we'll do that later in this hour. For now, understand that those web pages in the `Admin` folder are meant to be accessed only by users in the Administrators role, while those pages in the `Users` folder are meant to be accessed only by logged-on users.

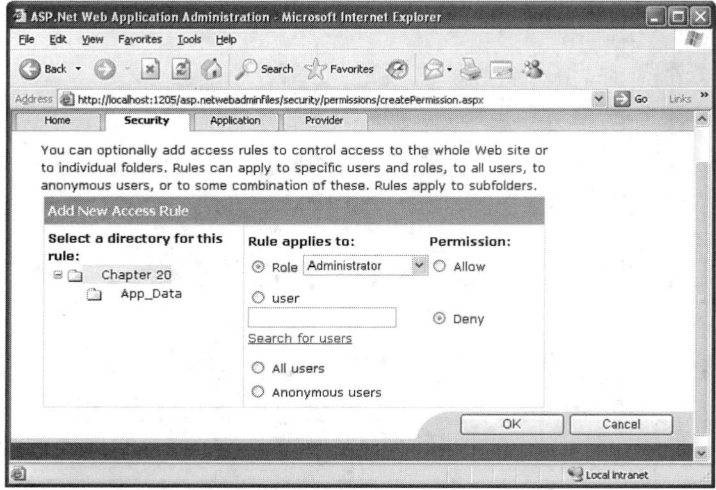

FIGURE 20.8 Define the access rules for the folders of your website.

To achieve these access rights, we would add the following rights via this screen:

- For the `Admin` folder, allow access for the Administrators role.
- For the `Admin` folder, deny access to all users.
- For the `Users` folder, deny access to anonymous users.

Notice that for the `Admin` folder we first allowed access for Administrators, but then denied access to all users. This might seem a bit confusing at first. Why not just allow access for Administrators and be done at that?

If you do not explicitly deny access to a particular role or user type, then those particular users can access that resource. So simply allowing Administrators to access the `Admin` folder would also permit others to view this folder because we did not explicitly deny access to these users who do not belong to the Non-Administrators role. At this point you may be wondering why we did not just simply deny access to the Non-Administrators role. This logic falls short because not every user must be in the Administrators or Non-Administrators role; users could be in no role. Therefore, we needed to both allow Administrators to access this folder and deny all users.

> Readers who are keen logicians may still see a bit of a paradox here because users in the Administrators role are still in the set of all users. Since there's the deny access to all users rule, won't even Administrators be denied access to the `Admin` folder?

When a user attempts to access a resource, ASP.NET processes the rules from the top down. So it says, "Is this user in the Administrators role? If so, she can access this folder." If the user is indeed in the Administrators role, then she is granted access. If she is not, ASP.NET proceeds to the next rule and asks, "Is this user in the set of all users? If so, then deny access."

To delete existing access rules or reorder the rules for a particular folder, click on the `Manage access rules` link from the Security screen. This will take you to a screen that lists the access rules for a selected folder. From here, you can remove any access rules or reorder the existing access rules.

By the Way

Whereas the user accounts and roles are stored in the `ASPNETDB` database, the access rights are stored in the configuration file, `web.config`. Specifically, a `web.config` file is added to each folder that has access rights specified, along with an `<authorization>` element that spells out the access rights for that folder.

At this point we have seen how to configure an ASP.NET website to support user accounts. Doing so automatically creates the needed database (`ASPNETDB`) and database tables (`aspnet_Users`, `aspnet_Membership`, `aspnet_Roles`, and `aspnet_UsersInRoles`). With the user account system set up, we can use ASP.NET's login Web controls in our website to allow visitors to create a new account and log in and out of the site. We'll examine these login controls throughout the remainder of this hour.

Configuring a Website's SMTP Settings

As we will see later in this hour, a number of the login Web controls provide built-in email features. For example, the CreateUserWizard control can be configured such that when a user creates a new account, he is automatically sent an email that includes his username, password, and other information. For the login Web controls to be able to send emails, the website must be configured to support sending email. This can be accomplished through the ASP.NET Website Administration Tool.

When you launch the ASP.NET Website Administration Tool, the start page lists three options:

- Security
- Application Configuration
- Provider Configuration

In the preceding sections we examined the Security option. To configure the website to send email, choose the Application Configuration option. From the Application Configuration screen, click the `Configure SMTP e-mail settings` link; this will display the screen shown in Figure 20.9. From here, you can provide the email server name, port, and authentication information (if required), along with the address that the email messages will be sent from.

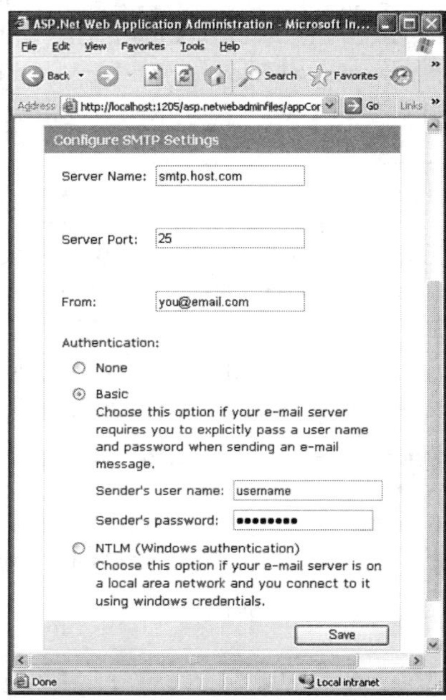

FIGURE 20.9
Configure your website's e-mail settings.

By the Way

Email messages are sent by sending the message to an **SMTP server**. The Configure SMTP E-Mail Settings screen prompts you for the requisite information needed to connect to an SMTP server. If you are hosting your website with a web-hosting company, it can provide you with the SMTP server, port, and authentication information needed. If you are not using a web-hosting company, you can configure the SMTP server settings to use the same SMTP server you use in your desktop email program.

After you have provided the appropriate values for the SMTP server through which emails will be sent, click the Save button. The settings specified in this screen are saved in the website's `web.config` file, in the `<mailSettings>` element; you can edit these values either directly through `web.config` or from the ASP.NET Website Administration Tool.

Allowing Visitors to Create New User Accounts

Although you can create user accounts through the ASP.NET Website Administration Tool, chances are you'll want to also allow users to create accounts on their own. This process can be handled by ASP.NET's CreateUserWizard login control, which provides a user interface very similar to that shown in the ASP.NET Website Administration Tool's Create User screen shown in Figure 20.4.

Let's create a new ASP.NET page in our website named `CreateAccount.aspx`. Add to the top of this page the text `Create an Account` and then drag the CreateUserWizard control from the Toolbox onto the page. (The CreateUserWizard control, along with the entire suite of login Web controls, can be found in the Login section of the Toolbox.) Figure 20.10 shows Visual Web Developer after this control has been added to the ASP.NET page.

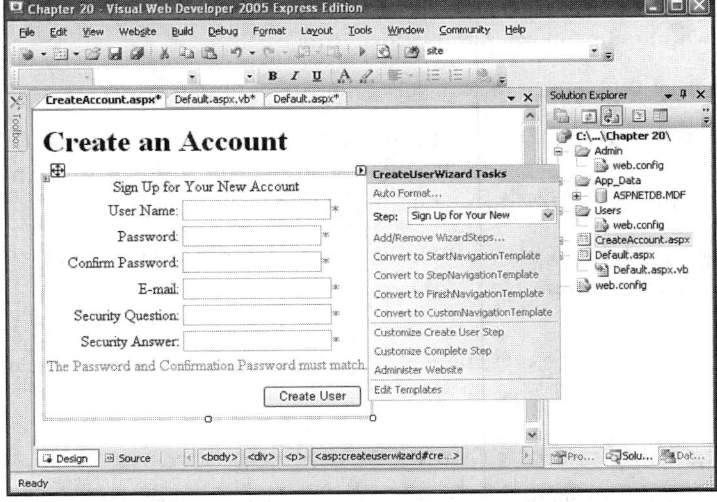

FIGURE 20.10 The CreateUserWizard login control allows the user to create an account.

The CreateUserWizard control is a **wizard Web control**. Wizard Web controls consist of a number of steps that the user progresses through. By default, the CreateUserWizard has two steps: Sign Up for Your New Account and Complete. The first step prompts the user to choose a username, password, email, and security question and answer, just as we did when creating the user through the ASP.NET Website Administration Tool. The user is taken to the Complete step after successfully creating an account; this step simply displays a `Your account has been created` message. You can toggle between the two steps through the CreateUserWizard control's smart tag.

Take a moment to try out the CreateUserWizard control in your browser. When you first visit the page, you'll see the Sign Up for Your New Account step. After entering your user account and clicking the Create User button, you'll be taken to the Complete step, informing you that your new account has been created. In addition to creating a new account, the user is also logged in as this newly created account.

Along with a message, the Complete step includes a Continue button. If you try to click it, you'll see that nothing happens. If you want the user to be whisked to a particular page after clicking this button, simply set the control's `ContinueDestinationPage` property to the appropriate URL. For our site, when the user clicks the Continue button, let's have him automatically sent back to `Default.aspx`; therefore, set the `ContinueDestinationPage` property to `Default.aspx`.

Customizing the CreateUserWizard Control

The CreateUserWizard control contains a cornucopia of properties that can be tweaked to customize the appearance. These appearance-related properties can be broken down into the following three classifications:

- Properties that dictate the control's colors, fonts, and borders.
- Properties that specify the text used for the user interface elements in the control. This includes elements like the labels preceding each text box, the default text in the text boxes, the text displayed in the buttons, and so on.
- Properties that indicate what bits of information are collected by the Create User Account Wizard.

Let's examine some of the more interesting properties from each of these classifications.

Adjusting the Control's Colors, Fonts, and Borders

Throughout this book we have seen many examples of properties that tweak a control's colors, fonts, and borders. Like virtually all other Web controls, the CreateUserWizard control has the common set of aesthetic properties, which include `BackColor`, `ForeColor`, `Font`, and so on. There are also a number of properties in the Styles section of the Properties window that define the appearance for various portions of the control.

For example, if you want to have each of the text box labels—User Name, Password, Confirm Password, E-mail, and so on—displayed in red using a bold font, you could set the `LabelStyle` property's `ForeColor` and `Font` subproperties accordingly. To customize the appearance of the text at the top of each step—Sign Up for Your New Account and Complete—use the `TitleTextStyle` property.

> Rather than manually setting these properties directly, I often start with the Auto Format option from the CreateUserWizard control's smart tag, which will set a number of these appearance-related properties. After Auto Format has done most of the work, I make any adjustments needed.

Specifying the Text for the Labels, Text Boxes, and Buttons

By default, the CreateUserWizard control labels each text box with text such as User Name, Password, Confirm Password, E-mail, and so on. Furthermore, it specifies default text for the error messages that may be displayed if the user enters an invalid email address or does not correctly duplicate her password in the Confirm Password text box. These defaults are all customizable through the control's properties, along with the text displayed in the Create User and Continue buttons. You can even provide default values for the text boxes in the create user step, if you so desire.

Table 20.1 lists a number of the properties that can be set to customize the labels, text boxes, and buttons in the control. For brevity, not all properties that fall into this classification are listed.

TABLE 20.1 The Text in the Labels, Text Boxes, and Buttons Can Be Customized

Property Name	Description
`UserNameLabelText`	Specifies the text displayed for the username text box label. (Defaults to `User Name:`.)
`UserName`	Provides the default value displayed in the username text box. (Empty, by default.)
`PasswordLabelText`	Specifies the text displayed for the password text box label. (Defaults to `Password:`.)
`ConfirmPasswordLabelText`	Specifies the text displayed for the confirm password text box label. (Defaults to `Confirm Password:`.)
`EmailLabelText`	Specifies the text displayed for the email text box label. (Defaults to `E-mail:`.)
`Email`	Provides the default value displayed in the email text box. (Empty, by default.)
`QuestionLabelText`	Specifies the text displayed for the security question text box label. (Defaults to `Security Question:`.)

TABLE 20.1 Continued

Property Name	Description
`Question`	Provides the default value displayed in the security question text box. (Empty, by default.)
`AnswerLabelText`	Specifies the text displayed for the security answer text box label. (Defaults to `Security Answer:`.)
`Answer`	Provides the default value displayed in the security answer text box. (Empty, by default.)
`CreateUserButtonText`	Specifies the text displayed in the Create User button.
`ContinueButtonText`	Specifies the text displayed in the Continue button.
`UserNameRequiredErrorMessage`	Specifies the error message that is displayed if the user does not provide a username. (Defaults to `User Name is required.`)
`PasswordRequiredErrorMessage`	Specifies the error message that is displayed if the user does not provide a password. (Defaults to `Password is required.`)
`EmailRequiredErrorMessage`	Specifies the error message that is displayed if the user does not provide an email address. (Defaults to `E-mail is required.`)

In addition to `UserNameRequiredErrorMessage`, `PasswordRequiredErrorMessage`, and `EmailRequiredErrorMessage`, there are a number of other error message properties. You can find all of them in the Validation section of the Properties window. In the next section we'll explore some properties that can prohibit certain questions from being asked, such as the user's email address. If the user is not prompted for his email address, then the `EmailRequiredErrorMessage` property becomes moot.

Dictating What Information Users Must Provide

By default, the CreateUserWizard control requires that the user provide a username, password, email address, and security question and answer to be able to create a new account. You can, however, decide whether to prompt the user for an email address or password. In the Behavior section of the Properties window, you'll find the `AutoGeneratePassword` and `RequireEmail` Boolean properties.

When `RequireEmail` is `True` (the default), the user is prompted to enter an email address when signing up. If you do not need to know the user's email address, you can set `RequireEmail` to `False`. I recommend leaving this property as `True` because it provides a communication channel between you and the user. Furthermore, various login Web controls, including the CreateUserWizard, provide the ability to email an informational message to the user. Of course, for this functionality to be utilized, the user's email address must be known.

The `AutoGeneratePassword` property, if `True`, does *not* prompt the user to enter and confirm a password; rather, the system automatically creates a random password. When `AutoGeneratePassword` is `False` (the default), the user chooses her own password.

A usability concern with assigning a random password is how to inform the user of this new password. That is, imagine that you set the `AutoGeneratePassword` property to `True`, thereby removing the Password and Confirm Password text boxes from the user interface. After the user enters his username, email address, and security question and answer, and clicks the Create User button, an account is created with a random password and the user is logged in. The problem is, the user doesn't know his password! How will he log back in to the site at some later point in time?

The common solution is to email the user his new, randomly selected password after he has created his account, along with instructions on how to change his password. To accomplish this, the CreateUserWizard control provides a `MailDefinition` property that can be configured to send an email to the user after he's created his account.

Emailing Users a Message After Creating Their Accounts

The CreateUserWizard control can optionally send an email message to the user who just created the account. This email message can provide the user with her username and password, along with any instructions and information necessary. To provide this functionality, the website must be configured to support sending email; we examined how to accomplish this earlier in this hour in the "Configuring a Website's SMTP Settings" section.

To send an email to new users, we must first define the content of the email message in a file. This file must exist within the website project and can be a text file or an HTML file, depending on whether you want the email message to be plain-text or HTML-formatted. In this file we can optionally use the placeholders `<%UserName%>` and `<%Password%>` to indicate where the user's username and password should appear.

Imagine that we wanted to send a user a plain-text email message that invited him to our site and contained just his username. We could accomplish this by creating a new text file in our website project with the contents shown in Listing 20.1. If, instead, we wanted to provide an HTML-formatted email that listed, say, both the user's username and password in a bulleted list, we could create an HTML file in our website project that contained the markup shown in Listing 20.2.

Did you Know?

> To add a text file or HTML page to your website, right-click on the project name in the Solution Explorer and choose the Add New Item menu option. In the Add New Item dialog box, you'll find Text file and HTML page file types.

LISTING 20.1 This Plain-text Email Includes the User's Username

```
Hello <%UserName%>!

You have just created a new account on MySite.com. Thanks!
You can login at any time by visiting http://MySite.com/Login.aspx

If you have any problems logging in, please contact help@mysite.com.
```

LISTING 20.2 This HTML-formatted Email Includes Both the Username and Password

```
<!DOCTYPE html PUBLIC "-//W3C//DTD XHTML 1.0 Transitional//EN"
➥"http://www.w3.org/TR/xhtml1/DTD/xhtml1-transitional.dtd">
<html xmlns="http://www.w3.org/1999/xhtml" >
  <head>
    <title>Welcome to My Website!</title>
    <style type="text/css">
      body { font-family: Verdana; font-size: medium; }
    </style>
  </head>
  <body>
    <h1>
      <span style="color: #990000; ">Welcome to My Website!</span>
    </h1>
    <p>
        According to our records you have created a new account on our
➥website. Your login
        information is:
    </p>
    <ul>
        <li>Username: <%UserName%></li>
        <li>Password: <%Password%></li>
    </ul>
    <p style="text-align: center">
        If you have any questions, please email me at </span>
        <a href="mailto:my@email.com"><em>my@email.com</em></a>
    </p>
  </body>
</html>
```

After the contents of the email message have been defined in a separate file, having the CreateUserWizard send the email message is as simple as setting a few subproperties in the control's `MailDefinition` property. The `MailDefinition` has four germane subproperties:

- `BodyFileName`—This is the name of the file that contains the email body of the message sent to the user who created the account.
- `From`—The from address of the email sent to the user. Recall that when the website was configured to support email, we specified a default from address. If you want this default from address used, simply leave this subproperty blank.
- `IsBodyHtml`—A Boolean property that indicates whether the email is sent as HTML-formatted or as plain-text. It defaults to `False`, meaning emails are sent as plain-text.
- `Subject`—The subject of the email message.

After these properties have been set, any newly created user will automatically receive an email. Figure 20.11 shows the email message received when the HTML-formatted email template from Listing 20.2 is used.

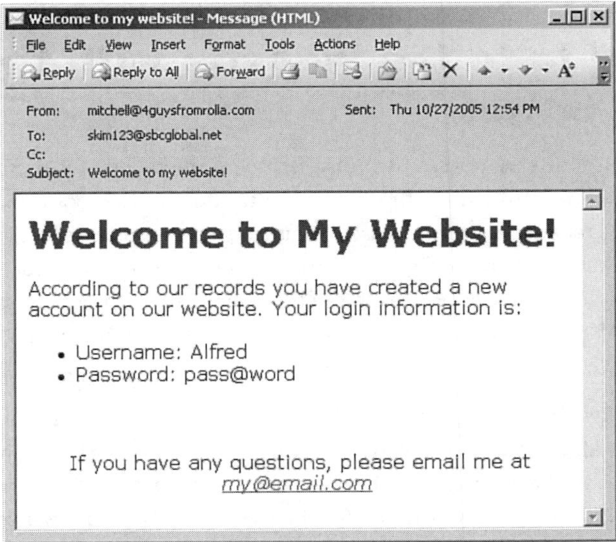

FIGURE 20.11
The email message sent to new user accounts.

Creating Inactive User Accounts

Whereas most sites allow users to create a new account by simply providing a username, password, and email address, some sites are more selective about their membership and want to make members **inactive** by default. An inactive member cannot log in to the site until she is made active. Recall that in the ASP.NET Website Administration Tool's Manage Users screen, shown in Figure 20.5, we could mark users active or inactive.

By default, newly created user accounts are active, but this is configurable through the CreateUserWizard control's `DisableCreatedUser` property. By default, this is set to `False`, which means the created user is *not* made inactive. However, to make the user inactive, simply set this property to `True`. As you may have guessed, when this property is set to `True`, the user is *not* automatically logged in after creating her account.

> If you make newly created users inactive, rather than redirecting them to the site's home page after creating a new account, you may want to send them to a page that explains that their account is currently inactive. This page should also include the policies used by your site to determine whether a user is marked as active.
>
> Furthermore, if you send an instructional email, as discussed in the "Emailing Users a Message After Creating Their Accounts" section, be sure to inform the users that their account is currently inactive.

Logging In to the Website with the Login Control

Any site that supports user accounts must include some means for the users to log in to the site. This is typically done through a **login page**. In the login page, the user is queried for his credentials—in our case, his username and password. Creating a login page in ASP.NET is quite simple thanks to the Login Web control, which renders the typical login user interface. To see this Web control in action, start by creating a new ASP.NET page named `Login.aspx`, adding the Login control to the page (see Figure 20.12).

As Figure 20.12 shows, the Login control contains two TextBox controls to capture the user's credentials. Additionally, there's a Remember Me Next Time check box. If the user logs on to the site without checking the Remember Me Next Time check box, she remains logged on to the site for the duration of her browser session; after she closes her browser and revisits the site, she'll need to log on again. If, however, the user checks this check box when signing on, she'll remain logged on across browser and computer restarts.

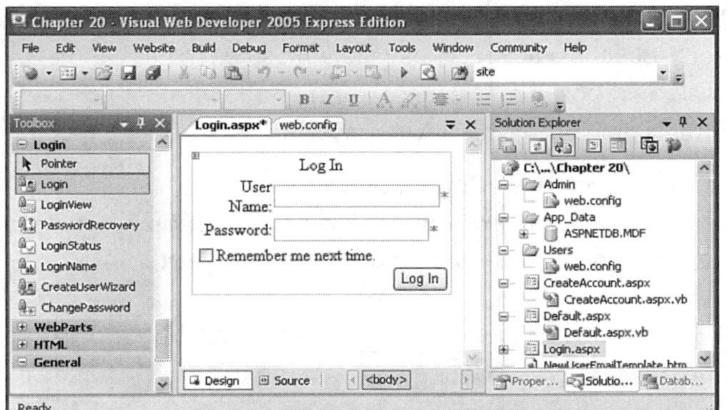

FIGURE 20.12
The Login control provides the standard login user interface.

Did you Know?

Online banking websites and other security-conscious sites often don't provide a Remember Me Next Time option to help prevent another person using the same computer from logging on to the first user's account. You can dictate whether this Remember Me Next Time check box appears through the Login control's `DisplayRememberMe` property.

When visiting this page, if a user enters invalid credentials or the credentials for an inactive account, he will be shown an appropriate message—`Your login attempt was not successful. Please try again.` by default. If he enters valid credentials, he will be logged on to the site and redirected to the URL specified by the Login control's `DestinationPageUrl` property. (If no value is specified for this property, the user will be sent to `Default.aspx`.) Try out this page on your own in a browser. Go to `Login.aspx` and observe what happens when you enter invalid credentials, or when you omit the username or password. Also, make sure to see what happens when you provide valid credentials.

By the Way

If the user attempts to visit a page that he does not have access to, he will automatically be redirected back to the login page. For example, earlier in this hour we created a `Users` folder and configured its access rights to disallow anonymous users. Take a moment to add a `Default.aspx` page to the `Users` folder and then, when logged out, try visiting this page. You'll find that you are automatically sent back to the login page, at which point you can enter your credentials. Upon being authenticated, you will be automatically sent back to the `Users/Default.aspx` page.

Customizing the Login Control

Like the Web controls examined in the preceding hour, the Login control has the usual suite of appearance-related properties. Furthermore, like the CreateUserWizard control, the Login control has properties—LoginButtonText, PasswordLabelText, UserName, UserNameRequiredErrorMessage, and so on—that can be used to customize the labels, text box content, and error messages. Rather than rehash them, let's focus on the Login control-specific properties.

The Login control properties worth noting include those in the Link and Behavior sections of the Properties window. Table 20.2 contains a listing of the control's more interesting properties, along with a brief description for each.

TABLE 20.2 Customize the Login Control Using These Properties

Property Name	Description
DestinationPageUrl	Indicates the URL the user is sent to after successfully logging in. Defaults to an empty value, which ends up sending the user to Default.aspx.
DisplayRememberMe	Specifies a Boolean value that indicates whether the Remember Me Next Time check box is present. Defaults to True.
RememberMeSet	Indicates a Boolean value that specifies whether the Remember Me Next Time check box is checked by default. Defaults to False.
VisibleWhenLoggedIn	Indicates whether the Login control is rendered when the page is visited by an authenticated user. Defaults to True.
Orientation	Has a Vertical orientation, by default, which causes the username text box to be placed above the password text box. You can have the text boxes laid side-by-side by setting this property to Horizontal.
TextLayout	Can be one of two values—TextOnLeft or TextOnTop. Specifies the position of the labels relative to the text boxes.
CreateUserText CreateUserIconUrl CreateUserUrl	Include a link from the Login control to the create account page by setting the CreateUserUrl and one or both of the CreateUserText and CreateUserIconUrl properties.
HelpPageText HelpPageIconUrl HelpPageUrl	Allow you to add a link to this page if you have created a help page, explaining the login process and policies.
PasswordRecoveryText PasswordRecoveryIconUrl PasswordRecoveryUserUrl	Provide a link to a web page from which the user can reset her password. (We'll examine the PasswordRecovery Web control in the "Recovering a User's Forgotten Password" section later in this hour.)

If you add a Login control to your site's home page, you likely want the control to appear only for unauthenticated users. That is, if a user is already logged in, there's no reason to show the Login control on the home page. To accomplish this, you can set the control's `VisibleWhenLoggedIn` property to `False`. Another option, though, is to use the LoginView Web control, which lets you define precisely what content is shown for logged-in users versus that shown for unauthenticated users. We'll discuss this control in more detail later in this hour in the "Displaying Content Based on Authentication Status" section.

Logging Out

While being able to log on to a site is important, it's also equally important to allow users to easily log off. This is usually accomplished through a Logoff link that, when clicked, signs the user out of the site. The LoginStatus Web control provides this functionality. When a user is logged on the site, the LoginStatus control displays a Logoff link; when a user is not logged on, the control renders a Login link.

Add the LoginStatus control to `Default.aspx`. In the control's smart tag, you'll see that there are two views: Logged In and Logged Out. Toggling between these views shows what visitors to the site will see depending on whether they're authenticated. The `LoginText` and `LogoutText` properties specify the text that's displayed for the Login and Logout links. If you would rather have these links displayed as clickable images, you can set the `LoginImageUrl` and `LogoutImageUrl` properties to the corresponding login and logout images.

Did you Know?

> You'll likely want to have the LoginStatus control appear on all of the pages in your website, thereby enabling users to log on or log off from anywhere on the site. Although this can be accomplished by manually adding a LoginStatus control to each and every page of the site, a better, more maintainable approach is to use **master pages**, which are the topic of our next hour.

By default, when the user clicks the logout link, he will be logged out but remain on the same page. If you want the person redirected to a specific URL after being logged out, use the `LogoutAction` and `LogoutPageUrl` properties. The `LogoutAction` property specifies what action is taken when the user clicks the Logout link, and can have one of three values:

- `Refresh`—The user is logged out and stays on the same page.
- `Redirect`—The user is logged out and redirected to the URL specified by the `LogoutPageUrl` property.
- `RedirectToLoginPage`—The user is logged out and redirected to the login page.

When an unauthenticated user visits a page with a LoginStatus control and clicks the Login link, he is taken to the login page with the URL of the page he was on passed along in the querystring. After the user successfully provides his credentials, not only is he logged on, but he is automatically redirected back to the page he came from.

Specifying the Login Page URL

If you scan the list of the LoginStatus control's properties, you'll notice that while there's a `LogoutPageUrl` property, there's no `LoginPageUrl` property. That is, there's no explicit way to tell the LoginStatus control where to send the user when she clicks the Login link. By default, the website uses the URL `Login.aspx` as its login page. If, however, you need to customize this, you can do so through the site's `web.config` file. Specifically, you need to find the `<authentication>` element and add a `<forms>` child element. In the `<forms>` element, use the `loginUrl` attribute to specify the URL of the site's login page.

For example, to create a site whose login page was at `SignOn.aspx` instead of `Login.aspx`, we'd go to the `web.config` file and locate the `<authentication>` element, which should look like this:

```
<authentication mode="Forms" />
```

We need to add the `<forms>` element as an inner element of the `<authentication>` element. Therefore, replace the preceding line with the following:

```
<authentication mode="Forms">
   <forms loginUrl="SignOn.aspx" />
</authentication>
```

To avoid having to muck around in the `web.config` file, I make sure to name my login page `Login.aspx`. If you decide to use a login page other than the default `Login.aspx`, keep in mind that the `web.config` file is case sensitive. Make sure to enter the `<forms>` element and `loginUrl` attribute with the correct casing.

Displaying Content Based on Authentication Status

Often we want to display different content based on whether the user is logged on. If the visitor is not logged on to the site, we might want to display the Login control; however, if the user has already been authenticated, in place of the Login control, we might want to display a short message like `Welcome back` *`username`*, where *`username`* is the name of the logged-on user.

As we saw in the preceding section, the Login control can be conditionally displayed based on the user's authentication status via the `VisibleWhenLoggedIn` property. Although setting this property to `False` will indeed hide the Login control from authenticated users, it doesn't provide a mechanism to replace the login control with a customized message. To accomplish that, we'll need to use the LoginView Web control.

Go to `Default.aspx` and add a LoginView control to the page. As the control's smart tag shows, the LoginView control provides two views: Anonymous Template, which is shown for unauthenticated users; and Logged In Template, which is shown for logged-in users. To add content that should appear only when the visitor is authenticated or not, simply add the content to the appropriate view.

Because we want `Default.aspx` to show a Login control for unauthenticated users, switch to the Anonymous Template view and then drag and drop a Login control from the Toolbox into the LoginView control. Next, switch to the LoginView control's Logged In Template. Whatever static HTML markup or Web controls we add here will appear for authenticated users. Begin by putting your mouse cursor inside the Logged In Template and click to give focus. Then type in the text `Welcome back`. Finally, drag the LoginName control from the Toolbox into the Logged In Template, preceding the text you just added (see Figure 20.13).

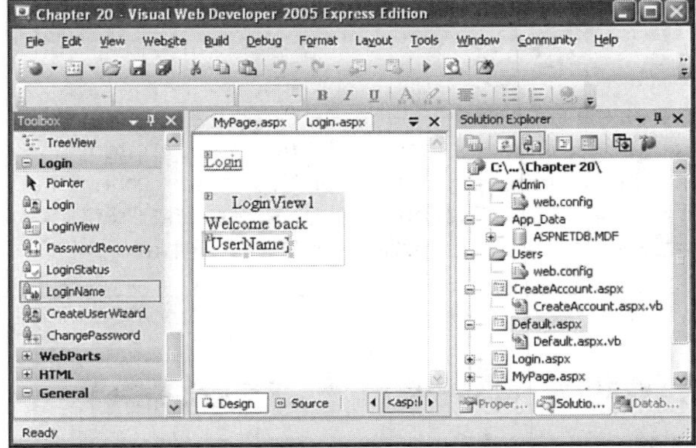

FIGURE 20.13 The LoginName control has been added to the LoginStatus control's Logged In Template.

As you may have guessed, the LoginName control displays the username of the logged-on user. If an anonymous user visits a page, the LoginName control displays nothing.

Figure 20.14 shows `Default.aspx` when viewed by an anonymous user, whereas Figure 20.15 shows the page when visited by a logged-on user.

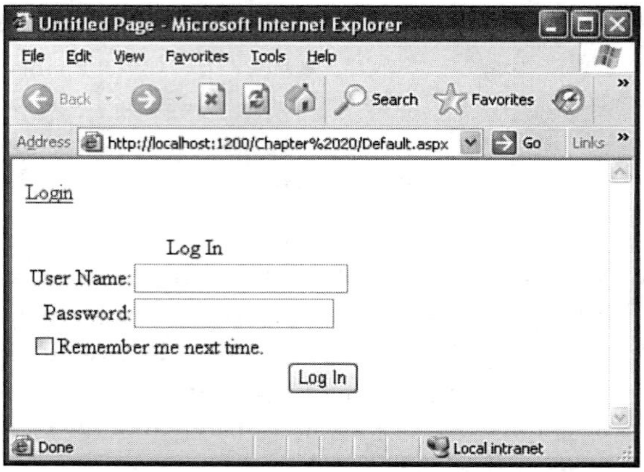

FIGURE 20.14 For anonymous users, the Login control is shown.

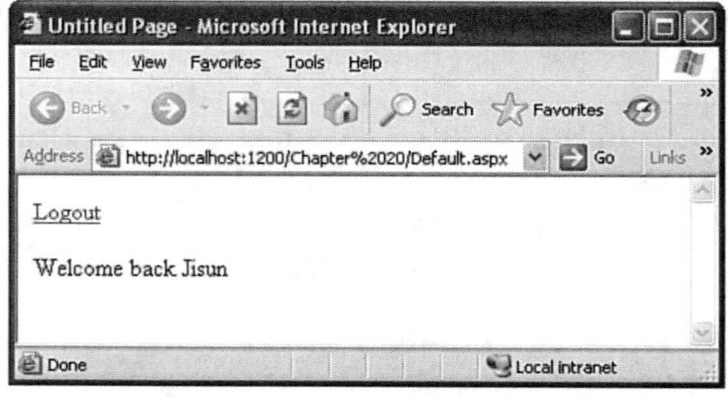

FIGURE 20.15 After Jisun has logged on, she sees a "Welcome back" message.

Did you Know?

> The LoginView control can also be configured to display content based on the logged-in user's role. For more information on this feature, check out Part 2 of my article "Examining ASP.NET 2.0's Membership, Roles, and Profile," available online at http://aspnet.4guysfromrolla.com/articles/121405-1.aspx.

Recovering a User's Forgotten Password

With the plethora of user accounts most people have these days, remembering all your different passwords can be difficult. To help those who have forgotten their password, sites that support user accounts typically include a way for users to retrieve their passwords. ASP.NET contains a PasswordRecovery Web control designed to help with this process. The PasswordRecovery control is a three-step wizard control that progresses through the following stages:

1. The user is asked for his username.
2. The user's security question is displayed, prompting the visitor for the answer to the question.
3. After the user provides the correct answer, the password is sent via email to the user's email address.

After the user completes these stages, the PasswordRecovery control sends the following email message:

```
Please return to the site and log in using the following information.
User Name: Username
Password: Password
```

You can send a more customized email message by creating a file and setting the PasswordRecovery control's `MailDefinition` property, just like with the CreateUserWizard control. For more on sending emails, refer to this hour's "Configuring a Website's SMTP Settings" and "Emailing Users a Message After Creating Their Accounts" sections.

Watch Out!

> Because the user is emailed her password, this process works only if you have collected the user's email address when she created her account. If the user's email address is not in the database, the user will not be able to proceed past step 2 of the password recovery workflow, regardless of whether she provides the correct answer to the security question.

If you try out the PasswordRecovery control on a page, you'll find that the password you are sent is a new, randomly generated password, and not the password you created the account with. The reason is that, by default, the ASP.NET user account system does not store the users' passwords in a plain-text format. Rather, it uses a **one-way hash** of the passwords.

Without getting into the technical details, a one-way hash is a function that takes in an input and modifies it in such a way that it is mathematically impossible to take the result and deduce the initial input. Because the database stores the hashed results of the passwords, rather than the plain-text, even if the database is compromised, the intruder will not be able to determine the plain-text passwords from the hashed versions.

At this point you may be wondering how, exactly, the system authenticates a user. If the database doesn't contain the user's plain-text password, but just a one-way hash of the password, how can we determine whether a user has provided valid credentials? The system takes the plain-text password sent by the user when providing his credentials and hashes it, and then compares the hashed results of the user's supplied password with the hashed value stored in the database. If they match up, the user is assumed to be valid.

By the Way

> For more background on hashing algorithms, check out the August 2003 edition of *MSDN Magazine*'s "Security Briefs" column, available online at http://msdn.microsoft.com/msdnmag/issues/03/08/SecurityBriefs/.

Because there is no way to take the hashed version stored in the database and convert it back into the plain-text form, the PasswordRecovery control has no option but to give the user a new, random password. The ASP.NET user account system can be configured to support plain-text passwords, however, in which case the PasswordRecovery control will email the user her plain-text password. A thorough discussion on configuring the system to allow for plain-text passwords is beyond the scope of this book. For more information, consult the "How To: Use Membership in ASP.NET 2.0" documentation at http://msdn.microsoft.com/library/en-us/dnpag2/html/PAGHT000022.asp.

By the Way

> Like the other controls we examined in this and the preceding hour, the PasswordRecovery control provides a bevy of properties for customizing the appearance and behavior.

Summary

Building a website that supports user accounts is trivial with ASP.NET, thanks to ASP.NET's built-in user account support and login Web controls. When we configure the ASP.NET website to use forms-based authentication, the ASP.NET Website Administration Tool automatically adds a database to our project, `ASPNETDB`. This database contains the tables needed to store user accounts and roles. Additionally, the ASP.NET Website Administration Tool simplifies adding and managing users, roles, and access rights.

After this database has been created, a host of Web controls can be used that interact with the data. The CreateUserWizard control allows users to create new accounts, whereas the Login control logs a user on to the site. The LoginStatus control displays a Login or Logout link, depending on whether the user is logged in, while the more flexible LoginView control allows us to specify a more generic user interface for both authenticated and anonymous visitors. We also looked at the PasswordRecovery control, which can be used to recover a user's forgotten password. Prior to ASP.NET 2.0, creating a website that supported user accounts was anything but trivial. It involved creating the appropriate database tables from scratch and creating web pages that could handle creating accounts, managing accounts, and logging in and out of a site. However, with ASP.NET 2.0's new user account features and login Web controls, supporting user accounts can be done with a minimal amount of time and effort.

Q&A

Q. ***I like how ASP.NET provides inherent user account support, but it seems to make a lot of assumptions for me. For example, passwords are stored as hashed digests, the user's password must be seven characters long and include nonalphanumeric characters, and so on. I want to change some of these defaults. Is this possible?***

A. Yes. The membership feature of ASP.NET is highly customizable through the website's `web.config` file. For more information, consult the "How To: Use Membership in ASP.NET 2.0" documentation at http://msdn.microsoft.com/library/en-us/dnpag2/html/PAGHT000022.asp.

Workshop

Quiz

1. What is authentication? How is authentication performed with forms-based authentication?
2. What three pieces of information do you need to provide when specifying an access right?
3. Imagine that on a web page you wanted to show anonymous users the user interface for logging in to the site as well as for creating a new user account, whereas for logged-on users you simply wanted to display a Logout link. What Web controls would you use to accomplish this?
4. What does the LoginName Web control do?
5. True or False: It's possible to convert a hashed digest back into its original form.

Answers

1. Authentication is the process of identifying a user. Forms-based authentication requires that the user provide her credentials through a Web Form.
2. To create an access right, you need to specify the following: the folder, the user or role, and whether the right is to allow or deny access.

3. Use the LoginView control. In the Anonymous Template view, add the Login and CreateUserWizard Web controls; in the Logged In Template view, add the LoginStatus control. Recall that the LoginStatus control displays a Login link for anonymous users and a Logoff link for authenticated users. Because the LoginView control's Logged In Template view is displayed only for authenticated users, the LoginStatus control will always show the Logoff link for an authenticated user.

4. The LoginName Web control displays the logged-in user's name. If the current user is not logged in, it displays nothing.

5. False.

Exercises

1. In Hour 16, "Deleting, Inserting, and Editing Data," we looked at displaying and editing the contents of the `Books` table through a GridView. If we were building a website to showcase our favorite books, we would want to make sure that only we could update the contents of the `Books` table, whereas other visitors could only view the results. For this exercise, create a website that supports user accounts and has an Administrator role defined. Next, add a folder named `Admin` to the website and then create two web pages: `BookList.aspx`, in the root folder; and `Default.aspx`, in the `Admin` folder. Have `BookList.aspx` list the contents of the `Books` table in a read-only GridView, with `Admin/Default.aspx` providing an editable GridView. Finally, configure the `Admin` folder to allow access only by those users who belong to the `Administrator` role.

2. Repeat Exercise 1, but instead of having a separate `Admin` folder, have only one page, `BookList.aspx`, in the root folder. Add a LoginView control and add a GridView to both the Anonymous and Logged In Templates. Finally, configure the GridView in the Logged In Template to allow editing, while keeping the GridView in the Anonymous Template read-only. With this setup, any authenticated user can edit the contents of the `Books` table, but anonymous users will be presented with a read-only interface.

3. Repeat Exercise 2, but this time instead of using two GridViews in a LoginView control, add just one GridView to the page. Configure the GridView to support editing. Next, turn the GridView's Edit, Update, Cancel column into a TemplateField through the Fields dialog box. This new TemplateField will have an ItemTemplate that contains a LinkButton with the text Edit and an EditItemTemplate with two LinkButtons: Update and Cancel.

Add a LoginView control to this new TemplateField's ItemTemplate, leaving the Anonymous Template empty and placing the Edit LinkButton in the Logged In Template. When an anonymous user visits the website, the field that normally contains the Edit button will be blank; when an authenticated user visits, however, he'll see the Edit button, which he can click to edit the contents of the corresponding record in the `Books` table.

(Both Exercises 2 and 3 allow any authenticated user to edit the `Books` table. You could restrict this functionality to users in the Administrator role by utilizing the LoginView's role-based features. For more information on customizing the LoginView control's output based on the user's role, refer to Part 2 of my article "Examining ASP.NET 2.0's Membership, Roles, and Profile," available online at http://aspnet.4guysfromrolla.com/articles/121405-1.aspx.)

HOUR 21

Using Master Pages to Provide Sitewide Page Templates

In this hour, we will cover

- Creating a master page
- Defining editable regions within a master page
- Associating a newly created page with an existing master page
- Making an existing page use a master page
- Adding source code to a master page

Virtually all professionally done websites have a very consistent look and feel across their pages. The common look and feel usually include both the layout of the page—where various user interface elements appear and how they are oriented with respect to one another—and the fonts, colors, and graphics used within the page. For example, if you visit sports channel ESPN's website, ESPN.com, you'll find that regardless of where you go on the site, at the top of the page you'll see the ESPN logo, a search box, and a menu listing the sports covered by ESPN. At the bottom of each page is another search box, along with the links to the most recently published stories.

When you are building the web pages in a site, it is important not to add the common sitewide features manually to each and every page. That is, the web designers at ESPN.com would be remiss to manually add the search box, logo, and common links to each and every page. Not only would this add significantly to the time required to build a page, but it would make updating the website's layout a nightmare. If the designers at ESPN.com wanted to remove the search box from the top or add to their menu of sports covered, they would have to visit and update each and every page of the site.

The approach used by professional web developers is to design some sort of site template that has the HTML content that should be present on each and every page. This is accomplished in ASP.NET through the use of a **master page**. A master page is a special ASP.NET page that, like regular ASP.NET pages, contains both a code portion and an HTML portion, with the HTML portion consisting of both static HTML content and Web controls. This master page contains the common layout content. Then, when you're creating a new ASP.NET page, this new page can be assigned to the master page, thereby inheriting its look and feel. With the master page model, updating the single master page automatically updates the common content in all of the pages that inherit that master page. With master pages, creating a unified site layout that can be easily updated is a snap!

An Overview of Master Pages

Ever since the first websites appeared on the World Wide Web, being able to define a consistent look and feel for all pages across a site has been an important part of the design process. Programs like Microsoft FrontPage and Macromedia's Dreamweaver—tools designed for designing websites and creating web pages—have long offered template features. With these tools, a designer can create a single template page that contains both common, sitewide content as well as regions that can be customized by each page that uses the template.

With ASP.NET 2.0 and Visual Web Developer, a page developer provides a sitewide template by creating a master page. Just like the template files in FrontPage and Dreamweaver, a master page consists of two pieces: content that appears on each and every page that inherits the master page and regions that can be customized by pages using the master page. The master page model in ASP.NET outshines simple HTML-based templates because master pages, like any ASP.NET page, can contain not only HTML markup, but Web controls and server-side source code as well.

Before we jump into creating our own master pages, let's first look at how the entire master page model works. Imagine that we wanted a website where each page on the site had the following four common user interface elements:

- The website's name on the top of the page
- A navigation breadcrumb at the top of the page
- A navigation treeview on the left of the page, showing the site's structure
- A copyright statement and a series of links—Legal, Privacy Policy, About Us, and so on—at the bottom of the page

The navigation treeview and breadcrumb on the pages in our site would ideally be implemented using the site navigation features and the SiteMapPath and TreeView Web controls examined in Hour 19, "Defining a Site's Structure and Providing Site Navigation."

Figure 21.1 shows the About page on this site.

FIGURE 21.1
Each page in the site will have the same look and feel.

The title at the top of the page (`"Welcome to My Website!"`), the treeview on the left, the breadcrumb, and the list of links at the bottom will exist on each page in our site precisely as they appear in the About page in Figure 21.1. The remaining portion of the page, the part that says `About Us` and `Lorem ipsum blah blah blah`, can be unique to each of the web pages on the site.

To accomplish this in an ASP.NET site, we would first create a master page. A master page needs to specify *both* the regions of the page that are common to all pages that inherit the master page as well as the regions that are customizable on a page-by-page basis. The content that is common to all pages that inherit the master page can simply be added to the master page just like you would add content to a regular ASP.NET page. You can enter the HTML markup and Web controls by hand, in the Source view, or use the WYSIWYG designer.

To indicate a region in the master page that is customizable on a page-by-page basis, use the ContentPlaceHolder Web control. As Figure 21.2 shows, this Web control simply renders as a box in the Design view of the master page. Later, when creating an ASP.NET page that inherits from this master page, we will be able to add content only to the page inside this box because the area outside is the user interface that is common to all pages that inherit the master page.

Did you Know?

> A master page may have multiple ContentPlaceHolder Web controls. Each ContentPlaceHolder control represents a location on the master page that can be customized by the ASP.NET pages that inherit it.

Figure 21.2 shows the master page used to create the common user interface shown in Figure 21.1. Note that the master page contains the common user interface elements—the title at the top of the page, the TreeView control (and SiteMapDataSource control), the SiteMapPath control, and the links at the bottom of the page—along with a ContentPlaceHolder control. (We'll look at the steps in creating a master page in greater detail later in this hour.)

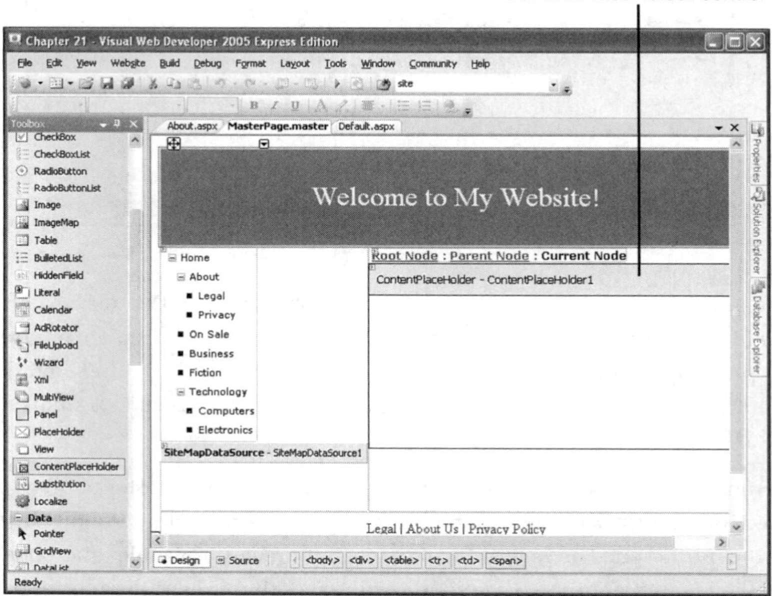

FIGURE 21.2 The master page has the common UI elements defined, along with a ContentPlace Holder control.

With this master page created, the next step is to create an ASP.NET page that inherits from the master page, a topic that we'll delve into later this hour. Once such a page has been created, the Design view for the ASP.NET page shows both the noneditable master page content as well as the editable content regions. Figure 21.3 shows the Design view of the About page.

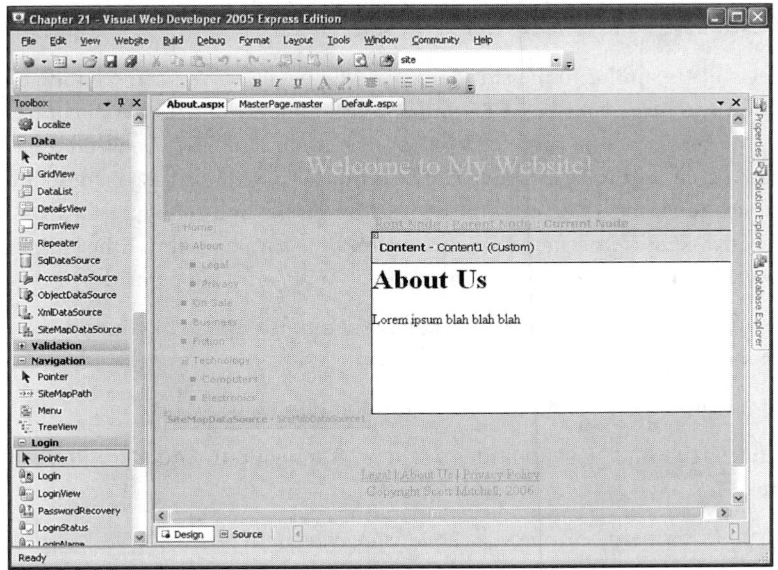

FIGURE 21.3 The About page's only editable region is the Content region.

We don't need to re-create the common page elements—the title, TreeView control, and so on. They are automatically shown in the page's Design view, inherited from the master page. Although it may not be particularly clear from the figures in this book, these common master page elements are grayed out and cannot be modified by the ASP.NET page. Rather, the only modifiable region o n the page is the Content region, which shows up precisely where the ContentPlaceHolder control was added to the master page.

With this master page setup, we can easily adjust the overall look and feel of the site by updating the master page. For example, if we wanted to change the text displayed at the top of the page or wanted to add new links to the bottom of this page, we could simply edit the master page. After the master page was modified and saved, those pages that inherited from the master page would immediately start showing the new look and feel.

To summarize, defining a sitewide template with master pages involves two steps, which should be done in the following order:

1. Create a master page that specifies the common, sitewide user interface elements along the regions that are customizable on a page-by-page basis.
2. Create the site's ASP.NET pages, with the pages configured to use the master page created in step 1.

The remainder of this hour examines these two steps in greater detail.

Creating a Master Page

A master page is similar to the standard ASP.NET pages we've been creating throughout this book. Like ASP.NET pages, master pages consist of Web controls, static HTML markup, and server-side code. The main difference between a master page and a standard ASP.NET page is that a master page's purpose is to define a template for the website. As we discussed earlier in this hour, the master page defines both the user interface elements common to all pages that inherit the master page as well as the regions that are editable on a page-by-page basis.

To get started defining a sitewide template, add a master page to your project using the following steps:

1. Right-click on the project name in the Solution Explorer.
2. Choose the Add New Item menu option, displaying the Add New Item dialog box.
3. From this dialog box, choose the Master Page item type.
4. Choose a name for the master page. By default, the name `MasterPage.master` is chosen. Feel free to leave it as this or change it to something else. Just be sure to keep the file extension as `.master`.
5. Check the Place Code in Separate File check box, if it's not already checked. As we discussed in previous hours, checking this check box places the master page's source code portion in a separate file.
6. Click the Add button to add the master page to your project.

After you add the new master page, the Design view shows a page with a single ContentPlaceHolder Web control (see Figure 21.4). This ContentPlaceHolder indicates the region that can be edited by the ASP.NET pages that inherit this master page. You can have multiple ContentPlaceHolders in your master page. To add a new ContentPlaceHolder, simply drag the ContentPlaceHolder control from the Toolbox onto the master page.

The ContentPlaceHolder Web control can be added only to master pages, not to ASP.NET pages. Therefore, when viewing a master page in Visual Web Developer, you will find the ContentPlaceHolder control in the Toolbox; however, when you're viewing a normal ASP.NET page, this control is not displayed in the Toolbox.

Take a moment to view the declarative markup of the master page by going to the Source view (see Listing 21.1). If you compare the default declarative markup for a master page to that of a regular ASP.NET page, you'll see two differences. The first is that the master page starts with a `<%@ Master %>` directive (line 1), whereas normal ASP.NET pages start with the `<%@ Page %>` directive. Furthermore, the master page contains, by default, a ContentPlaceHolder control (lines 12 and 13).

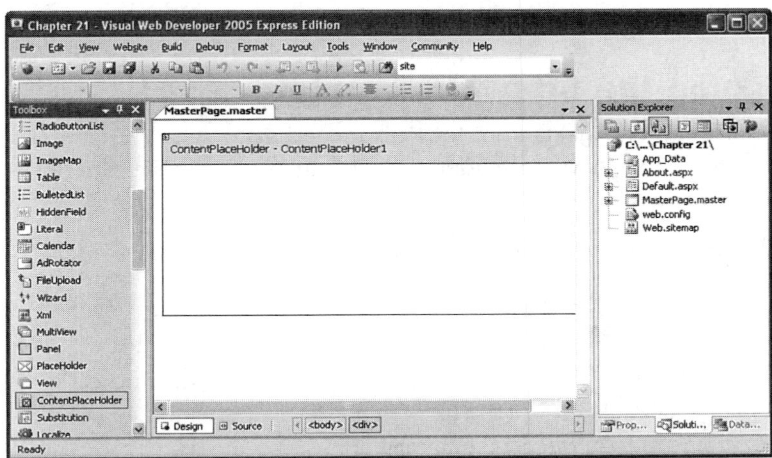

FIGURE 21.4 New master pages contain a single Content PlaceHolder control.

LISTING 21.1 The Default Declarative Markup for a Master Page

```
 1: <%@ Master Language="VB" CodeFile="MasterPage.master.vb"
➥Inherits="MasterPage2" %>
 2:
 3: <!DOCTYPE html PUBLIC "-//W3C//DTD XHTML 1.0 Transitional//EN"
➥ "http://www.w3.org/TR/xhtml1/DTD/xhtml1-transitional.dtd">
 4:
 5: <html xmlns="http://www.w3.org/1999/xhtml" >
 6: <head runat="server">
 7:     <title>Untitled Page</title>
 8: </head>
 9: <body>
10:     <form id="form1" runat="server">
11:     <div>
12:         <asp:contentplaceholder id="ContentPlaceHolder1" runat="server">
13:         </asp:contentplaceholder>
14:     </div>
15:     </form>
16: </body>
17: </html>
```

To create the sitewide look and feel, add the appropriate static HTML markup and Web controls to the master page. Again, you can do this by manually entering the HTML markup and control syntax through the Source view, or in a more graphical way through the Design view.

A website project can have multiple master page files, each one defining a different template. For example, a website may be broken into three different sections, with each section having its own unique look and feel. In this case we would create three different master pages for the site. When creating a new ASP.NET page, we would associate it with the appropriate master page.

Designing the Sitewide Template

Let's create a master page that has the look and feel first shown in Figure 21.1—a title at the top, a TreeView control along the left, and so on. This design has each page laid out into four regions:

- The header region, which displays the title of the website.
- The navigation region, which contains the TreeView control and appears on the left of the page beneath the header region.
- The main region, which contains the SiteMapPath control and the ContentPlaceHolder control. This region is located beneath the header region and to the right of the navigation region.
- The footer region, which contains the common links—Legal, About Us, and so on—along with the copyright statement.

To provide this page layout, let's use **tables**. A table is an HTML element that can be used to arrange a page into various columns and rows. For this site design, we want a table that takes up the entire page with two columns and three rows, with the top and bottom rows spanning two columns. Figure 21.5 illustrates this design concept graphically.

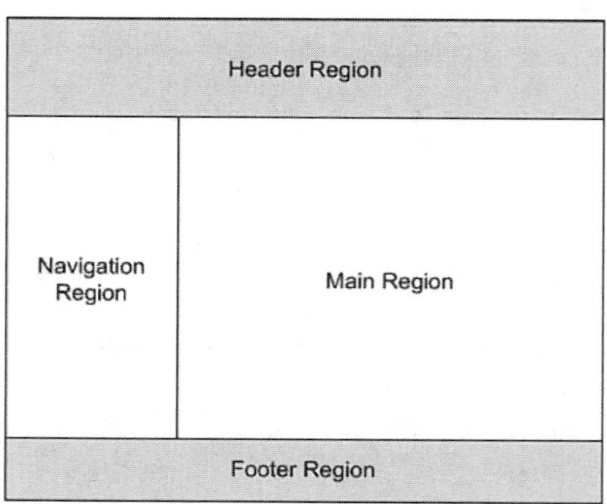

FIGURE 21.5 The site's design lays out pages using a two-column, three-row table.

To create such a layout in HTML, you can manually enter the appropriate HTML table markup, or you can use Visual Web Developer. If you are interested in entering the HTML markup by hand, feel free to do so; Listing 21.2, shown later, contains the complete markup for the master page.

If you are not an HTML aficionado and would rather have Visual Web Developer assist with creating the page's layout, follow these steps by going first to the master page's Design view. From the Layout menu, choose Insert Table, displaying the Insert Table dialog box (see Figure 21.6). From this dialog box, you can specify the precise table settings, indicating the number of rows and columns, the alignment, the width and height, and so on, or you can use a preexisting template. For our master page, go ahead and opt to use the "Header, footer, and side" template.

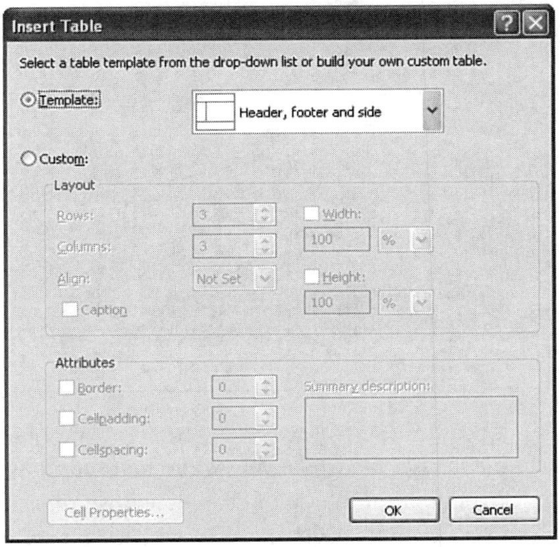

FIGURE 21.6
Add a table to the master page using the Insert Table dialog box.

The Insert Table dialog box adds the new table before the ContentPlaceHolder Web control. Because we want the ContentPlaceHolder control in the main region, take a moment to drag the ContentPlaceHolder from beneath the table into the second column in the second row of the table.

Creating the Header Region

In the header region, enter the site's title, such as `Welcome to My Website!` I've opted to have this title centered and displayed in a 24pt font size. These settings can be specified when typing in the website name, through the myriad of formatting options along the toolbar or through the Format menu.

These settings can also be made to apply to the entire content region, rather than just the particular piece of text being entered. To tailor the entire header region, perform the following steps:

1. Click inside the table cell and then go to the Properties window.
2. Click on the `Style` property, which will display a set of ellipses.
3. Click on these ellipses. This will display the Style Builder dialog box where you can set the font, background, layout, and other options that apply to the entire table row (see Figure 21.7).

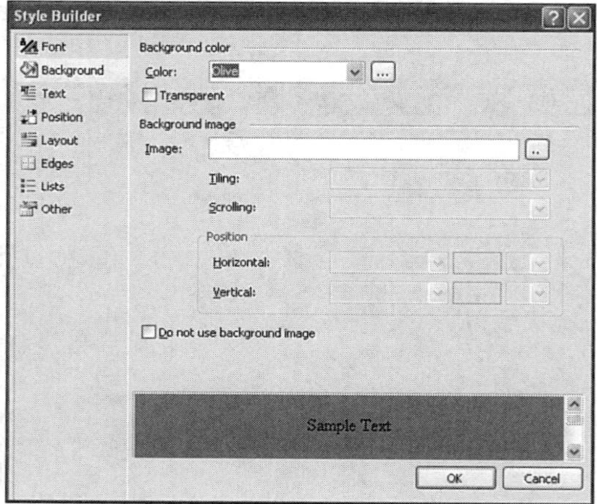

FIGURE 21.7
Customize the appearance of the header region through the Style Builder dialog box.

For example, to have the header region display white text on an olive background, from the Font tab, pick White from the Color drop-down list, and from the Background tab, pick Olive from the Color drop-down list. You can also specify font sizes, alignment, and a host of other settings through the Style Builder dialog box.

By default, the table rows that make up the header and footer regions have a height of 200 pixels. You can increase or decrease this amount by clicking on the border between the rows and, while holding down the button, move the mouse up or down.

Crafting the Navigation Region

The purpose of the navigation region is to provide the visitor with a complete listing of the site's structure, making it easy to quickly move to another page on the site. As we discussed in Hour 19, "Defining a Site's Structure and Providing Site Navigation," the ASP.NET TreeView Web control can be used in tandem with a SiteMapDataSource control to display the site's structure, assuming that there is a properly defined site map. For this hour, I am using the same site map used in Hour 19.

After you have created your site map, add the SiteMapDataSource and TreeView controls to the first column in the second row of the table, configuring the TreeView control to use the SiteMapDataSource.

By default, the content in a table cell is vertically placed in the middle of the cell. If the navigation region's row is particularly tall, which can happen in pages that include lengthy content in the main region, whitespace will appear between the header region and the TreeView control. In fact, if there is several pages' worth of content in the main region, the visitor may have to scroll down to see the TreeView.

Often the common sitewide elements are formatted so that their position is not affected by the page-specific content. To accomplish this, we need to have the navigation region's content appear at the top of the cell, rather than in the middle. This is configurable through the table cell's `valign` property. To set this property, click inside the cell that makes up the navigation region, go to the Properties window, and set the `valign` property to `top`. This will cause the navigation region's content to be vertically aligned with the top of the table cell, regardless of how much or how little content is in the main region.

Did you Know?

When you add a table using the "Header, footer, and side" template, the side column—the navigation region—is created with a width of 200 pixels. Like with the height of the header and footer regions, you can adjust this width by clicking on the border between the navigation and main regions and, while holding down the button, move the mouse to the right or left.

Creating the Main Region and Footer Region

At this point the only two regions remaining are the main and footer regions. The main region already has the ContentPlaceHolder control (dragged into it after adding the table) but still needs the SiteMapPath control, which shows a breadcrumb. Drag this control from the Toolbox into the main region, placing it above the ContentPlaceHolder control. Finally, set the main region's table cell's `valign` property to `top`, just as we did with the navigation region. This ensures that regardless of how little content is in the main region, it will appear at the top of the cell.

Finally, add the content for the footer region in the bottommost row. My footer region contains three links: Legal, About Us, and Privacy Policy. I manually typed in these links, although you could opt to use three HyperLink Web controls, if you'd prefer.

Refer back to Figure 21.2 to see the completed master page when viewed through the Visual Web Developer's Design view. Listing 21.2 contains the complete declarative markup of the master page when viewed through the Source view.

LISTING 21.2 The Master Page's Declarative Markup

```
<%@ Master Language="VB" CodeFile="MasterPage.master.vb"
➥Inherits="MasterPage" %>

<!DOCTYPE html PUBLIC "-//W3C//DTD XHTML 1.0 Transitional//EN"
➥"http://www.w3.org/TR/xhtml1/DTD/xhtml1-transitional.dtd">

<html xmlns="http://www.w3.org/1999/xhtml" >
<head runat="server">
    <title>Untitled Page</title>
</head>
<body>
    <form id="form1" runat="server">
    <div>
        <table border="0" cellpadding="0" cellspacing="0" style="width:
➥100%; height: 100%">
            <tr>
                <td colspan="2" style="height: 100px; color: #ffffff;
➥background-color: olive; text-align: center; font-weight: bold; font-size:
➥24pt;">
                    Welcome to My Website!</td>
            </tr>
            <tr>
                <td style="width: 200px" valign="top">
                    <asp:TreeView ID="TreeView1" runat="server"
➥ DataSourceID="SiteMapDataSource1" ImageSet="Simple" NodeIndent="10">
                        <ParentNodeStyle Font-Bold="False" />
                        <HoverNodeStyle Font-Underline="True"
➥ForeColor="#DD5555" />
                        <SelectedNodeStyle Font-Underline="True"
➥ForeColor="#DD5555" HorizontalPadding="0px"
                            VerticalPadding="0px" />
                        <NodeStyle Font-Names="Verdana" Font-Size="8pt"
➥ForeColor="Black" HorizontalPadding="0px"
                            NodeSpacing="0px" VerticalPadding="0px" />
                    </asp:TreeView>
                    <asp:SiteMapDataSource ID="SiteMapDataSource1"
➥runat="server" />
                </td>
                <td valign="top">
                     <asp:SiteMapPath ID="SiteMapPath1" runat="server"
➥ Font-Names="Verdana" Font-Size="0.8em"
                        PathSeparator=" : ">
                        <PathSeparatorStyle Font-Bold="True"
➥ForeColor="#1C5E55" />
                        <CurrentNodeStyle ForeColor="#333333" />
                        <NodeStyle Font-Bold="True" ForeColor="#666666" />
                        <RootNodeStyle Font-Bold="True"
➥ForeColor="#1C5E55" />
                    </asp:SiteMapPath>
                    <asp:ContentPlaceHolder ID="ContentPlaceHolder1"
➥runat="server">
```

LISTING 21.2 Continued

```
                    </asp:ContentPlaceHolder>
                </td>
            </tr>
            <tr>
                <td colspan="2" style="height: 50px; text-align: center;">
                    <a href="Legal.aspx">
                    Legal</a> ¦ <a href="About.aspx">About Us</a> ¦
➥<a href="Privacy.aspx">Privacy Policy</a><br />
                    Copyright Scott Mitchell, 2006</td>
            </tr>
        </table>
         
    </div>
    </form>
</body>
</html>
```

Creating an ASP.NET Page That Inherits the Master Page

With our master page created, the next step is to create an ASP.NET page that inherits from this master page. When we're creating such a page, our responsibility will be to define the content that belongs in the master page's ContentPlaceHolder controls. We *won't* be able to add any additional content outside these regions. To indicate that an ASP.NET page inherits a master page, when adding a new ASP.NET page to the project, simply check the Select Master Page check box (see Figure 21.8).

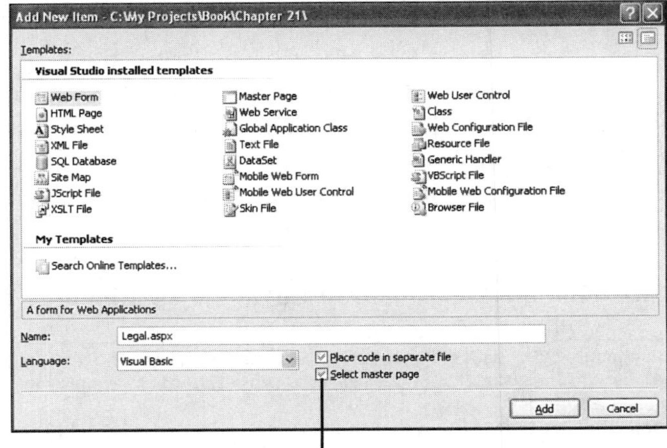

FIGURE 21.8 Associate the new ASP.NET page with a master page by checking Select Master Page.

After you check Select Master Page and click the Add button, the Select a Master Page dialog box will appear, as shown in Figure 21.9. This dialog box lists the master pages in the website project.

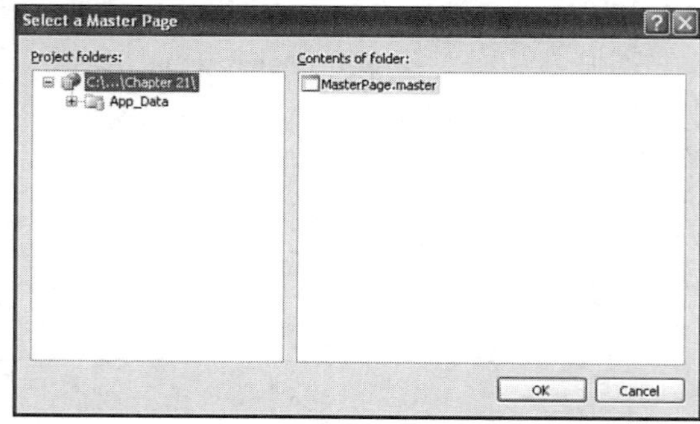

FIGURE 21.9 Select the new ASP.NET page's master page.

After you choose a master page, the new ASP.NET page's Design view shows the master page's sitewide markup as grayed-out, uneditable content (refer to Figure 21.3). Where the master page's ContentPlaceHolder controls were, however, are Content controls, which are editable regions whose content is unique to the particular ASP.NET page. You can type directly into the Content region or drag controls from the Toolbox.

If you prefer working through the Source view, entering the HTML markup and Web controls manually, you'll no doubt notice the default declarative markup for an ASP.NET page that inherits a master page (see Listing 21.3). The `<%@ Page %>` directive on line 1 includes a `MasterPageFile` attribute that indicates the path to the master page.

Rather than having the typical HTML markup, a new ASP.NET page that inherits a master page has, in its place, a Content control for each ContentPlaceHolder control in the associated master page (lines 2 and 3). The Content control's `ContentPlaceHolderID` property associates a Content control with a particular ContentPlaceHolder control in the master page.

LISTING 21.3 The Markup of an ASP.NET Page That Inherits a Master Page

```
1: <%@ Page Language="VB" MasterPageFile="~/MasterPage.master"
➥AutoEventWireup="false" CodeFile="Legal.aspx.vb" Inherits="Legal"
➥title="Untitled Page" %>
2: <asp:Content ID="Content1" ContentPlaceHolderID="ContentPlaceHolder1"
➥Runat="Server">
3: </asp:Content>
```

When you visit an ASP.NET page that inherits a master page through a browser, the ASP.NET engine grabs the associated master page's content. It then fuses in the markup and Web controls specified in the ASP.NET page's Content control into the corresponding master page's ContentPlaceHolder control. Because this infusion of master page and ASP.NET page occurs when the page is visited through a browser, any changes to the underlying master page are immediately reflected in the pages that inherit from it.

By the Way

An ASP.NET page does not lose any functionality when it inherits from a master page. All of the examples we have examined throughout this book would have worked just the same had we associated a master page with the ASP.NET page.

Having an Existing Page Inherit from a Master Page

Creating a *new* ASP.NET page that inherits from a master page is easy enough: Just check a check box and choose the master page. However, taking an existing, master page-less ASP.NET page and having it inherit from a master page is, unfortunately, not as simple. To take an existing page and have it inherit an existing master page, we must do two things:

- Add a `MasterPageFile` attribute to the page's `<%@ Page %>` directive.
- Create a Content control for each ContentPlaceHolder control in the master page, with the page's existing HTML markup and Web controls moved into the appropriate Content controls.

The first step is simple enough to accomplish. Start by opening the ASP.NET page that you want to have inherit a master page and go to the Source view. Next, place your cursor in the `<%@ Page %>` directive and type in `MasterPageFile=`. At this point, a drop-down list should appear containing the various master pages in your project. Simply choose which master page file you want to use and press the Tab key. In the end, the `<%@ Page %>` directive should include an attribute that looks like `MasterPageFile="~/`*`masterPageFileName`*`"`.

With the `MasterPageFile` attribute specified, the final step is creating a Content control for each of the master page's ContentPlaceHolders and moving over the appropriate markup. Assuming the existing page already has content, what I do is typically cut all of the content inside the Web Form and paste it into Notepad. After I have removed the content from inside the Web Form, I delete all the content in the web page except for the `<%@ Page %>` directive. (Recall that the Web Form is denoted by `<form runat="server">`.)

Finally, I go to the Design view of the ASP.NET page. Because the ASP.NET page now inherits the master page, it will show the master page's sitewide content as noneditable along with the content regions. To create the Content controls, right-click on the content regions in the Design view and choose the Create Custom Content menu option. After you have created the Content control for each of the ContentPlaceHolder controls in the master page, go back to the Source view and paste the code saved in Notepad back into the appropriate content regions.

To help make these concepts more concrete, let's look at a real-world example. Imagine that we had the page shown in Listing 21.4 and wanted to have it inherit from the `MasterPage.master` master page. (This markup shown in Listing 21.4 is the actual page content from an example we looked at in Hour 15, "Displaying Data with the Data Web Controls.")

LISTING 21.4 A Sample ASP.NET Page

```
<%@ Page Language="VB" AutoEventWireup="false"
➥CodeFile="AccessingData.aspx.vb" Inherits="AccessingData" %>

<!DOCTYPE html PUBLIC "-//W3C//DTD XHTML 1.0 Transitional//EN"
➥ "http://www.w3.org/TR/xhtml1/DTD/xhtml1-transitional.dtd">

<html xmlns="http://www.w3.org/1999/xhtml" >
<head runat="server">
    <title>Untitled Page</title>
</head>
<body>
    <form id="form1" runat="server">
    <div>
        <asp:SqlDataSource ID="SqlDataSource1" runat="server"
➥ConnectionString="<%$ ConnectionStrings:ConnectionString %>"
            SelectCommand="SELECT * FROM [Books]"></asp:SqlDataSource>
        <asp:SqlDataSource ID="SqlDataSource2" runat="server"
➥ConnectionString="<%$ ConnectionStrings:ConnectionString %>"
            SelectCommand="SELECT * FROM [Books]
➥WHERE (([BookID] <= @BookID) AND ([YearPublished] = @YearPublished))
➥ORDER BY [Price] DESC, [Title]">
            <SelectParameters>
                <asp:Parameter DefaultValue="3" Name="BookID"
➥Type="Int32" />
                <asp:Parameter DefaultValue="2005" Name="YearPublished"
➥Type="Int32" />
            </SelectParameters>
        </asp:SqlDataSource>
        <br />
        <asp:GridView ID="GridView1" runat="server"
➥AutoGenerateColumns="False" DataKeyNames="BookID"
            DataSourceID="SqlDataSource1">
            <Columns>
                <asp:BoundField DataField="BookID" HeaderText="BookID"
➥InsertVisible="False" ReadOnly="True"
                    SortExpression="BookID" />
```

LISTING 21.4 Continued

```
27:                 <asp:BoundField DataField="Title" HeaderText="Title"
➥SortExpression="Title" />
28:                 <asp:BoundField DataField="Author" HeaderText="Author"
➥ SortExpression="Author" />
29:                 <asp:BoundField DataField="YearPublished"
➥HeaderText="YearPublished" SortExpression="YearPublished" />
30:                 <asp:BoundField DataField="Price" HeaderText="Price"
➥SortExpression="Price" />
31:                 <asp:BoundField DataField="LastReadOn"
➥HeaderText="LastReadOn" SortExpression="LastReadOn" />
32:                 <asp:BoundField DataField="PageCount"
➥HeaderText="PageCount" SortExpression="PageCount" />
33:             </Columns>
34:         </asp:GridView>
35:
36:     </div>
37:     </form>
38: </body>
39: </html>
```

We would start by going to the `<%@ Page %>` directive on line 1 and adding the attribute `MasterPageFile="~/MasterPage.master"`. Next, we would cut and paste the content inside the Web Form—that is, the content spanning from line 11 through line 36—into Notepad. We would then remove all content from the ASP.NET page except for the `<%@ Page %>` directive on line 1. Then, from the Design view, we'd right-click on the master page's single content region and choose Create Custom Content. After we have completed all of these steps, our ASP.NET page's declarative markup would look like so:

```
<%@ Page Language="VB" MasterPageFile="~/MasterPage.master"
➥AutoEventWireup="false" CodeFile="Default.aspx.vb" Inherits="_Default" %>
<asp:Content ID="Content1" runat="server"
➥ContentPlaceHolderID="ContentPlaceHolder1">
     </asp:Content>
```

We'd complete this process by pasting in the saved content from Listing 21.4 (specifically lines 11–36) into the Content Web control.

Because having a new ASP.NET web page inherit a master page is much easier than having an existing page inherit a master page, I recommend you create a master page when starting on a new site. Keep the master page simple; I usually just have it contain the default ContentPlaceHolder.

When creating new web pages for the site, have them all inherit from the master page. At some later point, you can go back to the master page and actually implement the sitewide design. Since all pages inherit the master page, they'll all immediately reflect the update to the master page.

Providing Default Content in a Master Page

The ContentPlaceHolder controls in a master page represent the portions of the template that are editable on a page-by-page basis. Typically, an ASP.NET page that inherits the master page will customize these regions. However, in some circumstances a page may not want to customize a particular ContentPlaceHolder region, instead falling back on some default value specified by the master page.

For example, imagine that instead of having the title `Welcome to My Website!` displayed on each page in the header region, you wanted to allow each page to customize this title. However, you suspect that the majority of the pages will just be interested in using the value `Welcome to My Website!` To accomplish this, you could add a ContentPlaceHolder control in the header region and specify the default value of the ContentPlaceHolder as the title `Welcome to My Website!` Then, in the ASP.NET pages that inherited this master page, you could indicate whether the page should use the master page's default content or specify its own customized content.

To illustrate creating default value in a master page's ContentPlaceHolder control, let's create a new master page called `DefaultExample.master` that has the same layout as the `MasterPage.master` master page we created earlier.

To quickly copy the layout from `MasterPage.master` to `DefaultExample.master`, go to the Design view of `MasterPage.master`. Then select all content by going to the Edit menu and choosing Select All. After selecting all, go to the Edit menu and choose Copy. Return to `DefaultExample.master`'s Design view and select all content in this page and then go to the Edit menu and choose Paste.

Voila! You've just copied the content from one master page to another.

In the `DefaultExample.master` page, add a second ContentPlaceHolder control to the header region, removing the text `Welcome to My Website!` Set this ContentPlaceHolder control's `ID` property to `HeaderRegion`. To specify a default value for the `HeaderRegion` ContentPlaceHolder, simply add the default content to the ContentPlaceHolder, much like you would on an ASP.NET page to customize a particular content region. Because we want the default title to still be `Welcome to My Website!`, type this text into the ContentPlaceHolder in the header region. That's all there is to it!

Choosing to Use Default or Custom Content in an ASP.NET Page

An ASP.NET page that inherits from a master page can opt to provide custom content for a master page region or, instead, rely on the master page's default content for that region. To illustrate this, take a moment to add a new ASP.NET page that inherits from the `DefaultExample.master` page we just created. Because the master page has *two* ContentPlaceHolder controls in the Design view of the ASP.NET page, you'll see two content regions; similarly, the ASP.NET page's declarative syntax has, by default, two Content controls:

```
<%@ Page Language="VB" MasterPageFile="~/DefaultExample.master"
➥AutoEventWireup="false" CodeFile="DefaultContentTest.aspx.vb"
➥Inherits="DefaultContentTest" title="Untitled Page" %>
<asp:Content ID="Content1" ContentPlaceHolderID="HeaderRegion" Runat="Server">
</asp:Content>
<asp:Content ID="Content2" ContentPlaceHolderID="ContentPlaceHolder1"
➥Runat="Server">
</asp:Content>
```

To use the master page's default content for a region, rather than custom content, you need to remove the associated Content Web control from the ASP.NET page. To use the default content for the header region, simply delete the first Content control, the one whose `ContentPlaceHolderID` equals `HeaderRegion`. You can accomplish this by manually removing the Web control syntax from the Source view or by going to the Design view, right-clicking on the editable region, and choosing the Default to Master's Content option. Once this Content Web control has been removed from the ASP.NET page, the page will use the default content from the master page (`Welcome to My Website!`).

> To stop using the master page's default content and to create custom content for the page, you need to add back the Content Web control. You can do this manually, through the Source view, or by going to the Design view, right-clicking on the content region, and selecting Create Custom Content.

Working with a Master Page's Source Code Portion

A master page has all of the functionality found in a standard ASP.NET page. That means that it can have Web controls and static HTML markup. The Web controls in the master page can collect user input or retrieve data from a data source. For example, the master page created in the Creating a Master Page section had SiteMapDataSource and TreeView controls, which queried and displayed the site's structure based on the site map. We could have also added controls that collect user input. For example, sites that support user accounts often allow visitors to log in from any page on the site. We could accomplish this functionality by adding a Login control to the master page.

In addition to Web controls and static HTML markup, a master page can also have a server-side source code portion. This source code portion can contain event handlers for the Web controls added to a master page or code that is to run each time a page that inherits the master page is visited. To illustrate the server-side source code portion capabilities of master pages, let's create a new master page for our site, called `CodeDemo.master`.

In this master page, let's first add a Label Web control that displays the current date and time along with a mechanism to search the Internet from our site. Start by adding the Label Web control that will display the current date and time. Add this control above the ContentPlaceHolder control, clear out its `Text` property, and set its `ID` property to `currentDateTime`. Next, type in the word `Search` and, after that, add a TextBox Web control, setting its `ID` to `searchTerm`. Finally, add a Button Web control after the TextBox, setting its `ID` and `Text` properties to `btnSearch` and `Search`, respectively. After you have completed these steps, your screen should look similar to Figure 21.10.

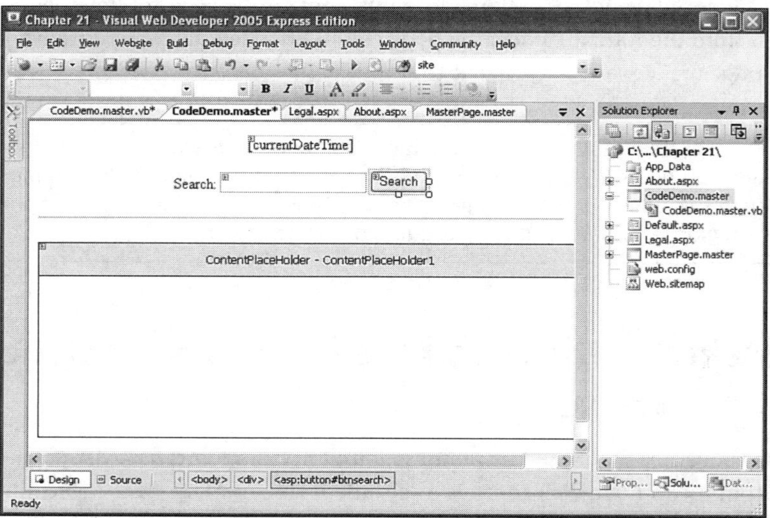

FIGURE 21.10 The master page includes three Web controls: a Label, a TextBox, and a Button.

With these Web controls in place, we're ready to add the server-side source code for the master page. Start by creating the `Page_Load` event handler. Recall from Hour 2, "Understanding the ASP.NET Programming Model," that the `Page_Load` event handler fires each and every time the page is visited. In this event handler we'll set the `currentDateTime` Label's `Text` property to the current date and time.

To create the `Page_Load` event handler, double-click in the Design view or go to the source code portion and select from the left drop-down list the (Page Events) option and, from the right drop-down list, the `Load` event. Add the following line of code to the `Page_Load` event handler:

```
currentDateTime.Text = "It is now " & DateTime.Now
```

For the search interface, when the user enters a search term and clicks the Search button, a postback will ensue, and the Button Web control's `Click` event will fire. For this example let's have the user search the Internet using Google. This can be accomplished by sending the user to http://www.google.com/search?q=*searchTerm*. To accomplish this, we'll create an event handler for the Button's `Click` event and then use `Response.Redirect(`*`url`*`)` to send the user to Google's site, passing in the user's search term through the querystring.

Start by creating an event handler for the Button Web control's `Click` event. You can either double-click the Button in the Design view or select the appropriate control and event from the drop-down lists at the top of the source code portion. After you have created the event handler, add the following line of code:

```
Response.Redirect("http://www.google.com/search?q=" & searchTerm.Text)
```

Listing 21.5 contains the complete source code portion for the master page.

LISTING 21.5 The Master Page Has Two Event Handlers

```
Partial Class CodeDemo
    Inherits System.Web.UI.MasterPage

    Protected Sub Page_Load(ByVal sender As Object,
➥ByVal e As System.EventArgs) Handles Me.Load
        currentDateTime.Text = "It is now " & DateTime.Now
    End Sub

    Protected Sub btnSearch_Click(ByVal sender As Object,
➥ByVal e As System.EventArgs) Handles btnSearch.Click
        Response.Redirect("http://www.google.com/search?q=" &
➥searchTerm.Text)
    End Sub
End Class
```

By the Way

You can use Google to search *just* the pages on your site by prepending the user-entered search term with `site:yourDomain+`. For example, if you wanted to search just www.YourSite.com for the term *lunch*, you could use the URL http://www.google.com/search?q=site:www.YourSite.com+lunch. Therefore, you can allow users to search just your site (versus searching the entire Internet) by changing line 9 in Listing 21.4 to

```
Response.Redirect("http://www.google.com/search?q=site:www.YourSite.com+" &
➥searchTerm.Text)
```

Testing the Master Page's Functionality

At this point we have created a master page that displays the current date and time along with an interface for searching the Web through Google. Unfortunately, we've yet to test this master page's functionality in a browser. To do so, we must create an ASP.NET page that inherits from this new master page.

Take a moment to create a new ASP.NET page, using `CodeDemo.master` as its master page. Add a short blurb to the Content region in the ASP.NET page and then load it in a browser. As Figure 20.11 shows, when visiting the page, you'll see the current date and time displayed at the top of the page. Furthermore, when you enter a search term into the text box and click the button, you are whisked to Google's search results for the entered search term. Figure 20.12 shows a user's browser after he has entered the term *Scott Mitchell* into the search text box and clicked the button.

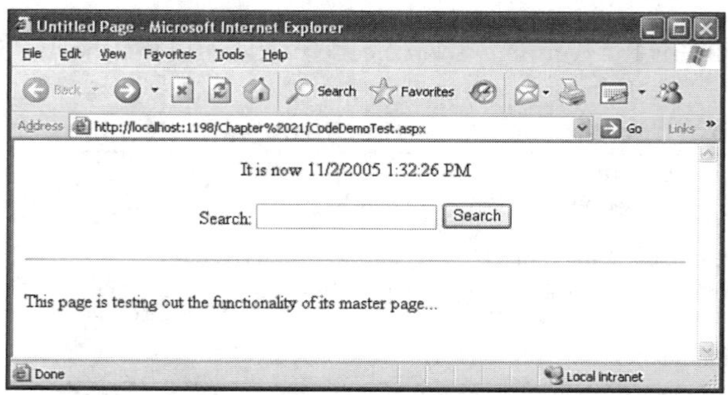

FIGURE 21.11
The current date and time is displayed at the top of the page.

FIGURE 21.12
Users can enter a search term and be taken to Google's results page.

Summary

When creating a website, designers strive to have all pages share a common look and feel. This includes a consistent color and font scheme along with consistent user interface elements. For example, most designers strive to have navigation controls and login-related controls available on all pages throughout the site. Implementing a consistent, sitewide design with ASP.NET is easy and hassle-free, thanks to master pages. A master page contains both sitewide user interface elements along with regions that can be customized on a page-by-page basis. These editable regions are indicated by ContentPlaceHolder controls.

Once a master page has been created, an ASP.NET page can inherit from this master page. This is accomplished by selecting the master page from a list of the site's master pages when adding the ASP.NET page to the project. When an ASP.NET page is associated with a master page, the ASP.NET page contains a Content Web control for each of the ContentPlaceHolder controls in the master page. The content placed in these editable regions is fused with the master page's content when the ASP.NET page is viewed through a browser. Because the melding of master page and ASP.NET page is done when the page is requested, any changes to a master page are automatically and instantly reflected in those pages that inherit from the master page.

As we saw throughout this chapter, Visual Web Developer provides rich design-time support for master pages. Creating a master page is tantamount to creating an ASP.NET page and can be done entirely through the Design view. When an ASP.NET page is associated with a master page, the Design view shows the master page's sitewide content grayed out, indicating that it cannot be modified on this page.

Q&A

Q. ***Can master pages be nested? That is, can a master page inherit a master page? For example, I want a very high-level sitewide look and feel defined by a parent master page. Then, for various sections of the site, I want a sectionwide template that borrows from the parent master page's look and feel, but defines some settings unique to the section. Is this possible?***

A. Yes, nested master pages are allowed. With nested master pages, the "root" master page can have HTML markup and Web control syntax, along with ContentPlaceHolders. A master page that inherits from that root master page can have only Content Web controls, just like a normal ASP.NET page that inherits from a master page. However, inside these Content Web controls can be additional ContentPlaceHolders.

For more information on nested master pages and master pages in general, check out "Master Pages in ASP.NET 2.0" at http://odetocode.com/Articles/419.aspx as well as Microsoft's official master page-related documentation, available at http://msdn2.microsoft.com/en-us/library/18sc7456(en-US,VS.80).aspx.

Workshop

Quiz

1. What is the purpose of a ContentPlaceHolder control in a master page?
2. True or False: A master page can have no more than one ContentPlaceHolder Web control.
3. What content is an ASP.NET page composed of when it is set up to inherit a master page?
4. What steps must be taken to create a new ASP.NET page that inherits a master page?

5. What steps must be taken to have an existing ASP.NET page inherit a master page?

6. How do you have an ASP.NET page use the master page's default content for a given region?

7. True or False: Master pages can contain a server-side source code portion.

Answers

1. The ContentPlaceHolder control indicates a region in the master page where ASP.NET pages that inherit the master page can optionally define the content. All other content in a master page is *not* editable by the inheriting ASP.NET page.

2. False. A master page can have an arbitrary number of ContentPlaceHolder controls.

3. ASP.NET pages that inherit master pages contain a reference to the master page in their `<%@ Page %>` directive (specifically, `MasterPageFile="`*`pathToMasterPage`*`"`) as well as a Content Web control for each ContentPlaceHolder region in the master page for which the page wants to provide a custom value.

4. To have a newly created ASP.NET page inherit from a master page, check the Select Master Page check box in the Add New Item dialog box. Doing so will bring up a list of the master pages in the project, from which you can select the one that the page inherits from.

5. If you have an existing ASP.NET page that you want to inherit from an existing master page, start by adding the appropriate `MasterPageFile` attribute to the page's `<%@ Page %>` directive. Next, replace the page's declarative markup portion with a Content Web control for each of the master page's ContentPlaceHolder controls. Some tips for accomplishing this step are discussed in the "Having an Existing Page Inherit from a Master Page" section.

6. An ASP.NET page that inherits a master page can opt to use the master page's default content for a given ContentPlaceHolder. To accomplish this, simply remove the ASP.NET page's Content control that corresponds to the ContentPlaceHolder for which you want to use the default content. You can do this by manually removing the Content control from the Source view or by going to the Design view, right-clicking on the Content region, and selecting the Default to Master's Content option.

7. True.

Exercises

1. In the preceding hour we looked at how to provider user account support in an ASP.NET website. Commonly, such sites have various user account-related Web controls on every page.

   Return to the examples from the preceding hour and create a master page that has a header region, left-side region, and main region. In the header region, put the website's title and the LoginStatus control. (Recall that the LoginStatus control displays a Login link for anonymous users and a Logout link for those who are logged in.) In the left-side region, use a LoginView control. In the control's Anonymous Template, put a Login Web control; in the Logged In Template, display the message `"Welcome back, username"` and include a Logout link. Figure 21.13 shows a diagram of the site template that your master page should implement.

   After you have created this master page, take a moment to convert the existing pages in the site to inherit this master page. Furthermore, create at least one new page that inherits from this master page.

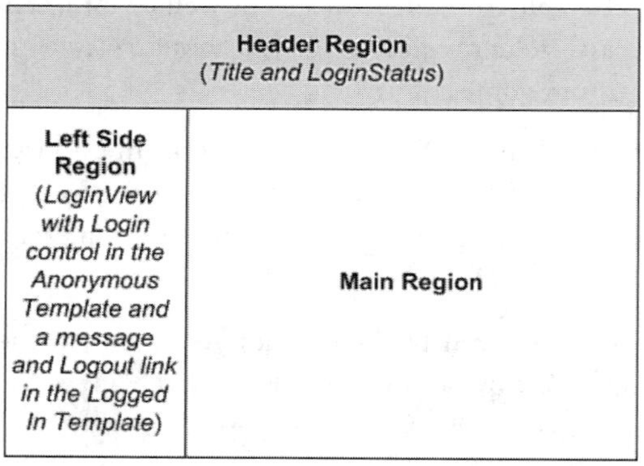

FIGURE 21.13
The site design contains three regions.

Header Region
(Title and LoginStatus)

Left Side Region
(LoginView with Login control in the Anonymous Template and a message and Logout link in the Logged In Template)

Main Region

PART V

Building a Photo Album Web Application with ASP.NET

HOUR 22

Devising a Plan for the Photo Album Application

In this hour, we will cover

- An overview of how web applications are commonly designed
- The requirements for our online photo web application
- Ways to use multiple tables in a database
- The photo album application's data model
- Foreign key constraints and their importance in ensuring database consistency

In the past 21 hours, we have looked at accomplishing a number of discrete tasks that are commonly performed in an ASP.NET website. In Hour 8, "ASP.NET Web Controls for Displaying Text," we examined how to display dynamic text in a web page using the Label and Literal Web controls. Hours 9 through 12 focused on collecting using input through Web Forms using controls like TextBoxes, DropDownLists, RadioButtons, and CheckBoxes. We also saw how to ensure data validity using the validation Web controls.

In Hours 13 through 18 we examined working with databases, from creating a SQL Server 2005 Express Edition database and defining its structure, to displaying, editing, inserting, and deleting database data through ASP.NET pages. We looked at how the SqlDataSource control provides an easy way to access and modify data, while the GridView and DetailsView Web controls make working with that data through an ASP.NET page a breeze. In the past three hours we looked at concepts that apply to entire websites: site navigation, membership, and master pages.

Although we've examined the important features of ASP.NET, we've yet to take these concepts and create a complete, end-to-end, fully functional website. That is the goal of the remainder of this book. Over the next three hours we will be creating an online photo album web application from the ground up. Our application will store user and picture information and user comments in a database. Our site will support user accounts and use master pages and ASP.NET's site navigation features. The GridView and DetailsView controls will be used on many pages, displaying and modifying data accessed through SqlDataSource controls.

Every journey starts with a first step. In this hour we will begin by defining the project's requirements and creating a database. We will actually begin creating ASP.NET pages in the next hour.

An Overview of the Design Process

Any nontrivial task requires some degree of planning before the task can begin. When building a house, an architect creates the blueprints, surveyors inspect the building site, and engineers ensure that the materials selected are sufficient. This process, which can take months or years, happens before the first brick is laid or the first nail hammered. You wouldn't want to live in a house that was built without any forethought, one whose design was decided on as the foundation was laid and the walls constructed.

While most web applications are not as complex as building a house from the ground up, they still warrant a sufficient amount of planning before the first web page is created or the first line of code is written. Applications that are started without a clear plan are typically buggier and more difficult to enhance or extend than those that were preceded with ample planning. Large and complex web applications—those with teams of dozens of developers—can take months of planning. For our much simpler online photo album application, however, an hour of planning should be sufficient.

The planning stage for any software application usually involves the following steps:

1. Collect design requirements from the customer.
2. For applications that need to persist data, implement the database schema necessary to capture the data spelled out in the design requirements.
3. Create mockups of the web application.

The goal of the first step is to understand the customer's needs for the application. What is the purpose of this application? What business requirements must be implemented by the system? How will the customer use the system on a day-to-day basis? What will the typical workflows be when using the system? Typically, this is the most challenging of the three steps because often a customer either doesn't know precisely what it is he wants to have the system accomplish, or there is some difficulty in fully explaining the requirements. Fortunately, we won't have this problem, since for this exercise we will be both the developer and customer!

By the Way

One way to help ascertain the customer's requirements is to ask her to provide **use cases**. A use case is a paragraph or two describing, in plain English, how a particular task would be accomplished. For example, a use case for our online photo album application might be as follows:

"Sally wants to upload an image to her photo album. She visits the website and can enter her login credentials from the home page. After she logs on, the `"Add Picture"` link is displayed. Clicking this, Sally is prompted to choose the picture from her hard drive that she wants to upload, along with a title for the picture, the category the picture belongs in, and a brief description."

The second step involves creating the database tables and defining their columns. The structure of the database will be highly dependent on the requirements gathered in step 1. The final step is to create a mockup of the application. This may be actual, working ASP.NET pages that have only a small subset of the functionality built in, or it may be something as simple as sketches on a piece of paper.

Commonly, the design process is iterative. That is, after creating the mockups, the customer is called back and shown the mockups. This provides an opportunity for the customer to refine the requirements or request changes to the appearance of the application. This cycle continues until the client is satisfied with the mockups and there is a solid understanding of the requirements between both the customer and the developers. When this point has been reached, the actual development of the working system can begin.

Over the next three sections, we'll perform each of these three software development steps. By the end of this hour, we'll have a solid understanding of the requirements of the system, along with the database structure defined. The final two hours take the concepts outlined in this hour and implement them.

The Photo Album Application's Design Requirements

An online photo album is a website that allows visitors to upload digital pictures from their personal computer to the website. These types of applications commonly allow users to include additional information about their pictures, such as a title, a description, whether other visitors can see the pictures, and so on. Many photo applications allow users to classify pictures into categories as well. After a picture has been uploaded, most sites will allow other visitors to view the pictures. When visitors view an image, some sites allow them to leave a comment or rate the picture.

For our online photo album application, we have the following requirements:

- The site must support user accounts.
- Both authenticated and anonymous users may visit the site and view others' pictures. However, only authenticated users can upload pictures.
- Users must be able to create, edit, and delete categories. A category has a name associated with it and is used to help organize a user's picture album.
- When uploading a picture, a user must provide the picture's title and a description for the picture. The user may optionally provide a category for the picture.
- Users need to be able to edit and delete their existing pictures.
- Authenticated users can view and leave comments for other users' pictures. Anonymous users can only view comments.
- Users should be able to view a particular user's pictures and filter the pictures by category.

Some of these requirements may sound a bit daunting. There are many requirements discussing "uploading a picture," but we've yet to see how, exactly, a visitor can upload a picture from her computer to the website. Furthermore, going from examples that focused on individual tasks to having a long and imposing list of requirements may be offputting. However, don't let the length of the list or the uploading concept scare you off. Whenever you first collect the design requirements, it always seems a bit overwhelming because the design requirements make up the *entire* project's needs, and any nontrivial project is going to have a pretty lengthy list of requirements.

When we begin to create the web application starting in the next hour, we'll tackle this long list one item at a time. Because we're breaking down the list into manageable chunks, the task ahead of us will seem much more doable.

Describing the Requirements as Use Cases

One way to help understand the design requirements is through **use cases**. A use case is a paragraph or two describing, in plain English, how a particular task would be accomplished. One big benefit of use cases is that they help keep the developers focused when creating the application because use cases spell out a particular way visitors will interact with the system. When creating that part of the system, the developers can turn to the use cases to judge whether the specific task can be completed.

Let's go over a few use cases for our online photo album application. They should help clear up any potential confusion you may have from the more terse requirements listed in the preceding section. Furthermore, when in the midst of development in the next two hours, we can return to these use cases to make sure we're on track.

Did you Know?

> Although this hour lists only four use cases, there's no reason we couldn't have more. Of course, a rather simple application like ours doesn't need dozens of use cases, but, as a general rule of thumb, the more use cases the better.

Supporting User Accounts

Jisun wants to create a user account for our online photo album application. To do so, she visits our site and sees a link titled `"Create Account"`. Clicking that, she is prompted for her desired username, a password, her email address, and a security question and answer. After she provides this information, an active account is created and she is logged on to the site.

Jisun may log out of the site by clicking the `Logout` link, which is available on every page in the site. She can log in to the site again by clicking the `Login` link, which is also available on every page in the site. Clicking the `Login` link takes Jisun to the Login page, where she is prompted for her username and password.

Each user account has its own album, which contains the pictures the user uploaded in the categories she has defined.

Configuring the Photo Album's Categories

After creating her account, Jisun decides to create some categories to help organize her photo album. She creates three categories with the names Animals, People, and Places. She then decides that she doesn't want the Animals category and promptly deletes it. Finally, she decides to rename the People category to Friends.

Uploading Pictures to the Website

Sam does not have an account on the website, nor does she want to create one. Therefore, as an anonymous user, she cannot upload pictures to the website.

Jisun, however, has created a user account and therefore can upload pictures. To upload a picture to her photo album, Jisun clicks on the `"Manage Photo Album "` link, which is displayed only to authenticated users. Clicking this link takes Jisun to a web page where she can choose an image file from her computer's hard drive and upload it to the website. Additionally, she is required to provide a title and description, and may optionally select a category for the picture.

After uploading an image, Jisun decides she doesn't like it and deletes it. She then uploads another one. After uploading the second one, she decides to rename the title and change the pictures category. This is accomplished by clicking an Edit button for the associated picture and changing the fields to the new, desired values.

Viewing Pictures and Leaving Comments

After Jisun has uploaded a number of her pictures, she gets an email from her friend and coworker Dave. Dave informs her that he, too, has created his own photo album on the website and has uploaded some pictures from the company's last happy hour. Jisun goes to the photo album website's home page, which lists all of the photo albums available. She quickly finds Dave's and visits it, seeing the pictures he referred to in his email. Seeing one of Dave standing on the balcony overlooking the ocean, she leaves a comment that reads, "What an amazing view!"

Sam, who does not have an account on the site, can also go to the site's home page and see the list of photo albums. Sam, too, can navigate to Dave's photo album and view the happy hour pictures, including reading Jisun's comment. Because Sam does not have an account on the site, however, she cannot leave her own message.

Creating the Database Structure

Most web applications use a database in some manner, and our photo album application is no exception. The precise structure of an application's database—what tables it consists of and the columns in those tables—depends precisely on the design requirements. The second task in the design phase is taking the requirements collected in the first step and translating them into the structure of the database. What tables and columns will we need to create to support the data needs of the photo album application?

When you're devising the database structure, it often helps to refer back to the use cases. Typically, the nouns represent the tables that need to be created. For example, the "Supporting User Accounts" use case started with the sentence "Jisun wants to create a *user account* for our online photo album application." This sentence implies that we will need some way to represent a user account in the database.

For user accounts, the precise set of tables and their columns is already defined for us by ASP.NET's membership feature, which was discussed in Hour 20, "Managing Your Site's Users." Therefore, we won't need to spend any more time defining the database requirements for user accounts.

In addition to the user account-related tables, we'll also need three additional tables:

- `Categories`—Because users can organize their albums using categories, we need a table that captures the categories created by each user.
- `Pictures`—As we will see in Hour 24, "Uploading and Displaying Images and Leaving Comments," when a user uploads a new picture to his album, the image file will actually be stored on the web server's file system; however, the meta-data about the picture—its title, description, and what category it belongs to—will reside in a database. This table will have one record for each uploaded picture in the system.
- `Comments`—Because users can leave comments for others' pictures, we need a table that stores these comments.

In the database examples we've examined thus far, we've focused on single table databases. However, most databases are composed of multiple, *related* tables. Two tables are said to be related if the data in one table is somehow dependent on the data in another table. For example, in the picture album data model, the `Comments` table's data is related to the `Picture` table's data because comments are left for a particular picture. There's a similar relationship between the `Pictures` and `Categories` tables.

Databases like SQL Server 2005 provide tools for enforcing relationships between tables. In the next section we'll examine some of these tools and their importance. Following that, we'll look at the individual table structure for each of the tables in the database.

Modeling Relationships in a Database

A good database design models each logical entity in the system as a table. In our photo album application, the entities in the system are categories, users, pictures, and comments; not surprisingly, our database will have a `Categories`, `Pictures`, and `Comments` table, along with the ASP.NET-defined tables for user accounts. Often, the entities in a system are related to one another in one of three ways:

- A one-to-one relationship
- A one-to-many relationship
- A many-to-many relationship

These relationships differ both conceptually and in implementation details. While the photo album application consists of only one-to-many relationships, let's take a moment to examine each of these three relationship types.

Examining One-to-One Relationships

If two tables share a one-to-one relationship, then for each record in the first table, there is at most one record in the corresponding table. A concrete example of this type of relationship can be seen between the ASP.NET-defined membership tables `aspnet_Users` and `aspnet_Membership`. The `aspnet_Users` table contains the `UserId` and `Username` values for each user account in the system. The `aspnet_Membership` table contains more detailed information about each account, including the user's password, email address, and security question and answer. As Figure 22.1 illustrates, for each record in `aspnet_User` there is precisely one matching record in `aspnet_Membership`.

aspnet_Users Table

UserID	UserName
1	Scott
2	Jisun
3	Sam
4	Todd
5	Dave

aspnet_Membership Table

UserID	Password	Email	IsApproved
1	Foo	scott@...	1
2	Bar	jisun@...	1
3	Terrier!	sam@...	1
4	60126	Todd-o@...	1
5	LaVitaMe	dave@...	0

FIGURE 22.1 The `aspnet_Users` and `aspnet_Membership` tables share a one-to-one relationship.

As Figure 22.1 shows, a relationship is set up by having the two tables share the same set of primary key columns. Recall that the primary key columns are the columns of a table whose values uniquely identify each row. Therefore, a given record in `aspnet_Users` can be associated with its related row in `aspnet_Membership` by finding the record in `aspnet_Membership` that has the same primary key column values.

Although Figure 22.1 shows the `UserId` column as a column with an integer data type, in actuality this column uses the `uniqueidentifier` data type. The `uniqueidentifier` data type is a very, very large number that is computed in such a way that it is guaranteed to be globally and temporally unique. That means that the `uniqueidentifier` chosen to uniquely identify a user account on your web server has never been used by any computer system in the past and will never be used by any computer system in the future.

Looking at One-to-Many Relationships

A one-to-many relationship (see Figure 22.2) occurs when a given record in one table can have zero to many related records in another table. Our photo album application has a number of such relationships. The `Pictures` table has a one-to-many relationship with the `Comments` table because each picture may have zero to many comments. Likewise, the `aspnet_Users` table has a one-to-many relationship with `Pictures` since each user may have zero to many pictures in the system.

By the Way

> The only type of relationship that is needed in the photo album application database is the one-to-many relationship. As we will see shortly, there are five such one-to-many relationships in our database.

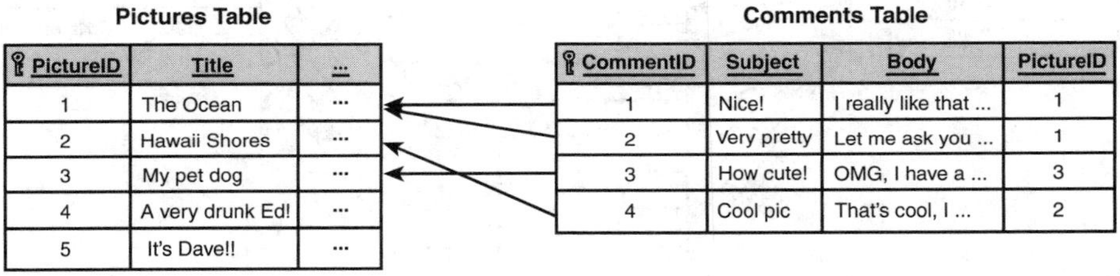

Pictures Table

PictureID	Title	...
1	The Ocean	...
2	Hawaii Shores	...
3	My pet dog	...
4	A very drunk Ed!	...
5	It's Dave!!	...

Comments Table

CommentID	Subject	Body	PictureID
1	Nice!	I really like that ...	1
2	Very pretty	Let me ask you ...	1
3	How cute!	OMG, I have a ...	3
4	Cool pic	That's cool, I ...	2

FIGURE 22.2 The `Pictures` and `Comments` tables share a one-to-many relationship.

A one-to-many relationship is implemented by having the "many" table include the columns that make up the "one" table's primary key. In Figure 22.2, the `Pictures` table's primary key column is `PictureID`; in the `Comments` table there is a `PictureID` column. This associates a particular comment with a particular picture. This design allows for a single picture to have multiple comments.

In Figure 22.2, two comments are associated with "The Ocean" picture, while one comment is associated with each the "Hawaii Shores" and "My pet dog" pictures. The "A very drunk Ed!" and "It's Dave!!" pictures have no comments associated with them.

By the Way

> Note that the "many" table has its own primary key, just like the "one" table. In Figure 22.2, the `Comments` table's primary key column is `CommentID`. `PictureID` is just a normal column in `Comments`; it's what ties a record in the `Comments` table back to a record in the `Pictures` table.

Understanding Many-to-Many Relationships

The last type of relationship, many-to-many, occurs when there are two tables and the tables' records may be cross-related in various combinations. The canonical many-to-many relationship is that between students and classes. A class may consist of several students, and each student may take several classes. Many-to-many relationships are implemented using a third table, one that associates each record from each table with a set of records from the other table, as shown in Figure 22.3.

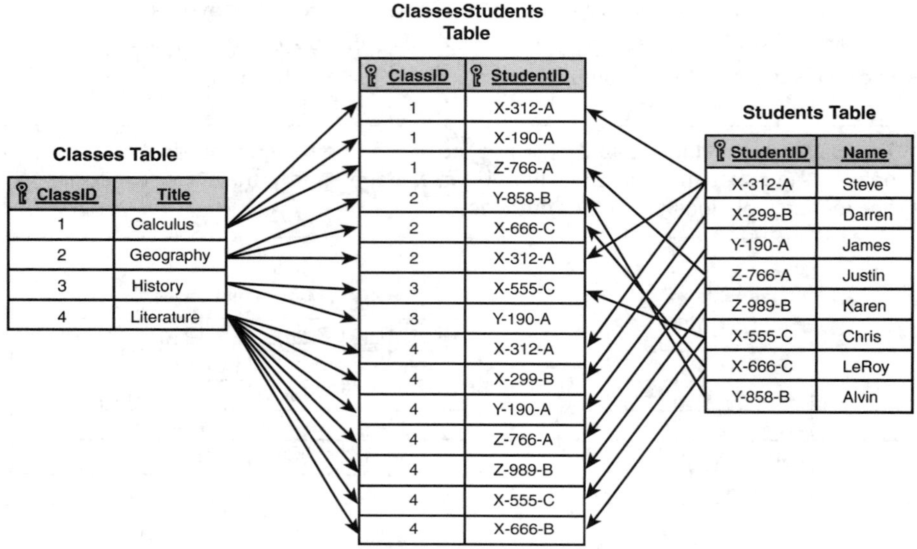

FIGURE 22.3
A many-to-many relationship is implemented using three tables.

The third table—`ClassesStudents` in Figure 22.3—contains the primary key columns from both of the "many" tables. Furthermore, the primary key columns in the third table are made the table's primary key.

A many-to-many relationship can be envisioned as two one-to-many relationships. For example, using Figure 22.3 you can easily construct a class's enrollment, which is a one-to-many relationship between the `Classes` and `Students` tables; similarly, you can also construct a student's schedule, which is a one-to-many relationship between the `Students` and `Classes` tables.

Enforcing Relationships with Foreign Key Constraints

The relationships between tables are encoded in the columns of the tables. In a one-to-many relationship, for example, the primary key columns of the "one" table are added as columns to the "many" table. While this enables a one-to-many relationship to exist between these two tables, it doesn't enforce **referential integrity**. Without care, the data in two related tables may become inconsistent. For example, in Figure 22.2 imagine that we changed the value of the `PictureID` column for the first comment from 1 to 100. After this modification, the first comment no longer is associated with a valid picture. Similarly, if we were to delete the first picture from the database, we'd still have comments in the `Comments` table that referred to the first picture.

Referential integrity ensures that the relationship between tables cannot become inconsistent; this integrity is implemented through the use of **foreign key constraints**. A foreign key constraint associates a column in one table with a primary key in another table. Once this constraint has been set up, whenever a new record is added or the foreign key column is updated, the value of the foreign key column must map to a value in the primary key table. If you attempt to insert a new record or change the foreign key column value to a value not in the primary key column, an error will occur and the change will not be accepted.

If you attempt to delete or change the associated primary column's value while there are foreign key values that map to this primary key column value, one of four things can happen, depending on how the foreign key constraint is configured:

- An error is raised and the deletion or modification of the primary key column value is rejected. This is the default behavior.
- The primary key column value is deleted or changed, and *all* corresponding records in the foreign key table are deleted. This behavior is referred to as **cascading deletes**.
- The primary key column value is deleted or changed, and the foreign key column values in the foreign key table are set to a value of Null. (For this option, the foreign key column must allow Nulls.)
- The primary key column value is deleted or changed, and the foreign key column values in the foreign key table are set to their default value. (For this option, the foreign key column must have a default value specified.)

To help hammer home this concept, let's look at a concrete example. In Figure 22.2 the `Pictures` and `Comments` tables were related with a one-to-many relationship. The `PictureID` column in the `Comments` table is a foreign key because its values should always map to the values of the primary key `PictureID` in the `Pictures` table. We would want to create a foreign key constraint between these two columns. After we did so, attempting to change the `PictureID` value in the `Comments` table to a nonexistent `PictureID` would fail. If we configured the foreign key constraint to cascade delete, deleting a picture would automatically delete the related comments.

When creating a database table through Visual Web Developer, you can indicate any foreign key constraints that exist along with the behavior when an associated primary key column value is changed or the record deleted. We'll see how to accomplish this when we look at how to create the database and tables.

Enumerating the One-to-Many Relationships in the Photo Album Application Database

Before we start creating the database and tables, let's first take a moment to list the one-to-many relationships that exist in our database. As mentioned previously, there are five such relationships:

- `aspnet_Users` to `Categories`—Because each user can create her own set of categories, each category in the `Categories` table needs to be associated with a particular user account.
- `aspnet_Users` to `Pictures`—Each picture uploaded to the system needs to be associated with a user account.
- `Categories` to `Pictures`—This application's requirements dictate that users should be able to categorize their photos into categories. Therefore, we need to associate each picture with a category.
- `Pictures` to `Comments`—Each picture can have an arbitrary number of comments.
- `aspnet_Users` to `Comments`—Each comment is associated with a particular user account.

The relationships among the tables of a database are often modeled using an **entity-relationship diagram**, also referred to as **ER diagrams**. ER diagrams show the **entities** in the database system (a fancy name for a database table), with lines between the tables highlighting the relationships. The ER diagram in Figure 22.4 shows the entities and relationships for the photo album application database.

> You can create ER diagrams through Visual Web Developer. From the Database Explorer, expand the Data Connections node and drill down into your database. Right-click on the Database Diagrams node and choose Add New Diagram. You will then be prompted for what tables you want to add to the diagram, after which the diagram will automatically be created. The diagram in Figure 22.4 was created in this manner.

Creating the User Account Tables

Before we can create the individual database tables for the photo album application database, we first need to create the actual database. In Hour 13, "An Introduction to Databases," we saw how to create a new SQL Server 2005 Express Edition database in the `App_Data` folder of our website. As we saw in Hour 20, "Managing Your Site's Users," when we configure an ASP.NET website to use user accounts, the `ASPNETDB` database is automatically created and placed in the App_Data folder. Rather than creating our own database, we'll instead use this autogenerated database. That is, the Categories, Pictures, and Comments tables will be added to ASPNETDB.

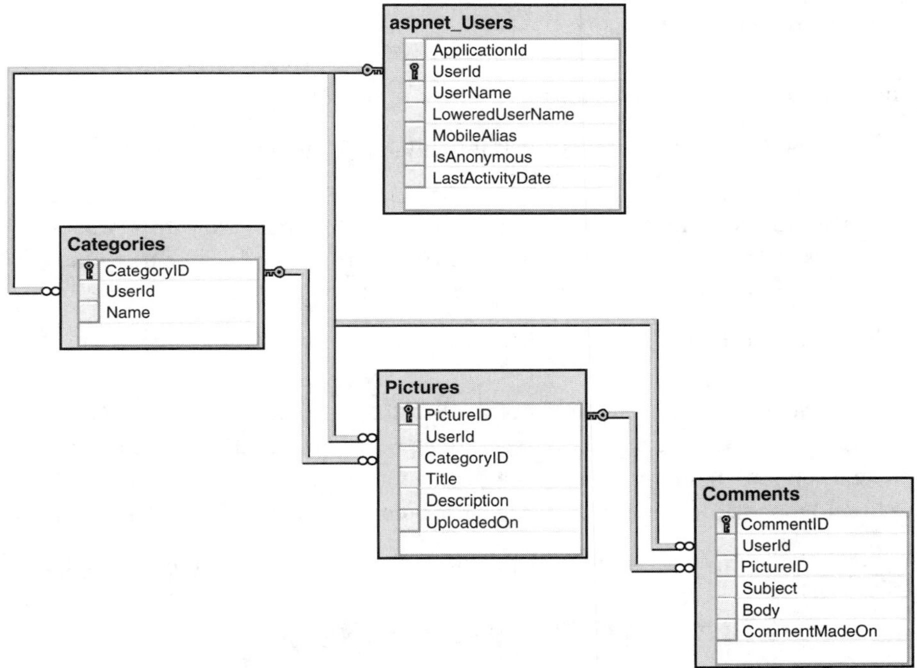

FIGURE 22.4 The five one-to-many relationships are shown in the database's ER diagram.

As we discussed in Hour 20, configuring the website to support user accounts involves launching the ASP.NET Website Administration Tool and changing the Security settings so that the authentication type used is for users coming over the Internet. Doing so creates the ASPNETDB database in our website's App_Data folder.

If you are following along, take a moment to complete these steps so that your website now has the appropriate user account-related database tables. Refer to Hour 20, if needed, for instructions on this process.

Creating the `Categories` Table

With the ASPNETDB database created, we're ready to start adding our tables unique to our photo album application. The first table we'll add is the Categories table, which will have one record for each category created by each user in the system. To add a table to the ASPNETDB database, go to the Database Explorer and drill down to the ASPNETDB database. Next, right-click on the Tables node and choose Add New Table.

The `Categories` table needs to capture the following information:

- A way to uniquely identify each category
- What user this category belongs to
- The name of the category

This translates into three columns:

- `CategoryID`—An auto-increment primary key column of type `int`, which uniquely identifies each category.
- `UserId`—A column of type `uniqueidentifier` that relates a category back to a user. This column must be of type `uniqueidentifier` because that's the type used to uniquely identify each account in the `aspnet_Users` table.
- `Name`—A column of type `nvarchar(50)`, used to store the name of the category.

None of these columns should allow Nulls. Recall that to mark a column as a primary key, you select the column and click the primary key icon in the Toolbar; to make a column an auto-increment, set the Identity Specification section in the Column Properties to Yes. Refer to Hour 13 for more information on these processes.

Figure 22.5 shows Visual Web Developer after this table's structure has been defined.

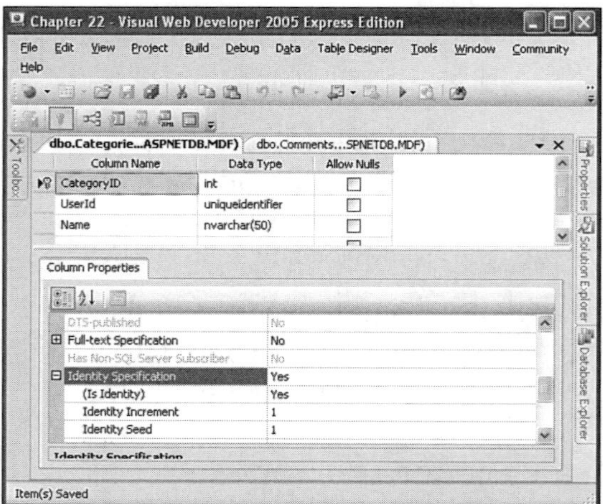

FIGURE 22.5
The `Categories` table has three columns.

Adding the Foreign Key Constraint

The `aspnet_Users` table has a one-to-many relationship with the `Categories` table. If we want to help protect the integrity and consistency of our database, it behooves us to add a foreign key constraint to ensure that the `UserId` values in `Categories` map to existing users. To accomplish this in Visual Web Developer, go to the Table Designer menu and choose Relationships. This will display the Foreign Key Relationships dialog box. Click the Add button to add a new foreign key relationship (see Figure 22.6).

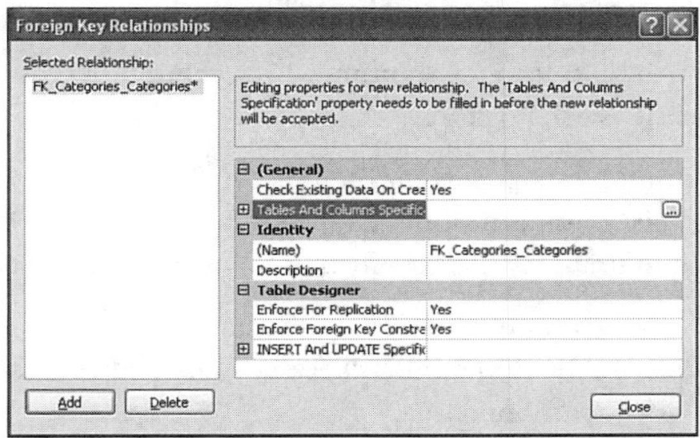

FIGURE 22.6 Configure a table's foreign key constraints through the Foreign Key Relationships dialog box.

In the foreign key constraint properties on the right, a Table and Columns Specifications property includes a pair of ellipses. Clicking on the ellipses displays the Table and Columns dialog box, where you can indicate the primary key and foreign key columns participating in the constraint.

For this particular foreign key constraint, the primary key is the `UserId` column in the `aspnet_Users` table, while the foreign key is the `UserId` column in the `Categories` table. Make these selections (as shown in Figure 22.7) and click the OK button.

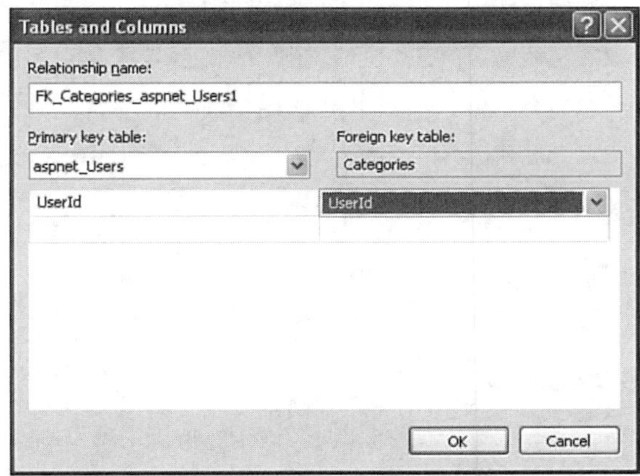

FIGURE 22.7 Map the `Categories` table's `UserId` column to the `aspnet_Users` table's `UserId` column.

After adding the foreign key constraint, click Close to close the Foreign Key Relationships dialog box. Finally, save the `Categories` table by going to the File menu and choosing Save Categories.

Defining the Structure of the `Pictures` Table

As we will see in Hour 24, when a user uploads a picture to the photo album site, the actual image file is saved on the web server's file system. The picture's additional information—the title, description, category, and so on—needs to be saved in the database. Therefore, the `Pictures` database will have the following columns:

- `PictureID`—An auto-increment, primary key column of type `int`, which uniquely identifies each picture.
- `UserId`—A column of type `uniqueidentifier` that relates a picture back to a user. Again, this column must be of type `uniqueidentifier` because that's the type used to uniquely identify each account in the `aspnet_Users` table.
- `CategoryID`—A column of type `int` that relates a picture back to a category. For this field, leave the Allow Nulls check box checked because assigning a picture to a category is optional.
- `Title`—An `nvarchar(50)` column used to store the title of the picture.
- `Description`—An `nvarchar(1000)` column used to store a description about the picture.
- `UploadedOn`—A column with a `datetime` data type that indicates when the picture was uploaded to the site.

Only the `CategoryID` column should have the Allow Nulls check box checked. Figure 22.8 shows the `Pictures` table after its columns have been created.

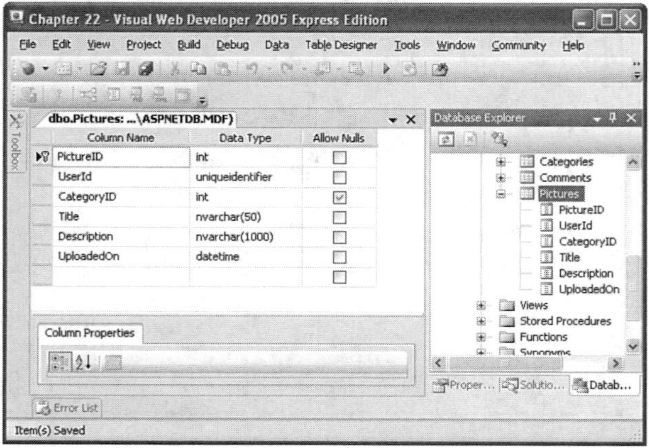

FIGURE 22.8 Each picture added to the system will be represented by a row in the `Pictures` table.

In addition to the columns, we need to add two foreign key constraints. The first constraint is identical to the sole foreign key constraint in the `Categories` table; it associates the primary key column UserId in the aspnet_Users table with the foreign key column UserId in the Pictures table.

The second foreign key constraint associates the primary key column CategoryID in the Categories table with the foreign key column CategoryID in the Pictures table. Recall that, by default, when a primary key column value is changed or the record is deleted, the change or deletion fails if there are existing foreign key records. With this default behavior, a user would be unable to delete a category if pictures were currently associated with that category.

For this application, let's allow users to delete categories, even if there are existing pictures associated with that category. If the user deletes such a category, we'll reset the associated pictures' CategoryID values to the Null value, which indicates that it does not belong to any category. To specify this through the foreign key constraint, select the INSERT and UPDATE Specification property in the Foreign Key Relationships dialog box and change the Delete Rule from No Action to Set Null (see Figure 22.9).

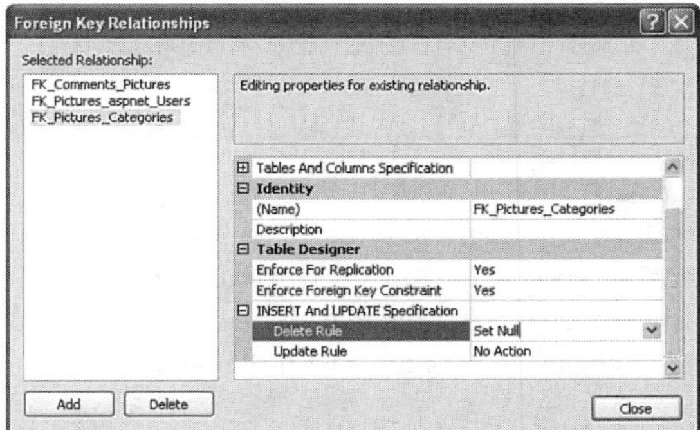

FIGURE 22.9
When a category is deleted, all associated pictures revert to the default category.

Creating the `Comments` Table

The final table in the photo album database is the Comments table, which will have one row for each comment left by a user for a picture. The Comments table has the following six columns:

- CommentID—An auto-increment, primary key column of type int, which uniquely identifies each comment.
- UserId—A column of type uniqueidentifier that relates a picture back to a user.
- PictureID—A column of type int that relates a comment back to a picture.
- Subject—An nvarchar(50) column used to store the subject of the comment.

- Body—An nvarchar(1000) column used to store the body of the comment.
- CommentMadeOn—A column with a datetime data type that indicates when the comment was made.

All columns in the Comments table should have the Allow Nulls check box unchecked. Figure 22.10 shows the table after its columns have been created.

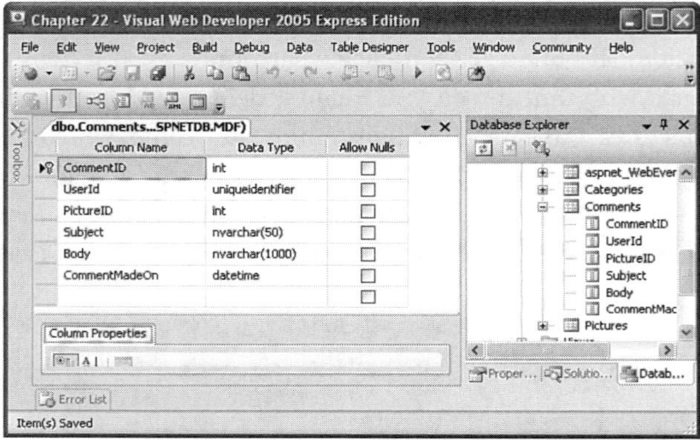

FIGURE 22.10 When a user leaves a comment, the comment will be added to this table.

In addition to the columns, we need to add two foreign key constraints. The first constraint is identical to the sole foreign key constraint in the Categories table and the first constraint we added to the Pictures tables; it associates the primary key column UserId in the aspnet_Users table with the foreign key column UserId in the Comments table.

The second one associates the primary key column PictureID in the Pictures table with the foreign key column PictureID in the Comments table. This constraint, by default, will prohibit a user from deleting a picture that has comments. Because a user can't edit or delete comments through the online photo album, it makes sense to have the comments for a picture automatically deleted when the picture is deleted. To accomplish this, set the Delete Rule for this foreign key constraint to Cascade (see Figure 22.11).

At this point we have created the entire database structure for the photo album application. The only step in the design process that remains is creating mockups for the application's user interface.

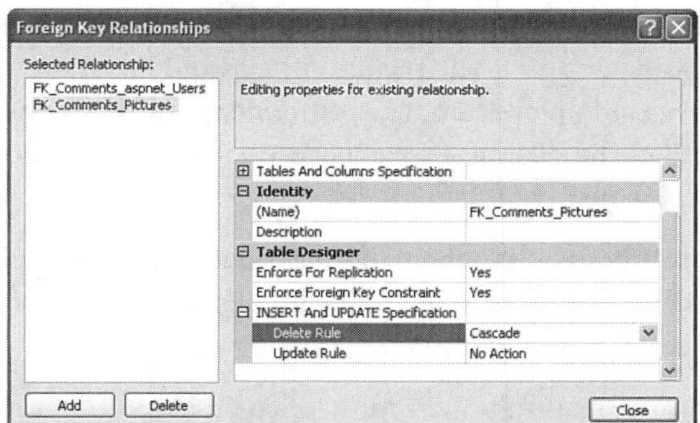

FIGURE 22.11 When a picture is deleted, all associated comments are automatically deleted as well.

Sketching Mockups for the Application's User Interface

The final step in the design process is creating mockups for the application's proposed user interface. The user interface is the forward-facing portion of an application, the means by which the end user interacts with the system. For web applications, the user interface is the set of the site's web pages.

Because end users judge the merit of an application by its usability, it's important to ensure that your application's user interface is intuitive. When trying to decide on a user interface, I often return to the use cases outlined in the earlier stages of the design process and ask myself, "What sorts of controls and layout would I need on this web page to make it easy for a user to accomplish this particular use case?"

The reason behind creating mockups is to generate ideas about the user interface, assess a proposed user interface's usability, and make sure that you and the customer are on the same page regarding the look and feel of the application. These mockups do not need to be functional web pages; in fact, many designers prefer to create their user interfaces using pencil and paper. Another option is to create dummy ASP.NET pages. These pages lack any sort of functionality, but include the Web controls that will make up their user interface.

The photo album application site will need the following web pages:

- **A home page**—From this page anonymous users should see a `Login` link, while authenticated users should be able to quickly jump to an administration page from which they can manage their photo album. Additionally, the home page should list all users in the system, with a link to view their photo album.

- **A photo album page**—The photo album page will list the categories and pictures for a particular user. The pictures listed would include the picture and its title, category, and uploaded date. Furthermore, the visitor viewing the photo album can filter the pictures by category. Clicking on a particular photo will take the user to the photo detail page.
- **A photo detail page**—From here, a user should see the picture, its title, category, uploaded date, description, and comments. Furthermore, if the user is authenticated, he can add a new comment.
- **A photo administration page**—Authenticated users can visit the photo administration page to upload new pictures to their account and to manage their existing pictures and categories.

I invite you to take a few minutes to sketch out some mockups for the proposed list of web pages. There's no right or wrong user interface, so feel free to try out various designs and ideas. When creating these mockups, try to put yourself in the shoes of the end user, asking yourself how you would accomplish the particular tasks outlined in the use cases. Strive to make your user interface as streamlined as possible for the use cases we identified earlier.

Did you Know?

To help assess the quality of your user interface design, recruit some people unfamiliar with your project to assist in evaluating your user interface.

Sit these volunteers in front of the mockups and read a use case to them. Then ask them how they would accomplish that task. If your use cases are simply sketches on paper, the volunteers might just show you where they would click or what functionality they'd expect to have happen when they performed some action.

Pay attention to the way the users interact with the user interface. Do certain aspects about the interface confuse or distract users? Are the volunteers having difficulty determining what they need to do to accomplish a given task? These are clues that can help you create a truly usable and intuitive user interface.

By the Way

When you're dealing with actual customers, remember that the design process is typically an iterative one. After creating the mockups, you'd return to the customers, presenting to them your understanding of the requirements and your mockups. At this point the customers may give you the green light to start implementing the system, but more than likely they'll have some refinements of the requirements and some ideas on how to tailor the user interface to fit the way they anticipate using the application.

Summary

This hour is the first of three hours during which we'll be building an online photo album application from the ground up. When we're beginning any nontrivial project, the first step is always a planning phase. The future success of the project can be predicted by the thoroughness and quality of the planning phase; a project that is insufficiently planned is almost certain to fail.

In software development, this typical design phase is iterative and involves three steps:

1. Collect design requirements from the customer.
2. For applications that need to persist data, implement the database schema necessary to capture the data spelled out in the design requirements.
3. Create mockups of the web application.

In this hour we worked through each of these three stages. In the first stage, the requirements for the photo album application were tersely defined, along with more palatable use cases.

Following that, we turned our attention to creating the database structure needed for this project. In previous database examples, we looked at working with databases with only a single table; however, the photo album application's database is constructed of several, related tables. In this hour we saw how one-to-one, one-to-many, and many-to-many relationships can be expressed, as well as how to use foreign key constraints to help ensure relational integrity.

This hour concluded with a discussion of the purpose and benefits of creating a mockup of the user interface. With the design phase complete, we're ready to start building our photo album application!

Q&A

Q. ***Why does the `CategoryID` column in the `Pictures` table have the Allow Null check box checked? What does it mean if a record in the `Pictures` table has a Null value for its `CategoryID` column, and is this allowed with the foreign key constraint?***

A. One of the design requirements for the system was that users could *optionally* place each picture in a category. This means that a given picture may be in a particular category or in no category at all. When a record in the `Pictures` table has a Null value for its `CategoryID` column, the picture does not belong to any category.

This is a common technique used when the records of the "many" table in a one-to-many relationship might not belong to any record in the "one" table. For this reason, Null values are allowed by the foreign key constraint.

Q. ***When a user uploads a picture, I want to capture additional information, such as whether the user wants this picture to be viewable by other users. Is it okay to add my own custom columns to the*** `Pictures` ***table?***

A. If you are comfortable adding your own columns and have some data you want to capture that isn't being captured by my suggested data model, then feel free to add the additional columns. (Of course, you'll need to also add additional Web controls to the user interface for uploading a picture.)

What I recommend, however, is that you first complete the photo album application exactly as I'm doing it so that you can follow along in the book. Then, after creating and testing the application, return to the design phase and augment the requirements to include the additional information you are in interested in storing.

Workshop

Quiz

1. What are the three stages of the design process in software development?
2. True or False: The design process for software development is usually an iterative process.
3. What is a use case, and how does it help in the design process?
4. Imagine that you have two tables—`Employees` and `Departments`—with the primary key columns `EmployeeID` and `DepartmentID`, respectively. If you wanted to establish a one-to-many relationship between `Departments` and `Employees`, what would you do?
5. How does a foreign key constraint guarantee referential integrity?

Answers

1. The three stages of the design process in software development are as follows: collect design requirements from the customer; for applications that need to persist data, implement the database schema necessary to capture the data spelled out in the design requirements; and create mockups of the web application.

2. True.

3. A use case is a paragraph or two describing, in plain English, how a particular task would be accomplished. Use cases help describe a system's functionality in everyday language and can be used to help with creating the database structure and ensuring that the user interface is usable.

4. To establish this relationship, you would add a `DepartmentID` column to the `Employees` table and then create a foreign key constraint, with the primary key column being the `DepartmentID` field in the `Departments` table and the foreign key column being the `DepartmentID` in the `Employees` table.

5. A foreign key constraint consists of a primary key column and a foreign key column. It ensures referential integrity by guaranteeing that the value in the foreign key column is either Null or maps to a value in the primary key column. With a foreign key constraint, an error will be raised and the modification will fail if the foreign key column value is changed to a value not in the set of values in the primary key column, or if a primary key column value is changed or the row is deleted and there are corresponding values in the foreign key column.

Exercises

There are no additional exercises for this hour or the remaining two. The creation of the photo album is our main exercise!

HOUR 23

Building the Photo Album Application Foundation

In this hour, we will cover

- **Looking in detail at the web pages that make up the online photo album application**
- **Creating a master page for the photo album site**
- **Adding dummy pages to the website project for each of the required pages**
- **Completing the majority of the ASP.NET pages associated with the application**
- **Adding common sitewide elements to the master page, including a site navigation control and a login Web control**

Now that we've worked our way through the design phase, we're ready to start building our online photo album application! But what do we start with? What web pages should we create first? What's the best way to start implementing this project? When we're creating any software application, it often helps to break down the task into small, manageable, independent chunks, which is the tactic we'll be taking when creating this application. Rather than rushing in and creating the web pages to complete a particular use case, we'll first step back and survey the project as a whole, mapping out our plan of attack.

For web applications, the manageable, independent chunks of a web application are typically web pages. In the preceding hour we identified a number of web pages that would be needed: a home page, a login page, a page to display the categories and pictures for a specified user's album, and so on. By the end of this hour, we'll have a number of these pages complete.

Rather than aimlessly picking a web page and starting development there, I find it helpful to list the web pages that will make up the site and create the actual ASP.NET pages in the website. At this early stage, these pages don't need to have any functionality. The mere act of thinking about the website's pages, creating these dummy pages, and understanding how users will move from one page to another helps in selecting where to start the development process.

By the end of this hour, we'll have the majority of the site's ASP.NET pages finished and fully functional. Those pages that we do not get to in this hour will be examined and implemented in the next and final hour.

Partitioning the Application into Manageable Tasks

If you have never worked on a decent-sized software application, you may be experiencing a plethora of emotions regarding the work that lies ahead of us. You may be a bit excited because this will be your first opportunity to create a fully functional, real-world ASP.NET application. You may also be a bit anxious because there is a good deal of work ahead, and only this hour and the next with which to complete it! At this point there is one very large task on our plate: "Create the photo album website."

In life, whenever you are faced with a task that seems overwhelming, break it down into smaller, more manageable tasks. As those who have had experience creating software applications know, this pearl of wisdom rings even more true when it comes to software development. When breaking down a complicated step into many smaller steps, I find it helpful to break down the task into just one step and then implement that substep before breaking down tasks any further.

For example, you might start breaking up the "Create the photo album task" into steps like "Create the home page," "Create the login page," "Create the photo album page," and so on. Then, rather than actually creating these ASP.NET pages, you may try to break down the task to another level. The "Create the home page" task can be broken down into "Displaying a welcome message" and "Showing the list of users who have photo albums." The "Showing the list of users who have photo albums" task can then be further broken down into "Use a SqlDataSource control to get the list of users in the database" and "Use a GridView control to list these users, with a link to the users' albums" tasks. At this point, however, you're likely to soon feel overwhelmed again because the list of to-do items keeps growing.

Instead, break down each step into substeps and then implement those substeps. In our example that would mean after breaking "Create the photo album task" into steps like "Create the home page," "Create the login page," and so on, we would actually create the web pages. Granted, these pages would not have any real functionality in them at this point, but implementing the substeps before drilling down further in any other step helps keep the list of steps on our plate at sensible levels.

When you're creating ASP.NET web applications, the implementation process typically adheres to the following pattern:

1. Create the site's master page.
2. Determine which web pages are needed in the site.
3. Create a dummy page for each of the required pages.
4. Determine which page to implement at this point and break down the page's requirements into manageable steps.
5. After the page chosen in step 4 is complete and fully functional, return to step 4 and choose another page. Repeat until the website is complete.

Although step 4 is written here as a single step, it may involve a large number of substeps, depending on the complexity of the page being implemented. In this hour we will start by proceeding through the first three steps. Following that, we'll implement a number of the site's pages, wrapping up the entire project by the end of the next hour.

Did you Know?

> When you're implementing a particular web page, there are no hard and fast rules regarding when you should break down the high-level task—implementing the web page—into simpler steps. My general rule of thumb is whenever a particular task either feels intimidating or is too complex to understand it in its entirety, I break it down.

Adding a Simple Master Page

As we discussed in Hour 21, "Using Master Pages to Provide Sitewide Page Templates," the first step to take when creating a multipage ASP.NET site is to create a master page. With the master page in place, we can start creating the individual web pages in the site. This initial master page need not be perfect and can later be modified. The idea is to get a master page created right off the bat because it's much easier to create a new page that inherits from a master page than to take an existing page and configure it to use a master page. Therefore, our first step is to create a master page.

Feel free to have your master page's look and feel be unique to your tastes, but do make certain that, at minimum, you have a ContentPlaceHolder control, a place to put a SiteMapPath control, and a place to put a LoginView control. As Figure 23.1 shows, my master page consists of a three-row table. The first row spans two columns, has a purple background, and displays the title of the website. The second row has two columns. The left column will eventually hold a SiteMapPath control; for now, I've just put the text `Breadcrumb will go here`. The right column will eventually contain a LoginView control that will display a `Login` link for anonymous users and a personalized message for authenticated users. For now, though, I've just put in the text *`Login information will go here`*. The bottom row—which, like the top row, spans two columns—contains the master page's sole ContentPlaceHolder control.

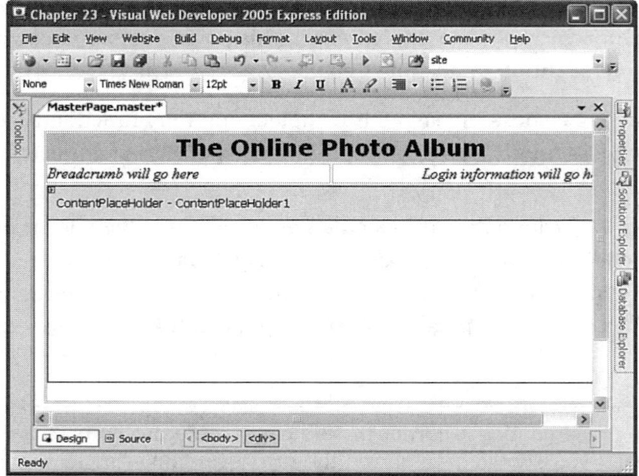

FIGURE 23.1
Start by creating your site's master page.

Creating the Dummy Web Pages

When you have the master page in place, the next step is to identify and create the site's web pages, having them inherit the master page we just created. Our site needs the following pages:

- `Default.aspx`—The site's home page.
- `Login.aspx`—The page a user will be taken to in order to log in to the site.
- `CreateAccount.aspx`—The page a visitor can access to create a user account.
- `PhotoAlbum.aspx`—The photo album page, which lists the categories and pictures for a particular user.
- `PhotoDetail.aspx`—The page that displays a single photo, including the interface for viewing and leaving comments.
- `Default.aspx` (in the `PhotoAdmin` folder)—When users want to administer their photo album, they'll come to this folder. The `Default.aspx` page allows users to add, edit, and remove pictures from their photo album.
- `ManageCategories.aspx` (in the `PhotoAdmin` folder)—Users can add, edit, and delete their photo album categories from this page.

For the photo album administration pages, first create a folder named `PhotoAdmin` and then add to that folder the files `Default.aspx` and `ManageCategories.aspx`; all other pages should be added to the website's root directory.

> **Did you Know?**
> Your website may already have the generic `Default.aspx` page. Rather than attempt to have the existing `Default.aspx` page inherit from the master page, it's quicker to simply delete this dummy page and re-create it, selecting a master page.

As we discussed earlier, at this point we're not worried about adding any functionality to these pages. We'll come back to these pages one at a time and add the necessary functionality; for now, we just want to focus on doing one task at a time. Rather than leaving these new pages without any content at all, I usually place the name of the page in the Content region.

At this point we have tackled the first three steps for creating the photo album application. Congratulations! We are now ready to actually implement the site's web pages.

Implementing the User Account-Related Pages

In the preceding hour we created the `ASPNETDB` database, which houses the database tables responsible for managing user accounts. These tables were automatically created by ASP.NET by using the ASP.NET Website Administration Tool and setting the authentication settings. To create a site that fully supports user accounts, however, generating these tables is only the first step. At minimum, we'll need to add a page that allows users with existing accounts to log back into the site. Depending on the application's requirements, we may also need web pages that allow visitors to create accounts and help them reset their forgotten passwords.

The design requirements laid out in the preceding hour for the online photo album application were a little vague as to what features needed to be supported. Specifically, the requirements stated that "The site must support user accounts." The use cases talk about a fictional user creating a new user account through the site but don't mention whether a user must be able to retrieve a forgotten password. Therefore, the online photo album application won't include a password reminder page. This is something, however, that you are encouraged to add on your own!

The photo album application has two web pages for working with user accounts:

- `CreateAccount.aspx`—Allows a visitor to create a new account.
- `Login.aspx`—Enables an existing user to log back on to the site

These two pages will use the login Web controls examined previously in Hour 20, "Managing Your Site's Users." If you need to brush up on these controls, feel free to skim through Hour 20 to refamiliarize yourself as needed.

Allowing Visitors to Create User Accounts

The process for implementing the `CreateAccount.aspx` page can be broken down into the following steps:

1. Add any instructional or header text to the page.
2. Drag and drop the CreateUserWizard control from the Toolbox onto the page's Design view.
3. Configure the CreateUserWizard control's properties.

For step 1, add whatever instructional or heading text you deem necessary. I decided to add `Create a New Account` at the top of the content region, followed by a short message explaining that only users with an account can add pictures to the site. After you have added the text you want to appear on the page, go to the Toolbox's Login section and locate the CreateUserWizard control. Drag and drop this control onto the `CreateAccount.aspx` page.

Finally, configure the CreateUserWizard control's properties. Again, feel free to use whatever property settings you like. For my implementation, I started by using the Auto Format Wizard and chose the Classic option. Next, I wanted to include a Cancel button on this page, so I set the `DisplayCancelButton` property to `True` and the `CancelDestinationPageUrl` property to `~/Default.aspx`. With these property settings, if users decided they do not want to create an account, they can click the Cancel button, at which point they'll be returned to the site's home page.

Recall that after users create an account, they are shown a confirmation message—`Your account has been successfully created`—along with a Continue button. The `ContinueDestinationPageUrl` property specifies where they are taken after creating an account. You can set this to the home page's URL, if you like; however, after users create an account, it might be nice to send them directly to the page where they can manage their photo album. Therefore, I set this property value to `~/PhotoAdmin/Default.aspx`.

Figure 23.2 shows `CreateAccount.aspx` when viewed through a browser. Take a moment to test your page in a browser and add a handful of new user accounts.

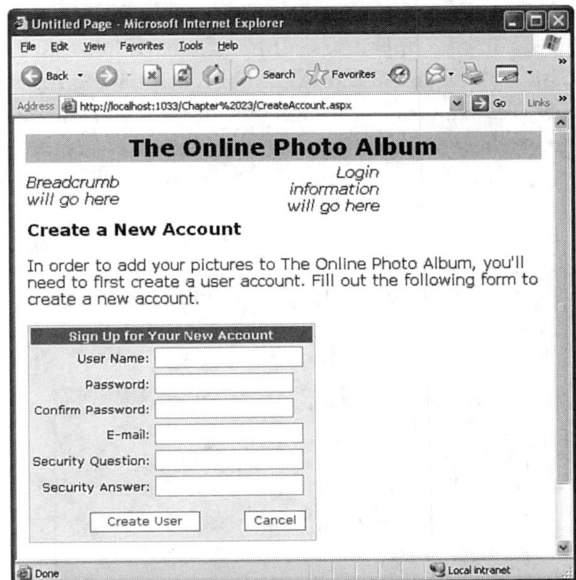

FIGURE 23.2 The `CreateAccount.aspx` page, when viewed through a browser.

By the Way

> Note that the master page still shows the ***`Breadcrumb will go here`*** and ***`Login information will go here`*** messages. This, of course, will be fixed eventually, after we set up the site navigation and create a login page.
>
> The beauty of master pages is that these additional user interface elements can be added at some later point and, upon doing so, are immediately reflected in all of the ASP.NET pages that inherit the master page.

Providing a Login Page

Similar to the `CreateAccount.aspx` page, the process for implementing the `Login.aspx` page can be broken down into the following steps:

1. Add any instructional or header text to the page.
2. Drag and drop the Login control from the Toolbox onto the page's Design view.
3. Configure the Login control's properties.

For step 1, I added a single header titled `Login to the Site` to the top of the content region. After you have added the text you want to appear on the page, go to the Toolbox's Login section and drag and drop the Login control onto the page's Design view.

As with the CreateUserWizard control in the previous section, I started step 3 by improving the Login control's appearance through the Auto Format Wizard, opting again for the Classic option. Because users might reach the login page but not have an account already created, I set the Login control's `CreateUserText` and `CreateUserUrl` properties to `Create an Account` and `~/CreateAccount.aspx`, respectively. This adds a link at the bottom of the Login control that the users can click to create an account.

Figure 23.3 shows `Login.aspx` when viewed through a browser. As with the `CreateAccount.aspx` page, be sure to take a few minutes to test the functionality; ensure that you can log in with an existing user's credentials.

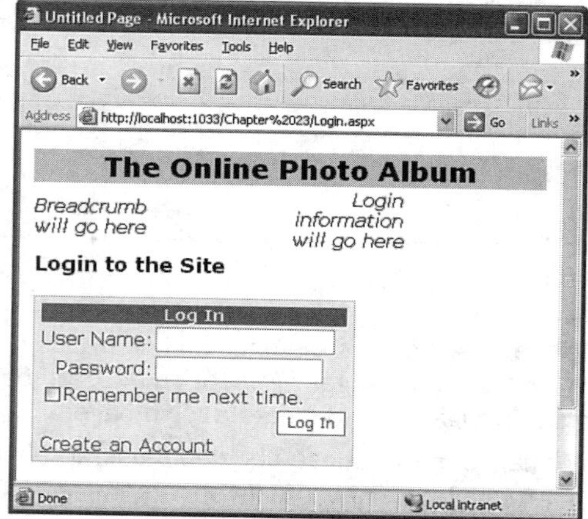

FIGURE 23.3 An existing user can log in to the site through the `Login.aspx` page.

Adding Login Information to the Master Page

Now that we have created the login page, let's go back to the master page and add in the login information in the header region. Specifically, we'll use a LoginView control. Recall that the LoginView control has two templates: AnonymousTemplate and LoggedInTemplate. When the visiting user is authenticated, the LoggedInTemplate's content is rendered; however, if the visiting user has not logged in, the AnonymousTemplate is displayed instead.

For anonymous users, let's display a link to the login page. For authenticated users, let's display a short message—`Welcome back, `*`username`*—along with a link to log out the users and a link to take them to the page where they can administer their photo album. The `Login` and `Logout` links in the two templates can both be added using the LoginStatus control. This control, which we examined in Hour 20, displays a `Login` link for anonymous users and a `Logout` link for authenticated users. To add the link for logged-in users to administer their photo album, use a HyperLink control in the LoggedInTemplate whose `NavigateUrl` property points to the `PhotoAdmin/Default.aspx` page.

To accomplish this, perform the following steps:

1. Go to the master page and drag and drop a LoginView control from the Toolbox onto the master page region that currently has the message *`Login information will go here`*.
2. In the AnonymousTemplate, add a LoginStatus control. This will display the `Login` link.
3. Switch the LoginView to the LoggedInTemplate.
4. Type into the template **`Welcome back,`** and then add a LoginName control.
5. After the LoginName control added in step 4, add the LoginStatus control to the template as well.
6. After the LoginStatus control added in step 5, add a HyperLink control to the template as well. Set its `Text` property to Manage Photo Album and its `NavigateUrl` property to `~/PhotoAdmin/Default.aspx`.

If you save the master page and view the site's home page, you will not be logged in and should therefore see a screen similar to Figure 23.4. Note that when you're not logged in, the `Login` link is shown. Finally, create a new user account. After doing so, you should notice that the login user interface has changed from a `Login` link to the message `Welcome back,` *`username`*, along with a `Logout` link (see Figure 23.5).

FIGURE 23.4
When you visit the home page as an anonymous user, the `Login` link is shown.

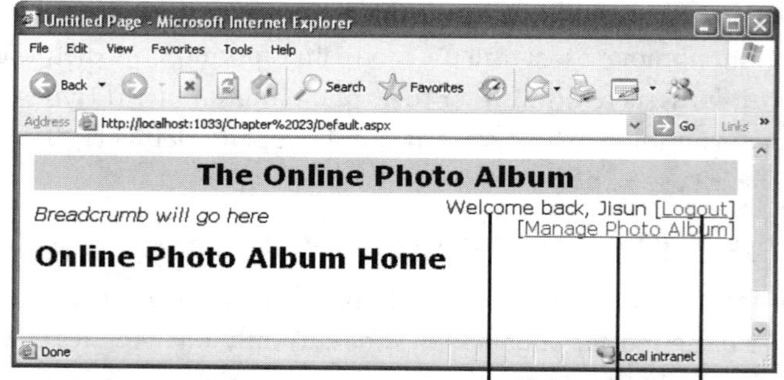

FIGURE 23.5 When users are authenticated, a welcome message is displayed along with two links.

Creating the Photo Album Website's Home Page

With the user account-related web pages out of the way, the next page we'll implement is the photo album website's home page. The purpose of this page is to list all of the photo albums hosted through our site, allowing visitors to quickly jump to a particular album. While I mentioned earlier that the `PhotoAlbum.aspx` page will be used to display the pictures in a particular user's photo album, we have yet to go into detail on how this will be accomplished. This may seem like a difficult task at first; after all, how will the page know what user's album to display?

In Hour 9, "Web Form Basics," we talked about various ways of passing information from one page to another. The mechanism used most frequently by ASP.NET applications is the postback, which occurs whenever a Button Web control is clicked. However, as discussed in Hour 9, there are other techniques for passing information. One common mechanism is to use the **querystring**. The querystring is an optional string that can be tacked on to the end of a web page's URL. Specifically, if a website URL has a question mark in it (?), everything after the question mark is considered the querystring.

You have probably seen web pages whose URL looks like

```
http://www.someserver.com/somePage.aspx?Name=Scott&Age=21
```

Here, the contents after the question mark are considered the querystring.

Therefore, to view a particular user's photo album, we'll use the URL `PhotoAlbum.aspx?ID=`*`UserId`*, where *`UserId`* is the unique identifier for the user in the `aspnet_Users` table. `PhotoAlbum.aspx` will then examine this querystring value and display the pictures that belong to that user. (We'll see how this is accomplished in the next hour.)

Therefore, we want to have our home page list all of the approved users in the `aspnet_Users` table, along with a link to `PhotoAlbum.aspx?ID=`*`UserId`*. To accomplish this, we will need to implement the following steps:

1. Include any instructional or header text to the page's content region.
2. Add a SqlDataSource control to the page that returns all approved users from the `aspnet_Users` table.
3. Add a GridView control to the page and associate it with the SqlDataSource from step 2.
4. Configure the GridView control to include a HyperLinkField that renders as a properly formatted link to `PhotoAlbum.aspx`, passing the particular user's `UserId` column value in the querystring.

For step 1, I added the header text `Online Photo Album Home` along with some instructions to the visitors, letting them know how to view an existing user's album as well as how to get started posting their own pictures.

Adding and Configuring the SqlDataSource Control

The next step in creating the photo album application's home page is adding a SqlDataSource control that retrieves those user accounts that are currently approved and have not been locked out. As we discussed in Hour 20, user accounts can be marked as not approved or locked out from the ASP.NET Website Administration Tool. Users who are not approved or who have been locked out should not appear in the list of albums on the home page.

To retrieve the list of applicable user accounts, start by adding a SqlDataSource control to the page, clicking the `Configure Data Source` link from its smart tag. From the Configure the Select Statement screen, you'll see a variety of **views** in the drop-down list, such as `vw_aspnet_MembershipUsers` and `vw_aspnet_Users`.

A view is, essentially, an alias for a more complicated `SELECT` query. For example, imagine that you had a rather involved SQL query that had a number of filter expressions and retrieved data from multiple tables. Rather than having to rewrite that SQL query every time you needed to use it, you could package it up into a view. Then the query could be executed by simply calling the view.

The `ASPNETDB` database contains a number of views to help make working with its underlying data easier. This is good news for us because the `ASPNETDB` contains multiple tables, and the queries for extracting data from multiple tables can be a bit unwieldy. By grouping these more intricate queries in a view, however, we can select the view from the SqlDataSource's wizard and work with that, bypassing the trickier SQL syntax.

The view we are interested in working with for the site's home page is the vw_aspnet_MembershipUsers view, which returns data from both the aspnet_Membership and aspnet_Users table. The aspnet_Users table contains just a list of UserIds and UserNames in the system; the additional user-related information, such as whether a user is approved or locked out, is stored in the aspnet_Membership table.

To configure the SqlDataSource control, perform the following steps:

1. From the Configure the Select Statement screen, choose the vw_aspnet_MembershipUsers view from the drop-down list.
2. From the column list, return just the UserId and UserName columns.
3. Click the WHERE button and add two filter expressions: one on the IsApproved column and the other on the IsLockedOut column. For both, use the Operator = and the Source of None, specifying a hard-coded value of True for IsApproved and False for IsLockedOut. This will ensure that only approved, non–locked-out users will be listed (see Figure 23.6).
4. Click the ORDER BY button and have the results ordered by the UserName column in ascending order.

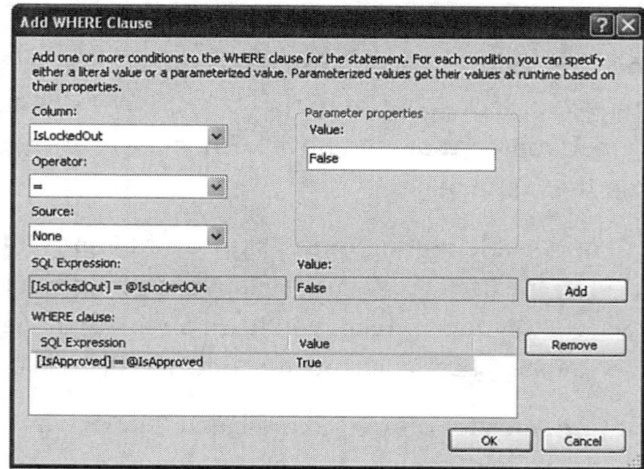

FIGURE 23.6
Add two filter expressions in the Add WHERE Clause dialog box.

After you perform steps 1 through 4, the resulting SQL SELECT query should read as follows:

```
SELECT [UserId], [UserName]
FROM [vw_aspnet_MembershipUsers]
WHERE (([IsApproved] = @IsApproved) AND ([IsLockedOut] = @IsLockedOut))
ORDER BY [UserName]
```

Furthermore, your screen should look like Figure 23.7.

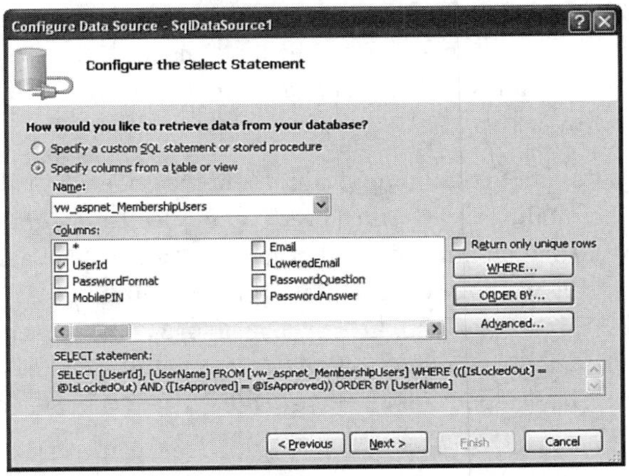
Configure Data Source - SqlDataSource1
Configure the Select Statement
How would you like to retrieve data from your database?
Specify a custom SQL statement or stored procedure
Specify columns from a table or view
Name:
vw_aspnet_MembershipUsers
Columns:
*
UserId
PasswordFormat
MobilePIN
Email
LoweredEmail
PasswordQuestion
PasswordAnswer
Return only unique rows
WHERE...
ORDER BY...
Advanced...
SELECT statement:
SELECT [UserId], [UserName] FROM [vw_aspnet_MembershipUsers] WHERE (([IsLockedOut] = @IsLockedOut) AND ([IsApproved] = @IsApproved)) ORDER BY [UserName]
< Previous
Next >
Finish
Cancel

FIGURE 23.7
The SqlDataSource control is configured to return all approved, non–locked-out users.

Displaying Links to the Photo Albums with a GridView

With the SqlDataSource control configured, the final steps are to add the GridView control, bind it to the SqlDataSource control, and configure the GridView to include a HyperLinkField. Start by dragging and dropping a GridView control from the Toolbox onto the home page in Visual Web Developer. Next, associate the GridView with the SqlDataSource control by selecting the SqlDataSource control `ID` from the drop-down list in the GridView's smart tag.

At this point, feel free to customize any of the GridView's properties. While not mandated by the design specifications, it might be nice to add sorting and paging support to the GridView. Furthermore, you might want to use the Auto Format Wizard to enhance the GridView's appearance or set the `EmptyDataText` property so as not to confuse users who are visiting a new photo album website that lacks any current accounts. (Recall that the value of the `EmptyDataText` property is displayed if no results are returned by the GridView's associated data source control.)

When you have the GridView looking the way you want, go to the GridView's smart tag and click the `Edit Columns` link, displaying the Fields dialog box. We need to add a HyperLinkField to display a link to the photo album for each user. First, though, take a moment to remove the UserId BoundField that is currently part of the GridView's fields listed in the bottom-left corner.

Next, add a new HyperLinkField and move it to the top of the column list. Finally, set the HyperLinkField's `Text` property to `View Album`, the `DataNavigateUrlFields` property to UserId, and the DataNavigateUrlFormatString property to PhotoAlbum.aspx?ID={0}. This combination of property values will add a hyperlink to each row in the GridView with the text of the link reading View Album. When visitors click on one of these links, they'll be taken to PhotoAlbum.aspx?ID=*UserId*, where *UserId* is the unique identifier of the user account whose row was clicked.

Figure 23.8 shows the photo album application's home page when viewed through a browser. This photo album site has three users' accounts: Jisun, Sam, and Scott. Clicking on the View Album link will send visitors to PhotoAlbum.aspx, passing in the particular user's UserId. For example, clicking on Jisun's View Album link will whisk the users to PhotoAlbum.aspx?ID=0fdeb883-0a34-443a-8e2d-50615308215f, whereas clicking on Scott's View Album link will lead to PhotoAlbum.aspx?ID=6b1835e1-5957-4c4e-9778-af9f1f4c5c86.

By the Way

As we discussed in the preceding hour, each user account is uniquely identified via the UserId column, which is of type uniqueidentifier. A uniqueidentifer is a very, very large number that is globally and temporally unique.

This large number is commonly represented in **hexadecimal format**, which uses 16 available characters to represent each digit (0 through 9 and *a* through *f*). The hexadecimal format is just another, more compact way to represent a large number.

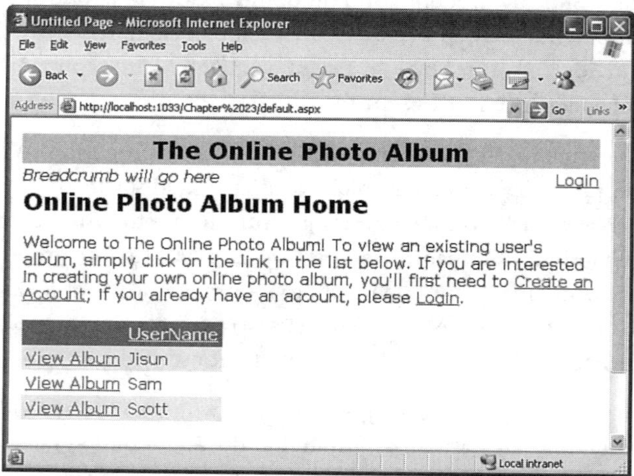

FIGURE 23.8 The home page lists each active, non–locked-out user, with a link to her album.

Managing Categories

One of the design requirements was that users be able to create, edit, and delete categories. The purpose of categories is to assist users in organizing their album. For example, users might add two categories to their album: Friends and Places. When adding a new picture to their album, they could optionally assign the picture with a given category. When visitors view a particular user's photo album, they will be able to filter the pictures by category.

The `PhotoAdmin` folder's two web pages—`Default.aspx` and `ManageCategories.aspx`—contain all of the functionality for managing a photo album, including managing categories and pictures. These pages are the most involved and complex pages in the website. It would benefit us, then, to break the involved task of managing a photo album into a series of simpler tasks:

1. Configure the ASP.NET website so that only authenticated users can visit the web pages in the `PhotoAdmin` folder.
2. Add the functionality to create new categories.
3. Allow users to edit an existing category.
4. Permit users to delete an existing category.
5. Provide the means for users to add a new picture to their album.
6. Make it possible for users to edit the information associated with a picture—its title, description, and so on.
7. Add functionality to allow users to delete existing pictures.

In this hour we'll knock out subtasks 1–4, with subtasks 5–7 left for the next hour.

Restricting Anonymous Users from Visiting the Administration Page

Because the web pages in the `PhotoAdmin` folder are used by authenticated users to manage their photo album, it's important that we restrict anonymous users from visiting the pages in this folder. As we discussed in Hour 20, the access rights for an ASP.NET website can be configured through the ASP.NET Website Administration Tool. Take a moment to load the Website Administration Tool by going to the Website menu and choosing the ASP.NET Configuration menu option.

After the ASP.NET Website Administration Tool loads, click on the `Security` link and then, from the Access Rules box, click on the `Create access rules` link. As Figure 23.9 shows, select the `PhotoAlbum` folder from the list on the left, choose the Anonymous Users and Deny radio buttons, and click OK. This will prevent unauthenticated users from visiting this page; if they attempt to do so, they'll be automatically directed to the login page.

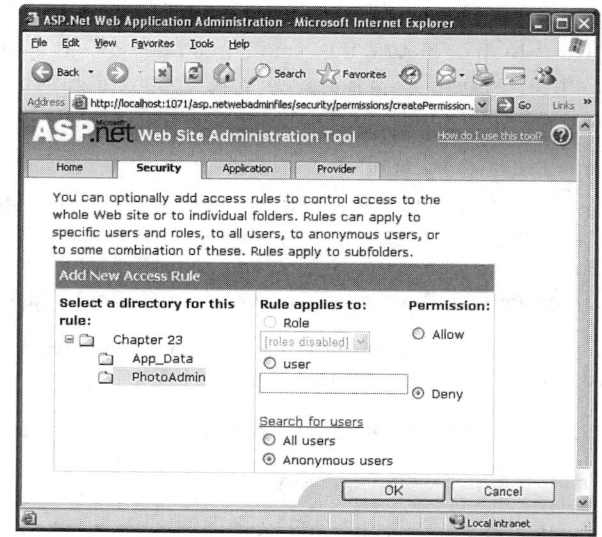

FIGURE 23.9
Configure the access rights to prevent anonymous users from visiting the administration page.

Retrieving the List of Categories for the Logged-On User

To display, edit, delete, and insert categories, we first need to add a SqlDataSource control to `PhotoAdmin/ManageCategories.aspx` that retrieves the appropriate records and also includes the `INSERT`, `UPDATE`, and `DELETE` statements. There are a few, new subtleties when adding this particular SqlDataSource control.

One such subtlety involves identifying the currently logged-on user. The `Categories` table contains *all* of the categories created by all users in the system. However, in `ManageCategories.aspx`, we want to show only the currently logged-on user's categories. The `UserId` column in the `Categories` table identifies which users have created what categories. Therefore, all we need to do is add a filter expression to the `SELECT` statement's `WHERE` clause to return only those `Categories` records whose `UserId` column equals the currently logged-on user's `UserId`.

Unfortunately, the SqlDataSource control wizard does not provide a way to create a `WHERE` clause parameter whose value is equal to the currently logged-on user's `UserId`. It does, however, allow us to set the `WHERE` clause parameter value based on a Web control on the page; therefore, we can add a Label Web control to the page whose `Text` property is assigned the currently logged-on user's `UserId` value and then use this Label control's value in the `WHERE` clause parameter.

To accomplish this, add a Label Web control to the content region in `ManageCategories.aspx`. Set the Label's `ID` property to `UserIdValue`, clear out its `Text` property, and set its `Visible` property to `False` so that the Label is not shown in the user's browser. Next, to assign the currently logged-on user's `UserId` value to the Label control, go to the page's source code portion and create the `Page_Load` event handler. (You can also create this by double-clicking in the content region.)

In the `Page_Load` event handler, add the following line of code:

```
UserIdValue.Text = Membership.GetUser().ProviderUserKey.ToString()
```

The `Membership` class provides a number of methods for working with ASP.NET's membership features. It has methods like `CreateUser()`, `GetUser()`, `GetAllUsers()`, `DeleteUser()`, and others. The `GetUser()` method, as you may have guessed, returns information about the currently logged-on user, and the `ProviderUserKey` property returns the user's `UserId` value. (The `.ToString()` method is called on the `ProviderUserKey` property value because this value is a unique identifier, and we need to convert it into a string to store it in the Label's `Text` property.) We assign this value to the Label control `UserIdValue`'s `Text` property.

Watch Out!

> If you forget to add the `.ToString()` method call, you'll get a `"Conversion from type 'Guid' to type 'String' is not valid"` error message when visiting the page.

Now that we have a Label Web control on the page that is assigned the currently logged-on user's `UserId` value, we can use this in the `WHERE` clause generated by the SqlDataSource control.

Start by dragging and dropping a SqlDataSource control from the Toolbox onto the Design view and setting its `ID` property to `categoriesDataSource`. Next, start the control's wizard and, from the Configure the Select Statement screen, choose the `Categories` table from the drop-down list and check the `CategoryID`, `UserId`, and `Name` columns. Click on the `ORDER BY` button and opt to have the results ordered by the `Name` column.

Because we need to allow the user to insert, edit, and delete categories, click the Advanced button and check the Generate `INSERT`, `UPDATE`, and `DELETE` Statements check box. You do not need to check the Use Optimistic Concurrency check box. Next, add a `WHERE` clause parameter so that only the currently logged-on user's categories are returned. Specifically, click on the `WHERE` button and, from the Add `WHERE` Clause dialog box, choose to add a parameter on the Column `UserId` with the Operator = and the Source set to the `UserIdValue` control (see Figure 23.10).

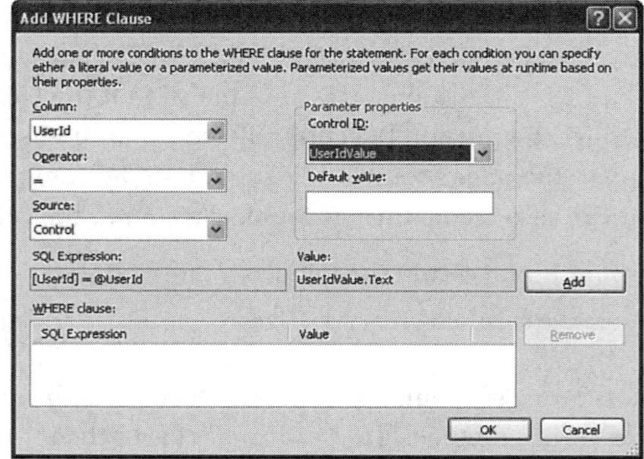

FIGURE 23.10
Add a WHERE clause filter to show only the logged-on user's categories.

Go ahead and complete the categoriesDataSource wizard. The final SQL SELECT statement should be as follows:

```
SELECT [CategoryID], [UserId], [Name]
FROM [Categories]
WHERE ([UserId] = @UserId)
ORDER BY [Name]
```

We still have one more important configuration issue with the SqlDataSource control. When working with a filter expression or an INSERT, UPDATE, or DELETE statement that contains a uniqueidentifier column, we need to manually change the SqlDataSource's parameter collections. Listing 23.1 shows the declarative markup you should see for the categoriesDataSource SqlDataSource control. (Note that many of the properties within the opening <asp:SqlDataSource> tag have been omitted for brevity.)

LISTING 23.1 The SqlDataSource Control's Declarative Markup

```
<asp:SqlDataSource ID="categoriesDataSource" runat="server" ...>
    <DeleteParameters>
        <asp:Parameter Name="CategoryID" Type="Int32" />
    </DeleteParameters>
    <UpdateParameters>
        <asp:Parameter Name="UserId" Type="Object" />
        <asp:Parameter Name="Name" Type="String" />
        <asp:Parameter Name="CategoryID" Type="Int32" />
    </UpdateParameters>
    <SelectParameters>
        <asp:ControlParameter ControlID="UserIdValue" Name="UserId"
➥PropertyName="Text" Type="Object" />
    </SelectParameters>
    <InsertParameters>
        <asp:Parameter Name="UserId" Type="Object" />
        <asp:Parameter Name="Name" Type="String" />
    </InsertParameters>
</asp:SqlDataSource>
```

The `UserId` `<asp:Parameter>` and `<asp:ControlParameter>` elements on lines 6, 11, and 14 have their `Type` property set to `Object`. For `uniqueidentifier` values, you need to remove the `Type` property altogether. That is, lines 6 and 14 should both be changed to `<asp:Parameter Name="UserId" />` and line 11 should be changed to

```
<asp:ControlParameter ControlID="UserIdValue" Name="UserId" PropertyName="Text"
/>
```

Watch Out!

> If you forget to remove the `Type` property for the parameters on lines 6 or 14, you'll receive an error with the message `"Implicit conversion from data type sql_variant to uniqueidentifier is not allowed. Use the CONVERT function to run this query"` when attempting to update or insert a value from the page. If you forget to remove the `Type` parameter on line 11, the SqlDataSource control won't return the expected results.

These two subtleties—having to express the currently logged-in user's `UserId` value through a Label control and having to manually remove the `Type` property from the SqlDataSource control's `UserId` parameters—must be performed to have this page function as expected and without error.

Adding a New Category

When visiting `ManageCategories.aspx`, a user needs to be able to view, edit, delete, and insert the categories specific to his photo album. Although all of these actions can be accomplished using the DetailsView, the DetailsView allows the user to view only one record at a time. Ideally, the user would be able to see all of the categories he has created. The GridView provides an interface for listing all categories, but it doesn't permit users to add new records. Because neither the DetailsView nor the GridView controls will suffice alone, we will use both a DetailsView and a GridView on this page—the DetailsView for adding new categories and the GridView for displaying, editing, and deleting existing categories. In this section we will examine adding and configuring the DetailsView; in the section "Viewing, Editing, and Deleting Categories," we'll look at adding the GridView.

To allow the user to add new categories, add a DetailsView to the page, set its `ID` property to `dvCategoriesInsert`, associate it with the SqlDataSource control `categoriesDataSource`, and check the Enable Inserting check box from the smart tag. By default, the DetailsView is displayed in a read-only mode, showing the value of a particular record from its associated SqlDataSource control. A user visiting the page can add a new record by clicking the Insert button, which renders the DetailsView in insert mode. Because, for this page, the DetailsView exists solely to add new records, we want it to be perpetually in insert mode, rather than requiring the user to click the `New` link. To accomplish this, set the DetailsView control's `DefaultMode` property to `Insert`.

The DetailsView's insert mode shows two TextBox controls: one for `UserId` and one for `Name`. However, we don't want to let the user choose the value of `UserId`; rather, the value of `UserId` should be the logged-on user's own `UserId`. Therefore, we need to remove the `UserId` field from the DetailsView's insert mode. Furthermore, because the DetailsView will always be displayed and always be displayed in insert mode, it doesn't make sense to have a Cancel button.

Go to the DetailsView control's smart tag and click on the `Edit Fields` link, bringing up the Fields dialog box. To remove the `UserId` BoundField from the insert interface, select the `UserId` BoundField from the list of fields in the lower-left corner and delete the field altogether. To hide the Cancel button, click on the New, Insert, Cancel command field and clear out the value of the `CancelText` property.

At this point your screen should look similar to Figure 23.11. In particular, note that the page has the `UserIdValue` Label, whose `Text` property is set to the currently logged-on user's `UserId` value; the SqlDataSource control `categoriesDataSource`, which returns the logged-on user's categories and provides `INSERT`, `UPDATE`, and `DELETE` support; and the `dvCategoriesInsert` DetailsView control, which is shown in its insert mode with just the Name BoundField.

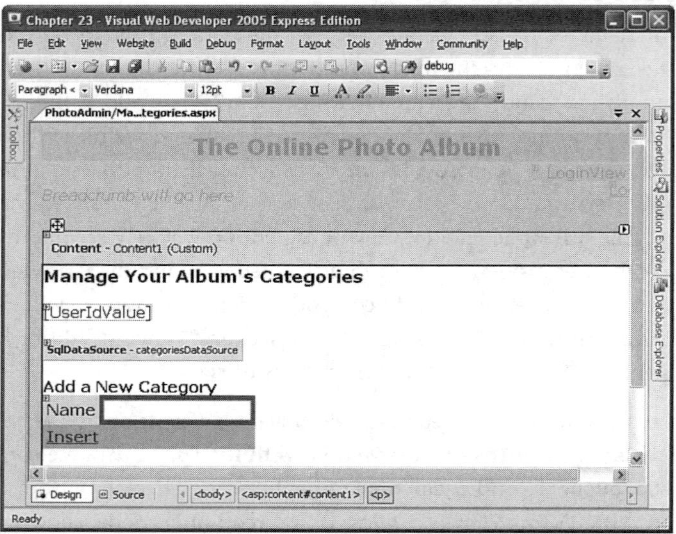

FIGURE 23.11
A DetailsView control has been added and configured to support inserting.

One more important step is still left. Right now, if you try to add a new category, you'll receive this error: "`Cannot insert the value NULL into column`

'UserId'". The reason is that we removed the UserId BoundField from the DetailsView; therefore, when the Insert button is clicked, the database INSERT fails because no value is specified for the UserId of the new category. To remedy this, we need to create an event handler for the DetailsView control's ItemInserting event. In this event handler we can programmatically set the value of the UserId to the currently logged-on user's UserId value.

To create this event handler, go to the code portion of ManageCategories.aspx and choose the DetailsView dvCategoriesInsert from the top-left drop-down list and the event ItemInserting from the top-right drop-down list. Then add the following single line of code in the event handler:

```
e.Values("UserId") = Membership.GetUser().ProviderUserKey
```

This sets the UserId value that will be inserted into the database to the value of the currently logged-on user's unique identifier.

By the Way

> The complete code listing for the ManageCategories.aspx web page is shown later in this hour in Listing 23.2.

With this one line of code, we can now add categories. Take a moment to view the page through a browser. When visiting PhotoAdmin/Default.aspx, you can add a new category for the logged-in user by entering a category name and clicking Insert. Currently, there's no display of existing categories on the page, but if you view the Categories table's data through Visual Web Developer, you can see any newly added categories.

Figure 23.12 shows PhotoAdmin/Default.aspx when viewed through a browser. Figure 23.13 shows the contents of the Categories table, viewed through Visual Web Developer, after five categories have been added by Jisun.

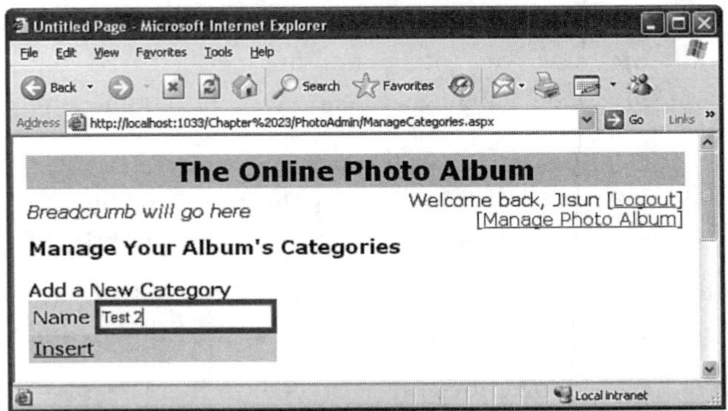

FIGURE 23.12 To add a new category, simply enter the name and click Insert.

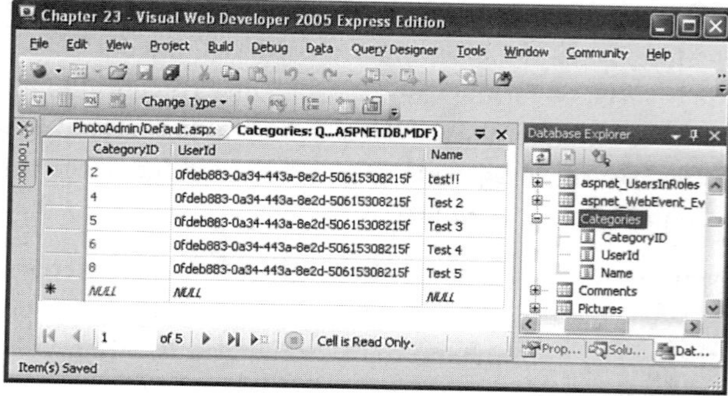

FIGURE 23.13 The categories added can be seen when listing the `Categories` table's data.

By the Way

> Clicking on the `Manage Photo Album` hyperlink takes users to `PhotoAdmin/Default.aspx`, which currently lacks any user interface. That means to test the `ManageCategories.aspx` page, you will either need to manually enter in the URL through your browser's Address bar or add a link from `PhotoAdmin/Default.aspx` to `ManageCategories.aspx`. When implementing `PhotoAdmin/Default.aspx` in the next hour, we'll add a link to `ManageCategories.aspx`, but you may go ahead and add it now to expedite testing the category administration.

Ensuring That the User Enters a Value for the Category Name

The `Categories` table requires that each record have a value for the `Name` column. Therefore, if you visit `ManageCategories.aspx` and click the Insert button *without* entering a category name, an error message will be displayed, explaining that the `Name` column cannot be assigned a Null value.

To remedy this situation, we need to use a RequiredFieldValidation control in the DetailsView's inserting interface. In Hour 16, "Deleting, Inserting, and Editing Data," we saw that the DetailsView's inserting interface can be customized by using TemplateFields; in Hour 12, "Validating User Input with Validation Controls," we looked at the validation Web controls, including the RequiredFieldValidator control, which checks that input has been entered into the specified Web control. To ensure that the user enters a value for the new category's name, complete the following steps:

1. Convert the Name BoundField to a TemplateField by going to the Fields dialog box and clicking the `Convert this field into a TemplateField` link.
2. Back in the Design view, click the `Edit Templates` link from the control's smart tag and pick the InsertItemTemplate for the Name TemplateField.
3. Add a RequiredFieldValidator control to the InsertItemTemplate.

4. Set the RequiredFieldValidator's `Display` property to `Dynamic`, its `ControlToValidate` property to the `ID` of the TextBox in the InsertItemTemplate, its `ValidationGroup` property to `CategoryInsert`, and its `ErrorMessage` property to `You must provide a name for the category`. (Depending on the background color of the DetailsView, you may need to change the `ForeColor` property from Red to a more complementary color.)

5. End template editing by clicking the `End Template Editing` link from the smart tag.

6. Click on the `Edit Fields` link in the DetailsView's smart tag and set the New, Insert, Cancel CommandField's `ValidationGroup` property to `CategoryInsert`.

By default, when a form is submitted, *all* validation controls on the page check to determine whether the control they are observing contains valid data. This behavior can be undesirable when we're working with a single page that has two separate user interfaces that each need their own validation logic. Specifically, our page will have *two* such separate user interfaces: one for adding a new category and one for listing, editing, and deleting existing categories.

By default, the validation controls added here in the Add a New Category user interface will still fire when the user is editing an existing category. Thankfully, ASP.NET provides a way to group validation controls and associate them with a particular Button. The `ValidationGroup` property—used in steps 4 and 6—creates a group of validation controls and associates that group with a Button control. All validation controls with the same `ValidationGroup` property value are considered grouped, and any Button control that has its `ValidationGroup` property set will cause only those validation controls with the same `ValidationGroup` property to fire when clicked. Step 4 creates a validation group named `CategoryInsert`, of which the RequiredFieldValidator is the sole member, and then associates the DetailsView's Insert Button with this validation group in Step 6.

After you have completed these steps, save the ASP.NET page and then view it through a browser. Now if you click the Insert button without providing a value for the new category's name, you should see an instructional message, as shown in Figure 23.14.

Viewing, Editing, and Deleting Categories

With the DetailsView for adding new categories in place, all that remains is to add the GridView control that will display the user's existing categories, as well as allow the user to update and delete these categories.

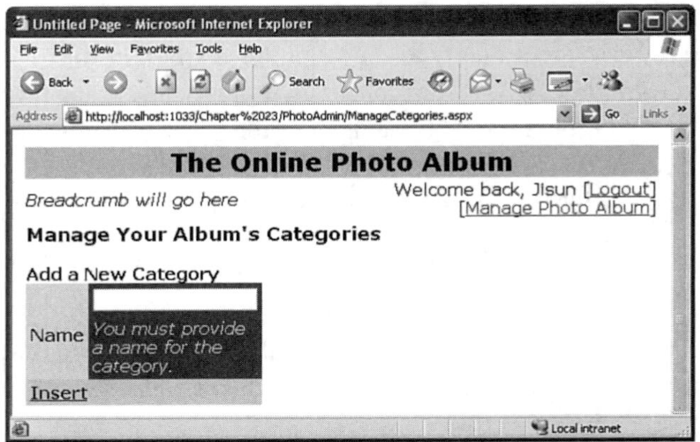

FIGURE 23.14 An instructional message is displayed if the user forgets to add a category name.

To accomplish this, add a GridView beneath the DetailsView control, associate it with the SqlDataSource control `categoriesDataSource`, and set its `ID` property to `gvCategories`. Because this GridView will list all categories and allow the user to edit and delete categories, from the smart tag, check the Enable Paging, Enable Sorting, Enable Deleting, and Enable Editing check boxes.

By the Way

> The sorting, paging, and deleting functionality works as is. Recall from our discussions in the preceding hour that when a category is deleted, all of its associated pictures are assigned to the default category. More specifically, if a particular category has a `CategoryID` value of, say, 23, and that category is deleted, all pictures with a `CategoryID` of 23 will have their `CategoryID` value set to Null instead.

By default, the GridView lists all of the columns from the associated SqlDataSource control, which includes the `CategoryID` and `UserId` columns. However, we don't want to allow the user to edit the `UserId` value for a given category, nor is there any real reason why we would want to show the `CategoryID` value. Therefore, from the GridView's smart tag, click the `Edit Columns` link and remove the `CategoryID` and `UserId` BoundFields.

When the user is editing the GridView, an error will occur if she does not provide a value for the category's name. To ensure that the user provides this value, we need to customize the GridView's editing interface by turning the Name BoundField into a TemplateField and adding a RequiredFieldValidator. Furthermore, this RequiredFieldValidator's `ValidationGroup` property must be set to some unique value—let's use `CategoryEdit`—and the GridView's CommandField's `ValidationGroup` property must be set to this same value.

As we saw in the "Adding a New Category" section earlier in this hour, when using the DetailsView to insert a new category, we needed to programmatically provide the currently logged-on user's `UserId` value. Because we removed the `UserId` BoundField from our GridView and because the SqlDataSource control's `UpdateCommand` expects a value for the `UserId` column, we need to provide this value programmatically when updating a record through the GridView. This is accomplished in much the same manner as with the DetailsView.

Start by creating an event handler for the GridView's `RowUpdating` event. In that event handler, add the following single line of code:

```
e.NewValues("UserId") = Membership.GetUser().ProviderUserKey
```

Listing 23.2 contains the complete source code portion of the `ManageCategories.aspx` page at this point in time. Lines 4–6 show the `Page_Load` event handler, where the currently logged-on user's `UserId` value is stored in a `UserIdValue` Label control so that we could use this value in the SqlDataSource control's wizard. Lines 8–11 show the DetailsView control's `ItemInserting` event handler, and lines 13–16 show the GridView's `RowUpdating` event handler, which we just added. These two event handlers both provide the currently logged-on user's `UserId` for inserting or editing purposes.

LISTING 23.2 **The Complete Source Code Portion for `ManageCategories.aspx`**

```
 1: Partial Class PhotoAdmin_ManageCategories
 2:     Inherits System.Web.UI.Page
 3:
 4:     Protected Sub Page_Load(ByVal sender As Object, ByVal e As
➥System.EventArgs) Handles Me.Load
 5:         UserIdValue.Text = Membership.GetUser().ProviderUserKey.ToString()
 6:     End Sub
 7:
 8:     Protected Sub dvCategoriesInsert_ItemInserting(ByVal sender As Object,
➥ ByVal e As System.Web.UI.WebControls.DetailsViewInsertEventArgs) Handles
➥dvCategoriesInsert.ItemInserting
 9:         'Set the UserId value to the currently logged on user's ID
10:         e.Values("UserId") = Membership.GetUser().ProviderUserKey
11:     End Sub
12:
13:     Protected Sub gvCategories_RowUpdating(ByVal sender As Object,
➥ByVal e As System.Web.UI.WebControls.GridViewUpdateEventArgs)
➥Handles gvCategories.RowUpdating
14:         'Set the UserId value to the currently logged on user's ID
15:         e.NewValues("UserId") = Membership.GetUser().ProviderUserKey
16:     End Sub
17: End Class
```

At this point you can further customize the GridView's properties. As with the other controls added throughout this hour, I used the Auto Format Wizard and selected the Classic option. I also set the GridView's `EmptyDataText` property to `"You currently do not have any categories"`. Furthermore, showing 10 records per page resulted in what seemed to me a too lengthy GridView, so I set the GridView's `PageSize` property to 5.

Congratulations! You have completed the functionality for adding, editing, viewing, and deleting categories! Take a moment to test this new functionality. Try adding some new categories and then editing, deleting, sorting, and paging through these newly created categories. Also, note that the categories displayed are user-specific. If you log off and then return to `ManageCategories.aspx` logged on as another user, you won't see the categories you just created.

Figure 23.15 shows how to edit an existing category.

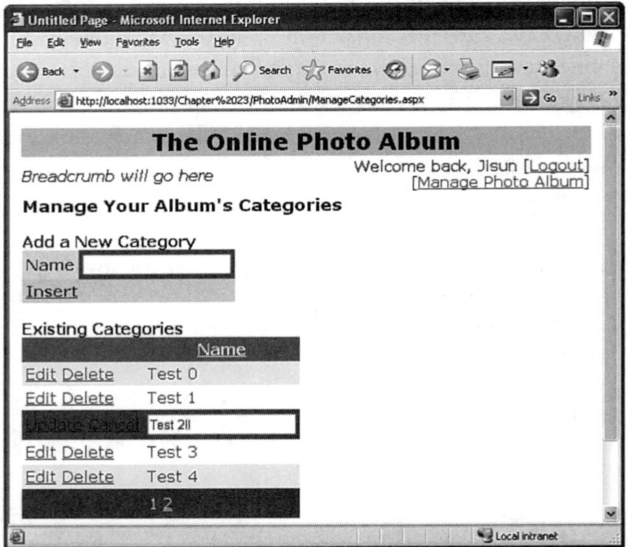

FIGURE 23.15
A user can change the name of his categories.

Summary

In this hour we started in the development phase for the online photo album application. We started by enumerating the pages needed in the project, which included a master page and six additional pages, and creating the actual files for these six pages.

After these dummy pages were created, we started implementing various pages. We began with the user account-related pages—`CreateAccount.aspx` and `Login.aspx`—which allow a user to create a new account and to log in to the site, respectively.

Following that, we created the site's home page, which listed all of the approved, non–locked-out users in the system, along with a link to their photo album.

Finally, we started work on the photo album administration web pages, which users visit to manage the categories and pictures of their album. In this hour we merely added the functionality to edit, insert, and delete categories. In the next and final hour, we'll work on the `PhotoAdmin/Default.aspx` page, which includes the capability for users to add, edit, and delete pictures. In the next hour we will also look at displaying the images in a particular user's photo album as well as leaving comments for a particular picture.

There are no quizzes or exercises for this hour.

Q&A

Q. ***From the home page the user is shown a GridView that lists all of the users in the system. Won't this list quickly become unwieldy when there are several dozen to hundreds of users?***

A. Yes, the user interface for the home page was not designed with the idea of a site with hundreds of photo albums in mind. If you expect to have 50 or more accounts on your site, it would behoove you to create an easier means of listing the albums on the site. You might include a search feature, where a visitor could enter some text and all users whose `UserName` contains that text would be returned.

Another option would be to include additional bits of information in the table, such as how many pictures are in each user's album and when the last picture was added. This type of information would help visitors determine if a particular album was recently updated or had any pictures.

To include this additional information for each user, you will need to set the SqlDataSource control's `SelectCommand` to

```
SELECT UserId, UserName,
       (SELECT COUNT(*) AS Expr1
        FROM Pictures AS p
        WHERE (UserId = u.UserId)) AS PictureCount,
       (SELECT MAX(UploadedOn) AS Expr1
        FROM Pictures AS p
        WHERE (UserId = u.UserId)) AS LastUpdateOn
FROM vw_aspnet_MembershipUsers AS u
WHERE (IsApproved = @IsApproved) AND (IsLockedOut = @IsLockedOut)
ORDER BY UserName
```

This change can be made either declaratively, through the Source view, or via the SqlDataSource's wizard, by opting to specify the SQL query manually.

Q. ***I understand why, when adding a new category in the*** `ManageCategories.aspx` ***page, we need to programmatically supply the currently logged-on user's*** `UserId` ***value, but I'm at a bit of a loss as to why this information must be provided when updating the categories through the GridView. When we're editing a record, the*** `UserId` ***is already set, and we don't want to change this, so why does it need to be set at all? Can't we have the editing update just the*** `Name` ***column for a particular category and leave the*** `UserId` ***column out of it altogether?***

A. When we created the SqlDataSource control in `ManageCategories.aspx`, we had it return the `CategoryID`, `UserId`, and `Name` column values. When we're configuring the SqlDataSource control to generate the `INSERT`, `UPDATE`, and `DELETE` statements, it automatically creates the `UPDATE` and `INSERT` statements to update and insert all nonprimary key columns. In this case, that's `UserId` and `Name`.

But, you're correct, the `UserId` value does not need to be updated when updating just the `Name` column, as through the GridView. You could manually adjust the SqlDataSource control's `UpdateCommand` and `UpdateParameters` properties to have the `UPDATE` statement update only the `Name` column; in that case, you wouldn't need to programmatically set the `UserId` value in the GridView's `RowUpdating` event handler.

If you wanted to go down this path, you would remove the reference to the `UserId` value and parameter, setting the SqlDataSource control's `UpdateCommand` property to

```
UPDATE [Categories] SET
  [Name] = @Name
WHERE [CategoryID] = @CategoryID
```

You would also remove the `<asp:Parameter Name="UserId" />` line from the SqlDataSource control's `<UpdateParameters>` section.

HOUR 24

Uploading and Displaying Images and Leaving Comments

In this hour, we will cover

- Uploading an image file from the user's computer to the web server's file system
- Editing and deleting existing pictures from a photo album
- Displaying all the pictures for a particular user's photo album
- Displaying the comments associated with a particular picture
- Allowing only authenticated users to add a comment to a picture
- Defining the photo album application's site structure and displaying a breadcrumb through the master page

At this point the development phase of our online photo album application is progressing nicely. In the preceding hour we implemented the user account-related pages, the site's home page, and began work on the photo album administration pages, allowing users to add, edit, and delete categories specific to their album.

We still have a good deal of work ahead of us for this final hour. We need to first complete the photo administration piece, allowing users to upload new pictures and manage their existing ones from the `PhotoAdmin/Default.aspx` page. Following that, we need to implement the `PhotoAlbum.aspx` and `PhotoDetail.aspx` pages. `PhotoAlbum.aspx` lists all of the pictures in a particular user's photo album, and `PhotoDetail.aspx` displays a particular picture and its comments.

By the end of this hour, we'll have the online photo album application complete. Of course, more features can always be added, and this hour concludes with a look at potential enhancements for the photo album application that you are invited to implement on your own.

Completing the Photo Album Administration Pages

In the preceding hour we completed the category administration page (PhotoAdmin/ManageCategories.aspx), from which users could manage the categories in their album. We still need to implement the PhotoAdmin/Default.aspx page, which enables users to upload new pictures and to manage existing ones.

When we added support for managing categories, we first added a SqlDataSource control that returned all of the currently logged-on user's categories. The user's particular categories were selectable through the UserId column in the Categories table. To determine the currently logged-on user's UserId value in the SqlDataSource SELECT statement, we added the UserIdValue Label to the page and, in the Page_Load event handler, assigned its Text property accordingly.

Like categories, pictures are also user-specific. Therefore, let's start by adding a SqlDataSource control to the PhotoAdmin/Default.aspx page. This SqlDataSource will retrieve the columns from the Pictures table whose UserId column value matches the UserId of the currently logged-on user. To complete this, perform the following steps:

1. Add a Label Web control to the page. Clear out the value of the Text property; then set the Visible property to True and the ID property to UserIdValue.
2. From the PhotoAdmin/Default.aspx page's source code portion, add the following line of code to the Page_Load event handler:

   ```
   UserIdValue.Text = Membership.GetUser().ProviderUserKey.ToString()
   ```

3. Add a SqlDataSource control to the page. Set the SqlDataSource control's ID property to picturesDataSource.
4. From the Configure the Select Statement screen of the Configure the Data Source Wizard, select the Pictures table from the drop-down list and select the asterisk in the column list, thereby returning all columns.
5. Click the ORDER BY button and have the results ordered by the UpdatedOn field in descending order. This will have the results initially ordered starting with the most recently added pictures.
6. Just like with the categories SqlDataSource control from the preceding hour, click the WHERE button and add a filter expression on the UserId column. Only records whose UserId column value equals the value of the UserIdValue control should be returned.
7. Click the Advanced button and check the Generate INSERT, UPDATE, and DELETE statements check box.

Remember that when we're using `uniqueidentifier` column types through the SqlDataSource wizard, it's imperative that we manually edit the control's parameters. Specifically, we need to go to the Source view and remove the `Type="Object"` properties from the parameters for the `picturesDataSource` SqlDataSource, just like we did in the previous hour for the `categoriesDataSource` SqlDataSource.

With the `picturesDataSource` SqlDataSource configuration complete, we're ready to implement the functionality for adding new pictures and managing existing ones.

Adding New Images to the Photo Album

For our application, users can add to their album only photos that exist on their computer. When users go to their photo album administration page and choose to add a new picture, they need to be prompted to select an image from their computer along with the image's title, description, and category. After they have selected an image; provided the title, description, and category; and clicked the Insert button, the image file's contents need to be **uploaded** to the web server where a copy of the image file will be saved. In addition, a new record will be added to the `Pictures` table with the title, description, and category values the users entered.

With the image file saved on the web server's file system, anyone who can access the web server can view the image. Figure 24.1 illustrates this concept. Keep in mind that the uploaded image file is saved on the web server's file system, in a particular folder in the website's location on disk. Some photo album implementations opt to store the actual binary contents of the uploaded file in the database itself. Our application, however, will use the file system instead.

By the Way

> If you are developing your web application locally, then when you test your website, your computer acts as both the user's computer and the web server. Therefore, uploading a file simply entails copying the selected image file from its current folder to the website's folder.

After the user selects a file from his computer; enters the picture's title, description, and category; and clicks the Insert button, the ASP.NET page must perform two distinct steps:

1. Add a new record to the `Pictures` table. This record captures the picture's title, description, and category.
2. Save the uploaded image to the web server's file system.

For reasons we'll see shortly, these two steps must be performed in this order. Furthermore, these two steps can be examined and implemented independently. In the next section, we'll create the inserting interface. Later, in the "Uploading and Saving the Image File" section, we'll see how to augment the inserting interface to enable users to pick a file from their computer and how to save the uploaded image to the web server's file system.

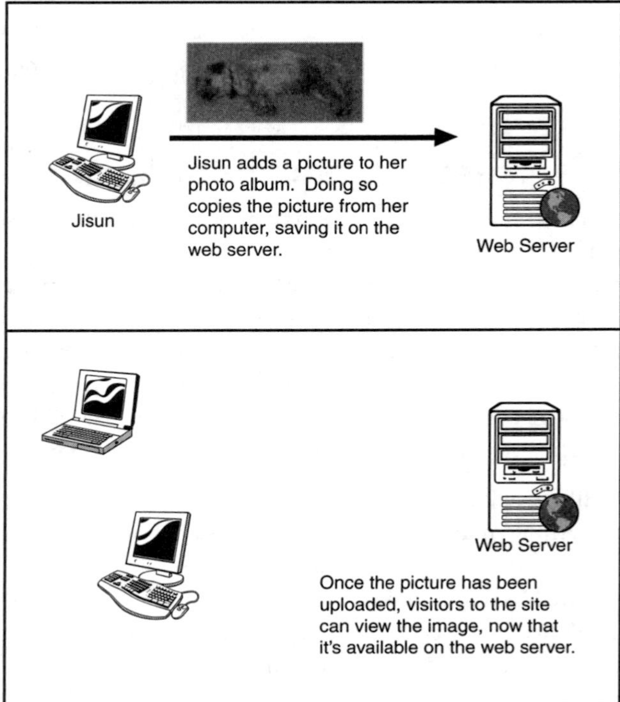
Jisun
Jisun adds a picture to her photo album. Doing so copies the picture from her computer, saving it on the web server.
Web Server
Web Server
Once the picture has been uploaded, visitors to the site can view the image, now that it's available on the web server.

FIGURE 24.1 When users add an image to a photo album, the image file is uploaded to the web server.

Inserting the Picture Information in the Database

Before we concern ourselves with the details of uploading and saving an image file from a user's computer, let's first build the interface for adding a new picture without worrying about the uploading requirements. To accomplish this, we'll use a DetailsView whose `DefaultMode` is set to `Insert`, just like with the interface for adding new categories explored in the preceding hour.

Start by adding a DetailsView control to the page, setting its `ID` property to `dvPictureInsert` and selecting the `picturesDataSource` control from the drop-down list in the DetailsView's smart tag. Next, set the `DefaultMode` property to `Insert` so that the DetailsView control is perpetually in insert mode.

At this point the DetailsView should show five fields: `UserId`, `CategoryID`, `Title`, `Description`, and `UpdatedOn`. Because the purpose of the `UpdatedOn` column in the

Pictures database table is to capture the date and time the picture was uploaded, we don't want to let the user enter this value; rather, we want this value to be set to the current date and time when the user clicks the Insert button. To accomplish this, we'll set the UpdatedOn value programmatically, in the DetailsView's ItemInserting event handler. Therefore, go to the smart tag, click on Edit Fields, and remove the UpdatedOn BoundField. Also remove the UserId BoundField because we don't want to let the user enter a UserId here; rather, we'll programmatically set this value to the currently logged-on user's UserId value, just like we did in the preceding hour when adding a new category.

At this point your screen should look similar to Figure 24.2. The categories that GridView added to this page in the preceding hour appear above the DetailsView.

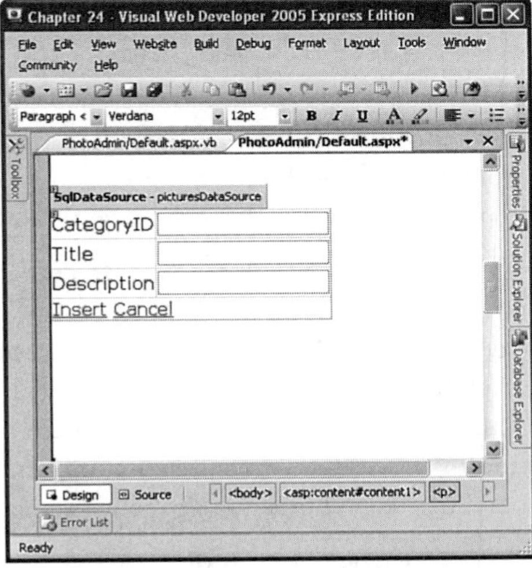

FIGURE 24.2
New pictures can be added through this DetailsView control.

When the user visits this page and enters the title, a description, and a category ID and clicks Insert, a postback will ensue and the DetailsView will work with its SqlDataSource control to attempt to insert a new record into the Pictures table. However, we need to programmatically provide two bits of information to have this interaction work successfully: the currently logged-on user's UserId value and the current date and time, for the UpdatedOn value.

As we saw in the preceding hour, the DetailsView's ItemInserting event fires before the actual INSERT statement is issued to the database. This event provides an opportunity for programmatically assigning the values to be inserted. Go to the ASP.NET page's source code portion and create an event handler for the dvPictureInsert DetailsView's ItemInserting event. Then add the following two lines of code:

```
e.Values("UserId") = Membership.GetUser().ProviderUserKey
e.Values("UploadedOn") = DateTime.Now
```

The first line of code sets the value being inserted into the `UserId` column to the currently logged-on user's `UserId`. The second line of code sets the value being inserted into the `UploadedOn` column to the current date and time.

With this code in place, you can visit `PhotoAdmin/Default.aspx` through a browser and add new records to the `Pictures` table. This interface, while working, leaves a lot to be desired. For starters, it doesn't allow the user to upload the associated picture. Rather, it just adds a new record to the `Pictures` database table. Another poor usability point is that if the user wants to associate a picture with a category, she must know the `CategoryID` value of the category. Finally, because there are no validation controls, if the user forgets or omits the title or description values, an exception will be raised since these columns do not accept Null values. We will address all of these woes over the next few sections.

Displaying a Drop-Down List of Categories

By default, the `CategoryID` BoundField, when in insert mode, is displayed as a TextBox. This requires that the user enter the appropriate `CategoryID` value, which assumes that the user somehow knows the IDs of his categories. Clearly, a better alternative would be to present the user with a drop-down list of his categories.

As we've seen in previous hours, customizing the inserting interface of the DetailsView involves turning a BoundField into a TemplateField. Take a moment now to convert the `CategoryID` BoundField into a TemplateField through the Fields dialog box. Next, from the DetailsView's smart tag, select Edit Templates and then select the `CategoryID` field's InsertItemTemplate. At this point the `CategoryID` field's InsertItemTemplate contains a TextBox. Delete this TextBox and, instead, drag in a DropDownList control, settings its `ID` property to `pictureCategory`.

The `pictureCategory` DropDownList needs to show those categories particular to the currently logged-on user. In the preceding hour we saw how to accomplish this in creating the `categoriesDataSource` SqlDataSource control. To replicate this functionality in `PhotoAdmin/Default.aspx`, add a SqlDataSource to the page, placing it before the `dvPictureInsert` DetailsView control. Next, configure it to return the `CategoryID` and `Name` columns from the `Categories` table for the currently logged-on user. Recall that this is accomplished by adding a `WHERE` clause using the `UserIdValue` Label control value. (For the `categoriesDataSource` control on this page, you do not need to generate the `INSERT`, `UPDATE`, and `DELETE` statements.)

Bind the `pictureCategory` DropDownList to this SqlDataSource control, having the DropDownList's text display the `Name` column and the value of the `CategoryID` column (see Figure 24.3).

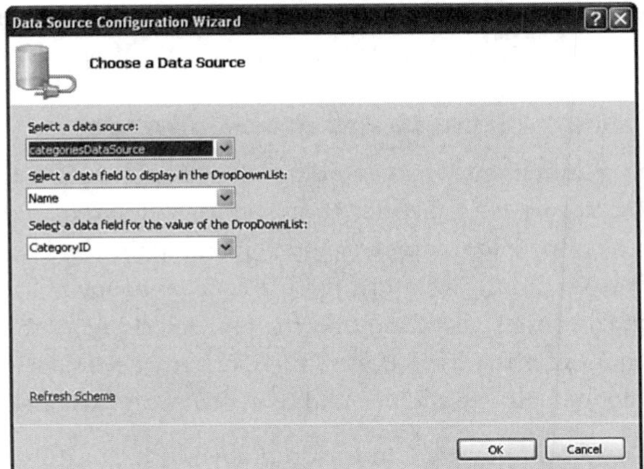

FIGURE 24.3 Choose the `categoriesDataSource` control as the DropDownList's data source.

With the `pictureCategory` DropDownList's data source configured, the user will see all of his categories listed here. To have the user's category selection saved upon clicking the Insert button, we need to configure the data bindings. Specifically, we must instruct the DetailsView to use the DropDownList's `SelectedValue` property for the `CategoryID` of the newly inserted record. We accomplish this by selecting the `Edit DataBindings` link from the DropDownList's smart tag and binding the `SelectedValue` property to the `CategoryID` field using two-way data binding, as shown in Figure 24.4.

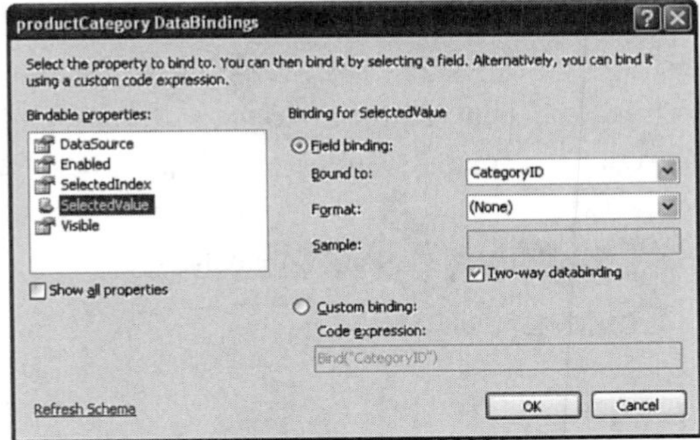

FIGURE 24.4 The DropDownList's `SelectedValue` indicates the picture's `CategoryID` value.

Be certain to check the Two-way Databinding check box in the `pictureCategory` DataBindings dialog box (see Figure 24.4). If you don't check this option, the category selected by the user won't be injected into the `INSERT` statement sent back to the database, and an exception may result.

Take a moment to view this page in your browser. When you visit this page, you should see the currently logged-on user's categories in the drop-down list.

Adding a `-- None --` Item to the Drop-Down List

One of the design requirements for the photo album application is that a user can *optionally* select a category for a picture. That is, a user should be able to add a new category that does not belong to any category. (Such pictures will have a Null value in their `CategoryID` column.) Currently, the `pictureCategory` DropDownList shows the user's existing categories, requiring that the user select one of them. But what if there are no categories for the user? Even if there are categories, how can a user select that the uploaded picture should not have a category assigned?

What we need is an additional item in the drop-down list, one that appears at the top and is labeled `-- None --`. With this additional drop-down list item, there will always be at least one item in the drop-down list, even if the user hasn't created any categories. Furthermore, the user can select this `-- None --` option to indicate that the uploaded picture does not have a category associated with it.

As we discussed in Hour 11, "Collecting Input Using Drop-Down Lists, Radio Buttons, and Check Boxes," a DropDownList's items can be specified through the `Items` property statically or dynamically. Currently, the values are specified dynamically, by associating the DropDownList with a SqlDataSource control. However, we can have the items specified *both* statically and dynamically. We'll leave the DropDownList associated with a SqlDataSource but add an additional `-- None --` option by statically specifying it through the `Items` property.

Go to the `pictureCategory` DropDownList's `Items` property and click on the ellipses to bring up the `ListItem` Collection Editor dialog box. From here, add a new item, setting its `Text` property to `-- None --`, and click OK (see Figure 24.5).

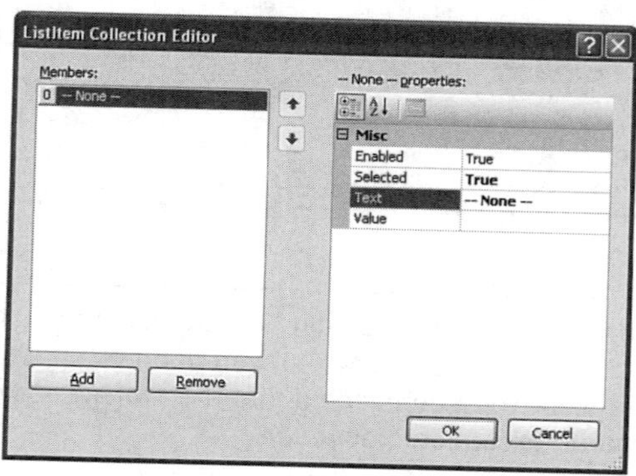

FIGURE 24.5 Add a "`-- None --`" option to the DropDownList's `Items` collection.

Regardless of what we set the Value property to, we need to go to the Source view and locate the ListItem instance just added in the declarative markup, which will look something like this:

```
<asp:DropDownList ID="pictureCategory" runat="server"
          DataSourceID="categoriesDataSource"
          DataTextField="Name"
          DataValueField="CategoryID"
          SelectedValue='<%# Bind("CategoryID") %>'>
    <asp:ListItem Selected="True" Value="value">-- None --</asp:ListItem>
</asp:DropDownList>
```

Here, the *value* in the <asp:ListItem> tag will depend on what value you entered in the ListItem Collection Editor dialog box; if you cleared out this property, the <asp:ListItem> tag will not have the Value property specified: <asp:ListItem Selected="True">-- None --</asp:ListItem>.

Regardless, you need to modify this <asp:ListItem> tag explicitly, setting the Value to the empty string, like so:

```
<asp:ListItem Selected="True" Value="">-- None --</asp:ListItem>
```

Watch Out!

If we omit the Value property from the <asp:ListItem> tag, the resulting item will use its Text property value as its Value property value. This is why we need to explicitly set Value="".

If we set Value="", when the user selects the -- None -- option, a Null value will be inserted into the database for the CategoryID column, which is what we are after. If we do *not* set Value="", an exception will be raised when the user attempts to add a new picture without assigning to an existing category.

The last step is to set the DropDownList's AppendDataBoundItems property to True. By default, when a DropDownList is bound to a datasource control, the DropDownList's existing items are cleared out and then the data binding takes place. This, however, would clear out the -- None -- option added in Figure 24.5. To keep the -- None -- option (or whatever ListItems have been added prior to data binding), simply set the AppendDataBoundItems property to True.

Ensuring That the User Enters a Title and Description

Because the Pictures table does not allow Nulls for the Title or Description columns, if the user fails to provide a value for either of these inputs in the DetailsView, an exception will occur. To overcome this problem, we need to customize the inserting interface for these two fields, adding RequiredFieldValidator controls. We performed this exact same process in the preceding hour to ensure that the user provided a name when adding a new category.

As in the preceding hour, to accomplish this, first convert the `Title` and `Description` BoundFields into TemplateFields. Then choose Edit Templates from the DetailsView's smart tag and configure the two TemplateFields' InsertItemTemplate sections. Specifically, add a RequiredFieldValidator, setting its `ControlToValidate`, `Display`, `ErrorMessage`, and `ValidationGroup` properties appropriately.

After adding and configuring these RequiredFieldValidators, be sure to set the `ValidationGroup` property of the DetailsView's New, Insert, Cancel CommandField to the same value as the two RequiredFieldValidators' `ValidationGroup` values. (I used `PictureAdd`.)

By the Way

While you're working on the DetailsView, feel free to add any additional customizations. For example, when editing the New, Insert, Cancel CommandField, you can clear out the `CancelText` property to remove the Cancel button from the insert interface. You can also clean up the appearance by setting the control's stylistic properties or by using the Auto Format Wizard.

At this point we have a completely functional interface for adding new records to the `Pictures` table. Granted, no actual image file is being uploaded to the web server, but entering a title, description, and category and clicking the Insert button would cause a postback and result in a new record being added to the table. Take a moment to try this out.

After you add some new pictures, return to Visual Web Developer and view the contents of the `Pictures` table. You should see a row for each picture added. When we get the uploading feature working, you're encouraged to delete these test records because no uploaded picture is associated with them. For now, though, don't worry about these junk records; just focus on testing and trying out the user interface.

Uploading and Saving the Image File

For adding new pictures, all that remains is providing the ability for the users to select an image from their computer and have it uploaded and saved to the web server's file system. Uploading an image from a user's computer to the web server's file system is relatively easy thanks to the FileUpload ASP.NET Web control. When a user visits a page with a FileUpload control, she sees a text box and a Browse button. Clicking the Browse button opens a dialog box that prompts the user to choose a file on her computer (see Figure 24.6).

After the user has selected a file and submitted the form, the actual contents of the file are sent to the web server. From the ASP.NET page's code portion, we can save the contents of the uploaded file to a folder on the web server.

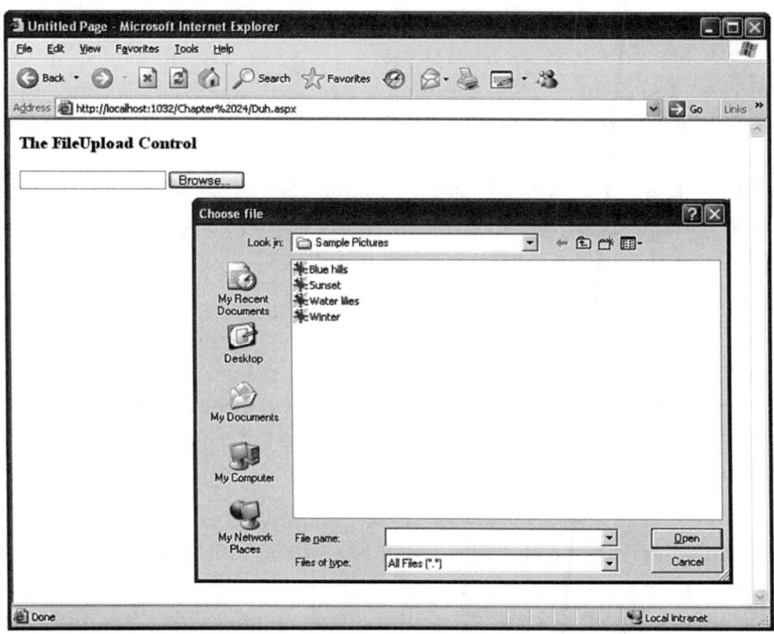

FIGURE 24.6
The FileUpload control, when viewed through a browser.

Let's start by adding a new TemplateField to the DetailsView, one that contains a FileUpload control. To accomplish that, perform the following steps:

1. From the DetailsView control's smart tag, click the `Edit Fields` link, opening the Fields dialog box.
2. Add a new TemplateField. From the upper-left corner, select the TemplateField and click the Add button.
3. Position the new TemplateField above the Category TemplateField. Next, set the new TemplateField's `HeaderText` property to `Picture`.
4. Returning to the Design view, click on the DetailsView's smart tag's `Edit Templates` link.
5. Go to the Picture TemplateField's InsertItemTemplate and drag the FileUpload control from the Toolbox into the template.
6. Set the FileUpload control's `ID` property to `imageUpload`.

With this addition, the DetailsView's inserting interface now includes a new row from which the user can pick the image file from his computer that he wants to add to his album.

While the FileUpload control automatically uploads the selected file from the user's computer to the web server, we need to write code to save the uploaded file. When we want to save user-uploaded content on a web server, a common challenge facing developers is how to name the uploaded files. Although the FileUpload control's `FileName` property indicates the name of the image uploaded by the user, if we use this filename, there is a chance for naming conflicts. For example, if Jisun uploads a picture named `MyDog.jpg`, and we save it on the web server as `MyDog.jpg`, what happens if, sometime later, Sam uploads a picture called `MyDog.jpg`?

The solution to this problem is to ensure that each uploaded image has a unique filename. We can guarantee this by saving the uploaded image with the filename *`PictureID`*`.jpg`, where *`PictureID`* is the `PictureID` column value of the corresponding record in the `Pictures` table. Because the `PictureID` column is a primary key, it's guaranteed to be unique; therefore, we can be certain that each uploaded image will have a unique filename.

This presents a sticky challenge: How do we determine what the `PictureID` will be for the uploaded image's corresponding record in the `Pictures` table? We need to wait until after the record has been added to the `Pictures` table before we save the uploaded image file because we won't know the `PictureID` value until after the record's been added to the table. The DetailsView's `ItemInserted` event fires *after* the record has been added to the database table. In this event handler we can query the database to determine the most recent `PictureID` value for the currently logged-in user and then save the uploaded file using this filename. Figure 24.7 illustrates this workflow.

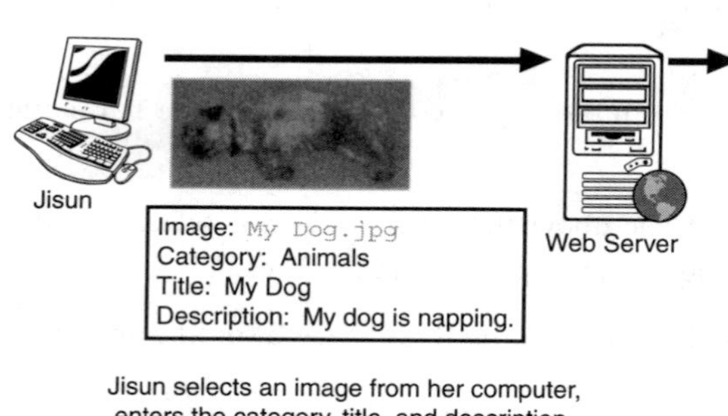
Jisun
Web Server
Image: My Dog.jpg
Category: Animals
Title: My Dog
Description: My dog is napping.
Jisun selects an image from her computer, enters the category, title, and description, and clicks the insert button.

(1) The DetailsView's `ItemInserting` event fires; the `UserId` and `UpdatedOn` values are set programmatically.

(2) The DetailsView invokes its SQlDataSource control, `INSERT`ing a new record to the `Pictures` table, capturing this image's category, title, and description.

(3) The DetailsView's `ItemInserted` event fires; the `PictureID` value of the just-inserted record is determined and the uploaded file is saved on the web server's file system as *`PictureID`*`.jpg`.

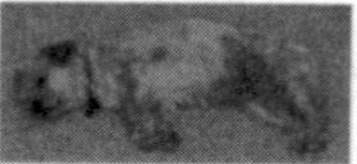

FIGURE 24.7
A new record is added to the `Pictures` table, after which the uploaded image is saved.

To determine the filename to use to save the uploaded image, we need to determine the PictureID value of the just-inserted record. We can accomplish this by grabbing the maximum PictureID value of the currently logged-in user. This logic works because the PictureID column is an Auto-increment column, meaning that each new record added to this table has a PictureID value greater than the preceding row. Because the currently logged-in user has just added a new row to the Pictures table, we can grab that PictureID value by simply getting the maximum PictureID for that user.

To accomplish this, we need to add yet another SqlDataSource control to the page. Set this SqlDataSource control's ID to maxPictureIDDataSource and start the control's Select Data Source Wizard. When you reach the Configure the Select Statement screen, select the Specify a Custom SQL Statement or Stored Procedure radio button and click Next. Then, in the SELECT tab, enter the following query:

```
SELECT MAX(PictureID)
FROM Pictures
WHERE UserId = @UserId
```

This will return the maximum PictureID value from the Pictures table for the user specified by the @UserId parameter. After you enter this query, click Next. Here, we are asked to provide the value for the @UserId parameter (see Figure 24.8). As we did with the categoriesDataSource and picturesDataSource SqlDataSource controls, select Control as the parameter source and then choose the UserIdValue Label from the ControlID drop-down list. (Recall that the UserIdValue Label's Text property is assigned the currently logged-on user's UserId value.)

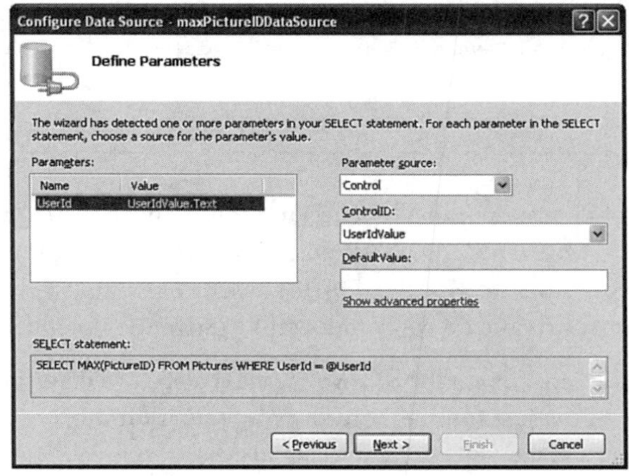

FIGURE 24.8 Assign the @UserId parameter's value to the Text property of the UserIdValue Label.

With this SqlDataSource complete, we can query it programmatically from the DetailsView's ItemInserted event handler. When we have the PictureID value, we can save the uploaded image using the FileUpload control's `SaveAs(path)` method. Listing 24.1 contains the complete code for the `ItemInserted` event handler.

The `ItemInserted` event handler uses the `DataView` class on lines 5 and 7. To use this class, you will need to add the following line of code to the top of the source code file, above the `Partial Class` declaration:

```
Imports System.Data
```

A complete listing of the `PhotoAdmin/Default.aspx` page's code portion can be found in Listing 24.3.

LISTING 24.1 The Uploaded File Is Saved in the `ItemInserted` Event Handler

```
 1: Protected Sub dvPictureInsert_ItemInserted(ByVal sender As Object,
➥ByVal e As System.Web.UI.WebControls.DetailsViewInsertedEventArgs)
➥Handles dvPictureInsert.ItemInserted
 2:    'If the record was successfully inserted, save the picture
 3:    If e.AffectedRows > 0 Then
 4:       'Determine the maximum PictureID for this user
 5:       Dim results As DataView =
➥ CType(maxPictureIDDataSource.Select(DataSourceSelectArguments.Empty),
➥DataView)
 6:
 7:       Dim pictureIDJustAdded As Integer = CType(results(0)(0), Integer)
 8:
 9:       'Reference the FileUpload control
10:       Dim imageUpload As FileUpload =
➥CType(dvPictureInsert.FindControl("imageUpload"), FileUpload)
11:
12:       If imageUpload.HasFile Then
13:          Dim baseDirectory As String = Server.MapPath("~/UploadedImages/")
14:
15:          imageUpload.SaveAs(baseDirectory & pictureIDJustAdded & ".jpg")
16:       End If
17:    End If
18: End Sub
```

The event handler begins on line 3 by checking the `AffectedRows` property of the `DetailsViewInsertedEventArgs` object passed into the event handler. This property indicates how many rows were affected by the insert. There may have been some error in inserting, in which case we do not want to save the uploaded file.

Assuming there's at least one affected row, the next step is to determine the `PictureID` value of the just-inserted record. This logic is handled by the `maxPictureIDDataSource` SqlDataSource; we just need to invoke the `SELECT` statement and retrieve the value. We accomplish this by calling the SqlDataSource control's `Select()` method, as shown on line 5. This method returns a `DataView`, which is an object that contains the data returned by the `SELECT` query. You can find the value of a particular row and column of the returned data using the syntax *`DataViewVariable`*`(`*`rowIndex`*`)(`*`columnIndex`*`)`, where both *`rowIndex`* and *`columnIndex`* are indexed starting at zero. This returned `DataView` object is assigned to the `results` variable. The actual `PictureID` value resides in the first column returned by the first row. This is accessed on line 7 by retrieving the value of `results(0)(0)` and casting it to an Integer.

After the `PictureID` value has been determined, we're ready to save the uploaded file. We start by grabbing a programmatic reference to the FileUpload control (line 10). Next, we check to ensure that the user picked a file to upload by checking the FileUpload control's `HasFile` property. If a file has been uploaded, we need to determine the path where we want to save the file.

We first need to determine in which folder to save the file. For our site let's save all user-uploaded picture files to the `UploadedImages` folder. (Take a moment to add this folder to your project.) To determine the path to a folder on the website, use the `Server.MapPath(`*`folderInSite`*`)` method, as shown on line 13. This method takes a **virtual path**, like `~/UploadedImages/`, and returns its corresponding **physical path**, like `C:\My Documents\My Websites\PhotoAlbum\UploadedImages\`. To save the uploaded image, we need to work in terms of a physical path.

We then concatenate the `baseDirectory` value, the newly inserted `PictureID` value, and the `.jpg` extension and save the uploaded file to the resulting, concatenated path using the FileUpload control's `SaveAs()` method (line 15).

By the Way

On line 15 we blindly save the uploaded image using the `.jpg` extension. This assumes that the uploaded image is a **JPEG image.** JPEG is a common image file format, and is the format virtually all digital cameras use. In the next section we'll see how to ensure that only JPEG images are uploaded.

By restricting our application to accept only JPEG images, we prohibit users from uploading other types of image files—GIF images, bitmap images, and so on. This limitation, along with some workarounds, is discussed in the Q&A section at the end of this hour.

Watch Out!

If you want to save the uploaded file to a folder on the web server's file system, the ASP.NET application must have write permissions on the specified folder. If these permissions are lacking, you'll receive a security-related exception when the `SaveAs()` method is reached in Listing 24.1.

The steps for granting write access to a folder and the actual user account used by the ASP.NET application differ depending on the operating system being used.

With this code in place, a user can now upload an image from her computer to the web server. Take a moment to test the page through a browser (see Figure 24.9). You should be able to select a file, choose a category, and enter a title and description. Clicking the Insert button causes a postback, during which a new record is added to the `Pictures` table and the uploaded image is saved to the `UploadedImages` folder in the website. Note that the filename of the uploaded image is equal to the `PictureID` value of the image's corresponding `Pictures` record. For example, the row added to the `Pictures` table for the image uploaded in Figure 24.9 happened to have a `PictureID` value of 7. Therefore, the uploaded image was saved in the `UploadedImages` folder with the filename `7.jpg`.

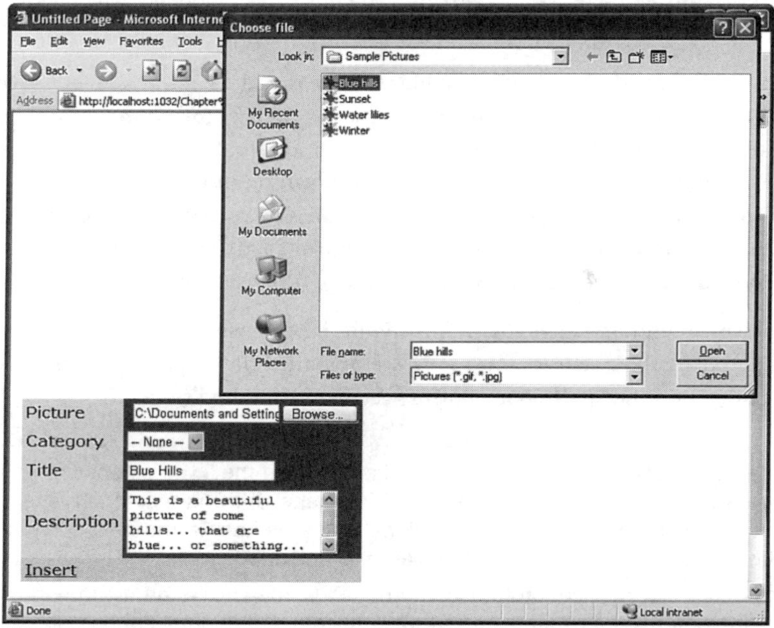

FIGURE 24.9 The user can select a picture from her computer to add to her album.

Ensuring That Only Image Files Are Uploaded

Currently, the photo album application doesn't ensure that the user has chosen a file to upload, nor does it require that the image uploaded be a JPEG image file. (That is, the user could upload a text file.) Let's examine how to both require that the user select a file to upload and that the file has the `.jpg` extension.

To ensure that the user has selected a file in the FileUpload control, we just need to add a RequiredFieldValidator to the Picture TemplateField, configuring its properties appropriately. As with the other RequiredFieldValidators added to the DetailsView's

TemplateFields, be sure to set its `ValidationGroup` property to the same value as the others.

With the RequiredFieldValidator, we can ensure that the user has uploaded some file, but how can we guarantee that he uploads a JPEG image, and not some other type of file? Ideally, when the user clicks the Browse button, the file dialog box will list only files with the `.jpg` extension; however, the FileUpload control cannot be configured in this manner. Rather, we have to wait until after the image is uploaded to determine its file extension.

Our test for determining whether a file is a JPEG image is a simple one: We simply check the file's extension. If the file's extension is `.jpg`, we assume that it's a valid JPEG image. If it does not have this extension, we assume that it's not a valid JPEG image.

By the Way

> Our approach for determining whether the file is a valid JPEG image is a rather naïve one. Because we are checking only the file extension, a user could simply rename a text file from `MyResume.txt` to `MyResume.jpg`, and our photo album application would accept the upload.

This check should be handled *before* a new row is added to the `Pictures` table. If the image uploaded is not an image file, we want to cancel the insert statement. Update the DetailsView's `ItemInserting` event handler so that it looks like the code in Listing 24.2.

LISTING 24.2 If an Invalid File Type Is Uploaded, the Insert Is Canceled

```
Protected Sub dvPictureInsert_ItemInserting(ByVal sender As Object,
➥ByVal e As System.Web.UI.WebControls.DetailsViewInsertEventArgs)
➥Handles dvPictureInsert.ItemInserting
    'Ensure that the uploaded image file has been specified and that
    'it's a valid image file
    Dim cancelInsert As Boolean = False

    'Reference the FileUpload control
    Dim imageUpload As FileUpload =
➥CType(dvPictureInsert.FindControl("imageUpload"), FileUpload)

    If Not imageUpload.HasFile Then
        'There was no file uploaded
        cancelInsert = True
    Else
        'There was a file uploaded, make sure it's a JPG file
        If Not imageUpload.FileName.ToUpper().EndsWith(".JPG") Then
           cancelInsert = True  'Invalid image file!
        End If
    End If

```

LISTING 24.2 Continued

```
19:     If cancelInsert Then
20:         'We can't proceed, cancel the insert and show the warning message
21:         e.Cancel = True
22:         cannotUploadImageMessage.Visible = True
23:     End If
24:
25:
26:     'Set the UserId value to the currently logged on user's ID
27:     e.Values("UserId") = Membership.GetUser().ProviderUserKey
28:
29:     'Set the UploadedOn value to the current date/time
30:     e.Values("UploadedOn") = DateTime.Now
31: End Sub
```

The `ItemInserting` event handler starts on line 4 with the creation of a local variable named `cancelInsert`. This variable indicates whether the insertion should be canceled. Initially, it is set to `False`, but checks from lines 9–17 might cause it to be set to `True`.

On line 7 the FileUpload control is programmatically referenced (just like we did on line 10 in Listing 24.1), and the `HasFile` property is checked to ensure that a file has been uploaded. If there is no file, the `cancelInsert` variable is set to `True`. If, however, a file has been uploaded, we proceed to check its extension (lines 14–16). The file extension check is performed with help from the `EndsWith()` method, which has the following form:

```
someString.EndsWith(substring)
```

`EndsWith()` returns `True` if the string *`someString`* ends with the passed-in *`substring`*, and returns `False` otherwise. Before calling the `EndWith()` method, the filename is capitalized by calling the `ToUpper()` method. This capitalization is performed because string comparisons are case sensitive. To skirt this issue, we simply capitalize the filename and then see whether it ends with the capitalized string `".JPG"` (line 14). If the extension of the uploaded file doesn't equal `.JPG`, `cancelInsert` is set to `True`.

If `cancelInsert` is `True` by the time line 19 is reached, the insertion is canceled by setting the `Cancel` property of the passed-in DetailsViewInsertEventArgs object (`e`) to `True` (line 21). If the insert fails, we need to alert the user that his attempted upload failed because the file uploaded was not considered a valid image file. In the HTML portion of the ASP.NET page, I've added a Label control with the ID `cannotUploadImageMessage` with a `Text` property value explaining the problem. Therefore, if the insertion fails, the `Visible` property of this Label control is set to `True` so that the informational message is displayed (line 22).

Lines 26–30 contain the code that programmatically sets the values of the `UserId` and `UploadedOn` values. Recall that we examined these lines of code earlier in this hour.

With this new code in place, if the user attempts to upload a file with an invalid file extension, the insert will cancel and he will see a message explaining the problem (see Figure 24.10). Canceling the insert prevents a new row from being added to the Pictures table and prevents the uploaded file from being saved to the web server's file system.

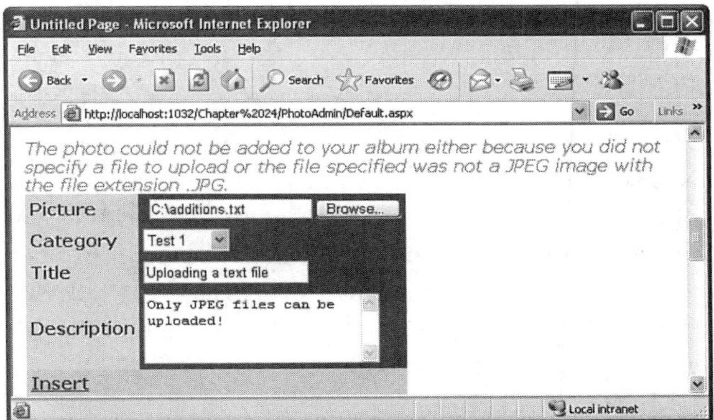

FIGURE 24.10
The user has attempted to upload a text file.

Viewing, Editing, and Deleting Existing Pictures

With the functionality to add new pictures and save the uploaded image complete, the last step for the photo album administration page is adding the GridView that allows the user to view, edit, and delete her existing pictures. To list the pictures, we'll use a GridView, much like we did in the preceding hour in the "Viewing, Editing, and Deleting Categories" section. Start by adding a GridView after the `dvPictureInsert` DetailsView control. Associate the GridView control with the `picturesDataSource` SqlDataSource; set its `ID` property to `gvPictures`; and check the Enable Paging, Enable Sorting, Enable Editing, and Enable Deleting check boxes.

Take a moment to clean up the GridView's fields, removing the superfluous ones and formatting the remaining ones. From the GridView's smart tag, click the `Edit Columns` link to bring up the Fields dialog box and remove the `PictureID` and `UserId` BoundFields. Next, set the `CategoryID` field's `HeaderText` property to `Category` and the `UploadedOn` BoundField's `HeaderText` property to `Date Added`.

Take a moment to test the page in a browser and attempt to edit an existing picture. Clicking the `Edit` link successfully displays the row in edit mode. However, if you try to save the values, the exception "Cannot insert the value NULL into column 'UserId'" is thrown. The reason is that the UPDATE statement issued by the GridView's underlying SqlDataSource control is expecting this value to be provided.

This same challenge faced us when working with the categories GridView in the preceding hour. Recall that we fixed this problem by programmatically assigning this value in the GridView's RowUpdating event handler. We can reapply this logic here. Create the RowUpdating event handler for the gvPictures GridView and add the following line of code:

```
e.NewValues("UserId") = Membership.GetUser().ProviderUserKey
```

With this event handler in place, changes to an existing picture can successfully be saved back to the database.

As we've done with the previous DetailsViews and GridView controls on this page, the next step is to convert the remaining BoundFields into TemplateFields to customize their editing interface. The Title and Description fields will need to be enhanced to include RequiredFieldValidators, while the CategoryID field should use a DropDownList just like was done in the dvPictureInsert DetailsView control. The UpdatedOn field needs to be made read-only because a user shouldn't be able to change it when she uploads a particular file.

In addition to turning the existing BoundFields into customized TemplateFields, we need to add a field that will show the actual picture. The next several sections examine how to accomplish these tasks.

Displaying a Drop-Down List of Categories with a -- None -- Option

Earlier in this hour, when implementing the interface for adding a picture, we saw how to display a drop-down list of the user's created categories to aid with choosing the category in which to place the new picture. In the GridView that displays the existing pictures, we want to use the same concept both when viewing the pictures in read-only mode and when editing a particular picture. The only difference between the read-only DropDownList control and the edit mode DropDownList control is that when a record is in read-only mode, the DropDownList's Enabled property will be set to False.

To accomplish this, we need to first convert the CategoryID BoundField into a TemplateField. Next, we need to replace the Label and TextBox controls in the ItemTemplate and EditItemTemplates with DropDownLists. In the ItemTemplate, set the DropDownList's ID property to pictureReadOnlyCategories and Enabled to False; in the EditItemTemplate, set the DropDownList's ID value to pictureEditCategories. Both DropDownLists will use the same datasource control—categoriesDataSource, which returns the currently logged-on user's categories—displaying the Name and CategoryID column values as the DropDownLists' text and value properties. Plus, both need to have their SelectedValue property bound to the CategoryID value using two-way data binding.

To add the -- None -- option to the DropDownList controls, set the AppendDataBoundItems properties to True and then add a new ListItem through the ListItem Collection Editor dialog box. After adding the new ListItem, don't forget to go to the Source view and explicitly add Value="" to the <asp:ListItem> tags for the two DropDownLists.

After you make these changes, take a moment to test the functionality in a browser. As Figure 24.11 shows, the list of pictures for the currently logged-on user is displayed with a disabled DropDownList for the read-only records. For the record being edited, the user can change the picture's category. Saving changes to a picture will work as long as you provide a value for the picture's title and description and use a valid date/time value for the UpdatedOn field.

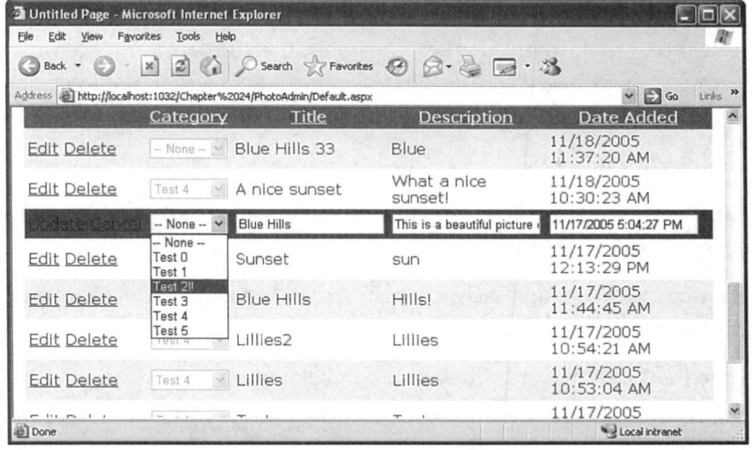

FIGURE 24.11
Each picture's category is shown as a drop-down list.

Ensuring that the User Enters the Title and Description

Because the Title and Description columns in the Pictures table do not allow Nulls, the user must provide values when editing a picture. To ensure that the user provides a value, we need to customize the editing interface for these two fields and include a RequiredFieldValidator, just like we did in the dvPictureInsert DetailsView control earlier in this hour.

Because we've discussed the process of adding RequiredFieldValidators in both this hour and the preceding one, I don't need to spell out the precise steps for adding the

RequiredFieldValidator controls. Just be certain to assign the `ValidationGroup` properties of both controls to some value (I chose `PictureEdit`). Whatever `ValidationGroup` value you choose, be sure to also set the GridView's CommandField's `ValidationGroup` property to the same value.

By the Way

> While working with the `Description` TemplateField's EditItemTemplate, I tweaked the appearance of the TextBox Web control, setting its `TextMode` property to `MultiLine` and the `Columns` and `Rows` properties to values of 25 and 4, respectively.

Making the `UpdatedOn` Field Read-Only

The GridView's `UpdatedOn` BoundField displays the date and time the picture was uploaded. Because the `UpdatedOn` field is a BoundField, when a GridView row is made editable, the `UpdatedOn` field will display a text box, allowing the user to edit the `UpdatedOn` value. However, we want to prevent the user from updating this value; after the photo has been uploaded, this value should *never* be changed.

To make this field uneditable, we need to convert the `UpdatedOn` BoundField into a TemplateField and replace the TextBox control in the EditItemTemplate with a Label control whose `Text` property is bound to the `UpdatedOn` column value using two-way data binding. To accomplish this, perform the following steps:

1. From the GridView's smart tag, click on the `Edit Columns` link.
2. From the Fields dialog box, select the `UpdatedOn` BoundField and click the `Convert this field into a TemplateField` link.
3. Returning to the Design view, click the `Edit Templates` link from the GridView's smart tag and select the `UpdatedOn` field's EditItemTemplate.
4. Delete the TextBox control and add a Label control.
5. Click the `Edit DataBindings` links from the Label control's smart tag and bind the `Text` property to the `UploadedOn` column value using two-way data binding.

After you complete these steps, test this page in a browser. When you click the Edit button for a row, the editable row's `UploadedOn` field should display the value as text rather than as a text box.

Showing the Associated Image

The `gvPictures` GridView lists the contents of the `Pictures` database table, allowing the user to manage the pictures in his album. While this functionality is sufficient, it would be nice to display a thumbnail image of the actual picture along with each GridView row (see Figure 24.13). This can be accomplished using an ImageField.

As we discussed in Hour 18, "Exploring Data Binding and Other Data-Related Topics," the ImageField displays an image whose URL is based, in part or in total, on one of the database columns bound to the GridView or DetailsView. We accomplish this by setting the following two properties:

- `DataImageUrlField`—The name of the database column whose value will appear in the image URL.
- `DataImageUrlFormatString`—The image URL; use `{0}` to inject the value of the database column specified in the `DataImageUrlField` property.

To see how these two properties work together, add an ImageField to the `gvPictures` GridView and set the `DataImageUrlField` property to `PictureID` and the `DataImageUrlFormatString` property to `~/UploadedImages/{0}.jpg` (see Figure 24.12).

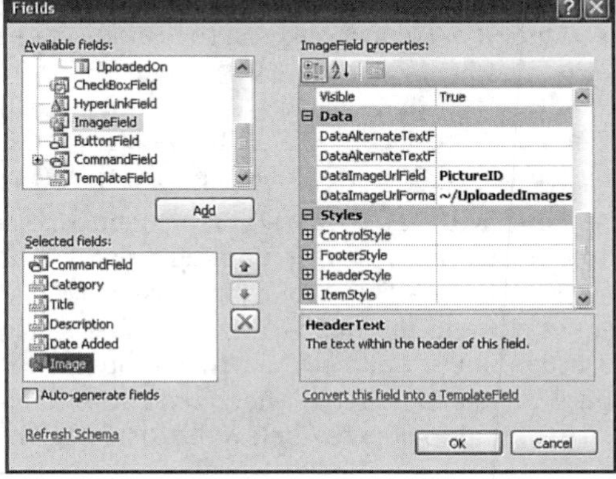

FIGURE 24.12
Add an ImageField to the GridView and set its properties.

The ImageField will display an image for each row in the GridView. The image URL for a particular row will be `~/UploadedImages/`*`PictureID`*`.jpg`, which is the location and filename where the uploaded file was saved. For example, in Figure 24.13 the first record—A nice sunset—has a `PictureID` value of 11; therefore, the ImageField renders the following markup:

```
<img src="../UploadedImages/11.jpg" />
```

The URL of the image is `11.jpg`. When I uploaded this particular picture to the website, it was saved in the `UploadedImages` directory as `11.jpg`.

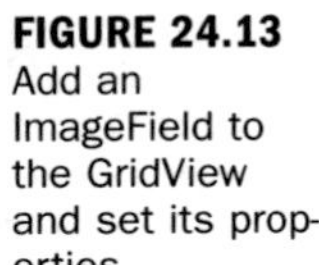

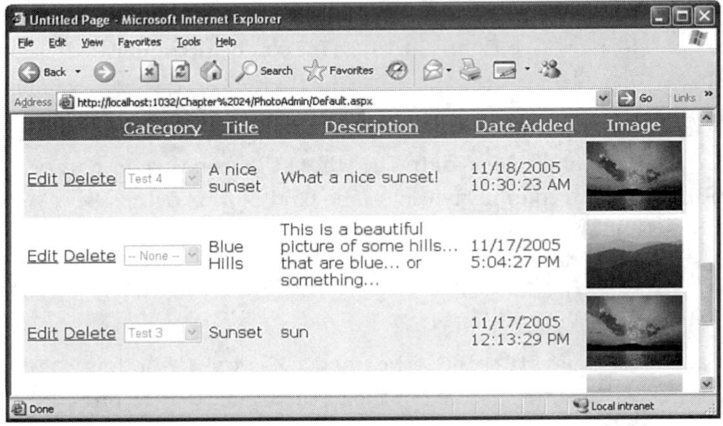

FIGURE 24.13 Add an ImageField to the GridView and set its properties.

Like the BoundField, by default an editable GridView's ImageField field is rendered as a TextBox for the editable row, displaying the value of the `DataImageUrlField` in the TextBox control. To prevent this, set the ImageField's `ReadOnly` property to `True`.

Did you Know?

> If you are following along at your own computer and have tested the ImageField, you have likely noticed that the various images associated with each row are shown at their full size. That is, if you have a very tall and wide image, it squishes the GridView's content. Contrast that to Figure 24.13, where each image has a width of 100 pixels. You can specify a static width or height for the images in an ImageField by setting the `ControlStyle` property's `Width` or `Height` subproperties.
>
> If you set *both* of the `ControlStyle` property's `Width` and `Height` subproperties, all images will be fixed height and width. The downside of this approach is that some images may appear distorted. This problem arises with pictures whose ratio of width to height is not close to the width-to-height ratio specified by the `Width` and `Height` subproperties. If you set just the `Width` or just the `Height` subproperty, all pictures will have the same `Width` (or `Height`), but they'll all automatically have a `Height` (or `Width`) that maintains their width-to-height ratio.

Deleting Pictures

The GridView contains a Delete button, and clicking it causes the corresponding record in the `Pictures` table to be deleted. It does not, however, cause the actual image file to be deleted from the web server's file system. When a user clicks the Delete button, a postback ensues, the underlying record is deleted, and the GridView's `RowDeleted` event fires. To delete the associated image file, we can create an event handler for the GridView's `RowDeleted` event and add code there that performs the file deletion.

To delete a file from the web server's file system, use the `File.Delete(`*`path`*`)` method, where *`path`* is the complete, physical path of the file to delete. To use the `File` class, add the following line of code to the top of the source code portion file:

```
Imports System.IO
```

After you add the `RowDeleted` event handler, add the following three lines of code:

```
Dim baseDirectory As String = Server.MapPath("~/UploadedImages/")
Dim fileName As String = baseDirectory & e.Keys("PictureID") & ".jpg"
File.Delete(fileName)
```

The first line gets the physical path to the `UploadedImages` folder and is identical to line 13 in Listing 24.1. The second line creates the full name of the file to be deleted by concatenating `baseDirectory` together with the `PictureID` value for the deleted row and the `.jpg` extension. In the third line, the file is deleted by calling `File.Delete(fileName)`.

The Complete Source Code Portion

We've at long last finished the photo album administration piece! Congratulations! Listing 24.3 contains the entire source code portion of the `PhotoAdmin/Default.aspx` page.

LISTING 24.3 The Complete Source Code Portion of the `PhotoAdmin/Default.aspx` Page

```
Imports System.Data
Imports System.IO

Partial Class PhotoAdmin_Default
    Inherits System.Web.UI.Page

    Protected Sub Page_Load(ByVal sender As Object,
➥ByVal e As System.EventArgs) Handles Me.Load
        UserIdValue.Text = Membership.GetUser().ProviderUserKey.ToString()
        cannotUploadImageMessage.Visible = False
    End Sub

    Protected Sub dvCategoriesInsert_ItemInserting(ByVal sender As Object,
➥ ByVal e As System.Web.UI.WebControls.DetailsViewInsertEventArgs)
➥Handles dvCategoriesInsert.ItemInserting
        'Set the UserId value to the currently logged on user's ID
        e.Values("UserId") = Membership.GetUser().ProviderUserKey
    End Sub

    Protected Sub gvCategories_RowUpdating(ByVal sender As Object,
➥ByVal e As System.Web.UI.WebControls.GridViewUpdateEventArgs)
➥ Handles gvCategories.RowUpdating
        'Set the UserId value to the currently logged on user's ID
        e.NewValues("UserId") = Membership.GetUser().ProviderUserKey
```

LISTING 24.3 Continued

```
    End Sub

    Protected Sub dvPictureInsert_ItemInserted(ByVal sender As Object,
➥ByVal e As System.Web.UI.WebControls.DetailsViewInsertedEventArgs)
➥Handles dvPictureInsert.ItemInserted
        'If the record was successfully inserted, save the picture
        If e.AffectedRows > 0 Then
            'Determine the maximum PictureID for this user
            Dim results As DataView =
➥ CType(maxPictureIDDataSource.Select(DataSourceSelectArguments.Empty),
DataView)

            Dim pictureIDJustAdded As Integer =
➥CType(results(0)(0), Integer)

            'Reference the FileUpload control
            Dim imageUpload As FileUpload =
➥CType(dvPictureInsert.FindControl("imageUpload"), FileUpload)

            If imageUpload.HasFile Then
                Dim baseDirectory As String =
➥Server.MapPath("~/UploadedImages/")

                imageUpload.SaveAs(baseDirectory &
➥pictureIDJustAdded & ".jpg")
            End If
        End If
    End Sub

    Protected Sub dvPictureInsert_ItemInserting(ByVal sender As Object,
➥ByVal e As System.Web.UI.WebControls.DetailsViewInsertEventArgs)
➥Handles dvPictureInsert.ItemInserting
        'Ensure that the uploaded image file has been specified and that
        'it's a valid image file
        Dim cancelInsert As Boolean = False

        'Reference the FileUpload control
        Dim imageUpload As FileUpload =
➥CType(dvPictureInsert.FindControl("imageUpload"), FileUpload)

        If Not imageUpload.HasFile Then
            'There was no file uploaded
            cancelInsert = True
        Else
            'There was a file uploaded, make sure it's a JPG file
            If Not imageUpload.FileName.ToUpper().EndsWith(".JPG") Then
                cancelInsert = True  'Invalid image file!
            End If
        End If

        If cancelInsert Then
            'We can't proceed, cancel the insert, show warning message
            e.Cancel = True
            cannotUploadImageMessage.Visible = True
        End If


        'Set the UserId value to the currently logged on user's ID
```

LISTING 24.3 Continued

```
        e.Values("UserId") = Membership.GetUser().ProviderUserKey

        'Set the UploadedOn value to the current date/time
        e.Values("UploadedOn") = DateTime.Now
    End Sub

    Protected Sub gvPictures_RowDeleted(ByVal sender As Object,
➥ByVal e As System.Web.UI.WebControls.GridViewDeletedEventArgs)
➥Handles gvPictures.RowDeleted
        Dim baseDirectory As String = Server.MapPath("~/UploadedImages/")
        Dim fileName As String = baseDirectory &
➥e.Keys("PictureID") & ".jpg"
        File.Delete(fileName)
    End Sub

    Protected Sub gvPictures_RowUpdating(ByVal sender As Object,
➥ByVal e As System.Web.UI.WebControls.GridViewUpdateEventArgs)
➥Handles gvPictures.RowUpdating
        'Set the UserId value to the currently logged on user's ID
        e.NewValues("UserId") = Membership.GetUser().ProviderUserKey
    End Sub
End Class
```

Displaying the Photo Album to All Visitors

With the photo album administration piece complete, we're entering the home stretch! There are only two more pages to implement:

- `PhotoAlbum.aspx`—Displays the pictures for a particular user's album
- `PhotoDetail.aspx`—Displays a particular image, allows visitors to view comments, and allows users to add comments

Let's start with `PhotoAlbum.aspx`. Recall that the photo album application home page lists all users with a link to their photo album. That link takes visitors here, to `PhotoAlbum.aspx`, passing in the `UserId` value through the querystring like so:

```
PhotoAlbum.aspx?ID=UserId
```

The pictures shown in the album should be filterable by category. That is, this page needs to include a DropDownList control that lists all of a user's custom categories (including an `-- All --` option). Only those pictures that belong to the selected category are displayed.

In addition to displaying each image in the selected category for the specified user, we need to enable visitors to go from this page to the `PhotoDetail.aspx` page. The

PhotoDetail.aspx page displays just the image specified along with any comments associated with the picture. Furthermore, authenticated users can leave comments.

While this list of tasks may sound a bit overwhelming, it shouldn't be too bad because we've already examined how to accomplish many of these tasks in this and previous hours. In Hour 17, "Working with Data-Bound DropDownLists, RadioButtons, and CheckBoxes," we saw how to use a DropDownList to filter the results displayed in a GridView. We just recently saw how to use ImageFields to display images in a GridView (as well as in Hour 18). There will be one new lesson learned: how to enhance the filtering DropDownList to allow a visitor to view *all* of the images in a user's photo album.

Filtering the User's Photo Album

Because this page needs to show the user's photo album, filtered by category, let's start by adding the DropDownList of categories through which the visitor can filter the results. Start by adding a SqlDataSource called `categoriesDataSource` to the page. Configure the SqlDataSource wizard using the following steps:

1. Select the `Categories` table from the drop-down list and return the `CategoryID` and `Name` columns.
2. Click the `ORDER BY` button and have the results sorted by the `Name` column in ascending order.
3. Click the `WHERE` button and add a filter expression on the `UserId` column based on the `QueryString` value `ID` (see Figure 24.14). We use `ID` because this is the name of the querystring value passed from the home page.
4. Finish the SqlDataSource wizard. Upon returning to the Design view, switch to the Source view and edit the SqlDataSource's `UserId` parameter, removing `Type="Object"`.

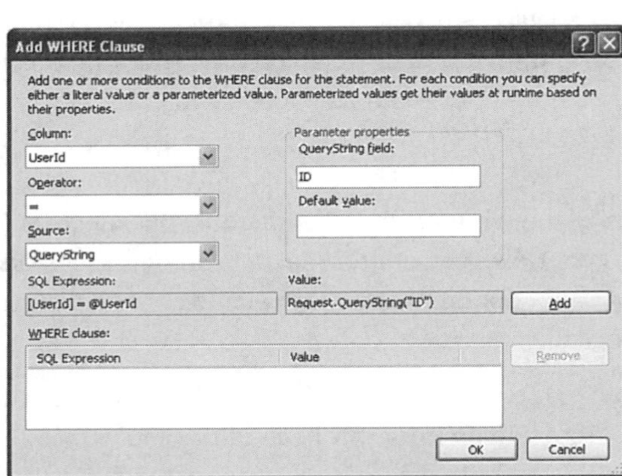

FIGURE 24.14 Add a filter expression on the `UserId` column based on the `ID` querystring value.

Watch Out!

Don't forget to remove `Type="Object"` from the SqlDataSource parameter (step 4). If you forget to omit the `Type` property, no records will be returned from the SqlDataSource, resulting in an empty DropDownList control.

With the SqlDataSource configured, we're ready to add the DropDownList control. Set this control's `ID` property to `categories` and assign it to the `categoriesDataSource` SqlDataSource. Because we want the list of pictures to update automatically when the user selects a new category from the list, set the DropDownList's `AutoPostBack` property to `True`.

We also need the DropDownList to include the `-- All --` option. When this option is selected, all pictures will be displayed, regardless of whether the picture belongs to a category. To accomplish this, set the DropDownList's `AppendDataBoundItems` property to `True` and add the `-- All --` option through the `ListItem` Collection Editor dialog box. After you add the `-- All --` option, don't forget to return to the declarative markup and ensure that the `<asp:ListItem>` just added has `Value=""` explicitly set.

Take a moment to view your progress by visiting the page through a browser. Figure 24.15 shows `PhotoAlbum.aspx`.

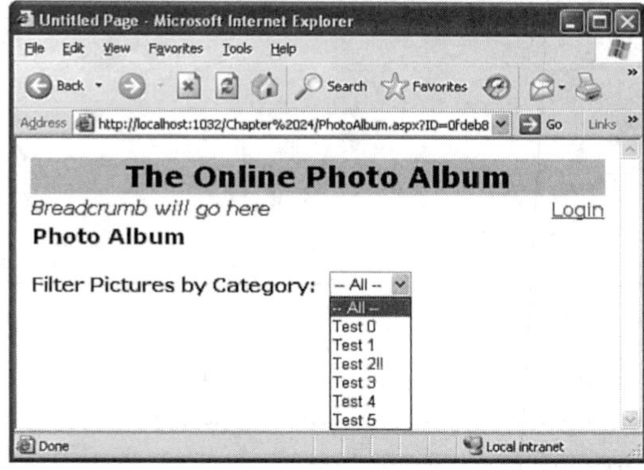

FIGURE 24.15
The drop-down list includes an `-- All --` option along with the user's categories.

Retrieving the Filtered Pictures

With the SqlDataSource and DropDownList for the categories complete, all that remains is creating the SqlDataSource for the pictures and the associated GridView. Start the process rolling by adding a SqlDataSource to the `PhotoAlbum.aspx` page named `picturesDataSource`. Because we want our filterable GridView to be able to show *all* pictures if the `-- All --` option is selected, we have to do a bit more work in setting up the SqlDataSource than we normally would have to.

For starters, we must provide a custom SQL statement. Open the SqlDataSource control's wizard and, from the Configure the Select Statement screen, choose the Specify a Custom SQL Statement or Stored Procedure radio button. Next, in the SELECT tab, enter the following query:

```
SELECT PictureID, Title, UploadedOn
FROM Pictures
WHERE UserId = @UserId AND
     (CategoryID = @CategoryID OR @CategoryID IS NULL)
ORDER BY UploadedOn DESC
```

Click the Next button and specify the parameter values. For the @UserId parameter, choose the QueryString option from the parameter source drop-down list and enter ID as the QueryString Field. For the @CategoryID parameter, set the parameter source to Control and choose the categories control from the drop-down list (see Figure 24.16).

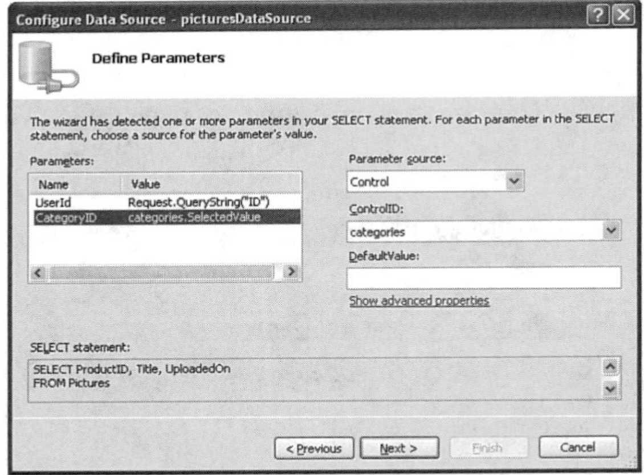

FIGURE 24.16 Specify the @UserId and @CategoryID parameter values.

This SELECT query returns the PictureID, Title, and UploadedOn columns from the Pictures table, where the UserId equals the UserId value passed through the querystring. The (CategoryID = @CategoryID OR @CategoryID IS NULL) filter expression returns *all* pictures for this user if the "-- All --" option is selected. Recall that an OR clause returns True if *either* of the statements is true, so if the @CategoryID parameter is assigned NULL (as it is when the -- All -- option is selected), the compound statement (CategoryID = @CategoryID OR @CategoryID IS NULL) returns True for every row evaluated. If @CategoryID is *not* NULL and is, instead, some valid CategoryID value, then the evaluation returns True only when the CategoryID equals the value of the @CategoryID parameter (which contains the value of the category selected from the drop-down list).

There's one more important step we need to take to have the picturesDataSource work properly. By default, a SqlDataSource cancels a SELECT query if any of the parameters are NULL. That means that, by default, when the -- All -- option is selected and the @CategoryID parameter is assigned NULL, the SqlDataSource will cancel the SELECT statement and no results will be returned. Quite the opposite of what we want! To remedy this situation, simply set the picturesDataSource SqlDataSource's CancelSelectOnNullParameter property to False.

Did you Know?

> Because a photo album can conceivably have categories to which no pictures have been assigned, it would be wise to enter a helpful message in the GridView's EmptyDataText property.

Displaying the Filtered Pictures

The last step for the PhotoAlbum.aspx page is to display the filtered results in a GridView. Add a GridView to the page, bind it to the productsDataSource SqlDataSource control, and check the Enable Sorting and Enable Paging check boxes. This will create three BoundFields in the GridView, one for each column returned by the SqlDataSource. Go to the Fields dialog box and remove the ProductID BoundField because we don't need to display that. While you're in the Fields dialog box, also set the UpdatedOn BoundField's HeaderText property to Date Added.

Currently, the GridView has two BoundFields: Title and UploadedOn. We need two additional fields: an ImageField to display the picture and a HyperLinkField that, when clicked, will whisk the user to ProductDetails.aspx, passing the PictureID value through the querystring. Add the HyperLinkField by performing the following steps:

1. From the GridView's smart tag, click the Edit Columns link, bringing up the Fields dialog box.
2. Add a HyperLinkField and move it so that it is the first field in the GridView.
3. Set the Text property to View Comments and the DataNavigateUrlFields and DataNavigateUrlFormatString properties to PictureID and ~/PhotoDetail.aspx?ID={0}, respectively.

The HyperLinkField property settings will result in a hyperlink titled View Comments with a link to PhotoDetail.aspx?ID=*PictureID*. PhotoDetail.aspx, which we'll implement in the next section, displays the photo whose PictureID equals the ID value passed in through the querystring. Additionally, it displays the picture's comments and allows authenticated users to add comments.

Complete the GridView by adding an ImageField, setting its `DataImageUrlField` and `DataImageUrlFormatString` properties to `PictureID` and `~/UploadedImages/{0}.jpg`, just like we did in the `gvPictures` GridView in the photo album administration page. I also suggest that you set the ImageField's `ControlStyle` property's `Width` or `Height` subproperties to appropriate values.

Figures 24.17 and 24.18 show Jisun's photo album when viewed by a visitor. In Figure 24.17 the user has opted to view all pictures; in Figure 24.18 the user has filtered the results to show only those pictures in the Test 4 category.

FIGURE 24.17
All of Jisun's pictures are shown.

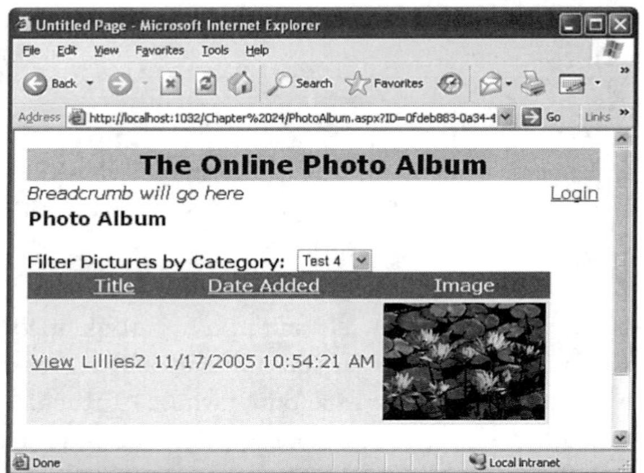

FIGURE 24.18
The photo album has been filtered and now shows only those pictures in category Test 4.

Viewing an Individual Picture and Its Comments

The final page left to implement is `PhotoDetail.aspx`. When users click the `View` link in the `PhotoAlbum.aspx` page, they are taken to this page, where the picture and its comments are shown. Anonymous users may view the picture's comments, but only authenticated users may leave a comment.

In the `PhotoAlbum.aspx` page we saw how to retrieve and display *all* pictures belonging to a particular user whose information was passed through the querystring. Rather than displaying all pictures, in `PhotoAlbum.aspx` we need to return information only about the picture whose `PictureID` value equals the `ID` value passed through the querystring.

To accomplish this, start by adding a SqlDataSource control to the page and set its `ID` property to `pictureDataSource`. Next, configure the wizard so that the `PictureID`, `Title`, and `Description` columns are returned from the `Pictures` table. Add a filter expression so that only the record whose `PictureID` value matches the `ID` querystring value is returned (see Figure 24.19).

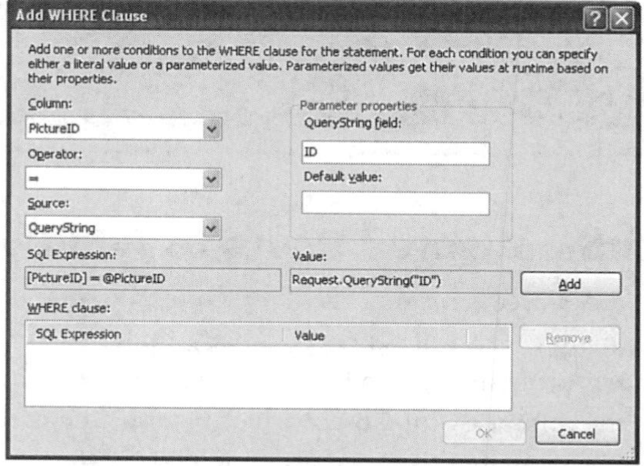

FIGURE 24.19 Return the one record whose `PictureID` value matches the `ID` querystring value.

After the `pictureDataSource` SqlDataSource has been configured, drag and drop a DetailsView control from the Toolbox onto the page and bind it to the SqlDataSource just added. This will add three BoundFields, one for each column returned by the SqlDataSource control. From the DetailsView's smart tag, click on the `Edit Fields` link and remove the `PictureID` BoundField, replacing it with an ImageField. Next, set the ImageField's `DataImageUrlField` and `DataImageUrlFormatString` properties to `PictureID` and `~/UploadedImages/{0}.jpg`, respectively.

In `PhotoDetails.aspx` I recommend using a DetailsView control to display the title, description, and picture. You could use a GridView control instead, but the GridView lays out its datasource's columns horizontally, whereas the DetailsView lays them out vertically, which more efficiently utilizes the screen real estate.

After these steps, take a moment to view the page through a browser. Figure 24.20 shows `PhotoDetails.aspx` when viewing the Blue Hills photo in Jisun's photo album.

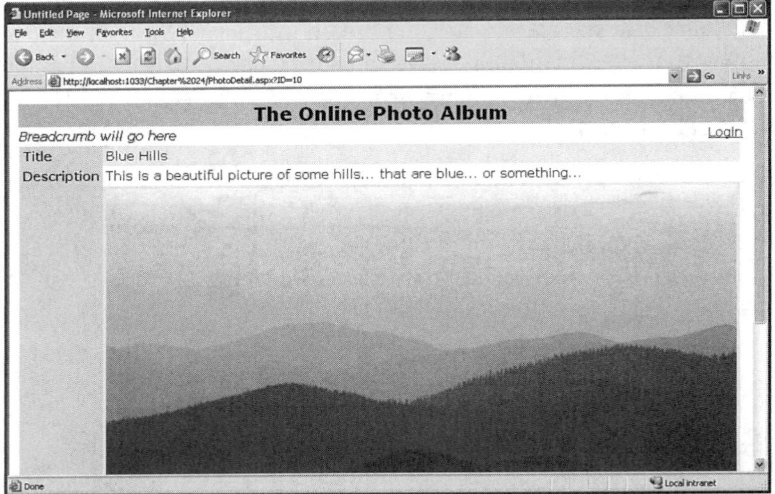

FIGURE 24.20
The title, description, and picture of the Blue Hills are displayed.

Allowing Authenticated Users to Add Comments

When an authenticated user views a particular picture, she should be able to leave a comment. A comment consists of a subject, a body, and the date and time the comment was made. Furthermore, a comment is associated with both a user—the person who made the comment—and a particular picture. The user making the comment will be able to enter both the subject and body of the comment through the ASP.NET page, but the comment's date and time, `UserId`, and `PictureID` values will be set programmatically, much like when adding a new picture to a photo album in the `PhotoAdmin/Default.aspx` page.

Because only authenticated users can leave comments, start by adding a LoginView control beneath the DetailsView added a moment ago. When an anonymous user visits this page, let's display the message `"Only logged in users can leave comments"`, along with a link to the login page. Enter this message into the AnonymousTemplate; for the login link, add a LoginStatus control.

Next, we need to add a SqlDataSource control that will retrieve the comments for the picture being viewed as well as provide capabilities for adding comments. Put this SqlDataSource outside the LoginView control because comments are viewable by both anonymous and authenticated users. Set this SqlDataSource control's `ID` property to `commentsDataSource` and configure the control to return all columns from the `Comments` table: `CommentID`, `UserId`, `PictureID`, `Subject`, `Body`, and `CommentMadeOn`. Add a filter expression on `PictureID` so that only the current picture's comments are returned (see Figure 24.19) and add an `ORDER BY` clause so that the results are sorted by `CommentMadeOn` in descending order. Click the Advanced button and check the Generate `INSERT`, `UPDATE`, and `DELETE` Statements check box. Finally, take a moment to go to the Source view and remove the `Type="Object"` attribute from the `UserId` `INSERT` parameter.

Next, add a DetailsView control to the LoggedInTemplate, set its `ID` to `dvAddComment`, and bind it to the `commentsDataSource` control. Configure the interface for adding new comments by performing the following steps:

1. From the DetailsView's smart tag, check the Enable Inserting check box.
2. Click on the `Edit Fields` link, opening the Fields dialog box, and remove the `CommentID`, `UserId`, `PictureID`, and `CommentMadeOn` BoundFields.
3. From the Properties window, set the DetailsView's `DisplayMode` to `Insert`.
4. Returning to the Fields dialog box, set the New, Insert, Cancel CommandField's `InsertText` property to `Add a New Comment` and clear out the `CancelText` property value.
5. To ensure that the user provides a subject and body, convert the `Subject` and `Body` BoundFields into TemplateFields and add RequiredFieldValidation controls to each TemplateFields' InsertItemTemplate.
6. Configure the `Body` TemplateField's TextBox control's `TextMode` property to `MultiLine`.

At this point the DetailsView control's user interface has been set up to correctly collect the subject and body of the user's comment. All that remains at this point is to programmatically set the `UserId`, `PictureID`, and `CommentMadeOn` values before the actual `INSERT` statement is sent to the database. As we saw in the photo administration page, the DetailsView control's `ItemInserting` event fires right before the `INSERT` statement is issued; an event handler for this event can programmatically set the values used in the `INSERT` statement.

Creating an Event Handler for a Nested Control

In Hour 7, "Working with Objects in Visual Basic," we saw how to create event handlers with Visual Web Developer: From the code portion, simply select the control from the left drop-down list and its event from the right drop-down list. Unfortunately, this technique cannot be used when working with controls that are **nested** within another control because the left drop-down list contains only non-nested controls. A nested control is a control that resides within the template of another control. In `PhotoDetails.aspx`, the `dvAddComment` DetailsView, for which we need to create an event handler for its `ItemInserting` event, is nested within a LoginView control.

To create event handlers for nested controls, we need to use the following steps:

1. From the Design view, select the control to add the event handler for; in this case, select the `dvAddComment` DetailsView control.
2. In the Properties window, click the lightning bolt icon, which will list the control's events (see Figure 24.21).
3. For the event to create a handler for, enter the name of the event handler. This can be any valid function name.

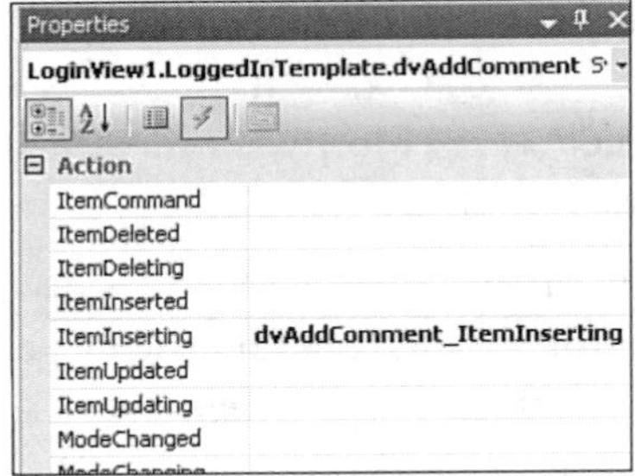

FIGURE 24.21
For nested controls, create event handlers through the Properties window.

After you complete these steps, an event handler will be added to the source code portion of the page. However, the event handler syntax lacks the `Handles` *`controlID.Event`* syntax that is present when you create an event handler through the drop-down lists. To see the difference, go to the photo administration page and note the `ItemInserting` event handler for the `dvCategoriesInsert` DetailsView:

```
Protected Sub dvCategoriesInsert_ItemInserting(ByVal sender As Object,
➥ByVal e As System.Web.UI.WebControls.DetailsViewInsertEventArgs)
➥ Handles dvCategoriesInsert.ItemInserting
  ...
End Sub
```

When you add the `ItemInserting` event handler for the `dvAddComment` DetailsView, the `Handles` statement is not present:

```
Protected Sub dvAddComment_ItemInserting(ByVal sender As Object,
➥ByVal e As System.Web.UI.WebControls.DetailsViewInsertEventArgs)
  ...
End Sub
```

As discussed in Hour 7, the `Handles` statement is what associates a particular control's event with a particular event handler. You may be wondering, then, how the event handler `dvAddComments_ItemInserting` is associated with the `dvAddComments` control's `ItemInserting` event. When you add an event handler through the Properties window, the event is tied to the control through the declarative HTML portion. If you go to the page's Source view, the DetailsView's declarative markup has been altered to include an attribute titled `OnItemInserting="dvAddComments_ItemInserting"`:

```
<asp:DetailsView ID="dvAddComment" runat="server"
                 OnItemInserting="dvAddComment_ItemInserting"
                 ...>
  ...
</asp:DetailsView>
```

This attribute associates the control's event with the event handler. More generally, the syntax is as follows:

```
OnEventName="EventHandler"
```

Setting the `INSERT`ed Values Programmatically

The `ItemInserting` event handler needs to programmatically set the `UserId`, `PictureID`, and `CommentMadeOn` values being inserted into the `Comments` table. To accomplish this, use the following three lines of code:

```
e.Values("UserId") = Membership.GetUser().ProviderUserKey
e.Values("PictureID") = Request.QueryString("ID")
e.Values("CommentMadeOn") = DateTime.Now
```

The first line of code sets the `UserId` value to the currently logged-on user's `UserId`; the second line of code assigns the `ID` value in the querystring to `PictureID`; the third and final line sets the `CommentMadeOn` field to the current date and time.

After you add these lines of code to the event handler, take a moment to add a new comment to a given picture. If you visit the page as an anonymous user, you should see a message instructing you to log on. When you are authenticated, you should see two text boxes for the subject and body. Go ahead and enter a comment. At this point we've yet to complete the user interface for displaying added comments, so you won't see the comment on the web page. However, you should see the added comment when viewing the contents of the `Comments` table through Visual Web Developer.

Watch Out!

> If you get an "`Implicit conversion from data type sql_variant to uniqueidentifier is not allowed. Use the CONVERT function to run this query`" exception when attempting to add a new comment, make sure that you've removed the `Type="Object"` attribute from the `commentsDataSource` SqlDataSource control's `UserId` `INSERT` parameter.

Displaying Comments

With the user interface for adding comments complete, all that remains for this page is displaying the existing comments. To display the appropriate comments, we just need to add a GridView control and bind it to the `commentsDataSource` control. Because both anonymous and authenticated users can view a picture's comments, add the GridView beneath the LoginView control.

Configure the GridView so that it supports paging and sorting; then edit its fields, removing all but the `Subject`, `Body`, and `CommentMadeOn` BoundFields. Finally, customize the `CommentMadeOn` BoundField, changing its `HeaderText` property to `Date`.

Figure 24.22 shows the two comments that have been left for the Blue Hills picture in Jisun's photo album.

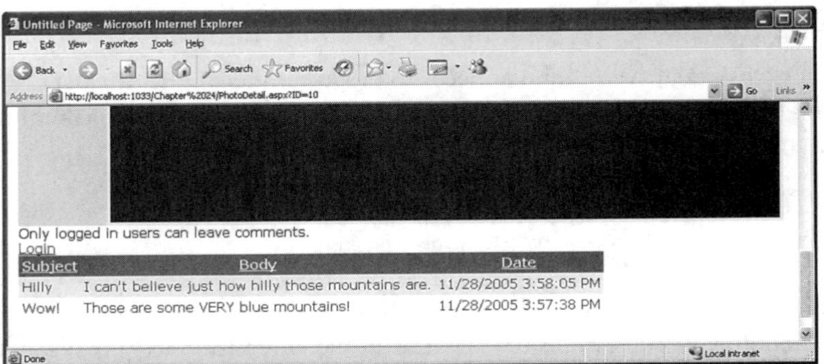

FIGURE 24.22 The picture's comments are shown at the bottom of the page.

Defining the Site's Structure and Providing Site Navigation

The final piece for our online photo album application is defining the site map. As we discussed in Hour 19, "Defining a Site's Structure and Providing Site Navigation," a website's structure can be defined using a **site map**, which is a static, XML-formatted file.

The static, XML-formatted file approach works well for sites whose site structure is predefined. However, with dynamic sites, the site's structure is more fluid. For example, the photo album application's structure includes several static pages—the home page, the login page, the photo administration page, and so on—but also includes dynamic pages, such as the photo album for a particular user or the comments page for a particular picture.

For dynamic websites like ours, the site map functionality can be customized by using a **custom site map provider**. Unfortunately, an exploration of this topic is beyond the scope of this book. Therefore, we will be creating a rather simple, static site map, one that does not include user-specific photo albums or pictures. If you are interested in implementing a dynamic site map through the use of a custom site map provider, check out my article, "Examining ASP.NET 2.0's Site Navigation," which begins at http://aspnet.4guysfromrolla.com/articles/111605-1.aspx.

The photo album application's site map is rather scant, having only five entries:

- **Home**—The site's home page, `Default.aspx`
- **Photo Album Administration**—The main photo album administration page, `PhotoAdmin/Default.aspx`
- **Manage Categories**—The manage categories page, `PhotoAdmin/ManageCategories.aspx`
- **Create an Account**—The create an account page, `CreateAccount.aspx`
- **Login**—The site's login page, `Login.aspx`

The two pages whose content is dynamically determined based on the querystring values—`PhotoAlbum.aspx` and `PhotoDetail.aspx`—are not included in the site map due to their dynamic nature. Listing 24.4 contains the site map's content.

LISTING 24.4 The Site Map Has an Entry for Each of the Four Static Pages

```
<?xml version="1.0" encoding="utf-8" ?>
<siteMap xmlns="http://schemas.microsoft.com/AspNet/SiteMap-File-1.0" >
    <siteMapNode url="~/Default.aspx" title="Home">
        <siteMapNode url="~/PhotoAdmin/Default.aspx"
➥title="Photo Album Administration">
            <siteMapNode url="~/PhotoAdmin/ManageCategories.aspx"
➥title="Manage Categories" />
        </siteMapNode>
        <siteMapNode url="~/CreateAccount.aspx"
➥title="Create an Account" />
        <siteMapNode url="~/Login.aspx" title="Login" />
    </siteMapNode>
</siteMap>
```

With the site map file created, the final step is to implement the site navigation user interface. Return to the master page and add a SiteMapPath control.

Figure 24.23 shows the Login page after the SiteMapPath control has been added. As you can see in the upper-left corner of the page, the SiteMapPath displays a breadcrumb based on the page being visited.

FIGURE 24.23
A SiteMapPath control has been added to the master page.

Summary

Congratulations, you have just completed your first real-world ASP.NET application! Over the past three intense hours we've created a multipage, fully functional website that has tied together the many lessons covered over the previous 21 hours. Give yourself a pat on the back; you deserve it!

I hope that working through this book has been both an enjoyable and educational experience, and that you're thoroughly impressed with the functionality of ASP.NET and Visual Web Developer. Despite the myriad of topics we've covered throughout these 24 hours, we've only just scratched the surface! That being said, we have covered the fundamental topics and in enough depth to build real-world, useful websites, as evidenced by the last three hours. But there's always more to learn and explore.

As you continue to use ASP.NET, sometimes you will get stuck when trying to solve a particular problem, and you won't find the answer in this book. Fortunately, surrounding ASP.NET is a huge community full of helpful individuals who are willing to help. I recommend that every ASP.NET developer check out Microsoft's ASP.NET Forums, available at http://forums.asp.net/. This online messageboard site boasts more than 200,000 registered users and far more than a million posts. It's a great place to ask your tough questions or help others work through their struggles.

In closing, thank you for reading this book. If you have any comments or suggestions, don't hesitate to email me at mitchell@4GuysFromRolla.com; you can also check out my blog at http://ScottOnWriting.NET/.

Happy Programming!

There are no quizzes or exercises for this hour.

Q&A

Q. ***Currently, the photo album application allows only JPEG images to be uploaded. How can I extend the application to allow for other image file formats to be uploaded?***

A. When an image is uploaded to a user's album, the picture's filename is saved using the `PictureID` value of the newly inserted record into the `Pictures` table. Although the `PictureID` value can be used to uniquely identify each picture, it cannot express the image's file extension—`.jpg`, `.gif`, `.bmp`, and so on.

You can resolve this problem in two ways: Either limit the application to allowing only one file extension or add an additional field to the `Pictures` table that captures the uploaded image's extension. Our application uses the former approach, but you can enhance the system to use the latter one by augmenting the `Pictures` table to include an `ImageExtension` column. When the user uploads an image, you would programmatically set the `ImageExtension` property to the extension of the uploaded file in the `dvPictureInsert_ItemInserting` event handler.

This approach introduces a new challenge when viewing the image files through an ImageField in the GridViews or DetailsViews, which is why I opted to restrict files of type JPEG for this application. Recall that the ImageField's image source URL can be configured via the `DataImageFieldUrl` and `DataImageFieldFormatString` properties, but only *one* databound column can be specified in the `DataImageFieldUrl` property, whereas now we need two—one for `PictureID` and one for `ImageExtension`.

There are a couple of ways to accomplish this. You can add a computed column to the `Pictures` table that will automatically concatenate the `PictureID` and `ImageExtension` columns, or you can customize the `SELECT` statement used by the SqlDataSource control to concatenate the two column values into one. Either way, these are slightly more advanced topics. If you are interested in exploring these options, consider asking for assistance on the ASP.NET Forums.

Q. ***In the* `PhotoDetails.aspx` *page, I'd like to include a back link to the user's photo album. How can I accomplish this?***

A. When the user clicks the `View` link from `PhotoAlbum.aspx`, he is taken to `PhotoDetails.aspx`, where he is shown the particular picture and its comments. Currently, there is no way to return to the particular user's photo album other than hitting the browser's Back button.

The challenge in providing a back link in `PhotoDetails.aspx` is that we must know the `UserId` of the user whose picture we are viewing. That is, when viewing Blue Hills (see Figure 24.20), we have to know that this is Jisun's picture, because to return to Jisun's album, we need to go back to `PhotoAlbum.aspx?ID=`*`Jisun'sUserID`*.

Because `PhotoDetails.aspx` is passed the `PictureID` of the photo to display, and because the `Pictures` table has a `UserId` associated with each picture, we could include the `UserId` column in the SqlDataSource. Then, in the DetailsView, we would add a HyperLinkField whose `Text` property was set to `"Back to the Photo Album"` and whose `DataNavigateUrlFields` and `DataNavigateUrlFormatString` properties were set to `UserId` and `PhotoAlbum.aspx?ID={0}`, respectively. This would add a back link to the DetailsView that would return the user to the correct photo album.

Q. ***In the comments displayed in the* `PhotoDetails.aspx` *page, the name of the person who made the comment is not shown. How can I add this?***

A. The `Comments` table doesn't contain the name of the person who made the comment; instead, it contains just the person's `UserId`. To retrieve the person's username, we would have to perform a **join** between the `Comments` table and the `aspnet_Users` table, which is the table that contains the username for each user in the system.

A join is a type of SQL query that retrieves records from two or more tables, joining the records based on relationships among the tables involved. Join syntax can be a bit tricky, but Visual Web Developer makes it easy when you are specifying a query manually in the SqlDataSource control wizard. Simply add the tables that you want to involve in the join and then check the columns to return from the tables. Visual Web Developer will automatically inject the correct join syntax.

If you decide to make this enhancement, do so with a new SqlDataSource control. That is, don't use the existing `commentsDataSource` SqlDataSource control in `PhotoDetail.aspx` because the DetailsView uses this datasource control for adding new comments. Instead, create a new SqlDataSource, configure it to join together the appropriate records from the `Comments` and `aspnet_Users` tables, and then bind this control to the GridView of comments.

Index

SYMBOLS

A

D

E

I

J - K - L

P

Q

R

S

T

U

V

W

X - Y - Z